D1738154

Israel's Past in Present Research

Sources for Biblical and Theological Study

General Editor:
David W. Baker
Ashland Theological Seminary

Israel's Past
in
Present Research

Essays on Ancient Israelite Historiography

edited by

V. Philips Long

Eisenbrauns
Winona Lake, Indiana
1999

Library of Congress Cataloging-in-Publication Data

Israel's past in present research : essays on ancient Israelite historiography /
    edited by V. Philips Long.
        p.   cm. — (Sources for biblical and theological study ; 7)
    Includes bibliographical references and indexes.
    ISBN 1-57506-028-0 (cloth : alk. paper)
        1. Jews—History—To 70 A.D.—Historiography.   2. Bible. O.T.—
    Historiography.   3. Palestine—History—To 70 A.D.—Historiography.
    4. Middle East—History—To 622—Historiography.   I. Long, V. Philips.
    II. Series.
    DS121.I85   1999
    933′.0072—dc21   99-044925
                                                                                         CIP

CONTENTS

Part 4
Writing Israel's History:
The Methodological Challenge

Part 5
The Historical Impulse in the Hebrew Canon:
A Sampling

Part 6
The Future of Israel's Past

Indexes

SERIES PREFACE

Old Testament scholarship is well served by several recent works which detail, to a greater or lesser extent, the progress made in the study of the Old Testament. Some survey the range of interpretation over long stretches of time, while others concern themselves with a smaller chronological or geographical segment of the field. There are also brief *entrés* into the various subdisciplines of Old Testament study included in the standard introductions as well as in several useful series. All of these provide secondary syntheses of various aspects of Old Testament research. All refer to, and base their discussions upon, various seminal works by Old Testament scholars which have proven pivotal in the development and flourishing of the various aspects of the discipline.

The main avenue into the various areas of Old Testament inquiry, especially for the beginner, has been until now mainly through the filter of these interpreters. Even on a pedagogical level, however, it is beneficial for a student to be able to interact with foundational works firsthand. This contact will not only provide insight into the content of an area, but hopefully will also lead to the sharpening of critical abilities through interaction with various viewpoints. This series seeks to address this need by including not only key, ground-breaking works, but also significant responses to these. This allows the student to appreciate the process of scholarly development through interaction.

The series is also directed toward scholars. In a period of burgeoning knowledge and significant publication in many places and languages around the world, this series will endeavor to make easily accessible significant, but at times hard to find, contributions. Each volume will contain essays, articles, extracts, and the like, presenting in a manageable scope the growth and development of one of a number of different aspects of Old Testament studies. Most volumes will contain previously published material, with synthetic essays by the editor(s) of the individual volume.

Some volumes, however, are expected to contain significant, previously unpublished works. To facilitate access to students and scholars, all entries will appear in English and will be newly typeset. If students are excited by the study of Scripture and scholars are encouraged in amicable dialogue, this series would have fulfilled its purpose.

DAVID W. BAKER, *series editor*
Ashland Theological Seminary

Publisher's Note

Articles republished here are reprinted without alteration, except for minor matters of style not affecting meaning. Page numbers of the original publication are marked with double brackets ([[267]], for example). Other editorial notes or supplementations are also marked with double brackets, including editorially-supplied translations of foreign words. Footnotes are numbered consecutively throughout each article, even when the original publication used another system. No attempt has been made to bring transliteration systems into conformity with a single style.

In the introductions to each part below, reference to works included in the respective "additional reading" sections is made by in-text citation; bibliographic information for all other works is provided in footnotes.

EDITOR'S PREFACE

More than once in the process of bringing the present volume to completion I found myself asking what could have prompted me to take it on in the first place. Perhaps a little naiveté and a healthy dose of wishful thinking about the busyness of my schedule played a part. Certainly, I was intrigued by the subject and welcomed the opportunity to immerse myself further in the pertinent scholarly literature. I had long been and am increasingly impressed by the importance of the questions that revolve around the study of Israel's past. And, like all others conversant in biblical studies, I had heard the repeated pronouncement that the historical study of ancient Israel is in a state of "crisis" or, put differently, at an impasse. And the temptation in such circumstances is always to want to have another look.

All of these factors combined to recommend the opportunity to bring together in one substantial volume a body of seminal or representative essays. As one who for a decade and a half has taught graduate-level courses in "Old Testament history" and who has penned a modest volume on issues surrounding the historical study of the Bible, I am keenly aware of the service that an anthology of selected readings could render to students and scholars alike who wish to find an entrée into this controversial area. The prospect of canvassing and including foreign language works that heretofore had not been translated into English made the project next to irresistible.

Having succumbed to these varied allurements, I found upon embarking on the project that it was even more challenging and raised more questions than I had anticipated. I catalogued more than 450 titles, consulted most of them, and considered many more than could ultimately be included in this volume. No doubt informed readers will question some of my inclusions and mourn some of my exclusions. Many worthy essays sparkled in places but were eliminated because of what I perceived as a (sometimes minor) blemish. Others just didn't quite seem to fit the criteria of the volume. Some didn't make the cut because, with all of their fine qualities, the ground they covered was adequately covered elsewhere. Some, undoubtedly, were overlooked because exhaustive reading nowadays is a virtual impossibility. And some were simply left out because of space constraints. As partial compensation, I have included in my introductions to each of the major sections of the volume a list of additional readings. But again, any who know the field will recognize how much has had to be omitted. (In the hopes of being of some use to scholarly as well as student readers, and space constraints notwithstanding, I have included in the additional reading sections a modest selection of foreign language works pertinent to our topic.)

Apart from the sheer mass of the literature to be canvassed, another challenge was to decide what kinds of publications should be consulted—scholarly journals and serious monographs only? magazines (such as *Biblical Archaeology Review* or *Bible Review*)? In the end, while the vast majority of essays come from the former recognized sources, a few contributions from more popular sources were chosen by virtue of one or more of the following: the reputation of their author, their pertinence to topic, their usefulness to readers, or their stylistic verve.

It was also necessary to consider what time frame should set the boundaries for the essays to be considered. In keeping with the general intent of the series, the emphasis falls on more recent work—the last twenty-five years or so, with the majority being even much more recent. I am aware, however, that "latest is not necessarily best," and so in my researches I have consulted older works and have not been averse to including a few classic expositions that seemed particularly apropos.

The question of how the anthology should be structured had also to be addressed. Early on I had the idea of simply determining who the current authorities in the field are, sending them a letter explaining the plan and purpose of the volume, and requesting that they submit an essay of their own choosing. While tempted by this idea (which likely would have yielded a useful volume), I chose to go a different route for several reasons. First, it is not always easy to determine just who should count as an authority. Publication rate is not always a good measure. The most vocal debaters are not necessarily the wisest. As in text-critical practice, witnesses should be weighed, not counted. And the measure by which a work, or an authority, is weighed is admittedly a somewhat subjective matter. This leads to my second reason for not deciding to formulate the volume by simply polling authorities. It seems to me, on the one hand, that some of the wisest perspectives on the vexed questions of Israel's history come from senior scholars whose net has been cast more broadly than just the area of historiography and who from this broader experience are able to provide sound counsel. On the other hand, there are a number of younger to midcareer scholars who have perhaps not gained the notoriety of their more senior (or, in some instances, more sensationalist) colleagues but whose solid contributions build a firmer foundation for future study and who deserve recognition.

The value judgments implied in phrases such as "it seems to me" and "firmer foundation" suggest my third reason for not simply soliciting contributions from the experts: it is hard to pursue any intellectual or academic question without the influence of one's own preferences and predispositions making itself felt. Or, to put the matter still more plainly, one's worldview (or control beliefs) inevitably carries significant weight when evaluative judgments must be made—even in questions as basic as which essays or excerpts to include in a volume such as this. The challenge I faced in planning the volume was whether I should chase the illusion of utter scientific objectivity or whether I should freely admit that some essays strike me as more convincing than others in part because they find a more-or-less comfortable place within the scheme of how I see things. This is not to say, of course, that my understandings of the issues surrounding this topic are fully formed and unchangeable. Nor is it meant to suggest that objectivity of a sort is not a desideratum. My conviction is simply that (1) the inevitable influence of our background beliefs is best controlled when we ourselves are aware of them and (2) our own positions are best understood by others when we allow them to know "where we are coming from."

Faced with these multiple challenges—the voluminous literature to be considered, the (in my view) mixed quality of some potential inclusions, the question of what kinds of publishing vehicles to consider, the time period in which to focus, the manner in which the volume should be constructed, and the awareness of my own subjectivity—I decided in the end that I would be most satisfied if I allowed myself the freedom to structure the volume in such a way that its overall shape conveyed some sense of my own "take" on the issues. This is not to say, of course, that I have included only essays with which I agree. I have consciously attempted to include representative voices from all sides. The question I kept before me was whether each essay included would be useful for students and fellow scholars to read, even if in some cases the chief benefit might lie in discovering the weaknesses of a particular position.

Having assumed the stance of redactor, or at least compiler, I sometimes felt myself to be working with recalcitrant material. Still, I hope that all of the inclusions usefully serve the overarching structure of the volume, which itself carries its own message. Quite apart from this overarching perspective, each individual essay stands on its own, and the reader will doubtless recognize that some of the essays could easily have filled more than one slot in the volume.

The following, then, in brief, is how the volume is structured: Six parts are organized around six areas of debate, with the first part being perhaps somewhat less hotly debated than the others. Since one can hardly expect to understand the current state of affairs without some knowledge of how the discipline has progressed to this point, part 1 focuses first on retracing *the path to the present*, followed by articulations of the *present crisis* in which history-of-Israel studies now find themselves. Part 2 provides necessary background to considerations of historiography in the Hebrew Bible and ancient historiography in general by discussing *the historical impulse among some of Israel's neighbors* in antiquity. Debates surrounding the proper use of comparative literatures and the comparative (contextual) method come to the fore in the essays included in this section. Part 3 then moves to a more focused consideration of the multiplex character of *Israel's history writing*—the very existence of which is today questioned by some. The essays are grouped under three rubrics that reflect significant issues in current debate: (1) Do the narratives in the Hebrew Bible that appear to exhibit a historiographical impulse have genuinely *antiquarian* intentions or do they not? (2) What about the obviously *aspectual* character of biblical narratives, where the theological slant makes itself felt so obviously that the so-called Historical Books (Joshua–Kings) have traditionally been dubbed the Former Prophets? Do theological and historical impulses represent mutually exclusive categories? (3) In a similar vein, can the literary *artistry* of many biblical narratives be reconciled with historiographical truth claims, or do artistic and historical impulses represent mutually exclusive categories?

Part 3 having considered the antiquarian, aspectual, and artistic nature of Israel's history writing, part 4 turns to the controversial matter of *writing Israel's history*. It begins with general discussions of method, which are then followed by a section devoted to social-science approaches and the battle over the Bible and a section exploring the relationship of literary study and historical reconstruction. Part 5 comprises sample essays that offer at least a hint of the historical impulse as it is felt in the major blocks of the Hebrew canon: the Law, the Prophets (Former and Latter), and the Writings. Where to place the datum point for the beginning of proper history writing in Israel is nowadays a hotly contested issue, and some scholars are pressing for ever later datings. Given the space available, it was not possible in the sampling of part 5 to represent all viewpoints adequately, or some even at all, so again my own preferences assert themselves.

Part 6, which concludes the volume, contains my own reflections on *the future of Israel's past*. That is, given the oft-remarked crisis in the study of Israel's history writing and in the writing of Israel's history, what developments is the future likely to witness? Here, of course, I can only hazard some guesses based on my own understanding of current trends, of the character of human nature and the academic enterprise, and of the penchants of personalities currently working in the field. Perhaps I may be forgiven if the same wishful thinking that helped me take on this project again reasserts itself from time to time as I seek to divine the road ahead.

Acknowledgments

Casting a glance back over the road I have traveled for the past several years, I realize that, although compiling this volume has at times seemed lonely work, I have in fact received help and encouragement from many people along the way. At an early stage, several scholars shared with me their own select lists of readings on the topic; thanks go to Robert Gordon, David Howard Jr., Edwin Yamauchi, and David Baker. A very special word of appreciation goes to Debora Kim, whose cheerful and skillful assistance on many administrative matters has significantly lightened my load from start to finish. Students in various courses have interacted with the substance of many of the essays in this volume; deserving of special mention are Tim Galage, Leon Pannkuk, and Daniel Santos. Thanks also to my teaching assistants, Bart Moseman, Pierce Yates, and Ewan Kennedy, as well as to Jim and Denise Pakala, Per Almquist, and others at the Covenant Seminary Library who have provided excellent resource support. To my faculty colleagues I express appreciation for their friendship and stimulation; thanks especially to Hans Bayer and Jack Collins, who graciously offered the occasional second opinion on linguistic matters. I am very grateful to Dean of Faculty Dan Doriani and the Board and Administration of Covenant Theological Seminary for granting me sabbatical leave to pursue this and other projects. For inviting me to compile a volume for the SBTS series, I express thanks to series editor David Baker, and for making the present volume a reality, heartfelt thanks go also to Jim Eisenbraun and his able editor, Beverly Fields. To my wife, Polly, and our four children: thanks for your love and encouragement and for making it well worthwhile to take a break from work now and then.

The volume is dedicated with deep respect and appreciation to my Doktorvater, Professor Robert P. Gordon, whose life and scholarship continue to inspire me in all the right directions.

V. Philips Long
Covenant Theological Seminary

ABBREVIATIONS

AB	Anchor Bible
ABC	A. K. Grayson, *Assyrian and Babylonian Chronicles*
ABD	*Anchor Bible Dictionary*
ABRL	Anchor Bible Reference Library
ACF	*Annuaire du Collège de France*
AfeT	Arbeitskreis für evangelikale Theologie
AfO	*Archiv für Orientforschung*
Ag. Ap.	Josephus, *Against Apion*
AHR	*The American Historical Review*
AION	*Annali dell'Istituto Universario Orientali di Napoli*
AJA	*American Journal of Archaeology*
AK	*Archiv für Kulturgeschichte*
AmSc	*American Scholar*
AnBib	Analecta Biblica
ANEH	W. W. Hallo and W. K. Simpson, *The Ancient Near East: A History*
ANET	J. B. Prichard (ed.), *Ancient Near Eastern Texts Relating to the Old Testament* (3d ed.)
AnOr	Analecta Orientalia
AnSc	*Annals of Science*
AnSt	*Anatolian Studies*
Ant.	Josephus, *Antiquities*
AOAT	Alter Orient und Altes Testament
A(r)Or	*Archiv Orientální*
AR(AB)	D. D. Luckenbill (ed.), *Ancient Records of Assyria and Babylonia*
ARINH	F. M. Fales, ed., *Assyrian Royal Inscriptions: New Horizons in Literary, Ideological and Historical Analysis*
ARM	Archives royales de Mari
AS	Assyriological Studies
ASA	Association of Social Anthropologists
ASOR	American Schools of Oriental Research
ASTI	*Annual of the Swedish Theological Institute*
ATANT	Abhandlungen zur Theologie des Alten und Neuen Testaments
ATD	Das Alte Testament Deutsch
ATS	Arbeiten zu Text und Sprache im Alten Testament
BA	*Biblical Archaeologist*

BAReader	*Biblical Archaeologist Reader*
BAR(ev)	*Biblical Archaeology Review*
BASOR	*Bulletin of the American Schools of Oriental Research*
BBB	Bonner biblische Beiträge
BEATAJ	Beiträge zur Erforschung des Alten Testaments und des antiken Judentums
BETL	Bibliotheca ephemeridum theologicarum lovaniensium
BGBH	Beiträge zur Geschichte der biblischen Hermeneutik
BH	Biblical Hebrew
B(ib)I(nt)	*Biblical Interpretation*
BIFAO	*Bulletin de l'institute français d'archéologie orientale*
BJRL	*Bulletin of the John Rylands University Library of Manchester*
BK	*Bibel und Kirche*
BKAT	Biblischer Kommentar: Altes Testament
BOT	Boeken van het Oude Testament
BRev	*Bible Review*
BSac	*Bibliotheca Sacra*
BTB	*Biblical Theology Bulletin*
BWANT	Beiträge zur Wissenschaft vom Alten und Neuen Testament
BZ	*Biblische Zeitschrift*
BZAW	Beihefte zur *Zeitschrift für die Alttestamentliche Wissenschaft*
CBC	Cambridge Bible Commentary
CBQ	*Catholic Biblical Quarterly*
CHM	*Cahiers d'histoire mondiale*
CSSH	*Comparative Studies in Society and History*
CTM	*Concordia Theological Monthly*
DBS	L. Pirot, A. Robert, H. Cazelles, and A. Feuillet (eds.), *Dictionnaire de la Bible, Supplément*
DOTT	D. W. Thomas (ed.), *Documents from Old Testament Times*
EAEHL	M. Avi-Yonah (ed.), *Encyclopaedia of Archaeological Excavations in the Holy Land*, 4 vols.
Ebib	Études bibliques
EnBr	*Encyclopaedia Britannica*
E(r)I(sr)	*Eretz Israel*
ESHM	European Seminar in Historical Methodology
EstBib	*Estudios Bíblicos*
EvT(h)	*Evangelische Theologie*
ExpTim	*Expository Times*
FCI	Foundations of Contemporary Interpretation
FGLP	Forschungen zur Geschichte und Lehre des Protestantismus
FRLANT	Forschungen zur Religion und Literatur des Alten und Neuen Testaments
FSTRP	Forschungen zur systematischen Theologie und Religionsphilosophie
FT	*Faith and Theology*
FTS	Freiburger theologische Studien

GS	*Gesammelte Studien*
GTS	Gettysburg Theological Studies
HAT	Handbuch zum Alten Testament
HHI	H. Tadmor and M. Weinfeld (eds.), *History, Historiography, and Interpretation*
HSM	Harvard Semitic Monographs
HSS	Harvard Semitic Studies
HTh	*History and Theory*
HTR	*Harvard Theological Review*
HUCA	*Hebrew Union College Annual*
ICC	International Critical Commentary
IDBSup	K. Crim (ed.), *Interpreter's Dictionary of the Bible Supplementary Volume*
IEJ	*Israel Exploration Journal*
Int	*Interpretation*
IOSOT	International Organization for the Study of the Old Testament
ISLL	Illinois Studies in Language and Literature
JAAR	*Journal of the American Academy of Religion*
JAOS	*Journal of the American Oriental Society*
JBL	*Journal of Biblical Literature*
JCS	*Journal of Cuneiform Studies*
JDT	*Jahrbücher für deutsche Theologie*
JETh	*Jahrbuch für evangelische Theologie*
JETS	*Journal of the Evangelical Theological Society*
JHI	*Journal of the History of Ideas*
JNES	*Journal of Near Eastern Studies*
JPOS	*Journal of the Palestine Oriental Society*
JR	*Journal of Religion*
JSOT	*Journal for the Study of the Old Testament*
JSOTS(up)(S)	Journal for the Study of the Old Testament Supplement Series
JSS	*Journal of Semitic Studies*
JTC	*Journal for Theology and the Church*
JTS	*Journal of Theological Studies*
JTSA	*Journal of Theology for Southern Africa*
J.W.	Josephus, *The Jewish War*
JWCI	*Journal of the Warburg and Courtauld Institutes*
KAI	H. Donner and W. Röllig, *Kanaanäische und aramäische Inschriften*
KTU	M. Dietrich, O. Loretz, and J. Sanmartín (eds.), *Die keilalphabetischen Texte aus Ugarit*
KuD	*Kerygma und Dogma*
LCL	Loeb Classical Library
NCB	New Century Bible
NEAEHL	E. Stern (ed.), *The New Encyclopedia of Archaeological Excavations in the Holy Land*
OA	*Oriens antiquus*
OBO	Orbis biblicus et orientalis

OIP	Oriental Institute Publications
OLP	*Orientalia lovaniensia periodica*
Or	*Orientalia*
OrAnt	*Oriens antiquus*
OTL	Old Testament Library
OTS	*Oudtestamentische Studiën*
PEGLMBS	*Proceedings, Eastern Great Lakes and Midwest Biblical Societies*
PEQ	*Palestine Exploration Quarterly*
Pjb	*Palästina-Jahrbuch*
PMLA	*Proceedings of the Modern Language Association of America*
Proof	*Prooftexts: A Journal of Jewish Literary History*
RA	*Revue d'assyriologie et d'archéologie orientale*
RB	*Revue biblique*
RGG(^{3})	*Die Religion in Geschichte und Gegenwart* (3d ed.)
RHPhR	*Revue d'histoire dt de philosophie religieuses*
RiBib	*Rivista biblica*
RLA	G. Ebeling et al. (eds.), *Reallexikon der Assyriologie*
RR	*Radical Religion*
SBLDS	Society of Biblical Literature Dissertation Series
SBLSPS	Society of Biblical Literature Seminar Papers Series
SBT(h)	Studies in Biblical Theology
SCCNH	D. I. Owen and M. A. Morrison (eds.), *Studies on the Civilization and Culture of Nuzi and the Hurrians*, 2 vols.
SJOT	*Scandinavian Journal of the Old Testament*
SKGG	Schriften der Königsberger Gelehrten Gesellschaft
SR	*Studies in the Renaissance*
SSEA	Schriften der Studiengemeinschaft der Evangelischen Akademien
STT	O. R. Gurney, J. J. Finkelstein, and P. Hulin (eds.), *The Sultantepe Tablets*, 2 vols.
SVT	Vetus Testament Supplements
SWBA	The Social World of Biblical Antiquity
TAVO	*Tübinger Atlas des Vorderen Orients*
TB	*Tyndale Bulletin*
TBC	Torch Bible Commentary
TB(ü)	Theologische Bücherei
THAT	E. Jenni and C. Westermann (eds.), *Theologisches Handwörterbuch zum Alten Testament*
T(h)LZ	*Theologische Literaturzeitung*
ThR(u)	*Theologische Rundschau*
ThStud	*Theologische Studiën*
T(h)WAT	G. J. Bottwerweck, H. Ringgren, and H. J. Fabry (eds.), *Theologisches Wörterbuch zum Alten Testament*
ThZ	*Theologische Zeitschrift*
TRHS	*Transactions of the Royal Historical Society*
TrinJ	*Trinity Journal*
TUAT	*Texte aus der Umwelt des Alten Testaments*

TUMSR	Trinity University Monograph Series in Religion
TynB	*Tyndale Bulletin*
UF	*Ugarit-Forschungen*
VT	*Vetus Testamentum*
VTS(up)	Vetus Testamentum Supplements
WBC	Word Biblical Commentary
WF	Wege der Forschung
WMANT	Wissenschaftliche Monographien zum Alten und Neuen Testament
WO	*Die Welt des Orients*
WTJ	*Westminster Theological Journal*
ZA	*Zeitschrift für Assyriologie*
ZAW	*Zeitschrift für die alttestamentliche Wissenschaft*
ZDMG	*Zeitschrift der Deutschen Palästina-Vereins*
ZEE	*Zeitschrift für evangelische Ethik*
ZT(h)K	*Zeitschrift für Theologie und Kirche*

Part 1

Israel's Past in Present Research

Introduction

Not to know the way forward is to be lost. To have forgotten how one has come is to be doubly lost. If students and scholars today, amidst the bewildering variety of opinion being expressed about even the possibility of writing a history of Israel, feel a bit lost, speak of "crisis" or "impasse," and wonder aloud if there is a way forward, some excuse can perhaps be made. Less excusable, however, is the double lostness that results when insufficient effort is expended to retrace the path that has led to the current situation. The place to begin the present volume, then, is with a look backward.

Among the many essays that seek to describe the history of the study of the history of Israel, one of the best in terms of clarity, scope, and conciseness is John H. Hayes's introductory chapter in the 1977 volume that he jointly edited with J. Maxwell Miller (*Israelite and Judaean History*). In its full published form, Hayes's survey ranges from "the earliest treatments of Israelite and Judaean history" right up to "current approaches" as they existed in 1977; for the present volume, however, space considerations mean that only an excerpt of Hayes's survey can be included. Since, as Hayes puts it, "the foundations of modern historiography were laid in the Renaissance," this is where our excerpt begins (found on pp. 7–42 below).

During the Renaissance, typified by "intellectual and technological accomplishments" and also "militant humansim" (p. 8), there arose what Hayes calls " 'middle-range explanations'—what we today would call sociological, economical, geographical, climatic considerations" (p. 13). During the seventeenth century, thinkers such as Grotius, Hobbes, and Spinoza drew attention to what they regarded as discrediting features in the biblical texts—literary inconsistencies, repetitions, and the like. This period saw the abandonment of many traditional beliefs about the Bible, but, if Hayes is correct, this abandonment did not so much *result from* the application of more advanced, critical methods but, rather, *preceded* them. He writes: thinkers such as those just mentioned "had [already] moved away from the typical Jewish and Protestant view of religious authority and

2

revelation," so that "their criticism was probably the result rather than the cause of such a move" (p. 19).

Continuing his survey into the eighteenth century, Hayes describes what he terms "an unprecedented and trenchant examination and critique" of Christianity and the Bible at the hands of the deists. Essentially— though there was considerable variety among them—the deists "sought to distil the biblical traditions, to siphon off the supernatural, the miraculous, and the unbelievable, and to leave behind the pure essence of a reasonable faith" (p. 21)—the standard of what counted as "reasonable" being, of course, the naturalistic and rationalistic assumptions of the Enlightenment.

Among major trends of the nineteenth century, Hayes highlights the general increase in religious liberalism, the development of "a positivistic approach to history," the decipherment of and enthusiasm for the languages and literatures of Israel's ancient Near Eastern neighbors, the rise of keen interest in the historical geography of the Near East, and the ascendancy of literary theories such as Wellhausen's highly influential Documentary Hypothesis. All of these nineteenth-century trends have made themselves felt in the twentieth-century study of Israelite history, not least the latter, because, as Hayes observes, "the primary influence on Wellhausen's reconstruction of Israelite *history* was . . . the results and consequences of his *literary* study of the Old Testament" (p. 36; italics mine).

Hayes develops his survey of the current situation under four headings: "the orthodox or traditional approach," "the archaeological approach," "the traditio-historical approach," and "socio-economical" approaches. Perhaps because this part of his survey deals with a time more familiar to current readers, one may wish to quibble with some of Hayes's choices, such as the scholars he chooses to represent the "orthodox view" (there are other, more notable luminaries) and the decision to give "practically no attention" to conservative writers on the ground that their work aims merely "to support and elucidate the adequate history which the Bible already provides" (p. 39). Apart from the fact that just such histories have wide appeal among believing Jewish and Christian communities, Hayes's assessment overlooks the fact that many contemporary scholars who hold a high view of scripture are as keenly aware as any of the challenge they face in rightly interpreting the biblical texts. Apart from quibbles such as these, Hayes's survey offers a fine overview of the path that has led to the present—or almost present. As noted, Hayes published his survey in 1977.

The second inclusion below (pp. 43–50)—an excerpt from the first chapter of Mark Z. Brettler's 1995 book entitled *The Creation of History in Ancient Israel*—serves to give a flavor of trends in the more recent present. In describing "the new biblical historiography," Brettler does of course take the occasional glance backward, but his main emphasis is on the latest publications, of which his own work is an example. Brettler seeks to show how various recent developments (for example, heightened interest in the ideological nature of the so-called Deuteronomistic History [Joshua–Kings], increased use of social-science methods, trends in the secular study of history ["New History," "annales school"], improved awareness of the rhetorical character of historiography, and the Bible as literature movement) "have acted in concert to alter radically the way in which we study biblical texts concerned with Israel's past." Brettler writes:

> Until the early 1970s, there was a general consensus that the best way to study texts such as Judges and Kings was to use the tools of the historian, for these texts are in some sense "historical." For many American scholars . . . the texts were "historical" in the sense of being reasonably accurate depictions of the history of ancient Israel. American scholarship has now moved quite far from this position, but there is no single unifying figure or position which has replaced the Albright school. The old consensus is gone, and there is no indication that a new one is developing to replace it. (p. 50)

Perhaps it would be more accurate to say that *much of* American scholarship (and not only American) has moved away from the view that texts such as Judges and Kings give "reasonably accurate depictions of the history of ancient Israel." But even such an observation evokes many questions that need to be addressed. What all is involved in the recognition that historiography involves depictions (or representations)? What kind of accuracy should be expected in depictions? What determines what is *reasonable* accuracy? For his part, Brettler in the end distances himself somewhat from "the radical skepticism of some scholars" (he mentions as an example Thomas L. Thompson, and elsewhere he cites also N. P. Lemche, P. R. Davies, and others). Brettler believes, rather, that "particular reconstructions may be . . . 'rationally justifiable,' though lacking in outside verification" (222 n. 53, not reproduced here).

If Brettler speaks of lack of *consensus*, Rolf Rendtorff, author of the final essay included in part 1, speaks of *crisis*. In "The Paradigm is Changing: Hopes—and Fears" (pp. 51–68 below), Rendtorff states his belief that, "in the terminology of Thomas Kuhn, Old Testament scholarship is 'in crisis'" (p. 60). Rendtorff traces the unraveling of older critical certainties, such as Wellhausen's Documentary Hypothesis, elucidates early witting or unwitting departures from the Wellhausen schema in the writings of, for example, Gunkel, Noth, and von Rad, and highlights what he regards as hopeful signs in some of the more recent developments in scholarship of the Hebrew Bible. Among these hopeful signs Rendtorff cites those studies that seek to combine diachronic and synchronic concerns. In particular he urges that "we go beyond diachronic observations of diversity to the search for the inner, or even overarching unity" of the biblical texts (p. 67). As for the place of the biblical texts in the reconstruction of Israelite history, Rendtorff writes: "I do not understand the *raison d'être* of a history of Israel that is not carried out in close contact with the Hebrew Bible" (p. 63). That Rendtorff can make such a statement in a time when so many others are trumpeting the general irrelevance of the biblical texts to the task of reconstructing a history of ancient Israel is testimony to just how open the field is at present.

Additional Reading

The Path to the Present

Miller, J. M.
  1985   Israelite History. Pp. 1–30 in *The Hebrew Bible and Its Modern Interpreters*. Edited by D. A. Knight and G. M. Tucker. Philadelphia: Fortress / Chico: Scholars Press.
  1994   Introduction to the History of Ancient Israel. Pp. 244–71 in vol. 1 of *The New Interpreter's Bible*. Edited by L. E. Keck et al. Nashville: Abingdon.
Pienaar, D. N.
  1990   Bybelse argeologie en Ou-Testamentiese gesckiedskrywing. *Nederduits Gereformeerde Teologiese Tydskrif* 31: 310–18.
Porter, J. R.
  1979   Old Testament Historiography. Pp. 125–62 in *Tradition and Interpretation: Essays by Members of the Society for Old Testament Study*. Edited by G. W. Anderson. Oxford: Clarendon.
Reventlow, H. G.
  1982   Ist das Alte Testament ein Geschichtsbuch? Pp. 121–37 in *Hauptprobleme der alttestamentilichen Theologie im 20. Jahrhundert*. Darmstadt: Wissenschaftliche Buchgesellschaft.
Vaux, R. de
  1965   Method in the Study of Early Hebrew History. Pp. 15–29 in *The Bible and Modern Scholarship*. Edited by J. P. Hyatt. Nashville: Abingdon. [Also worthy of note are the replies to de Vaux by G. E. Mendenhall and M. Greenberg in the same work, pp. 30–36 and 37–43, respectively.]

The Present Lack of Consensus

Dever, W. G.
  1996   Archaeology and the Current Crisis in Israelite Historiography. *Eretz-Israel* 25 (Aviram volume): 18–27.

Herrmann, S.
  1992   Observations on Some Recent Hypotheses Pertaining to Early Israelite
          History. Pp. 105–16 in *Justice and Righteousness*. Edited by H. G. Reventlow
          and Y. Hoffman. Journal for the Study of the Old Testament Supplement
          Series 137. Sheffield: Sheffield Academic Press.
Hess, R. S.
  1994   Recent Studies in Old Testament History: A Review Article. *Themelios* 19:
          9–15.
Miller, J. M.
  1987   In Defense of Writing a History of Israel. *Journal for the Study of the Old
          Testament* 39: 53–57.
  1989   New Directions in the Study of Israelite History. *Nederduits Gereformeerde
          Teologiese Tydskrif* 30: 152–60.
Weippert, M.
  1993   Geschichte Israels am Scheideweg. *Theologische Rundschau* 58: 71–103.
Yamauchi, E.
  1994   The Current State of Old Testament Historiography. Pp. 1–36 in *Faith,
          Tradition, and History: Old Testament Historiography in Its Near Eastern Con-
          text*. Edited by A. R. Millard, J. K. Hoffmeier, and D. W. Baker. Winona
          Lake, Ind.: Eisenbrauns.

The History of the Study of Israelite and Judaean History

From the Renaissance to the Present

JOHN H. HAYES

From the Renaissance to the Enlightenment

[[33]] D. C. Allen, *The Legend of Noah: Renaissance Rationalism in Art, Science, and Letters*, ISLL 33/3–4, 1949, ²1963; K. W. Appelgate, *Voltaire on Religion: Selected Writings*, New York: Frederick Ungar 1974; K. Barth, *Die Protestantische Theologie im 19. Jahrhundert*, Zollikon/Zürich: Evangelischer Verlag 1947 = *Protestant Theology in the Nineteenth Century: Its Background and History*, London/Valley Forge: SCM Press/ Judson Press 1972; I. Berlin, "Herder and the Enlightenment," *Aspects of the Eighteenth Century*, ed. E. R. Wasserman, Baltimore: Johns Hopkins Press 1965, 47–104; P. Burke, *The Renaissance Sense of the Past*, London: Edward Arnold 1969; H. Butterfield, *The Origins of Modern Science 1300–1800*, London/New York: G. Bell & Sons/Macmillan 1949, ²1957; G. R. Cragg, *Reason and Authority in the Eighteenth Century*, London: Cambridge University Press 1964; L. Diestel, *Geschichte des Alten Testamentes in der christlichen Kirche*, Jena: Mauke's Verlag 1869; H. W. Frei, *The Eclipse of Biblical Narrative: A Study in Eighteenth and Nineteenth Century Hermeneutics*, New Haven: Yale University Press 1974; E. B. Fryde, "Historiography and Historical Methodology," *EnBr* 8, 1974, 945–61; P. Gay, *Deism: An Anthology*, Princeton: Van Nostrand 1968; E. Grant, "Late Medieval Thought, Copernicus, and the Scientific Revolution," *JHI* 23, 1962, 197–220; E. M. Gray, *Old Testament Criticism: Its Rise and Progress from the Second Century to the End of the Eighteenth*, New York: Harper & Brothers 1923; C. Hartlich and W. Sachs, *Der Ursprung des Mythosbegriffes in der*

Reprinted with permission and excerpted from "The History of the Study of Israelite and Judaean History," in *Israelite and Judaean History* (ed. John H. Hayes and J. Maxwell Miller; Philadelphia: Westminster, 1977) 33–69.

modernen Bibelwissenschaft, SSEA 2, 1952; P. Hazard, *La Crise de la Conscience Européene*, Paris: Boivin 1935 = *The European Mind (1680–1715)*, London: Hollis & Carter 1953; J. M. Headley, *Luther's View of Church History*, New Haven: Yale University Press 1963; R. Hooykaas, "Science and Reformation," *CHM* 3/1, 1956, 109–39; G. Hornig, [[34]] *Die Anfänge der historisch-kritischen Theologie. Johann Salomo Semlers Schriftverständnis und seine Stellung zu Luther*, FSTRP 8, 1961; D. R. Kelley, *Foundations of Modern Historical Scholarship: Language, Law, and History in the French Renaissance*, New York: Columbia University 1970; D. A. Knight, *Rediscovering the Traditions of Israel*, SBLDS 9, 1973, [2]1975; H.-J. Kraus, *Geschichte der historisch-kritischen Erforschung des Alten Testaments*, Neukirchen-Vluyn: Neukirchener Verlag 1956, [2]1969; W. G. Kümmel, *Das Neue Testament: Geschichte der Erforschung seiner Probleme*, Freiburg: K. Alber 1958 = *The New Testament: The History of the Investigation of Its Problems*, Nashville/London: Abingdon Press/SCM Press 1972/3; S. F. Mason, "The Scientific Revolution and the Protestant Reformation," *AnSc* 8, 1952, 64–87, 154–75; D. R. McKee, "Isaac de la Peyrère: A Precursor of Eighteenth-Century Critical Deists," *PMLA* 59, 1944, 456–85; A. Momigliano, "Ancient History and the Antiquarian," *JWCI* 12, 1950, 285–315 = his *Studies in Historiography*, London: Weidenfeld and Nicolson 1966, 1–39; [[H. Prideaux, *The Old and New Testament Connected in the History of the Jews and Neighbouring Nations, from the Declension of the Kingdoms of Israel and Judah to the Time of Christ* 1–2, London: R. Knaplock 1717–18; quoted from edition of 1823–24;]] C. K. Pullapilly, *Caesar Baronius; Counter-Reformation Historian*, Notre Dame: University of Notre Dame Press 1975; A. Rabil, *Erasmus and the New Testament: The Mind of a Christian Humanist*, TUMSR 1, 1972; H. Reventlow, "Die Auffassung vom Alten Testament bei Hermann Samuel Reimarus und Gotthold Ephraim Lessing," *EvTh* 25, 1965, 429–48; B. R. Reynolds, "Latin Historiography: A Survey 1400–1600," *SR* 2, 1955, 7–66; J. W. Rogerson, *Myth in Old Testament Interpretation*, BZAW 134, 1974; K. Scholder, "Herder und die Anfänge der historischen Theologie," *EvTh* 22, 1962, 425–40; idem, *Ursprünge und Probleme die Bibelkritik im 17. Jahrhundert: Ein Beitrag zur Entstehung der historisch-kritischen Theologie*, FGLP 10/33, 1966; [[S. Schuckford, *The Sacred and Profane History of the World Connected, From the Creation of the World to the Dissolution of the Assyrian Empire at the Death of Sardanapalus, and to the Declension of the Kingdom of Judah and Israel under the Reigns of Ahaz and Pekah* 1–2, London: R. Knaplock & J. Tonson 1728–30; quoted from edition of 1810; R. W. Southern, "Aspects of the European Tradition of Historical Writing, 2: Hugh of St. Victor and the Idea of Historical Development," *TRHS* 21 (1971) 159–79;]] L. Stephen, *History of English Thought in the Eighteenth Century* 1–2, London/New York: Smith, Elder & Co./G. P. Putnam's Sons 1876, [2]1881; E. G. Waring, *Deism and Natural Religion: A Source Book*, New York: Frederick Ungar 1967; R. Weiss, *The Renaissance Discovery of Classical Antiquity*, Oxford: Basil Blackwell 1969; T. Willi, *Herders Beitrag zum Verstehen des Alten Testaments*, BGBH 8, 1971.

The foundations of modern historiography were laid in the Renaissance which began in Italy in the fourteenth century and spread northward. The militant humanism of this period certainly had its roots in medievalism, in spite of its scorn for the Middle Ages; but its intellectual and technological accomplishments were revolutionary both in themselves and in their implications. One of the products of the Renaissance was history as an independent discipline. A second result was a critical approach to many of the problems and issues of life. The radical consequences of these two developments for the study of Israelite and Judaean history, however, were not to be developed fully until the nineteenth century.

During the Renaissance, four elements which pervaded much of the intellectual activity were generative of momentous consequences [[35]] for future historiography. These were a true sense of anachronism, a renewed interest in antiquarianism, a critical stance towards the literary evidence from the past, and the attempt to understand the causation of historical events through reason (see Burke). One must not, of course, assume that a majority of the educated and scholarly figures of the Renaissance period shared these perspectives, any more than one should assume that after the publication of Darwin's *Origin of Species* everyone gave up the idea that God created man in a paradise state.

As we noted earlier, medieval writers as a rule lacked a historical perspective on the past as past, as different in space and time from the contemporary. In the fourteenth century, a historical sensibility began to develop. This appears, for example, in Giotto's fresco painting in the Arena Chapel at Padua (about 1305) which depicts Pontius Pilate clean-shaven, with garlanded head, and wearing a Roman robe embossed with a golden, imperial eagle. He appears as a figure from the past, not as a contemporary. Petrarch (1304–74) was well aware of the differences between his own day and those of his beloved Rome before the conversion of Constantine. So much so, that he described his own times as barbarian and wrote "nostalgic" letters to the classical authors expressing his longing to escape from the present and to find solace in those happier bygone days of old. Renaissance authors slowly recognized that everything had changed over time—laws, words, clothes, customs, arts, and buildings (see Burke 1969: 39–49). There was, in other words, a historical relativity to all things.

Antiquarianism was a natural accompaniment to the revived interest in the past (see Momigliano 1950 and Weiss 1969). In the Renaissance, men like Petrarch were not only interested in ancient literary works but in what would be called archaeological remains. Coins, inscriptions, and ancient ruins were of interest not just as relics from the past but as means to reconstruct the past. Petrarch used coins to discover what Roman emperors looked like and in his epic poem *Africa* drew upon the ruins of Rome, which he had visited, in describing the city at the time of the Carthaginians' visit. In 1446, Flavio Biondo produced a topographical description of Rome dependent upon both the literary sources and his personal visits to the ruined sites. The fact that Renaissance scholars frequently misinterpreted antiquities or distorted their antiquarian knowledge is beside the point, for the issue is not their correctness in detail but their methodological procedure.

The discipline of documentary criticism was a specialty of many [[36]] Renaissance scholars. The most outstanding and influential early Renaissance literary critic was Lorenzo Valla (about 1406–57). Petrarch, however, had already (in 1355) used internal and external evidence to prove that a document exempting Austria from the jurisdiction of the Emperor Charles IV was a forgery (see Burke 1969: 50–54). In 1439, Valla disproved the authenticity of the Donation of Constantine in which Constantine had supposedly assigned temporal power over Italy to Pope Sylvester I and his successors. (Otto of Freising and other medieval authors had suspected that the document was a forgery, as did Valla's contemporaries Nicholas of Cusa and Reginald Pecock, independently.)

> The significance of Valla's declamation was neither in applying philological criteria, for Petrarch and others, including canonists, had taken this step, nor in denying the authenticity of the document, which had already been placed in doubt; rather it was in exhibiting the whole array of humanist weapons—polemic and personal vituperation as well as criticism stemming from grammar, logic, geography, chronology, history, and law. (Kelley 1970: 38)

Valla and others applied their literary criticism to numerous documents, both classical and Christian, to prove their inauthenticity or to elucidate their origin and history.

> In 1460, Nicholas of Cusa wrote the *Sieving of the Koran* (cribratio Alcoran) which treated the Koran as Nicholas had already treated the *Donation.* He identified three elements in its composition: Nestorian Christianity, a Jewish adviser of Muhammad, and the corruptions introduced by Jewish "correctors" after Muhammad's death. This was to treat the Koran as a historical document, and to write the history of its leading ideas. (Burke 1969: 59)

The status of the Bible as the word of God exempted it from such treatment for the moment.

The literary legends about national origins and hagiographic legends about the saints were open to criticism by the humanists. Two examples will suffice. The Italian historian, Polydore Vergil, published a history of England in 1534 in which he took up the older attack on Geoffrey of Monmouth's depiction of the Trojan Brutus as the founder of Britain. His basic argument rested on an appeal to the ancient sources: none of the ancient Roman authors and sources make any reference to this Brutus. (Similar attacks were made on other national and foundational legends;

see Burke 1969: 71–75.) In a short biography prefaced to his edition of Jerome's works, Erasmus (in 1516) argued that many of the legendary traditions "contaminate the saints with their old wives' tales, which are childish, ignorant, and [[37]] absurd" and that the best source for knowledge about Jerome was the man himself.

> For who knew Jerome better than Jerome himself? Who expressed his ideas more faithfully? If Julius Caesar is the most reliable source for the events of his own career, is it not all the more reasonable to trust Jerome on his? And so, having gone through all his works, we made a few annotations and presented the results in the form of a narrative, not concealing the fact that we consider it a great enough miracle to have Jerome himself explaining his life to us in all his famous books. If there is anyone who must have miracles and omens, let him read the books about Jerome which contain almost as many miracles as they do sentences. (text in Burke 1969: 70)

The literary study of the early Renaissance humanists was not oriented merely to the detection of forgery and exposure of many venerated traditions as non-historical legends. There was a very positive side to the focus on documentary evidence. "The mere problem of gaining access to the past began to supersede the problem of how to make use of it" (Kelley 1970: 24). The humanists stressed that the recovery of the past through documentary sources had to depend upon philology and grammar. This meant a literal and realistic reading of the sources and at times textual criticism to restore the sources. Valla, in his *Annotations on the New Testament* published by Erasmus in 1505, came close to placing the biblical sources on the same footing with other ancient documents. Valla had also concluded that "none of the words of Christ have come to us, for Christ spoke in Hebrew and never wrote down anything" (quoted in Fryde 1974: 952). Erasmus, who argued for a "return to the sources" (*versetur in fontibus*), defended Valla's position on the need for textual criticism to restore the sources of theology (see Rabil 1972: 58–61). This meant that the reliability of the Old Testament versions must be established on the basis of Hebrew and the New Testament versions on the basis of Greek. (Pope Clement V at the Council of Vienne in 1311–12 had called for the training of teachers in three languages—Greek and Hebrew in addition to Latin.) In interpreting the Bible, Erasmus argued that the role of the grammarian was more important than that of theologian.

> Nor do I assume that theology, the very queen of all disciplines, will think it beneath her dignity if her handmaiden, grammar, offers her help and the required service. For even if grammar is somewhat lower in dignity than other disciplines, there is no other more necessary. She busies herself

with very small questions, without which no one progresses to the large. She argues about trifles which lead to serious matters. If they answer that theology is too important to be limited by grammatical rules and that this [[38]] whole affair of exegeting depends on the inspiration of the Holy Spirit, then this is indeed a new honor for the theologian that he alone is allowed to speak like a barbarian. (quoted in Rabil 1972: 59)

In spite of Erasmus' emphasis on grammar in the understanding of the biblical text, he refused to disavow allegorical interpretation, although he warned that it should not be overdone, should apply everything to Christ, and requires a pious mind (see Rabil 1972: 109–13). Here he shows himself closer kin to Augustine than to Valla.

The trivial concerns of the grammarian or the "very small questions" grammar asks—to use Erasmus' terminology—were part of a major revolution in thought. The difference between the medieval interpretative gloss on a text and the grammatical analysis of a text is enormous; they belong to two different worlds of thought. The humanists of the Renaissance openly broke with the scholastic method, caustically opposed it, and asserted the superiority of their new methods. Valla declared:

> The discourse of historians exhibits more substance, more practical knowledge, more political wisdom . . . , more customs, and more learning of every sort than the precepts of any philosophers. Thus we show that historians have been superior to philosophers. (quoted in Kelley 1970: 19)

The difference between scholasticism and humanism in the Renaissance period has been described in the following terms:

> By proliferating abstractions and superfluous distinctions, scholastic philosophy had lost contact with concrete reality. It had cut men off from meaning, hence from their own humanity. Valla's philosophy, on the other hand, emphasized precisely these standards—concreteness, utility, and humanity. . . . Indeed, a return to reality may be taken as the slogan of Valla's entire philosophy. (Kelley 1970: 29)

The quest or return to reality was not only the source of the humanistic or historical revolution of the Renaissance but also the basis for the scientific revolution which had its roots in the same period (see Grant). Science had to overcome the legacy of Aristotelian scholasticism. It is difficult to overstate the importance of the scientific revolution, which reached a climax in the sixteenth and seventeenth centuries, for all aspects of life including biblical studies, although Butterfield seems to have been successful in this regard:

> Since that revolution overturned the authority in science not only of the middle ages but of the ancient world—since it ended not only in the eclipse

[[39]] of scholastic philosophy but in the destruction of Aristotelian physics—it outshines everything since the rise of Christianity and reduces the Renaissance and Reformation to the rank of mere episodes, mere internal displacements, within the system of medieval Christendom. (Butterfield 1949: vii)

Mechanics and astronomy were the first scientific disciplines to develop.

These new approaches to reality were concerned with questions of explanation and causation in both natural and human orders. The way was opened for a view of the world which operated according to "natural law" even if that law be understood as the will of God. The historical implication of such a view is enormous: man can understand past events as analogous to present events. Human, climatic, geographical, and other factors could be viewed as causal elements in historical events both past and present. This rise of explanation in historical studies marked a significant development in historiography.

> In medieval historical writing there are explanations of an extremely specific kind, in terms of the motives of individuals; there are also explanations of an extremely general kind, in terms of the hand of God in history, or the decay of the world; but middle-range explanations are lacking. (Burke 1969: 77)

These "middle-range explanations"—what today we would call sociological, economical, geographical, climatic considerations—have their beginnings in the Renaissance (see the collection of texts in Burke 1969: 77–104).

The Protestant Reformation of the sixteenth century, which in many ways represents merely a radical and religious application of Renaissance principles and aims, made at least four significant contributions that were ultimately of great importance in the history of Hebrew historiography.

First of all, the reformers placed the Bible at the centre of the theological enterprise. *Sola scriptura* [['scripture only']] was the keynote of the Reformation (see Kraus 1956: 6–9). In emphasizing the Bible as the rule and norm of faith, the reformers stressed a literal interpretation of the scriptures. Luther wrote:

> The Holy Spirit is the plainest writer and speaker in heaven and earth, and therefore His words cannot have more than one, and that the very simplest, sense, which we call the literal, ordinary, natural sense.
>
> All heresies and error in Scripture have not arisen out of the simple words of Scripture. . . . All error arises out of paying no regard to the plain words [[40]] and, by fabricated inferences and figures of speech, concocting arbitrary interpretations in one's own brain.
>
> In the literal sense there is life, comfort, strength, learning, and art. Other interpretations, however appealing, are the work of fools.

In addition to an emphasis on the literal reading of scripture, the reformers argued that scripture is its own interpreter. Luther declared:

> Scripture itself by itself is the most unequivocal, the most accessible, the most comprehensible authority, itself its own interpreter, attesting, judging, illuminating all things.

(For the above texts, see Kümmel 1972–73: 20–23.) This emphasis upon a literal reading of the scriptures, which had earlier been stressed in Judaism over against a christocentric reading of the Old Testament, did not immediately produce any critical-historical approach to the Bible. Even Luther retained a prophetic-christocentric attitude towards the Old Testament. The idea of the divine inspiration of scripture or the Bible as the word of God halted the reformers short of any really critical approach, although Luther relegated Hebrews, James, Jude, and Revelation to an appendix in his New Testament translation primarily because of theological reasons which he buttressed with an appeal to the dispute over these documents in the early church (see Kümmel 1972–73: 24–26). Matthias Flacius Illyricus' *Clavis scripturae sacrae* (1567), one of the first handbooks on biblical hermeneutics, is representative of Protestantism's stress on the importance of the literal or grammatical sense, but warns that there are no contradictions in scripture and that exegesis must be in agreement with faith (for excerpts from his work, see Kümmel 1972–73: 27–30). This emphasis on the literal reading of the biblical materials was ultimately to make literary-critical analysis not only possible but also necessary.

A second contribution of the reformers was an iconoclastic attitude towards tradition. This phenomenon was widely current in many circles during the times as previous examples have shown. The reformers sought to restore the purity of the church and return to the origins; components and traditions which appeared to have intervened extraneously could be repudiated. Such attitudes, however, fostered a sense of criticism although it was much easier to be critical of post-biblical than biblical traditions. An example of a significant critique of an ancient and venerated tradition is represented by Carolus Sigonius who challenged the traditional Jewish view of the origin of the synagogue. An expert on Greek and Roman institutions, Sigonius, in his *De republica Hebraeorum libri VII* (1583), argued as follows regarding the antiquity of the synagogue:

> [[41]] The origin of the synagogue is by no means an old one. We find, indeed, no mention of it [in scripture] either in the history of the Judges or in the history of the Kings. If it is at all admissible to venture a conjecture in this kind of antiquity, I would surmise that synagogues were first erected in the Babylonian exile for the purpose that those who have been deprived of the temple of Jerusalem, where they used to pray and teach,

would have a certain place similar to the temple, in which they could assemble and perform the same kind of service. (quoted by I. Sonne, *IDB* 1.478)

Many concepts, positions, and traditions, however, were taken over uncritically by the reformers. Both Luther and Melanchthon accepted the four monarchies approach to world history. The Frenchman Jean Bodin, in his *Method for the Easy Understanding of Histories* (1566), thus sensed he was breaking new ground when he included an essay on the "refutation of those who postulate four monarchies and the golden age."

A third contribution of the Reformation and the Catholic Counter-Reformation can be seen in the fact that the history of the church became a dominant issue in the struggles within the church in the sixteenth and seventeenth centuries. Historiography was a major weapon in both arsenals. Protestants argued that the teachings of Jesus and the faith of the primitive church had become distorted by the hierarchy of the church. (They differed among themselves as to the precise date at which the apostasy occurred.) Catholics sought to prove that the church at the time was the true successor of primitive Christianity and that the church was basically the same as it had always been. Luther and Calvin's writings reflect the general Protestant view of church history (on Luther, see Headley) although Luther wrote in the introduction to Robert Barnes' *Vitae Romanorum pontificum* (1535) that it was a wonderful delight and the greatest joy to see that history, as well as scripture, could be used to attack the papacy. In Eusebian fashion, historians on both sides turned again to the extensive study and employment of documents, to even a greater extent than many humanist historians, who, especially in Italy, were more interested in literary form than documentation, being strongly influenced by the rhetorical tradition (see Reynolds). The greatest monuments to this historical controversy are the thirteen-volume *Historia ecclesiae Christi* (1559–74) produced by the Magdeburg Centuriators, under the leadership of Matthias Flacius, and the twelve-volume rejoinder, *Annales ecclesiastici*, by Caesar Baronius. (On the historical controversy, see Pullapilly 1975: especially 144–77.) As a result of this use of historiography as a battlefield, ecclesiastical history in the sixteenth and [[42]] seventeenth centuries displayed a greater erudition, a more minute analysis of sources, and a more historiographic sophistication than secular history. Unfortunately none of this energy and insight was applied to the study of Israelite and Judaean history, although the issue established history as an important element in religious controversy.

The fourth significant development which grew out of the Reformation was religious freedom which allowed for enormous theological diversity. The rejection of authoritarianism in tradition, priesthood, and religious practice permitted an increased appeal to private judgment,

often, of course, uncompromisingly certain that it reflected the true biblical and Christian point of view. Thus theological positions were capable of
absorbing modernity while claiming to be founded upon true antiquity.
This permitted significant shifts on the questions of authority and revelation which made biblical criticism not only possible but sometimes desirable. "The exercise of private judgment permitted the Protestant not
so much to avoid as to conclude compromises: he could come to terms
with the new ideas around him" (Gay 1968: 19). Protestantism thus had a
built-in flexibility which made accommodation possible.

> It is to Calvin's great credit that he recognized the discrepancy between
> the scientific world system of his days and the biblical text, and secondly,
> that he did not repudiate the results of scientific research on that ac-
> count. (Hooykaas 1956: 136)

The Italians, Lelio (1525–62) and Faustus Socinus (1539–1604), with their
moderate unitarian theology and their assumption that the veracity of
scripture should be subjected to rational judgment, were among the first
to formulate a view of religion whose modernity even antagonized the reformers (see Scholder 1966: 34–55; Kraus 1956: 41–43).

Following the Council of Trent (1545–63), which reaffirmed the Vul-
gate canon and text of the Bible but recommended the latter's revision, a
long debate ensued between Catholics and Protestants and among Protestants themselves over which Old Testament text—Latin, Greek, or Hebrew—was authoritative. Even the inspiration of the Hebrew vowel points
became involved (see Diestel 1869: 253f., 326–28; Allen 1949: 39–65). The
attempts to decide such issues led to heated controversy and, though perhaps not widely recognized, to humans sitting in judgment over the text.

The reformers had argued that a person could interpret the scriptures aided by divine light or *fides divina*. Luther, at the Diet of [[43]]
Worms (1521), had spoken of being "convinced by the testimony of the
scriptures or by clear reason" (text in Kümmel 1958: 20). Gradually the
fides divina had to give more and more to "clear reason" and the divine or
inward light tended to become "really the *Lumen naturale* [['light of nature']] under a mask" (Allen 1949: 45). The seventeenth century witnessed
the dethronement of the Bible as the authoritative source of knowledge
and understanding and saw biblical interpreters and historians utilizing
the products of the *lumen naturale* (see Scholder for seventeenth-century
developments and biblical studies).

The heliocentric theory in astronomy, expounded in Copernicus' *De
revolutionibus orbium coelestium* and opposed by Luther and Melanchthon,
was undergirded by Kepler's mathematical work and Galileo's theory of
dynamics and his invention of the telescope. Kepler suggested that sci-

ence should be used in understanding the Bible and proposed (in 1606) that the Bethlehem star was due to the unusual conjunction of Mars, Saturn, and Jupiter in the sign of Taurus in 6 B.C.E. The discovery and exploration of new lands brought to attention the existence of peoples beyond the purview of the biblical texts. Travel accounts reported on the life and customs of distant lands. For the first time—in the writings of figures like Pietro della Valle and Michael Nau—reports on monuments, sites, and life in Palestine became known. The scientific revolution possessed its philosophical counterpart in the thought of Francis Bacon and René Descartes. Based on an empirical and critical approach to all knowledge, the new philosophy sought, as Bacon stated, "a total reconstruction of sciences, arts, and all human knowledge, raised upon proper foundations." The establishment of history as an independent discipline in the major universities necessitated the self-consciousness of the field as a "science." The earliest professors of history were primarily commentators on the writings of ancient historians. The first professor of history at Cambridge University was dismissed in 1627 because his comments on Tacitus were considered politically dangerous. (Hobbes in *Leviathan*, written in 1651, commented: "As to rebellion in particular against monarchy, one of the most frequent causes of it, is the reading of the books of policy, and histories of the ancient Greeks, and Romans. . . . From the reading, I say, of such books, men have undertaken to kill their kings" [chap. 29].) Historians produced manuals on the art of history writing and the use and criticism of documents. The most important of the latter was Jean Mabillon's *De re diplomatica* (1681). Generally, in the seventeenth century, antiquarian or archaeological and historical concerns were pursued separately. The former was undertaken, with some [[44]] exceptions, by dilettantes possessed by an abundance of leisure and some interest in the arts and travel. Much energy and money were expended to secure artifacts for the adornment of museums and living rooms. Near the end of the century efforts were made to combine historical and antiquarian interests; some scholars went so far as to claim the superiority of archaeological over literary evidence in reconstructing history (see Momigliano 1950: 14). The seventeenth century was also a time of general questioning of authority, both political and religious, as the Puritan movement and the Cromwellian revolution in England demonstrate.

The impact of the intellectual climate of the seventeenth century upon the study of biblical history can be illustrated through the selection of three examples: the desire to produce a definitive biblical chronology, the attempt to defend a literal interpretation of biblical events through the use of the new sciences, and the growing literary-critical approach to Old Testament documents.

In 1583, Scaliger (1540–1609), the most outstanding philologist of his day, published his *De emendatione temporum*, which provided a synchronized world chronology incorporating Greek, Roman, and Jewish calculations and utilizing recent astronomical discoveries. In 1606, he published his *Thesaurus temporum*, a collection of every chronological relic extant in Greek and Latin. The most influential biblical chronology in the English-speaking world was published in 1650–54 by the Irish bishop James Ussher (1581–1656). In the preface to his *Annales Veteris et Novi Testamenti*, Ussher confidently assured the reader:

> If anyone well seen in the knowledge not only of sacred and exotic history, but of astronomical calculation, and the old Hebrew calendar, should apply himself to these studies, I judge it indeed difficult, but not impossible, for such a one to attain, not only the number of years, but even of days from the creation of the world.

Of the date of creation, he wrote:

> In the beginning, God created Heaven and Earth, Genesis 1, verse 1, which beginning of time, according to our chronologers, fell upon the entrance of the night preceding the 23rd day of October in the year of the Julian Calendar, 710 . . . Marginal note: the year before Christ, 4004. (texts in Burke 1969: 47f.)

Subsequently, Ussher's chronological calculations were placed in the margin of the King James Version of the scriptures. Chronographers, [[45]] of course, differed in their calculations, but many of the scientific minds of the seventeenth century sought to establish scientifically the biblical chronological data. Even so great a mathematical mind as that of Isaac Newton, in a work published posthumously in 1733, sought to demonstrate the accuracy of the predictions in Daniel when applied to papal power. He also sought to make biblical chronology agree with the course of nature, astronomy, sacred history, and the classical histories, especially Herodotus.

One of the most debated topics in the seventeenth century was Noah's flood—its historicity, nature, and extent. In a classical study, Allen has shown how all the sciences of the time were drawn upon to expound the flood in a literal sense and to explain it in rational terms. Scholars discussed the chronology of the flood, the size of the ark, the number and names of the animals, the amount of food needed to feed the ark's passengers, and so on. The most vexing problem was, of course, the question of the origin of sufficient water to flood the entire earth to a depth of fifteen cubits. With the discovery of new lands and new animals, living quarters on the ark became more crowded. Even astronomical phenomena, such as comets, were brought into the picture as explanations. A local flood theory developed when reasonable arguments for a universal flood wore thin. Such an enormous superstructure of arguments was developed to support a literal flood until the whole thing was doomed to topple from its own weight. What resulted from such attempts to support the literal historicity of biblical narratives was a "rational exegesis, a form of pious explanation that innocently damned the text that is expounded." "Theologians now required the Bible to conform to the reason of men" (Allen 1949: 65, 89f.).

A third seventeenth-century development was the application of literary and documentary criticism to the Old Testament, especially the pentateuch. Documentary criticism meant that questions about the origin, nature, and historical reliability were to be asked of the biblical materials. Earlier scholars, such as Isaac ben Suleiman in the tenth century, Ibn Ezra in the twelfth century, [[A. B.]] Carlstadt and others in the sixteenth century, had raised questions about the Mosaic authorship of the pentateuch. The significant biblical critics of the seventeenth century were Thomas Hobbes (1588–1679), an English philosopher, Benedict de Spinoza (1632–77), a Dutch-Jewish philosopher, Hugh Grotius (1583–1645), a Dutch jurist and theologian, and Richard Simon (1638–1712), a French Catholic priest (see Gray 1923: 75–115; Knight 1973: 39–54, and bibliography given there).

Spinoza outlined the programme of biblical criticism.

[[46]] The history of the scriptures should . . . teach us to understand the various vicissitudes that may have befallen the books of the prophets whose tradition has been handed down to us; the life, character and aim of the author of each book; the part which he played; at what period, on what occasion, for whom and in what language he composed his writings. Nor is that enough; we must know the fortune of each book in particular, the circumstances in which it was originally composed, into what hands it subsequently fell, the various lessons it has been held to convey, by whom it was included in the sacred canon, and, finally, how all these books came to be embodied in a single collection. (Spinoza, *Tractatus theologica-politicus*, 7)

Several assumptions can be discerned in this newly budding biblical criticism. (1) The Bible is to be subjected to critical study just as any other book. (2) The biblical material has a history of transmission which can be elucidated by determining the various circumstances through which it passed. (3) Internal statements, styles, and repetitions make it possible to deny single and Mosaic authorship of the pentateuch. It should be noted that Grotius, Hobbes, and Spinoza had moved away from the typical Jewish and Protestant view of religious authority and revelation and that their criticism was probably the result rather than the cause of such a move.

The most important and influential seventeenth-century biblical critic was Simon (see Hazard 1935: 180–97, for a perceptive essay on him). As a Catholic, Simon sought to show that Protestantism's reliance upon the Bible was not as sound a principle as the Catholic reliance upon Bible, tradition, and the church. He stressed the importance of a thorough knowledge of Hebrew for Old Testament study as well as textual criticism and philology. Simon emphasized the process by which the biblical materials were transmitted, pointing to their supplementation and alteration. Claiming inspiration for the revisers of the materials, on the analogy of church tradition, Simon argued that those who had the power to write the sacred books also had the power to revise them. Simon deliberately stressed the word "critic" and "criticism" in his writing, using it in the title of practically all his works. He explained the usage this way:

> My readers must not be surprised if I have sometimes availed myself of expressions that may sound a little strangely in their ears. Every art has its own peculiar terminology, which is regarded more or less as its inviolable property. It is in this specialized sense that I have employed the words *critic* and *criticism* . . . together with some others of the same nature, to which I was obliged to have recourse in order to express myself in the terms proper to the art of which I was treating. These terms will come as no novelty to [[47]] scholars, who have for some time been accustomed to their use in our language. (quoted from Hazard 1935: 182)

Simon addressed his writings to the general educated audience, and wrote in French, not Latin, and his *Histoire critique du Vieux Testament*, published in 1678, had, by 1700, gone through four Latin, two English, and seven French editions. The object of multiple attacks for its questioning of venerated traditions and positions, the book was condemned by the Congregation of the Index in 1683.

The humanists' and reformers' insistence on a "return to the sources" and a literal reading of the text had been based on the conviction that there one could find the pristine faith, piety, and history. This confidence was to be shattered on the rocks of biblical criticism. What literary criticism found in the Bible was to produce a quagmire that was increasingly to absorb scholarly attention.

In the eighteenth century, and for the first time in Western history, a diversity of philosophical-theological systems with scholarly respectability competed in the intellectual market-place. These included a variety of approaches to Christian theism ranging from scholasticism to experiential pietism, Pyrrhonic agnosticism, atheism, and pragmatic rationalism (see Hazard 1935 for the general background and Barth 1972: 33–173, for a descriptive analysis). The sanctity of tradition, the customs of culture, and the regulations of the market-place all favoured the theistic option; however, Christianity and the Bible were subjected to an unprecedented and trenchant examination and critique. The agent of this activity was deism.

Deism's roots can be traced to various earlier influences and anticipatory figures. McKee has done this in the case of Isaac de la Peyrère, who in 1655 published a work advancing such hypotheses as the existence of men before the creation of Adam and the non-Mosaic authorship of the pentateuch. Gay provides a good description of the exponents of the movement:

> All deists were . . . both critical and constructive. . . . All sought to destroy in order to build, and reasoned either from the absurdity of Christianity to the need for a new philosophy or from their desire for a new philosophy to the absurdity of Christianity. . . . Deism . . . is the product of the confluence of three strong emotions: hate, love, and hope. The deists hated priests and priestcraft, mystery-mongering, and assaults on common sense. They loved the ethical teachings of the classical philosophers, the grand unalterable regularity of nature, the sense of freedom granted the man liberated from superstition. They hoped that the problems of life—of private conduct and public policy—could be solved by the application of unaided human reason, and that the mysteries of the universe could be, if [[48]] not solved, at least defined and circumscribed by man's scientific inquiry. (Gay 1968: 13)

Various stances towards the Bible were taken by the deists, but as a rule, they sought to distil the biblical traditions, to siphon off the supernatural, the miraculous, and the unbelievable, and to leave behind the pure essence of a reasonable faith. (On deism, see the readings in Waring 1967 and Gay 1968; for descriptive discussions, see Stephen 1876 and Cragg 1964.)

During the height of the deistic controversy in England (1700–1750), two major studies of Israelite and Judaean history were published. Prideaux's work, which covers the period from the reign of Tiglath-pileser III to the lifetime of Jesus, comprises three volumes which totalled almost 1,400 pages. The work went through over a score of editions and was translated into German and French. Prideaux relied primarily upon the biblical traditions and Josephus, but made use of practically every known literary document from antiquity. Only occasionally did Prideaux take a critical attitude towards his sources. He challenged the authenticity of the letter of Aristeas and its account of the origin of the LXX and provided the reader with a history and description of the study of the LXX (Prideaux 1824: 2.264–98). Prideaux disagreed with Josephus on Alexander's route to Jerusalem (2.132) and argued that the synagogue had its origin in the days of Ezra (2:12f.).

Shuckford wrote his volumes to present the history from creation to the point where Prideaux had begun. Like his predecessors, from the fourth century on, Shuckford presented universal history in a biblical perspective, beginning with Adam and Eve. This was still the classical model. Sir Walter Raleigh had started at this point in his widely used *History of the World*, published in 1614, and although unfinished it covered history down to the Roman period. Basically the same model was employed in the multi-volume *An Universal History from the Earliest Time to the Present*, written by a consortium of scholars, mostly from Oxford and Cambridge, and published in 1736–50 (see Southern 1971: 178f.). Shuckford, like Prideaux, was thoroughly familiar with all the ancient sources as well as the history of research. Both, for example, used, quoted, and opposed Spinoza and Simon. Shuckford's work, which was never completed beyond the time of Joshua, was, perhaps because of the biblical material covered, more influenced by the deistic controversy than that of Prideaux. In describing the magicians at the court of Pharaoh, Shuckford presents them as deistic philosophers:

> [[49]] In Moses' time, the rulers of the Egyptian nation, . . . were then the most learned body in the world, *beguiled by the deceit of vain philosophy*. . . . The Pagan divinations, arts of prophecy, and all their sorceries and enchantments, as well as their idolatry and worship of false gods, were founded, not upon superstition, but upon learning and philosophical study; not upon too great a belief of, and adherence to revelation, but upon a pretended knowledge of the powers of nature. Their great and learned men erred in these points, not for want of freethinking, such as they called so; but their opinions upon these subjects were in direct opposition to the true revelations which had been made to the world, and might be called the deism of these ages; for such certainly was the religion of the governing and learned part of the Heathen world in these times. (Shuckford 1810: 1.565–66)

Like his predecessors, Shuckford stretched his intellectual powers in defence of the biblical chronology, arguing that the antediluvians enjoyed longevity because before the flood the earth was situated so as to have a perpetual equinox, thus sparing its inhabitants the rigours of seasonal change (Shuckford 1810: 1.20f.). He argued that "at the flood, the heavens underwent some change: the motion of the sun was altered, and a year, or annual revolution of it, became, as it now is, five days and almost six hours longer than it was before" (1.iii). However, Shuckford, who was thoroughly familiar with the problems of textual criticism, was occasionally willing to amend the Hebrew text on the basis of the Greek (for example, Deut 34:6 should read 'they buried him'; Shuckford 1810: 2.229; thus Moses did not write the account of his death). He sensed the problem of the divine names in Genesis and Exodus, and devoted an extended discussion to the use of the names Jehovah, El Shaddai, and Elohim (1.517–30).

His solution to the problem was not to postulate a multiplicity of documents but to theorize about the diversity of persons in the godhead.

Outside England, the deist impulse led to some very scathing attacks on Christianity and the Bible. The Frenchman Voltaire (1694–1778) never tired of pointing out what he called the absurdities, inconsistencies, and low morality found in the Bible. To claim that God was its author was to make "of God a bad geographer, a bad chronologist, a bad physicist; it makes him no better a naturalist" (quoted in Appelgate 1974: 26). To claim that Moses wrote the pentateuch was to claim Moses to be a fool. Voltaire suggested that much of the Old Testament was borrowed by the Jews from other peoples, and proposed that Moses may have never lived: "If there only were some honest and natural deeds in the myth of Moses, one could believe fully that such a personage did exist" (quoted in Appelgate 1974: 102). The significance of Voltaire was his popularization, [[50]] in caustic language, of many of the issues which had previously been the concerns of erudite scholars. Voltaire, however, approached the Bible and its historical materials not so much as a critic but as an assassin.

In Germany, the impact of deism can be seen in the work of H. S. Reimarus (1694–1768) who, at his death, left behind what the philosopher Lessing published as the *Wolfenbüttel Fragments*. One of these fragments was an essay on "the passage of the Israelites through the Red Sea" (for a selection, see Gay 1968: 158–63; for a study of Reimarus and the Old Testament, see Reventlow 1965). Reimarus sought to show the impossibilities in a literal interpretation of the biblical description of the crossing of the sea. According to Exod 12:37f., about six hundred thousand Hebrew men left Egypt not counting the women, children, and mixed multitude and animals which accompanied them. Reimarus says this would give a figure of about three million people, three hundred thousand oxen and cows, and six hundred thousand sheep and goats. Approximately five thousand wagons would have been needed to carry provisions and three hundred thousand tents would have been required to house the people at ten per tent. Had the multitude marched ten abreast, the three million would have formed a column one hundred and eighty miles long. It would have required nine days as a minimum for such a group to march through the parted sea. Reimarus' arguments, and there were others who made similar points, hit at the very heart of those who took the Bible as literally inspired and as factually infallible.

Among the founding fathers of the United States were many with deistic leanings. Jefferson edited a version of the New Testament devoid of any miracles and concluding with the death of Jesus. Thomas Paine, an Englishman who spent several years in the U.S. supporting the Revolutionary War and some time in France in exile, was a brutal controversialist in his attack upon the Bible. "Paine's peculiarity consists in the freshness with which he comes upon very old discoveries, and the vehemence with which he announces them" (Stephen 1876: 1.461). In his book *The Age of Reason*, Paine wrote:

> Whenever we read the obscene stories, the voluptuous debaucheries, the cruel and torturous executions, the unrelenting vindictiveness, with which more than half the Bible is filled, it would be more consistent that we called it the word of a demon than the word of God. It is a history of wickedness that has served to corrupt and brutalize mankind; and, for my part, I sincerely detest it, as I detest everything that is cruel. . . . Speaking for myself, if I had no other evidence that the Bible is fabulous than the [[51]] sacrifice I must make to believe it to be true, that alone would be sufficient to determine my choice. (see the selection from Paine in Gay 1968: 164–76)

The significance of the deistic movement and the enlightenment of the eighteenth century was not in the area of historiography *per se*. The deists, in their discussions of the Bible and the history portrayed in the Bible, presented the issues of biblical criticism to the general public. In addition, their scathing attacks on the defences supporting a factual, literal reading of the text were devastating. It would never again be easy to present Israelite and Judaean history by simply retelling and amplifying the biblical narratives.

Several developments, in addition to the deistic controversy, occurred in the eighteenth century which should be noted since they were greatly to affect the study of Israelite and Judaean history. The use of ancient literature in comparative studies of the Old Testament became more common and less apologetic. In 1685, John Spencer, of Corpus Christi College in Cambridge, published his *De legibus Hebraeorum ritualibus et earum rationibus* in which he compared the ritual laws of the Old Testament with relevant material from Egypt, Greece, and Rome. Comparative study, as the deists demonstrated, could cut in two directions; it could be used to support either the uniqueness or the dependency of the biblical materials. The study of Palestinian geography was advanced by Hadrian Reland's *Palaestina ex monumentis veteribus illustrata* (1714) and the pioneer work in Palestinian antiquities, *Compendium antiquitatum Hebraeorum*, by Johann David Michaelis, appeared in 1753.

The basic elements in the documentary criticism of the Old Testament were established during this time. The German pastor Henning Bernhard Witter (1683–1715) and the French physician Jean Astruc (1684–1766) laid down some of the criteria for source criticism of the pentateuch. The classic four-source theory of the pentateuch was to be worked out in the nineteenth century but the five pillars of documentary criticism were established in the eighteenth. These pillars are (1) the use of different names for the deity, (2) varieties of language and style, (3) contradictions and divergences, (4) repetitions and duplications, and (5) indications of composite structure.

A third phenomenon to be noted is the maturation of the science of Old Testament introduction. Pioneers in this area were Michaelis and Johann Salomo Semler (see Kraus 1956: 97–113; Kümmel 1958: 62–73; and on Semler, see Hornig 1961). Both of these men were influenced by English deism (see Kümmel 1958: 415 nn. 59, 63). With Johann Gottfried Eichhorn's [[52]] *Einleitung in das Alte Testament* (1780–83), the basic problems of Old Testament introduction—growth of the canon, history of the text, and origin and nature of the individual books—were discussed in handbook form. With Eichhorn, the humanistic argument that the literature of the Old Testament should be investigated like any other literature was integrated into the mainstream of Protestant biblical study.

A fourth factor in the eighteenth century was the poetic or "romantic" reaction to the classicism and rationalism of the enlightenment. In Old Testament studies, this movement is most closely associated with the work and thought of Johann Gottfried Herder (1744–1803), who was influenced by such figures as Jean-Jacques Rousseau (1712–78), Johann Georg Hamann (1730–88), and Robert Lowth (1710–87). The latter's *De sacra poesi Hebraeorum* (1753) studied Hebrew poetry along the lines of research applied to Greek and Latin poetry, arguing that poetry represented man's earliest form of speech and was as expressive of truth as philosophy. The pietist Hamann had also expressed an emphasis on poetry as the mother-tongue of the human race, and like most pietists, stressed the reader's immediacy to the biblical materials. Rousseau glorified primitive man as a free and happy being living in accordance with nature and instinct, and for whom language was his basic expression of the natural and communal spirit. (On Herder's broad concerns and their relationship to enlightenment thought, see Berlin 1965; on his hermeneutics, see Frei 1974: 183–201.) Herder emphasized the necessity of entering empathetically into the human world out of which the Bible had come, rather than seeking understanding merely through critical and technical analysis. He was more interested in the group than the individual and in the manner in which the group gave expression to its distinctive culture, not necessarily according to any universal laws. Cultures are like plants which grow in unique ways dependent upon the situation of the place, the circumstances of the times and the generative character of the people. Whatever can take place among mankind does take place; life does not operate along rationalistic lines. Herder's approach to the human past stressed an appreciative and imaginative relationship to the "spirit" and not a rational, judgmental relationship. (See Scholder 1962; and Willi 1971 on Herder's general contributions to Old Testament study.)

A final development in eighteenth-century Old Testament research was the introduction of mythological study. The systematic study of classical mythology originated with the German classicist Christian Gottlob Heyne (1729–1812) who argued that myth was [[53]] one of primitive man's basic modes of expressing his experiences and understanding of life and nature. The first application of mythological studies to the Old Testament was made by Eichhorn, a student of Heyne at Göttingen, who published a work on Genesis 1–3 entitled *Die Urgeschichte* (1779). Eichhorn's work, which was greatly influenced by Lowth, was taken up by Johann Philipp Gabler (1753–1826). The concept of myth, when applied to parts of the Old Testament, greatly affected the manner in which scholars examined these materials and naturally led directly to the question of the historical factuality of their content. Later, what could be labelled as mythical was removed from the arena of the historical. (On the early stages of mythological research on the Old Testament see Hartlich and Sachs 1952: 1–53, and Rogerson 1974: 1–15.)

The Nineteenth Century

S. W. Baron, *History and Jewish Historians*, 1964; F. J. Bliss, *The Development of Palestine Exploration*, New York: Charles Scribner's Sons 1906; F. G. Bratton, *A History of Egyptian Archaeology*, New York: Thomas Y. Crowell 1968; C. A. Briggs, *The Higher Criticism of the Hexateuch*, New York: Charles Scribner's Sons 1893, ²1897; [[J. Bright, *A History of Israel*, Philadelphia/London: Westminster Press/SCM Press 1959, ²1972;]] J. E. Carpenter, *The Bible in the Nineteenth Century*, London: Longmans, Green and Co. 1903; T. K. Cheyne, *Founders of Old Testament Criticism*, London: Methuen & Co. 1893; [[H. G. A. Ewald, *Geschichte des Volkes Israels bis Christus* 1–5, Göttingen: Dieterichschen Buchhandlung, 1843–55, ²1851–59, ³1864–68 (seven volumes) = *The History of Israel* 1–6, London: Longmans, Green, and Co. 1869–83;]] G. P. Gooch, *History and Historians in the Nineteenth Century*, London: Longmans, Green & Co. 1913, ²1952; [[H. H. Graetz, *Geschichte der Juden von den ältesten Zeiten bis auf die Gegenwart* 1–11, Leipzig: O. Leiner 1861–75 = *History of the Jews* (abridged) 1–6, Philadelphia: The Jewish Publication Society of America 1891–98; S. Herrmann, *Geschichte Israels in alttestamentlicher Zeit*, Munich: Chr. Kaiser 1973 = *A History of Israel in Old Testament Times*, London/Philadelphia: SCM Press/Fortress Press 1975;]] H. V. Hilprecht, *Explorations in Bible Lands during the Nineteenth Century*, Philadelphia/Edinburgh: A. J. Holman & Co./T. & T. Clark 1903; E. G. Kraeling, *The Old Testament since the Reformation*, London/New York: Lutterworth Press/Harper & Brothers 1955; New York: Schocken Books 1969; H.-J. Kraus, *Geschichte der historisch-kritischen Erforschung des Alten Testaments*, Neukirchen-Vluyn: Neukirchener Verlag, 1956, ²1969; S. Lloyd, *Foundations in the Dust: A Story of Mesopotamian*

Exploration, London: Oxford University Press 1947; Harmondsworth/Baltimore: Penguin Books 1955; R. A. S. Macalister, *A Century of Excavation in Palestine*, London: Religious Tract Society 1925; [[H. H. Milman, *The History of the Jews, from the Earliest Period down to Modern Times*, London: John Murray 1829; quoted from Harper's Family Library edition, New York 1834;]] L. Perlitt, *Vatke und Wellhausen*, BZAW 94, 1965; [[H. Prideaux, *The Old and New Testament Connected in the History of the Jews and Neighbouring Nations, from the Declension of the Kingdoms of Israel and Judah to the Time of Christ* 1–2, London: R. Knaplock 1717–18; quoted from edition of 1823–24; S. Shuckford, *The Sacred and Profane History of the World Connected, From the Creation of the World to the Dissolution of the Assyrian Empire at the Death of Sardanapalus, and to the Declension of the Kingdom of Judah and Israel under the Reigns of Ahaz and Pekah* 1–2, London: R. Knaplock & J. Tonson 1728–30; quoted from edition of 1810;]] R. J. Thompson, *Moses and the Law in a Century of Criticism since Graf*, SVT 19, 1970; J. Wellhausen, *Geschichte Israels* 1, Berlin: Georg Reimer 1878 = *Prolegomena zur Geschichte Israels*, Berlin: Georg Reimer 1883 = *Prolegomena to the History of Israel*, Edinburgh: A. & C. Black 1885; idem, "Die Composition des Hexateuchs," *JDT* 21, 1876: 392–450, 531–602; 22, 1877: 407–79 = *Die Composition des Hexateuchs und die historischen Bücher des Alten Testaments*, Berlin: Georg Reimer 1899; idem, "Israel," *EnBr* 13, [9]1880, 396–420 = *Prolegomena to the History of Israel*, 427–548; [idem, *Israelitische und jüdische Geschichte*, Berlin: Georg Reimer 1894, [2]1895, [3]1897; reprinted, Berlin: Walter de Gruyter 1958;]] idem, "Heinrich Ewald," [[54]] *Festschrift zur Feier des 150 jährigen Bestehens der Königlichen Gesellschaft der Wissenschaften zu Göttingen*, Berlin: Weidmannsche Verlagsbuchhandlung 1901, 61–81 = idem, *Grundrisse zum Alten Testament*, ed. R. Smend, TB 27, 1965, 120–38; J. A. Wilson, *Signs and Wonders upon Pharaoh: A History of American Egyptology*, Chicago: University of Chicago Press 1964.

Major developments in the nineteenth century which form the background for Israelite historiography may simply be noted since they have been so frequently discussed. In the first place, more liberal stances in theology came to characterize many segments of the religious communities. This liberalism was less dogmatic in its theological orientation, more progressive in its relationship to contemporary culture and thought, and more humanistic in its perspectives than previous generations. This gradual shift can be seen, for example, in the rise of the so-called *Wissenschaft des Judentums* movement which sought "to see in Jewish history the gradual progression of Jewish religious or national spirit in its various vicissitudes and adjustments to the changing environments' (Baron 1964: 76). This liberal spirit, which was now located within the life of the religious communities themselves, was willing to break with traditional beliefs and approaches and to take a more critical attitude towards the biblical materials.

Secondly, major advances were made in general historiography. The nineteenth was the century of history. Of special importance was the development of what has been called a positivistic approach to history, which not only attempted but also believed it possible to reconstruct past history 'as it had actually happened' (*wie es eigentlich gewesen*). The most prominent of these outstanding positivistic historians were Barthold Georg Niebuhr (1776–1831), Leopold Ranke (1795–1885), and Theodor Mommsen (1817–1903). Practically every aspect of human life was subjected to historical exploration in the nineteenth century (for the major developments and historians, see Gooch 1913).

Thirdly, the decipherment of ancient Near Eastern languages—especially Egyptian hieroglyphics and Akkadian cuneiform—opened the long-closed literary remains of Israel's neighbours to study and interpretation (see Lloyd 1947; Bratton 1968; and Wilson 1964). The full impact of these new fields of learning was not to be felt fully until the last years of the nineteenth and the first decades of the twentieth century. Nonetheless, for the first time scholars could examine the literary products of these cultures at first hand and thus were no longer dependent upon the ancient, secondary sources.

[[55]] Fourthly, the exploration of the Near East and Palestine raised historical geography to a level of real competence. Explorers like the Swiss Johann Ludwig Burckhardt (1784–1817) and the American Edward Robinson (1794–1863) whose three-volume work, *Biblical Researches in Palestine, Mount Sinai and Arabia Petraea* (1841), based on his travels in 1838, reported on sites, place-names, and customs and used modern names to identify many places mentioned in the Bible. In 1865, the Palestine Exploration Fund was established and, in 1872–78, it sponsored a geographical survey of western Palestine (the Conder and Kitchener expedition). Other national societies were begun to encourage and finance exploration. Archaeological excavations at several sites in Palestine were undertaken (see Bliss 1906; Hilprecht 1903; and Macalister 1925).

Fifthly, the isolation and dating of the "documents" which went to make up the pentateuch continued apace. The so-called four-source hypothesis which argued that four major documents (J, E, P, D) were redactionally combined to produce the pentateuch gradually came to dominate discussions after mid-century. The character, content, and date of the individual documents were considered of great significance in understanding the religious development of Israelite and Judaean life and in evaluating the historical reliability of the documentary materials. (On the development of critical research, see Briggs 1893; Carpenter 1903; Kraus 1956: 152–308, 242–74; Thompson 1970.)

A survey of Israelite and Judaean history in the nineteenth century can best be made by examining some innovative works from the period. The first work to be noted, and perhaps the first really critical history of Israel ever written, is that by Henry Hart Milman (1791–1868). Milman, a graduate of Oxford University, was ordained in 1816. During his early

days, he wrote poetry and plays and from 1821 to 1831 held a professor-
ship of poetry at Oxford. In 1849, he was appointed dean of St. Paul's.
Most of Milman's rather extensive literary output were works in church
history. His *History of the Jews* was first published in 1829 and met with significant opposition. The work, however, was issued in a number of editions by various publishers until the first decade of the present century.
Of the twenty-eight books in his three-volume history, the final ten are
concerned with the history of the Jews following the Bar-Kochba War.

Milman's history was addressed to the general reading public and
tends to be rather sketchy and to avoid any detailed discussion of controversial points or of methodology. The extent of his familiarity with Old
Testament studies cannot be really determined. Only a few [[56]] isolated
references are made to significant figures, although Milman was acquainted with travel reports on the Near East and Palestine and makes
rather frequent reference to these. Milman adopted a developmental approach to Jewish history:

> Nothing is more curious, or more calculated to confirm the veracity of
> the Old Testament history, than the remarkable picture which it presents
> of the gradual development of human society: the ancestors of the Jews,
> and the Jews themselves, pass through every stage of comparative civili-
> zation. (Milman 1834: 1.v)

Excepting only their knowledge of God and their custodianship of the
promises, "the chosen people appear to have been left to themselves to
pass through the ordinary stages of the social state" (Milman 1834: 1.vi;
see 3.346). Milman approached the Bible with a very limited view of inspiration and noted that "much allowance must . . . be made for the essentially poetic spirit, and for the Oriental forms of speech, which pervade so
large a portion of the Old Testament" (1.viii) and that God "addressed a
more carnal and superstitious people chiefly through their imagination
and senses" (1.vi). He warned his readers that miracle would play little
role in his interpretation of history, noting that those who have criticized
the belief in revelation are "embarrassing to those who take up a narrow
system of interpreting the Hebrew writings; to those who adopt a more rational latitude of exposition, none" (1.xi). Whereas Prideaux and Shuckford were unwilling to accommodate their historical discussions to the
views of the biblical critics, for Milman, there was no other option.

Milman began his history with the patriarchs and made no reference
to the materials in Genesis 1–10. Abraham is described as an "independent
Sheik or Emir" (1.10) or "the stranger sheik" who is allowed "to pitch his
tent, and pasture his flocks and herds" in Canaan (1.20). Milman considered the different stories of the endangering of the wife to be "traditional

variations of the same transactions" (1.20). "Abraham is the Emir of a pastoral tribe, migrating from place to place. . . . He is in no respect superior to his age or country, excepting in the sublime purity of his religion" (1.22f.). In describing patriarchal society, Milman wrote:

> Mankind appears in its infancy, gradually extending its occupancy over regions, either entirely unappropriated, or as yet so recently and thinly peopled, as to admit, without resistance, the new swarms of settlers which seem to spread from the birthplace of the human race, the plains of central Asia. They are peaceful pastoral nomads, travelling on their camels, the ass the only other beast of burthen. . . . The unenterprising shepherds, from [[57]] whom the Hebrews descended, move onward as their convenience or necessity requires, or as richer pastures attract their notice. (Milman 1834: 1.29f.)

The description of the patriarchs as "the hunter, the migratory herdsman, and the incipient husbandman," suggests that the record draws upon "contemporary traditions" (1.32). The Israelite ancestors are thus a *Volk* who differ from their contemporaries only in their theological view of God.

In discussing the stay in Egypt, Milman argued against identifying the period with the Hyksos era but dated it later, refusing however to hypothesize a specific time (1.40–42). He noted that biblical tradition assigns either 430 (MT) or 215 (LXX) years to the stay, but that both of these are irreconcilable with the mere two generations which separated Moses from Levi, a factor which also raised uncertainty about the number of Israelites leaving Egypt (1.48f., 119). Milman described the plagues and the crossing of the Red Sea, but spoke of the "plain leading facts of the Mosaic narrative, the residence of the Hebrews in Egypt, their departure under the guidance of Moses, and the connexion of that departure with some signal calamity, at least for a time fatal to the power and humiliating to the pride of Egypt" (1.73). In describing the crossing of the sea, he refers to a report by Diodorus Siculus concerning the erratic behaviour of the water in the area (1.72; see Herrmann 1975: 63). The quails and manna in the desert are explained in naturalistic terms and the changing of bitter water to sweet is explained chemically. In footnotes in the second edition, Milman reports on the chemical analysis of water especially secured from a Palestinian spring called Marah which suggested high concentrations of "selenite or sulphate of lime" which could be precipitated by "any vegetable substance containing oxalic acid . . . and rendered agreeable and wholesome." He also reports that a traveller had brought him a sample of manna produced by the tamarisk tree (Milman 1834: 1.117).

The pentateuchal legislation—"the Hebrew constitution" (1.79)—is attributed to Moses, "the legislator constantly, yet discreetly, mitigating the savage usages of a barbarous people" (1.113).

The laws of a settled and civilized community were enacted among a wandering and homeless horde who were traversing the wilderness, and more likely, under their existing circumstances, to sink below the pastoral life of their forefathers, than advance to the rank of an industrious agricultural community. Yet, at this time, judging solely from its internal evidence, the law must have been enacted. Who but Moses ever possessed such authority as to enforce submission to statutes so severe and uncompromising? Yet, as Moses incontestably died before the conquest of Canaan, [[58]] his legislature must have taken place in the desert. To what other period can the Hebrew constitution be assigned? To that of the judges? a time of anarchy, warfare, or servitude! To that of the kings? when the republic had undergone a total change! To any time after Jerusalem became the metropolis? when the holy city, the pride and glory of the nation, is not even alluded to in the whole law! After the building of the temple? when it is equally silent as to any settled or durable edifice! After the separation of the kingdoms? when the close bond of brotherhood had given place to implacable hostility! Under Hilkiah? under Ezra? when a great number of the statutes had become a dead letter! The law depended on a strict and equitable partition of the land. At a later period it could not have been put into practice without the forcible resumption of every individual property by the state; the difficulty, or rather impossibility, of such a measure, may be estimated by any reader who is not entirely unacquainted with the history of the ancient republics. In other respects the law breathes the air of the desert. Enactments intended for a people with settled habitations, and dwelling in walled cities, are mingled up with temporary regulations, only suited to the Bedouin encampment of a nomad tribe. (Milman 1834: 1.78f.)

Milman certainly realized that the dating of the law was the central issue in Old Testament interpretation and that when one dates the law is highly determinative for how one writes the history. Also, he raised practically all the possible options for dating the law.

Milman follows the basic biblical account of the conquest and division of the land. The judges of early Israel, whose title is associated with "The Suffetes of the Carthaginians," are described as "military dictators" operating in emergencies within the "boundaries of their own tribe." Their qualifications were their "personal activity, daring, and craft," and they appear "as gallant insurgents or guerilla leaders." In the case of Deborah, several tribes came together in "an organized warlike confederacy." The tribes were disunited because of their disobedience to the Mosaic law and were compelled to arms in furthering the incomplete conquest in "war of the separate tribes against immediate enemies" (Milman 1834: 1.155f.). Although the Bible speaks of the judges being raised up by the Lord, "their particular actions are nowhere attributed to divine action" (1.158f.). The absence of Judah and Simeon from the song of Deborah (Judges 5) suggests that perhaps they "had seceded from the confederacy, or were occupied by enemies of their own" (1.160).

Enough has been said of Milman's work to suggest his approach since many of the basic issues arise in treating the period prior to David. Although Milman was probably the first to treat Israelite and Judaean history from a secular orientation and in the same terms one would write a history of Greece or Rome, his name and an [[59]] exposition of his position are seldom mentioned in surveys of Old Testament studies.

A second innovative work was the lengthy, multi-volume history by Heinrich Georg August Ewald (1803–75), one of the most outstanding Oriental and Semitic scholars of the nineteenth century (on Ewald, see Wellhausen 1901; Cheyne 1893: 66–118; Kraus 1956: 199–205). He was a student and successor of Eichhorn at Göttingen. Ewald's history is as verbose and dull as Milman's is crisp and entertaining.

Almost one half of the first volume of Ewald's history is devoted to the problem of the sources for Israelite history (1843: 1.11–203). Ewald says his "ultimate aim is the knowledge of what really happened—not what was only related and handed down by tradition, but what was actual fact" (1.13). Tradition thus preserves an image of what happened but it is also formed by imagination, which may blur the details or form of the event it remembers, and is shaped by the memory, which tends to obliterate details and contract the overall content (1.14–16). Chronological distance from the events reduces the extent and trustworthiness of the tradition:

> The Hebrew tradition about the earliest times—the main features of which, as we have it, were fixed in the interval from the fourth to the sixth century after Moses—still has a great deal to tell about Moses and his contemporaries; much less about the long sojourn in Egypt, and the three Patriarchs; and almost nothing special about the primitive times which preceded these Patriarchs, when neither the nation, nor even its "fathers," were yet in Canaan. So, too, the Books of Samuel relate many particulars of David's later life passed in the splendour of royalty, but less about his youth before he was king. (Ewald 1869–83: 1.17)

Tradition has supports in songs, proverbs, and personal names, and in visible monuments such as altars, temples, and memorials (Ewald 1869–83: 1.17–21). The strongest support of tradition, however, is the institution such as annually recurring festivals which recall the incidents (1.21f.). Foreign elements also enter traditions: names are added, numbers lose exactness, events shift their chronological moorings, and similar traditions become associated (1.22–26). Tradition rests in imagination and feeling more than understanding and thus is closely associated with nationalistic sentiments (1.26–31). Different events are remembered in different styles of traditions and since tradition is very plastic it may be moulded by religious interests, aetiological concerns, and mythological perspectives (1.31–41).

The earliest Israelite historians found the tradition that they used as "a fluctuating and plastic material, but also a mass of unlimited extent" (1.41). At the writing-down stage, tradition went through [[60]] further change. The modern historian must "distinguish between the story and its foundation, and exclusively . . . seek the latter with all diligence" (1.45).

> Tradition has its roots in actual facts; yet it is not absolutely history, but has a peculiar character and a value of its own. . . . It is our duty to take the tradition just as it expects to be taken—to use it only as a means for discovering what the real facts once were. (Ewald 1869–83: 1.44)

Thus, Ewald has a high regard for tradition's relationship to historical facts and for the historian's ability to use the tradition to discover the facts. By the Mosaic era, writing was known in Israel and a historiography possible (1.49–51).

Ewald divides the historical books into three groups: the Great Book of Origins (the hexateuch), the Great Book of Kings (Judges–Kings + Ruth), and the Great Book of Universal History down to the Greek Times (Chronicles–Ezra–Nehemiah + Esther). Ewald then analyses these great books as to their sources. The basic source of the hexateuch was what Ewald called the "Book of Origins" (what is today called P) which he dated to the period of the early monarchy (1.74–78). This book incorporated older fragments and materials and was subjected to various modifications, prophetic and Deuteronomistic, before it attained its final form at the end of the seventh or the beginning of the sixth century (1.131). In similar manner, Ewald proceeds to analyse the other two historical complexes, their origin, components, modifications, and history.

Before beginning his reconstruction of the history, Ewald discussed some problems of chronology (1.204–13) and general geographical matters (1.214–55). Ewald follows the four-age theory of P and speaks of the three ages of the preliminary history of Israel: creation to Noah, Noah to Abraham, and Abraham to Moses. In discussing the first two ages, Ewald compares the traditions with those of other peoples, discusses the ages of the characters, and avoids any real straightforward statements about the factuality of the materials. Behind the patriarchal figures are to be seen tribal groups. The oldest extant tradition about Abraham is Genesis 14 (1.307). The patriarchal ancestors spoke and thought monotheistically but not quite in the Mosaic form (1.320f.). The Hebrews are pictured entering Egypt at different times in various migrations, beginning in the Hyksos period, but the exodus is not to be associated with the expulsion of the Hyksos (1.388–407).

The Hebrew nation as a theocracy came into being under Moses in the wilderness. The event of the exodus, which inaugurated this period, cannot be fully reconstructed:

> [[61]] Whatever may have been the exact course of this event, whose historical certainty is well established; its momentous results, the nearer as well as the more remote, were sure to be experienced, and are even to us most distinctly visible. (Ewald 1869–83: 2.75)

Under Moses, the golden theocratic age of Israel began, the law was given, and the age reached maturity under his leadership and that of Joshua. From Joshua to the monarchy was a time of the decay of the pure theocracy and the relaxation of the national bond.

Enough has been said of Ewald's work to suggest its general approach. His work was innovative in that it sought to base the discussion of the history on a systematic study of the biblical traditions and sources. Ewald, however, basically adhered to the theological perspective of the biblical text while modifying the miraculous element. As in the Bible, the golden age of Israelite history is the age of Moses. After wading through Ewald's presentation, one possesses the impression of having read a historical commentary on the historical books, but not of having read a history of Israel.

A third innovative history of the nineteenth century was the work by Heinrich Graetz (1817–91). His work is not of major significance *per se* but because it represents the first modern history of ancient Israel and Judah written by a Jew. Graetz had been preceded by his younger Jewish contemporary, Isaac Marcus Jost (1793–1860), whose nine-volume history of the Jews from Maccabaean times until the nineteenth century was the first major Jewish history in modern times (on Jost, see Baron 1964: 240–75). The first volume of Graetz's work covered the period from Moses to the death of Simon in 135 B.C.E. (on Graetz and his history, see Baron 1964: 263–75). The work is primarily a rather free—at times rather romanticized—narration built upon the biblical materials. Very few of the problems are given any detailed treatment. The real importance of Graetz's work is the fact that it depicts the history free from any overriding theological stance or biblical orthodoxy.

A final nineteenth-century historian to be noted was Julius Wellhausen (1844–1918), who was the most influential and significant Old Testament scholar of the time. Before producing a reconstruction of Israelite history, Wellhausen carried out a detailed examination of the literary traditions in the hexateuch. He accepted and supported the documentary criticism which argued that there were four sources in the pentateuch which originated in the order J, E, D, P. In his *Prolegomena*, Wellhausen supported this theory with an incisive analysis of the history of worship and religion, which sought to demonstrate that Israelite religious life had gone through [[62]] various states which are reflected in the documents of the pentateuch. Some of Wellhausen's major conclusions on the literary and religious history were the following. (1) The theocratic organization of Israel and the priestly laws of the pentateuch were the basis not for life in the age of Moses but for post-exilic Judaism. (2) The eighth century was the age of real literary activity in Israel: "The question why it was that Elijah and Elisha committed nothing to writing, while Amos a hundred years later is an author, hardly admits of any other answer than that in the interval a non-literary had developed into a literary age" (1885: 465). (3) The Yahwistic (J) and Elohistic (E) sources came into being during the early days of classical prophetism and reflect the pre-prophetic religion of Israel (1885: 360f.). (4) Under the influence of the prophets, Deuteronomy was produced in the seventh century (1885: 487–88). (5) Deuteronomy was strictly a law-book and J was a history-book; the combination of these two was the beginning of the combination of law and narrative which was the pattern followed by P (1885: 345). (6) The priestly work derives from post-exilic times and reflects the atmosphere of theocratic Judaism. (7) The presentations of the earliest phase of Israelite history, the patriarchal period, in the various sources were coloured by the times in which the sources were written and thus cannot be used for historical purposes:

> We attain to no historical knowledge of the patriarchs, but only of the time when the stories about them arose in the Israelite people; this later age is here unconsciously projected, in its inner and outward features, into hoar antiquity, and is reflected there like a glorified mirage. (Wellhausen 1885: 318f.)

It should be noted that Wellhausen makes such a statement only for the patriarchal period, and not for the following ones. (8) Wellhausen saw Israelite religion developing through three phrases: (a) the stage of primitive religion characterized by popular sentiments, a spontaneous and simple faith, and a nature orientation; (b) the stage of ethical concerns and consciousness initiated by the prophets; and (c) the stage of ceremonial and ritual religion influenced by the priestly legislation and further separated from the orientation to nature. Wellhausen seems to have sympathized most with the religion of the earliest phase, although he shared in the general nineteenth-century excitement over the "rediscovery" of the prophets as creative individuals and exponents of personal and ethical religion (Wellhausen 1885: 464–70; 1958: 78–103).

Various attempts were, and still are, made to counter Wellhausen's position by arguing that he imposed Hegelian [[63]] philosophy or evolutionary thought on the Old Testament (see Thompson, 35–49, and bibliography there). This attempt to condemn by association has really no foundation in fact (see Perlitt). The basic influences upon Wellhausen were the emphasis laid by Herder and by Romanticism on primitivism, with its opposition to cultic ceremonial and things priestly, the positivistic approach to history exemplified in Niebuhr, Ranke, and Mommsen, the general nineteenth-century concern with stages in the history of practically everything, which most frequently argued for progressive development (in a good sense), although this was not completely the case with Wellhausen, the Lutheran theological position *vis-à-vis* the problem of law and gospel, and the general philosophy of history inherent in Christianity. (Even Bright [[1959]], who criticizes Wellhausen for his evolutionary thought, calls the epilogue to his history "Toward the Fullness of Time.") The primary influence on Wellhausen's reconstruction of Israelite history was, of course, the results and consequences of his literary study of the Old Testament.

Wellhausen's article on Israel, published in the ninth edition of the *Encyclopaedia Britannica* in 1880, was his basic statement on the topic. His later publications expanded the content but made no substantive changes; thus this article in its 1885 reprint can serve to present his views. For him, the ancestors of Israel were part of a Hebrew group, which included the ancestors of the Edomites, Moabites, and Ammonites, which settled in southeastern Palestine. Sometime in the fifteenth century B.C.E., a part of this Hebrew group left southern Palestine and moved into Goshen in Egypt. They were later subjected to forced labour until Moses reminded them of the God of their fathers and taught them self-assertion against the Egyptians. When Egypt was scourged by a plague, the Hebrews fled secretly to return to their old home. The fleeing Hebrews were pursued by the Egyptians but were able to ford a shallow sea which had been blown back by a high wind. A struggle ensued between the Egyptians and Hebrews but the former in their chariots were at a disadvantage and were annihilated by the returning waters (Wellhausen 1885: 429f.).

After visiting Sinai, the emigrants settled at Kadesh for many years and there had their sanctuary and judgment-seat. Some attempts to move northwards into Canaan may have been made while the Hebrews pastured their flocks over an extended area around Kadesh. They left Kadesh to aid their kinsmen against Sihon in Transjordan, being joined by kindred elements. At this stage some groups—the six Leah clans and Joseph, a Rachel clan—may have already existed as organized tribes (1885: 430–32). From the historical [[64]] tradition in the pentateuch, Wellhausen argued that some picture of Moses can be seen: he was the founder of Torah, called into activity the feeling for law and justice, and was the founder of the nation, but presented the Hebrews with no new concept of God (1885: 432–40).

The first movement into Palestine was led by Judah; the second wave by Joseph. There the divisions of Israel and Judah developed. Joshua was the leader of the Joseph and Benjamin groups (1885: 441–44). After some united effort at conquest, the tribes and families fought for their own land. Much of the indigenous population was absorbed. Gradually Israel advanced from pastoralism to agriculture (1885: 441–46). Yahweh was the god of Israel and Israel the people of God in its earliest days. In origin, the name Yahweh was a special name of the god El; Yahweh was the warrior El (1885: 443f.). For a time, Baalism and Yahwism existed side by side. Gradually Yahwism absorbed elements of Baalism including the main elements in the cult (1885: 447f.).

This summary of Wellhausen's reconstruction of the early history of Israel sufficiently demonstrates his approach. Wellhausen refused to understand Israel's history by postulating a golden period at some point early in its history, from which subsequent generations degenerated.

Current Approaches

W. F. Albright, "Archaeology Confronts Biblical Criticism," *AmSc* 7, 1938, 176–88; idem, "The Ancient Near East and the Religion of Israel," *JBL* 59, 1940, 85–112; D. M. Beegle, *The Inspiration of Scripture*, Philadelphia: Westminster Press 1963; J. Bright, *Early Israel in Recent History Writing: A Study in Method*, SBT 19, 1956; M. Buss, "The Study of Forms," in *Old Testament Form Criticism*, 1974, 1–56; J. Dus, "Mose oder Josua? (Zum Problem des Stifters der israelitischen Religion)," *AOr* 39, 1971, 16–45 = "Moses or Joshua? (On the Problem of the Founder of Israelite Religion," *RR* 2, 1975, 26–41; [[H. G. A. Ewald, *Geschichte des Volkes Israels bis Christus* 1–5, Göttingen: Dieterichschen Buchhandlung, 1843–55, ²1851–59, ³1864–68 (seven volumes) = *The History of Israel* 1–6, London: Longmans, Green, and Co. 1869–83;]] D. N. Freedman, "Archaeology and the Future of Biblical Studies, 1: The Biblical Languages," in *The Bible in Modern Scholarship*, 1965, 294–312; P. Haupt, "Midian und Sinai," *ZDMG* 63, 1909, 506–30; [[S. Herrmann, *Geschichte Israels in alttestamentlicher Zeit*, Munich: Chr. Kaiser 1973 = *A History of Israel in Old Testament Times*, London/Philadelphia: SCM Press/Fortress Press 1975;]] W. Keller, *Und die Bibel hat doch recht: Forscher beweisen die historische Wahrheit*, Düsseldorf: Econ-Verlag 1956 = *The Bible as History: A Confirmation of the Book of Books*, London/New York: Hodder & Stoughton/William Morrow & Co. 1956; D. A. Knight, *Rediscovering the Traditions of Israel*, SBLDS 9, 1973, ²1975; H. Lindsell, *The Battle for the Bible*, Grand Rapids: Zondervan 1976; G. E. Mendenhall, "The Hebrew Conquest of Palestine," *BA* XXV, 1962, 66–87 = *BAR* 3, 1970, 100–126; idem, *The Tenth Generation*, Baltimore: Johns Hopkins Press 1973; idem, [[65]] "The Monarchy," *Int* 29, 1975, 155–70; [[E. Meyer, *Geschichte des Altertums* 1–5, Stuttgart: J. G. Cotta 1884–1902; Basle: Benno Schwabe 1953 (5 volumes in 8);]] M. Noth, *Das System der zwölf Stämme Israels*, BWANT 4/1, 1930; idem, *Die Gesetze im Pentateuch (Ihre Voraussetzungen und ihr Sinn)*, SKGG 17/2, 1940 = his *GS* 1, 1957, 9–141 = "The Laws in the Pentateuch:

Their Assumptions and Meaning," in his _Laws in the Pentateuch_, 1966, 1–107; idem, _Überlieferungsgeschichtliche Studien_, 1957; idem, _History of the Pentateuchal Traditions_, 1972; G. von Rad, _Das formgeschichtliche Problem des Hexateuch_, BWANT 4/26, 1938 = his _GS_ 1, 1958, 9–86 = _Problem of the Hexateuch_, 1966, 1–78; idem, [["Der Anfang der Geschichtsschreibung im alten Israel," _AK_ 32, 1944, 1–42 =]] "The Beginnings of Historical Writing in Ancient Israel," _Problem of the Hexateuch_, 1966, 166–204; R. J. Thompson, _Moses and the Law in a Century of Criticism since Graf_, SVT 19, 1970; [[R. de Vaux, _Histoire ancienne d'Israel: Des Origines à l'Installation en Canaan_, Paris: J. Gabalda 1971; _La Periode des Juges_, Paris: J. Gabalda 1973 = _The Early History of Israel: To the Period of the Judges_, London/Philadelphia: Darton, Longman & Todd/Westminster Press, 1976;]] M. Weber, _Gesammelte Aufsätze zur Religionssoziologie, III: Das antike Judentum_, Tübingen: J. C. B. Mohr 1921, ²1923 = _Ancient Judaism_, Glencoe: The Free Press 1952; J. A. Wilcoxen, "Narrative," _Old Testament Form Criticism_, 1974, 57–98; [[L. J. Wood, _Survey of Israel's History_, Grand Rapids: Zondervan 1970]].

Subsequent chapters in this volume [[in the original volume]] discuss the modern history of research on particular periods of Israelite history. At this point, a brief comment on the general methodology of the major current approaches to the history will be made to provide some background for later discussions.

One approach which is still used by conservative scholars is the orthodox or traditional approach. This position operates on the assumption that the Bible is of supernatural origin and in its autograph form (which is no longer available) was totally free of any error (on this view of the Bible, see Lindsell). Other scholars who would classify themselves as conservative would not take so rigid a view of biblical inspiration (see Beegle 1963). The orthodox view, similar to mainline biblical studies of the seventeenth and eighteenth centuries, works primarily from the evidence of the biblical text, supplying this with illustrative and supportive material drawn from extra-biblical texts and archaeological data. At points, the biblical texts need to be harmonized where apparent contradictions seem to appear. This view of the biblical materials is sometimes extended to the seven-day creation scheme, to be dated about 4000 B.C.E., and to the flood. Wood's history supplies a good representation of this approach. He is able to supply exact dates for biblical events which are all taken as historically accurate: Abraham was born in 2166 B.C.E., Isaac married Rebekah in 2026 B.C.E., Jacob was seventy-seven years old when he went to Haran and hired himself to Laban for fourteen years, the exodus occurred in 1446 B.C.E., and so on. Biblical figures are accurate; over two million Hebrews left Egypt. Miracles happened as described, although God normally employed natural law when this was available: the sea was opened to approximately a mile in width [[66]] to allow passage of the fleeing Hebrews (1970: 132f.) and the earth "slowed, in its speed of rotation on its axis, approximately to half that of normal" in order to provide Joshua with additional daylight in his battle near Gibeon (1970: 181). Sufficient has been noted to illustrate this approach. In the following chapters, practically no attention will be given to this view since it does not assume that one has to reconstruct the history of Israel; one has only to support and elucidate the adequate history which the Bible already provides.

A second approach to Israelite history is what might be called the archaeological approach, since it seeks to substantiate much of the biblical data by appeal to evidence external to but supportive of the biblical text. This approach to Israelite history, built on the earlier antiquarian interests, became a fully conscious approach in the late nineteenth century as a reaction to documentary criticism of the pentateuch and the historical approaches, such as that by Wellhausen, built on documentary criticism (see Thompson 1970: 91–96, 132–39, and bibliography there). In recent years, this approach has been associated in a special way with William Foxwell Albright (1891–1971) and his students (but see the widely popular book by Keller 1956), although there are many archaeologists who would not share his methodological approach. Albright formulated his approach to the history and religion of Israel in the 1920s and 1930s and this remained basically unchanged throughout his career. His methodology rests on two basic arguments. (1) The traditions of the Old Testament are generally quite reliable. One should assume that these traditions embody historical memory and that the tendency to preserve traditions rather than create them was a fundamental characteristic of Near Eastern life, including Israelite, where one finds "a superstitious veneration both for the written word and for oral tradition" (Albright 1938: 183). (2) Archaeological remains—both literary and artifactual—provide a source of material external to the Bible which can be used as a control against the unnecessary dependency upon literary, philosophical, or fundamentalist hypotheses. Since archaeology "is concrete, not speculative," it can play this role (Albright 1938: 179; see Bright 1956: 11–33, 111–26). Albright and his students operated on the assumption that archaeology had and would support the historicity of the biblical traditions.

> Archaeological and inscriptional data have established the historicity of innumerable passages and statements of the Old Testament; the number of such cases is many times greater than those where the reverse has been proved or has been made probable. (Albright 1938: 181)
> Before archaeology there was no adequate alternative to the creation of [[67]] hypothetical frameworks for the biblical narrative; but as the factual evidence has become available, there is less and less excuse for such exercises in ingenuity, and in due course there will be none. (Freedman 1965: 298)

Probably few, if any, of Albright's students would go as far as the following statement of Mendenhall on the role of archaeology, but an emphasis on external evidence points in this direction:

> We have an abundance of documentation from excavations comprised of primary, contemporary, and datable sources that yield all kinds of information about the social, political, ethnic, and religious traits of man in the Near East. . . . Unless biblical history is to be relegated to the domain of unreality and myth, the biblical and the archaeological must be correlated. Methodologically, the archaeological documents, especially the written ones, must be given priority and considered seriously. (Mendenhall 1973: 142)

A third typological approach to Israelite history may be called the traditio-historical approach (see Knight 1973 for the history and description of this methodology). This methodology is most closely associated with Albrecht Alt (1883–1956), Martin Noth (1902–68), and Gerhard von Rad (1901–71). The impetus for this approach goes back to Hermann Gunkel (1862–1932) who was the pioneer in Old Testament form-critical studies (on Gunkel, see Buss 1974: 39–52; Wilcoxen 1974: 57–79). Gunkel's work was postulated upon a number of perspectives which were ultimately of significance in the traditio-historical study of the Old Testament. (1) The writing down of Old Testament traditions in the form of documents was a late stage in a long process, and the writers of the documents were more like redactors or editors than authors. (2) Old Testament traditions had a long history of usage in an oral stage before they were written down. (3) Traditions may be divided into genres according to the content and mood of the materials, their formal language of expression, and their setting in life. (4) The basic form of the tradition is the individual unit or genre. (5) In the patriarchal traditions, the primary unit is the saga. (6) The individual sagas had their particular function in the setting in which they were used and the function of many of these was aetiological; they were used to "explain" the origin of some physical feature, custom, practice, or ethnic relationship. (7) The individual sagas could be combined to produce cycles of traditions. (8) History writing in Israel developed out of this saga tradition.

Von Rad contributed four perspectives that were to be influential in traditio-historical studies in the latter's impact on the study of [[68]] Israelite history. (1) He isolated the small summaries of Israel's pre-monarchic history and related the usage of these to cultic celebrations (von Rad 1966: 1–50). (2) The Sinai tradition was not originally a part of the historical summaries but had a different setting in the cult. (3) The cultic summaries were seen as the basis of the Yahwist's (J) history of early Israel which incorporated the Sinai theme and was prefaced by the primeval history. (4) The time of David and Solomon was the period when Israelite historiography developed out of the narrative art of the saga (von Rad 1966: 166–204; so Meyer 1884–1902: 2/2.285f.).

A number of preliminary stages led to Noth's history of Israel along traditio-historical lines. In 1930, he used the concept of the Greek amphictyony to explain the organization of the tribes in pre-monarchical Israel (so already, in limited ways, Ewald 1869–83: 1.370; and Haupt 1909). The unity of the twelve tribes during this period was primarily religious but with some legal basis as well. In 1940, Noth published his study of pentateuchal law, whose origin he associated with the life of the tribal amphictyony. Noth's study of the Deuteronomistic history (1943) stressed the later editorial work in the book of Joshua and its account of the conquest. His study of the pentateuchal traditions (1948) argued that the major traditions in the pentateuch can be divided into five major themes: guidance out of Egypt, guidance into the land, promise to the patriarchs, guidance in the wilderness, and revelation at Sinai. Each of these themes was originally independent of the others. These themes were first combined during the time of the tribal league—the pre-monarchical source "G" in which these were combined was the basis for the later sources such as J from the Davidic–Solomonic period.

When these concepts are applied to the history of Israel, Noth has to begin his treatment with the tribal league. Since the early themes have only been associated secondarily, their historical outline is unreliable. Nothing substantial can be known about Moses since he has been introduced secondarily into the thematic traditions. The patriarchal traditions cannot be penetrated to discover anything of real historical value. The dominant account of the conquest is Deuteronomistic, although some early, primarily aetiological, materials are found in the accounts. Since the tribes moved into Palestine separately, no united leadership of the tribes can be ascribed to Joshua. It was the amphictyonic Israel which first imposed the "all Israel" concept upon what were originally independent traditions and independent pasts. This time of the sacral amphictyonic organization is, for Noth, something like a golden age from which the later ages deviated.

[[69]] A further approach to the early history of Israel is the attempt to understand early Israelite life in socio-economical categories. The first scholar to work along these lines was the sociologist Max Weber (1864–1920) in his *Ancient Judaism* (1952) although he was not an Old Testament specialist. This approach has been taken up recently by Mendenhall, Dus, Gottwald, and others. Although there are some major differences within this approach, the following are generally shared convictions. (1) Israel as a people or tribal confederacy originated in the land of Canaan. (2) Her origin was primarily the product of an internal revolt within Canaan against the Canaanite city-states' economic and political structures. The peasants and pastoralists involved in this revolt sought liberation and freedom from their oppressive overlords. (3) Israel created a new order of society in its tribal and covenant relationships. (4) The idea of Israel's origin in nomadic culture and the concept of a general conquest from outside the land must be given up. (5) The establishment of the monarchy was in many ways a return to the pre-revolutionary state of affairs and thus represents a paganization of the life and faith of liberated Israel.

These four approaches represent the basic alternatives at present employed in reconstructing Israelite history. The crucial period is, of course, the pre-monarchic times. Obviously, different scholars utilize insights and evidence from other approaches than that which is dominant in their own methodology. Some historians, especially Herrmann and de Vaux, cannot be said to be dominated by any exclusive methodology but are more eclectic.

The New Biblical Historiography

Mark Zvi Brettler

[[2]] My analysis builds upon the newer views that have developed over the last two decades concerning the way in which texts which purport to narrate the Israelite past have been understood. Biblical books that were previously viewed as history in the sense of a generally accurate depiction of the Israelite past are now seen as historiography, literally "history writing," a term typically used to emphasize the creative nature of historical texts.[1] This change is not entirely new; in many ways, it is a return to the position espoused by Julius Wellhausen over a century ago. Wellhausen's position, however, was relatively short-lived due to the tremendous influence of scholars such as Albrecht Alt and William Foxwell Albright.[2]

The more recent return to the skepticism of Wellhausen can be traced by comparing the three Bible survey volumes published this century by the Society for Old Testament Study. The relevant section in *Record and Revelation,* published in 1938, is entitled "The History of Israel," and attempts a short reconstruction of the history of Israel.[3] The comparable chapter in *The Old Testament and Modern* Study, published in 1951, is entitled "The Historical Books" and is primarily concerned with the date and

Reprinted with permission and excerpted from *The Creation of History in Ancient Israel* (London/New York: Routledge, 1995) 2–6 (plus notes from pp. 146–49).

1. For a different description of the shift from history to historiography, see Thomas L. Thompson, *The Origin Tradition of Ancient Israel: I. The Literary Formation of Genesis and Exodus 1–23*, JSOTSup 55 (Sheffield: Sheffield Academic Press, 1987) esp. 11–24.

2. Thompson, *Early History of the Israelite People [[from Written and Archaeological Sources* (Studies in the History of the Ancient Near East 4; Leiden: Brill, 1992)]] 1–76.

3. W. L. Wardle, Theodore H. Robinson, and H. H. Rowley, "The History of Israel," *Record and Revelation*, ed. H. Wheeler Robinson (Oxford: Oxford University Press, 1938) 110–86.

sources of these books.[4] The most recent chapter, in *Tradition and* [[3]] *Interpretation*, published in 1979, is entitled "Old Testament Historiography";[5] it probes the relation between biblical and ancient Near Eastern historiography and explores the theology of large blocks of biblical historiographic material. These changes reflect a movement from history in the sense of a reconstruction of the past to history as a narrative which is influenced by its authors' religious and political ideologies.

The change reflected in the titles and contents of these surveys may be seen in other ways. For example, in the last twenty years, scholars have begun to write articles on topics which are fundamentally different from those of their predecessors. Typical works from the middle portion of this century attempted to reconstruct the actual history of Israel, and sometimes used ancient Near Eastern texts toward this purpose. Classic articles such as Roland de Vaux's "The Prophets of Baal on Mount Carmel"[6] or Albrecht Alt's "The Monarchy in the Kingdoms of Israel and Judah"[7] typify this genre. While similar works continue to be written, especially in Europe, these have been supplemented by studies such as W. Lee Humphreys's "From Tragic Hero to Villain: A Study of the Figure of Saul and the Development of 1 Samuel"[8] and Lillian R. Klein's *The Triumph of Irony in the Book of Judges*.[9] Works of this sort, dealing with literary or rhetorical aspects of texts such as Judges, Samuel and Kings, are now regularly published in the mainstream scholarly journals; they were largely absent before the 1970s.

A further significant indication of the changes of the last decades may be seen in the reactions to *A History of Ancient Israel and Judah* by J. Maxwell Miller and John Hayes, published in 1986.[10] More than fifty pages of review articles on Miller and Hayes were published in a leading journal, most of which questioned the working assumptions of the authors in their attempt

4. N. H. Snaith, "The Historical Books," *The Old Testament and Modern Studies: A Generation of Discovery and Research*, ed. H. H. Rowley (Oxford: Oxford University Press, 1951) 84–114.

5. J. R. Porter, "Old Testament Historiography," *Tradition and Interpretation*, ed. G. W. Anderson (Oxford: Oxford University Press, 1979) 125–62.

6. Roland de Vaux, *The Bible and the Ancient Near East*, trans. Damian McHugh (Garden City, New York: Doubleday, 1971) 238–51; this article first appeared in French in 1941.

7. Albrecht Alt, *Essays on Old Testament History and Religion*, trans. R. A. Wilson (Garden City, New York: Doubleday, 1967) 311–35; this article was first published in German in 1951.

8. W. Lee Humphreys, "From Tragic Hero to Villain: A Study of the Figure of Saul and the Development of 1 Samuel," *JSOT* 22 (1982) 95–117.

9. Lillian R. Klein, *The Triumph of Irony in the Book of Judges*, JSOTSup 68 (Sheffield: Almond Press, 1989).

10. J. Maxwell Miller and John Hayes, *A History of Ancient Israel and Judah* (Philadelphia: Westminster).

to recreate the ancient Israelite past.[11] Many reviewers wondered if a history of Israel could be written or is worth writing. The book's authors were especially criticized for paying too much attention to the biblical text and too little attention to sociological modeling. These criticisms were seen as so fundamental to the traditional venture of writing the history of Israel, that one of the book's authors entitled his response "In Defense of Writing a History of Israel."[12] This is the first time that the publication of such a volume evoked such questions. It is possible that this book's explicit treatment of methodological issues created a new awareness of the basic methodological problems involved in the writing of Israelite history, inviting scholars to criticize it. The criticism continues. Thompson's recent *Early History of the Israelite People from Written and Archaeological Sources* has "deconstruction" as its *Leitwort* [['key word']], and another recent work has claimed that the genre History of Israel "is probably obsolete."[13]

The changes of the last several decades may be symbolized by the contrasting treatments in 1944 and 1985 of the biblical narrative about [[4]] King David. In Gerhard von Rad's classic 1944 essay, "The Beginning of History Writing in Ancient Israel,"[14] he calls the succession narrative, the biblical story in Samuel and Kings concerning the fight for the throne of David, "The oldest piece of ancient Israelite historical writing,"[15] by which he means that it contains "acute perception of the realities of a nation's situation" and use of "historical contingency [and] . . . cause and effect."[16] Much more recently, Walter Brueggemann introduces his book *David's Truth in Israel's Imagination and Memory* with the following: "First of all it should be understood that we are not here interested in the 'historical David,' as though we could isolate and identify the real thing. That is not available to us."[17] These two studies typify the changing attitudes over the last half-century.

11. *JSOT* 39 (1987) 3–63. The importance of this book and these reviews is also highlighted by Thompson, *Early History of the Israelite People*, 104.

12. [[J. Maxwell Miller,]] *JSOT* 39 (1987) 53–57.

13. [[Philip R.]] Davies, *In Search of "Ancient Israel,"* [[JSOTSup 148; Sheffield: JSOT Press, 1992]] 11.

14. Gerhard von Rad, "The Beginning of History Writing in Ancient Israel," *The Problem of the Hexateuch and Other Essays* (London: SCM, 1984) 166–204.

15. Von Rad, "The Beginning of History Writing," 176.

16. Von Rad, "The Beginning of History Writing," 166.

17. Walter Brueggemann, *David's Truth in Israel's Imagination and Memory* (Philadelphia: Fortress, 1985) pp. 13–14. Brueggemann's work is not the first to shy away from von Rad's position; cf. Lienhard Deleket, "Tendenz und Theologie der David–Salomo-Erzählung," *Das ferne und das nahe Wort: Festschrift Rost*, BZAW 105 (Berlin: Töpelman, 1967) 26–36, esp. 29 and Ernst Würthwein, *Die Erzählung von der Thronfolge Davids—theologische oder politische Geschichtsschreibung*, ThStud 115 (Zürich: Theologischer Verlag, 1974). More recently, see esp. Keith Whitelam, "The Defence of David," *JSOT* 29 (1984) 61–87.

The changes reflect a shift away from concern with texts as a source for the social, political or religious history of the Israelite past to an interest in the literary merits or ideological underpinnings of the texts.[18] Several factors working together are responsible for this shift.

Over the last few decades, scholars have paid more attention to questions concerning the Deuteronomist, the supposed author or editor of the books Deuteronomy through Kings. Until the nineteenth century, most Bible readers saw the first five books of the Bible, namely the Pentateuch or Torah, as a unit. As a result of the critical study of the Bible, which saw the Pentateuchal sources continuing into the book of Joshua, it became customary to speak of the Hexateuch, that is the six books from Genesis through Joshua.[19] This was changed with the publication in 1943 of Martin Noth's *Überlieferungsgeschichtliche Studien*,[20] which remains a classic of biblical scholarship, and suggests that the first four books of Genesis through Numbers are a unit, and must be distinguished from Deuteronomy through Kings, which are labeled the Deuteronomistic History. Noth's study is essential in that the attribution of such a large corpus, namely Deuteronomy though Kings, to a single hand must be defended by examining how the editor reworked earlier materials[21] using a consistent ideology. As a result, the ideology of a historical work became a more central focus of attention than the text's historicity or sources. This was a catalyst for a debate concerning the text's ideology and the extent of its pervasiveness.[22] As other scholars began to cast doubts on the unity of this corpus, they advanced their arguments by noting the multiplicity of ideologies within the

18. On the current interest in ideology, which has replaced recent literary perspectives, see David J. A. Clines, "Possibilities and Priorities of Biblical Interpretation in an International Perspective," *BI* 1 (1993) 82–86.

19. See, for example, A. T. Chapman, *An Introduction to the Pentateuch*, CBC (Cambridge: Cambridge University Press, 1911) which, despite its title, actually concerns itself with the Hexateuch.

20. Reprinted Tübingen: Max Niemeyer, 1967. The first half of this work was translated by various scholars as *The Deuteronomistic History*, JSOTSup 15 (Sheffield: JSOT Press, 1981). The second half of Noth's study concerns the Chronicler, who until recently has played a much less significant role in biblical studies than the Deuteronomistic History. That half appears in English as *The Chronicler's History*, trans. H. G. M. Williamson, JSOTSup 50 (Sheffield: JSOT Press, 1987).

21. Note the work's subtitle: *Die sammelnden und bearbeitenden Geschichtswerke im Alten Testament*.

22. This debate continues. See, for example, the debate concerning the authorship of the last four verses of Kings: Jon D. Levenson, "The Last Four Verses in Kings," *JBL* 103 (1984) 353–61; Christopher Begg, "The Significance of Jehoiachin's Release: A New Proposal," *JSOT* 36 (1986) 49–56; and Bob Becking, "Jehojachin's Amnesty, Salvation for Israel? Notes on 2 Kings 25, 27–30," *Pentateuchal and Deuteronomistic Studies: Papers Read at the XIIIth IOSOT Congress Leuven 1989*, ed. C. Brekelmans and J. Lust (Leuven: Leuven University Press, 1990) 283–93.

Deuteronomistic History.[23] Thus, the isolation of the Deuteronomistic History as a separate corpus and the debate concerning the number and provenience of the Deuteronomistic Historians has helped to accentuate the role of ideology in the writing of biblical historical texts.[24]

A second factor responsible for the shift of focus from history to historiography is the introduction of social scientific models into biblical studies. While there were some early experiments in this direction at the turn of the century, George Mendenhall's 1962 article on "The Hebrew Conquest [[5]] of Palestine"[25] has served as a catalyst for further studies which apply social scientific methods to biblical texts.[26] The authors of these studies vary widely in terms of their methodologies, but they frequently emphasize the lack of historicity of major blocks of the biblical text.

This negative assessment has been centered around the claims of archeologists that the predominant biblical account of Joshua conquering Canaan should be rejected in favor of the peaceful settlement of Canaan.[27] Some biblical scholars are now moving beyond the early history of Israel, and are questioning the historicity of an ever-increasing number

23. See the summaries of Richard D. Nelson, *The Double Redaction of the Deuteronomistic History*, JSOTSup 18 (Sheffield: JSOT Press, 1981); Mark A. O'Brien, *The Deuteronomistic History Hypothesis: A Reassessment*, OBO 92 (Freiburg: Universitätsverlag, 1989); Steven L. McKenzie, *The Trouble with Kings: The Composition of the Book of Kings in the Deuteronomistic History*, SVT 42 (Leiden: E. J. Brill, 1991) 1–19; and most recently, Baruch Halpern and David S. Vanderhooft, "The Editions of Kings in the 7th–6th Centuries B.C.E.," *HUCA* 62 (1991), 179–224.

24. For a discussion of additional aspects of Noth's significance in the creation of the new biblical historiography, see Thompson, *Early History of the Israelite People*, 81–82. Stephen Geller (letter of August 1, 1991) has suggested to me that this debate concerning the Deuteronomistic History is symptomatic of the general state of biblical studies in the early 1960s, when the consensus position that was developed and refined in Germany began to fall apart. The dissolution of this consensus opened the field to newer methodologies, such as the literary study of the Bible. For an essay which expresses the attitude toward the disintegration of the standard views, see John Bright, "Modern Study of the Old Testament Literature," *The Bible and the Ancient Near East: Essays in Honor of William Foxwell Albright*, ed. G. Ernest Wright ([[reprinted]] Winona Lake, IN: Eisenbrauns, 1979 [f.p. 1961]) 13–31. More recently, see Rolf Rendtorff, "Between Historical Criticism and Holistic Interpretation," SVT 40 (Leiden: E. J. Brill 1988) 289–303.

25. *BA* 25 (1962) 66–87, reprinted in *BAReader* 3 (1970) 100–120.

26. See esp. *Palestine in Transition: The Emergence of Ancient Israel*, SWBA 2, ed. David Noel Freedman and David Frank Graf (Sheffield: Almond, 1983), Niels Peter Lemche, *Early Israel: Anthropological and Historical Studies on the Israelite Society before the Monarchy*, SVT 37 (Leiden: E. J. Brill, 1985) and Robert B. Coote and Keith Whitelam, *The Emergence of Early Israel in Historical Perspective*, SWBA 5 (Sheffield: Almond Press, 1987). For a summary, see Lowell K. Handy, "The Reconstruction of Jewish History and Jewish-Christian Relations," *SJOT* (1991/1) 11–16.

27. Israel Finkelstein, *Archaeological Discoveries and Biblical Research* (Seattle: University of Washington, 1990) 37–84 and Amihai Mazar, *Archaeology of the Land of the Bible 10,000–586 B.C.E.*, AB (Garden City, New York: Doubleday, 1990) 328–38.

of texts. For example, Thomas L. Thompson notes in reference to the reconstruction of Israelite history, including that of the monarchy, "One cannot but question any alleged 'reliable pool of information.'"[28] He follows a position advocated by Niels Peter Lemche, "I propose that we decline to be led by the biblical account and instead regard it, like other legendary materials, as formally ahistorical; that is, as a source which only exceptionally can be verified by other information."[29] While the positions of Lemche, Davies,[30] and Thompson have not gained general assent, these three scholars have begun to make contemporary scholars who attempt to reconstruct ancient Israelite history much more aware of the fundamental problems involved in their task.

Two external developments have begun to change the direction of study of biblical historical texts. The "New History" or "*annales* school," which emphasizes social rather than political history,[31] has recently begun to influence the work of several biblical scholars.[32] This has happened especially in the United States, as biblicists have moved away from theological models and interests and have become a more integral part of the university, open to newer developments outside of the theological disciplines.[33]

---

28. *Early History of the Israelite People*, 115.

29. Thompson, *Early History of the Israelite People*, 132.

30. See his *In Search of "Ancient Israel."*

31. For a summary of the "new history" and other contemporary approaches to writing history, see Georg G. Iggers, *New Directions in European Historiography*, revised edition (Middletown, CT: Wesleyan University Press, 1984). and *New Perspectives on Historical Writing*, ed. Peter Burke (University Park, PA: Pennsylvania State University Press, 1992).

32. See, for example, the critique of Miller and Hayes by Fredric R. Brandfon, "Kingship, Culture and '*Longue Durée*,'" *JSOT* 39 (1987) 30–38, and note the new series entitled The Social World of Biblical Antiquity, appearing from Almond.

33. Earlier, history and theology were closely connected, esp. under the influence of Gerhard von Rad. For an American example, see G. Ernest Wright, *God Who Acts: Biblical Theology as Recital*, SBT 8 (London: SCM, 1952). For a general discussion, see Gerhard Hasel, *Old Testament Theology: Basic Issues in the Current Debate* (Grand Rapids, MI: Eerdmans, 1979) 57–75 ("The Question of History, History of Tradition, and Salvation History") and the important comments of Matitiahu Tsevat, "Israelite History and the Historical Books of the Old Testament," *The Meaning of the Book of Job and Other Biblical Studies: Essays on the Literature and Religion of the Hebrew Bible* (New York: Ktav, 1980) 177–83. On the status of the Bible in contemporary American universities, see Bruce Zuckerman, "Choosing among the Schools: Teaching Old Testament Survey to Undergraduates at a Secular University," *Methodology in the American Teaching of Judaism*, ed. Zev Garber (Lanham, MD: University Press of America, 1986) 91–115 and the essays in *Hebrew Bible or Old Testament? Studying the Bible in Judaism and Christianity*, ed. Roger Brooks and John J. Collins (Notre Dame: University of Notre Dame Press, 1990). The earlier, predominantly theological, approach is captured by Gösta W. Ahlström's *The History of Ancient Palestine from the Paleolithic Period to Alexander's Conquest* [JSOT Sup 146; Sheffield: Sheffield Academic Press, 1993] 52:

> The intention of this book has not been to write a theological history of Bible lands. There are already too many of these. My goal has been to write a history of

The second external development is the rise of the study of rhetoric within general historiography. This movement is especially associated with Hayden White in the States and Paul Veyne in France, and has produced works such as "The Fictions of Factual Representation"[34] and "Plots, Not Facts . . . ,"[35] which defend the literary and ideological nature of all history writing. To the extent that biblical scholars are becoming more attuned to the intellectual world of the university, they are increasingly influenced by these general developments.[36]

A final factor influencing the changing viewpoints of scholars concerning texts narrating Israel's past is the rise of the movement to study the Bible as literature.[37] This movement began to develop in the 1960s under the influence of such figures as Meir Weiss,[38] Luis Alonso Schökel,[39] and James Muilenburg.[40] The movement gained momentum and extensively dealt with prose texts in the mid-1970s. The publication in 1975 of J. P. Fokkelman's *Narrative Art in Genesis: Specimens of Stylistic and Structural Analysis*,[41] the first book-length study in a European language to apply new-critical insights to biblical narrative texts, is an important landmark in this respect. [[6]] Two of the earliest applications of this method to longer historical episodes are by David Gunn, who wrote literary analyses

---

ancient Palestine in the same way that the history of any other nation country and all of its people is normally written.

34. Hayden White, *Tropics of Discourse: Essays in Cultural Criticism* (Baltimore: Johns Hopkins University Press, 1978) 121–34.

35. Paul Veyne, *Writing History*, trans. Mina Moore-Rinvolucri (Middletown, CT: Wesleyan University Press, 1984) 31–46.

36. I do not mean to imply, however, that the issues facing modern biblical historians are identical to those encountered by historians of the more recent past. In studying the history of ancient Israel, the nature of the sources has caused disagreements concerning the basic outlines of the events. The facticity of events such as the exodus, the conquest of Canaan and the reforms of Hezekiah and Josiah have been extensively debated. In contrast, major debates concerning the facticity of major recent events are much less common. On these issues, see the Conclusions below [[not reprinted here]].

37. For a brief summary, see Luis Alonso Schökel, "Some Recent Developments in Old Testament Studies: Trends: The Plurality of Methods, the Priority of Issues," SVT 40 (Leiden: E. J. Brill, 1988) 286–88. Many important articles in this field have been collected in *Beyond Form Criticism: Essays in Old Testament Literary Criticism*, Sources for Biblical and Theological Study 2, ed. Paul R. House (Winona Lake, IN: Eisenbrauns, 1992).

38. *The Bible from Within: The Method of Total Interpretation* (Jerusalem: Magnes, 1984); the first Hebrew edition appeared in 1962.

39. A recent summary of his approach is *A Manual of Hebrew Poetics*, AnBib 11 (Rome: Pontifical Biblical Institute, 1988).

40. See his selected essays: *Hearing and Speaking the Word: Selections from the Works of James Muilenburg*, ed. Thomas F. Best (Chico, CA: Scholars Press, 1984).

41. J. P. Fokkelman, *Narrative Art in Genesis: Specimens of Stylistic and Structural Analysis* (Assen: Van Gorcum, 1975).

of the stories of King David and Saul.[42] The literary treatment of biblical historical texts reached broader audiences with the publication in 1981 of Robert Alter's *The Art of Biblical Narrative*.[43] Thus, by the early 1980s, literary, largely new-critical methodologies were applied to narrative texts that were previously considered historical. This movement has gained many adherents, causing a massive shift in how texts narrating Israel's past are studied.[44]

The various changes suggested above have acted in concert to alter radically the way in which we study biblical texts concerned with Israel's past. Until the early 1970s, there was a general consensus that the best way to study texts such as Judges or Kings was to use the tools of the historian, for these texts are in some sense "historical." For many American scholars, especially those sympathetic to the work of William Foxwell Albright, the texts were "historical" in the sense of being reasonably accurate depictions of the history of ancient Israel.[45] American scholarship has now moved quite far from this position, but there is no single unifying figure or position which has replaced the Albright school. The old consensus is gone, and there is no indication that a new one is developing to replace it.[46]

42. David Gunn, *King David: Genre and Interpretation*, JSOTSup 6 (Sheffield: JSOT Press, 1978) and *The Fate of King Saul: An Interpretation of a Biblical Story*, JSOTSup 14 (Sheffield: JSOT Press, 1980).

43. Robert Alter, *The Art of Biblical Narrative* (New York: Basic, 1981).

44. To some extent, literary scholars are also beginning to move away from new-critical models and are beginning to explore newer ("post-modernist") approaches to biblical texts, including biblical historical texts; see the collection of essays in J. Cheryl Exum and David J. A. Clines, eds., *The New Literary Criticism and the Hebrew Bible*, JSOTSup 143 (Sheffield: JSOT Press, 1993).

45. Note the summary of Albright's position by his student, David Noel Freedman: "W. F. Albright as an Historian," *The Scholarship of William Foxwell Albright: An Appraisal*, HSS 33, ed. Gus W. Van Beek (Atlanta: Scholars Press, 1989) 30, "In any case, he [Albright] opted for an older and simpler solution: the essential historicity of the biblical narrative going all the way back to patriarchal times." Cf. Handy, "The Reconstruction of Jewish History," 4–6 and the summary and critique of Albright in Thompson, *Early History of the Israelite People*, 11–26. Most recently, see the essays on Albright in *BA* 56 (1993), *Celebrating and Examining W. F. Albright*, esp. Burke O. Long, "Mythic Trope in the Autobiography of William Foxwell Albright," 36–45, which relies heavily on the Albright papers.

46. Other factors might also be considered, especially the role of etiology in biblical historical consciousness. However, it is noteworthy that etiologies have played a diminished role in recent biblical scholarship on historical texts; cf. P. J. van Dyk, "The Function of So-Called Etiological Elements in Narratives," *ZAW* 102 (1990) 19–33; and John Van Seters, *Prologue to History: The Yahwist as Historian in Genesis* (Louisville, KY: Westminster/John Knox, 1992) 28–30. An important earlier study which they fail to mention is I. L. Seeligmann, "Aetiological Elements in Biblical Historiography," *Zion* 26 (1961) 141–69 (Hebrew with English summary).

The Paradigm Is Changing: Hopes—and Fears

ROLF RENDTORFF

[[34]] This has been a great century in Old Testament scholarship. At its dawn we find a number of names that have left their stamp on the whole century, and the ideas of these scholars still serve as guidelines in many areas of Old Testament studies. I name three of them: Julius Wellhausen, Bernhard Duhm, and Hermann Gunkel.

Wellhausen, in a sense, represented the conclusion of one epoch of research and, at the same time, the opening of a new one. The question how to interpret the history of the origins of the Pentateuch was discussed throughout the whole of the nineteenth century, and different models were proposed and applied. Now one model gained the upper hand: the "newer documentary hypothesis." It was not invented by Wellhausen. His own contemporaries, for example, Heinrich Holzinger in his famous *Einleitung in den Hexateuch* (1893), called it the "Graf Hypothesis," because Karl Heinrich Graf was the first to publish the new hypothesis.[1] But Wellhausen was so fascinated by it, and his impact on Old Testament scholarship of his time was so overwhelming, that during the following decades it became more and more the Wellhausen hypothesis, as it is to this day.

Let us consider for a moment what happened when, after a short while, this new theory became commonly accepted. In a more technical sense, it was the victory of the "documentary hypothesis" over the earlier "fragment hypothesis," and in particular over the "supplementary hypothesis" that had been widely accepted in the decades before Wellhausen. But it is obvious that the main reason for this victory was not the purely literary question of dividing sources. Wellhausen himself explained quite clearly the main reason for the fascination with this new theory. In

Reprinted with permission from *Biblical Interpretation* 1 (1993) 34–53.

1. K. H. Graf, *Die geschichtlichen Bücher des Alten Testaments: Zwei historisch-kritische Untersuchungen* (Leipzig: T. O. Weigel, 1866).

the introduction to his famous *Prolegomena to the History of Israel*,[2] he told
the reader how, as a young [[35]] scholar, he had loved the stories about
Saul and David, Ahab and Elijah, and the early prophets, but how he had
felt it to be impossible to understand the Pentateuchal law as the basis of
all this literature. Then,

> in the summer of 1867 [when he was 23 years old], I learned . . . that Karl
> Heinrich Graf placed the Law later than the Prophets, and, almost with-
> out knowing his reasons for the hypothesis, I was prepared to accept it: I
> readily acknowledged to myself the possibility of understanding Hebrew
> antiquity without the book of the Torah.[3]

That was what fascinated Wellhausen, and then the majority of European
Protestant Old Testament scholars: to liberate Hebrew antiquity from the
burden of the later Jewish law. Therefore it becomes clear that the acceptance of the "newer documentary hypothesis" included a particular view of
the history of Israelite religion. This view was not new. Already De Wette
had divided his "Biblical Dogmatics" (1813) into two parts which he called
"Hebraism" and "Judaism." The latter he viewed as "the unsuccessful restoration of Hebraism . . . : a chaos which is longing for a new creation"
(§142).[4] Together with this concept Wellhausen inherited from De Wette
an emphatic romantic view of earlier Israelite history: "the history of the
ancient Israelites shows us nothing so distinctly as the uncommon freshness and naturalness of their impulses. The persons who appear always act
from the constraining impulse of their nature, the men of God no less than
the murderers and adulterers: they are such figures as could only grow up
in the open air."[5] In contrast, the Torah belonged to the era of Judaism:
"the warm pulse of life no longer throbbed in it to animate it. . . . The soul
was fled; the shell remained, upon the shaping out of which every energy
was now concentrated."[6]

This new hypothesis had fundamental consequences for the reconstruction of the history of Israel. And this was Wellhausen's leading interest, as the title of his foundational book, *History of Israel*, demonstrates,
and as is apparent from the second edition, *Prolegomena* [[36]] *to the History*

---

2. J. Wellhausen, *Geschichte Israels* (Berlin: G. Reimer, 1878); 2nd edn: *Prolegomena zur
Geschichte Israels* (1883); English translation from the 2nd edn: *Prolegomena to the History of
Israel* (Edinburgh: Adam & Charles Black, 1885) = *Prolegomena to the History of Ancient Israel*
(New York: Meridian Books, 1957).

3. English edition, pp. 3–4.

4. With this view of post-exilic Israel, compare R. Rendtorff, "The Image of Post-exilic
Israel in German Bible Scholarship from Wellhausen to von Rad," in *"Sha'arei Talmon": Stud-
ies in the Bible, Qumran, and the Ancient Near East Presented to Shemaryahu Talmon* (Winona
Lake, Ind.: Eisenbrauns, 1992).

5. English edition, p. 412.

6. English edition, p. 78.

of Israel.[7] It is thus only half the truth to call Wellhausen the representative of the "newer documentary hypothesis." For him, and for his adherents in the following decades, the question of the sources of the Pentateuch was indissolubly connected with their respective historical settings. Dividing sources and dating sources were two sides of the same coin. Dating meant, however, relating the sources to a certain point in Israel's history, in particular in the history of its religion. And that constituted the fundamental difference between the older sources, the Yahwist (J) and the Elohist (E), on the one hand, and the later Priestly Code (P), on the other.[8]

This was true until one or two decades ago, and in a sense it still is. Viewed as a whole, Old Testament scholarship still lives in the era of Wellhausen. This brings me to a question of definition. In the title of this paper, I use the word "paradigm." I mean it in the sense of Thomas Kuhn's famous analysis of *The Structure of Scientific Revolutions*.[9] According to Kuhn, a paradigm is, to simplify it somewhat, a methodological model that, for a distinct scholarly field, has won common acceptance, with the result that scholarly research and discussion in this particular field is performed inside the frame established by the paradigm and dependent on the paradigm. This is exactly what happened in Old Testament scholarship.[10] For decades everybody could use the abbreviations "J" or "P" without explaining them, and without explicitly mentioning the implications with regard to the dating and setting of the texts labeled by these letters. The connotations of "early" and "late," and even of "Hebrew" or "Israelite," and "Jewish" were always tacitly implied. Of course, the whole thing continued to be a pure hypothesis. But common acceptance made it a quasi fact. Nobody had to give reasons for building upon this theory, but to question it was, and still is, almost like denying a fact.

The case is similar with some of the main theses of Bernhard Duhm. [[37]] Most of what he published and what was of great influence in his time is now more or less forgotten. But in the interpretation of the book of Isaiah, we still find today two key terms that were coined by Duhm: the one is "Trito-Isaiah," the other, "The Servant Songs."[11] Duhm invented the

---

7. See the interesting volume, *Julius Wellhausen and His Prolegomena to the History of Israel* (ed. D. A. Knight; *Semeia* 25 [1982]).

8. Wellhausen originally called the Priestly Code "Q" from 'quattuor' (four), because he saw it as the 'book of the Four Covenants' (*Vierbundesbuch*).

9. T. Kuhn, *The Structure of Scientific Revolutions* (Chicago: University of Chicago Press, 1962; 2nd edn, 1970).

10. I am aware of Kuhn's reservations about using his concept for fields other than the sciences, as expressed in the postscript of the 2d edition. But I find the parallelism too striking, in particular with regard to the period of crisis, so that I gratefully accept his understanding for such a use.

11. B. Duhm, *Das Buch Jesaja* (Göttinger Handkommentar zum Alten Testament 3/1; Göttingen: Vandenhoeck & Ruprecht, 1892; 4th ed., 1922).

term "Trito-Isaiah" in 1892, when he declared chaps. 56–66 of Isaiah to be the work of an author different from that of chaps. 40–55. Time and again there was some discussion of this thesis, but in general it was accepted, and today it is still used with a self-evidence similar to that of the Pentateuchal sources. And again, as in the Pentateuch, by the positing of a Trito-Isaiah, the book of Isaiah represents the two main epochs of Israelite history: the "early" Isaiah, characterized by the spirit of the Hebraic times, and the "late," Jewish Trito-Isaiah, showing all the signs of this "unsuccessful restoration of Hebraism," to quote De Wette again.

Between these two contrasting elements of Israelite history, we find the second key term introduced by Duhm's commentary, the "Servant Songs" in Deutero-Isaiah. Again it was Duhm who ascribed this group of texts to a separate author. It is interesting to see how, in the scholarship of the following century, there appeared an overwhelming flood of literature on the question who this *'ebed* [['servant']] might be. Yet, until recently, almost no one questioned, or even discussed, the literary independence of this group of texts from the rest of Deutero-Isaiah.[12] Duhm belongs therefore to the great figures that shaped Old Testament scholarship in this century. And perhaps even today his hypotheses are less questioned than Wellhausen's. (In the framework of the Society of Biblical Literature there is now a seminar on these questions first raised by Duhm.)

Hermann Gunkel's case is different. A younger contemporary of Wellhausen and Duhm,[13] he published his first fundamental book, *Schöpfung und Chaos*, in the last decade of the previous century (1895).[14] This book gave him an honorable place in the ranks of the *Religionsgeschichtliche Schule* [['history of religions school']]. But his impact on the whole century was based on the establishment of the new methodological approach to the texts of the Hebrew Bible that he himself first called *Literaturgeschichte* [['history of literature']] or *Gattungsforschung* [['genre study']], and that later developed under the name of *Formgeschichte* or 'form criticism'.

Possibly some non-German readers might find it a bit strange to rank Gunkel so high in the scholarship of our century. I must explain, therefore, why, in my view, he deserves that distinction. At first glance, Gunkel belongs to the majority of Old Testament scholars at the beginning of this century, who, without hesitation, followed the principles of the "newer documentary hypothesis." His commentary on Genesis (first edition 1901)

---

12. But see, now, T. N. D. Mettinger, *A Farewell to the Servant Songs: A Critical Examination of an Exegetical Axiom* (Lund: Gleerup, 1983).

13. Wellhausen (1844–1918); Duhm (1847–1928); Gunkel (1862–1932).

14. H. Gunkel, *Schöpfung und Chaos in Urzeit und Endzeit: Eine religionsgeschichtliche Untersuchung über Gen 1 und Ap Joh 12* (Göttingen: Vandenhoeck & Ruprecht, 1895).

seemed to be in full accord with the spirit of that age. But it only seemed to be so. My first thesis is that, from the outset, Gunkel's approach actually was incompatible with the idea of literary "sources" or "documents." The introduction to his Genesis commentary, which in the revised edition from 1910 covers almost a hundred pages, is entitled, *Die Sagen der Genesis* (the sagas of Genesis). Here Gunkel explains the different kinds of sagas (*Arten der Sagen*), their artistic form (*Kunstform der Sagen*), and their oral transmission, and only then does he finally reach their literary stage. Here he mentions the documents or sources in the commonly accepted form, with a polite bow towards Wellhausen. But then he goes on to tell the reader that these documents are collections of oral traditions, and that their authors were not individuals but schools of narrators (*Erzählerschulen*).

Possibly Gunkel was too much a child of his time to realize the basic difference between the two approaches. But others already felt it in his own time. In a review of Gunkel's Genesis commentary in the same year (1901), Friedrich Giesebrecht expressed his amazement that Gunkel, along with his own new approach, continued as well to divide sources.[15] Some decades later, in 1934, in a report on literature on Genesis, Paul Humbert declared that "Gunkel by his methodological effort to dissolve the large contexts and to go back to the smaller circles of sagas and to the single sagas as the primary units, is responsible for the downfall of the documentary hypothesis."[16] I believe that there are good reasons for such a thesis. The further development of Old Testament scholarship, in my view, shows clearly that Gunkel inaugurated a methodological approach [[39]] that moved into a direction quite different from that established by Wellhausen. In order not to be blamed for too limited a Germanophile view, I quote from a well-known American book, *The Hebrew Bible and Its Modern Interpreters*: "It would be fair to say that Gerhard von Rad and Martin Noth have offered the most significant comprehensive work on the Pentateuch in modern biblical scholarship."[17] It is obvious that both von Rad and Noth were deeply influenced by Gunkel. Von Rad, in 1938, used the term *Formgeschichte* [['form criticism']] in a broader sense (*Das formgeschichtliche Problem des Hexateuchs*),[18] while Noth, in 1943, introduced the

---

15. F. Giesebrecht, Review of H. Gunkel, *Genesis, Deutsche Literaturzeitung* 22 (1901) 1861–66.

16. P. Humbert, "Die neuere Genesis-Forschung," *TRu* NF 6 (1934) 208.

17. D. A. Knight and G. M. Tucker, *The Hebrew Bible and Its Modern Interpreters* (Philadelphia: Fortress Press, 1985) 265.

18. G. von Rad, *Das formgeschichtliche Problem des Hexateuchs* (Stuttgart: Kohlhammer, 1938); reprinted in *Gesammelte Studien zum Alten Testament* (München: Kaiser, 1958) 9–86; English translation: "The Form-Critical Problem of the Hexateuch," *The Problem of the Hexateuch and Other Essays* (Edinburgh and London: Oliver & Boyd, 1966) 1–78.

term *Überlieferungsgeschichte* (history of transmission).[19] Both declared explicitly that their work was a consistent, further development of Gunkel's approach. To the readership of this journal [[Rendtorff's reference is to the readers of the journal *Biblical Interpretation*]] there is no need to explain the work of these two authors. My question is how it is related to the Wellhausen paradigm.

At first glance, both authors seemed to be good Wellhausenians. They seemed to agree to the ruling system of sources and to work with it. But again, as was the case with Gunkel, it only seemed to be so. Like Gunkel, both von Rad and Noth used the results of the newer Documentary Hypothesis in the commonly accepted way. But actually, they asked questions that Wellhausen never would have asked, so that their main field of concern lay beyond the area of Wellhausen's hypotheses. Their leading common interest was the question of the origin of the Pentateuchal material. Noth, in particular, dealt mainly with the earliest pre-literary stage of the traditions, before they became shaped as narratives or as other genres. One could almost call it a pre-Gunkel stage, because in the main parts of his book Noth never spoke about actual texts, but only about "themes" and "narrative materials" (*Erzählungsstoffe*). But then, in [[40]] a highly surprising move at the end of his book, he jumped over to the "sources." And here he was more orthodox than many of his predecessors by declaring that the authors of the sources had been individuals. In my view, this is a classic example of the working of the paradigm. Obviously Noth thought bona fide that he worked within the Wallhausenian system, simply because he had no alternative way of thinking. What he did had nothing to do with sources and the like, but he felt the need to put his own work in the commonly accepted framework of source criticism. Here he had the interesting idea of an earlier source, a kind of pre-source, that he called "G" (*gemeinsame Grundlage* 'common base'); but he never explained in what sense the authors of the later sources, the "real" sources J and E, could be called "authors," after everything had been shaped before they began to work. This only shows that for Noth the whole matter of sources was an *opus alienum* [[alien work]]. In the core of his book,[20] he dealt with matters beyond the field of source criticism.

Von Rad shared with Noth an interest in the early stage of Pentateuchal traditions. Actually, he was the first to ask this question by pos-

---

19. M. Noth, *Überlieferungsgeschichtliche Studien: Die sammelnden und bearbeitenden Geschichtswerke im Alten Testament* (Halle: Niemeyer, 1943); *Überlieferungsgeschichte des Pentateuch* (Stuttgart: Kohlhammer, 1948); English translation: *A History of the Pentateuchal Traditions* (Englewood Cliffs, N.J.: Prentice-Hall, 1972; reprinted: Chico, Calif.: Scholars Press, 1981).

20. In his book on the Pentateuch (see n. 19), in particular §§6 to 10, in a broader sense also §§11 to 14.

iting an early "creed" that Noth developed further (and changed, in my view) into what he called "themes." Von Rad's main concern, however, was the growth of the Pentateuch as a whole, up to its final form. In this process, according to von Rad, mainly one major collector, narrator, and theological interpreter was at work. Von Rad called him "J," the Yahwist. But what kind of Yahwist was that? Was he one of a number of authors of sources? At the end of his book, von Rad, like Noth, turned to the question of sources. Unlike Noth, he did not claim to have an overall concept. On the contrary, he admitted that he did not understand the matter:

> Not that the conflation of E and P with J would now appear to be a simple process, nor one which could be altogether explained to one's satisfaction! The problem of the origin and purpose of these two works, their derivation, and the readers for whom they were destined, is as much an open question now as it was before, and will probably remain so. But these problems are generically different from the ones we have been dealing with in our present study.[21]

Again, the paradigm worked, and von Rad paid his tribute to it. [[41]] But in passing, he declared that this was not his problem. I feel that even the choice of the name "Yahwist" for the great theologian who, according to von Rad, shaped the Pentateuch, was a tribute to the paradigm, if only an unconscious one. Von Rad could as well have taken another name. Thus my second thesis is that von Rad and Noth confirm my first thesis, namely that Gunkel opened a way of reading Old Testament texts different from Wellhausen's and finally leading in a different direction. But like Gunkel, von Rad and Noth were not aware—in the case of von Rad I would prefer to say, not fully aware[22]—of the fundamental tension between the purely literary analysis of source criticism and their own intentions, which they explicitly related to Gunkel's work.

Von Rad, in particular, drew the line beginning with Gunkel much further; namely, to the final stage of the shaping of the Pentateuch (or Hexateuch, as he called it, or Tetrateuch, according to Noth). I believe that this was not only a logical further development but, at the same time, a fundamental change in Gunkel's approach. Gunkel's interest was concentrated on the smallest units, and at most on some larger units that could be understood as collections of originally smaller ones. He never looked at those larger entities that had to be explained as the result of some kind of literary process, however, and that means he never dis-

---

21. G. von Rad, *The Problem of the Hexateuch and Other Essays,* 74.

22. In his last essay, on Exodus 1–14, he pleaded for a much more holistic approach: "Beobachtungen an der Moseerzählung Exodus 1–14," *EvT* 31 (1971) 579–88; reprinted in *Gesammelte Studien* 2 (München: Kaiser, 1973) 189–98.

cussed the way that eventually led to the book or books as we have them before us. Precisely this was von Rad's starting point. His question was: how did the Pentateuch (or Hexateuch) reach its final form? His theory is well known and need not to be explained here in detail. Von Rad saw the development in four stages: first the basic credal connection of Israel's exodus from Egypt and its settlement in the promised land; then the insertion of the Sinai tradition; thirdly, the unfolding of the patriarchal story; and, finally, the placement of the primeval history at the beginning of the whole edifice.

The main achievement of this new approach was—or at least could have been—to shift the focus from the internal literary problems to an understanding of the organizing structures and ideas of the books. And I believe it is not a mere coincidence that only a few years after von Rad's book on the Hexateuch (1938), Noth put [[42]] the same question to the historical books (or former prophets in the Hebrew canon) in his *Überlieferungsgeschichtliche Studien* (1943). That was the hour another quasi paradigm was born, the "Deuteronomistic Work." It is extremely interesting to see how, at this very moment, the assumption of a deuteronomistic redaction of the books from Joshua to Kings, that had been generally accepted for decades, was turned into the question of the organizing structure of this whole series of books as one huge literary and theological work. From now on the Deuteronomistic Work could be seen as the second great literary entity alongside the Pentateuch.

It is also interesting that in the following years, and even decades, there was almost no methodological relation between the observations made about the Pentateuch and those made about the Deuteronomistic Work. Apparently scholars felt the starting points of both hypotheses to be too far apart. In other words, the paradigm worked again. The problems of the Pentateuch are not to be mixed with those of any other part of biblical literature.

The parallelism is evident, however. Noth declared that the Deuteronomist "was not only a 'redactor,' but the author of a historical work that combined the transmitted tradition materials, which were of very different character, stringing them according to a definite plan. In doing so, Dtr generally gave the final word to the sources he had at his disposal, and only linked the individual pieces by a connecting text."[23] According to some scholars, myself included,[24] this is exactly what could be said about the so-called "P" stratum, at least in some parts of the Pentateuch. Several

---

23. M. Noth, *Überlieferungsgeschichtliche Studien*, [p. 11], p. 53.
24. See R. Rendtorff, *Das überlieferungsgeschichtliche Problem des Pentateuch* (BZAW 147; Berlin: de Gruyter, 1977); English translation: *The Problem of the Process of Transmission in the Pentateuch* (Sheffield: JSOT Press, 1990).

years ago, I tried to discuss this similarity with scholars of my teachers' generation, with Noth, von Rad, Zimmerli and others, who regularly met in the framework of the *Biblischer Kommentar* series. I received no response. The uniqueness of the Pentateuchal sources was still a taboo. Nevertheless, looking back, it is obvious that here the Wellhausen paradigm had been undermined in a far-reaching manner. Thus my third thesis is that the traditio-historical approach, as an offspring of form criticism, consistently led to the question of the final shape, be it of a book, or even of a larger entity like the Deuteronomistic Work. Again, not many were aware of this fact, and new impulses [[43]] from other sides were needed to develop this new approach to the final shape. Now, however, as we reach this era of discussion, I feel these connections to be evident. Let me quote from the first paragraph of von Rad's book on the Hexateuch:

> A process of disintegration on a large scale has taken its course [that has a] deep corroding effect. Almost everywhere the final form of the Hexateuch has become only a point of departure that itself is not regarded as worth any specific discussion, but the debate has to get away from that as quickly as possible in order to arrive at the real problems lying behind it.

It is interesting that von Rad, here in 1938, used the term *Letztgestalt*, that in the current discussion is used for 'final form' or 'final shape'. His complaint about the disregard of the *Letztgestalt* could even have been formulated today.

I have sought to demonstrate that Old Testament scholarship in this century was, and still is, deeply determined by the methods of *Literarkritik*, in the form of the Documentary Hypothesis. At the same time, this paradigm was continually undermined by form criticism and its continuation in tradition criticism and, in a certain sense, in redaction criticism—a development that finally led to a new interest in the final form of books, and even larger entities, within the Old Testament. There is a continuity with the present discussion about the final shape of the text, canon criticism, and the like. This is where I would locate my own scholarly interests and endeavors. But I think it would be an inappropriate harmonization of the history of research to draw too straight a line from Gunkel through von Rad and Noth to the present discussion, because there are obvious elements of discontinuity, in particular since the mid-seventies.

In what follows, I will not mention names. On the one hand, I will speak mainly about developments and tendencies that are represented by more than one specific name. On the other hand, I want to avoid being accused of mentioning some names and not mentioning others (some names may be found in the footnotes). In the chapter on the Pentateuch of the book quoted earlier, *The Hebrew Bible and Its Modern Interpreters*,

D. A. Knight writes that there "occurred a serious departure from the Wellhausen/von Rad/Noth schema."[25] Indeed, these three names belong together particularly in one central [[44]] point, the dating of the sources, especially the date of the so-called Yahwist. Until the mid-seventies the dating of "J" in the period of the early monarchy had been widely accepted. But since then, scholars have begun to question that dating and to vote for a much later date for the "Yahwist," such as even the exilic period.[26] The existence of a "Yahwist" seemingly is kept up, but actually one of the basic elements of the Wellhausen hypothesis, the setting of "J" in the early monarchic period, is given up. I believe this late dating does at least as much harm to Wellhausen's ideas as the general denying of the existence of sources. An exilic "Yahwist," in my view, has nothing to do with Wellhausen's position—and even less with that of von Rad. Such a Yahwist loses his meaning for a reconstruction of Israel's history in the time of the monarchy, and, even worse, the temporal gap between the "Yahwist" and the "Priestly code" dwindles away, and with it one of the main arguments for the deep discrepancy between the earlier "Israel" and the later "Judaism" that had been of such great importance for Wellhausen.

I believe that the traditional Documentary Hypothesis has come to an end. Of course, there are still attempts to save the Yahwist, and even the Elohist, whose existence had been questioned much earlier. But I do not see any new arguments that could turn back the wheel. Therefore I think that, in the terminology of Thomas Kuhn, Old Testament scholarship at present is "in crisis." The Wellhausen paradigm no longer functions as a commonly accepted presupposition for Old Testament exegesis. And, at present, no other concept is visible that could replace such a widely accepted position. On the contrary, the shift in dating texts makes it obvious that the shaking of this paradigm is part of a more far-reaching shaking of the centuries-old fundamentals of Old Testament scholarship. Von Rad and Noth could still ask whether a certain text was pre-amphictyonic or post-amphictyonic. Today not only is the amphictyony dead, but the question is rather whether the texts are pre-exilic or post-exilic. Almost half a thousand years have faded away.

In this respect, the problems of interpreting the Pentateuch are closely connected to the general problems of reconstructing Israel's [[45]] history and the history of its religion. The late dating of texts is an indication of the loss of confidence in their historical credibility. The later the

---

25. P. 271.

26. In particular are to be named J. Van Seters, *Abraham in History and Tradition* (New Haven: Yale University Press, 1975), and H. H. Schmid, *Der sogenannte Jahwist: Beobachtungen und Fragen zur Pentateuchforschung* (Zürich: Theologischer Verlag, 1976); cf. also the discussion in *JSOT* 3 (1977).

texts are, the farther remote they are from the events they are talking about, and the less they can be expected to provide historical information. It is therefore no accident that one of the most fundamental changes occurred with the hypotheses about the origins of Israel. In the fifties, there was the great fight, or even war, between the Albright school and the Alt school. It was a fight that touched certain basic elements of scholarship and even of credibility when, for example, Noth was called by some Albrightians a "nihilist." But in spite of all that, a common basis existed for all of these scholars—a basis founded on the biblical account that the Israelites had been nomads who, within a certain historical period, entered the land of Canaan to settle there, be it by conquest or by *Landnahme* [['annexation']]. Today, any consensus is gone. It is not only questioned when and how the Israelites came into the land, but whether or not they came at all. The theory of an internal social revolution or upheaval in Canaan not only added a third model to those offered earlier by the two great schools, it also questioned certain basic assumptions of the generally accepted view of Israel's history.

One of the main points of uncertainty is the question of Israel's identity. Of course, the political and national structure of premonarchic Israel has always been subject to discussion. But now the Israelites themselves have become a matter of dispute. Who were the Israelites? Are they distinguishable from the Canaanites? And how? And what about Israelite religion? In the Old Testament, the religious distinction from other people, not only from the Canaanites, is the main criterion for Israelite identity. Is that an original element of Israel's history—or is it only a late development, or even a priestly construct? In recent years an increasing number of scholars declare that Israel's religion did not differ from the type of religion common to other peoples or groups in Canaan. Originally it was polytheistic; Yhwh was a god of the Baʿal- or Hadad-type, or even identical with the Canaanite Baʿal, and, of course, he had a spouse, who, however, was not always the same—sometimes Asherah, but sometimes even Anat, who for that purpose had to be fetched from afar.[27] Only [[46]] later some people had the idea of differentiating this god from other Baʿals, which led to a struggle against the worshippers of other gods and finally to a rigorous monotheism.[28]

---

27. Cf. M. Weippert, "Synkretismus und Monotheismus: Religionsinterne Konfliktbewältigung im alten Israel," in *Kultur und Konflikt* (ed. J. Assmann and D. Harth; Frankfurt/M: Suhrkamp, 1990) 143–73, esp. 156–57.

28. One of the books frequently quoted in this context is M. Smith, *Palestinian Parties and Politics That Shaped the Old Testament* (New York and London: Columbia University Press, 1971; reprinted, London: SCM Press, 1987). But it is interesting that in the preface to the

One of the main characteristics of those hypotheses is that in certain cases they maintain exactly the opposite of what the biblical texts say. That this is in fact the intention of some scholars becomes clear by the recent remark of one of them. "The biblical (and scholarly) 'dogma' that Yahweh never had a *paredros* [['mate']] has been nullified by the finds from Kuntillet ʿAjrûd"; that is, from inscriptions from "a desert station in northern Sinai dating from about 800 B.C.E.," asking for a blessing from "Yahweh of Shomeron (Samaria) and his Ashera/ashera" and from "Yahweh of Teman and his Ashera/ashera."[29] Of course, these are interesting inscriptions, and they need careful interpretation. But, in my view, they have to be interpreted, not against biblical texts but in relation to them, in order to determine their specific value for reconstructing the history of Israel's religion, in particular the quite unique development that led to a religion without parallels in the ancient Near East. I doubt that inscriptions like those from Kuntillet ʿAjrûd and Khirbet el-Qom are able simply to "nullify" the broad and unanimous biblical testimony.

In this particular case some new sources could be quoted. This is, however, a rare exception. For the rest, the sources are the same as they have always been. What has changed is the scholarly attitude to the sources, in particular to the main core of sources, namely the texts of the Old Testament itself. The change becomes particularly [[47]] obvious in a recent debate about the question, "Is it possible to write a history of Israel without relying on the Hebrew Bible?"[30] In this case, again, the members of the great schools of the fifties and sixties would have been unified: they would not have understood the question. On what else should one rely if not on the Hebrew Bible? And what else could be the purpose of studying the history of Israel if not to increase the understanding of the Hebrew Bible? All these scholars of the fifties and sixties understood themselves first of all as Bible scholars, critically using all kinds of methods and information to reconstruct Israel's history. Therefore one of the basic changes

---

second edition the author writes: "I must call the readers' attention to one important book, J. Tigay's *You Shall Have No Other Gods* (Atlanta: Scholars Press, 1986). By collection of epigraphic and other data Tigay has shown that from monarchic times on Yahweh was by far the most often mentioned god of the Israelites. Worship of other gods has left comparatively little evidence. How Tigay's facts relate to those set out in this book is a problem for further research." One wonders whether all those quoting and translating Smith have been aware of this warning. Cf., e.g., B. Lang (ed.), *Der einzige Gott: Die Geburt des biblischen Monotheismus* (München: Kösel, 1981), where parts of Smith's book are translated; however, this book appeared before the reprint of Smith's book.

29. G. Ahlström, "The Role of Archaeological and Literary Remains in Reconstructing Israel's History," in *The Fabric of History: Text, Artifact and Israel's Past* (ed. D. Edelman; Sheffield: JSOT Press, 1991) 116–41, esp. 127.

30. J. M. Miller, in Edelman (ed.), *The Fabric of History*, 93–102.

in the field seems to be the separation of the history of Israel from the Hebrew Bible by some scholars relying exclusively on archaeology.[31] I have a high regard for archaeology, and I try to follow its main developments. But I do not understand the *raison d'être* of a history of Israel that is not carried out in close contact with the Hebrew Bible, whose very existence in my view is now, as before, the main, if not the only reason to study the history of ancient Israel at all.

The subtitle I have given this essay is "Hopes—and Fears." I suppose that my readers have realized that, in the meantime, I have entered the chapter on "fears," in particular because I have the feeling that some of the discussions in the area mentioned above are unnecessarily polemical. Sometimes representatives of this new kind of history writing declare their own method to be the only correct one, and accuse other people who still work with the Bible when doing history of being biblicists or even fundamentalists. I do not think that this is the right field in which to declare each other heretics. There are many scholarly approaches and methods, in Bible studies as well as in history writing. Nobody will forbid any scholar or group or school to believe their own method to be the best one. Many will be interested in seeing the results and checking their validity and usefulness. But in scholarship, by definition, there is no heresy. We should rather practise and accept methodological pluralism.

[[48]] Let me return to the problem of the late dating of biblical texts. This tendency has taken possession of great parts of Old Testament exegesis. It would go far beyond the scope of this paper to go through all the problems involved. Therefore I want to single out two main points. The first one seems, at first glance, to be only a question of terminology. Since Martin Noth redefined the term "deuteronomistic," it became more and more common practice to label by this expression any text or formulation that seems to be somehow dependent on the ideas of Deuteronomy. Now, the more texts are dated in post-Deuteronomic times, the more texts are called "deuteronomistic." As a result, this term loses its concreteness and tends to become a rather vague expression for post-Deuteronomic, post-exilic, or simply for "late" as compared to assumed older texts. Some scholars ironically coined the word "deuteronomisticism," and when written with "y," it expresses something of the mystic darkness of texts of a late time. Indeed, Deuteronomy played a fundamental role in the history

---

31. See, e.g., T. L. Thompson, *The Origin Traditions of Ancient Israel: I. The Literary Formation of Genesis and Exodus 1–23* (Sheffield: JSOT Press, 1987) 40: "The following chapters make abundantly clear the necessity of separating biblical interpretation from modern historiography. This, once achieved, ends the crisis in biblical scholarship which we have discussed in the pages of this chapter." The reader will be aware that this is a different view of the character of the present crisis, and therefore of the appropriate means for its solution.

of biblical thought and biblical literature. But I suspect that in post-exilic times the ideas and the language of this school of thought became widely accepted and used, while in many cases there is no immediate relation to Deuteronomy or to a certain group of deuteronomistic theologians or writers. This is particularly evident in texts whose language contains certain deuteronomistic elements, together with other elements that are characteristic, for example, of the priestly layer in the Pentateuch, of Ezekiel, or of Isaiah 40–66, to name just some of the peculiar language or styles of late pre-exilic or exilic times that every trained biblical scholar can easily recognize. In my view this kind of "mixed" language is a characteristic element of certain texts formulated in post-exilic times. To avoid making the term so broad as to be meaningless, we should restrict the use of the term "deuteronomistic" mainly to the so-called Deuteronomistic History.

It is not only a question of terminology. The more texts are dated in post-exilic times, the more differentiated we have to imagine the spectrum of Israel's life, thinking, and belief in this time. Calling texts of this period "deuteronomistic" means seeing them as dependent on an earlier piece of literature instead of trying to understand them as independent and original expressions of their own time. I see a possible danger of all this late dating: it threatens to make a great deal of Old Testament literature non-original and even second-rate. I wonder to what degree scholars still have in mind the [[49]] traditional hierarchy of "early" and "late," or even of "Israelite" and "Jewish," as it dominated the thought of Wellhausen and his followers. I have to confess that I am in a permanent conflict, because although I see good reasons for dating certain texts in post-exilic times, I also suspect that this could easily entail a diminution of their value.

The latter aspect is related to my second point. Dating texts in the post-exilic period means dating them in a dark period. From the rebuilding of the temple in Jerusalem in 515 B.C.E. until the appearance of Alexander the Great in the Near East around 333 B.C.E., the only information we have about Israel (or Judah) is to be found in the books of Ezra and Nehemiah. Of course, these books provide very interesting information; but they are so isolated from the murky periods before and after them, that with regard to the life of the Jewish people in the land of Israel during the time of the Persian empire, more questions are raised than can be answered. I am always amazed by the sureness, not to say boldness, of some scholars, who feel able to date with precision all kinds of texts within this period, even within specific decades. It is even more amazing when certain historical events are mentioned in texts that, according to their interpreters, were written much later. One interesting example is the interpretation of the first part of the book of Isaiah by some recent commentators who do not believe that any of the material in Isaiah 1–12 was written in the period of Isaiah, let alone by the historical prophet himself. That means that texts like Isaiah 7 and others mentioning the so-called Syro-Ephraimite War are only expressions of the ideas of certain post-exilic people, dependent on deuteronomistic war-theology, and have nothing to do with the historical situation of that war.[32] Here the interpreters create a whole series of new problems, whose solution would need a detailed knowledge of post-exilic times. How can we know what people thought and believed in this dark period? Perhaps we can learn something by a reconstruction based on scrutinizing the image we get from the texts that we believe to be dated in this period. This would mean working in an almost classical hermeneutical circle of dating texts and using the same texts for reconstructing the time in [[50]] which they are dated. I hope that scholars familiar with this period will take up the challenge of this task. Then we will have to redesign our image of Israel's history and the history of it religion. This brings me back to some of my earlier remarks about the reliability of biblical texts for reconstructing history. The value of texts can no longer depend on their early dating, as it did for Wellhausen and many others, or on their usefulness as historical sources, as some modern scholars claim. We have to learn to take biblical texts seriously for their own sake, from whatever period and in whatever context they appear.

Let me add a remark on a certain Christian attitude toward the later parts of the Old Testament. There is a widespread practice of moving as fast as possible from the prophets to the New Testament, from Deutero-Isaiah to Jesus. Now, the more texts are dated in post-exilic times, the more we will have to deal with the centuries in between; and the more we will realize that the Old Testament is not so much "Israelite," in the Wellhausenian sense, as "Jewish." Here another wide and fruitful hermeneutical field is opening.

In conclusion, I want to return to hope. I have tried to show that some reasons for fear lie in certain consequences of dating texts. Of course, in some cases dating will be useful in order to understand a particular text better. But sometimes one has the feeling that dating becomes an end in itself. And in some cases one might ask what benefit all the efforts at dating will have for an appropriate understanding of the respective text. There are many texts in the Old Testament whose meaning and message are not dependent on information about their dating.

---

32. So, e.g., O. Kaiser, *Das Buch des Propheten Jesaja: Kapitel 1–12* (ATD 17; Göttingen: Vandenhoeck & Ruprecht, 5th edn, 1981; English translation: London: SCM; Philadelphia: Westminster Press, 1983); cf. also J. J. Vermeylen, *Du prophète Isaïe à l'apocalyptique*, 2 (Paris: Gabalda, 1977–78).

There are also methods of reading and interpreting biblical texts that are not concerned with problems of dating. This is true for the whole range of approaches related to the newer literary criticism. It is, I might add, sometimes disturbing for a German scholar today to feel unable to use the classical word *Literarkritik* in its English translation as 'literary criticism' without running the risk of being misunderstood. In the language of German Old Testament scholarship there is, however, no word for the newer literary criticism, because the methods coming from more recent general studies of literature have not yet been taken up by German Old Testament scholars. One could see this as a specifically German problem, arguing that the Germans are behind international scholarship. In a sense that would be true. But there is another reason for the divergence [[51]] between German and American, or even Anglo-Saxon scholarship, namely the fact that in Germany study of the Bible is conducted almost exclusively in the framework of Theological Faculties or Schools. This situation brings German Bible scholars much less in contact with scholars of other fields of literature, and the same is true for students. One could complain of this isolation, which remains a fact.

I mention this divergence mainly for two reasons. One is simply to say that in this field I am only an observer and reader, but not an active participant. Nevertheless, some of the developments in this area contain for me signs of hope. (I shall return to this point.) The other reason is that the different developments in our countries result in different relations to the scholarly tradition. By taking up new methods from other disciplines, some scholars seem not to feel the need of maintaining a relationship to older methods used earlier in their field. When reading books and articles on Old Testament topics based on new literary methods, I sometimes ask myself whether there is any continuity with classical Old Testament scholarship at all. I believe that it would be harmful to our common scholarly endeavours not to acknowledge the relation of newer approaches to the history of modern Old Testament scholarship. Therefore our somewhat old-fashioned German Bible scholarship might have the positive function of maintaining a certain continuity.

Let me say now why I see some hope in some of these new approaches. It is because here the text is taken as it is. I do not want to enter into a theoretical discussion of "the text itself" or the like. But looking from the point of view of traditional Old Testament scholarship, I realize that interpreters using these new approaches do not begin by analyzing the text from a diachronic point of view according to its different levels or sources and the like, as the majority of scholars trained in the older methods still do. On the contrary, they want to interpret the text as we have it before us, in its given form. Some of these new approaches could thus offer real alternatives to the traditional methods of Old Testament exegesis that, in a sense, have come to an end. Again, the question would be whether or not and how we could establish connections between new approaches and the tradition of Old Testament exegesis. I believe that not too many scholars trained in the older methods would be ready just to jump over the ditch and to begin anew. And who knows how long the current methods will be in vogue?

[[52]] What will continue, I hope, is the attitude of taking the text seriously in its given form, in its final shape. In this respect there are close connections between some of the new literary approaches and so-called canon criticism. It would require another paper to explain in detail how I see the similarities as well as the differences between these approaches. But, first of all, I want to stress that taking a synchronic approach to the text in its given shape is a task Old Testament scholarship has neglected too long and too intentionally. Scholars still seem to be proud of knowing things better than the final redactors or compilers. This is a kind of nineteenth-century hubris we should have left behind us. The last writers, whatever we want to call them, were, in any case, much closer to the original meaning of the text than we can ever be. From time to time we should remember what Franz Rosenzweig taught us: that the letter "R," as usually taken for the "redactor," actually should be read as "Rabbenu," "our master." For we receive the text from the hands of these last writers, and they are the ones whose voice and message we have to hear first.

At this point I want to say again that we should try to relate new, mainly synchronic aspects, to older, mainly diachronic insights, for what was observed in careful studies during the last two centuries was not entirely wrong. It is obvious that some, or even many, of the observations that led to diachronic decisions had a certain validity. The question is how to handle those observations and what consequences to draw from them. Even the most committed synchronic exegete today would not argue that the first two chapters of the book of Genesis were written by the same author. But how to read them in their interrelation and in their wider context needs a much more sophisticated approach than just dividing them into two different sources. Moreover, the consequences for reading the book of Genesis as a whole, the Pentateuch as a whole, and the canon of the Hebrew Bible as a whole will be more fascinating if we go beyond the diachronic observation of diversity to the search for the inner, or even overarching unity. Such a unity in some cases might appear to be full of tensions. But even this tension was surely not hidden from the later writers, so that we can try to follow their guidance in reading their texts.

The paradigm is changing. I believe it has changed already. But the field is open. Many new and fruitful approaches are visible that will lead

Old Testament scholarship into the twenty-first century. At [[53]] the moment there is no new model that could be expected to achieve common acceptance as a paradigm, and there will probably be none in the near future. This will give considerable freedom to those who are looking for new approaches and who are ready to move ahead. They are many, and therefore there will be hope.

Part 2

The Historical Impulse among Israel's Neighbors

Introduction

Few contemporary scholars of the Hebrew Bible would deny the value of the study of ancient Near Eastern literatures as an aid to understanding the Bible, for it stands to reason that just as cognate languages can often shed light on the workings of a particular language (such as Hebrew), so cognate literatures can often shed light on the workings of a particular literary corpus (such as the Hebrew Scriptures). The general agreement in principle regarding the value of comparative study, however, does not mean that most scholars of the Hebrew Bible have delved very deeply into this study; as Alan Millard notes in the third essay reproduced below, such study has in fact barely begun. Nor is there a consensus regarding what, in fact, comparative study has so far demonstrated with respect to ancient Israelite historiography. Some scholars believe that the ancient Near East was lacking in historiographical texts until a fairly late period, and they conclude from this that biblical history writing such as is found in the so-called "Deuteronomistic History" must be of quite late origin. John Van Seters (1983), for example, is of the opinion that we do not encounter historiography comparable to that found in the DH until Herodotus, and he concludes from this that the DH must be quite late in origin. Further, since he believes that the Deuteronomist was Israel's earliest historian, the remaining historiographical texts must be later still. Other scholars hold a very different view: "Whether it has to do with historiography, law, or prophetic pronouncements, everything points to the Bible not having developed in a ghetto but in serious engagement with the great religious cultures of its time. There are literary models, already in the second millenium, that the Bible used" (Cazelles 1989: 42; my translation). Put succinctly, "Israel was heir to already established ideas of history and practices of history-writing."[1]

---

1. J. R. Porter, "Old Testament Historiography," in *Tradition and Interpretation: Essays by Members of the Society for Old Testament Study* (ed. G. W. Anderson; Oxford: Clarendon, 1979) 127.

What accounts for this wide diversity of opinion? As W. W. Hallo points out in a seminal essay (pp. 77–97 below), it is not a question of one scholar's taking a comparativist approach and another's refusing: "In fact, some of their strongest arguments [Hallo has in mind John Van Seters, Thomas L. Thompson, and others] are based on the comparison of biblical data with neo-Assyrian and neo-Babylonian or even with classical Greek and Roman sources. What they rule out is only the comparison with older Near Eastern materials" (p. 80).

To adopt a comparativist approach can, of course, be risky. There is always a danger of minimizing the special character of the Hebrew Bible. But this reductionistic tendency should be avoided, since the Hebrew Bible is distinctive in various ways, as the following observation by J. R. Porter illustrates:

> [I]n the cultures surrounding Israel, these [historiographic] literary forms are found almost entirely as separate units. In this sense it would be true to say that they are the raw materials of history, rather than history proper, although many of them are genuine historiography, in so far as they present interpretations and understanding of history and an aware-ness of direction within it. By contrast, in the Old Testament, all these ele-ments, as far as the Pentateuch and the Former Prophets are concerned, are embedded in a chronologically added narrative. Nowhere else in the ancient Near East is there to be found anything strictly comparable to this collecting and arranging of traditions and documents as successive ele-ments in larger corpora and ultimately, into a single corpus.[2]

As Millard has succinctly stated, "The Hebrew histories are unrivalled for their continuous view of the nation's affairs, and to compare them with the incomplete and episodic compositions available from their neigh-bours may be misleading. . . . Nevertheless," Millard adds, "where com-parisons are possible they should be made, otherwise the Hebrew writings have to be treated in a vacuum and the results of that can be, in fact often have been, extremely misleading" (Millard 1985: 75). Bertil Albrektson, whose landmark 1967 publication, *History and the Gods*, did much to cor-rect false or facile claims about the distinctiveness of faith in the Hebrew Bible, continues to regard the Hebrew Bible as "something *sui generis* in the ancient Near East."[3] That which most distinguishes Hebrew faith from its neighbors' faith, according to Albrektson, "is, in the last resort, derived from what the Old Testament represents as a divine revelation through the word."[4]

---

2. Ibid., 130–31.
3. B. Albrektson, *History and the Gods: An Essay on the Idea of Historical Events as Divine Manifestations in the Ancient Near East and in Israel* (Lund: CWK Gleerup, 1967) 7.
4. Ibid., 122.

A first danger, then, of the comparative method is that it may lapse into a kind of reductionism that allows the comparative to become imperative, which is to say, the Hebrew Bible is reduced to the status of its assumed parallels. Perhaps in an effort to avoid such reductionism, Hallo and others prefer to speak of the "contextual method" rather than the "comparative method," for the Hebrew Bible and its literary counterparts should be both compared and contrasted (see Hallo 1991: 148–49).

A second danger of the comparative method is the tendency of some biblical scholars "to convert parallels into influences and influences into sources."[5] But again, Hallo offers a helpful perspective by noting that "in many cases [parallels] owe more to a common ancient Near Eastern heritage—shared by Israel—than to any direct dependence of one body of literature on the other" (Hallo 1988: 38).

A third danger is the notion that where parallels are lacking in the Hebrew Bible's ancient Near Eastern environment (or for that matter in the experience of the modern scholar), this lack of parallels is sufficient grounds for dismissing the claims of the text of the Hebrew Bible. But as Millard contends, "lack of comparable data alone is never an adequate basis for rejecting ancient statements. Nothing should be dismissed simply because the modern critic finds it unbelievable!"[6]

A fourth danger is that the ancient Near Eastern texts themselves may be misunderstood. After all, the interpretation of extrabiblical ancient Near Eastern literature is often at least as challenging as the interpretation of the biblical literature. In a recent essay, for example, Antti Laato challenges the widespread assumption that Assyrian inscriptions are more reliable than the biblical traditions. Focusing on the inscriptions of Sennacherib, Laato highlights "typical literary and stylistic devices . . . which are used when there is reason to believe that an attempt has been made to veil a military setback." Laato's study, and others like it, "raise questions on the larger historiographical problem of how the ancient sources are to be used (Assyrian, Babylonian, Egyptian, etc. royal inscriptions) in the reconstruction of the historical events of the ancient Near East" (Laato 1995: 199).

Awareness of the dangers that attend the comparative (or, better, contextual) method is a first step toward avoiding them. Their presence should not be allowed to diminish the considerable gains that comparative study can achieve for biblical interpretation. Millard, in the essay reproduced below (pp. 129–40), makes a good case for the judicious use of

---

5. So E. E. Ellis, cited in D. R. Hall, *The Seven Pillories of Wisdom* (Macon, Ga.: Mercer University Press, 1990) 69.

6. A. Millard, "The Old Testament and History: Some Considerations," *Faith and Thought* 110 (1983) 34–53; quotation from p. 36.

the comparative method, arguing for instance that a comparison of the third-person narratives of Samuel–Kings with the generally first-person Aramean inscriptions suggests that the former should be considered a kind of "transformational history-writing." More than anything else, the goal of interpreters (whatever their personal presuppositions) should be to read the biblical texts *on their own terms*, and the comparative materials provide valuable assistance toward that end.

While much remains to be explored in regard to the relevance of ancient Near Eastern literatures to the Bible, examples of the profitable use of the comparative/contextual method are beginning to appear. One thinks, for instance, of a number of works by K. L. Younger, especially his *Ancient Conquest Accounts*, or H. J. Tertel's *Text and Transmission*.[7] With respect to the present volume's focus on history and historiography, useful surveys are provided by, among others, A. K. Grayson (on the Assyrians and Babylonians), H. A. Hoffner and A. Malamat (on the Hittites), and S. B. Parker (on Ugarit), each listed below. More comprehensive surveys include, of course, J. B. Pritchard's *Ancient Near Eastern Texts Relating to the Old Testament*, W. Beyerlin's *Near Eastern Texts Relating to the Old Testament*, and the currently appearing multivolume work *The Context of Scripture*, edited by W. W. Hallo and K. L. Younger. Also useful are the recent compendia by P. K. McCarter, K. A. D. Smelik, and V. H. Matthews and D. C. Benjamin, as well as a couple of nice introductions to the subject by J. H. Walton, all listed below.

---

7. K. L. Younger, *Ancient Conquest Accounts: A Study in Ancient Near Eastern and Biblical History Writing* (Sheffield: JSOT Press, 1990); H. J. Tertel, *Text and Transmission: An Empirical Model for the Literary Development of Old Testament Narratives* (Beihefte zur Zeitschrift für die alttestamentliche Wissenschaft 221; Berlin: de Gruyter, 1994).

Additional Reading

Beyerlin, W., ed.
  1978   *Near Eastern Religious Texts Relating to the Old Testament*. Old Testament Library. London: SCM.
Cazelles, H.
  1989   Die biblische Geschichtsschreibung im Licht der altorientalischen Geschichtsschreibung. Pp. 38–49 in *XXIII. Deutscher Orientalistentag vom 16. bis 20. September 1985 in Würzburg: Ausgewählte Vorträge*. Edited by E. von Schuler. Zeitschrift des deutschen morgenländischen Gesellschaft Supplement 7. Stuttgart: Franz Steiner.

Cogan, M. and I. Eph'al, eds.,
   1991   *Ah, Assyria: Studies in Assyrian History and Ancient Near Eastern Historiography Presented to Hayim Tadmor.* Scripta Hierosolymitana 33. Jerusalem: Magnes.
Grayson, A. K.
   1980   Histories and Historians of the Ancient Near East: Assyria and Babylonia. *Orientalia* 49: 140–94.
Hallo, W. W.
   1988   Sumerian Literature: Background to the Bible. *Bible Review* 4: 28–38.
   1990   The Limits of Skepticism. *Journal of the American Oriental Society* 110: 187–99.
   1991   The Death of Kings: Traditional Historiography in Contextual Perspective. Pp. 148–65 in *Ah, Assyria: Studies in Assyrian History and Ancient Near Eastern Historiography Presented to Hayim Tadmor.* Edited by M. Cogan and I. Eph'al. Scripta Hierosolymitana 33. Jerusalem: Magnes. [Biblical and Mesopotamian historiography]
Hallo, W. W., and K. L. Younger, Jr., eds.
   1997   *The Context of Scripture*, Vol. 1: *Canonical Compositions from the Biblical World.* Leiden: Brill.
Hess, R. S., and D. T. Tsumura, eds.
   1994   *"I Studied Inscriptions from before the Flood": Ancient Near Eastern, Literary, and Linguistic Approaches to Genesis 1–11.* Sources for Biblical and Theological Study 4. Winona Lake, Ind.: Eisenbrauns.
Hoffmeier, J. K.
   1994   The Structure of Joshua 1–11 and the Annals of Thutmose III. Pp. 165–79 in *Faith, Tradition and History: Old Testament Historiography in Its Near Eastern Context.* Edited by A. R. Millard, J. K. Hoffmeier, and D. W. Baker. Winona Lake, Ind.: Eisenbrauns.
Hoffner, H. A., Jr.
   1980   Histories and Historians of the Ancient Near East: The Hittites. *Orientalia* 49: 283–332.
Kitchen, K. A.
   1988   Egypt and Israel during the First Millenium B.C. Pp. 107–23 in *Congress Volume: Jerusalem 1986.* Edited by J. A. Emerton. Supplements to Vetus Testamentum 40. Leiden: Brill.
   1991   Israel Seen from Egypt: Understanding the Biblical Text From Visuals and Methodology. *Tyndale Bulletin* 42: 113–26.
Laato, A.
   1995   Assyrian Propaganda and the Falsification of History in the Royal Inscriptions of Sennacherib. *Vetus Testamentum* 45: 198–226.
Malamat, A.
   1955   Doctrines of Causality in Hittite and Biblical Historiography: A Parallel. *Vetus Testamentum* 5: 1–12.

1988 Pre-monarchical Social Institutions in Israel in the Light of Mari. Pp. 165–76 in *Congress Volume: Jerusalem 1986*. Edited by J. A. Emerton. Supplements to Vetus Testamentum 40. Leiden: Brill.

Matthews, V. H., and D. C. Benjamin
1997 *Old Testament Parallels: Laws and Stories from the Ancient Near East*. 2d ed. New York: Paulist.

McCarter, P. K., Jr.
1996 *Ancient Inscriptions: Voices from the Biblical World*. Washington, D.C.: Biblical Archaeology Society.

Millard, A. R.
1985 Sennacherib's Attack on Hezekiah. *Tyndale Bulletin* 36: 61–77.

Millard, A. R., J. K. Hoffmeier, and D. W. Baker, eds.
1994 *Faith, Tradition, and History: Old Testament Historiography in Its Near Eastern Context*. Winona Lake, Ind.: Eisenbrauns.

Parker, S. B.
1989 *The Pre-biblical Narrative Tradition: Essays on the Ugaritic Poems Keret and Aqhat*. Society of Biblical Literature Resources for Biblical Study 24. Ed. W. L. Humphreys. Atlanta: Scholars Press.
1994 The Ancient Near Eastern Literary Background of the Old Testament. Pp. 228–43 in vol. 1 of *The New Interpreter's Bible*. Edited by L. E. Keck et al. Nashville: Abingdon.
1997 *Stories in Scripture and Inscriptions: Comparative Studies in Biblical and Epigraphic Narratives*. Oxford: Oxford University Press.

Pritchard, J. B., ed.
1969 *Ancient Near Eastern Texts Relating to the Old Testament*. 3d ed. Princeton: Princeton University Press.

Roberts, J. J. M.
1976 Myth versus History: Relaying the Comparative Foundations. *Catholic Biblical Quarterly* 38: 1–13.

Schmid, H. H.
1986 The Notion of History in the Old Testament and in the Ancient Near East. *Old Testament Essays* 4: 14–27.

Smelik, K. A. D.
1991 *Writings from Ancient Israel: A Handbook of Historical and Religious Documents*. Translated by G. I. Davies. Edinburgh: T. & T. Clark.

Tadmor, H.
1981 History and Ideology in the Assyrian Royal Inscriptions. Pp. 13–33 in *Assyrian Royal Inscriptions: New Horizons in Literary, Ideological and Historical Analysis*. Edited by F. M. Fales. Orientis Antiqui Collectio 17. Rome: Istituto per l'Oriente.

Tadmor, H., and M. Weinfeld, eds.
1983 *History, Historiography and Interpretation: Studies in Biblical and Cuneiform Literatures*. Jerusalem: Magnes.

Van Seters, J.
1983   *In Search of History: Historiography in the Ancient World and the Origins of Biblical History.* New Haven: Yale University Press. Reprinted, Winona Lake, Ind.: Eisenbrauns, 1997.

Walton, J. H.
1989   *Ancient Israelite Literature in Its Cultural Context: A Survey of Parallels between Biblical and Ancient Near Eastern Texts.* Grand Rapids: Zondervan.
1994   Cultural Background of the Old Testament. Pp. 255–73 in *Foundations for Biblical Interpretation.* Edited by D. S. Dockery et al. Nashville: Broadman & Holman.

Younger, K. L., Jr.
1991   Heads! Tails! Or the Whole Coin?! Contextual Method and Intertextual Analysis: Judges 4 and 5. Pp. 109–46 in *The Biblical Canon in Comparative Perspective.* Edited by K. L. Younger Jr., W. W. Hallo, and B. F. Batto. Scripture in Context 4. Lewiston: Edwin Mellen.

Biblical History in Its Near Eastern Setting

The Contextual Approach

WILLIAM W. HALLO

I

[[1]] "The Reverend Ebenezer Brewer, in his *Dictionary of Phrase and Fable*, tells of a little old seventeenth-century lady who used to say to her pastor that she 'had found great support in that blessed word Mesopotamia.'" True or not, this tale reads well. It serves as title and peroration of a speech originally delivered in 1956 by Henry Allen Moe, and published in a posthumous collection of essays by the late president of the Guggenheim Memorial foundation.[1]

The acoustical powers of "that blessed word" continued undiminished into the next century, to judge by a brief biographical sketch of the eighteenth century evangelist George Whitefield, which avers: "His voice had the range of an organ and with it he could reduce grown men to tears by the mere pronunciation of the word 'Mesopotamia.'"[2]

Reprinted with permission from *Scripture in Context: Essays on the Comparative Method* (ed. C. D. Evans, W. W. Hallo, and J. B. White; Pittsburgh: Pickwick, 1980) 1–18 (plus notes from pp. 18–26).

Author's note: This paper was first presented to the Institute for Advanced Studies, Hebrew University, Jerusalem, May 10, 1979. I am indebted to my colleagues at the Institute and to other scholars in Israel for many fruitful discussions.

1. Henry Allen Moe, *The Power of Freedom in Human Affairs* (Philadelphia: American Philosophical Society, 1977) 97–112: "That Blessed Word Mesopotamia: A Lawyer's Reflections." For the quotation in question, see pp. 111–12.

2. Peter J. Gomes, "Vita: George Whitefield, Flamboyant Revivalist: 1714–1770," *Harvard Magazine* 79/7 (May–June 1977) 36.

Presumably the word finally lost some of its magic in the nineteenth century with the successful decipherment of the cuneiform scripts, first of Persia and then of Mesopotamia itself. Now fantastic and baseless speculations about the Mesopotamian past gradually gave way to more sober assessments grounded in the cuneiform texts. Even earlier, the decipherment of Egyptian hieroglyphics had begun to discredit the naive and often mystical interpretations long attached to the surviving monuments in the valley of the Nile. Subsequent [[2]] discoveries have added many more scripts, languages and bodies of texts to the arsenal of the ancient historian, and the pace of discovery shows no sign of abating.[3]

The discipline of biblical history has inevitably responded to these intellectual developments. True, the mere mention of Mesopotamia no longer reverberates with the elusive echo of an enigma. But it, and indeed the entire ancient Near East, is still a concept to conjure with—only now in a scholarly sense. The day is long past when the history of Israel could be written solely or largely on the basis of the biblical text; now one must take into account the evidence, particularly the written documentary testimony, of the civilizations rediscovered throughout the surrounding Near East.

On this dictum there is today fairly universal scholarly agreement. But when it comes to applying the dictum, the consensus quickly breaks down. The remarks that follow will therefore address some of the considerations involved in the attempt to study biblical history in its ancient Near Eastern matrix, to see "scripture in context."[4] The intention is not to repudiate the comparative approach, but to define it, refine it and broaden it, notably by wedding it to the "contrastive approach."[5] The resulting blend can perhaps avoid both of these somewhat controversial labels and qualify instead as a "contextual approach." The allusion here is not to the "sociological context . . . visible behind the [literary] material" as in Hanson's "contextual-typological" method,[6] but rather to the literary context itself, broadly interpreted as including the entire Near Eastern literary milieu to the extent that it can be argued to have had any conceivable impact on the biblical formulation.

3. Maurice Pope, *The Story of Decipherment: From Egyptian Hieroglyphic to Linear B* (London: Thames and Hudson, 1975). Cf. also M. S. Dandamaev, *Persien unter den ersten Achämeniden (6. Jahrhundert v. Chr.)*, translated by H.-D. Pohl (= Beiträge zur Iranistik 8, 1976), chap. 1: "Aus der Geschichte der Erforschung der Behistun-Inschrift," 1–22.

4. I owe this title to John B. White. Meantime I have become aware of K. A. Kitchen's *Old Testament in Its Context* (1973), but have not seen the book.

5. William W. Hallo, "New Moons and Sabbaths: A Case-Study in the Contrastive Approach," *HUCA* 78 (1977; appeared 1979) 1–17.

6. Paul D. Hanson, "Jewish Apocalyptic against Its Near Eastern Environment," *RB* 78 (1971) 33.

II

"The Use of Ancient Near Eastern Materials in the Study of Early Hebrew History" was the subject of a session of the Society of Biblical Literature some four years ago.[7] S. Dean McBride covered the question at length, and I agreed to respond to him.[8] Then as now, however, the topic hardly lent itself to true debate. This is clear if one changes just one word in the chosen title: let us suppose for a moment that the subject was "The Use of Ancient Near Eastern Materials in the Study of Early Mesopotamian History." Would anyone care to debate the validity, not to say the legitimacy, of such an [[3]] enterprise? I heartily doubt it. Then why should the use of ancient Near Eastern materials still be debatable enterprise in the study of early Hebrew (or I would say early Israelite) history? Why is it facing a frontal assault from such authorities as Morton Smith, John Van Seters, and Thomas L. Thompson? And why is it that after passing in quick review all the different narratives deriving Israel variously from Egypt, Sinai, Transjordan, Syria, Mesopotamia or Canaan, Thompson can conclude: "Of these narratives as well as all of the narratives of the pentateuch, the historical problem is not so much that they are historically unverifiable, and especially not that they are untrue historically, but that they are radically irrelevant as sources of Israel's early history"?[9]

This rather skeptical view of matters is not universally shared. Among biblical historians, for example, Abraham Malamat has been a conspicuous advocate of the judicious use of comparative data, notably from Mari, to illuminate the origins and formative stages of Israel—and vice versa.[10] On the Egyptological side, a rather ringing rebuttal to the views of Van Seters, Thompson and, for good measure, Donald B. Redford, has recently been offered by K. A. Kitchen[11] who had earlier expressed himself in sympathy with those who, like myself, "are sceptical of traditional literary-critical methods . . . preferring objective comparative data to unverifiable hypotheses."[12]

---

7. Hudson-Delaware Section, Philadelphia, May 4, 1975, Jeffery H. Tigay presiding.

8. This and the next section represent a revised version of my remarks at that time.

9. "The Narratives about the Origin of Israel" in John H. Hayes and J. Maxwell Miller, eds., *Israelite and Judaean History* (Philadelphia: Westminster, 1977) 210–12. This book with its exhaustive and critical survey of the secondary literature provides an excellent introduction to the subject, and served as textbook for the seminar (below, n. 37). Cf. the perceptive review by Robert North, *Bib* 59 (1978) 423–26.

10. See most recently his "Origins and the Formative Period," in H. H. Ben-Sasson, ed., *A History of the Jewish People* (Cambridge: Harvard University, 1976), Part 1 (pp. 1–87).

11. *The Bible in Its World: The Bible and Archaeology Today* (Exeter: Paternoster, 1977), chap. 4: "Founding Fathers in Canaan and Egypt." Cf. also below, n. 87.

12. Kitchen, *Ancient Orient and Old Testament* (London: Tyndale, 1966) 125 n. 52.

As an Assyriologist, I indeed feel disposed to approach these questions from an admittedly comparativist position without, however, conceding that the critics are *not* comparativists. In fact, some of their strongest arguments are based on the comparison of biblical data with neo-Assyrian and neo-Babylonian or even with classical Greek and Roman sources. What they rule out is only the comparison with older Near Eastern materials. Therefore, let us avoid such labels as orthodox (or pseudorthodox) and nihilist, comparativist and anti-comparativist, or Albrightian and Alt-Nothian.[13] If we must resort to labels at all, let it be the fairly innocuous maximalist and minimalist;[14] no doubt most of us can then happily place ourselves somewhere in the golden middle. And let us return to a moment to the relatively non-controversial ground of early Mesopotamian history.

The materials for that history obviously consist (apart from such relative constants as physical geography) of artifactual remains and textual discoveries. The latter, in turn, can best be divided into three broad categories, namely what I like to call monuments, archives and canons.[15] All of these [[4]] classes of evidence must be invoked in any historical reconstruction worthy of the name. If we had only canonical texts such as the Sumerian King List, the epics, and the royal hymns, our picture of Sumerian history would today be sadly distorted. We would have little or no basis for establishing a firm chronology, none at all for tracing the evolution of social and economic institutions, and whole areas of Sumerian experience such as the rise and fall of Lagash or Umma would be left largely out of account. How does this compare with the biblical situation?

In textual terms, we deal here almost exclusively with a canon in the sense in which that term is sometimes applied on the cuneiform side, i.e., with the final literary formulation of a record which is itself later, sometimes later by far, than the documents on which it may have been based, documents which in turn must often have been later than the events which they presume to record. Generally these documents are themselves held to have been literary in character; their reconstruction is the subject of the "documentary hypothesis" which, as its very name implies, is

13. "Pseud-orthodox" was coined by Morton Smith in his opening salvo, "The Present State of Old Testament Studies," *JBL* 88 (1969) 19–35. The charge of "nihilism" was first levelled against Martin Noth by W. F. Albright, echoed repeatedly by John Bright, and escalated to Nihilimismus by J. Hempel, as pointed out by Noth, "Der Beitrag der Archäologie zur Geschichte Israels," VTSup 7 (1960) 262–82 [= Aufsätze 1 (1971) 34–51]; see especially p. 263.

14. I find that W. G. Dever (int. al.) uses the same terms in the same sense in Hayes and Miller, *Israelite and Judean History*, 77. Dever's survey of the issues in the debate (ibid., 70–79) is instructive.

15. William W. Hallo and William K. Simpson, *The Ancient Near East: A History* (New York: Harcourt Brace Jovanovich, 1971) 154–56. Hereafter: *ANEH*.

doomed to remain hypothetical—that is to say, beyond demonstrable proof.

On rare occasions, the "documents" may be hypothetically described as monumental (e.g., the Psalm of Hezekiah)[16] or archival (e.g., Numbers 7)[17] but the form in which they have reached us is nevertheless canonical or literary. Of course, archaeology supplies a second component here too: an occasional monument, inscribed as in the case of the bulla of Berachyahu (= Baruch?) ben Neriyahu[18] or uninscribed as in the case of the alleged Assyrian royal standard newly unearthed at Tell-es-Shariʿah (ancient Ziqlag);[19] more rarely still, a precious archival scrap like the "letter-prayer" from Meṣad Ḥashavyahu,[20] or the ostraca from Samaria, Lachish and Arad.[21] Such finds as these are universally admitted as relevant for Israelite history, but only because they date from the Iron Age. When it comes to "early Hebrew history," i.e., the Bronze Age, the opinions diverge. To quote Noth:

> The material remains of historical life, together with the innumerable inscriptions (*Schriftdenkmäler*) recovered from the ancient Near East, have created for the history of Israel such a lucid background that our knowledge of Israel's history and its integration into ancient Near Eastern history as a whole appears to be assured at least in its basic outlines. And this is in fact the case for the later and latest history of Israel—not, however, for the early history.[22]

It is only the maximalist position which holds that *all* monuments, archives and canons of the Bronze Age Near East [[5]] are potential building blocks in the reconstruction of early Israelite history. In this respect, the

16. William W. Hallo, "The Royal Correspondences of Larsa: I. A Sumerian Prototype for the Prayer of Hezekiah?" *Kramer Anniversary Volume* (= AOAT 25, ed. B. L. Eichler; Neukirchen-Vluyn: Neukirchener Verlag, 1976) 209–24.

17. B. A. Levine, "The Descriptive Tabernacle Texts of the Pentateuch," *JAOS* 85 (1965) 307–18. Cf., however, A. F. Rainey, "The Order of Sacrifices in OT Ritual Texts," *Bib* 51 (1970) 485–98.

18. Nahman Avigad, "Baruch the Scribe and Jerahmeel the King's Son," *IEJ* 28 (1978) 52–56 and pl. 15; *BA* 42 (1979) 114–18.

19. E. D. Oren, "Esh-Shariʿa, Tell (Tel Seraʿ)" in Michael Avi-Yonah and Ephraim Stern, eds., *Encyclopedia of Archaeological Excavations in the Holy Land* 4 (London: Oxford University, 1978) 1059–69. See p. 1062 for a description and p. 1069 for a photograph of the "socketed, crescent-shaped bronze (Assyrian) standard . . . found on the brick-lined floor of the northern basement" of the Assyrian citadel dating from the seventh century B.C.E.

20. Dennis Pardee, "The Judicial Plea from Meṣad Hashavyahu (Yavneh-Yam): A New Philological Study," *Maarav* 1/1 (1978) 33–66, with previous literature.

21. André Lemaire, *Inscriptions Hebraïques I: Les Ostraca* (= Littératures Anciennes du Proche-Orient 9, 1977).

22. "Beitrag der Archäologie," 262. (Translation mine.)

maximalist position is in agreement with the Bible itself which, in incorporating so many ancient Near Eastern motifs, obviously regarded it as legitimate to draw on all the available sources (whether written or oral). That in itself does not justify the position. And indeed the minimalist would counter that, even when some kind of correlation can be established between an ancient Near Eastern source and the biblical appropriation of it, what it amounts to is some kind of misappropriation. For him, the history of Israel begins with the Conquest, the Iron Age, if you like, with Pharaoh Merneptah ca. 1220 B.C.E.

III

Between these extreme positions, where can the historian of Egypt or Mesopotamia take his stand? Speaking as an Egyptologist, Kitchen has stated

> that principles found to be valid in dealing with ancient Oriental history and literature will in all likelihood prove to be directly applicable to Old Testament history and literature and conversely, that methods or principles which are demonstrably false when applied to first-hand ancient Near Eastern data should not be imposed upon Old Testament data either.[23]

I myself phrased matters from the Assyriologist's point of view thus:

> We should neither exempt biblical literature from the standards applied to other ancient Near Eastern literatures, nor subject it to standards demanded nowhere else. On this basis, Israelite traditions about its own Bronze Age, though these traditions were written down in the Iron Age, have to be given as much credence as Middle and neo-Assyrian notions about the Old Assyrian past.[24]

As much—and no more. For the very point of the analogy is that many of these notions, as enshrined in canonical texts like the Assyrian King List, must be sifted critically in the light of the monuments, archives and older canons. When this is done, it will be seen that Assyrian historiography provides an instructive parallel to biblical historiography. In order to stress the antiquity and continuity of Assyrian institutions, Assyrian king lists and royal inscriptions appropriated the legendary past of the Sumerians as a common heritage; viewed Sargonic overlords as predecessors; claimed ethnic affiliation to the Amorite tribes of all of Mesopotamia;

---

23. *Ancient Orient*, 28. Cf. ibid., 115 and 169–70.

24. William W. Hallo, "Problems in Sumerian Hermeneutics," in *Perspectives in Jewish Learning* 5 (ed. B. L. Sherwin; Chicago, 1973) 4. Cf. idem, "Assyrian Historiography Revisited," in *H. L. Ginsberg Volume* (= Eretz-Israel 14, 1978), Hebrew summary, p. 191.

raised subservient governors to royal status; and incorporated into Assyrian royal genealogies those foreign overlords whose memory they could not suppress.[25]

[[6]] Egyptian historiography is said to have pursued directly opposite means, but to an essentially identical end. It illustrates the principle that the

> collective historical memory of the nation (accepts) an acclimatized foreigner who adopts the culture of the natives and tries to become one of them (while) a foreign war-lord who reduces the country through war and rules it, not on the strength of traditional practice, but on the strength of his army, is never accepted as a native, but is forever after remembered as an alien.[26]

In other words, interludes of subservience to foreign domination are not glossed over, but simply denied legitimacy except on native terms.

What these examples suggest is that historiography is a subjective enterprise in which each culture ultimately defines the ethnic parameters of its own past for itself. Or, as it has been said in a pregnant definition: "History is the intellectual form in which a civilization renders account to itself of its past."[27] I would like to put the emphasis in Huizinga's definition on the two words "to itself." I would, in fact, argue that *each* civilization or ethnic entity is entitled to render account of the past *to itself* by appropriating *to itself* that portion of the past which it chooses *for itself.* I wold submit further that such appropriation can, by this very definition of history, never be misappropriation. A few examples may illustrate the point.

The Quranic view of the pre-Islamic past, for instance, includes both reasonably authentic memories of the Arabian Peninsula in the early centuries of the Christian era, and thoroughly garbled "appropriations" of biblical traditions, both from the New Testament and from the Old, the latter often filtered through the aggadic versions preserved among the Jewish communities of Arabia. Both the pagan Arabian past and the Judaeo-Christian traditions are linked to the Islamic present by various means, including genealogies, and we are often in a position to evaluate these links.

25. Hallo, "Assyrian Historiography Revisited," 1*–7*.

26. Donald B. Redford, "The Hyksos Invasion in History and Tradition," *Or* 39 (1970) 1–51, esp. 9–10. Cf. also Gun Björkman, "Egyptology and Historical Method," *Orientalia Suecana* 13 (1964) 9–33, who argues that literary evidence can be used for historical reconstruction only with the greatest caution.

27. J. Huizinga, "A Definition of the Concept of History," in Raymond Klibansky and H. J. Paton, eds., *Philosophy and History: Essays Presented to Ernst Cassirer* (Oxford, 1936) 1–10, esp. 9, quoted by J. J. Finkelstein, "Mesopotamian Historiography," *Proceedings of the American Philosophical Society* 107 (1963) 462 and n. 4. (Note that Finkelstein wrote: "of the past.")

But we are not free to invalidate the claims based on them. Rather, we are bound to admit the reality of Islamic claims to kinship, in one form or another, with a variety of pre-Islamic ethnic entities as these claims are conceived and formulated within Islam.[28]

Again, the Roman view of the Roman past as formulated particularly under the Principate differs considerably from that of the modern historian. We would not regard the Aeneid as an unimpeachable source for the history of the Sea Peoples or of the colonization of Italy. Yet we have adopted one of its major tenets (which it shares with Livy and Roman historians generally), i.e., that the focus of Roman history is the [[7]] city of Rome and not, say, the province of Latium, the Latin-speaking area, or the Italian peninsula.[29] Indeed we speak in terms of Roman history, not Latin or Italian history, when we deal with the Western Mediterranean in classical times. At least equal respect, then, should be accorded to Roman claims for its Trojan ancestry, even if that does not imply uncritical acceptance of Dido and every other episode preserved in this connection.[30]

To shift the analogy once more, American civilization can choose (and usually does choose) to appropriate much of English history or European history in pre-revolutionary or pre-colonial times. Black Americans may prefer to do likewise with African history, while Native Americans can with equal justice relate to the Western hemisphere in pre-Columbia times. But by and large, the "canonical" view of American history conceives of the United States as a nation of immigrants from Europe, perpetuating in cultural, legal and political institutions and above all in language the heritage of Europe in general and of England in particular. And if the English tradition, including that of America's English colonists, happened to regard itself as indebted to classical and biblical models, then the American tradition may claim the same derivation by right of inheritance. Of course, we must draw the line somewhere: the further notion of the "British Israelites" that Britons are lineally descended from one of the Ten

28. In this connection I have noted but not studied the following: Abraham I. Katsch, *Judaism in Islam: Biblical and Talmudic Backgrounds of the Koran and Its Commentaries, Suras II and III* (New York: New York University, 1954); Tor Andrae, *Der Ursprung des Islams und das Christentum* (Uppsala: Almqvist & Wiksell, 1926; French trans. Jules Roche, Paris: Adrien-Maisonneuve, 1955); Richard Bell, *The Origin of Islam in Its Christian Environment* (London: Macmillan, 1926).

29. Cf. Michael C. J. Putnam, "Italian Vergil and the Idea of Rome," in Louis L. Orlin, ed., *Janus: Essays in Ancient and Modern Studies* (Ann Arbor: University of Michigan, 1975) 169–99.

30. Moshe Weinfeld calls my attention to *Iliad* 20:306–7: "and now verily the mighty Aeneas will rule over the Trojans, and his sons' sons that are hereafter to be born" where some traditions substitute 'all' (*pántessin*) for 'Trojans' (*Trôessin*) according to Strabo, *Geography* 13:1:53 (608); cf. Ludolf Malten, "Aineias," *Archiv für Religionswissenschaft* 29 (1931) 33–59, esp. 53.

Lost Tribes can be dismissed as a minority view.[31] But who is to deny those claims which rest on the collective judgment of the civilization as a whole? And who is to deny the validity, the legitimacy of the biblical claim to certain ancient Near Eastern traditions?[32]

In this light, the issue can no longer be phrased in terms of "historicity." The historicity of the Chaldeans, the Arameans, the Habiru, the Amorites and (at least until recently)[33] even the Sumerians is not in question, and every new piece of evidence permits us to be more certain and more precise about them. And the biblical claim to some of the traditions of all of these peoples is likewise not open to question on the factual level—i.e., no one can deny that the biblical texts make the claim. Sometimes the claim is phrased in genealogical terms, sometimes in geographical ones, sometimes simply in terms of literary affinities as when Ezekiel invites his listeners to consider Noah, Daniel and Job as three ancient worthies of their own (Ezek 14:14, 20), though the first is clearly drawn from Babylonian traditions and the second from "Canaanite" ones.[34] Nor are we, I submit, free to question the claim on the level of its legitimacy, given Huizinga's definition of history.

[[8]] But once the claim is granted, the significance of the Bronze Age evidence assumes a new light, and can be assessed more dispassionately. We can then begin to argue, for example, that the primeval history of Genesis 1–11 was appropriated virtually in its entirety from external sources, or the casuistic legislation of Exodus and Deuteronomy selectively. We can ponder specific clues like the case of the goring ox which includes in the biblical formulation at least one law buried in Tell Harmal since Old Babylonian times;[35] or the possibility that the "Road to Emar"

31. Cecil Roth, *The Nephew of the Almighty: An Experimental Account of the Life and Aftermath of Richard Brothers, R.N.* (London: Edward Golston, 1933); idem, *Magna Bibliotheca Anglo-Judaica: A Bibliographical Guide to Anglo-Jewish History* (2nd ed.; London: Jewish Historical Society of England, 1937) B. 17: "British Israel and Lost Ten Tribes," 379–89. Note that this entry no longer appears in the newer editions of this work by Ruth P. Lehman (1961, 1973).

32. For an analogy between American and biblical historiography that has become a classic of its kind, see John Bright, "The School of Alt and Noth: A Critical Evaluation," in his *Early Israel in Recent History Writing* (= SBT 19; London: SCM, 1956) 79–110; reprinted in Samuel Sandmel, ed., *Old Testament Issues* (New York: Harper & Row, 1968) 159–95. For a response see Noth, "Beitrag der Archäologie," esp. 280–82.

33. F. R. Kraus, *Sumerer und Akkader: Ein Problem der altmesopotamischen Geschichte* (Amsterdam: Koninklijke Akademie der Wetenschapen, 1970); J. S. Cooper, "Sumerian and Akkadian in Sumer and Akkad," *Or* 42 (1973) 239–46.

34. S. Spiegel, "Noah, Daniel and Job, Touching on Canaanite Relics in the Legends of the Jews," *Louis Ginzberg Jubilee Volume* 1 (1945) 305–55; M. Noth, "Noah, Daniel and Hiob in Ezechiel XIV," *VT* 1 (1951) 251–60.

35. J. J. Finkelstein, "The Goring Ox," *Temple Law Quarterly* 46 (1973) 169–290; B. S. Jackson, "The Goring Ox Again," *Journal of Juristic Papyrology* 18 (1974) 55–93, reprinted in *Essays in Jewish and Comparative Legal History* (Leiden: E. J. Brill, 1975) 108–52.

has "passed into the patriarchal narrative of the defeat of Amora."[36] And we may have to conclude that when the biblical authors appropriated Bronze Age sources for early Israelite history, they did so intelligently, purposefully and selectively. The surviving traditions were sifted and weighed. Their reflexes in biblical literature are neither free creations *de novo*, nor uncritical imitations of everything available.

The case for the use of ancient Near Eastern materials is thus the same whether we are studying early Hebrew history or early Mesopotamian or Egyptian history; it serves to tell us whether the form in which those civilizations rendered account of their past to themselves accords with the form in which we would do so for them. The seminar which generated the papers published in the present volume studied the history of Israel on the basis of these considerations, that is, in the light of literary traditions preserved in the Bible and in the ancient Near Eastern texts.[37] Defenders of the comparative approach were read and evaluated alongside its critics. Emphasis was put on the major phases of ancient Near Eastern history; on Israel's place in each phase; and on the validity of the literary traditions enshrining these phases in each of the major cultures. The seminar papers published herewith reflect some of these same concerns, and fill in a few of the numerous lacunae left by my own presentations. These ranged widely but selectively over three millennia of biblical history and its Near Eastern setting, and it would be futile to attempt to summarize them here. But it may be appropriate to consider the more general epistemological problems of the comparative approach, and the challenges raised against it.

IV

[[9]] The challenges against the comparative approach to biblical literature in general, and to biblical historiography in particular, have in recent years escalated to the level of a frontal assault. A useful summary of the indictment has just appeared from the pen of J. Alberto Soggin, and may serve as point of departure for the discussion. Soggin entitles his essay "The History of Ancient Israel: A Study in Some Questions of Method."[38] As the subtitle indicates, he is at pains to find a proper methodology for

36. William W. Hallo, "The Road to Emar," *JCS* 18 (1964) 86. See in greater detail the paper by N.-E. A. Andreasen below [[i.e., in *Scripture in Context: Essays on the Comparative Method*]], 59–77.

37. "Biblical History in Its Near Eastern Setting," Summer Seminar for College Teachers sponsored by the National Endowment for the Humanities, Yale University, June 19–August 11, 1978.

38. *H. L. Ginsberg Volume*, 44*–51*.

the evaluation of biblical historiography. His own prescription is to determine a "datum point" for Israelite history, that is to say a *starting-point*, or perhaps we should say a *turning-point* from legend to more or less "objective" historiography. In early Mesopotamian historiography, such a transition can be observed in the Sumerian King List at the point where impossibly long reigns give way to more nearly plausible ones.[39] It would seem to have an obvious parallel in Genesis where the life span progressively diminishes from the incredible longevity of the antediluvians to the standard or ideal figure of 110 or 120 years, more or less, among the postdiluvians.[40] But Soggin does not cite this parallel, which he would find irrelevant for his purpose. For he considers the comparative approach altogether inadequate from the point of view of methodology: it operates with parallels that antedate his starting-point, and indeed has hitherto neglected to determine a starting-point in the first place. The only previous scholar who at least recognized the importance of such a determination is said to be Noth, though even he was too generous in his evaluation of early Israelite historiography when he began his history of Israel with the Iron Age and the Conquest.[41]

Soggin himself lowers the starting-point to the reign of David, or at the earliest Saul. It is far from clear what motivates his choice. The apodictic statement is made that "this new datum point has the advantage of offering a succession of events whose historicity is accepted beyond doubt,"[42] and again:

> With the foundation of a united kingdom under David, the history of Israel leaves the realm of pre-history, of cultic and popular tradition and enters the arena of history proper. The kingdom under David and Solomon constitutes a datum point from which the investigation of Israel's history can safely be begun.[43]

But it is not averred that we have explicit archaeological or epigraphic testimony to this "succession of events," or allusions to them in extra-Israelite [[10]] sources. On the contrary, as Soggin himself admits, "archaeological

39. Note that a strictly historical figure like Mebaragesi still rules for 900 years! For the Egyptian parallel, see W. K. Simpson, *ANEH*, 193.

40. Cf. Gen 6:3; 50:22; Deut 34:7. Later texts lower the optimal figures to 100 (Isa 65:20) or less (Ps 90:10). For Egyptian analogies to a 110-year life-span and other explanations of some of these figures, see Stanley Gevirtz, "The Life Spans of Joseph and Enoch . . . ," *JBL* 96 (1977) 570–71. For the Mesopotamian view of the "ages of man" and a 90-year life-span, see J. Nougayrol, *RA* 62 (1968) 96 ad *STT* 400; cf. Hallo, *Assur* 1/4 (1975) 1.

41. *H. L. Ginsberg Volume*, 45*–46*.

42. Ibid., 51*.

43. Soggin, "The Davidic-Solomonic Kingdom," in Hayes and Miller, eds., *Israelite and Judean History*, chap. 6, p. 332.

evidence for the Davidic and Solomonic period is fragmentary and, on the whole, disappointingly scarce."[44] Where Jerusalem is concerned, there are still no discoveries "which can be dated with any certainty to the time of David and Solomon."[45] Whether the current excavations of the "City of David" will change this picture, remains to be seen. Outside Jerusalem, the assignment of important strata at Arad and Beer Sheva to David and at Gezer, Megiddo, Hazor and possibly Lachish to Solomon has been widely but not universally accepted.

What then is Soggin's criterion for making these reigns his "datum point"? From his other writings, it is clearly the emergence of a true historiography. "Israel achieved mature historiography at the beginning of the period of the monarchy."[46] Or again: "From the time of David and Solomon onwards, we see that in court circles there are not only traces of remarkably developed annals (we only have notes of them, the texts have been lost), but organic history-writings are beginning to take shape."[47] But the argument is circular: history begins where historiography begins, and historiography begins—or becomes "mature" or "organic"—where history is said to have its datum point. I prefer to maintain the proposition that history begins where writing begins[48] and see no reason to exempt Israel from this working hypothesis.

Admittedly, then, the comparative approach is open to criticism, but critique must go beyond fault-finding. To be constructive it must pose alternatives, and the alternatives are themselves vulnerable—notoriously so. As if to dramatize the arbitrariness of Soggin's starting-point, we may note that in the very same volume Morton Smith proposes what amounts to an even later one when he uses "East Mediterranean Law Codes or the Early Iron Age"[49] to date most of the Pentateuch to the period ca. 750–450 B.C.E., or what he somewhat impishly (albeit on good "classical" authority) refers to as the "archaic period."[50] John Van Seters, though approaching the biblical material from the opposite geographical direction, similarly dates most of the patriarchal legal precedents by analogy to neo-Assyrian and especially neo-Babylonian parallels.[51] Interestingly enough, Thomas L. Thompson, who joins Van Seters in so much of his critique of estab-

44. Ibid., 340.

45. Ibid., quoting G. E. Wright; cf. North, *Bib* 59 (1978) 425.

46. Soggin, *Introduction to the Old Testament*, trans. John Bowden (London: SCM, 1976) 50.

47. Ibid., 51.

48. Below, n. 58.

49. *H. L. Ginsberg Volume*, 38*–43*.

50. Ibid., 43*.

51. *Abraham in History and Tradition* (New Haven: Yale University, 1975); idem, "The Childless Wife in Assyria and the Stories of Genesis," *Or* 44 (1975) 485–86 (with A. K. Grayson).

lished positions,[52] parts company with him precisely over these and other suggested alternatives.[53]

The basic weakness of all these proposals, it can be argued, is their discriminatory character. Call them ad hoc, ad hominem or ad corpus, they single out biblical historiography in a manner inconsistent with the principle enunciated [[11]] above (p. 5 [[82]]). Soggin's starting-point, for example, is not applied to the history of any other people, nor is it claimed as a methodological standard for any other historiographic corpus. But a standard worthy of the name must be widely if not universally applicable and applied. Such a standard is, in my opinion, available. The history of a given entity, national or otherwise, as reconstructed by the modern historian from "external" evidence, can be confronted with the formulations as preserved by that entity itself. Most often, these formulations take the form of literary traditions. It is thus possible to take full account of ancient historiography when reconstructing the history of ancient literate societies. More, it is impossible to ignore literature in the enterprise, or to divide it hermetically from "objective history." The modern historian should aspire to write a history that is at the same time "a commentary on ancient history and historiography."[54] This is true whether his subject is ancient Mesopotamia and Egypt or ancient Israel.

V

"History as reconstructed confronted with the (native) formulations as preserved" is, then, the common standard proposed here. But confrontation does not, of course, imply uncritical equation; on the contrary, the term is chosen deliberately to stress the need for critical evaluation of the two terms of the equation. What is important, and to some extent even novel, is the choice of the terms. For hitherto the comparative method has generally implied a different sort of confrontation, namely between the biblical text and the external data, the "objective" facts recovered by archaeology from the excavations of the surrounding Near East. This was, however, a confrontation between unequals, an attempted equation between two essentially incommensurable quantities. It inevitably aroused skepticism. One need only cite the Nuzi texts in this connection. A whole generation of biblical scholars employed these texts to explain and even to date the patriarchal narratives on the basis of common juridical practices allegedly found in both. American scholars such as E. A. Speiser and

---

52. *The Historicity of the Patriarchal Narratives* (= BZAW 133; Berlin: de Gruyter, 1974).
53. "A New Attempt to Date the Patriarchal Narratives," *JAOS* 98 (1978) 76–84.
54. Hallo, *ANEH*, vi. Differently Björkman, "Egyptology and Historical Method."

C. H. Gordon led the way since American expeditions were responsible for the excavations at Nuzi. But a second generation of biblical scholars, disciples of the first prominent among them, has demolished the putative parallels one by one.[55] Does that discredit the entire attempt to evaluate patriarchal law by Bronze Age parallels? Hardly, *pace* Van Seters [[12]] and Thompson. Rather, it invites a reconsideration of the terms of the comparison. The biblical canon should be weighed, *not* against the archival data excavated from a distant corner of the Mitanni empire, but rather, on the one hand, against the occasional scrap of archival evidence recovered from the soil of Palestine itself[56] and, on the other and far more important, against the literary formulations of the surrounding Near East. Only then will one be comparing the commensurate quantities, and only then will one be operating with a standard equally applicable to the other cultures of the ancient Near East. The entire historiographic spectrum lends itself to this treatment, but it cannot be traversed even in a cursory fashion here. The relevant bibliography is enormous; the mere sampling provided in the present volume is drawn in part from a syllabus for the seminar, which also included a working chronology. The latter may serve as the basis for a broad overview of the methodological problems at issue (fig. 1).[57]

The context of biblical literature is at once spatial and temporal. In spatial terms, the biblical authors all shared with the land of Israel its central location. That is to say, they were potentially exposed to the surrounding Near East in the same high degree as was their native soil; some of them, indeed, lived and wrote in the lands of the Dispersion. A map of the Near East should therefore be kept in mind in what follows. Some might wish to include the Aegean world in such a map, but all would agree on its broad outlines. No comparable degree of agreement, however, characterizes the temporal context, not even its outer limits. As is clear from the chart, that context is here regarded as spanning three millennia (ca. 3100–100 B.C.E.). This long epoch is more or less co-terminous with the life-spans of the cuneiform and hieroglyphic systems of writing in Mesopotamia and Egypt. It may be treated as some sort of continuum if one accepts the central importance of written documentation in the reconstruction—indeed in the very definition—of history, a view of matters not universally shared.[58]

---

55. For a partial list, see Kitchen, *The Bible in Its World*, 68–71 and 144–45, esp. nn. 64–66.

56. William W. Hallo and Hayim Tadmor, "A Lawsuit from Hazor," *IEJ* 27 (1977) 1–11 and pl. 1.

57. See also Hayes and Miller, eds., *Israelite and Judean History*, for extensive bibliography.

58. *ANEH*, 4–5. For a critique of this position, see Ray L. Cleveland, review of *ANEH*, in *JNES* 32 (1973) 252–53.

Fig. 1. Comparative Chronology of the Ancient Near East

(1)	(2)	(3)	(4)	(5)	(6)	(7)
3100 B.C.E.						
3000 B.C.E.		Jemdet Nasr	Ante-diluvians	Dyn. I	Early Dynastic	
2900 B.C.E.						
2800 B.C.E.		Early Dynastic I	"Flood" etc.	Dyn. II		
2700 B.C.E.						
2600 B.C.E.		Early Dynastic II	Confusion of Tongues	Dyn. III–IV		Early Bronze
2500 B.C.E.						
2400 B.C.E.	Old Sumerian	Early Dynastic III	Line of Shem	Dyn. V	Old Kingdom	
2300 B.C.E.						
2200 B.C.E.		Sargonic	?	Dyn. VI–VIII		
2100 B.C.E.	Neo-Sumerian	Ur III		Dyn. IX–XI	1st Int. P.	
2000 B.C.E.						
1900 B.C.E.		Early Old Babylonian	Patriarchs?	Dyn. XII	Middle Kingdom	Middle Bronze
1800 B.C.E.	Old Babylonian					
1700 B.C.E.		Late Old Babylonian		Dyn. XIII (+ XIV)		
1600 B.C.E.						
1500 B.C.E.	Middle Babylonian	Kassite	Slavery?	Dyn. XV–XVIII	2nd Int. P.	Late Bronze
1400 B.C.E.					New Kingdom	
1300 B.C.E.			Exodus and Wanderings	Dyn. XIX–XX		
1200 B.C.E.	Middle Assyrian		Conquest and Judges			
1100 B.C.E.		Post-Kassite				
1000 B.C.E.						
900 B.C.E.	Neo-Assyrian		First Common-wealth	Dyn. XXI–XXV	3rd Int. P.	(Early) Iron
800 B.C.E.		Neo-Assyrian				
700 B.C.E.						
600 B.C.E.	Neo-Babylonian	Neo-Babylonian	Exile	Dyn. XXVI	Saïte	
500 B.C.E.						
400 B.C.E.		Achaemenid	Second Common-wealth	Achaemenids, etc.	Late Dynastic	Graeco-Persian
300 B.C.E.	Late Babylonian					
200 B.C.E.		Seleucid		Ptolemies		
100 B.C.E.						

The thirty centuries involved (col. 1) can be grouped in various ways, to begin with by major archaeological periods (col. 7). The names and dates of these periods have been gradually arrived at in connection with excavations in the Levant and the Aegean; their extension to Mesopotamia and (to a lesser extent) Egypt[59] rests on the observation that fundamental technological developments quickly spread from one end of the ancient Near East to another, and that they therefore provide a significant basis for synchronizing the material finds from widely scattered excavations.[60] Thus the terms "Stone Age," [[14]] "Bronze Age" and "Iron Age" are more than merely designations of convenience: they actually serve to define the periods in which these materials were the principal mediums for tools and weapons throughout the Near East.[61] The subdivisions of these Ages similarly are based in the first instance on technological innovations whose impact was swift and widespread, such as the large-scale introduction of the horse both as a mount and for drawing chariots at the beginning of the Late Bronze Age,[62] or the official adoption of the "alphabetic" (Aramaic) script by the Achaemenids and their (in part perhaps resultant) unification of the Near East in the Late Iron Age (here the "Graeco-Persian Age").

A partially co-terminous but finer breakdown of the continuum is provided by "cultural" periods. In the case of Egypt (col. 6), the resort is to the conventional periodization; for Mesopotamian (col. 2), it is to a scheme advanced and defended in greater detail elsewhere.[63] It is based on a succession of 300-year periods which, though schematic to the point of appearing mechanical, nevertheless dates and identifies the "dominant cultural factor" in each period (except possibly the neo-Assyrian one) in fairly remarkable agreement with assessments arrived at by more traditional means. The lacuna at the beginning of this column again reflects the importance attached to written sources and the consequent difficulty in labelling periods for which these sources are scarce or impenetrable.

---

59. Systematically first in *ANEH*; cf. also Hallo, "Mesopotamia, History," *Encyclopedia Judaica* 16 (Jerusalem: Keter Publishing House, 1971), cols. 1483–1505.

60. James D. Muhly, *Copper and Tin: The Distribution of Mineral Resources and the Nature of the Metals Trade in the Bronze Age* (Connecticut Academy of Arts and Sciences Transactions 43, 1973 and 46 [*Supplement*], 1976). Although the author himself is extremely cautious about drawing the above conclusion, it can in my judgment be inferred from the massive data he has assembled.

61. *ANEH*, 6–7, 29–33, 123.

62. Cf., e.g., J. A. H. Potratz, *Die Pferdetrensen des Alten Orient* (= AnOr 41, 1966), chap. 1: "Das domestizierte Pferd." Potratz (p. 4) credits the Mitanni Kingdom with this innovation.

63. William W. Hallo, "Toward a History of Sumerian Literature," in S. J. Lieberman, ed., *Sumerological Studies in Honor of Thorkild Jacobsen* (= Assyriological Studies 20, 1976) 181–203, esp. 196–201.

Political considerations provide a still more detailed periodization. For Egypt (col. 5), the native system of dynasties furnishes the obvious scale; for Mesopotamia (col. 3), modern historical reconstructions must serve. In all cases, dates are necessarily approximate and in some debatable.[64] But the approximations serve as the "contextual frame" for locating the grand subdivisions of biblical history (col. 4; no attempt is made there to differentiate between subdivisions arrived at primarily on literary grounds from those suggested by political history). At the same time, they show at a glance the extent of the overlap between chronological boundaries arrived at primarily on technological, literary and political grounds, i.e., if one prefers, between archaeological, cultural and "historical" periods.

This overlap is most conspicuous in the precise center of the continuum: in or about 1600 B.C.E. we may date the capture first of Memphis by Salitis and the Hyksos and then of Babylon by Mursilis and the Hittites.[65] These "escapades" were presumably paralleled by "many of the ruling houses in Levantine states during the Late Bronze Age (who) traced their [[15]] descent from a Middle Bronze founder," including Ugarit, Tunip, Alalakh, Qatna, Mitanni, Hanigalbat and possibly Aleppo; they represent a kind of "knight-errantry" on the analogy of William the Conqueror and differ markedly from the *Völkerwanderungen* [['mass migrations']] at the end of the Late Bronze Age.[66] But they were equally effective in bringing about the virtually simultaneous conclusion of the Middle Kingdom in Egypt, the Old Babylonian Dynasty in Mesopotamia, and the Middle Bronze Age in the intervening areas of the Levant. The chronological conjunction in question may thus be said to embrace the entire geographical extent of the Near Eastern setting, and one is entitled to ask whether biblical historiography recognized an equally decisive temporal watershed and a comparable spatial sweep.

Phrased thus, the question suggests its own answer: the Book of Genesis involves the entire area, moving in succession over Mesopotamia (chaps. 1–11), Syria–Palestine (chaps. 12–36) and Egypt (chaps. 37–end).[67] And it embraces the entire time span here equated with the Early and Middle Bronze Periods. It is the only biblical book to paint history in such broad strokes; the others focus instead much more narrowly on a restricted theater of action over a century or two in time. In Genesis, it has

64. See *ANEH* for details.

65. Redford, "The Hyksos Invasion," 2–3 and 23 associates the fall of Memphis with the founding of the 15th (Hyksos) Dynasty which he dates between 1660 and 1649 B.C.E.

66. Ibid., 16–17.

67. See in somewhat greater detail: William W. Hallo, "Genesis and Ancient Near Eastern Literature," in W. Gunther Plaut, ed., *The Torah: A Modern Commentary*, vol. 1: *Genesis* (New York: Union of American Hebrew Congregations, 1974) xxix–xxxiv.

been argued, the creation myth "serves merely as background, furnishing the physical context within which Israel's religion originated."[68] One may extend this idea to suggest that all of the first chronological half of ancient Near Eastern history was drawn on by biblical historiography to provide the geographical context for the subsequent unfolding of Israelite history within its Near Eastern setting.

VI

"This (i.e., biblical) idea of history represents a true historiography, for it traces the events of Israel's experience from a distinct beginning point, follows them down through a progression in time, and looks to a future unfolding of that history."[69] This characterization is meant to distinguish "the prophetic idea of history" from other schools of biblical historiography, and even more emphatically from the rest of ancient Near Eastern historiography. But the idea of the starting-point is inherent in all of them. For prophetic historiography it is the call of Abraham, for priestly historiography it may have been Creation, for others the Exodus from Egypt.[70] Thus Soggin's methodological desideratum is worth returning to. The concept of a starting-point is grounded in biblical [[16]] historiography, not imposed on it by modern scholarship. But nowhere, not even in the "royal theology" as preserved particularly in the "royal psalms,"[71] does the Bible itself date the beginnings of national identity to the introduction of monarchy. On the contrary, that event occurred relatively speaking very late in the evolution of Israel's national consciousness, well after the constitutive events—attributed to the deity—which shaped that consciousness: the deliverance from slavery, the giving of the law, and the conquest of the land.[72] A starting-point for Israel's history, for its awareness of a "group identity," should indeed be sought, but it should be selected from among those offered by the text itself, i.e., by one of the schools of biblical historiography.

One proposal that meets this criterion is that of Malamat who argues persuasively that Israelite history begins once the tribes demonstrably occupy the areas consistently assigned to them as their final area of settlement in all historiographical traditions. The tribe of Asher and especially Dan is a case in point.[73] Since their tales unfold in the Book of Judges, this

---

68. Hanson, "Jewish Apocalyptic," 41.
69. Ibid., 40.
70. Ibid., and n. 23, citing H. Ringgren.
71. Ibid., 43–44.
72. Ibid., 42.
73. Malamat, "The Canite Migration and the Pan-Israelite Exodus-Conquest: A Biblical Narrative Pattern," *Bib* 51 (1970) 1–16.

theory implies that Israelite historiography began there, and that the Hexateuch preserves, rather, what may be called the proto-history of Israel.[74]

The proposal here set forth is that Israelite history begins with the Egyptian oppression when the consciousness of a collective destiny first dawned on an aggregate of discrete and, in origin, perhaps diverse groups. Israelite historiography, as distinguished, say, from the royal historiography of the Davidic court or the universal historiography of the priesthood, begins, by the test of a collective focus, with the Book of Exodus which formulates the emergence of that consciousness. Certain corollaries which it is impossible to pursue here follow from this postulate. In literary terms, it implies a questioning of conventional groupings of the textual material into tetrateuch (Genesis–Numbers), pentateuch (Genesis–Deuteronomy) or hexateuch (Genesis–Joshua) in favor of a more qualitative caesura after Genesis and a new beginning in Exodus—perhaps of a triteuch[75] that ran from Exod 1:8 through Numbers and originally included the death of Moses in Deuteronomy 34.[76] In historical terms, it implies the essential historicity of the Egyptian oppression, as well as its sequel throughout the pre-monarchic period as related and sequentially ordered in the historical books of the Bible: the exodus, wanderings, conquest and period of the judges.[77] It does not imply that all that preceded the oppressions is utterly devoid of historicity, let alone "radically irrelevant as source(s) of Israel's early history" (above, p. 3 [[79]]), only that it has a different character: a broader geographical and temporal scope, a liberal acceptance [[17]] or appropriation of universal or non-Israelite traditions as the background for the emergence of a discrete Israelite ethnic consciousness, and a deliberate *Tendenz* [['bias']] to narrow the focus of

74. I am grateful to Professor Malamat for showing me the manuscript of his Haskell Lectures (1979) which deal with many of these questions.

75. The term is borrowed from Athanasius' Letter to Marcellinus (*Patrologia Graeca* 27, 1887, col. 12) who applied it to the sequence Joshua-Judges-Ruth, as is clear from his Festal Epistle 39, for which see most recently Sid Z. Leiman, *The Canonization of Hebrew Scripture* (Connecticut Academy of Arts and Sciences Transactions 47, 1976) 157 n. 207. It is entered in older editions of Liddell and Scott, *Greek-English Lexicon*, but not in the newer ones, nor in Guido Miller, *Lexicon Athanasianum* (Berlin: de Gruyter, 1952).

76. Martin Noth, *Überlieferungsgeschichtliche Studien I: Die Sammelnden und Bearbeitenden Geschichtswerke im Alten Testament* (Halle: M. Niemeyer, 1943) 39–40 et passim. Sigmund Mowinckel, *Tetrateuch-Pentateuch-Hexateuch: Die Berichte über die Landnahme in den drei altisraelitischen Geschichtswerken* (= BZAW 90, 1964).

77. Insistence on the biblical sequence might seem superfluous but for a new theory calling it in question: Seán Warner, "The Period of the Judges within the Structure of Early Israel," *HUCA* 47 (1976) 57–79; idem, "The Dating of the Period of the Judges," *VT* 28 (1978) 455–63. Warner would date the Judges before the Wanderings and Conquest. Cf. also Yohanan Aharoni, "Nothing Early and Nothing Late: Rewriting Israel's Conquest," *BA* 39 (1976) 55–76. Contrast Kitchen, *The Bible in Its World*, 87 and nn. 44–47.

the selected traditions, funnelling them to the putative bearers of that consciousness. Given these characteristics, the comparative approach is as relevant for the traditions preserved in Genesis as it is for the priestly historian of Exodus–Numbers, the Deuteronomist, the "prophetic historian" or the Chronicler.

On this view of matters, the primeval histories of Genesis 1–11 illustrate the widespread "practice of beginning an ethnic history in primordial times . . . a practice extending from the Sumerian King List to Berossos and Manetho," and as such bear comparison with numerous other "ethnic histories" both early and late.[78] And on the other side of the patriarchal traditions, a special new significance attaches to the cycle of Joseph stories which concludes Genesis. The cycle has long proved troublesome to all interpretations of Israelite historiography because (with the exception of some intrusive elements[79] such as the story of Judah and Tamar in Genesis 38)[80] it resists facile literary analysis into separate strands which would link it to those identified by one means or another elsewhere in Genesis or the tetrateuch.[81] On the contrary, it contains late technical terms—neo-Assyrian[82] or Saite[83]—and late literary motifs[84] which call into question its ostensible early Egyptian coloring and literary models.[85] It seems then, to constitute a discrete literary unit best described as

78. Paul D. Hanson, "Rebellion in Heaven, Azazel, and Euhemeristic Heroes in 1 Enoch 6–11," *JBL* 96 (1977) 196 and n. 4.

79. Herbert Donner, *Die literarische Gestalt der alttestamentlichen Josephsgeschichte* (= Sitzungsberichte der Heidelberger Akademie der Wissenschaften, ph.-hist. Kl., 1976/2) esp. 24–35. For Genesis 49, cf. B. Vawter, "The Canaanite Background of Genesis 49," *CBQ* 17 (1955) 1–18; differently Donald B. Redford, *"A Study of the Biblical Story of Joseph (Genesis 37–50)* (= VTSup 20; Leiden: E. J. Brill, 1970) esp. 234.

80. M. C. Astour, "Tamar the Hierodule," *JBL* 85 (1966) 185–96; differently Umberto Cassuto, "The Story of Tamar and Judah," in *Biblical and Oriental Studies* 1 (Jerusalem: Magnes, 1973) 29–40.

81. Redford, *Biblical Story of Joseph*, esp. chap. 1. (Redford thinks that all of Gen 37:2–46:7 is an interpolation in the *tōlᵉdôt Yaᶜᵃqōb* [['history of Jacob']].) Differently Otto Eissfeldt, *The Old Testament: An Introduction*, trans. P. R. Ackroyd (New York: Harper and Row, 1965) 186.

82. J. S. Croatto, *"'Abrek* 'Itendant' dans Gen. XLI 41, 43," *VT* 16 (1966) 113–15.

83. Redford, *Biblical Story of Joseph*, chap. 9.

84. A. Meinhold, "Die Gattung der Josephgeschichte und des Estherbuches: Diasporanovelle," *ZAW* 87 (1975) 306–24; 88 (1976) 72–93; S. Niditch and R. Doran, "The Success Story of the Wise Courtier: A Formal Approach," *JBL* 96 (1977) 179–93. Cf. also W. L. Humphreys, "A Life-Style for Diaspora: A Study of the Tales of Esther and Daniel," *JBL* 92 (1973) 211–23.

85. J. Vergote, *Joseph en Égypte: Génèse ch. 37–50 à la lumière des études égyptologiques récentes* (Louvain: Publications Universitaires, 1959). Cf. J. Janssen, "Egyptological Remarks on the Story of Joseph," *Jaarboek Ex Oriente Lux* 14 (1956) 63–72; S. Morenz, "Joseph in Ägypten," *TLZ* 84 (1959) 401–16.

a novella[86] which was only slightly modified in order to be ingeniously inserted into the seam between the (primeval and patriarchal) traditions of Genesis and the more vivid memories of the oppression.[87] It thus initiates the subtle transformation of the personal biographies of the patriarchs into the ethnic histories of the several tribes, a process in which the twelve eponymous sons of Jacob became the one collective entity known to the Bible as the Children of Israel and to Merneptah simply as Israel. This process was carried further in the record of the wanderings, particularly in Numbers, and consummated in the purely tribal account of the conquest and settlement, notably in Judges.[88]

The stories of Joseph, so difficult to justify on other grounds, thus achieve a lucid purpose as the turning-point from tradition to history. Their smooth integration between two bodies of text so disparate in character and so disproportionate in size constitutes a literary achievement of considerable magnitude. Mesopotamian historiography failed to match it when confronted by a corresponding problem, for [[18]] at the turning-point from primordial legend to a real if remote antiquity, its principal document offered no such help to the reader. The biographies of the early kings are barely alluded to in the Sumerian King List even when they are known to have existed in separate literary traditions.[89] Here as elsewhere, comparison and contrast are alike legitimate tools in providing the essential context of biblical historiography; they are the twin components in a contextual approach to biblical literature.

86. Redford, *Biblical Story of Joseph*, chap. 4, calls it a "novelette." For the corresponding genre in cuneiform, see for now Hallo, "Toward a History of Sumerian Literature," 196, with nn. 102–3.

87. For a different view, see Kitchen, review of Redford, *Biblical Story of Joseph*, in *Oriens Antiquus* 12 (1973) 233–42.

88. See in somewhat greater detail my "Numbers and Ancient Near Eastern Literature," in Plaut, ed., *The Torah: A Modern Commentary*, vol. 4: *Numbers* [[New York: Union of American Hebrew Congregations, 1979, pp. xxi–xxx.]]

89. For the Egyptian situation, see Redford, "The Hyksos Invasion," 28–29.

Biblical and Prebiblical Historiography

H. CAZELLES

[[481]] Several years ago an article by M. de Certeau, entitled "To Do History," appeared. The title reveals a primarily literary interest. How, given the existence of preserved documents and facts known by one means or another, does one present these facts or documents to [[482]] the modern reader in a way that makes them intelligible? The focus of study may be shifted from the modern reader's point of view to that of the ancient reader, whence the collective work edited by R. Dentan, *The Idea of History in the Ancient Near East,* [1] or the more recent individual work by J. Van Seters, *In Search of History.* [2] This focus also underlies the essay by P. Gibert, *La Bible à la naissance de l'histoire* [[The Bible at the Birth of History]]. [3]

This interest can also direct itself not only toward a literary treatment of a work that presents itself as history but also toward the events, customs, or oral traditions that were at the source of the accounts. The same P. Gibert, in his recent work *Vérité historique et esprit historien* [[Historical Truth and the Spirit of History]], [4] makes a happy methodological distinc-

Reprinted, translated, and revised with permission from "Historiographies bibliques et prébibliques," *Revue biblique* 98 (1991) 481–512. Translated by David W. Baker.

1. R. Dentan, *The Idea of History in the Ancient Near East* (New Haven: Yale University Press, 1955). Considering the magnitude of the subject, my bibliography is restrained and, as much as possible, recent. There are, of course, many other works from which I have derived important data in order to produce this essay, without discussing all of their propositions.

2. J. Van Seters, *In Search of History: Historiography in the Ancient World and the Origins of Biblical History* (New Haven: Yale University Press, 1983; repr. Winona Lake, Ind.: Eisenbrauns, 1997).

3. P. Gibert, *La Bible à la naissance de l'histoire: Au temps de Saül, David et Salomon* (Paris: Fayard, 1979).

4. Idem, *Vérité historique et esprit historien—L'historien biblique de Gédéon face à Hérodote: Essai sur le principe historiographique* (preface by A. Caquot; Paris, 1990). B. Halpern has published a parallel reaction, but concerning the Deuteronomistic History: *The First Historians: The Hebrew Bible and History* (San Francisco: Harper & Row, 1988).

tion between the reported events and the intention of truth.[5] This intention of truth is the intention of an author vis-à-vis a reader. What is the truth in which the reader is interested that the writer addresses? It appears to me that this is the major difficulty with biblical criticism. The author can allow himself to be seen through the text that he leaves us, but the reader can only be indirectly discovered, not only his personality but also his surroundings and the concerns of those surroundings. The modern reader is continuously disposed toward projecting his own concerns into the biblical text, now placed at his disposal through a multiplicity of editions and translations.

We have, however, a certain point of departure: the corpus of the Hebrew Bible, historiographical or not, was edited during the course of the first millennium before our era, even if it utilized traditions and even some earlier texts. Several great cultures preceded it, after the invention of writing.[6] John Van Seters has provided us with a fine literary analysis of different types of historiography. He discusses Egypt, relying almost exclusively on Breasted's translations in [[483]] *Ancient Records of Egypt*,[7] and Mesopotamia, relying on Grayson's[8] translations of the Mesopotamian chronicles, and he does not ignore Hittite historiography, in particular, the annals.[9] He also takes into account the fragments of the Annals of

---

5. Gibert, *Vérité historique*, 233. Its exact rendering is: the reality of truth and the intention of truth.

6. P. Amiet, "La naissance de l'écriture ou la vraie révolution," *RB* 97 (1990) 525–41.

7. Hereafter *ARE* (5 vols.; Chicago: University of Chicago Press, 1906–8). He also is aware of the synthesis of E. Otto, "Geschichtsbild und geschichtsschreibung in Ägypten," *WO* (1966) 161–76; and the well-documented work, now published, of D. Redford, *Pharaonic King-Lists, Annals and Day-Books: A Contribution to the Study of the Egyptian Sense of History* (Mississauga: Benben, 1986). The notion of 'annals' [[Egyptian]] *gnwt* (idem, *Studien zu Sprache und Religion Ägyptens: Zu Ehren von Wolfhart Westendorf überreicht von seinen Freunden und Schülern* [Göttingen: Hubert, 1984] 327–41) is not identical to that of 'annals' in Mesopotamia and relates to the study of 'annals' cited in the book of Kings. See also, concerning biographies, E. Otto, *Die biographischen Inschriften der ägyptischen Spätzeit* (Leiden: Brill, 1954); for a Middle Kingdom biography, see A. Gasse, *BIFAO* (1988) 84–85. A selection of texts is translated in C. Lalouette, *Textes sacrés et profanes de l'ancienne Égypte*, vol. 1 (Paris: Gallimard, 1984); J. B. Pritchard, *Ancient Near Eastern Texts Related to the Old Testament* (3d ed.; Princeton: Princeton University Press, 1969) 227–28.

8. Grayson, *Assyrian and Babylonian Chronicles* (hereafter *ABC*; Locust Valley: Augustin, 1975); idem, *Assyrian Royal Inscriptions* (2 vols.; Wiesbaden: Harrassowitz, 1972–76). Add R. Kutscher, *Royal Inscriptions: The Brockman Tablets of the University of Haifa* (Haifa: University of Haifa, 1989); the German translations and introductions of R. Borger, *Texten aus der Umwelt des Alten Testament* (TUAT) 1/4; and the synthesis of W. W. Hallo, "Assyrian Historiography Revisited," *ErIsr*14 (1978) *1–*7.

9. Translations and introductions by H. M. Kummel, TUAT 1/5, and his synthesis in *Or* 49 (1980) 283–432; see also the study by H. Cancik, *Grundzüge des hethitischen und alttestamentlichen Geschichtsschreibung* (Wiesbaden: Harrassowitz, 1976). The article by H. Güterbock,

Tyre that Josephus transmitted to us, as well as historical texts of the eastern coast that do not have much historiographical breadth.[10] Finally, he
treats the beginnings of Greek historiography. It is indeed curious that
this is his first chapter, even though, chronologically speaking, it should
come in last place. With good reason, he reckons that Babylonian historiography offers a better approach than Hittite (second millennium B.C.)[11]
for a comparison with ancient Hebrew prose. The Neo-Babylonian chronicles to which Van Seters often returns are from a century before Herodotus,[12] who did not travel and write until after numerous great dramas of
Israelite history.[13] [[484]]

Prebiblical Historiographies

Mesopotamia and Hittite Anatolia

Prebiblical historiography begins in Sumer with the royal inscriptions,[14]
whether dedicatory or commemorative. They celebrate the great deeds of
Utu-hegal, his victories and his treaties fixing the frontiers, and finally the
protection of the gods that permitted him to repulse an invasion by the
barbarian Guteans. This historiographical horizon went beyond the sovereign to become dynastic[15] and in no time was confronting the problem of

---

"Die historische Tradition und ihre literarische Gestaltung bei Babylonien und Hethitern bis 1200" (*ZA* 42 [1934] 1–91; 44 [1938] 45–149), remains a foundational work.

10. Texts and bibliographies by Dietrich and Loretz, TUAT 1/5. See also J. M. Sasson, "On Idrimi and Šarruwa," in *Studies on the Civilization and the Culture of Nuzi and the Hurrians . . . to E. Lacheman* (SCCNH 1; Winona Lake, Ind.: Eisenbrauns, 1981) 309–24.

11. Van Seters, *In Search of History*, 105. With good cause, he debates Cancik's thesis.

12. In case of debate, one should prefer the dates proposed by Grayson, who is the spe-cialist; see also below, [[p. 128 n. 107]].

13. Perhaps it is not without malice that P. Gibert subtitled his book "face à Hérodote" [['facing Herodotus']]. Van Seters probably addresses an audience better versed in Hellenism than in Semitics. The paratactic style that assembles little units into a conglomeration is found in the Bible and earlier historiographies (annals) or epics (Gilgamesh). This is not the only case where Greek literature adapted earlier models. Hesiod did the same with his myths: V. Fritz, "Weltalter und Lebenszeit: Mythische Elemente in der Geschichtsschreibung Israels und bei Hesiod," *ZTK* 87 (1990). Fritz also shows how Israel wrote history as a func-tion of the realities that structure the present. Likewise, H. C. Schmitt, *ZAW* 102 (1990) 344: "alttestamentliche Geschichtsschreibung kein primär antiquarisches Interesse besitzt" [['Old Testament historical writing does not have a primarily antiquarian interest']].

14. E. Sollberger, *Inscriptions royales Sumériennes et Akkadiennes* (LAPO; Paris: Du Cerf, 1971); W. H. P. Römer in TUAT 1/4. 289–353; S. N. Kramer, "Sumerian Historiography," *IEJ* 3 (1953) 217–32; E. Sollberger, *JCS* 21 (1967) 279–91.

15. M. de Jong Ellis, "Observations on Mesopotamian Oracles and Prophetic Texts: Lit-erary and Historiographic Considerations," *JCS* 41 (1989) 127–86.

conflicts and succession between dynasties.[16] From that royal Sumerian list, edited in Sumerian either during the Third Dynasty of Ur (about 2100 B.C.) or, more likely, during the First Dynasty (Semitic) of Babylon (about 1900 B.C.), came a much later "Dynastic Chronicle."[17]

The Semitic Akkadians (about 2300–2100) themselves went, it is reported, either on a royal campaign (Sargon or Naram-Sin in the west) or to erect a monument.[18] The reigns of this period were recalled and judged in the "Weidner Chronicle," which covered approximately the years 2600–2050.[19] The period covered by the Chronicle may go back to the First Dynasty of Babylon, but the three extant copies are Neo-Assyrian or Neo-Babylonian. It seems to have been used by the "Chronicle of the Ancient Kings," which covers the reigns from Sargon of Agade (about 2300) until Agum III (approximately 1640).[20] These royal lists and chronicles have their own special tendencies, but they seem to be based on other documents. As early as the Ur III period (about 2100), each year was designated by an event, thus allowing the possibility of dating events [[485]] for practical purposes. It became necessary to make lists of these date-events. Furthermore, at the end of each reign, annalists began giving the total of the years of the reign. Later, king lists were inaugurated, of which one (List B)[21] goes from the Dynasty of Akkad all the way to the fifteenth century B.C. The Assyrian lists date the year by the name of a *līmu* (high official) and a corresponding event; the king was generally given a place in the list in the second year of his reign.

The chronicles also used other kinds of lists. These, not arranged in chronological order, are lists of portents (omens). They are of all kinds, but some mention a historical event (in the protasis) and say (in the apodosis) whether it is "good or ill." A number of them were precisely recorded by the diviners of the Akkadian period. Many of the events mentioned in the protasis are "of the highest historical value."[22] The same

---

16. "Königlisten und Chroniken," *RLA* 6.77–86 (D. O. Edzard on the Sumerian), 6.86–135 (A. K. Grayson on the Akkadian). The Sumerian King List (TUAT 1/4. 328–37) gives the duration of reigns and, as in the Bible, the length of the reigns is unrealistic before the Flood but becomes realistic afterward.

17. A. K. Grayson, *Assyrian and Babylonian Chronicles* [[hereafter *ABC*]], number 18, "Who was king? Who was not king?" asks the Sumerian King List (VII,1).

18. For example, Sollberger, *Inscriptions royales*, 44.

19. J. J. Finkelstein, "Mesopotamian Historiography," in *Proceedings of the American Philosophical Society* 107 (1963) 461–72; Grayson, *ABC*, Chronicle 19. [[See B. Arnold, "The Weidner Chronicle and the Idea of History in Israel and Mesopotamia," in *Faith, Tradition, and History: Old Testament Historiography in Its Near Eastern Context* (ed. A. R. Millard, James K. Hoffmeier, and David W. Baker; Winona Lake, Ind.: Eisenbrauns, 1994) 129–48.]]

20. Grayson, *ABC*, Chronicle 20.

21. See *ANET*, 271; and the article "Datenlisten" (Ungnad), *RLA* 2.131–94.

22. Van Seters, *In Search of History*, 77.

does not hold true of the interpretation that the apodosis gives or of their application by the chronicles.

In effect, from these ancient records proceed the more developed works of Assyria and Babylonia. They are not independent of each other. Royal inscriptions often developed into annals. The oldest annals actually known are those of Adad-nirari I (1306–1274).[23] These annals do not limit themselves to relating a great deed of the king but recount a series of campaigns. The celebration of the erection of a monument (a stele, a temple, or a palace) comes at the end, without chronological precision. They have reached us in the form of many recensions, some abbreviated and others completing the earlier annals.[24] Yahdun-lim of Mari (approximately 1800) and Shamshi-Adad of Assyria, soon thereafter, sum up briefly but not without concrete details, their two expeditions as far as the Mediterranean. Tiglath-pileser I (twelfth century), who "crossed the Euphrates twenty-eight times," summarized his campaigns and victories over the Arameans in his annals. The annals of Ashurnasirpal (884–859) inform us of Syria and the tribute that the chiefs of Syria (referred to as Hatti) had to pay. The Annals of Shalmaneser III, with its various exemplars, [[486]] variously inscribed, are the first to record contacts with Israel (854 B.C.) and with Hazael of Damascus. On the occasion of the campaigns of such-and-such a year of their reign, Adad-nirari III, then Tiglath-pileser III and his successors (Shalmaneser V, Sargon II, Sennacherib, Esarhaddon) are said to have encountered Samaria, Judah, or its kings (Jehu, Joram, Menahem, Ahaz, Manasseh). Finally, Ashurbanipal left annals in various recensions, which were buried, along with his library full of labeled copies, at the time of the fall of Nineveh (612).

Babylon also had its royal lists and annals. What has been called "The Genealogy of Hammurabi"[25] starts with "seventeen kings who lived in tents," a paragraph that partially borrows from the Assyrian King-List. It concludes with the First Dynasty of Babylon. Assur often pillaged Babylon and took documents found there to Nineveh. There was a chronicle (no. 25) concerning the Kassite Dynasty and the Isin II Dynasty (approxi-

23. Concerning this king, see P. Garelli, *Le Proche-Orient Asiatique I: Des origines aux invasions des Peuples de la Mer* (Paris: Du Cerf, 1969) 178, 187–89, 322–35. Texts are in Grayson, *Assyrian Royal Inscriptions*, I, 59ff. The texts are very fragmentary.

24. A. L. Oppenheim, *Ancient Mesopotamia: Portrait of a Dead Civilization* (Chicago: University of Chicago Press, 1964) 144–53.

25. J. J. Finkelstein, *JCS* 20 (1966) 95–118, reinterpreted by W. G. Lambert, *JCS* 22 (1968) 1–2; A. Malamat, "King Lists of the Old Babylonian Period and Biblical Genealogies," *JAOS* 88 (E. A. Speiser festschrift; 1968) 163–73; P. Garelli in *Miscellanea Babylonica: Mélanges offert à Maurice Birot* (ed. J.-M. Durand and J.-R. Kupper; Paris: Éditions recherche sur les civilisations, 1985) 91–95.

mately 1200–1050)[26] and one of King Nabu-nasir (eighth century). We also have Neo-Babylonian chronicles (Nabopolassar, Nebuchadnezzar II, Nabonidus). It would be difficult to distinguish them from annals, if it were not that the chronology is generally less precise.

One hesitates about the classification of these texts: Are they historical documents or "historiography"? One might consider the two divergent versions of the reconstruction of the Sin Temple in Harran by Nabonidus to be historiographical[27] because they include this event in the context of other events and give them different interpretations. In the eighth campaign of Sargon to the Caucasus, which appears in the form of a letter to the national god Assur, so many episodes are included that the campaign is even comprised of episodes.[28] One would be more hesitant when it comes to the triumphal steles that summarize the glories of someone's reign or celebrate the erection of a [[487]] monument. One would hesitate even more about historical epics, such as the Epic of Tukulti-Ninurta I[29] or Adad-shumu-usur (1218–1189),[30] or astronomical agendas concerned with the cost of buying, such as the "Chronicle of the Cost of Buying,"[31] or *ex eventu* [['after the event']] prophecies,[32] or the numerous letters from state archives. These texts all treat an event in their own way and are useful for history, but they are not historiography.

26. Chronicle 25, which goes from 1216 to 1047, joins two previously known chronicles, Chronicle P (22) and the "Eclectic Chronicle" (24), corresponding from a Babylonian point of view to the "Synchronistic Chronicle" (21), which presents events from an Assyrian point of view. See C. Walker in *Zikir Shumi: Assyriological Studies Presented to F. R. Kraus* (ed. G. van Driel et al.; Leiden: Brill, 1982) 398–447.

27. C. J. Gadd, "The Haran Inscriptions of Nabonides," *AnSt* 8 (1958) 35–92; and the interpretations of W. Moran, *Or* 28 (1959) 130–40; H. Tadmor, "The Inscriptions of Nabunaid," AS 16 (1965) 351–64; P. Garelli, "Nabonide," *DBS* 6 272–80; Van Seters, *In Search of History*, 62–64.

28. F. Thureau-Dangin, *Une relation de la huitième Campagne de Sargon* (Paris: Geuthner, 1912).

29. P. B. Machinist, "Literature as Politics: The Tukulti Ninurta Epic and the Bible," *CBQ* 38 (1976) 455–82. It is advisable to avoid the term *epic* in the Bible. Joshua is an epic person, but the narratives of Genesis concerning the patriarchs are not epic, apart from Genesis 14.

30. A. K. Grayson, *Babylonian Historical-Literary Texts* (Toronto Semitic Texts 3; Toronto: University of Toronto, 1975) 56–77.

31. Grayson, *ABC*, Chronicle 23.

32. Examples in *ANET*, 451–52, 606–7. A. K. Grayson and W. G. Lambert, "Akkadian Prophecies," *JCS* 18 (1964) 7–30; W. Moran, "New Evidence from Mari on the History of Prophecy," *Bib* 50 (1969) 15–56; F. Ellermeier, *Prophetie in Mari und Israel* (Theologische und Orientalische Arbeiten 1; Herzberg: Jungfer, 1968); R. D. Biggs, "Babylonian Prophecies, Astrology and a New Source for 'Prophetic Text B,'" in *Language, Literature and History: Philological and Historical Studies Presented to Erica Reiner* (ed. F. Rochberg-Halton; New Haven, Conn.: American Oriental Society, 1987) 1–14.

Like Van Seters, I consider Hittite historiography to be dependent on
Mesopotamian historiography,[33] just as cuneiform script came to Hatti
from Mesopotamia. Through the merchant colony at Kanesh (2000–1900),
Akkadian culture penetrated Asia Minor, which came to be dominated by
the Hittite Empire around 1800. This Hittite literature nevertheless was
not without its own character, before disappearing about 1200 B.C.[34] First
and foremost, it consisted of annals. The oldest of these concerns Anitta
of Kussar, a contemporary of the Assyrians of Kanesh, prior to the foundation of the Empire,[35] probably an Assyrian-style compilation of great
deeds, building projects, myths, legends, and imprecations. The royal annals were called the "Manly actions of Hattusilis, Mursilis, Suppiluliumas.
. . ." They appear in many forms: Hittite and Akkadian versions for Hattusilis, decennial and extensive annals for Mursilis. Though we do not have
a "letter to the god," as we do for Sargon of Agade, we [[488]] do have a
prayer by Mursilis II on the occasion of a plague[36] and some narratives
concerning a single campaign. Finally, there are some important texts concerning the legitimacy of the monarch (Apology of Hattusilis III, the revolt
of Maduwatta) and problems with succession (order of Telepinus).[37]

Treaties

It is necessary to create a separate category for treaties, especially Hittite and Assyrian treaties, though we also have Akkadian, Eblaite, Egyptian, and Babylonian examples. After giving the titulary of the monarch
(there are but few parity treaties), the texts are comprised of a historical
prologue in which various events, consisting of many kindnesses of the
monarch toward his vassal, are recounted. The prologues do not constitute real historiography. They select events concerned with the gratitude
of the vassal, the stipulations imposed on him, and his oath of fealty before the gods of the contractual parties. Mursilis II recalls to Duppi-
Teshub of Amurru the revolt of his grandfather, the faithfulness of his

33. There is a Hittite translation of the exploits of the eldest Sargon and of Naram-Sin:
H. Hoffner, "Histories and Historians of the Ancient Near East: The Hittites," *Or* 49 (1980)
318–20; A. Kammenhuber, "Die hethitische Geschichtsschreibung," *Saeculum* 9 (1958) 136–
55; see also the works of Güterbock and Cancik cited above.
34. Even if one grants priority to Babylonian historiography, the texts such as the political testament of Telepinus, the double recension of the Acts of Mursilis, and the "Autobiography of Hattusilis" hold great interest for biblical historiography (see Cancik). For the
treatises, see below.
35. E. Neu, *Der Anitta Text* (Wiesbaden: Harrassowitz, 1974).
36. Text in *ANET,* 394. Bibliography in E. Laroche, *Catalogue des Textes Hittites* (2d ed.;
Paris: Klincksieck, 1971) no. 378.
37. Cf. ibid., nos. 1–216, and the other royals texts, 1–39. They include a "palace chronicle" and a "siege of the town of Urshu."

father, and the way in which he himself reestablished him on the throne when he was ill. Likewise, he recounts to Manapa-Datta (of the land of the Seha River) his revolt and the grace he had shown to him. Before dictating stipulations to Shatti(?)waza, son of Tushratta of Mitanni (located at the bend of the Euphrates), Suppiluliumas (a Hittite king) reminds him of the wars that his father had waged with him, of his defeats, and of his own victories prior to placing him on the throne of Mitanni and making him his son-in-law.

These historical prologues are less pronounced in Syrian and Assyrian treaties from the first millennium, but the same schema obtains in the treaty of Ashurbanipal with Qedar. "While they are common in the Hittite treaties, such citations were not particular to them."[38]

Historiography among the Semites of the West

In Syria, influenced by Assyrian or Hittite politics and culture, records and inscriptions also have historiographical aspects without being historiography proper, whether [[489]] the texts are in cuneiform (second millennium), Phoenician, or Aramaic (ninth century). The treaty between Abban of Aleppo and Yarim-Lim of Alalah is preceded by a historical prologue:[39] conquest of the village of Irrid and exchange of towns between the two monarchs (seventeenth century). Two centuries later, Yarim-Lin's successor, Idrimi, recounts in something like a biography his expulsion from Alalah, his flight to Emar on the Euphrates,[40] his passage through Canaan, his seven years with the Hapiru, his return to Alalah thanks to a coalition, his victories in Hatti, and finally the construction of his palace. At Ugarit, a list of kings deified after their deaths has been found among several kinds of archives, as well as a dynastic text going back to the Amorite ancestor Ditanu.[41]

Egyptian Historiography

A treaty between Muwatalli of Hatti and Ramses II after the battle of Qadesh (ca. 1280) shows how the same subject can be treated differently—

38. D. McCarthy, *Treaty and Covenant* (2d ed.; Rome: Pontifical Biblical Institute, 1978) 120.

39. Cf. H. Klengel, *Geschichte Syriens* (Berlin: Akademisches Verlag, 1965) 1.136.

40. Now well known from the campaigns of J. Margueron and the publication of the texts by D. Arnaud, *Recherches au Pays de Ashtata* (4 vols.; Paris: Éditions recherche sur les civilisations, 1985–87). Concerning Idrimi, see above, n. 10.

41. List published by C. Schaeffer, *AfO* 20 (1963) 214–15; studied by K. Kitchen, *UF* 9 (1977) 131–42. On the dynastic list: A. Caquot, *ACF* 75 (1975) 427–28; M. Heltzer, *OLP* 9 (1978) 15–16; P. Bordreuil and D. Pardee, *Syria* 59 (1982) 121–28. Text transliterated by O. Loretz, *KTU*, 1.161.

as both a high achievement and a defeat. This same battle is recounted in two extremely different ways even in the Egyptian sources (a "report" and a "poem"[42]). This is not to say that it did not take place. On the contrary! The Egyptians took pleasure in recording these events,[43] on commemorative stelae (e.g., the stele of the fifth year of Merneptah that mentions Israel),[44] on dedicatory monuments (Abydos), in annals (Thutmoses III, Amenophis II, 15th century B.C.), in autobiographies, and in historical "novellas." There are a number of possible definitions of these "novellas": some see a specific schema [[490]] in which the king is seated in the midst of his council. I willingly take the term in a more general sense: they are the recital of a great royal deed in laudatory rhetoric with legendary and poetic flourishes. This kind of recital occurs in other cultures.

These texts center on the person of the king. However, the question of legitimacy and dynastic succession have occasioned the redaction of royal lists. The Palermo Stone lists kings from the prehistoric period until the end of the fifth dynasty (ca. 2350).[45] It mentions, through the First Dynasty, one or two political or cultural events per year and, from the Second Dynasty on, the annual or biennial census of livestock. The *Turin Papyrus*, a manuscript of the thirteenth century, begins with a dynasty of "demi-gods" (the "glorified") and continues until the beginning of the Eighteenth Dynasty.[46] Four other little lists are more selective and filled with gaps.[47] Hatshepsut the usurper and Akhenaton the heretic are excluded from one of these lists. The Egyptians also had a taste for genealogies, and not just royal genealogies, with generations extending to several centuries. The work of Manetho, drawn up in the third century B.C. at the request of the Ptolemies, is dependent on old Egyptian lists.[48]

---

42. A. Gardiner, *The Ḳadesh Inscriptions of Ramesses II* (Oxford: Griffith Institute, 1960).

43. Even certain palettes (Narmer) prior to the invention of hieroglyphic writing seem to refer to a victory or a siege.

44. Recently studied by J. Yoyotte, "La campagne palestinienne du pharaon Mérnephtath: Données anciennes et récentes," in *La Protohistoire d'Israël de l'exode à la monarchie* (ed. E. M. Laperrousaz; Paris: Du Cerf, 1990) 109–21. The "Voyage of Wenamun" and "The Adventures of Sinuhe" elevate the romanticized biography even higher, though they remain useful for knowledge of an epoch and its customs (especially the court and temple).

45. It is completed by some fragments now deposited in Cairo. The name of the king is written above the regnal years (facsimile in A. Gardiner, *Egypt of the Pharaohs* [Oxford: Oxford University Press, 1981] 62, pl. 3).

46. A. Gardiner, *The Royal Canon of Turin* (Oxford: Griffith Institute, 1959).

47. Facsimiles of the Tables of Abydos and Saqqarah in Gardiner, *Egypt of the Pharaohs*, 49, fig. 8; D. Redford, *Pharaonic King Lists, Annals and Day Books* (Mississauga, Ont.: Benben, 1986) 18–24.

48. Ibid., on Manetho, 231–32.

Conclusion

Near Eastern historiography is thus abundant and varied and poses many questions.

(1) Is it prompted by a taste for antiquity, for the past? Or is it not, rather, for purposes of the present that it interrogates past events? It is centered on the king because his life and victories, until his postmortem exaltation, are the life of the nation and even more directly of the court. The royal court and functionaries had a direct interest in preserving the events of the past.

Because jealousies and disputes are the lot of humanity, the problem of royal legitimacy was often posed and, consequently, the problem of royal and dynastic succession arose.[49] Even the [[491]] redactor of the *Turin Papyrus* became interested in the Semitic Hyksos dynasties when the problems of the Canaanite revolts arose during the Nineteenth Dynasty. The Ugaritic Legend of Keret treats the rebellion of the firstborn and the substitution of another child in his place.[50] The autobiography of Hattusilis III is the account of a succession conflict with Urhi-Teshub. The Assyrian King-List attempted to resolve the problem by grouping all of the kings into a single dynasty, despite the fact that there were usurpers, and the Sumerian King List sought to establish the unity of Mesopotamia in the period of the First Dynasty of Babylon by presenting some contemporary dynasties as successive.

(2) This problem of royal legitimacy is a religious problem, and it is treated as such in the histories. The king, whether divine or not, belongs to a sacral order: he is "servant" of the national god—possibly his son—and vested with a supernatural power.[51] To obey the holder of the throne, or not, is a matter of faith, which is why kings require vassals and soldiers to take an oath before the gods.[52] It is not until the Deuteronomist, or even better, Ezekiel, that the distinction between sacred and profane, between prince and priest, is recognized. In the ancient Near East, the king is a

49. This since the first dynasty; cf. N. Grimal, *Histoire de l'Égypte Ancienne* (Paris: Fayard, 1988) 62; English trans., *A History of Ancient Israel* (Oxford: Blackwell, 1992). Concerning the political testament of Hattusilis I, see S. de Martino, *OrAnt* 28 (1989) 1–24.

50. A. Caquot and M. Sznycer, *Textes Ougaritiques I* (Paris: Du Cerf, 1974) 541. The god El says to Keret concerning the youngest of his sons, "I will make him the firstborn." Cf. H. Cazelles, "Ras Schamra und der Pentateuch," *Tübinger Theol. Quartalschrift* 138 (1958) 26–39.

51. H. Frankfort, *Kingship and the Gods* (Chicago: University of Chicago Press, 1948); Egyptian texts in C. Lalouette, *Textes sacrés et profanes de l'ancienne Égypte* (Paris: Gallimard, 1984) 27–160. For Mesopotamia, M. J. Seux, "Königtum," *RLA* 6.145–52, 155–59, 166–72. H. Cazelles, *Le Messie de la Bible: Christologie de l'Ancien Testament* (Paris: Desclée, 1978) 31–58 and texts, 227–33.

52. Text in *ANET*[3], 353.

priest, even when he performs cultic functions through the clergy. The enthronement ceremonies allow the assembled people to gaze on the election of the sovereign by the national god.

(3) It is also necessary to pay attention when the historical narratives or dynastic syntheses (which I have summarized too briefly above) are classified as "royal propaganda."[53] In that time, the spread of ideas was not accomplished by writing.[54] The ordinary person [[492]] knew how to read neither hieroglyphics nor cuneiform, with its hundreds of signs. One had to be an Ashurbanipal to brag of knowing how to read and write. Even when there were many hieratic copies of a royal text or many exemplars of Assyrian, Babylonian, and Hittite annals, these copies or duplicates were for the use of the court or future scribes. It is appropriate to see in these texts an affirmation of a doctrine or royal election that served as the basis for functioning of the administration or for negotiations with other powers. Because the intended audience of a writing was an omniscient deity, one should not be surprised occasionally to find that the text was buried, for example, a votive nail in the temple of Mari, or in Egypt, painted on the walls of some necropolis, where the public had no access.

This situation would be altered about 1500 B.C. by the invention of the alphabet. This democratic tool reduced the number of letters to thirty signs or less.[55] But this instrument was more a means of recording information (reports, contracts, decrees, computations) than a means of spreading it. It would become indispensable to the scribes and merchants of the Levant. The workers at Serabit-el-Khadim used it for their steles in honor of "Baalat." But we have still not arrived at the degree of dissemination of ideas that was true in Greek times (thinking of the writings of Aristotle), let alone what is possible with use of paper and printing. No, during this period it was the great cultic ceremonies that served as royal propaganda.

53. The term was used by G. Posener, *Littérature et Politique dans l'Égypte de la XIIe dynastie* (Paris: Champion, 1956) and is often taken up by Van Seters (*In Search of History*, 172, 190–91, 193, 244, etc.). See also N. Grimal, *Études sur la propagande royale égyptienne* (2 vols.; Cairo: Institut Francais d'Archaeologie Oriental, 1981); idem, *Les termes de la propagande royale égyptienne de la XIXe dynastie à la conquête d'Alexandre* (Paris, 1990); M. Liverani, "Hattushili alle prese con la propaganda ramesside," *Or* (1990) 207–17.

54. Concerning writing and libraries, C. B. F. Walker, *Reading the Past: Cuneiform* (London: British Museum / Berkeley: University of California Press, 1987). A. L. Oppenheim, after having noted that steles were placed in accessible places, quickly added that one buries them like cylinders (*Mesopotamia*, 234). The *kudurrus* that served as boundary markers were more divine symbols than they were texts.

55. The invention of the alphabet especially suited scribes and their schools. A. Lemaire, *Les Écoles de scribes et la formation de la Bible dans l'Ancien Israël* (OBO 39; Fribourg: Éditions universitaires, 1981). We do not, however, have other examples of the diffusion of thought by this means.

Biblical Historiography

History and Organization of Israel

Israel came into being at the end of the second millennium.[56] Due to discoveries in areas of the ancient Near East during the past two centuries, one cannot treat Israel's religious literature in isolation. The Bible was born among earlier religious cultures that [[493]] had profoundly permeated Canaan before the Bible freed itself from their influence. The prophetic oracles, like the Pentateuchal narratives and the Deuteronomistic History (Joshua–2 Kings), constantly show these people being influenced by or in battle with their great neighbors.

The great difference that leaps out at us during any literary analysis of the texts is that biblical history is centered *on law and not on royal personages*. This difference raises the problem of institutions to a matter of first priority. These institutions had their origins in the surrounding cultures. The organization of Israel as a monarchic institution "like the other nations" (1 Sam 8:5, 20) would therefore pose a painful problem for the faith of the Israelites, given their religious ideology.

Since the specialists' rejection of M. Noth's hypothesis of a premonarchic amphictyony of twelve tribes,[57] no evidence remains of an Israel consisting of twelve tribes before David and prior to the Solomonic system of twelve administrative districts.[58] According to this amphictyonic principle, each district (in which one tribe resided among many other peoples)

---

56. H. Gunkel, more than any other, studied the way in which legend developed into narrative, but Van Seters has shown that his presentation is too systematic (*In Search of History*, 210ff.); see Van Seters, "History and Historians in the Ancient Near East: The Israelites," *Or* 50 (1981) 137–98. Gressmann seems to me to make more room for the appearance of historical recital in legend. Other recent studies: M. Weippert, "Fragen der israelitischen Geschichtsschreibung," *VT* 23 (1973) 415–42; H. Cazelles, "Die biblische Geschichtsschreibung im Licht der altorientalischen Geschichtsschreibung" (XXIII Deutscher Orientalistentag, 16–20 Sept 1985; Stuttgart, 1989) 38–49; B. G. Boschi, *Le origini di Israele nella Bibbia fra storia e teologia: La questione del metodo e la sfida storiografica* (Suppl. alla Revista biblica 20; Bologna: Dahoniane, 1989). For the questions of history and traditions in the Pentateuch, there is an excellent bibliography, classified and annotated, in S. J. DeVries, "A Review of Recent Research in the Tradition History of the Pentateuch," *SBL 1987: Seminar Papers* (SBLSP 26; Atlanta: Scholars Press, 1987) 459– 502.

57. This idea is rejected by R. de Vaux, G. W. Anderson, and the majority of specialists. See the study and bibliography in A. Soggin, *Storia d'Israele* (Brescia, 1984) 258–67; English trans.: *A History of Israel: From the Beginnings to the Bar Kochba Revolt* (Louisville: Westminster/ John Knox / London: SCM, 1989).

58. A. Caquot, "Préfets," *DBS* 8 273–86. W. F. Albright showed that the territory of these districts corresponded approximately with the places where the tribes had settled, generally as minorities among peoples of other, Canaanite races (*JPOS* 5 [1925] 17–54).

in turn maintained the sanctuary and adjacent palace for one month. Prior to that time, the tribes lived independently, while contracting many different sorts of unions with others. Even the reign of Saul was not able to achieve a durable institutional unity.[59] It was because of the eclipse of the great empires—Hatti, Assyria, Babylonia, and Egypt (from whom the Philistines inherited a part of Canaan in the twelfth century)—that the small West Semitic monarchies could burst forth (including the Phoenician maritime nation). This was the case with Israel, though not without both external (Ammonite, Midianite, Philistine) and internal tensions (Ephraim, jealous of Gideon of Manasseh, of Jepthah of Gilead, and even of Benjamin).[60] At this juncture it would be possible to draw up an [[494]] Israelite history showing the formation of this new monarchic state in the context of other nations (Table of Nations, Genesis 10). In order to overcome the intertribal tension, particularly between the recent Judah and the ancient, conquering Ephraim–Benjamin, would it be possible to appeal to the premonarchic traditions? As a matter of fact, Judah does not take part in the combat of the ten tribes who, under the direction of the Naphtalite Barak, 'volunteered' or mobilized themselves (*mitnaddĕbîm*) into an *ʿam* ('army, people') at the call of the Ephraimite prophetess (Judg 5:9). Would it be in Judah or in Benjamin that a king would be elected by Yahweh? David would be recognized by all of the Israelite and Judean tribes (2 Sam 5:1–3), but upon the death of his son Solomon, would it be the Judean Rehoboam or the Ephraimite Jeroboam that people would obey in the name of Yahweh?

---

59. Monographs concerned with the life of each tribe have multiplied since the synthesis of R. de Vaux, *Histoire ancienne d'Israël* (2 vols.; Paris: Lecoffre, 1971–73) 1.487–620, 2.19–66 (Eng. trans., *The Early History of Israel* [Philadelphia: Westminster / London: Darton, Longman & Todd, 1978] 523–680, 683–749). Concerning the formation of Judah, see 1.507–10 (Eng., pp. 546–50).

60. In E. M. Laperrousaz (ed.), *La Protohistoire d'Israël*, A. Lemaire (author of "Deux origines d'Israël: La montagne d'Éphraïm et le territoire de Manassé," 183–292; and of "La montagne de Juda," 293–98), while relying on biblical, Egyptian, and archaeological data, looked at the origin of Israel in the alliance at Shechem of the *bĕnê Jacob* [['sons of Jacob']] coming from the North and the *bĕnê Israel* [['sons of Israel']] coming from the South as bordering on an Israelite confederation (*La Protohistoire d'Israël de l'exode à la monarchie* [ed. E. M. Laperrousaz; Paris: Du Cerf, 1990]). While being in agreement with the final dates proposed, I (ibid., "Peut on circonscrire un événement Exode," 30–55) would allow a more complex process to be at work in institutions like the *ben ʿameh*, the *ʿam* [['people, army']], and the *qāhāl* [['assembly/audience']]. It is Asriel (Israel) that appears to me to settle in Shechem (Gen 33:20; 48:21–22). Jacob would belong to some vague earlier period (Hyksos scarabs) and would leave its ties with Isaac from the south (Lahai-roi, Beer-sheba) in order to ascend toward Bethel (Gen 28:19) and join Israel on the Jabbok (Gen 32:29) at the time of the Aramean expansion.

Provoked by conflicts between pretenders to the royal throne, as was the case in Egypt[61] and in all of the kingdoms of the time, this history would be religious, taking into account the sacral character of the monarchies of the period.[62] Under the action of the prophetic schools, the Israelite monarchy would be desacralized. But, in the beginning, it would be the king who organized the cult, chose the clergy, blessed the people and prayed for them. His word was an "oracle" (Prov 16:10ff.). He delivered decrees (*ḥuqqîm*), as did the deified Pharaoh of Egypt (Gen 47:22, 26), because he was a *mĕḥôqēq* [['legislator']].[63] Now the Law, or the laws on which the biblical history would be oriented, would not be covered by the sacral authority of the kings but by the divine authority of other institutions.

[[495]] The Law, or "Torah," must necessarily be analyzed according to the codes that make up the Pentateuch. At first reading, one sees the Passover and Unleavened Bread laws (Exodus 12–13), the "Covenant Code" (*sēper habbĕrît* Exod 24:7 = 20:24–23:19), the code called "covenant renewal" (Exod 34:12–26), the Deuteronomic Code (Deuteronomy 12–26), and the composite collection of the "legislation given at Mount Sinai" (Lev 26:48) completed in Moab (Num 36:13), the "Priestly Code" (Exodus 25–31, 35–40; all of Leviticus; Numbers 1–10:19; 15–19; 25–36). This is not the place to return to the precise analyses of the literary-critical school (Graf, Kuenen, Wellhausen, Reuss, and Driver), delineated accurately by Lagrange. By comparing the resolutions of concrete legal cases on the same subject (murder, theft, rape, liturgical cycle, and so on), it is possible to establish the relative age of these codes.[64] Though the literary critics

61. In Egypt, "the very idea of opposition is unthinkable. No alternative to political power existed. It was replaced by competition between pretenders to the same office" (Grimal, *Termes de la propagande royale*, 648). In Mesopotamia these were "the competitions around the throne" (P. Garelli in *La voix de l'opposition en Mésopotamie* [Brussels: Institut des Hautes Études de Belgique, 1973] 213; contributions by A. Finet, C. Wilcke, E. Cassin, and J. Bottéro).

62. The sacral character of the Israelite monarchy was established by the endeavors of the Scandinavian school (Engnell, Widengren), perhaps in too systematic a manner, and the English school (Hooke, A. Johnson); it was contested by J. de Fraine and K. Bernhardt. This sacral character was never admitted without correction by the Bible, but the historical facts are summarized by R. de Vaux, *Les Institutions de l'Ancien Testament* (2d ed.; Paris: Du Cerf, 1989) 1.155–77 (Eng. trans., *Ancient Israel 1: Social Institutions* [New York: McGraw-Hill / London: Darton, Longman & Todd, 1961] 100–114); Cazelles, *Le Messie de la Bible*, 60–86.

63. On the term for a leader who "inscribes" decrees, cf. my *Autour de l'Exode: Études* (Paris: Lecoffre/Gabalda, 1987) 18.

64. The list provided by S. Driver (*Introduction to the Literature of the Old Testament* [9th ed.; Edinburgh: T. & T. Clark, 1913] 73–75) remains a model, as does the distribution of vocabulary and phraseology presented by H. Holzinger, *Einleitung in den Hexateuch* (Leipzig: Mohr, 1893).

tied the Passover laws either to the Priestly Code or to the code of Exodus 34, they showed by another route the connections between these codes and other parts of the Bible, such as Deuteronomy with the book of Kings and the reform of Josiah, and the legislation of Joshua 21 with the Priestly Code.

It was analysis of the vocabulary and style that permitted recognition of the connections between the codes and the narratives of the biblical histories. Eventually, it led to discernment of the importance of institutions in the composition of *this* historiography. At this point, we should say, "of *these* historiographies," because, for example, the historiography of the Priestly Code is very different from the history in which the code of Exodus 34 appears. Here the contribution of ancient Near Eastern studies was decisive. The deciphering of the Code of Hammurabi by P. Scheil (1902) and of its casuistic style ("If . . .") essentially was the deciphering of the *mišpaṭîm* (judicial decisions) of the so-called Covenant Code. Additional clarification came from the Near Eastern covenant treaties, which evidence a link between the report of events and the stipulations imposed in direct address ("You . . .").

Just as the importance of the royal institution was cast into relief by the Scandinavian and English schools, the discoveries at Mari by A. Parrot led to discovery of the importance of the prophetic institution. The institution of judge was already better known through the Phoenician-Punic culture (the suffetes), and that of the priest was clarified by every ancient culture. These are the four great institutions of the Deuteronomic Code [[496]] (Deut 16:18–18:22). The Priestly Code retained only the institution of priest (as distinct from prince and Levite) as foundational. The "elder" played only a secondary, though not negligible, role. Finally, the institution of "sage," strongly assailed by the prophets but appreciated by the Deuteronomist, could be analyzed more closely thanks to texts from the ancient Near East: Egypt, Mesopotamia, Ugarit, and the West Semitic inscriptions.

All of these codes and institutions have a religious character, even the Hittite collections that lack prologues and colophons.[65] However, one could say that they do not have the same sacral character as a king, except when the king takes responsibility for collections of legal material (Ur-Nammu; Hammurabi, etc.). Neither the judge nor the "sage"[66] scribe who

---

65. Hittite Laws I 75; II 54; cf. TUAT 1/1. 109, 118. These are collections of jurisprudence; the judicial institution is not sacral like the institution of royalty. The *mišpaṭîm* [['judicial decisions']] in Exod 22:6–9 are as discretely religious as the Hittite articles.

66. One must not forget that the 'sage' (*ḥākām*) is a suspect scribe in the dynastic history and with the prophets. The Deuteronomist respects him and, after the exile, he is a repository of divine wisdom.

pronounced or recorded a sentence or sentences was a mediator between god and man, not even when there was a protector god such as Thoth in Egypt or Nabu in Mesopotamia. In contrast, the treaties concluded between monarchs with the gods of the contracting parties as witnesses were of a sacral order, and their stipulations were the object of an oath (*adê*).[67] This religious or sacral character of the codes that, in the biblical history, took the place of the king in the histories of the period demands a theological analysis of its presuppositions. All of the biblical codes are said to come from the national God, except for the Deuteronomic Code (Deut 12:1).

The older historiographies were centered on royal ideology in order to inculcate into the reader the fact that "so-and-so" was chosen by the national god, in spite of problems of dynasty and succession. It was necessary to give him fealty and trust. It is true that biblical historiographies are drafted according to the essentials of Israelite faith[68]—faith in YHWH. But who was YHWH? What did he want? Who was his representative whom one must obey? Was it Jeroboam the Ephraimite or Rehoboam the Judean? Was it the YHWH of Josiah and the Deuteronomic reform or the YHWH of the [[497]] high places and of Jehoiakim, who affirmed his loyalty by changing his name (Eliakim) to a Yahwistic name? When it is a question of opting between a national storm-god—Hurrian or Canaanite of a Baal or Teshub type—and a solar type of national god (Egyptian Re or the Hittite goddess Arinna), it is difficult to speak of "theology." These are two aspects of royal ideology. However, when it is a question of opting between a YHWH of the Baal type and the God of Deuteronomy, defined by an ethic, one can speak of "theology." The authority of law takes the place of an older royal authority, and biblical history thus will be centered on a theology.

Biblical Historiographies

The Deuteronomistic History (DH)

It is with the *Deuteronomistic History*[69] that modern theological spirit feels most at ease. It is a monotheistic theology that casts into relief the

---

67. Concerning this much-studied term borrowed by the Assyrians from the Arameans (Wiseman, Weinfeld, de Vaux, etc.), see my *Autor de l'Exode*, 19.

68. M. Noth, *Überlieferungsgeschichtliche Studien*, (Halle: Niemeyer, 1943) 4 [[English trans. of pp. 1–110: *The Deuteronomistic History* (JSOTSup 15; Sheffield: JSOT Press, 1981)]], according to his analysis of "themes" essential to Israelite faith.

69. This history has been the subject of many works, in addition to those dealing generally with biblical history (see n. 56 above). See the introductions of W. H. Schmidt, *Einführung in das A. T.* (3d ed.; Berlin: de Gruyter, 1985) 136–40; A. Soggin, O. Kaiser, and the *Entstehung* of Smend. I will content myself with citing here: Z. Zevit, "Deuteronomic Historiography in

transcendence and tenderness of the God of the fathers. He proposes his
laws so that one may find life and avoid death (Deut 30:15–20). It is by
personal faithfulness or infidelity to the decrees, maxims, and commandments of YHWH, united in a single *Torah*, that humans are judged. It has
long been observed that the book of Kings was inspired by this theology.
This is true also for the Deuteronomistic Historian, even if he does not
use exactly the same vocabulary as the Deuteronomist.[70] However, one
should recognize, along with M. Noth,[71] the hand of the Deuteronomistic
Historian in the collection [[498]] that runs from Genesis to Kings. By
closely inspecting the manner in which he works, it becomes clear that the
text is the result of the hand of an editor, not an author. By making certain additions he imprinted a new coloration on predeuteronomic texts.

This is also apparent in the book of Kings. It seems certain to me that
a preexilic edition, prior to the death of Josiah (see 2 Kgs 22:19, celebrating the king's Deuteronomic reform, 23:1–25), was recast at the time of
the exile. Critical theory tends to go further and to postulate a historical
foundation (DtrG) completed by a DtrP with a prophetic spirit and a DtrN
who judged according to the Law.[72] It is the latter who gave his/their mark
to the Book. I will only remind the reader that there are three evident
doublets in which the theology reveals itself.

---

1 K 12–2 K 17 and the Reinvestiture of the Israelite Cult," *JSOT* 32 (1985) 57–73, which takes
careful account of Near Eastern culture; J. Mejia, "The Aim of the Deuteronomistic History:
A Reappraisal," in *Proceedings of the Sixth World Congress of Jewish Studies* (Jerusalem: Magnes,
1977–78) 291–98; U. Koppel, *Das deuteronomistische Geschichtswerk und seine Quelle* (Berne:
Lang, 1979); Mark A. O'Brien, *The Deuteronomic History Hypothesis: A Reassessment* (OBO 92;
Fribourg: Universitätsverlag / Göttingen: Vandenhoeck & Ruprecht, 1989); R. D. Nelson,
The Double Redaction of the Deuteronomistic History (JSOTSup 18; Sheffield: JSOT Press,1981);
R. Albertz, "Die Intentionen und die Träger des deuteronomistischen Geschichtswerk," in
Schöpfung und Befreiung . . . , Festschrift C. Westermann 80. Geburtstag (ed. R. Albertz; Stuttgart:
Calwer, 1989) 37–53.

70. H. Weippert, "Die deuteronomistische Bearbeitungen der Könige von Israel und
Juda, und das Problem der Redaktion der Königsbücher," *Bib* 53 (1972) 301–39; idem, *Die
Prosa Reden des Jeremiasbuches* (BZAW 132; Berlin: de Gruyter, 1973); "Das deuteronomis-
tische Geschichtswerk: Sein Ziel und Ende in der neue Forschung," *ThRu* 50 (1985) 213–49;
J. Roy Porter, "The Supposed Deuteronomic Redaction of the Prophets: Some Considera-
tions," in *Schöpfung und Befreiung . . . , Festschrift C. Westermann 80. Geburtstag* (ed. R. Albertz;
Stuttgart: Calwer, 1989) 69–78.

71. M. Noth, *Überlieferungsgeschichtliche Studien* (Halle: Niemeyer, 1943); *Die Überlieferungsgeschichte des Pentateuch* (Stuttgart: Kohlhammer, 1948). Also see F. Langlamet, "Affinités
sacerdotales, deutéronomiques, élohistes dans l'histoire de la Succession (2 S 9–20; 1 R 1–2),"
in *Mélanges Bibliques et Orientaux . . . H. Cazelles* (ed. A Caquot; AOAT 212; Neukirchen-Vluyn:
Neukirchener Verlag, 1981) 233–46.

72. E. Würthwein gives some examples that seem characteristic to him (*Die Bücher der
Könige* [ATD; Göttingen: Vandenhoeck & Ruprecht, 1984] 498). I fear that the text he proposes for DtrG (505–15) might not be sacral enough for the period, but the "annals" are
hardly sacral.

(1) In 2 Kgs 17:18, YHWH condemns Israel in regard to his cult and for turning away from him; Judah remains. In v. 19, YHWH "their God" also condemns Judah for not having kept his prescriptions and having followed the decrees of Israel.

(2) In 1 Kgs 2:12 and 46b, it is said that the kingship of Solomon was (solidly) 'established' (*kwn*). The conclusion of v. 46b does not lead to any moral or theological consideration. The conclusion of 2:12, on the contrary, leads to a Deuteronomic insertion on the paternity of David, the length of his reign (10–11), and in 3–4, to the moral demands of the Law of Moses. This is an insertion into the "Succession Narrative."

(3) A curious doublet repeats the dialogue of YHWH-Elyon in 1 Kgs 19:13b–14 from vv. 9b–10. The Deuteronomist wishes to desacralize the cave according to the law of the single sanctuary. He sets the divine dialogue outside the cave. The Elijah cycle, from the Carmel sacrifice to the dialogue at Horeb, the mountain of God, ignores the centralization law of Deuteronomy 12. The same Deuteronomist, in 1 Kgs 3:2, had thought it appropriate to justify the sacrifices that had been offered on the high place at Gibeon instead of at Zion.

(4) M. Noth has noted that there are Deuteronomic additions in the books of Samuel, although they are less numerous.[73] What better place would there be for the oracle of Nathan than in 2 Sam 7:19, in a passage about Solomon's construction of the Temple "for my Name"?[74] The Deuteronomist's hand is especially recognizable at the end and at [[499]] the beginning of the book. Chapters 21–24 interrupt the Succession Narrative and attribute the establishment of the Yahwistic cult in the Temple area to David (chap. 24). The Deuteronomist placed this precisely next to the sacrifice on "the mountain of YHWH" at Gibeah (chap. 21, especially v. 6). These two chapters (21 and 24) bracket a song of David with his last words. He is surrounded by his fighting men and rescued from Saul (22:1) and from the sons of Belial (23:6).

The introduction to the book (1 Samuel 1–3) also carries traces of Deuteronomic modification of the ancient narrative of the Ark. Samuel is the true prophet (3:19) who makes and unmakes kings; he is now the subject of a song that announces the *māšîaḥ* ('Messiah', 2:10), *šā'ûl* the 're-quested one' (*šā'al*, 1:27). The priesthood of Shiloh is rejected, and the offerings (*'iššê*, 2:28; cf. Deut 18:1) will be the lot of a "faithful priest" and his house (2:35). This can only be the Jerusalem priesthood.

(5) The book of Judges is not based on Deuteronomistic theology and phraseology (one God, one people and one king, one Temple) but on the

---

73. Noth, *Überlieferungsgechichtliche Studien*, 103–14.
74. R. de Vaux (*Bible de la Jérusalem*, fasc. Samuel, ad loc.) notes that this insertion changes the sense of 'house', which is here not 'dynasty' but 'temple'.

cycles of sin, punishment, appeal, and rescue by judges,[75] who correspond approximately to the twelve tribes. However, a doublet reveals the hand of the Deuteronomist: Judg 2:20–3:4 takes up the theme of the punishment and irritation of YHWH (developed in 2:11–19) regarding the breach of covenant and the instructional testing by God in order to teach war to any inexperienced descendants (3:1–2; cf. Deut 8:1–5). It was the marriages with the Canaanite women that perverted the men of Israel (3:6; cf. Deut 7:1–4). Finally, in the narratives of Gideon/Jerubbaal (Judges 6–9), Gideon's refusal of the kingdom (8:23) must be attributed to the Deuteronomist, in contradiction to the context (8:18; 9:1–6). It is the Deuteronomist who fuses two earlier traditions: that of Gideon and that of Jerubaal, a process that we shall meet again.

(6) In the book of Joshua, the part played by the Deuteronomist is much more considerable. He is credited with an edition of the book, even if it might be necessary to acknowledge a second, priestly edition (Mowinckel, contra Noth; see chap. 21). Furthermore, he used some earlier narratives concerning Gilgal, Jericho, Bethel, and Gibeon, all Benjaminite holy places in which the Jerusalem priesthood was not held dear.

(7) We will rediscover traces of Deuteronomic additions in the Pentateuch. One of the most characteristic, analogous to the addition observed above in 1 Kings 19, is found in Deut 27:1b–3. In 27:4–7, Moses again orders Joshua to dress stones and smear them [[500]] with lime in order to set up an altar to YHWH, according to the prescriptions of the code and the covenant (Exod 20:24–25). This order is taken up in vv. 1b–3, but without further mention of an altar, because this would be contrary to the law of the singleness of the sanctuary found in Deuteronomy.

In Exodus 33, the Deuteronomist finds himself in the presence of two divergent traditions. In 33:1–4 YHWH refuses to accompany the people to "go up" toward the Promised Land: it is an angel (*malʾāk*) that will be sent before Moses. However, in 33:12–17 YHWH kindly deigns to accompany him. In 33:5–6, the Deuteronomist reconciles the two traditions by transforming the absolute refusal into a conditional one, and the rite of mourning (stripping off of ornaments, v. 4) becomes a rite of penitence (5b–6, doublet of 4). The Deuteronomist's hand is encountered also at the ends of the two codes found in Exodus 34 and 20–23. One concludes the Sinai Covenant with Moses at Sinai (34:2, 4) and the other concludes the covenant with the people at the base of the mountain (24:4). The cultic calendar of Exod 23:15–17 (v. 13 is a doublet of v. 17) presents itself as a Deuteronomic addition in 34:18ff.,[76] making the latter text a code of "re-

---

75. This is similar to the predeuteronomic schema proposed by W. Richter, *Die Bearbeitungen des "Retterbuches" in der deuteronomischen Epoche* (BBB 21; Bonn: Hanstein, 1964).

76. See *Études sur le code d'alliance* (Paris: Letouzey et Ané, 1946) 97–99. But the feast of 23:18 is not the Feast of Passover.

newal" of the covenant that was completed by Deuteronomic additions.[77] And, in the conclusion of the so-called Covenant Code, 23:27–33 (Deuteronomic complement of 23:20–26, which refers to the *mal'āk* [['angel']] of 33:2)[78] prepares for Judg 2:20–3:6, itself a complement of Judg 2:11–19 (see above): the people will not be driven out immediately.

H. H. Schmid made an interesting comment concerning the structure of the Mosaic call in Exod 3:7ff.[79] Even more interesting, it seems to me, is the manner in which the Deuteronomist produced this structure, the study of which allows us to analyze vocabulary and repetitions. The Deuteronomist found himself in the presence of two traditions. In the one, Yhwh sends Moses to the Israelites in order to make them "go up toward the land" that was promised and tells him, "I will be with you" (3:7–8, 12a). In the other, Elohim gives him his Name and sends him with the elders to the king of Egypt (14:16–29; the list of 8b makes a doublet with that of v. 17). In 3:9–10, 17b, v. 9 is a doublet of v. 7: the Deuteronomist unites the two traditions: he alters the northern "go up" of conquest to a Deuteronomic "go out."

This is not the place to take up in detail the other Deuteronomic additions to the Pentateuch, by which the "Jehovist" desired to unite the [[501]] divergent traditions. Let us note, however, the way he does it in Genesis 15, a tradition concerning the lineage of Abraham (by night, oppression of 400 years in Egypt), another the possession of the land (at twilight, iniquity of the Amorites during four generations). The Deuteronomic additions are visible not only in v. 1[80] but also in vv. 18–19: the Israelite frontiers will extend as far as the "great river, the Euphrates" (cf. Deut 1:7; Josh 1:4). Altogether exceptionally in the texts of Genesis prior to P, God's covenant with a Patriarch corresponds to the oath made to the Fathers according to Deut 1:8 (ten times).

These examples are sufficient to see that the so-called Jehovist is a Deuteronomist who found himself in the presence of earlier divergent traditions. He wanted to unite them into a common history for *a single* people of *a single* God who ordered it by *one* Law, even if drafted in several codes. His history has a completely different orientation from Herodotus's. Herodotus set out to "learn by inquiry in order that so the memory of the past may not be blotted out from among men by time, and that great and marvellous deeds done by Greeks and foreigners . . . may

---

77. Exod 34:24b (with "Yhwh your God") is a doublet of v. 23 ("the Lord Yhwh, God of Israel"). See my *Autour de l'Exode*, 175–88 (reprinted in *Mélanges Delcor*).

78. Concerning the 'hornet' (*sr'ah*), see Deut 7:20. Concerning the 'snare', Deut 7:16; Josh 23:13.

79. H. H. Schmid, *Der sogenannte Jahwist: Beobachtungen und Fragen zur Pentateuch Forschung* (Zurich: Theologischer Verlag, 1976) 19–31.

80. The textual analysis in *RB* 69 (1962) 321–49 needs revision at this point.

not lack renown."[81] When the Deuteronomist set to work, these events were already fixed in writing, and the Deuteronomist had a difficult time arranging them. He oriented them toward the gift of a Law from YHWH, applying the ten words of Horeb (Gen 34:28; cf. Deut 4:13; 10:4). The lists of conquered peoples end with the Jebusites, the inhabitants of Zion. After the fall of Samaria and the subjugation of the ten tribes to foreign gods and a foreign king, it is in the dynasty of David and the cult of the Temple of YHWH at Zion that there is hope.

The Yahwistic History

The Yahwistic History (J) (or dynastic history) is one of the divergent traditions that the Deuteronomist had to include in the project. We cannot take up here the analyses of vocabulary, expression, and perspective that have been done and redone.[82] It only remains to specify the orientation and methods of the history.

Like the Deuteronomistic History, the Yahwistic History comprises the gift of a Law from YHWH to his people. This is the code of Exodus 34, presented, like the stipulations of one of the covenants at Sinai, not directly with the people [[502]] but with a leader: Moses (v. 27).[83] This "personal" covenant during a theophany of YHWH, identified as El-qannah,[84] is nothing other than an episode analogous to the patriarchal theophanies. Moses is presented in effect as a patriarch: his birth and the etymology of his name (Exod 2:1–10), his marriage and childhood (2:16–22), the divine promise (3:7–8, 12a), his negotiations, his wandering. He also has

---

81. Herodotus *Histories* 1.1 (trans. A. D. Godley; LCL; Cambridge: Harvard University Press / London: Heinemann, 1966) 3, cited by Van Seters who, in other respects, often leads his ancient history back to an "antiquarian interest" (cf. *In Search of History*, 71, 76, 91). This is what is in question. The author appears to me more felicitous when he invokes (p. 72) the problems of legitimacy and usurpation.

82. See, for example, Schmidt, *Einführung*, 72–81; O. Kaiser, *Einleitung in das A.T.* (4th ed.; Gütersloh: Gütersloher, 1984) 90–101; A. Soggin, *Introduzione* [[*all'Antico Testamento* (4th ed.; Brescia: Paideia, 1987) 146–50 = Eng. trans.: *Introduction to the Old Testament* (trans. John Bowden; 3d ed.; London: SCM / Philadelphia: Westminster, 1989) 114–21]]; R. Smend, *Die Entstehung* [[*des Alten Testaments* (3d ed.; Stuttgart: Kohlhammer, 1984) 86–93]].

83. "I have made a covenant with you." After this direct object, the Deuteronomist added "and with Israel" in order to harmonize the text with other covenant formulas, in particular the one in Exod 24:3–8. Verse 10 of the MT (in distinction from the LXX) makes no mention of "with whom" YHWH made covenant, which is abnormal. It is not always "with the people," but it is "before the people" that YHWH "will do with you" wonders. On this text, see my *Autour de l'Exode*, 177. But Elyon is mentioned at Sefire, not at Karatepe.

84. This divine name is of the same form of ancient divine names: El-olam, El Shaddai, El Elohei-Israel, El-berith, El-bethel, El-elyon . . . , probably a Yahwistic adaption of the Canaanite-Phoenician El-qoneh (Gen 14:22; cf. ibid., 61; *DBS* 7 146).

in hand a staff *maṭṭeh* (Exod 4:2, 17; 7:15), analogous though not identical to the royal staff/scepter (Gen 49:10).

Centered on the question of the ruler and his legitimacy, this history is much closer to prebiblical histories than the Deuteronomistic History. The king is not suspect here, as he is in the royal law of Deut 17:14–20 and in the critique of Gideon and of the dynasties of the books of Kings. Having a king is a benefit in Gen 49:10, as in Num 24:7, 15. However, the royal institution poses great problems for Israelite faith. They are problems of legitimacy and problems of succession, similar to the problems we have seen in Babylonian, Hittite, Egyptian, and Canaanite histories. The Ugaritic Legend of Keret transfers the right of the firstborn (*bkr*) from the firstborn to the last daughter. It is as a function of this royal *theologoumenon* [['theological formulation']] in a still-sacral monarchy that our Yahwist will interpret the old tribal and local traditions. What appears familial is in fact of dynastic interest. Cain is the firstborn of Eve, "mother of all living," who, like the mother of a king, must have a descendant who will break the head of the symbolic serpent. But Seth is substituted (Gen 4:25) for the brother who was killed, as Solomon is substituted for the firstborn of David and Bathsheba. Among all peoples, a descendant of Shem (of whom Canaan/Ham is slave and Japheth the guest in his tents) had the blessing (and not Babel). By him the blessing will extend to all the families of the earth. The heir of the benediction will not be the firstborn of Abram (Ishmael) but Isaac. Similarly, Rebeccah will pass the heritage of Esau (Edom) to Jacob (Israel), and Jacob in his benediction will grant the royalty to Judah, not to his three elder brothers. Thus [[503]] Bathsheba will secure a promise from David that the throne will be given to his tenth son, Solomon, and not to his older brothers.

After having established the place of Israel vis-à-vis Canaan, Babel, Ishmael, Aram, and Edom, the Yahwist in effect had to choose from among the traditions the one that legitimated before YHWH (more of a religious problem than a judicial one) a submission of peoples (Gen 49:10) to the Judean dynasty. The incest of Reuben (Gen 35:22) and the violence of Simeon and Levi (Genesis 34) transferred the royal benediction of Jacob to Judah. The situation is different for the Joseph tribes (Ephraim, Manasseh, Benjamin), especially since the clan of Ephrata, into which David was born in Bethlehem, owes its name to Ephraim (Ephrata is the adjectival form). This is the *nazîr* [['prince']] of the brothers (Gen 49:26). But our historiographer J recalls that it is Joseph who denounced the four sons of Bilhah and Zilpah (37:2). He practiced magic, lied in order to keep Benjamin for himself, and profited from the famine in order to acquire all of the land of Egypt for Pharaoh. It was Judah who intervened to save Joseph (37:26f.), then Benjamin (44:12–34). This occurs after chap. 38, which relates the birth of Perez, ancestor of David according to Ruth 4:17–22.

This history supporting the legitimacy of the Judean monarchy, heir of YHWH's promises to Abraham, Isaac, and Jacob, understandably is accompanied by the failure of the Manassite monarchy of Abimelech, son of Jerubbaal, and the failure of the Benjaminite monarchy of Saul. The so-called narrative of Saul's kingship is in fact inserted into "the accession of David" and with it forms a "Succession Narrative" in which, by alliance with David, Jonathan legitimates David's kingship (not to speak of David's marriages to Michal and Merab). Finally, the succession of David concludes this history in 1 Kgs 2:46b: "The kingdom was established in the hands of Solomon."

This thematic unity should not conceal the literary disparities. The Yahwist is a collector of traditions and narratives[85] that already had a history before our historiographer marked them [[504]] with his theology of the sacral heritage of the promises. In prebiblical history, the divine promises were made to the king: descendants, land, and prosperity.[86] However, our historian centers his history on a Judean monarchy of recent vintage, contested on the one hand by the Benjaminite Shimmei, faithful to the dynasty of Saul (2 Sam 16:5–14), and on the other by the Ephraimites of Jeroboam or by Baasha of Issachar. Also, for him, the divine promises were not made to the dynasty's founder but rather to Israel, to whom the twelve tribes are attached. Even more, the promises were made to Isaac (for Edom) and to Abram (from whom arise the Ishmaelites, the Midianites, and also, through his nephew Lot, Ammon and Moab). This very extensive horizon corresponds to the universal pretensions of the pharaohs, for whom all foreign power is rebellious, and to those of the Babylonian kings, who claimed to be "kings of the four regions [[= the entire earth]]."[87]

---

85. Narrative analyses have shown a great upsurge in the last few years. See L. Alonso Schökel, "Arte narrativa en José-Jueces-Samuel-Reyes," *EstBib* 48 (1990) 145–69 and the bibliography on pp. 168–69 (Conroy, Polzin, Fokkelman, R. Alter, D. Jobling, etc.) [[the article by Alonso-Schökel is now translated and appears in this volume, pp. 255–278]]; and C. Westermann attempted a classification (*Arten der Erzählungen in der Genesis* [Forschung am Alten Testament; Munich, 1964] 9–91). These analyses are very effective when they treat each tradition and its literary development in isolation. They run an occasional risk of obliterating the bumpiness of vocabulary and the insertion of some episode into the concrete history of Israel, in the midst of its internal and external tensions. D. Daube had occasion to show that this or that biblical narrative was constructed according to a problem of law (*Studies in Biblical Law* [Cambridge: Cambridge University Press, 1947]; idem, *Ancient Jewish Law* [Leiden: Brill, 1981]).

86. All of the promises were made to the king. See above, n. 51; *DBS* 7 143–44; M. J. Seux, *Épithètes royales: Akkadiens et sumériens* (Paris: Letouzey et Ané, 1967) 19ff.

87. Ibid., 26, 244, 291, 350, etc.

The divine promises, made to the kings and founders of the dynasty, pass to Abraham, Isaac, and Jacob, and finally to Moses. The Judean dynasty is heir to the promises of prosperity made to Abraham and the other patriarchs. It is thus relativized. However, it is even more conditioned by the Sinai Covenant and its stipulations.

These stipulations are of a cultic order, essentially the connection between the Passover festival and the three seasonal feasts of the sedentary Canaanites (Exodus 34, apart from the Deuteronomistic additions, but with the cultic preamble of Exod 19:10–15, the 'whoever' (*hmh*) of v. 13 announcing the sacred banquet of 24:1, 9–11). Like the Weidner Chronicle, centered on the Marduk cult in Babylon, and many other Near Eastern histories, this first biblical history needed to confront problems raised by local cults that were often observed by the patriarchs (Shechem, Salem, Beer-sheba, Bethel, etc.), and the cult of the national God prior to the Ark of the Covenant, "YHWH enthroned on the cherubim" (1 Sam 4:4, etc.). Our historian does not attack local cults and their theophanies. However, following a Canaanite model,[88] the local deities are nothing but a *mal'āk* [['messenger, angel']] of YHWH, the God of Israel (Exod 34:23), whose throne is now in the Temple built by Solomon and before whom all males should present themselves three times a year.

[[505]] This history therefore has its own theological coherence and seeks to respond to the faith of Israel. YHWH is the national God for the South (Gen 4:26) just as for the North (Judg 7:20). But are David and his dynasty really the heirs of the promise made to Abraham and Israel? And are Solomon or his son Rehoboam more entitled than the Ephraimite Jeroboam to demand "the obedience of the people" in the name of the blessing of Jacob, when one knows the conditions under which the elderly David designated his successor?

Unity of theological design in a work does not correspond to literary unity, even if certain expressions ("good and evil," the politically-suspect "wisdom") and anthropomorphisms do run throughout the work. There is no common standard among certain anecdotes inserted into the genealogical schema of the Table of Nations (Gen 10:9, 25, with the same literary phenomenon in the Sumerian King List), brief notations (Gen 5:29) or court scenes (Gen 25:29–34), and the "novellas" developed on an Egyptian model (the marriage of Isaac, Genesis 24; blessing of Isaac, Genesis 27; Judah and Joseph, etc.). Our historian stitched together some traditions (actually, some narratives) of extremely different origin, using several

---

88. H. Cazelles, "Essai sur le pouvoir de la divinité à Ugarit et en Israël," *Ugaritica* 6 (Mélanges Schaeffer) 32–36; idem, "Fondements bibliques de la théologie des anges," *Revue Thomiste* 98 (1990) 181–93; J.-L. Cunchillos, *Cuando los ángeles eran dioses* (Salamanca: Universidad Pontificia, 1976).

seams, in order to achieve his dynastic aims. It is fitting to give a large place
to the local sanctuaries. After all, where does the schema of Atra-ḫasis (revolt, creation, multiplication of humanity, deluge, etc.) come to him from
if not from a Canaanite sanctuary (Tel Megiddo, where a fragment of Gilgamesh was found)? Don't theophanies, in particular those of Lahai-roi or
Beer-sheba, presuppose a sanctuary? Each narrative should then be studied according to laws of narrative[89] and folklore,[90] without forgetting that
prebiblical history always takes as its point of departure an event, even if
it does not entail respecting either the chronology or the historical sequence. With our Yahwist, the event might have been either the encounter
of a tribe with a cult or a conflict with an Abimelech or a conflict between
tribes (Gen 37:2). Problems arising from intertribal competition do not appear after the fall of Samaria, nor does the problem of [[506]] local sanctuaries after the Deuteronomic reform. After the exile, it was levitical
problems (Aaron and Korah) and those of wisdom that would plague the
faith of Israel. The problems confronting the dynastic history pose themselves at the beginning of the united monarchy, either during the old age
of Solomon or, as I now think, during the time of Rehoboam and Asa
(1 Kgs 13:22): Benjamin is disputed between the North (Joseph) and
Judah. This would demand a broader investigation, especially since the
"Joseph" tradition comes from the North, and the J redaction (from the
South) appears prior to the E redaction (from the North).

The Elohistic History

The Elohistic History (E), or prophetic, rests on analyses already undertaken by Ilgen and Hupfeld, summarized in modern introductions.[91]
There are narratives and laws that duplicate J's and are not Deuteronomistic (plurality of sanctuaries). They form the second series of divergent
traditions that the Deuteronomist had to bring into harmony with his
perspective.

The historiographical orientation is different: not dynastic but prophetic; not cultic but moral. The prophetic institution was known in the

---

89. See n. 85 above.

90. J. G. Frazer was one of the first to assemble ethnographic evidence on the subject
(*The Golden Bough: A Study in Comparative Religion* [New York: Macmillan, 1890]). Gunkel
and Gressmann pursued this line of research. Over time, its methods were improved, particularly in the study of etiologies; so Burke O. Long, *The Problem of Etiological Narratives in
the Old Testament* (BZAW 108; Berlin: Alfred Töpelmann, 1968). One should equally take
note of the astonishing capacity for tribal memory; cf. A. Jaussen, *Coutumes palestiniennes*
(Paris: Geuthner, 1927) 417–32: "l'Exode des Azeizat"; B. Couroyer, "Histoire d'une tribu
semi-nomade de Palestine," *RB* 58 (1951) 75–91.

91. Schmidt, *Einführung*, 82–90; Kaiser, *Einleitung*, 101–10; Soggin, *Introduzione*, 150–
54; Smend, *Entstehung*, 82–85.

ancient Near East (Mari, Wenamon, Zakur), but it played only a secondary role for the kings to whom the prophet brought a divine response or whom the king could summon. In the E narratives, Abraham is a prophet, even for a foreign king (Genesis 20). Moses is more of a prophet (Numbers 12) than a patriarch. It is he who has the Spirit and communicates it to the elders who are judges with him (Exod 18:13–27; Num 11:16–17, 24–25). He is also a Levite (Exod 2:1) who received the divine Words in the cloud, either on the mountain of God, Horeb (Exod 3:2; 20:18; 24:12), or in the Tent outside the camp (Exod 33:7–11). Joshua is his assistant (Exod 24:13; 33:11; Num 11:28) instead of being the warrior (Exod 17:9, 13). The allusions to the king in Numbers 24 (J) hide from the oracles of Balaam in chap. 23 (E). No allusion is made to the Judean or Davidic monarchy.

Moses transmits the Words of God to the people (24:3) and it is to these words that the people bind themselves in the covenant with God (24:3, 8). This covenant at the foot of the mountain has some characteristics that are very different from the Sinai Covenant of Exodus 34. It is not concluded by God with Moses but with the people, a people made up of 12 tribes represented by 12 steles and 12 young men. It is they who sacrifice, [[507]] even if it is Moses, the Levite, who sprinkles the altar (where God showed himself) with blood (Exod 20:24b), and the people bind themselves with a single voice. This covenant is also very different from the covenant on the plains of Moab in Deut 28:69; 29:9–14. The "Elohist" ritual was closely tied to the "words" of Horeb. In the current Deuteronomistic edition, the 'words' (*dĕbārîm*) are joined to the *mišpāṭîm* [['judgments']] of Exod 22:1ff. as a part of the *sēper habbĕrît* [['The Book of the Covenant']] of 24:7.[92]

In this nonroyal history, the part played by narrative diminished to the benefit of commandments and laws. As noted, these often are repeti-

---

92. This chapter is complex. The Deuteronomist joined the conclusion of the covenant to a meal in the presence of God, very probably the covenant meal of J. The Deuteronomic stamp is noticeable in the doublet of vv. 7 and 3. In 7 the "words" have become a "book" (only mentioned in vv. 3 and 8), with a reference to "listening"—very Deuteronomic but very surprising: one "puts into practice" before even "listening." Equally absent from v. 8, the *mišpāṭîm* [['judgments']] are suppletive in v. 3 and refer to the *mišpāṭîm* of 21:1, therefore referring to the code that precedes the existing redaction. But this *sēper habbĕrît* [['Book of the Covenant']], previously known solely from 2 Kgs 23:2, 21 (Deuteronomist), can be nothing other than Deuteronomy (with a law concerning Passover unknown from Exodus 20–23). *Pārîm* [['young bulls']] also appear as suppletive in Exod 24:5, which is also Deuteronomic, its source being the large Passover animal of Deut 16:2, which is unknown in the regular Passover ritual (Exodus 12). With Kuenen, one must admit that it is the Deuteronomic addition at the end of the Pentateuch that led the Deuteronomist to transfer "to the bottom of the mountain" the code of Exodus 20–23 and the concluding commitment of the people to the covenant of E at Horeb.

tions of Yahwistic narratives concerning Abraham and Jacob, with a more moral, less anthropomorphic coloration. But this is not always the case, as in the covenant ritual of Exod 24:3–6, 8, in the story of the substitution of the ram for Isaac (Genesis 22), and especially in the narrative of the flight of Jacob from Laban. Here again the Deuteronomist must have united two traditions concerning two Aramean-Israelite accords: one familial (J) in Gilead, and one political (E) fixing a frontier.[93] The E narratives of the Mosaic period are even more complex and appear to arise from two traditions: one levitical and the other Transjordanian.

The fragmentary, scattered character of these narratives raises doubts that their amalgamation constitutes a history of Israelite origins; it seems to be a supplement to the Yahwistic history, a development of those traditions. Certainly it is possible that many redactions took place in isolation from each other but, on the other hand, it is difficult to contest the unity of style and perspective of these alterations (Eissfeldt).

It seems that the solution should be found in the fact that, abandoning the plan of royal history, the Elohist fell back on the historiography of the treaty prologues. The [[508]] change itself was traced by the Yahwist himself, who had given priority to the divine Mosaic Covenant (Exodus 34) over the dynastic election. The Elohist takes up this theology as structure for the life of the 12 tribes united as one people. The suzerain presents himself (Gen 15:6) as "God (LXX) who brought Abram out of Ur of the Chaldees" in order to give him the land of the Amorites (whose sin is not "complete") as a possession. Then comes a series of scenes that recalls the benevolence of God to Abraham, Isaac, Jacob, Joseph (without a shadow this time), Moses and Aaron, who meet at the "mountain of God" (Exod 4:13–17, 27–31, etc.), and this despite the "murmurings"[94] of the people of Horeb (Exod 17:7; cf. 33:6). This people was punished after Moses had received and broken the tablets of stone containing the "words" of God. Moses conducted the people to the plains of Moab "at the foot of the mountain," and it is there that the stipulations of the so-called Covenant Code were given, followed by the commitment of the people before the 12-stone altar.[95] Knowing the Yahwistic history, the Elohistic historian must give much more space to this historical prologue than do the treaties of the period. However, as in the treaties, this history

93. J. Briend, "Genèse 31,43–54: Traditions et rédactions," in *De la Torah au Messie: Études d'exégèse et d'herméneutique bibliques offertes à Henri Cazelles* (ed. M. Carrez et al.; Paris: Desclée, 1981) 107–12.

94. G. W. Coats, *Rebellion in the Wilderness: The Murmuring Motif in the Wilderness Traditions of the Old Testament* (Nashville: Abingdon, 1968).

95. These can only be the 12 stones of Gilgal from Josh 4:9, 21, associated with the altar of Josh 22:10, suspected by the Deuteronomist as being contrary to the singleness of the sanctuary at Jerusalem.

ends with the curses of Shechem (Deuteronomy 27) and the blessings of the 12 tribes by Moses (Deuteronomy 33). These are two predeuteronomic texts, which form a doublet with the Deuteronomic blessings and curses found in Deuteronomy 28–29.

The majority of specialists attribute this prophetic and nonroyal history to the Northern Kingdom. It corresponds to the covenantal theology of Hosea,[96] which does not recognize the religious legitimacy of kings (8:4) and makes allusion to the putting into writing of "my law" (8:12). The objections that have been made to this attribution were summarized by O. Kaiser[97] but are not convincing. With Elijah and Elisha, prophecy played a major role in the accession of the dynasty of Jehu and enjoyed considerable prestige. The interest directed toward the Aramean frontier is well explained by the rapprochement that comes about between Damascus and Samaria in the face of the Assyrian menace. The entirety is optimistic and does not have in mind the catastrophe of 722. The absence of any [[509]] allusion to the Judean monarchy cannot be easily explained if the composition follows the Deuteronomic movement. Finally and above all, instead of siding with Judah, the Elohist demands for Judah: "restore him to his people" (Deut 33:7). The Elohist grouped components having different characteristics, coming from different local sanctuaries, according to the schema of a covenant between God and the tribes united into an *'am* [['people']].

This historiography has at its base the premonarchical "word" of God, of which the levitical clergy are trustees (Deut 33:8–11). Moses, first prophet and first judge (Exod 2:14; 18:13), is the ancestor of the levitical clergy of Dan (Judg 18:30) and probably of Bethel (by Eliezer, Exod 18:4). The book of Judges, in its first edition, was redacted in the same spirit: the savior is not the king, but the judge, a soldier according to Exod 18:25b–26. However, a soldier such as the conquering Ephraimite Joshua is no more than the companion of the Levite Moses. In spite of the support of authentic historical traditions, the care of the institutions carries it away.

The Priestly History

The Priestly History (P) is even more removed from the ancient Near Eastern models of history than those preceding. It presupposes, in effect,

---

96. To be sure, the Elohist and the Deuteronomistic movement are temporally and philosophically close. L. Perlitt (*Bundestheologie im Alten Testament* [WMANT 36; Neukirchen-Vluyn: Neukirchener Verlag, 1969]) does not want to see the beginning of covenant "theology" before the Deuteronomistic movement in the Northern Kingdom and sees additions in all of the texts where Hosea speaks of *bĕrît* [['covenant']]. This understanding forgets the very special nature of the *bĕrît* in Exod 34:10 and does violence to some texts in Hosea, such as 6:7; 8:1; cf. my *Autour de l'Exode*, 162.

97. Kaiser, *Einleitung*, 82; Soggin, *Introduzione*, 150; Smend, *Entstehung*, 47–58.

the distinction made by Ezekiel between the "prince" and the "priest" (Num 27:12–23) and the distinction between the priests and Levites.

Its literary characteristics are distinctly marked: its numbers[98] and its judicial and cultic terminology. Because it incorporates a mass of legislative texts, either earlier[99] or later,[100] one hesitates concerning the narrative line of this history. Based especially on the Yahwistic history (Sinai and not Horeb, antediluvian genealogies of Genesis 4, taken up though transformed in Genesis 5), it accents the dissimilarities: here some very brief summaries with [[510]] short identifications such as Mamre and Hebron (Gen 35:27), there some more developed scenes (deluge, Abrahamic Covenant, burial of Sarah, call of Moses, consecration of the sanctuary and of Aaron, etc.).

The Deuteronomistic Historian had gathered into a single history a succession of codes that led to a single *Torah* composed of *dĕbārîm*, [['words']], *mišpāṭîm* [['laws']], *miṣwâ* [['commandment']], *ʿēdôt* [['testimonies']], and so on. The Priestly History would become a history of institutions (Sabbath in Gen 1:1–2:4a; circumcision in Genesis 17; ownership of the field and the cave of Machpelah in Genesis 23; Passover in Egypt according to Exod 12:1–15; cult of the Tent in Sinai) in order to lead to a single *ʿedût* [['testimony']][101] given at Sinai. The Ark of the *bĕrît* [['Covenant']] becomes the Ark of the *ʿēdût* [['Testimony']] (Exod 25:22).

These institutions, which constitute Israel's identity, are those of an Israel that lives in exile among the nations. All of humanity is created in the image and likeness of God. All of humanity is a sinner and exiled, and P

---

98. Following the work of M. Barnouin (*RB* 76 [1969] 351–64; 77 [1970] 347–65) and of E. M. Bruins, D. W. Young has taken up the analysis of these numbers according to Babylonian mathematics; cf. "The Influence of Babylonian Algebra on Longevity among the Antediluvians," *ZAW* 102 [1990] 321–35, and the same principle applied to the dynasty of Kish in the Sumerian King List (*JNES* 50 [1991] 23–36), the importance of which as a historiographical model we have already seen (see above, [[pp. 101, 107]]).

99. This is the case with the first edition of the Holiness Code (Leviticus 17–26), where the old liturgical cycle was based on the three seasonal feasts of Exod 34:23 and Deuteronomy 16. It has been completed by a liturgical cycle based on the Sabbath and a purely numerical calendar of the days and months. The calendar appears in Numbers 28–29. A new conclusion (vv. 37–38) separates the ritual of the Feast of Succoth into two parts.

100. So the Torah of the sacrifices (Leviticus 1–5, 6–7) interrupts the execution of the orders given by God in Exodus 25–30. The narration of this performance, suspended in Exodus 40, takes up again in Leviticus 8–9. See also J. L. Ska, "Quelques remarques sur Pg et la dernière rédaction du Pentateuque," in *La Pentateuque en question: Les origines et la composition des cinq premiers livres de la Bible à la lumière des recherches récentes* (ed. A. de Pury; Geneva: Labor et Fides, 1989) 95–125.

101. Concerning *ʿēdût* [['testimony']]: "Les structures successives de la 'bérît' dans l'Ancien Testament" (*Mél. Martin-Achard* [Bull. Centre Protestant; Geneva, 1984] 33–46); reprinted in my *Autour de l'Exode*, particularly pp. 151–52.

takes up in his own way the deluge and the Table of Nations of J in order to lead to the eternal Noahic Covenant, parallel to the Covenant, no less eternal, with Abraham, "who walks blamelessly before God" (Genesis 17) and is father of a multitude of nations. The Mosaic cultic Covenant at Sinai is nothing but the renewal[102] of the Abrahamic Covenant (Exod 6:5; 19:5) by which the land of Canaan is given as a perpetual possession.

Once assured of the presence of God in the midst of his people by the glory descending on the Tent (Exod 40:35) and by the consecration of Aaron and his sons, charged with the liturgy of that Tent (Leviticus 8–9), the people move off in a grand procession through the desert.[103] In Numbers 1–10, the numerical and geometrical schemas of the Torah of Ezekiel (40–48) again appear, and they lead to the division of the Promised Land in Joshua 14–21, a more concrete adaptation of the geometrical schema of Ezekiel 48. It is brought to fruition under the control of Eleazer the priest and of the (prince) Joshua (Josh 14:1).

It is with this history that it is legitimate to speak of the Hexateuch. It is centered on the possession of the land of Canaan [[511]] by a people that had lost its political independence but had assured its religious autonomy around a sanctuary where the glory of God dwelled, served by the Aaronic priesthood, assisted by the Levites. This history will be taken up for the later period by the book of Chronicles, which knows but transforms the Deuteronomistic History.

Conclusion

Biblical historiography is thus in fact a plurality of historiographies. They progressively free themselves from the ancient royal history, in which protection was given to the people by the king. He was sole mediator between the national god and his people, but his religious legitimacy often caused problems. The historians knew the problem and resolved it by presenting some familiar events from their own perspectives. These are the court writings, redacted according to the belief in the sacral character of the king.

---

102. This is the position of W. Zimmerli, "Sinaïbund und Abraham Bund," *ThZ* 16 (1960) 268–80, a position that I supported in *Beiträge zur alttestamentliche Theologie: Festschrift für Walther Zimmerli zum 70. Geburtstag* (ed. H. Donner; Göttingen: Vandenhoeck & Ruprecht, 1977); cf. my *Autour de l'Exode*, 199–309.

103. Already Isaiah 40–55 describes the return of exiled Israel as a new exodus, joyful and triumphant. Incidentally, P describes the crossing of the sea in Exodus 14 in the language of oracles such as Isa 51:9–10, where the Babylonian myth of the "divided" waters of the great Abyss (Tiamat) at creation becomes an image of Israel's redemption as they pass with dry feet through the depths of the sea.

Biblical history would place into question the sacral character of the
king and his dynasty. Quite different from the rational history of the
Greeks and from modern history, in which history becomes the study of
the human past,[104] in biblical history the deity remains an actor in the
present.[105] But it is not just any deity. The God of Abraham and Israel is
not an Ammon or a Marduk, even less a Baal. Royal mediation makes way
for mediation by Moses, then by the prophets and judges, before going on
to a sanctuary served by a levitical priesthood. A moral and liturgical Torah
controls these mediatorial institutions. Finally, the Aaronic institution, the
last to survive the exile, is the most circumscribed of them all. Not only
does it not have the political power that belonged to the prince (he can be
a foreigner until the hope in the Son of David is realized), but the Aaronic
institution is not the mistress of a Mosaic cultic legislation, fixed in the Torah, of which the scribes of [[512]] the Ezra type supervise the execution. It
remains to be seen what the divine mediation will be when the Temple, the
dwelling of the name of God according to the Deuteronomistic History,
will disappear, along with its glory, according to the Priestly History.[106]
However, this is no longer the historiography of the Hebrew Bible.[107]

104. F. E. Deist ("Biblical and Modern Historiography: On Presuppositions and
Hermeneutics," *Old Testament Essays* 3/1 [1990] 7–22) and J. H. le Roux ("Biblical and Modern Historiography: The Widest Horizon," ibid., 23–42) seem reasonable to me in their
analysis of the hermeneutical presuppositions that differentiate biblical and modern historiography. Le Roux approaches the text from different points of view, interested in human,
psychological, social, and economic causes in the series of events. As Van Seters has shown,
this was initiated in antiquity. However, biblical historiography is differentiated in another
sense. It affixes itself to God's personal and national action in organizing the chain of events.

105. It is interesting that the language concerning the invisible God evolved from the
anthropomorphisms of the Yahwist to the mathematical and geometric symbols of P, while
passing through the "dreams" of E and the humanism of D.

106. Concerning the range of symbols used by P to express the presence of God, King,
and holiness in the Temple, see M. Haran, *Temples and Temple-Service in Ancient Israel: An Inquiry into Biblical Cult Phenomena and the Historical Setting of the Priestly School* (2d ed.; Oxford:
Clarendon, 1978; repr., Winona Lake, Ind.: Eisenbrauns, 1985).

107. Since the preparation of this essay, I have received T. Abusch, J. Huehnergard,
P. Steinkeller (eds.), *Lingering Over Words: Studies in Ancient Near Eastern Literature in Honor
of William L. Moran* (HSS 37; Atlanta: Scholars Press, 1990), with four important studies on
our subject: J. A. Brinkman, "The Babylonian Chronicle Revisited," 73–104 (especially Chronicles 1, 14, 15); Stephen J. Lieberman, "Canonical and Official Cuneiform Texts: Towards an
Understanding of Assurbanipal's Personal Tablet Collection," 305–36; N. Lohfink, "Welches
Orakel gab den Davididen Dauer? Ein Textproblem in 2 Kön 8,19 und das Funktionieren der
dynastischen Orakel im deuteronomistischen Geschichtswerk," 349–70; J. M. Sasson, "Mari
Historiography and the Yahdun-Lim Disc Inscription," 439–49.

Israelite and Aramean History in the Light of Inscriptions

A. R. MILLARD

[[261]] "Comparisons are odious" we are told, yet analogies are the historian's staple diet! Ancient Israel is often treated as unique in world history, yet at the same time many scholars try to fit her history into an acceptable mould by adducing analogies from other times and nations. While both approaches can be supported, there should be no doubt that the most positive and most productive essays in understanding the history of Israel will be those which view it in the terms of Israel's contemporaries before attempting any assessment. That is a large task, barely begun. The following paragraphs try to show some lessons from comparison of Israel and Judah with the Aramean states.

Sources

Israel's history can be read in a continuous narrative in Samuel-Kings from the establishment of the monarchy to its fall. In this Israel is unique. Despite the accumulation of monuments and manuscripts from Egypt, Mesopotamia and Syria over the past two hundred years, nothing approaches the Hebrew narrative in its range or variety, the nearest approaches are to be found in the Hellenistic compilations of Manetho and Berossus.[1] For the first millennium B.C. almost all the extra-biblical texts are contemporary inscriptions, often relating to a single occasion and frequently presented as the speeches of the kings whose names they bear. Through the sack and desertion of Assyrian cities, numerous royal records

Reprinted with permission from *Tyndale Bulletin* 41 (1990) 261–75.
    1. Manetho: W. G. Waddell, *Manetho*, LCL (London, 1940); Berossus: S. M. Burstein, *The* Babyloniaca *of Berossus*, Sources from the Ancient Near East 1.5 (Malibu, 1978).

have been preserved from the Assyrian empire.[2] It should be remembered that for many small states of the Near East those inscriptions are the [[262]] only contemporary sources of historical information (e.g., Tyre, Media). Indeed, it is a salutary exercise to discover how little would be known of ancient Israel and Judah were they the only sources for that history. No text earlier than about 850 B.C. names either of those kingdoms, and the first to do so, inscriptions of Shalmaneser III of Assyria (858–824 B.C.), would leave an insoluble puzzle were it not for the complementary biblical reports. Shalmaneser lists Ahab the Israelite among his opponents at the battle of Qarqar, then in subsequent texts reports tribute paid by Jehu, son of Omri. It would be logical to conclude rulers of two different states—Israel and Beth Omri—were in view, logical, but wrong. (For these and the following texts see Appendix 1.) Thereafter Joash, Menahem and Hoshea of Israel (called Beth-Omri), Ahaz, Hezekiah and Manasseh of Judah appear in Assyrian royal monuments. The Babylonian Chronicle gives a date for the fall of Samaria, which Sargon of Assyria reports, and the Chronicle notes Nebuchadnezzar's capture of Jerusalem in 597 B.C. That is all. David and Solomon, Jehoshaphat, Jeroboam II, Josiah, and many others, are known only from the Hebrew Scriptures; the famous list of Palestinian places Pharaoh Shishak's army visited names neither the state in which they lay nor its ruler.[3] As everyone knows, Hebrew royal monuments are yet to be found; their absence is due to the hazards of survival and discovery.

The situation of the Hebrew kingdoms is not unusual. The neighbouring states are represented in an equally haphazard way in the Assyrian records, and native monuments, though available from some places and hailed with delight by modern scholars, are really very rare. Damascus, sometimes the leader of Aramean leagues, occurs about two dozen times in Assyrian royal inscriptions and related documents, some of them being duplicates.[4] No monument at all can be attributed to any of the kings of Damascus with certainty. There are five [[263]] texts which may relate to them. The Melqart Stele was erected by a Bar-Hadad, king of Aram, but his father's name cannot be read, as the disagreement between recent at-

2. Complete translations available in *ARAB* and, to the end of the reign of Ashurnasir-pal II, in A. K. Grayson, *Assyrian Royal Inscriptions* 2 (Wiesbaden, 1976); extracts relating to Syria and Palestine in *ANET.*

3. See K. A. Kitchen, *The Third Intermediate Period in Egypt* (Warminster, 1986²) 293–302, 432–47, 575, 587.

4. For a concordance of place-names see S. Parpola, *Neo-Assyrian Toponyms*, Alter Orient und Altes Testament 6 (Kevelaer-Neukirchen, 1970); the majority of the texts concerning Syrian kingdoms are set out in H. Sader, *Les états araméens de Syrie depuis leur fondation jusqu'à leur transformation en provinces assyriennes*, Beiruter Texte und Studien 36 (Beirut and Wiesbaden, 1987).

tempts demonstrates, and Aram need not mean Damascus; two ivory plaques engraved "for our lord Hazael" probably refer to the king of Damascus whom Elisha anointed (2 Kings 8),[5] as do two bronze horse trappings also inscribed "for our lord Hazael."[6] (Note that these bronzes were found in Samos and Euboea, far from Hazael's home, and were probably looted from a shrine after an Assyrian attack, then passed from hand to hand until they found their way to two Greek temples. One might compare the stone bead found in Ashur which carries a cuneiform text declaring it is booty from the temple of Shahar in Malaha, a city of Hazael, brought to Assyria by Shalmaneser.[7]) The Bible offers a dozen passages on the history of Damascus in connection with Israel and Judah. Further north, the city of Hamath on the Orontes was the centre of a state which Assyrian texts mention a little more frequently, no doubt because it was slightly nearer to Assyria on the route through the Levant towards Egypt. Thirty or so notices refer to Hamath, again some of them are duplicates. The greater distance from Israel results in the biblical references being fewer, three. Local kings have left a dozen or so inscriptions in Hieroglyphic Hittite, celebrating their construction works or marking their property. One king of Hamath is known by his Aramaic monument, the Stele of Zakkur (which was originally a statue of the king, only the footstool and the text below it now surviving).[8] One more Aramaean state deserves attention here, the principality of Sam'al in the Amanus mountains, with its capital at modern Zinjirli. Five Assyrian inscriptions deal with it, but local documents are more abundant. Three exist in [[264]] Phoenician, a dozen or so in Aramaic, including ownership labels, and one seal is engraved with a king's name in Hittite Hieroglyphs. The greater number of stone monuments found there is, most likely, the result of light occupation in later centuries. While this survey could be extended further, these three kingdoms provide adequate sources for this study. It can be seen that the Hebrew kingdoms and the Aramean states are treated equally in the Assyrian texts; the focus of this paper is the native recording.

5. Treated recently by E. Puech, "L'ivoire inscrit d'Arslan-Tash et les rois de Damas," *RB* 88 (1981) 544–62.

6. H. Kyrieleis, W. Röllig, "Ein altorientalischer Pferdeschmuck aus dem Heraion von Samos," *Mitteilungen des Deutschen Archäologischen Instituts, Athenische Abteilung* 103 (1988) 37–75; Fr. Bron, A. Lemaire, "Les inscriptions araméennes de Hazael," *RA* 83 (1989) 35–44; I. Eph'al, J. Naveh, "Hazael's Booty Inscriptions," *IEJ* 39 (1989) 192–200.

7. *ANET* 281; H. Sader, op. cit., 237f. VI Aa 2c.

8. A stele in Aleppo Museum is carved in low relief with a standing male figure whose feet rest on a stool identical with the one on the Stele of Zakkur.

Hebrew and Aramean Records

There is a contrast between the native sources available for Israelite history and those available for the Aramean states. The former are continuous narratives in the third person put in their present form long after the events, the latter are first person recitations composed for a specific moment. A number of simple comparisons of individual points in the Hebrew and Aramaic documents have been made during this century on literary and conceptual levels, but a further step may be taken which, borrowing a term from modern linguistics, may be termed transformational history-writing. An ancient royal inscription may be transposed into a third person narrative in the manner of Samuel–Kings; contrariwise, segments of the Hebrew text may be reconstituted as royal monuments.

The stele of Zakkur, (Appendix 2) set up soon after 800 B.C.,[9] could be transformed along the following lines:

> Zakkur was king over Hamath and Lu'ash. He was a man of 'Anah (or a humble man[10]) whom Ba'lshamayn [chose] and supported. He made him king in Hadrach. Then Bar-Hadad, son of Hazael, king of Aram, leagued against him with [1]7 kings, Bar-Hadad and his army. . . . Then Zakkur prayed to Ba'lshamayn and Ba'lshamayn answered him, speaking through seers and diviners. Ba'lshamayn said to him, "Do not be afraid. It was I who made you king and I shall support you and deliver you from all [these kings who] have laid siege to you. . . ."

Regrettably, the sequel is destroyed. Zakkur obviously saw his enemies retreat, for the remainder of the stele describes [[265]] the defences and shrines he built, and curses anyone who should damage his memorial. Nevertheless, the text which remains is, as presented, little different from passages in the Bible: divine selection and support, raising to the throne, prayer when enemies threatened, divine response through prophetic oracles, the enemy defeated and the triumphant king strengthening and beautifying his realm. Viewing this monument in biblical terms, Zakkur may be compared with David. Neither was heir to a throne—Zakkur does not name his father, which may suggest he was not a member of a royal line—each was selected by his god, and gained his throne with divine aid, each ruled a composite state, Zakkur over Hamath, Lu'ash and Hadrach, David over Judah, Israel and principalities to the east and north. Oracles encouraged Zakkur to resist his powerful foes, and David was likewise emboldened to face the Philistine attack (2 Sam 5:17–25). Other parallels could also be produced.

---

9. For the date see H. Sader, op. cit., 216–20.
10. See A. R. Millard, "The Homeland of Zakkur," *Semitica* 39 (1989) 60–66.

Further north, the state of Sam'al provides a most interesting illustration of the politics of the time through its monuments. The dynastic line can be followed from the ancestor Gabbar about 900 B.C. through perhaps nine other kings to Bar-Rakib about 730 B.C. A man named Kilamu who became king about 835 B.C., left a Phoenician inscription as his memorial (Appendix 3). It opens with a list of preceding kings, each dismissed as 'ineffectual' (*bl pʿl*). Notice in passing that the second one, Hayya son of Gabbar, can be identified with Hayan, son of Gabbar, "living at the foot of the Amanus" listed as a tributary of Shalmaneser III of Assyria. Kilamu makes no secret of his land's weakness among its neighbours and the way he overcame it by buying the king of Assyria's aid to fight his foes. Consequently Kilamu's kingdom prospered, he became a father to his people "a man who had never seen the face of a sheep I made the owner of a flock. . . ."

Again, comparisons with Hebrew texts become more striking when the first person account is transformed into the third person. There is a row of unsuccessful kings, maybe like those who "did evil in the Lord's sight" (although failure or success were not rigidly decided by conduct), there is a new king who changes policy, preferring distant Assyria's suzerainty to domination by a nearby bully, and then there is prosperity. [[266]] The alliance of Ahaz with Tiglath-pileser III is comparable, when Damascus and Samaria threatened Jerusalem (2 Kings 16; Isaiah 7, 8). Is the picture of prosperity to be likened to Isaiah's oracles at that time? Kilamu's descriptions of the prosperity of his rule recall the comment on Solomon's reign, "silver was not reckoned valuable in the days of Solomon" (1 Kgs 10:21). They are notable as typical hyperbole and as the realization of blessings the gods were expected to pour on their devotees, in contrast to the curses commonly listed which wish want and hardship on enemies. The curses which close this text associate the gods of the city with specific ancestors. Such allocation of gods to different ancestors was not possible for Israelite historians, but the attitude revealed in Kilamu's inscription is comparable to the expression "the God of your father David" used in oracular contexts to kings of Judah (2 Kgs 20:5; 2 Chr 21:12; cf. 2 Chr 34:3).

Later Sam'al experienced a palace revolt. A king and seventy 'brothers' or 'kinsmen' (*'yhy 'bh*) were killed, but one of the royal line survived to secure the throne with Assyrian help as Panammu II. Sustaining the local dynasty so long as it remained loyal may have been an Assyrian promise in the agreement setting out the relationship of the two states. That would let the local kings continue to rule in their own right, erecting monuments in their own names and retaining their own royal seals. As vassals, they were required to support the Assyrian king against his enemies and it was in that role, fighting beside his master, Tiglath-pileser, against Damascus, that Panammu II of Sam'al died, as his son unashamedly recorded. That son, Bar-Rakib, tells in his own inscription of his greatest moment when, like his father, he ran beside the chariot of his Assyrian overlord. Since the Assyrian texts concentrate on triumphs over enemies and rebels and listing the submissive, sources like these which illuminate the behaviour and attitudes of acquiescent kings are most valuable complements.

As always, the first person recitations need critical reading no less than the third person narratives. Biblical historians may observe the scepticism expressed about one of Kilamu's claims, that he "hired (*skr*) the king of Assyria" [[267]] against the king of the Danunim who was dominating him.[11] Surely the prince of so small a state as Sam'al would not have expected so powerful a ruler to do as he asked! That opinion, in fact, seems to show too narrow an appreciation of the politics of the time, for obviously the Assyrian emperor would only comply if it suited him to do so, which it evidently did. Assyrian intervention need not mean the king himself appeared in Sam'al; his generals customarily acted for him and, as they were extensions of his power, their successes were reckoned as his. Another objection is raised, that Kilamu's admission of his need for external help would belittle him in the eyes of his own subjects. The way Bar-Rakib who ruled the same state about a century later proudly proclaimed how his father and he had places in the Assyrian emperor's retinue shows such an objection is groundless. If the Danunim were a longstanding hostile neighbour, as appears to be the case, obtaining decisive intervention against them could be a matter for congratulation. The ancient context gives the proper perspective for interpreting these records.

At first glance, the contemporaneity of the Aramaic monuments might appear to ensure their accuracy as records of their times and the events that took place in them. Consideration of their nature may throw some doubt on that impression, quite apart from ill-founded objections of the type noted already. These inscriptions are bombastic public declarations designed to ensure continued respect for the kings and veneration of their names by subsequent generations. Now the names of several of the kings and their realms are attested independently, so they cannot be dismissed as inventions, nor is there any reason to suppose they did not build the defences or palaces or shrines they boast about. Yet several of them happily speak of their gods placing them on their thrones, saving them, and giving them success. In cases like the Zakkur Stele the expres-

---

11. For the objections and discussion of them and the themes of Kilamu's monument, see F. M. Fales, "Kilamuwa and the Foreign Kings: Propaganda vs. Power," *Die Welt des Orients* 10 (1979) 8–22.

sions are more than polite piety—all is due to Baʿlshamayn. Such an inscription is religious propaganda; its aim is to glorify the gods of Zakkur as well as the king. He and [[268]] the other ancient kings believed the gods were on their side, and they said so! If a calamity befell one of these rulers, he would only report it when it was overcome, as the Panammu I inscription shows. The statements about divine aid need to be taken seriously, for to dismiss them as the clothing of an antique ideology which modern scientific investigation can ignore is to throw away some of the ancient evidence which is always a rare and precious heritage. Zakkur's Stele is damaged at the point where it might have related how Baʿlshamayn answered his prayer and saved him from the coalition of hostile kings. Possibilities can be multiplied: the leaders of the coalition quarrelled (cf. 2 Kgs 3:23); plague broke out in the armies of the besiegers; rumour of an Assyrian advance sent each king to secure his own capital (cf. 2 Kgs 7:6). (The possibility of Assyrian intervention, long ago suggested, is strengthened if Zakkur's home was at ʿAnah on the mid-Euphrates, a region under Assyrian control. That intervention may then be identified with the saving of Israel from Aramean oppression, 2 Kgs 13:3–5.) Whatever explanations may be advanced, the fact is to be accepted that something did happen which released Zakkur from his predicament, and which he attributed to the action of his god on his behalf. In contrast, the inscription of Kilamu has no religious element, except in the closing curses. He claims the credit for his success through his own policy of buying Assyrian aid. There is no reason why ancient kings should have had a uniform attitude. Later, it may be mentioned, Panammu I of Samʾal believed the god Hadad and the other gods of Samʾal had placed him on the throne and established his rule, while Panammu II was saved from the slaughter of the royal family by the city's gods, yet placed on the throne by Tiglath-pileser of Assyria, according to the memorial his son Bar-Rakib composed for him. Fluctuations in acknowledging divine guidance or support can be traced in the biblical records, too. Near the beginning of his reign, David asked for oracles in the face of the Philistine threat, as quoted above, although reports of later campaigns are silent on this matter, as if the king acted on his own initiative and in confidence of his own ability. That is a possible reading of the text; the insult offered by Hanun the Ammonite and the coalition he formed may have provided a [[269]] sufficient *casus belli* [['occasion of war']], yet here divine aid might be thought essential for David with so extensive an opposition (2 Samuel 10). More plausible is the supposition of narrative economy; the king habitually sought his god's direction and blessing, but the narrator included only those occasions when the detail was appropriate for the sake of the story, or the circumstances required the explanation.[12] (In 2 Samuel 2 it is important that David's move to Hebron had divine sanction and was not solely a human decision.)

Zakkur not only reported that his god responded to his appeal, he gave the words of the response, commencing "Do not be afraid!" That encouragement and the following phraseology have much in common with oracles and religious poetry in Hebrew.[13] If a greater amount of Aramaic literature survived, these would almost certainly be seen to belong to a common tradition shared by both languages, a tradition also embracing Mesopotamia.

These religious expressions join other idioms and phrases which are not unique to a particular monument or narrative. When Panammu I tells of the killing of his father Bar-Ṣur and seventy of his kinsmen, Jehu's massacre of the seventy sons of Ahab comes to mind (2 Kings 10), and the survival of Panammu is reminiscent of the rescue of Joash when Athaliah slaughtered the Judean royal house (2 Kings 11). The motif of a king threatened by stronger neighbours, shared by Zakkur and Kilamu, is common elsewhere, and with the triumph of the weak. Such features may be part of a scribal or court tradition, with set phrases learnt in training. Certainly old royal inscriptions were used in this way in Babylonia a millennium before, and the inclusion of stock titles and phrases in Babylonian and Assyrian royal inscriptions is obvious. If the interpretation of Ostracon 88 from Arad as a pupil's copy of a [[270]] Judean royal report is correct,[14] then the same process may be assumed for Judah. The arrangement of set phrases, the repetition of certain acts by one king after another, or the recurrence of certain situations is not necessarily a sign of scribes or historians lazily copying the work of their forbears. Protocol would demand certain formulae, no king would deprecate his own achievement, and each monument should end on a note of success. Yet when these stereotypes present themselves in the Aramaic royal monuments, they stand in unique settings, which gives reason to suppose they were deliberately selected as the most apt expressions of the actual activities of the various rulers. These are episodic and isolated texts, as already remarked, so there is little repetition within them. Where there is a long series of inscriptions,

---

12. The same economy may be observed in the matter of interpreters. One is specified in the account of Joseph meeting his brothers because the story demands mention of an intermediary, Gen 42:23. In other cases the reader can assume interpreters were operating although they are not introduced in the text to avoid unnecessary complication. Thus, the Rab-shakeh is likely to have employed an interpreter to speak Hebrew to the people of Jerusalem, 2 Kgs 18:19ff., and so is Solomon in negotiating his alliances, e.g., 1 Kgs 3:1.

13. See J. C. Greenfield, "The Zakir Inscription and the Danklied," *Proceedings of the Fifth World Congress of Jewish Studies* 1 (Jerusalem, 1972) 174–91.

14. A. R. Millard, "Epigraphic Notes, Aramaic and Hebrew," *PEQ* 110 (1978) 232–36.

as in Assyria, or a continuous narrative, as for Israel and Judah, repetition is likely to occur as successive kings faced the same enemies in the same areas, or repaired the same temples in the same towns. Attempts to reduce to single incidents accounts of different kings doing the same things (as some commentators do with biblical narratives) are misconceived.

Being contemporary records, the Aramaic monuments may have had no sources except the memories of the kings and their officers. The compilers of Samuel and Kings refer to some earlier records which were at their disposal; whether or not they also drew on royal stelae written in Hebrew it is impossible to say. Nevertheless, much of their writing resembles quite closely portions of the Aramaic inscriptions from Syria, a resemblance which suggests Samuel–Kings is a compilation drawn from contemporary records, not a largely theological fabrication to establish a particular ideology.

Here is a matter of method. Comparing the Aramaic monuments with the records of Israel's history seems to indicate that both describe the same sort of politics and similar attitudes to events. In assessing either, proper regard to the context is essential, as this essay has begun to show. With those, and other, ancient texts available, it is, surely, unscientific and very subjective to treat the Hebrew records [[271]] from the start as if they are totally different creations. Only when indubitable inconsistencies or errors are traced and found to be contrary to ancient practices should the suspicion of later editorial shaping be entertained. Whatever the presuppositions of the modern reader, whatever the religious beliefs, or lack of them, the biblical writings demand a readiness to read them in their own terms, and extensive study of the ancient Levant and adjacent cultures leads to a clearer understanding of those terms.

Appendix 1
Kings of Israel and Judah in Assyrian Royal Inscriptions

Ahab at the Battle of Qarqar (ca. 853 B.C.)

^1a-*ḫa-ab-bu* ^{māt}*sir-ʾi-la-a-a* 'Ahab the Israelite'
Shalmaneser III (ca. 858–824 B.C.), Kurkh Stele, III *R* 8 ii 92; English Translations *ARAB* I §611, *ANET* 279, *DOTT* 47(a).

Jehu a tributary (ca. 841 B.C.)

^1ya-*ú-a mār* ^{1}*ḫu-um-ri-i* 'Jehu the Omride'
Shalmaneser III, Black Obelisk, A. H. Layard, *Inscriptions in the Cuneiform Character* (London, 1851) pl. 98.ii, *ARAB* I §590, *ANET* 281, *DOTT* 48(c); Kalah Fragment, III *R* 5.6 25; *ARAB* I §672, *ANET* 280,

DOTT 48(b); Kurbaʾil Statue, J. V. Kinnier Wilson, *Iraq* 24 (1962) 94, pls. xxxiv, xxxv 29, 30; *¹ya-a-ú mār ¹ḫu-um-ri-i*, Ashur Stone, F. Safar, *Sumer* 7 (1951) 12 iv 11, cf. E. Michel, *WO* 2 (1954–59) 38.11.

Joash a tributary (ca. 796 B.C.)
   ¹ya-ʾa-su ᵐᵃᵗsa-me-ri-na-a-a 'Joash the Samarian'
   Adad-nerari III (ca. 810–783 B.C.) Tell al-Rimah Stele, S. Dalley, *Iraq* 30 (1968) 142, 143, pl. xxxix 8. a tributary state *ᵐᵃᵗḫu-um-ri-i* 'Omri-land' Nimrud Slab, I *R* 35 1 12, H. Tadmor, *Iraq* 35 (1972) 148f., *ARAB* I §739, *ANET* 281f.; *DOTT* 51(a).

Menahem a tributary (ca. 738 B.C.)
   ¹me-ni-ḫi-im-me ᵃˡsa-me-ri-na-a-a 'Menahem the Samarian' [[272]]
   Tiglath-pileser III (ca. 744–727 B.C.), "Annals" III *R* 9.3 50, *ARAB* I §772, *ANET* 283, *DOTT* 54(a); *¹mi-ni-ḫi-im-me ᵐᵃᵗsa-me-ri-na-a-a* Stele, L. D. Levine, *Two Neo-Assyrian Stelae from Iran* (Toronto, 1972) 18, fig. 2, pl. v ii 5.

Pekah and Hoshea (ca. 732 B.C.)
   [The people of Beth-Omri] *pa-qa-ḫa šarru-šú-nu is-ki-pu-ma ¹a-ú-si-ʾ* [*ana šarrūti ina muḫḫi*]-*šú-nu áš-kun* 'They overthrew their king Peqah, and I set Hoshea as king over them'
   Tiglath-pileser III, Nimrud Tablet, III *R* 10.2 28, 29, *ARAB* I §§815, 816, *ANET* 283, *DOTT* 55(b)

Ahaz a tributary (ca. 732 B.C.)
   ¹ya-ú-ḫa-zi ᵐᵃᵗya-ú-da-a-a 'Jehoahaz the Judean'
   Tiglath-pileser III, Nimrud Slab, II *R* 67 r. 11, *ARAB* I §801, *ANET* 282, *DOTT* 55(c)

Sargon II (ca. 721–705 B.C.) refers to the revolt and capture of Samaria often, without naming a king, note, among others,
   ᵃˡsa-me-ri-na al-me ak-šud 27,290 nišē a-šib libbi-šú áš-lu-la 'I surrounded and conquered Samaria and carried away 27,290 people living in it'
   Display Inscription, H. Winckler, *Die Keilschrifttexte Sargons*, 2 (Leipzig, 1889) 30 23–25, *ARAB* II §55, *ANET* 284f., *DOTT* 60(c).
   Sargon . . . *ka-šid ᵃˡsa-me-ri-na ù gi-mir ᵐᵃᵗbīt ⁽¹⁾ḫu-um-ri-a* 'conqueror of Samaria and all the land of Beth Omri'
   Pavement Slab iii 31, 32, H. Winckler, op. cit., 38, *ARAB* II §99, *ANET* 284, *DOTT* 60(d).
   He also calls himself *mu-šak-niš ᵐᵃᵗya-ú-du ša a-šar-šú ru-ú-qu* 'conqueror of Judah which is far away'
   Nimrud Inscription 8, H. Winckler, op. cit., 48, *ARAB* II §137, *ANET* 287, *DOTT* 62(i), and lists *ᵐᵃᵗya-ú-di* as a tributary state, Winckler, op. cit., 44 D 26′, *ARAB* II §194, *ANET* 287, *DOTT* 61(f). [[273]]

Hezekiah a tributary (ca. 701 B.C.)

^{1}*ḫa-za-qí-ya-ú* ^{māt}*ya-ú-da-a-a* 'Hezekiah the Judean'
Sennacherib (ca. 704–681 B.C.), "annals" iii 37ff. and other texts, D. D. Luckenbill, *The Annals of Sennacherib* (Chicago, 1924) 33 etc., *ARAB* II §240 etc., *ANET* 287f., *DOTT* 66f.

Manasseh a tributary (ca. 674 B.C.)

^{1}*me-na-si-i šar* ^{āl}*ya-ú-di* 'Manasseh king of Judah'
Esarhaddon (ca. 680–669 B.C.) R. Campbell Thompson, *The Prisms of Esarhaddon and of Ashurbanipal* (London, 1931) v 55, pl. 11, *ANET* 291, *DOTT* 74.

^{1}*mi-in-se-e šar* ^{māt}*ya-ú-di* 'Manasseh king of Judah'
Ashurbanipal (ca. 668–627 B.C.) Prism C ii 27, M. Streck, *Assurbanipal*, II (Leipzig, 1916) 138, *ARAB* II §876, *ANET* 294, *DOTT* 74.

Appendix 2
The Stele of Zakkur

Face A

The monument which Zakkur, king of Hamath and Lua'sh, set up for El-wer [in Hadrach (?)]. I am Zakkur, king of Hamath and Lu'ash. I was a man of 'Anah[15] and Ba'lshamayn [raised] me and stood beside me, and Ba'lshamayn made me king over Hadrach. Then Bar-Hadad, son of Hazael, king of Aram, united against me s[even]teen kings: Bar-Hadad and his army, Bar-Gush and his army, the king of Que and his army, the king of 'Amuq and his army, the king of Gurgum and his army, the king of Sam'al and his army, the king of Melid and his army [   ] seven[teen], they and their armies. All these kings laid siege to Hadrach. They raised a wall higher than the wall of Hadrach, they dug a ditch deeper than [its] ditch. Now I raised my hands (in prayer) to Ba'lshamayn, and Ba'lshamayn answered me. Ba'lshamayn [spoke] to me through seers and diviners (?). Ba'lshamayn said to me, "Do not be [[274]] afraid! Since I made [you king, I will stand] beside you. I will save you from all [these kings who] have besieged you." [Ba'lshamayn] also said to [me "   ] all these kings who have [besieged you   ] and this wall ["]

Face B

[   ] Hadrach[   ] for chariot [and] horseman [   ] its king within it(?) I [built] Hadrach and added [to it] all the surrounding [   ] and I set it up [   ] these defences on every side [I] built shrines in   [every place (?)] I built [   ] Apish and [   ] the house

---

15. Or 'a humble man'; see n. 10.

[   ] and I set up this monument before [El-wer] and wr[ote] on it my [achievements. In future (?)] whoever removes (?) from this monument what Zakkur king of Hamath [and Luʿash] has [accomplished] and who[ever re]moves this monument from [before] El-wer and takes it away from its [place], or whoever throws it [May· Baʿ]lshamayn and El[wer   ] and Shamash [and Shahar [   ] and the gods of heaven and the god]s of earth and BaʿlX [   ] x and x [   ] xx [   ]

Face C

[   ] the name of Zakkur and the name of [   ]

Appendix 3
The Inscription of Kilamu of Samʾal

I am Kilamu son of Hayy[aʾ]. Gabbar was king over Yaʾudi and he achieved nothing. Then there was Bamah, and he achieved nothing. Then there was my father Hayyaʾ, and he achieved nothing. Then there was my brother Shaʾal, and he achieved nothing. Now I, Kilamu son of Tam[ ],[16] whatever I have achieved none of my predecessors had achieved. My father's house was among mighty kings and each undertook to make war, so I was under the control of the kings like one who chews his beard, and like one who gnaws his hand, for the king of the Danunites was stronger than me. Then I hired the king of [[275]] Assyria for my side, who can give a maiden in exchange for a sheep and a warrior for a robe.

I, Kilamu son of Hayyaʾ, sat upon my father's throne. The *mushkabim*[17] were treated badly (?) like dogs before the previous kings, but I became a father to one and a mother to another, and a brother to a third. One who had never seen a sheep I made owner of a flock, and one who had never seen an ox I made the owner of a herd of cattle, and of silver and of gold. He who had never seen a tunic of linen from his childhood, in my days he was clad in byssus. I supported the *mushkabim* and they looked on me as an orphan to his mother. Whoever among my sons succeeds me, should he damage this inscription, may the *mushkabim* not respect the *baʿararim*, and may the *baʿararim* not respect the *mushkabim*. Whoever destroys this inscription, may Baʿal-semed who belongs to Gabbar destroy his head, and may Baʿal-hamman who belongs to Bamah destroy his head, and Rakab-el, the lord of the dynasty, too!

---

16. Perhaps his mother's name.
17. *mushkabim* and *baʿararim* were apparently social classes.

Part 3

Israel's History Writing: Its Multiplex Character

Introduction

In the current climate of scholarly opinion, it may seem naive or presumptuous to entitle a section simply "Israel's History Writing." Most scholars, to be sure, are willing to admit that much of the Hebrew Bible—particularly the bulk of its narratives—has a "history-like" quality. Many are even willing to ascribe genuine antiquarian intentions to the biblical writers; Baruch Halpern, for instance, contends strongly that some of the Bible's authors "had authentic antiquarian intentions," which is to say, "they meant to furnish fair and accurate representations of Israelite antiquity" (Halpern 1988: 3); similarly, Rudolf Smend maintains that the biblical authors "wrote generally in good faith that the events which they were narrating had actually happened" (Smend 1977: 54). But some scholars remain unconvinced. Some contend that the Hebrew Bible only *appears* to be concerned with history. R. J. Coggins writes of the Chronicler's history, for instance, that it indeed "appears to be explaining to its readers the reality of their own situation by reminding them of certain salient points in their past," but since it "does not make the distinction essential for a modern historian between the legendary elements of stories and those parts which might have a more solid historical foundation," it cannot be said to contain history writing proper. He explains, "Divine and human actions can be inextricably bound together without any sense of impropriety—which may be an admirable thing, but is clearly not history" (Coggins 1979: 36, 43). Such comments occur fairly often (for example, in the writings of James Barr, J. J. Collins, and others), but they are at best confusing. In what sense can it be an "admirable thing" for that which "is clearly not history" to be presented as if it were? And is Coggins justified in simply equating references to divine actions with "legendary elements," as the parallelism in his words just quoted suggests? Surely theists, among whom are many practicing biblical scholars, must reflect on whether they are quite prepared to reduce God, or at least God's actions, to the status of legend.

Because of the high level of debate over whether the Hebrew Bible even intends to write narratives that can be broadly described as historical, the first subdivison below will deal with this issue of *antiquarianism*. The general view espoused by Coggins, and by Barr before him, is represented in the present volume by J. J. Collins's "'Historical Character' of the Old Testament in Recent Biblical Theology" (pp. 150–69 below). The other essays selected for this subsection, though they touch on many subjects, are included here to provide the reader with a sampling of the debate over whether Israel of the biblical period had a genuinely antiquarian, historiographic tradition. Joining Collins in his negative verdict, though for different reasons, are John Van Seters and Philip Davies. More positive appraisals are offered by Norman Whybray and Gerhard Maier.

Among reasons given for denying the essential antiquarianism of the bulk of the narratives of the Hebrew Bible, two are particularly prominent. Briefly stated, they are the fact that the biblical narratives are both *aspectual* and *artistic* in character. As to their aspectual nature, the biblical narratives view events from a theological, or prophetic, standpoint; they often speak without embarrassment of divine involvement in the affairs of men, whether overt or covert. As D. N. Freedman has noted, it is "this conviction concerning the reality and authority of Yahweh" that is "the fixed point of departure for any presentation or evaluation of the biblical idea of history. . . . That the God who initiated the order of the universe and the history of man would also bring them to fruition, climax and end, was axiomatic for biblical writers" (Freedman 1967: 38). In fact, as Gerhard Maier observes in the essay translated and reprinted below, "the Old Testament cannot speak of God without telling of the history brought about by him, nor can it speak of history, without bringing it into relation with God" (below, p. 203). In short, the Hebrew Bible's view is that there can be no true understanding of God that does not involve history, and there can be no true understanding of history that does not involve God.

The problem that this raises, of course, is that according to the historical-critical method as commonly practiced, "God-talk" is by definition "unhistorical" (Coggins's words quoted above). Chief among the hindrances to writing a truly objective history of Israel, according to J. M. Miller, "is the overriding problem that our modern historical-critical methodologies presuppose a quite different understanding of historical reality than does the Hebrew Bible, which in turn is our primary source of information about ancient Israel."[1] Miller believes, in fact, "that historical-critical methodology would collapse altogether if the traditional Judeo-Christian understanding of God's dynamic involvement in human history were even taken as a possibility."[2] Given this level of tension between the Hebrew Bible and the historical-critical method, it would seem that some rethinking is in

---

1. See J. M. Miller, "New Directions in the Study of Israelite History," *Nederduits Gereformeerde Teologiese Tydskrif* 30 (1989) 152–53.
2. Ibid., 153.

order. Miller describes as "non-negotiable" historical criticism's assumption "that anything historical can be explained without reference to overt, direct intrustion,"[3] but it must be asked whether such an assumption should indeed be nonnegotiable, and if so, by what right. Miller is, of course, aware that the application of the historical-critical method to the biblical texts is fraught with "epistemological and methodological problems," but he is inclined to defer them and get on with the business of doing history: "If we wait for the theoretical issues to be resolved, . . . we will never get anywhere with the more practical matters of research and teaching."[4] It seems to me, however, that if we don't at least clarify the "theoretical issues," our research and teaching will lack perspective, we will not identify true areas of agreement and disagreement, and although by leaving theoretical issues unresolved we may get somewhere, we may in fact get to the wrong place and draw the wrong conclusions.

In the light of these kinds of concerns, the second section below deals with the *aspectual* character of biblical historiographical texts—namely, their theological perspective and didactic intent. J. A. Soggin addresses the distinction between "history as confession" and "history as object of scientific research." His conclusion is that confessional histories are not by nature primitive (they are still around today!) and are legitimate for the nurture of the community of faith, though they are to be distinguished from scientific histories, which strive to capture a "critically assured minimum." Soggin's essay (pp. 207–19) raises some interesting questions. For instance, who today (or ever, for that matter) has written a history of Israel that consists solely of the "critically assured minimum"? Or are not all histories in some sense didactic or confessional? Do they not all exhibit some perspective on the subject treated? In this sense, are not all histories *aspectual*? A second question, which Soggin does not address, is how a wedge came to be driven between "confessional" and "scientific" histories in the first place. Here C. Westermann's essay, "The Old Testament's Understanding of History in Relation to That of the Enlightenment" (pp. 220–31), sheds some light. Westermann's exposure of some of the Enlightenment's restrictive notions of what can count as history begins to offer some of the epistemological and methodological reflection that was noted above as a desideratum.

If history writing can be, and indeed generally is, *aspectual* in one way or another (didactic, confessional, ideological, and so on), then the fact that Hebrew biblical narratives are aspectual in some of these senses

3. Ibid.
4. Ibid., 155

should not be cited as undercutting their apparently *antiquarian* intent. Simply put, the fact that biblical historiography clearly is written from a certain perspective (call it theological or prophetic) is not in itself grounds for dismissing it as genuine history writing. As Maier notes, "*nowhere are facts simply narrated without interpretation.* The only question is, which is the 'correct' interpretation" (below, p. 203).

But even if the *aspectual* character of biblical narratives is not a problem, another reason is often given for rejecting their apparent antiquarian intentions. This reason revolves around *literary* issues, and it comes in at least two different forms. The first asserts that traditional *Literarkritik* (as distinct from modern literary approaches) has shown the biblical narratives to be in places self-contradictory and incoherent, the result of editorial stitching together of sources (as detected by source criticism and the like). It is further argued that this old-style literary criticism has demonstrated the late date of much of the corpus of the Hebrew Bible. Thus, given the limited coherence and late dating of the bulk of biblical narratives, surely little confidence can be placed in these narratives, whatever their apparently antiquarian intent. Among those scholars who express minimal confidence in the Hebrew Bible as a source of historical information, many justify their minimalism by simply citing the "assured results" of the older literary criticism. But here the more sophisticated approaches of some strains of modern literary criticism indicate that serious rethinking is in order. Looking at the very same textual phenomena that formerly led to a verdict of narrative incoherence, modern literary interpreters are increasingly finding narratorial competence and finesse. In the place of disjointed composite authorship, they are finding authorial competence. If lack of attention to or understanding of the literary artistry, the rhetorical workings, the "poetics," of biblical narratives led past scholars to draw many false conclusions, it is no longer acceptable simply to cite the older positions as adequate grounds for dismissing the potential historical importance of the texts of the Hebrew Bible. It can be hoped that the future will see increased dialogue between old-style and new-style literary criticisms. But the latter come in a wide variety, and not all are conducive to taking the Hebrew Bible seriously as a source of *history*. This brings us to the second "literary" reason given for rejecting the apparent antiquarian intentions of biblical narratives.

Simply put, the argument is that since many narratives in the Hebrew Bible are finely wrought works of literary *art*, they are untrustworthy as *history*. Lemche's recent comment on the pentateuchal narratives illustrates the art-versus-history dichotomy: "A literary analysis of the Pentateuch proves incontrovertibly that its narratives are not reliable sources for the study of antiquity; rather, they are works of art."[5] It is true of course that many biblical narratives are rightly regarded as masterful works of art. As Robert Alter notes, many display "the kind of subtle cogency we associate with the conscious artistry of the narrative mode designated prose fiction."[6] But does this disqualify these same narratives as history? While Alter does not always sound a clear note, he does in places indicate that his response to the question would be in the negative:

> In all this, as I have said, it is quite possible that the writer faithfully represents the historical data without addition or substantive embellishment. The organization of the narrative, however, its lexical and syntactic choices, its small shifts in point of view, its brief but strategic uses of dialogue, produce an imaginative reenactment of the historical event, conferring upon it a strong attitudinal definition and discovering in it a pattern of meaning. *It is perhaps less historicized fiction than fictionalized history*—history in which the feeling and the meaning of events are concretely realized through the technical resources of prose fiction.[7]

The basic point can be clarified with an analogy. In an oil portrait, which is clearly a historical work, the visage and character of the subject are "concretely realized through the technical resources" of oil painting, but the artistic form does not negate historical import. What is true of visual artistry is true also of verbal (literary) artistry. Indeed, among secular historians there is renewed interest in narrative explanation as a historical mode. As H. M. Barstad recently put it, "The return to narrative history . . . is *not* completely a return to 'fiction.'"[8] To address the issues raised above, the final section below deals with the *artistic* character of Israel's history writing. More general, theoretical issues are treated in my "History and Fiction: What is History?" (pp. 232–54) and more specific issues are addressed in our English translation of L. Alonso Schökel's "Arte narrativa en Josué-Jueces-Samuel-Reyes" (pp. 255–78).

In sum, the three sections—*antiquarian, aspectual,* and *artistic*—are meant to highlight three dominant features of Israel's history writing. Attention to each of these impulses is fundamental to a responsible exploration of Israel's history writing for, as Brettler succinctly comments, "Biblical historical texts reflect a combination of genuine interest in the past, strong ideological beliefs and refined rhetorical devices."[9]

---

5. N. P. Lemche, *Prelude to Israel's Past: Background and Beginnings of Israelite History and Identity* (trans. E. F. Maniscalco; Peabody, Mass.: Hendrickson, 1998) 61.

6. R. Alter, *The Art of Biblical Narrative* (New York: Basic Books, 1981) 32.

7. Ibid., 41; italics mine.

8. H. M. Barstad, "History and the Hebrew Bible," in *Can a 'History of Israel' Be Written?* (ed. L. L. Grabbe; JSOTSup 245/European Seminar in Historical Methodology 1; Sheffield: Sheffield Academic Press, 1997) 54.

9. M. Brettler, *The Creation of History in Ancient Israel* (London: Routledge, 1995) 138.

Additional Reading

Antiquarian

Barr, J.
1976   Story and History in Biblical Theology. *Journal of Religion* 56: 1–17.
Barstad, H. M.
1997   History and the Hebrew Bible. Pp. 37–64 in *Can a 'History of Israel' Be Written?* Edited by L. L. Grabbe. Journal for the Study of the Old Testament Supplement Series 245/European Seminar in Historical Methodology 1. Sheffield: Sheffield Academic Press.
Coggins, R. J.
1979   History and Story in Old Testament Study. *Journal for the Study of the Old Testament* 11: 36–46.
Halpern, B.
1988   *The First Historians: The Hebrew Bible and History.* San Francisco: Harper & Row.
Licht, J.
1989   The Hebrew Bible Contains the Oldest Surviving History. *Bible Review* 5: 22–25, 38.
1990   Biblisches Geschichtsdenken und apokalyptische Spekulation. *Judaica* 46: 208–24.
Nicholson, E. W.
1994   Story and History in Biblical Theology. Pp. 135–50 in *Language, Theology and the Bible.* Edited by S. E. Balentine and J. Barton. Oxford: Oxford University Press.
Smend, R.
1977   Tradition and History: A Complex Relation. Pp. 49–68 in *Tradition and Theology in the Old Testament.* Edited by D. Knight. Philadelphia: Fortress.
Strange, J.
1989   Heilsgeschichte und Geschichte: Ein Aspekt der biblischen Theologie. *Scandinavian Journal of the Old Testament* 3/2: 100–13.
Weippert, M.
1973   Fragen des israelitischen Geschichtsbewusstseins. *Vetus Testamentum* 23: 415–41.

Aspectual

Aiken, D. W.
1991   History, Truth and the Rational Mind: Why It Is Impossible to Separate Myth from History. *Theologische Zeitschrift* 47: 226–53.
Albrektson, B.
1967   *History and the Gods: An Essay on the Idea of Historical Events as Divine Manifestations in the Ancient Near East and in Israel.* Lund: CWK Gleerup.
Deist, F. E.
1990   Biblical and Modern Historiography: On Presuppositions and Hermeneutics. *Old Testament Essays: Journal of the Old Testament Society of South Africa* 3: 7–22.

Freedman, D. N.
   1967   The Biblical Idea of History. *Interpretation* 21: 32–49.
Gnuse, R. K.
   1987   Holy History in the Hebrew Scriptures and the Ancient World: Beyond the Present Debate. *Biblical Theology Bulletin* 17: 127–36.
Lemke, W.
   1982   Revelation through History in Recent Biblical Theology. *Interpretation* 36: 34–46.
Lohfink, N.
   1982   Gesellschaftlicher Wandel und das Antlitz des wahren Gottes: Zu den Leitcategorien einer Geschichte Israels. Pp. 119–31 in *Dynamik im Wort: Lehre von der Bibel, Leben aus der Bibel.* Stuttgart: Katholisches Bibelwerk.
Millard, A. R.
   1983   The Old Testament and History: Some Considerations. *Faith and Thought* 110: 34–53.
Saebø, M.
   1981   Offenbarung in der Geschichte und als Geschichte: Bemerkungen zu einem aktuellen Thema aus alttestamentlicher Sicht. *Studia Theologica* 35: 55–71.
Trompf, G. W.
   1979   Notions of Historical Recurrence in Classical Hebrew Historiography. Pp. 213–29 in *Studies in the Historical Books of the Old Testament.* Edited by J. A. Emerton. Supplements to Vetus Testamentum 30. Leiden: Brill.
Tsevat, M.
   1980   Israelite History and the Historical Books of the Old Testament. Pp. 177–87 in *The Meaning of the Book of Job and Other Biblical Essays.* Edited by M. Tsevat. New York: Ktav.
Yamauchi, E. M.
   1987   History and Hermeneutics. *Evangelical Journal* 5: 55–66.
Zakovitch, Y.
   1983   Story versus History. Pp. 47–60 in *Proceedings of the Eighth World Congress of Jewish Studies, August 16–21, 1981.* Jerusalem: Magnes.

Artistic

Alter, R.
   1981   *The Art of Biblical Narrative.* New York: Basic Books.
Axtell, J.
   1987   History as Imagination. *The Historian: A Journal of History* 49: 451–62.
Bar-Efrat, S.
   1989   *Narrative Art in the Bible.* Translated by D. Shefer-Vanson. Sheffield: Almond.
Berlin, A.
   1983   *Poetics and Interpretation of Biblical Narrative.* Sheffield: Almond. Reprinted, Winona Lake, Ind.: Eisenbrauns, 1994.

Degenaar, J.
  1986   Historical Discourse as Fact-Bound Fiction. Pp. 65–80 in *Facts and Values.* Edited by M. C. Doeser and J. N. Kraay. Dordrecht: Martinus Nijhoff.
Fokkelman, J.
  1995   *Vertelkunst in de bijbel: Een handleiding bij literair lezen* [*Narrative Art in the Bible: A Guide for Literary Reading*]. Zoetermeer: Boekencentrum.
Gossman, L.
  1978   History and Literature: Reproduction or Signification. Pp. 3–39 in *The Writing of History: Literary Form and Historical Understanding,* edited by R. H. Canary and H. Kozicki. Madison, Wisc.: University of Wisconsin Press.
Gordon, R. P.
  1988   Simplicity of the Highest Cunning: Narrative Art in the Old Testament. *Scottish Bulletin of Evangelical Theology* 6: 69–80.
Lasine, S.
  1984   Fiction, Falsehood, and Reality in Hebrew Scripture. *Hebrew Studies* 25: 24–40.
Longacre, R. E.
  1995   Genesis as Soap Opera: Some Observations about Storytelling in the Hebrew Bible. *Journal of Text and Translation* 7: 1–8.
Rigney, A.
  1991   Narrativity and Historical Representation. *Poetics Today* 12: 591–605.
Sasson, J. M.
  1984   The Biographic Mode in Hebrew Historiography. Pp. 305–12 in *In the Shelter of Elyon: Essays in Honor of G. W. Ahlström.* Edited by W. Barrick and J. Spencer. Journal for the Study of the Old Testament Supplement Series 31. Sheffield: JSOT Press.
Ska, J. L.
  1990   *"Our Fathers Have Told Us": Introduction to the Analysis of Hebrew Narratives.* Subsidia Biblica 13. Rome: Pontifical Biblical Institute.
Stambovsky, P.
  1988   Metaphor and Historical Understanding. *History and Theory* 27: 125–34.
Sternberg, M.
  1985   *The Poetics of Biblical Narrative: Ideological Literature and the Drama of Reading.* Bloomington: Indiana University Press.
White, H.
  1980   The Value of Narrativity in the Representation of Reality. *Critical Inquiry* 7: 5–27.
  1984   The Question of Narrative in Contemporary Historical Theory. *History and Theory* 23: 1–33.

The "Historical Character" of the Old Testament in Recent Biblical Theology

JOHN J. COLLINS

[[185]] Ever since the famous inaugural address of Johann Philipp Gabler in 1787 there has been widespread agreement that biblical theology should be distinguished by its "historical character" from the didactic and philosophical interests of dogmatics.[1] Biblical theology and biblical studies in general have been dominated by historical critical methods, and indeed there has been a recurring debate as to whether biblical theology can be distinguished from the history of Israelite religion and early Christianity.[2] While the rise of historical-critical methodology can be correlated with the general modern concern for scientific critical inquiry and the decline of religious authority,[3] it is also true that the biblical material lent itself readily to historical examination. This is particularly true of the OT, which gives great prominence to allegedly historical events and reflects

Reprinted with permission from *Catholic Biblical Quarterly* 41 (1979) 185–204.

1. J. P. Gabler, "Oratio de iusto discrimine theologiae biblicae et dogmaticae, regundisque recte utriusque finibus," *Kleine theologische Schriften* (eds. Th. A. Gabler and J. G. Gabler; Ulm: Stettin, 1831) 2.179–98 [[translated by J. Sandys-Wunsch and L. Eldredge as "An Oration: On the Proper Distinction between Biblical and Dogmatic Theology and the Specific Objective of Each," in *The Flowering of Old Testament Theology: A Reader in Twentieth-Century Old Testament Theology, 1930–1990* (SBTS 1; Winona Lake, Ind.: Eisenbrauns, 1992) 492–502]]. See R. Smend, "J. P. Gablers Begründung der biblischen Theologie," *EvT* 22 (1962) 347–67; H.-J. Kraus, *Die biblische Theologie* (Neukirchen-Vluyn: Neukirchener Verlag, 1970) 52–59; G. F. Hasel, *Old Testament Theology: Basic Issues in the Current Debate* (Revised ed.; Grand Rapids: Eerdmans, 1975) 21–22.

2. Kraus, *Die biblische Theologie*, 114–25; 160–69. See the classic formulation of the problem by W. Wrede ("The Task and Methods of New Testament Theology," *The Nature of New Testament Theology* [ed. R. Morgan; SBT 2/25; Naperville: Allenson, 1973] 68–116).

3. E. Krentz, *The Historical-Critical Method* (Philadelphia: Fortress, 1975) 6–32 and the literature there cited.

the history of ancient Israel over a [[186]] period of several hundred years.[4] Undoubtedly, von Rad's blunt assertion that "the Old Testament is a history book"[5] was an over-simplification and the theological category "revelation in history" was ambiguous and problematic.[6] Yet the fact remains that a great part of the OT is concerned with allegedly historical events, and any theology of the OT must take account of this fact. Even James Barr, perhaps the most persistent critic of the theology of "revelation in history," affirms "the central and dominant importance of the great mass of narrative material within the Old Testament" and believes that "the presence and the dominance of this material in the religious tradition made a quite decisive (though not absolute) difference as against many other religious and cultural traditions."[7] He also grants that this narrative material "had *certain* of the features that belong to history."[8] Two of these features are especially important: "The story is, broadly speaking, a unitary story, as distinct from separate anecdotes about people who might have lived at any time" and "The story is provided with a chronological framework which sets it against a time scale."[9] Barr might have added that the prophetic material, which is seldom narrative in form, is integrated into the chronology of Israel's history and is addressed to specific historical situations. While it would be incorrect to claim that historical narratives constitute the exclusive medium of revelation in the OT and while the Pentateuchal narratives might be more appropriately described as "stories" than as history,[10] it is clear that the chronological sequence of events is an important factor in the OT. One major task, then, of any theological appreciation of the OT is to elucidate and account for the "central and dominant importance" of what Barr calls "history-like" material.[11]

The discussion of this material in recent biblical theology has gradually shifted from an insistence on its historical reliability to an appreciation of its literary form. It has become increasingly clear that the

4. G. von Rad, *Old Testament Theology* (2 vols.; New York: Harper & Row, 1962–65) 2.417.

5. Ibid., 357.

6. J. Barr, *Old and New in Interpretation* (London: SCM, 1966) 65–102; "Revelation in History," *IDBSup* (Nashville: Abingdon, 1976) 746–49; B. S. Childs, *Biblical Theology in Crisis* (Philadelphia: Westminster, 1970) 62–66. See now also A. H. J. Gunneweg, *Understanding the Old Testament* (Philadelphia: Westminster, 1978) 173–217.

7. J. Barr, "Story and History in Biblical Theology," *JR* 56 (1976) 6.

8. Ibid. See also R. Smend, *Elemente alttestamentlichen Geschichtsdenkens* (Zürich: EVZ-Verlag, 1968) and "Tradition and History: A Complex Relation," *Tradition and Theology in the Old Testament* (ed. D. Knight; Philadelphia: Fortress, 1977) 49–68.

9. Barr, "Story," 6.

10. Ibid., 5.

11. Ibid. Barr adapts the term from H. Frei, *The Eclipse of Biblical Narrative* (New Haven: Yale, 1974) chap. 1.

narratives of the [[187]] OT do not provide a guaranteed corpus of historical facts that can be taken as a fixed and certain basis for faith. Barr's category "story" is more appropriate than "history," insofar as it allows that the material may be fictional, and suggests that it should be appreciated as literature. However, the category "story" gives little positive indication of the nature or perspective of these narratives since stories are of many kinds. If the discussion is to move beyond Barr's contribution, it is necessary to specify the nature of the OT story by attending to its "history-like" character.

The purpose of this essay is to review the central issues of the discussion and suggest how the "history-like" character of the OT might be better appreciated. The first section reviews the problem that accompanied the theological attempt to regard the OT as "history" in the work of de Vaux, Wright and von Rad. The second section considers the contribution of James Barr to understanding the theological significance of the biblical narratives as story or literature. The third and final section attempts to move beyond Barr by considering the implications of the "history-like" character of the OT story.

The Narratives as History

De Vaux

The traditional view of the "history-like" narratives of the OT has been most clearly set forth by Roland de Vaux in his critique of von Rad.[12] De Vaux agrees with von Rad "that there is a world of difference between the history of Israel as it is reconstructed by modern historical science and the salvation history written by the authors of the Bible." He continues, however: "But salvation history depends on facts which the historian with his positive methods should be able to check."[13] While von Rad doubts that the biblical facts can be verified and suggests that in any case they make no difference, de Vaux insists that "It makes all the difference in the world, since it involves the truthfulness of God and the foundation of our faith."[14] So, for de Vaux: "God reveals himself in history. His choosing of the people of Israel, their salvation, the promises made to them and the punishments imposed on them are reported as facts. In the New Testament, the Incarnation is a fact, and the Resurrection is a fact. These facts have to be true, because as St. Paul says "If Christ has not been raised to

---

12. R. de Vaux, "Is it Possible to Write a 'Theology of the Old Testament'?" *The Bible and the Ancient Near East* (Garden City: Doubleday, 1971) 49–62.

13. Ibid., 59.

14. Ibid.

life, our faith is in vain."[15] While the relevance of Paul's statement to the OT might be [[188]] questioned, the logic of de Vaux's position is quite clear. Certain things have to be true because they involve "the foundation of our faith." One begins with faith, and the historicity of the biblical narratives follows deductively. The inductive work of the critical historian may corroborate, clarify, or even correct in minor details, but the main historical questions are not open to dispute. Theology is "the science of faith; its material object (i.e., what it studies) and its formal object (i.e., the aspect under which the material is studied) and the criteria it employs (*lumen sub quo*) are all known by faith. *Fides quaerens intellectum* [['Faith in search of understanding']]. . . ."[16]

De Vaux's position is a classic expression of what has been called the traditional "morality of knowledge." The gulf that separates such a position from the morality of knowledge presupposed in modern critical historiography has been lucidly demonstrated by Van Harvey. Traditional Christian morality "celebrated faith and belief as virtues and regarded doubt as sin." The new morality "celebrates methodological skepticism. . . . The old morality was fond of the slogan 'faith seeking understanding'; the new morality believes that every yes and no must be a matter of conscience."[17] It is important to realize that the alternatives here are not an open universe that allows the possibility of divine action, on the one hand, and a closed secular universe on the other.[18] The choice is not between religious dogma and the equally dogmatic views of secular historians. Rather what is at issue is whether the historicity of specific events can be guaranteed by faith and so removed from the sphere of possible critical debate. From the viewpoint of a critical historian any event or conclusion may in principle be questioned in the light of new evidence or argumentation. An historian may believe and assert that Joshua captured Jericho, but if that belief is questioned in the light of archeological or other evidence, the only rational response is to show how that evidence can be explained. It is not sufficient to assert that the historian believes the account in Joshua 6 to be true. An assertion cannot be used to justify itself. This point has been clearly shown by Harvey: "A lawyer may have faith that his client is innocent, but his arguments in court are logically independent of this trust. The lawyer will have to show why his inner trust is justified, and he will have to appeal to data and warrants that are acceptable to those who remain to be convinced. . . . It is precisely this distinction between an

---

15. Ibid., 57.
16. Ibid., 56–57.
17. V. A. Harvey, *The Historian and the Believer* (New York: MacMillan, 1966) 103. Harvey draws heavily on the work of Ernst Troeltsch.
18. So Krentz, *The Historical-Critical Method*, 61.

assertion and its justification that the appeal to faith most often obscures."[19] In short, faith [[189]] cannot, logically, be invoked as a justification for faith.

De Vaux believed that critical scholarship was more supportive of the biblical account than von Rad allowed. The different evaluation of critical scholarship was, however, only a subsidiary argument; his main point was that historical accuracy was demanded by faith. Further, we should note that the issue was not simply whether one ought to base one's faith on facts—i.e., whether faith should be based on knowledge rather than on emotion or will. In that case one should presumably begin by establishing the facts and then decide what to believe. Rather, de Vaux begins with a traditional faith, and accepts the specific biblical statements as facts on the authority of that faith. In this sense de Vaux's position has rightly been labelled "confessional."[20] De Vaux differed from many confessional theologians insofar as his faith was indeed *quaerens intellectum* [['in search of understanding']] and eager to reconcile itself with critical historiography. The word "confessional" must not be thought to imply an indifference to rational knowledge. However, the scope of critical inquiry in de Vaux's theology was clearly limited: "The paradox of faith, which flows from its very essence, is that these facts of history are incapable of being grasped by historical methods."[21] We must question here whether that "which cannot be grasped by historical methods" can be called "historical fact." De Vaux's position offers no common basis for dialogue with a critical historian who does not share his faith. Critical historiography is welcome insofar as it supports the tenets of faith, but in case of disagreement de Vaux evidently does not regard critical method as a final court of appeal. Insofar as de Vaux's claim that the narratives are historically reliable ultimately rests on faith, it must forfeit the claim to objectivity that might be derived from a thorough reliance on commonly accepted critical methods.

Wright

A position closely related to de Vaux's is that articulated by G. E. Wright. Wright correctly perceived the weakness of de Vaux's confessional approach and insisted that biblical theology must start from the descriptive work of the historian, not from the tenets of faith.[22] Yet, in his earlier book, *God Who Acts*, Wright had written:

---

19. Harvey, *The Historian and the Believer*, 112–13.
20. Hasel, *Old Testament Theology*, 41.
21. De Vaux, "Is it Possible to Write a 'Theology of the Old Testament'?" 57.
22. G. E. Wright, *The Old Testament and Theology* (New York: Harper & Row, 1969) 53–57.

Now in Biblical faith everything depends on whether the central events actually occurred. . . . To assume that it makes no difference whether they are facts or not is simply to destroy the whole basis of the faith. Or even to infer that these facts, if they are such, [[190]] are irrelevant, would to the Biblical mind be a form of faithlessness and harlotry. Consequently, to the Biblical viewpoint it makes a great difference whether the events are really events or not.[23]

Wright does not claim that the historicity of the central biblical events is guaranteed by faith, although we may wonder how critically a theologian can assess the evidence for, say, the Exodus when threats of faithlessness and harlotry hang over him.[24] Yet Wright claimed that the historicity of the main biblical events could be established by historical methods, especially with the aid of archeology. If these events could be established to the historian's satisfaction, they need not appeal to faith as their guarantee but could provide a basis for faith. This position might seem to present a viable framework for biblical theology, so long as a scholarly consensus supported the basic reliability of the biblical account. However, the most recent comprehensive history of Israel makes amply clear that whatever consensus there may have been about the early history of Israel has by now thoroughly dissipated.[25] The sceptical views of Thompson[26] and Van Seters[27] should, of course, by no means be taken as definitive, but at least they show the limits of the evidence and the fragility of any reconstruction of early Israelite history. If the biblical theologian is guided by the critical ideal of "not entertaining any proposition with greater assurance than the proofs it is built on will warrant,"[28] then the controversial evidence for early Israelite history can hardly inspire deep conviction. If "in biblical faith everything depends on whether the central events actually occurred," then OT faith, at least, must be said to rest on a very fragile basis.

---

23. G. E. Wright, *God Who Acts: Biblical Theology as Recital* (SBT 8; London: SCM, 1952) 126–27.

24. See Harvey's remarks on "the falsifying influence of the demand for belief" (*The Historian and the Believer*, 106–11).

25. *Israelite and Judean History* (eds. J. H. Hayes and J. M. Miller; Philadelphia: Westminster, 1977).

26. T. L. Thompson, *The Historicity of the Patriarchal Narratives* (BZAW 133; Berlin: de Gruyter, 1974).

27. J. Van Seters, *Abraham in History and Tradition* (New Haven: Yale, 1975). See the critique of Thompson and Van Seters by J. T. Luke ("Abraham and the Iron Age: Reflections on the New Patriarchal Studies," *Journal for the Study of the Old Testament* 4 [1977] 35–47).

28. Harvey, *The Historian and the Believer*, 123. The formulation of this ideal is taken from John Locke, *An Essay concerning Human Understanding* (ed. A. S. Pringle-Pattison; Oxford: Oxford University, 1934) book 4, chap. 19.

However, the attempt to establish a positive basis for faith by historical methods is beset by difficulties of a more fundamental order. Even the
most resolute defenders of "revelation in history" agree that "acts of God"
are not simply history, such as might be verified by historical research, but
[[191]] "history interpreted by faith"[29] that involves a "projection of faith
into facts that is then considered as the true meaning of the facts."[30] In
short, the interpretation of an event as an act of God depends on the perspective of the interpreter, whether the interpreter in question is an individual or an entire community. Any of the alleged acts of God, such as the
Exodus, could also be explained from other perspectives, without appeal
to divine intervention. This perspectival dimension of historical revelation is readily admitted, and is indeed inevitable. However, if the events
in question can only be seen as acts of God from the particular perspective of faith, they evidently cannot be established as such by critical historiography, and so they forfeit the claim to objectivity that might be
derived from independent verification. "Facts of history" can only be established by historical methods, and whatever cannot be established by
these methods cannot be called historical fact. This is not to say that only
those things that can be verified by historians can have actually happened.
Historical criticism can never deny the possibility that a particular event
(natural or supernatural) may have taken place. The point is that a mere
possibility should not be classified as "historical fact."

Any attempt to treat the OT narratives as reliable historical information is beset by the problem that there is a gulf between anything that can
be established by critical historiography and the confession of divine activity that is central to the biblical texts.[31] It is true of course that the possibility that the biblical account is historical is strengthened if it can be
shown to have some historical basis. However, we must admit that what is
central to the OT is not just that a group of Hebrews escaped from Egypt
but that Yahweh brought them out, and that this claim cannot possibly be
established by historical methods. Wright's affirmation that the central
events of the OT are historical is therefore ultimately confessional, despite his resolute attempt to avoid any confessional appeal to faith, and
his criticism of de Vaux on this point. In the case of both Wright and de
Vaux, the appeal to historical verification only confuses the theological issue, since it is admitted that the central affirmations of the OT are not
amenable to such verification.

29. Wright, *God Who Acts*, 128.
30. Ibid., 117.
31. This has been conclusively shown by L. Gilkey ("Cosmology, Ontology and the Tra-
vail of Biblical Language," *JR* 41 [1961] 194–205 and *Naming the Whirlwind* [New York:
Bobbs-Merrill, 1969] 91–95).

Von Rad

One of the many contributions of Gerhard von Rad to biblical theology [[192]] has been to focus scholarly attention on the gulf between the modern critical view of Israelite history and the view presupposed in the OT itself.[32] Despite the widespread and heated criticism evoked by this position,[33] the gulf to which he points is inescapable. The point at issue here is not "the size of the discrepancy between the two pictures."[34] Obviously John Bright's *History* diverged less from the biblical account than Martin Noth's, while the recent volume edited by Hayes and Miller shows perhaps the greatest divergence to date. The significant point, however, is that even a rather conservative reconstruction like that of Bright still modifies the biblical account[35] and, most importantly, can offer no historical corroboration of divine activity. Further, von Rad's dichotomy of the two pictures does not presuppose that we have one definitive modern picture of Israel's history. Rather, the very multiplicity of modern views underlines his basic point that the confessional account found in the OT does not provide a critically acceptable history by modern standards. The biblical narratives cannot be regarded as a reliable source of historical information. This, again, is not to say that there is no historically accurate material in the OT, but that the biblical narratives are not necessarily factual and the extent to which they are historical is a debatable matter on which scholarly opinions fluctuate. The more important events, such as the Exodus, are by no means the most firmly established historically, and insofar as they posit divine activity they cannot be established historically at all. Consequently any biblical theology that regards the OT narratives as a reliable source of factual information has only limited and uncertain validity and cannot be said to deal adequately with those aspects of the narratives that cannot be established historically.

Von Rad's clear-cut distinction between the two pictures of Israel's history highlights the problem of describing biblical faith as "historical." While the prominence of "history-like" materials suggests that "the Old Testament's historical understanding is as intense as our own," it is not "historical" in the modern, critical, sense of the term but "confronts our modern way of thinking about history with a different one."[36] Von Rad rightly

---

32. Von Rad, *Old Testament Theology*, 1.105–15; 2.417–25.

33. For references see Hasel, *Old Testament Theology*, 57–75 and D. G. Spriggs, *Two Old Testament Theologies* (SBT 2/30; London: SCM, 1974) 50–56.

34. Spriggs, *Two Old Testament Theologies*, 51.

35. E.g., Bright espouses the theory of Mendenhall that "The conquest was to some degree . . . an 'inside job' " (*A History of Israel* [2nd ed.; Philadelphia: Westminster, 1972] 134).

36. Von Rad, *Old Testament Theology*, 2.417.

saw here a central problem for biblical theology, but he cannot be said to have resolved it. By continuing to use "salvation history" as his central [[193]] category, von Rad increased rather than lessened the confusion attached to the terms "history" and "historical."[37] The reaction of de Vaux is understandable, even if not entirely justified: "In his view 'sacred history' is not 'true' history, it is the changing and false interpretation—as far as the historian is concerned—which the holy men of Israel gave to the events of history. The only conclusion which we can draw from this standpoint . . . is that the faith of Israel is an 'erroneous faith.' "[38] Von Rad, however, resisted the implication that the biblical view was false. "The kerygmatic picture too (and this even at points where it diverges so widely from our historical picture) is founded in the actual history and has not been invented."[39] However we understand this statement[40] it is evidently difficult to reconcile with the sharp dichotomy between the kerygmatic and critical pictures of history. The assertion that the kerygmatic picture is founded in "the actual history" can only be defended if it can after all be fitted into "our historical picture." If it can in no way be reconciled with the critical reconstruction, then its relation to "actual history" must be presumed to be a purely confessional tenet of faith. In fact, von Rad seems to be misled here by his reliance on the term "history." He rightly sees that a kerygmatic statement that is unhistorical by modern standards should not for that reason be dismissed as without any value, or categorized as "false." However, he still appears to judge "truth" or "falsehood" in terms of relation to "the actual history." He fails to consider the possibility that a "history-like" narrative might be "true" in other ways than by reference to historical events.

The three theologians we have considered here represent three attempts to account for the "history-like" character of the OT narratives. De Vaux and Wright, from their different perspectives placed great emphasis on the historical reliability of the narratives. The difficulty with this emphasis is that the central biblical claim of divine activity is simply not accessible to historical verification. Accordingly the historicity of that claim becomes a matter of confessional faith. Whatever the merits of confes-

---

37. Spriggs (*Two Old Testament Theologies*, 34–59) effectively shows the confusion that has resulted from von Rad's use of *Heilsgeschichte*, but fails to discriminate between those criticism of von Rad that are substantial and those that are not.

38. De Vaux, "Is it Possible to Write a 'Theology of the Old Testament'?" 57.

39. Von Rad, *Old Testament Theology*, 1.108.

40. Spriggs (*Two Old Testament Theologies*, 55) suggests that "the events described in the biblical picture (the referent) need not be the events which gave rise to the picture (the source). An account of the Exodus might reflect Israel's experience with God in the tenth century. . . ." It is not clear, however, whether this is what von Rad had in mind.

sional faith, it does not carry weight as historical evidence or establish historical [[194]] facts in any objective sense. The central revelatory events of the OT cannot, then, be regarded as objective history, and the attempt to regard them so only obscures their real character.

Von Rad was far less concerned with the factual accuracy of the biblical narratives than were Wright and de Vaux, but he caused considerable confusion by retaining the term "history" as a central category in his theology. The root of the problem, however, was that the term "history" inevitably carries with it some implication of factual accuracy. Progress in the theological appreciation of the OT "acts of God" could only be made by recognizing that "history" is not the appropriate category for these narratives.

The Narratives as Literature

The Category "Story"

In view of the problems in von Rad's work it was inevitable that biblical theology should move away from "history" as a central category. This move can be seen most clearly in James Barr's thesis that "the long narrative corpus of the Old Testament seems to me, as a body of literature, to merit the title of story rather than that of history. Or, to put it another way, it seems to merit entirely the title of story but only in part the title history; or again we may adopt the term used by Hans Frei and say that the narrative is "history-like."[41] Barr has not as yet fully developed the implications of the category "story" but they may in some part be inferred from his discussion of the Bible as literature.[42] There he distinguishes between

> two sorts of writing. The first is intended as informational; its value can be assessed from the accuracy of its reports about entities ("referents," things referred to) in the outside world. The second has a different kind of meaning and value. Its meaning lies rather in the structure and shape of the story, and in the images used within it. It is valued as literature, aesthetically, rather than as information.[43]

41. Barr, "Story," 5. Note also the shift away from the category "history" reflected in the volume *Tradition and Theology* (above n. 8). The category "tradition" is both closer to von Rad and applicable to more of the biblical material than "story." However, its breadth of application inevitably makes it less specific. As the Editor, Douglas Knight, remarks, "What cannot be considered a matter of tradition?" ("Introduction: Tradition and Theology," 2). While the discussion of tradition is highly important for biblical theology in general, it does not bear directly on the specifically "history-like" traditions that are the focus of our discussion here.

42. J. Barr, *The Bible in the Modern World* (New York: Harper & Row, 1973) 53–74. See also his "Reading the Bible as Literature," *BJRL* 56 (1973) 10–33.

43. *The Bible in the Modern World*, 55.

While the category "history" most readily refers to the [[195]] first kind of writing, "story" evidently refers to the second. As Barr further remarks "much of literature, to put it bluntly, is fiction."[44] To read the OT narratives as stories is for all practical purposes to read them as fictions. Fictional narrative may of course be based on actual historical events. There very probably was a siege of Troy which prompted Homer's epics and Caesar was certainly murdered before Shakespeare wrote his play. However, the historical references in Homer or Shakespeare are not of decisive importance for the appreciation of their work. Similarly, the fact that some Hebrew slaves may have escaped from Egypt is not necessarily what is important about the Exodus story. Many biblical stories are readily accepted as fictional—the opening chapters of Genesis, Job, the parables of Jesus—and their value is none the less for that. Barr suggests that the so-called "historical" books should be read in the same way, not only or primarily because these books cannot be shown to be historical, but because "the story has its main effect anyway before the question of historical events or external realities is answered; and that, even when this latter question has been answered, it has not added to the effectiveness of the story."[45]

It should be stressed that this approach does not at all dispense us from the historical examination of the OT. Since the biblical narratives have the appearance of history, the question whether, or how far, they should be read as informational inevitably arises. In view of the widespread assumption that the biblical accounts are factual, the question of historicity cannot be simply ignored. Barr rightly warns that, "The study of the Bible as literature might then result in a kind of unholy alliance between a quite secular and non-theological study on the one hand, and on the other hand the prejudices of all those who out of religious motives are hostile to historical criticism."[46] In recent years Karl Barth has frequently been invoked as a model for a literary-theological (as opposed to historical) approach to the Bible.[47] So David Kelsey writes that "it is as though Barth took scripture to be one vast loosely structured non-fictional novel— at least Barth takes it to be non-fictional."[48] However, the assertion that the biblical narrative is non-fictional involves historical claims and these can only be validated by historical criteria. A literary approach to the text

44. Ibid.
45. Ibid., 57–58.
46. Ibid., 65.
47. Frei, *The Eclipse of Biblical Narrative*, vii–viii; D. H. Kelsey, *The Uses of Scripture in Recent Theology* (Philadelphia: Fortress, 1975) 39–50. Compare Childs' defense of Barth (*Biblical Theology in Crisis*, 110–11).
48. Kelsey, *The Uses of Scripture*, 48.

cannot be allowed to screen [[196]] historical assumptions from critical examination.[49]

The literary approach to the Bible advocated by Barr is not the only valid or even necessary way of treating this material. There is no reason why historians should not draw on whatever evidence these narratives have to offer for historical reconstruction. It is clear, however, that a literary approach to these narratives has wider and firmer validity than one that regards them as reliable historical information. In the past the literary approach has been applied mainly to books like Job, which are not usually classified as historical. However, we have seen that the central saving events or "acts of God" that dominate the "history-like" sections of the OT cannot be adequately explained by historical categories. It is precisely in these central aspects of the OT revelation that a literary approach can be most illuminating for biblical theology. Specifically, the nature of "acts of God" such as the Exodus may be illuminated by regarding them as paradigmatic stories or myths, whose significance lies in their expression of some recurring aspect of the human condition.

"Saving Events" as Paradigmatic Stories

As we have seen already, even the most adamant defenders of the historical reliability of the biblical narratives agree that "acts of God" are not simply history, such as might be verified by historical research, but "history interpreted by faith" which involves a "projection of faith into facts."[50] An event such as the departure of the Hebrews from Egypt is interpreted in terms of divine causality, although it could admittedly be explained in terms of "natural" causes. Barr comments: "Where this is so, it is not unfair to say that the 'event' of the biblical narrative is a mythical representation of an actual saving event which is however of quite a different character," and concludes that "the concept that the Bible depends for its status on 'saving events' is not nearly so far removed as has generally been believed from the function of the Bible as literature or as myth. . . . Whatever the nature of the real events, it seems to be on *the telling of the story in this form* that the effective status of the Bible depends."[51] Barr's statement that the saving event is "of quite a different character"

---

49. This point is also relevant to the canonical approach advocated by B. S. Childs. If "To do Biblical Theology within the context of the canon involves acknowledgement of the *normative* quality of the biblical tradition" (*Biblical Theology in Crisis*, 100) then we must ask whether it involves the unquestioning acceptance of the apparently historical claims found in the Bible. If this question is not clarified, the appeal to the canon can too easily become a screen for unexamined historical assumptions.

50. Wright, *God Who Acts*, 117.

51. Barr, *The Bible in the Modern World*, 83–84.

seems to suggest unnecessarily that the biblical account is inappropriate, and in general he seems to make an [[197]] unwarranted distinction between "the real events" and their interpretation. We must surely allow that an imaginative, poetic or mythical, elaboration can often capture the "real" character of an event more adequately than a purely factual, verifiable, account. The significant point however is that such an elaboration should not be assessed as information, for the historical accuracy of its details, but for "the structure and shape of the story and the images used within it."

The biblical way of describing an event such as the Exodus is evidently an attempt to express the significance of that event, from the perspective of the Israelite community. By affirming that the event in question is an act of God, the biblical account is claiming that it had an abiding significance for the community since it provides, in effect, a revelation of God. The significance of such an event cannot be adequately appreciated by merely asking whether it happened. We must also ask in what way the event illuminates the subsequent experience of the community, and indeed, what implications it may have for humanity at large. This point has long been appreciated even by theologians who work with an historical model of revelation. H. Richard Niebuhr "suggests that revelation might best be understood as an event that so captures the imagination of a community that it alters that community's way of looking at the totality of its experience. It is an event that strikes the community as illuminatory for understanding all other events."[52] For Alan Richardson, the central biblical events are "disclosure situations" that are "rooted in the particular predicaments of Israel's actual history" but "illuminate the truth concerning the predicament of all nations in every age."[53] If we follow this line of approach, however, it is apparent that the reference to "Israel's actual history," is neither a necessary nor a constant factor. The revelatory power of the stories of creation and fall is no less for their mythic and legendary character. The historical basis for the story of Abraham is quite uncertain and even the Exodus and Conquest are keenly debated.[54] The status of any of these stories cannot and need not lend any weight to their historical probability and, conversely, their revelatory status need not depend on their supposed historicity. In short, the imagination of a community can be captured by a story no less than by an event. Moreover, even where a story had an historical basis, it was still the story that lived on and influenced the life of the community.

52. Harvey, *The Historian and the Believer*, 253, paraphrasing H. R. Niebuhr, *The Meaning of Revelation* (New York: MacMillan, 1946) 93.
53. A. Richardson, *History, Sacred and Profane* (Philadelphia: Westminster, 1964) 226.
54. See Hayes and Miller, *Israelite and Judean History*, 70–212.

We may then affirm Barr's conclusion that the stories of "saving events" in the OT are not far removed from the role of myth or of literary [[198]] paradigm. In each case the function of the story is to illuminate other areas of experience. This paradigmatic function is fundamental to the re-presentation of the "saving history" in the Israelite cult.[55] It is also evident in the prophetic expectation of a new Exodus, where the story of the wilderness and the deliverance from Egypt is used as a paradigm for the future. The affinities of historical and mythic paradigms can be seen clearly in the frequent association of the imagery of Canaanite mythology with the Exodus.[56] Second Isaiah provides a striking example:

> Awake as in ancient times, primeval generations.
> Was it not thou who smote through Rahab?
> Who pierced Tannīn (the dragon)?
> Was it not thou who dried up Sea,
> the waters of the abysmal Deep?
> Who makes the deep places of the sea a way
> for the redeemed to pass over.
> The redeemed of Yahweh shall return
> and come with shouts of joy to Zion.[57]

The prophet is primarily concerned with the imminent return of the exiles from Babylon. His understanding of this event is shaped by the application of two paradigms, one purely mythical and the other an "historical" reference to the Exodus. However there is no reason to suppose that the historicity of the Exodus is of any concern here. Whether Yahweh actually dried up the sea is no more an issue than whether he actually slew Rahab. In each case the prophet is recalling a story that provides a paradigm for the new event that is about to take place.

In this section we have noted two ways in which Barr's category "story" illuminates the "history-like" narratives of the OT. First, the term "story," unlike "history," does not imply that the events actually happened. To read the OT as story is to read it as literature, in terms of its structure and imagery, rather than as factual information or as a record of events that can be otherwise substantiated. Second, the "acts of God" such as the Exodus, which are problematic for historical categories, can be appropriately regarded as paradigmatic stories or myths, which are significant for the light they shed on recurring aspects of the human condition.

---

55. M. Noth, "The Re-presentation of the O.T. in Proclamation," *Essays on Old Testament Hermeneutics* (ed. C. Westermann; Richmond, VA: John Knox, 1963) 76–88.
56. F. M. Cross, *Canaanite Myth and Hebrew Epic* (Cambridge: Harvard, 1973) 91–144.
57. Isa 51:9–11. Trans. Cross, *Canaanite Myth*, 108.

[[199]] However, the value of the category "story" for appreciating the OT narratives is limited by its lack of specificity. "Story" covers a multitude of forms of expression, and may be applied to such diverse material as ancient myths, fairy tales, epics and realistic fiction such as we find in modern novels. The problem here may be focused by reference to the familiar contrast between the myths of the ancient Near East and the history-like narratives of the OT. We have noted in this section that the "saving events" of the OT may be appropriately regarded as myths. Yet there are at least apparent differences between the biblical stories and the myths of the ancient Near East. We must consider then whether there are not different kinds of myths and stories, and attempts to specify the "history-like" character of the stories of the OT.

"History-Like" Narratives and the Temporality of Experience

Myths and Archetypes

Few generalizations about the ancient world are more widespread (even outside the domain of biblical theology) than that which contrasts the "historical" character of the Old Testament with the "mythic" conceptions of Israel's neighbours. This statement by Mircea Eliade is typical: "The God of the Jewish people is no longer an Oriental divinity, creator of archetypal gestures, but a personality who ceaselessly intervenes in history, who reveals his will through events."[58] Literary critic Herbert Schneidau asserts: "The Bible's 'influence' is not to give us genres or archetypes which can be endlessly refilled with extraneous materials; instead it plays a role that demands that we acknowledge how precarious is our grasp of any meaning in the world at all."[59] Schneidau describes the role of the Bible as "demythologizing,"[60] and attributes this role to its "historicizing style."[61] We need not dwell here on the debate about the distinctiveness of the Hebrew conception of history. Undoubtedly the contrast between Israel and the other Near Eastern peoples has been greatly exaggerated at this point.[62] For the present we are not concerned with the question of

---

58. M. Eliade, *The Myth of the Eternal Return* (New York: Pantheon Books, 1954) 104.

59. H. N. Schneidau, *Sacred Discontent: The Bible and Western Tradition* (Berkeley: University of California, 1976) 255.

60. Ibid., 12.

61. Ibid., 215.

62. H. Gese, "The Idea of History in the Ancient Near East and the Old Testament," *JTC* 1 (1965) 49–64; B. Albrektson, *History and the Gods* (Lund: Gleerup, 1967); J. J. M. Roberts, "Myth *versus* History: Relaying the Comparative Foundations," *CBQ* 38 (1976) 1–13.

distinctiveness but with the understanding of the "history-like" biblical narratives implied in the contrast.

The quotations from Eliade and Schneidau highlight one common way in which the "historical" character of the Old Testament is defined, over [[200]] against the ancient myths. Myths are said to provide archetypes that are endlessly refilled. Historical narratives on the other hand are thought to have a once-for-all quality and emphasize the particularity of events rather than recurring patterns. We should note that Schneidau, at least, is under no illusion that the biblical narratives are "actual history." The point is "that the historicizing style . . . dominates even passages which are undoubtedly unhistorical . . . because of the Hebrew reluctance to homogenize . . . they take on a historical shape in spite of themselves."[63]

In the light of our discussion in the previous section, however, this distinction cannot be maintained. As we have seen the Exodus functions repeatedly as a paradigm for a recurring pattern. Scholars who have commented on this phenomenon have usually felt obliged to add a disclaimer that "the 're-presentation' at the periodical feasts of ancient Israel does not involve some timeless myth, but something which is by nature a unique historical event."[64] However, it is not apparent that this lessens the archetypal role of the Exodus or that the once-for-all character of the Exodus is any more definitive than the defeat of Tiamat in the *Enuma Elish*. In both cases the stories of allegedly ancient events can be used as paradigms for the interpretation of recurring situations. The difference between the mythical stories of the Mesopotamians and the history-like stories of the Israelites is not that the one expresses recurring patterns and the other does not, but must be sought in the nature of the patterns expressed.

Stories of Anti-structure

The contrast between myth and history has usually been made on the assumption that mythic archetypes posit fixed and unchanging structures and so a static or cyclic view of the world. Whether this assumption does justice to ancient Near Eastern myth is a debatable question that lies beyond the scope of this essay. However, paradigmatic stories and recurring patterns do not necessarily presuppose fixed and unchanging structures. As the anthropologist Victor Turner has argued at length: "There are symbols of structure and symbols of anti-structure."[65] There are stories that

63. Schneidau (*Sacred Discontent*, 215) draws on the famous discussion of Genesis by E. Auerbach (*Mimesis: The Representation of Reality in Western Literature* [Garden City: Doubleday, 1957] 1–20).

64. Noth, "The 'Re-Presentation,'" 85.

65. V. Turner, *Dramas, Fields and Metaphors* (Ithaca: Cornell, 1974) 46.

suggest that the world is founded on an unchanging order and stories that suggest [[201]] that no order is permanent or beyond change. The "history-like" character of the OT narratives lends itself ultimately to symbolizing anti-structure and change rather than order and permanence.

As we noted at the beginning of this essay, the OT narratives are "history-like" in the sense that they tell a story that is more or less continuous (as opposed to isolated anecdotes) and follows a chronological outline. The focal points of these narratives (e.g., the Exodus) might be called mythical rather than historical in style, insofar as they purport to describe divine or supernatural actions. However, these episodes are integrated into the human story of Israel and are said to be encountered in the human experience of the people, at specific times and places. Accordingly, they are subject to the relativity of all human experience. They are not absolutely given, before the dawn of history, and their consequences are neither definitive nor unambiguous. The revelation of God is located in historical time and in Langdon Gilkey's words: "To be in time, as we in our world are, is to be subject to changing moments as day replaces day, to new relations between the moving things in our world, to new and so to surprising combinations of what is around us."[66] Consequently, the God of Israel remains "a hidden God" who can never be fully or definitively known.

The point here is not, of course, that there are no myths or fixed structures in the OT, but that any structure is relativized when it is viewed in the context of historical change. So Schneidau writes:

> whenever mythology developed in Hebrew history, it was inherently more unstable than the mythologies of the surrounding cultures, and those of other cultures generally, because it had a tendency to turn against itself. ... Each form of mythologizing aroused its generation of critics—i.e., prophets—sooner or later. Even such institutions as the Law, which was manifestly an attempt to stabilize and sacralize the social ideology and thus substitute for myth, eventually became liable to demythologization. When Paul determined that the holiness of the Law was contingent and not innate, his work was the culmination of a long process, a cultural tradition which is, in effect, a culture-questioning tradition.[67]

The Exodus may have seemed to guarantee the favor of God to the Israelites, but the prophets could turn such a myth against itself. A God who brought the Israelites out of the wilderness could take them back there

---

66. L. Gilkey, *Reaping the Whirlwind* (New York: Seabury, 1977) 1.
67. Schneidau, *Sacred Discontent*, 13–14.

again.[68] The covenant with David may have seemed to promise eternal security for the Davidic line but such a promise would have to be radically reinterpreted in the light of the Babylonian exile. If revelation [[202]] is located in historical experience, no particular revelation can be taken as final, because it can always be qualified or even contradicted by further experience.[69]

However, the significance of the "historicizing style" in the Old Testament does not lie only in this relativizing effect. The unpredictability of historical experience is itself celebrated as a revelation of the transcendent power of Yahweh. It is Yahweh who kills and gives life, makes poor and makes rich,[70] who makes fools of diviners and reverses the predictions of the wise.[71] In particular the Exodus stands as a powerful symbol for the possibility of change. The formulation of Second Isaiah is striking: "Thus says the Lord who makes a way in the sea, a path in the mighty waters. . . . Remember not the former things nor consider the things of old. Behold I am doing a new thing."[72] The Exodus for the prophet is not primarily past history, an established fact. It is a paradigm for the possibility that Yahweh can do "a new thing" at any time.

The Exodus was depicted in the Pentateuchal narratives as an event in the historical sequence. It was not an absolute beginning. The story recorded that before the Exodus the Hebrews had been slaves in the land of Egypt and that their deliverance came about in an unexpected way, which was not subject to their control. Such a story had a twofold implication: first, the chastening thought often evoked by the prophets that the God who gave them their independence could take it away again—if they had been slaves before, they could be slaves again—and second, the basis for hope, since any situation, no matter how desperate it appeared, could be reversed. The transcendent power of God is the converse of human creaturehood, which is at once contingent and hopeful.

---

68. Hos 11:5: "They shall return to the land of Egypt and Assyria shall be their king." Compare also the prophecy of return to the wilderness in Hosea 2.

69. Compare the comment of W. J. Ong ("Maranatha: Death and Life in the Text of the Book," *JAAR* 45 [1977] 440): "The Bible's basically historical cast, contrasted by Auerbach with Homer's basically fictional structures, of course accounts in part for the relative lack of closure in its narratives." The open-ended character of biblical revelation inevitably leads to the well-known phenomenon of contradictions in the biblical text. For a recent treatment of this problem see P. D. Hanson, "The Theological Significance of Contradiction within the Book of the Covenant," *Canon and Authority* (eds. G. W. Coats and B. O. Long; Philadelphia: Fortress, 1977) 110–31.

70. 1 Sam 2:6.

71. Isa 44:25. Compare Dan 2:20–22.

72. Isa 43:16–18.

The familiar contrast between Near Eastern myth and biblical history cannot be maintained in the form in which it is usually made. The central biblical stories, like the ancient myths, express human situations that are typical and recurring, rather than unique. However, the fact that the biblical stories are told in a "history-like" form and integrated into a chronological [[203]] sequence does make a significant difference. The truth to which they point is not timeless or static but is precisely the truth of historical change, which is the root at once of human contingency and human hope.

Conclusion

The narratives of the OT are not indeed historical in the sense of providing an assured corpus of facts. Their "history-like" character is however significant because it represents the temporal character of human experience and asserts that divine revelation shares the relativity of everything temporal. On the one hand this involves a recognition that Yahweh is a hidden God and that no revelation is absolute or final. On the other it suggests a view of human existence that is at once contingent, and so vulnerable to the changes of time, and hopeful since even desperate situations are not final.

The theological implications of such a view of the human situation are manifold and lie beyond the scope of this essay. We may close however with two observations. First, the older biblical theology that was oriented to salvation history was perennially embarrassed by the wisdom literature because "it does not fit into the type of faith exhibited in the historical and prophetic literatures. In it there is no explicit reference to, or development of, the doctrine of history, election or covenant."[73] However, proverbial wisdom shows an acute awareness that no one can boast about the morrow[74] and that there is a time and a season for everything.[75] The orientation to experience in its temporal variability constitutes an extensive common ground between wisdom and the "historical" books of the Old Testament. The fact that such an orientation to temporal experience is characteristic of the international wisdom of the ancient Near East should caution against any exaggeration of the distinctiveness of the "historical" character of the Old Testament.

---

73. Wright, *God Who Acts*, 103.

74. Prov 27:1. See further J. J. Collins, "Proverbial Wisdom and the Yahwist Vision" (forthcoming in an issue of *Semeia* on the topic *Gnomic Wisdom*) [[now available in *Semeia* 17 (*Gnomic Wisdom*; ed. J. D. Crossan; 1980) 1–17]].

75. Qoh 3:1.

Second, the more recent approaches to the Bible as literature often suggest an antithesis between literary and historical critical study.[76] Insofar as historical-critical study has been narrowly concerned to establish factual history, such an antithesis is justified. However, the main impact of historical-critical study has not been to establish definitive historical results but to show that "the Old Testament is wholly and in every respect a product of history" and that even the canon "exists in a variety of historically conditioned [[204]] forms."[77] In this respect we may agree with the literary critic Schneidau that historical criticism "appears founded on firmly biblical premises"[78] since an appreciation of the historical character of all human experience, including revelation, is also fundamental to the "historicizing style" of the Old Testament from a literary point of view.

76. E.g., D. Patte, *What Is Structural Exegesis?* (Philadelphia: Fortress, 1976). However, not all scholars who advocate literary criticism imply such an antithesis.

77. Noth, "The Re-presentation," 76.

78. Schneidau, *Sacred Discontent*, 267.

Joshua's Campaign of Canaan and Near Eastern Historiography

JOHN VAN SETERS

Introduction

[[1]] Nowhere has modern historiography, in its reconstruction of the history of ancient Israel, experienced a greater sense of frustration than in its attempts to come to terms with the accounts of military conquest in the Book of Joshua. The use of archaeology to illuminate and evaluate the various episodes has produced conflicting results.[1] The archaeological remains of the three most important cities in the conquest narratives, Jericho, Ai, and Gibeon, all create major problems for the historical presentation of the conquest. No amount of chronological juggling or interpretation of the stories can overcome these difficulties. What is lacking in the approach by scholars who appeal to archaeology is any attempt to come to terms with the historiographic form of the biblical text. These historians, such as John Bright,[2] are unable to explain how the participants in the events of the conquest passed on their accounts or memories to later generations and how they came to take the form they now have in the biblical text. It therefore becomes difficult to engage in a discussion about the historiographic problem of the conquest accounts in Joshua.

Reprinted with permission from *Scandinavian Journal of the Old Testament* 4/2 (1990) 1–12.

1. Compare the following works: John Bright, *A History of Israel* (3rd ed.; Philadelphia, 1980); M. Weippert, *The Settlement of the Israelite Tribes in Palestine* (London, 1971); J. Maxwell Miller, "The Israelite Occupation of Canaan," in *Israelite and Judaean History* (ed. by John Hayes and J. Maxwell Miller; Philadelphia, 1977), chap. 4; J. J. Bimson, *Redating the Exodus and Conquest* (Sheffield, 1978). This latest attempt at redating has not been well received; see the review by J. Callaway, *BA* 44 (1981) 252–53.

2. Cited in the note above.

By contrast the approach of M. Noth has been quite otherwise.[3] He [[2]] has attempted to make an assessment of the literary growth of the Book of Joshua and of the traditions that lie behind its earliest written stages, and on this basis to build his historical reconstruction of early Israel. A number of scholars, particularly in Germany, have followed his lead with similar historical conclusions.[4] It is not necessary for our purpose to review the current debate on the literary character of the Book of Joshua, since Noth's work has become an important point of departure for so much of this scholarship today. This paper will, therefore, address itself to the essential points of Noth's thesis about Joshua 1–12.

Noth's Literary Reconstruction

Noth broke with earlier Hexateuchal studies by making the Book of Joshua part of a larger Deuteronomistic history (DtrH) from Deuteronomy to 2 Kings and dissociating Joshua with any of the Pentateuchal sources. However, the actual contributions of DtrH in Joshua 1–12 are viewed as rather limited, being observed primarily in chapter 1 and the summary of the conquest in chap. 12, with one episode concerning the building of the altar at Shechem in 8:30–35. For the rest DtrH merely added some glosses to a preexisting literary work.[5]

The pre-DtrH work is regarded as a collection of etiological legends in chaps. 2–9 combined with military narratives in chaps. 10–11. This work was created to give an account of the conquest of Canaan west of the Jordan. The "compiler" of this work was responsible for giving to these local stories an all-Israelite orientation and for introducing into them the figure of Joshua. This Judean compiler created his work sometime around 900 B.C. Noth proposes that even before the compiler's work the various etiological stories had become fixed in written form and for this reason they still contain something of their original character.[6]

While many scholars have followed this general literary scheme, the [[3]] question must still be raised as to whether Noth has made a good case for an early "compiler" before the time of DtrH.[7] Above all, Noth has not

---

3. *Das Buch Joshua* (3rd ed.; Tübingen, 1971). See also the same, *Überlieferungsgeschichtliche Studien* (2nd ed.; Tübingen, 1957), translated, in part, as *The Deuteronomistic History* (Sheffield, 1981); see especially chap. 6.

4. E.g., S. Herrmann, *A History of Israel in Old Testament Times* (Philadelphia, 1975), chap. 4. The same basic schema is followed in the recent book by A. D. H. Mayes, *The Story of Israel between Settlement and Exile* (London, 1983) 40–57.

5. *Das Buch Joshua*, 9–10.

6. *Das Buch Joshua*, 11–13; Mayes, *Story of Israel*, 53.

7. See Otto Kaiser, *Introduction to the Old Testament* (Minneapolis, 1975) 138.

addressed the question of literary form. What would be the point of an author-compiler who created the work of Joshua 2–11 out of such odd fitting pieces without giving a clear indication as to its purpose? Lists and compilations are certainly not unknown in the ancient Near East, e.g., omen texts. But they are always of a specific kind and for a particular purpose. The notion of a compiler is more an attempt to solve certain literary problems about the relationship of certain story units to the whole than it is to explain literary form of the growth of the work.

Furthermore, Noth was so convinced, following Gunkel and Alt, that etiological stories ought to belong to the most primitive level of the tradition's creation, he allowed this to unduly influence his literary analysis. Once he began with the separate etiological legends in chaps. 2–9 he was forced to construct a complex, hypothetical process to achieve the final form of the text. However, an entirely different literary analysis is possible, yielding quite different results.

DtrH's Campaign Account

The first task in understanding the limits, form and character of DtrH's account of Joshua's campaign is to identify a number of additions that have been made to it.[8] The story of Rahab the harlot and the spies (chap. 2) is not the beginning of the earliest conquest account but a later addition and fits rather awkwardly within its context. The instructions given in 1:10–11 suggest that 3:2–3 should be understood as a direct continuation of chap. 1 and the chronology does not allow for an additional three or more days for the spying episode (2:16). Furthermore, the mission of the spies, presumably to gain valuable information for the taking of Jericho, plays no role in the destruction of the city. On the other hand, the spy story must presuppose the story of the fall of Jericho and its connection with the [[4]] latter in 6:17b, 22–23, 25 is clearly secondary. This means that the etiological statement in 6:25, which is the basis for judging the story to be early, also belongs to the secondary additions to the story of Jericho's capture. Consequently, one must regard the whole of the story of Rahab as a late tale added to the earlier Dtr history in order to modify the Deuteronomic principle of the *herem*, the complete destruction of the non-Israelite inhabitants, and to allow for conversion to Israel's faith.[9]

---

8. For a more detailed literary analysis see J. Van Seters, *In Search of History: Historiography in the Ancient World and the Origins of Biblical History* (New Haven and London, 1983 [[reprinted, Winona Lake: Eisenbrauns, 1997]]) 324–31.

9. The recent study by J. P. Floß, *Kunden oder Kundschafter?* (ATS 16, 26; St. Ottilien, 1982–86), seeks to preserve Noth's scheme for Joshua 2 by introducing several redactional levels into the story. But a division of the text in which the early story consists primarily of

Another major addition is the story of the sin of Achan (chap. 7). At the conclusion of the Jericho episode the author expresses divine approval: "So Yahweh was with Joshua, and his fame was in all the land" (6:27). One is therefore surprised to find in chap. 7 that God was displeased with his people and permitted their defeat at Ai. Furthermore, 8:1–2 forms the original introduction to the conquest of Ai as a direct continuation after chap. 6. Only in 8:3–9 is there a connection made with the earlier defeat in 7:2–5, but 8:3–9 is clearly a doublet of what follows, inserted into the text to create a better transition with the Achan story.

Throughout the recounting of the Jordan crossing (chaps. 3–4), the encampment on the west side (chap. 5), and the taking of Jericho by a procession with the ark, there are a number of embellishments having to do with priestly interests, which create numerous problems and duplications in the story. These additions have to do with the special arrangements for the priests who bear the ark at the crossing of the Jordan, concern for the memorial stones at Gilgal, the rite of circumcision and the keeping of the passover, and the elaboration of the march around Jericho which transforms it into a great cultic procession. Finally, there is the episode of the reading of the law at Mt. Ebal with the special ceremony of blessing and cursing (8:30–35) which is linked to the instructions of Moses in Deuteronomy 27. This too fits poorly within its context. Noth identified all these additions as the work of DtrH even though they often do not reflect the thought and [[5]] outlook of Deuteronomy. The attribution to DtrH is quite inappropriate. The additions must belong to a priestly writer/editor.

The author of this original conquest narrative is easily identified; it is DtrH. This is evident in the introduction in chap. 1 which has so many obvious connections with Deuteronomy. The emphasis in chap. 3 on the "ark of the covenant" also points in this direction. The complete destruction of Jericho and Ai by means of the ban, *herem*, is an example of Deuteronomic policy. The story of the Gibeonites' ruse makes no sense unless it presupposes the law of warfare in Deut 20:15–16. The portrayal of the victories and the summarizing statements in chaps. 10 and 11 are all typically Dtr. One cannot remove all these signs of the DtrH's hand as if they were a few incidental glosses and argue for a pre-DtrH account. The whole narrative is entirely the work of DtrH.

Once the additions to the DtrH narrative of the conquest are identified then the basic form and structure of Joshua's campaign becomes clear.

---

the narrative action in vv. 1–6, 15–16, 22–23, and the later theological modification in the dialogue of 8–14, 17–21 seems arbitrary. The old story, thus reconstructed, is a meaningless fragment without the broader narrative context and the problem of its place in the larger structure of Joshua is not addressed.

1. Joshua receives instructions and a word of encouragement by God about the coming military campaign (1:1–11). The eastern allies join with the rest and swear loyalty (1:12–18).
2. The people break camp and cross the Jordan, which is in flood, the waters being temporarily blocked up stream.[10]
3. Israel lays siege to Jericho. The people march about the wall for seven days and on the seventh at the signal of a single blast on the shofar the people raise a shout and the walls come down. The city is completely destroyed.[11]
4. After Jericho the people proceed to Ai and capture it by means of special military strategies.[12]
5. The people at Gibeon send a delegation, pretending to be from a distant region, and enter into a covenant of subjugation.[13]
6. The people next engage and defeat a southern coalition with the public execution of five kings and the destruction of a series of cities [[6]] in rapid succession. In the same way a northern coalition is also defeated.[14]
7. The account ends with a summary statement of the campaign's accomplishments.

Assyrian Campaign Reports

In this form and manner of presentation the account of Joshua's conquest has striking resemblances to descriptions of military campaigns in Assyrian royal inscriptions. The following features are noteworthy:

1. Many inscriptions, especially those of Esarhaddon and Ashurbanipal, mention the encouragement given the king through an oracle of the deity before the campaign begins. Note the following example:

   Esarhaddon, king of the lands, fear not! . . . I am the goddess Ishtar of Arbela, she who has destroyed your enemies at your mere approach. What order have I given you which you did not rely upon? . . . I shall lie in wait for your enemies, I shall give them to you. I, Ishtar of Arbela, will go before you and behind you. Fear not.[15]

---

10. The original account is reconstructed as Josh 3:2–3, 4b (beginning with לְמַעַן [['that']]), 6–7, 9–11, 13a, 14–16; 4:11–14.

11. 6:1–3, 4a, 5, 6a, 7, 10–11, 14–16ab, 20b, 21, 24a, 26–27; on 5:13–15 see below.

12. 8:1–2, 10–29.

13. Chap. 9 but omitting vv. 14, 15b, 17–21, 23 as a later priestly addition.

14. Chaps. 10–11.

15. *ANET*[3], 605. This one is from a collection of oracles taken from their original contexts. The *Sitz im Leben* of this oracle as an oracle of confidence before battle is obvious.

This corresponds rather closely in language and themes to Joshua:

> Moses my servant is dead; now therefore arise, go over this Jordan, you
> and all this people, into the land which I am giving to them, to the people
> of Israel. . . . No man shall be able to stand before you all the days of
> your life; as I was with Moses, so I will be with you; I will not fail you or
> forsake you. . . . Having I not commanded you? Be strong and of good
> courage; be not frightened, neither be dismayed. (1:2, 5, 9)

2. The march is described with special attention given to the overcoming of great physical obstacles, especially rivers at flood stage. The following example is typical:

> I, Sargon [crossed] the Tigris and Euphrates at the highest flood, the
> high water of the spring of the year . . . and made my way on the dry
> land.[16] [[7]]

One interesting example from Ashurbanipal's time reads:

> The troops saw the Idide, a raging torrent, and were afraid to cross. Ish-
> tar, who dwells in Arbela, in the nighttime revealed a dream to my
> armies, thus she addressed them: "I will go before Assurbanipal, the king
> whom my hands have formed." My armies put their trust in that dream,
> crossed the Idide in safety.[17]

The account in Joshua makes much of the crossing of the Jordan as an important event at the initial stage in the campaign. But elsewhere in the
Old Testament there seems to be no problem with crossing the Jordan at
one of its several fords. Even in the spy story of Joshua 2 it is assumed that
the spies could easily cross the Jordan at a ford near Jericho (vv. 7, 23).
The special emphasis on the crossing can only be explained as a topos
taken from the Assyrian military accounts.

3. Usually a few major battles are described in detail, especially in the
   capturing of important cities. The rest of the victories are given in a
   more summary fashion.[18] Thus Joshua treats the taking of Jericho and
   Ai in detail but the cities of Judah in a series of easy victories as in
   Joshua 10.
4. Special attention is sometimes given to the capture and execution or
   humiliation of the foreign kings in the presence of the Assyrian

---

16. D. D. Luckenbill, *Ancient Records of Assyria and Babylonia* (Chicago, 1926–27) II, #195.
17. Luckenbill, *AR* #807.
18. See Sargon's eighth campaign in Luckenbill, *AR* ##139–78; also the treatment of
this text by A. L. Oppenheim, "The City of Assur in 714 B.C.," *JNES* 19 (1960) 133–47.

king.[19] Similarly the five kings of Judah are executed before Joshua in Josh 10:22ff.

5. The fame and terror of the Assyrians and their king spreads quickly from land to land. It often results in a delegation from a distant region coming to the king to offer their willing submission to Assyrian rule.[20] This topos must be understood as lying behind the ruse of the Gibeonites who pretend to be from a distant place until they make a treaty with the Israelites which will spare them from slaughter. In exchange for their lives they become enslaved to Israel (chap. 9). [[8]]

6. The Assyrians usually encounter coalitions of peoples or princes that have come together to withstand them but they are always defeated.[21] Joshua faces two coalitions, a southern one in the Judean region (chap. 10), and a northern one (chap. 11).

7. Very frequently the decimated region is repopulated by peoples brought in from another region.[22] In the case of the Joshua story, the Israelites themselves repopulate the region.

8. The inscriptions regularly conclude with summary statements about the extent of the conquests and the amount of booty taken. Such summary statements are found in Joshua 11 and the list of defeated kings in chap. 12.

9. In Assyrian texts from the time of Sennacherib onward the whole region of Syria-Palestine is known as "the land of the Hittites." In the geographic description of the land to be conquered in Josh 1:4 DtrH has taken over this usage from the Assyrian royal inscriptions.[23]

10. Before or during their campaign the Assyrian kings frequently made use of omens. These may be of various kinds but one common type has to do with the observation of the position of heavenly bodies. J. S. Holladay has suggested that the reference to the sun standing still in Joshua 10 is really based upon omen literature.[24] The appearance of the right omen is a sign that the god has given heed to the petition of the king.[25]

---

19. Luckenbill, *AR* ##520, 528 (Esarhaddon), ##831, 865, 866 (Ashurbanipal). The expression, "to stand on the neck of one's enemies" (cf. Josh 10:24) is also common in these inscriptions.

20. See Luckenbill, *AR* ##149, 909–10; *ANET*[3], 284b.

21. See *ANET*[3], 276–301.

22. The policy is also known from the Bible. See 2 Kgs 17:6, 24.

23. See J. Van Seters, "The Terms 'Amorite' and 'Hittite' in the Old Testament," *VT* 22 (1972) 64–81.

24. J. S. Holladay, "The Day(s) the Moon Stood Still," *JBL* 87 (1968) 166–78.

25. A. Leo Oppenheim, *Ancient Mesopotamia* (Chicago, 1964) 206–27, esp. 225.

All these correspondences in form and detail would seem to point rather strongly to a dependence by DtrH upon the Assyrian royal inscription tradition. That the capitals of both Israel and Judah contained examples of such inscriptions is quite likely since the Assyrian kings frequently mention setting up such monuments on foreign soil.[26]

The Mysterious Figure in Josh 5:13-15

[[9]] The account of the appearance of the divine figure in Josh 5:13-15 calls for special treatment. It serves as a suitable test case for the problem of genre and the thesis being proposed here.

The view expressed by M. Noth is typical of many commentaries on this passage and is widely followed.[27] Noth suggests that the episode is a fragment out of an unknown source that was used by the "compiler" as a part of his materials for the conquest account, but that only the fact of the heavenly appearance was preserved and nothing more. He regards it as based upon an ancient tradition that was connected with a holy place "that certainly stems from the previous Canaanite period" and that was used to legitimize the sanctity of the place. Since the identification of Jericho seems unlikely as such a holy place, some have regarded the reference to Jericho in v. 13 as secondary and have suggested Gilgal[28] or Shiloh[29] as alternatives.

Recently some new suggestions have been put forward. G. Ernest Wright states that the story is "unique and without parallel" and that "it is surely not a composition of Dtr."[30] Yet he takes exception to Noth's position that attachment to a specific place plays any role in the story and proposes instead that the story derives from the holy war traditions. J. M. Miller and G. Tucker suggest the possibility "that the tradition once reported the vocation of Joshua."[31] This proposal is based on the similarity of v. 15 with Exod 3:5 in the story of the call of Moses. But if this similarity is based upon a direct literary quotation of one source by the other, as

---

26. On the presence of foreign monuments and texts in Israel/Judah see R. Frankena, "The Vassal-Treaties of Esarhaddon and the Dating of Deuteronomy," *Oudtestamentische Studien* 14 (1965) 150–54.

27. *Das Buch Joshua*, 23–24. See also 39–40.

28. H. W. Hertzberg, *Die Bücher Josua, Richter, Ruth* (Göttingen, 1953) 35–36.

29. K. Möhlenbrink, "Die Landnahmesagen des Buches Josua," *ZAW* NF 15 (1938) 263–64.

30. G. E. Wright and R. G. Boling, *Joshua* (*The Anchor Bible*; Garden City, N.Y., 1982) 72.

31. J. M. Miller and G. Tucker, *The Book of Joshua* (Cambridge, 1974) 49–50. So also T. W. Mann, *Divine Presence and Guidance in Israelite Tradition: The Typology of Exaltation* (Baltimore, 1977) 200. It is noteworthy that Mann, who extensively surveyed the motif of the divine presence in the Assyrian Annals, failed to make any connections with this text.

Miller and Tucker believe, then the notion of an old call narrative is hardly possible. Furthermore, even these new proposals share with Noth the opinion that in 5:13–15 we have to do with a fragment of ancient pre-DtrH tradition, whatever its significance might have been.

[[10]] The grammatical and literary arguments put forward for the separation of 5:13–15 from what follows in chap. 6 are not particularly convincing.[32] On the grammatical side the case rests upon viewing עתה באתי [['I have now come']] (v. 14) as separate from what precedes and therefore incomplete. But this can only be the case if עתה [['now']] is construed as ועתה [['and now']] but this is quite unnecessary.[33] The entire sentence may be a little awkward and unusual because it is inverted for special emphasis but without emendation it must be construed: "Neither, but I (as) captain of the host of Yahweh, have now come." Nothing is missing from the text.

On the literary side, the fact that nothing further is said about the "captain of the host of Yahweh" but instead Yahweh speaks directly in 6:2 is no problem. In parallel examples where the angel of Yahweh appears in a theophany the account often resumes by indicating that it is Yahweh himself who is meant. So it is in the theophany to Moses in Exodus 3. Nor must the statement in 6:1 be taken as a new beginning. In fact it is more appropriate to construe it as a parenthetical statement within the conversation because it does not even contain a finite verb.

The fact remains that all the judgments about the unit 5:13–15 representing a fragment of ancient tradition have rested entirely upon certain general preconceptions about what that pre-literary traditional material was like. The unit itself does not give any direct indication that it is either fragment or ancient, i.e., pre-DtrH.

The question of how to understand this text can be decided, however, on the basis of a Near Eastern parallel, as pointed out in a study of the text by M. Rose.[34] In the account of Ashurbanipal's seventh campaign dealing with his war against Elam the king tells how he offered a prayer before the campaign in the temple of Ishtar of Arbela.[35] As a consequence a seer received a nocturnal vision and reported to the king the following description:

> The goddess Ishtar who dwells in Arbela came in. Right and left quivers were suspended from her. She was holding a bow in her hand, and a

---

32. See B. J. Alfrink, *Josue* (BOT III; Roermond, 1952) 37–38; also Möhlenbrink, *ZAW* 15, 263.

33. See Noth, *Das Buch Josua*, 23 and the translation on 34.

34. *Deuteronomist und Jahwist* (ATANT 67; Zürich, 1981) 55–64, esp. 59–60.

35. See Luckenbill, *AR* II, #858ff.

sharp sword was drawn to do battle. You (the king) were standing in front of her and she [[11]] spoke to you like a real mother. Ishtar called to you . . . giving you the following instructions: "Wait with the attack; (for) wherever you intend to go, I am ready to go."[36]

The text goes on to indicate how the goddess gave additional words of comfort to the king and then proceeded to defeat his enemies without the king needing to do anything.

The parallel with the text in Josh 5:13–15 is obvious. In both cases the theophany of the divine warrior appears at the beginning of the campaign to give encouragement and assure the leader of victory by divine power. There is no reason whatever, on this basis, to separate the appearance of the captain of Yahweh's host from the subsequent overthrow of Jericho. On the contrary, the scene becomes one more confirmation that the basic genre used by the author is that of a campaign report as in Assyrian royal inscriptions.[37]

Conclusion

The above literary and form-critical analysis of the Book of Joshua has led to results quite different from those of M. Noth. I have argued that the DtrH's work is not limited to the final touches of the book but that DtrH is the author and creator of the conquest story. He began with a simple origin tradition about the migration and conquest of the aboriginal inhabitants of the land. Such origin traditions were common among Israel's neighbors[38] and the antiquarian traditions of Greece and Rome. DtrH has interpreted this tradition in terms of a great military campaign using the model offered by the Assyrian royal inscriptions. His historiographic method is to write past history in the form and style of contemporary [[12]] historical texts. The identification of the basic genre of Joshua 1–12 as a campaign report also confirms the literary analysis because those passages that were suspect as secondary on other grounds do not fit the form of the campaign report.

---

36. The translation follows *ANET*[3], 606; see also 451. However, the translations in *ANET* do not make it clear that the excerpts are taken from a larger campaign report.

37. Rose's study (n. 34 above) differs from mine in that he does not consider the full range of Assyriological parallels throughout the Dtr account and therefore comes to somewhat different conclusions. Nevertheless, he concludes that (1) the scene in Josh 5:13–15 does not represent a separate tradition of a theophany, (2) that it functions to introduce a military engagement such as the present context suggests, and (3) the text in Exod 3:5 is dependent upon the text in Joshua and not the reverse (pp. 71–92).

38. Amos 9:7; Deut 2:10–12, 20–33.

This means that it is incorrect to see the conquest narrative as a collection of local oral traditions. The story of the spies in chap. 2 and the account of Achan's sin in chap. 7 are theological and didactic tales that depend upon, and embellish, the DtrH narrative. Similarly, the notion that the tradition about the crossing of the Jordan was preserved and ritually reenacted at the Gilgal sanctuary from hoary antiquity is called into question.[39] It rests entirely upon references to cultic acts and procedures that are all secondary expansions of the text, including the setting up of the "memorial" stones at Gilgal. In the primary account the marches of the people are military, not cultic, and Gilgal is just a military camp. The Jordan crossing is a topos of the military campaign scheme introduced by DtrH. Other etiological elements in the Joshua narrative are explicable, not as evidence of old oral traditions, but as reflecting a regular technique of ancient historiography, that of supplying the account with numerous monuments to give the history credibility.[40]

Likewise, it should be clear that there is no justification for trying to associate archaeological ruins of the end of the Late Bronze Age with a conquest narrative written 600–700 years later. DtrH did not have any records from Israel's earliest period, nor did he follow old oral traditions. The invasion of the land of Canaan by Israel under Joshua was an invention of DtrH. The conquest narrative is a good example of ancient historiography but it cannot pass for historical by any modern criteria of historical evaluation.

39. H.-J. Kraus, "Gilgal," *VT* 1 (1951) 181–99.
40. B. S. Childs, "A Study of the Formula 'Until This Day,'" *JBL* 82 (1963) 279–92. See also *In Search of History*, 24–25.

What Do We Know about Ancient Israel?

R. N. WHYBRAY

[[71]] Recently a group of scholars has been telling us that the Old Testament is almost (if not quite) useless as a source of information about the history of ancient Israel.[1] Since the Old Testament is in fact the *only* ancient source of information that we possess about the history of ancient Israel, this judgment, if true, would appear to wipe out an entire nation from world history; indeed, some scholars appear now to question whether there ever existed a kingdom (or kingdoms) with the name Israel.[2]

Is it, then, impossible to write a history of ancient Israel? While some of the scholars referred to above think not, others point to and employ other ways of looking for evidence than the use of the Old Testament. Three methods in particular have been employed for this purpose. One of these, the attempt to correlate the biblical data with written material from outside the Bible, has long been employed, and, as far as it goes, has

Reprinted with permission from *The Expository Times* 108/3 (1996) 71–74.
    1. Notable examples of this tendency are K. W. Whitelam, "Recreating the History of Israel" (*JSOT* 35, 1986) 45–70; N. P. Lemche, *Ancient Israel: A New History of Israelite Society* (The Biblical Seminar, JSOT Press, 1988); G. Garbini, *History and Ideology in Ancient Israel* (SCM Press, 1988); P. R. Davies, *In Search of 'Ancient Israel'* (JSOTSup 148, JSOT Press, 1992); G. W. Ahlström, *The History of Ancient Palestine: From the Palaeolithic Period to Alexander's Conquest* (JSOTSup 146, JSOT Press, 1993).
    2. Davies (op. cit., 22) concedes that at the time of writing this questioning was not yet really on the agenda of biblical scholarship: "Rarely if ever is it asked whether there really existed a social and political entity" called "Ancient Israel." For him, however, "The 'Israel' of the biblical literature is at least for the most part not an historical entity at all," and "most of the 'biblical period' consists not only of unhistorical persons and events, but even of tracts of time *that do not belong to history at all*" (p. 26, his italics).

achieved results; but these are very meagre: there are only a handful of references by name to Israelite kings who also appear in the Old Testament, mainly on Assyrian and Babylonian inscriptions. No continuous history can be inferred from these, although they have often been taken to "prove" the historicity of the biblical account of the period of the monarchy as a whole.

A second method is the use of archaeological data, that is, buildings and other artefacts extracted from the soil of Palestine in modern times. It is generally agreed that such data can be useful to some extent, but that even if correctly interpreted—and there is frequently no such [[72]] agreement among the archaeologists—they cannot possibly provide the information needed for the writing of a continuous history. Moreover, any conclusions that are drawn from them are necessarily only provisional, being subject to modification or even refutation when further discoveries are made. A further limitation of their usefulness is that most of what has been excavated is "mute," that is, it cannot be identified as having belonged to or been associated with any particular person. In fact, apart from the buildings, there is usually no reason to suppose that any such object was historically significant.[3]

A third method is that of comparative anthropology. In the case of a relatively unknown society like that of ancient Israel this normally takes the form of a comparison of what little is certainly known about that society with modern tribal societies that are deemed to be at a comparable stage of social and political development, in order to enable conclusions to be drawn about the society under study. This method, though it may have a limited usefulness, is very subjective in that the initial assumption of similarity between the two societies may be mistaken. Also, like the archaeological methods, it is open to a variety of conflicting interpretations.[4] If none of these methods can provide an adequate basis for the writing of a history of Israel, it would seem that if such a history is to be written the biblical text, however liable to correction, must be taken as a foundation.[5]

---

3. See Ahlström, op. cit., 21–22; Lemche, op. cit., 71–73.

4. The method is defended by F. S. Frick, "Social Science and Theories of Significance for the Study of the Israelite Monarchy: A Critical Review Essay" *(Semeia* 37, Scholars Press, 1986) 9–52. This essay is remarkable for the fact that the Old Testament is hardly mentioned in it at all. K. W. Whitelam, "Sociology or History: Towards a (Human) History of Ancient Palestine?" (in J. Davies, et al., eds., *Words Remembered, Texts Renewed: Essays in Honour of John F. A. Sawyer* [JSOTSup 195, JSOT Press, 1995] 149–66) is critical; Lemche, op. cit., 68–69, is also critical but hopeful of future positive results.

5. See J. H. Hayes, "On Reconstructing Israelite History" *(JSOT* 39, 1987) 5–9.

Clearly not everything in the so-called "historical books" of the Old Testament should be accepted as historical fact. We now know that bias-free historiography is an impossibility. All history writing reflects the point of view of the historian, who consciously or unconsciously "bends" the facts in a particular direction by selecting, emphasizing, understating, or omitting them as he sees fit, and by making judgments about causes and effects. The ideological bias of ancient historians may often have been more marked and more blatant than is the case with modern "scientific" historians, though the propaganda composed in the present century in dictatorial regimes may be even more blatant than that of the ancient world. However this may be, there is no doubt that the authors of Old Testament narrative literature presented the history of Israel in terms of their own theological (or ideological, if modern jargon is preferred) beliefs. But it by no means necessarily follows from this that they deliberately falsified or invented statements of fact to such an extent as to distort them beyond recognition. At the same time it must be recognized that it was not their intention to write a "secular" history in the modern sense or to record every event which might be politically important but was not relevant to their purpose.

How important is it for the Jewish or Christian reader to know in precise detail the political history of ancient Israel? This is debatable; but since both Judaism and Christianity are faiths that attach great importance to God's involvement in human affairs, the history of ancient Israel *in its main lines* cannot be brushed aside as a matter of no significance for these faiths. Although the biblical scholar's interests may not coincide entirely with those of the "scientific" historian, all who are concerned with Israel's history should be concerned to assess the extent to which Israel's historians "embellished" the material that lay to their hands in order to support their theological purpose. No doubt this depended on a variety of factors. One of these was the literary form in which their material came to them. In writing about human origins and the early history of the nation (in the Pentateuch and the books of Joshua and Judges) they necessarily depended on traditional material of a legendary or "heroic" character. Even the accounts of the early Israelite monarchy (Saul, David, Solomon) clearly contain some material of this kind. So much is now familiar and widely accepted. But with the account of the division of the kingdom and of the histories of the separate kingdoms of Israel and Judah (from 1 Kings 12 onwards) there comes a change, both in style and content and also, it appears, in the intention of the authors. What begins here is in intention an organized systematic history of the kingdoms of Israel and Judah. It is not free from the above mentioned theological bias, nor entirely free from patently legendary material; but the methodical chronological arrangement

of the successive reigns and the careful interlacing of the histories of the
two kingdoms proclaim an intention to set down in order a series of historical events—admittedly not as a purely political or dynastic history but
for theological reasons, seeking to demonstrate a divine influence operating within the events, expressing itself in both blessing and judgment on
particular kings and on the nation itself.

Is it possible to identify this theological "bias" in the books of Kings,
to separate it from the rest, and so to obtain a residue of "historical facts"?
Those who believe that these books are useless as a historical source obviously think that it is not: *nothing* in them can be relied on apart from those
few statements—e.g. the names of certain kings; Sennacherib's attack on
Judah in 701 B.C. [[73]]—that can be checked from outside sources.[6] Most
modern historians of Israel disagree; and this is true not only of books entitled *A History of Israel* but of a mass of detailed studies of particular passages that have been published during the last 150 years and more. All of
these scholars have supposed that the books of Kings give a basically reliable account of the Israelite kingdoms and one that accords with what is
known of the general history of the ancient Near East in that period. To
regard as useless for the historian's purposes the only account of a nation's history written by its own nationals is, to say the least, extraordinary.
It is difficult to find a parallel. The fact that histories of other peoples of
the ancient Near East—Egypt, Babylonia, Phoenicia—were written in Hellenistic or Roman times offers no genuine parallel: the works in question,
as far as can be known from what has been preserved of them,[7] do not in
any way resemble the books of Kings. One unique feature of both Kings
and the Old Testament books that purport to recount Israel's earlier history is that in them Israel is mainly, and in the end wholly, treated with dis-
favour. Far from trumpeting the glorious past, these writers chronicle the
ignominious slide of their own ancestors into a fully merited disaster.
Such a portrayal is unlikely to have been simply invented and corrobo-
rated with such detail.

The fact that the ancient Israelite kings, in contrast to those of Egypt
and Mesopotamia, have left behind them no monumental inscriptions recording their deeds has been taken to indicate that in fact there was no
sequence of Israelite and Judahite kings.[8] It is perhaps remarkable that

6. So Garbini, op. cit., 16.

7. Manetho's *Aegyptiaca* is lost and only brief summaries giving the names and reigns
of Egyptian kings and dividing the history of Egypt into thirty dynasties are preserved, in
works by later writers. Only fragments of the history of Babylonia by Berossus are preserved;
the *Phoenician History* of Philo of Byblos, supposedly a Greek translation of an earlier work
by Sanchuniathon, is preserved only in short excerpts in Eusebius's *Ecclesiastical History*.

8. E.g. Garbini, op. cit., 16–19.

none such have been preserved; various arguments have been used to account for this. But it must be remembered that even on its own showing the nation of Israel was, at least after the death of Solomon and the division of the united kingdom, only a very minor power in the Near Eastern world. In fact, during a very large part of the period of the monarchy the native kings of both northern Israel and Judah were without real power, being no more than vassals, at various times, of the really great powers—Assyria, Babylon, and Egypt. In such circumstances the setting up of monumental inscriptions praising their rulers' glorious triumphs would have been extremely inappropriate if not suicidal.

Another objection that has been made against the historical value of the books of Kings is their supposedly late date. It is argued that writers living several hundred years after the supposed events that they describe would have had insufficient knowledge of their remote past to be capable of giving any reliable account of it.[9] One difficulty with this argument is that it makes an assumption about the date of Kings—the late Persian or the early Hellenistic period—which is far from being generally accepted. As with much of the Old Testament literature, there is no scholarly agreement about the date of Kings—or of the so-called Deuteronomistic History of which it is commonly supposed to be a part. That its final edition is to be dated not long after the last event that it records (561 B.C.; 2 Kgs 25:27–30)—that is, during the Babylonian Exile though not necessarily by one of the Jewish deportees—is a widely held view that may be right. Its author, if resident in or near Jerusalem at that time, would have had first hand experience of the events of the final years of the city before its destruction, and may well have had access to written records relating to the earlier periods of the monarchy. The claim of some modern scholars living two and a half millennia after the events to be competent to judge the accuracy of that ancient historian is somewhat ironical.

It is important to take into account the fact that the historical books are not the only Old Testament witnesses to the existence and history of the Israelite monarchies. In particular, many of the Psalms and large parts of the prophetical books make frequent reference to persons, notably kings, and events which correspond to similar references in Kings. To meet this difficulty, P. R. Davies suggested that not only the historical books of the Old Testament but the Old Testament as a whole was compiled, by post-exilic scribes as an "exercise in self-definition"—that is, to provide the Persian province of Yahud, whose population in his view had little or nothing to do with an earlier people of Israel, with an identity. To this end they made up, in addition to a fictional history, "a 'wisdom tradition', a cultic

---

9. See Davies, op. cit., chap. 6 on this question.

repertory and other kinds of literature which any state should have in order to gain credibility and accountability."[10]

This astonishing theory, for which there appears to be no solid evidence, reduces the Old Testament to a lengthy and complex pastiche, whose authors successfully imitated a great variety of styles (but if they had no models, how could they do this?) in order to give a false impression of antiquity. All distinctions of style and content in the Old Testament, usually attributed to developments of thought and language, are thus flattened out by this theory. The very existence of development is denied; there is no such thing as "tradition." Proverbs and Ecclesiastes, Kings and Chronicles, Amos and Ezekiel are all the creations of post-exilic scribes. The motive put forward for such remarkable activity is based on a conjectural picture of the post-exilic province of Yahud, [[74]] on which is erected a hypothesis about the composition of the entire Old Testament. Among its improbabilities is the brushing aside of the history of language. If, for example, the "wisdom tradition" of the Old Testament is entirely a post-exilic fiction, the Hebrew of the book of Proverbs becomes contemporary with that of Ecclesiastes; and if that is so, as Delitzsch famously remarked,[11] there is no history of the Hebrew language. That these two books cannot be contemporary can be confirmed even by beginners in Hebrew who, having been trained in the "classical" language, find the language of Ecclesiastes to be almost unrecognizable.

There is no space in this article to take up the consequences of these theories for the study of the history of the religion of Israel except to note that they cast doubt on the possibility of our knowing anything about it, though it may be surmised that that religion was in reality very different from what is portrayed in the Old Testament.

What are the reasons for such extreme radicalism? Is it the result of disinterested scholarship? Do the radical proponents of such views feel forced by the evidence to reach their conclusions? It has been alleged that the study of the history of ancient Israel has reached a point at which the old methods can make no progress and that an entirely new approach is needed.[12] But is this so? The methods that have been employed up to the present to investigate the Old Testament accounts of that history appear to this writer to be, on the contrary, satisfactory; and the continued appearance of new histories of Israel and of related studies in journals in re-

10. Davies, op. cit., 130.

11. Delitzsch's remark was directed against the opinion that Ecclesiastes was written by Solomon; but the principle involved is the same: that whenever these two books respectively were composed, there must have been several centuries between them.

12. This is implied, for example, by the subtitle of Lemche's *Ancient Israel—'A New History of Israelite Society'—*and in the title of Davies's *In Search of Ancient Israel* (my emphasis).

cent years suggests that only a minority of scholars, who are determined to move on to something new and more radical with perhaps just a touch of iconoclastic zeal, think otherwise. Though such studies will no doubt continue to be made, I suggest that the future lies not with them but with the painstaking critical methods that have hitherto been employed.

"Ancient Israel" and History
A Response to Norman Whybray

PHILIP R. DAVIES

[[211]] The recent article by my respected colleague Norman Whybray (*ET* 108, pp. 71–74) is not untypical of reaction to recent suggestions, including my own, that the Old Testament is not a direct testimony to "pre-exilic" Israel but essentially a set of compositions from the "post-exilic" period. But his comments misrepresent, I am sure unintentionally, both the basis of mine and others' arguments as well as their impact.

First, the arguments: Whybray starts off by saying that since nonbiblical literary and artifactual data are inadequate to write a history of pre-exilic Israel, and comparative anthropological data are too subjective, the biblical text must be taken as a foundation for Israelite history. But it is a very dubious general principle that any story should be accepted as a basis for history if it happens to be the only source available. How many epics, myths and legends fall into this category? Even within the Bible, what about the stories of Adam and Eve, the Tower of Babel, Abraham and Sarah, Jonah, Ruth or Esther? Or the parables of Jesus? Those scholars (the majority) who regard such examples as being fictional historical are not following this principle at all. Critical biblical scholarship has always paid much more attention to the origin, genre and plausibility of biblical stories in deciding whether they are historical or not. This is certainly true of the view that the books of Samuel and Kings are largely historiographical while the exploits of Elijah and Elisha they contain are mainly legendary. In the case of the books of Genesis to Judges, most scholars, including Whybray, believe that a great deal is not historical and that most of the material is epic, mythical or legendary.

Reprinted with permission from *The Expository Times* 108/7 (1996) 211–12.

The question is: if so much of the Old Testament is, by general agreement, not historical, why do they believe the rest? I do not mean this question in a rhetorical sense, but quite earnestly. Since the majority of scholars accept that much of what looks like historical reporting is actually unhistorical, what reasons can we give for believing that the rest of it is historical? Whybray says that it was not the intention of the authors of these accounts "to write a 'secular' history in the modern sense or to record every event which might be politically important but was not relevant to their purpose." That is agreed. But how does Whybray (or anyone) know what their intention was? Such judgments often turn out to be impressionistic or rationalizations. For example, Whybray's appeal to a difference between the "legendary" character of some writing on the one hand and an "organized systematic history" on the other is based on an entirely subjective judgment: the genealogies of Chronicles 1–9 are much more organized and systematic than the regnal formulae of 2 Kings, which to most scholars still pose serious chronological difficulties. But most scholars dismiss the former as unhistorical and the later as historical. I simply cannot see much reason in this approach. We cannot do history on the basis of subjective assessments of this kind. In any case, whatever the intention of the writer(s) of Kings was, it did not preclude making things up or using legendary sources. So how far did the fictionalizing go? No one knows; but a skepticism that assumes a high degree of fictionalizing is every bit as justifiable as a credulity that assumes a low level.

The point is not, of course, whether or not certain details are historical. I know of no one who suggests the book of Kings is written entirely out of an author's head. But the historicity of Jonah (on which I give no opinion) does not make the story of the great fish and the repentance of Nineveh into fact rather than fiction. Now, since both those represented by Whybray and those who share my view accept that the Old Testament contains a lot of fiction, the important thing is to find explanations for the fiction. I have decided for a more systematic explanation: Whybray, if I understand correctly, prefers a more ad hoc one. Whybray prefers systematic accounts in the Old Testament; I prefer systematic explanations.

The issue at stake has, then, a lot to do with historical method. But the debate itself—which is raging quite fiercely in some quarters—may have to do with attitudes towards a sacred text. Whybray puts his finger closer to the nub when he talks about "brushing aside" the historicity of ancient Israel as a matter of no significance to Judaism and Christianity. Note the emotive language, and ask honestly whether religious faith, which may be able to move mountains, can *make* things historical or unhistorical. We are all attached to sacred stories, even the most secular of us; different sacred stories divide the terrorists of Ireland, the Jews and Palestinians, and countless other warring groups. Postmodernists call these "master narratives," since they organize our social and personal beliefs and actions. Do we want to affirm the right of historical research to ask its questions independently of explicit religious claims, or not? Or do we allow secular histories of everything except ancient Israel? Frankly, I am not sure if Whybray is arguing for a secular history or not.

Other suggestions he makes are equally beside the point. That the history of pre-exilic Israel is drawn unfavorably does not point, as Whybray claims, to its reliability. It could as well, if not better, suggest that a post-exilic generation wanted to contrast a bad past with a reformed present (my view). And since Kings ends with the exile of Judaeans, I can at least prove that it is a post-exilic [[212]] work. That does not, of course, make it necessarily unhistorical. As Whybray says, the pre-exilic history may have been written by an eyewitness of the destruction of Jerusalem. He may even have had access to earlier records. But equally, he *may* have written later and *may* have had no access. Neither I nor Whybray knows, one way or the other. Why he calls my explanation "astonishing" I cannot say, and he does not explain. It seems to me as likely as his (more so, I would argue). Whybray has tradition on his side, and a majority. But that is always the case when older views are confronted with new ones, and it tells us nothing about the relative merits of either.

Finally, Whybray asks "what are the reasons for such radicalism?" and suggests iconoclastic zeal. Perhaps—for no scholar should deny that nonscholarly motives are present. What about his motives? Maybe he is driven by reactionary conservatism or religious attachment to Christian scripture. Yet I would rather not debate on this level, lest we bring scholarship as a whole into disrepute. I would rather encourage readers to look at arguments rather than attribute motives. I would say that the reasons for the "new histories" are mostly methodological; that they have a great deal of plausibility and raise questions that need to be raised—and answered. Who is closer to the "truth" (and there are no "true" histories) remains to be seen, and will probably never be determined to the satisfaction of all.

In the meantime, however, let each side continue to discuss in a collegial manner, looking to expose rather than conceal the vast tracts of common ground, and, above all, try to explain to nonscholars what the debate is really about and why differences of opinion exist. The most difficult task may be insisting to believers that, while Christianity and Judaism have a stake in history, historical agendas cannot be driven by any kind of religious piety. Jews, Christians, and Muslims, on the other hand, may remain confident that historical research cannot rule on the meaning of history, the existence of God, or the reality of religious experience. However factual or fictional the Old Testament may be viewed, it is on these more basic metaphysical questions that it addresses the believer, and indeed, my own experience is that the average churchgoer has little knowledge of or interest in the content of Old Testament history. Are they less Christian for that, I wonder?

Truth and Reality in the Historical Understanding of the Old Testament

GERHARD MAIER

[[9]] Jörn Rüsen, one of today's leading historians, holds that historical science essentially has to do with storytelling. For him storytelling is "a basic human form of . . . interpretation."[1] *Interpretation*, in turn, is thought to involve the notion that through it our understanding and behavior are regulated or guided. For engaging the science of history, then, three elements are essential: fact, interpretation, and contemporary relevance.[2]

This brings us close to what we must deal with in treating our theme of "truth and reality in the historical understanding of the Old Testament." This concerns two theologically fundamental aspects of the narratives of the Old Testament. The first, what we are here calling *truth*, is intended to reveal an intellectual context that determines, or at least influences, our future behavior.[3] The second aspect, which here we are calling *reality*, establishes this intellectual context in factual events in the past.

Our theme concerns the relationship between the two aspects. Their relationship in the Old Testament will be considered specifically. I propose to proceed in three steps. First, the theological-historical problem will be sketched. Second, I will draw in the present-day conversation

Reprinted and translated with permission from "Wahrheit und Wirklichkeit im Geschichtsverständnis des Alten Testaments," in *Israel in Geschichte und Gegenwart* (ed. Gerhard Maier; Wuppertal and Giessen: Brockhaus / Basel: Brunnen, 1996) 9–23. Translated by Peter T. Daniels.

1. J. Rüsen, *Zeit und Sinn* (Frankfurt, 1990) 18.
2. Ibid., 12.
3. Cf. ibid., 92.

about the science of history. Last, the relationship between truth and reality in the narrative texts of the Old Testament itself will be discussed.

The Theological-Historical Problem

Only from the vantage point of post-modernity does the full significance of the Enlightenment in the shaping of modern thought become clear.[4] The Enlightenment, seen from the standpoint of posthistory, appears as the baseline for the following modern age, which extends to the present. [[10]] To that extent, the theological-historical problem cannot be discussed without reference to the Enlightenment.

Allow me nonetheless to point out that "truth and reality in the historical understanding of the Old Testament" had already provided food for thought much earlier. This was so at least since the time of the early Christian apologists. One of their tasks was to establish the factuality of the Old Testament miracles in the face of opponents of Christianity such as Celsus and Porphyry. Schlingensiepen went so far as to put it this way: "The historical question emerges as one of the most important for the apologists."[5] Conversely, early Christian theologians inveighed against heathen miracles, since they were not "consistent with scientific knowledge."[6]

On the whole, however, our problem came into focus in a new way with the Enlightenment. This is also understood for the science of history in general.[7] The degree of focus can be seen for example in Gotthold Ephraim Lessing's short essay "Über den Beweis des Geistes und der Kraft" [['On the Proof of the Spirit and of Power']], published in 1777. One of its lapidary statements reads: "The accidental truths of history can never become the proof of necessary truths of reason." This means: a past event as such can never constrain the present. *Truth* in the sense of "necessary rational truth" can only be something that is established as a metaphysical or moral conviction in the here and now—what "enlightens" modern man.[8] But this is in principle distinct from tradition and history. As for miracles, whose testimonial power constituted one of the central points of dispute, Lessing will accept only what can "be evidenced through

---

4. On this notion, cf. *Postmoderne und Dekonstruktion* (Stuttgart, 1990) (Reclam Universal-Bibliothek No. 8668), especially the chapter by Jean-François Lyotard.

5. H. Schlingensiepen, *Die Wunder des Neuen Testaments* (Gütersloh, 1933) 33. Cf. also pp. 47, 76–77.

6. Cf. G. Petzke, *Die Traditionen über Apollonius von Tyana und das Neue Testament* (Leiden, 1970) 7, as well as my chapter, "Zur neutestamentlichen Wunderexegese im 19. und 20. Jahrhundert," in *The Miracles of Jesus* (ed. D. Wenham and C. Blomberg; Gospel Perspectives 6; Sheffield, 1986) 49ff.

7. Cf. Rüsen, *Zeit und Sinn*, 37.

8. Cf. the English term 'Enlightenment' for *Aufklärung*.

miracles still occurring in the present." This amounts to nothing more than Lessing's making present-day plausibility into the standard for reality. And this in turn depends on the repeatability of the principal analogy.

A hundred years earlier, Baruch Spinoza had already let modern plausibility, in the guise of "reason," decide about the reality of biblical stories. In his *Theological-Political Tractate* of 1670, he proposed the rule "that the power of nature is itself divine [[11]] power and might."[9] What is *contra naturem* [['against nature']] is also *contra deum* [['against God']]: "If, therefore, something took place in nature that goes against its general laws, then it would also go against the will, the understanding, and the nature of God as well."[10] But since the general laws of nature are established in the light of reason, the contents of the Bible must be susceptible to reason, or else they must be rejected. With regard to the miracles of the Old Testament, this means that either they must be understood in harmony with the general laws of nature; or they can be understood as adaptation (accommodation) to contemporary ideas; or—if neither of these alternatives is possible—they are "inserted into the Holy Scriptures by sinful hands"[11] and thus should be expunged.

Since the Enlightenment, the theologians in any case have had to—and this strikes me as one of the most important repercussions—justify themselves, if they insisted on the reality of the events as described in the Old Testament texts. This pressure toward self-justification intensified again through the establishment of classical history in the nineteenth century. One of the fathers—indeed the long-influential hermeneut of this science of history that was growing independent—was Johann Gustav Droysen. In 1989 Hans-Joachim Gehrke composed a sensitive portrait of this great historian in the Berlin series of biographical sketches.[12] Therein the biographical and intellectual-history connection between this sort of historical science and nineteenth-century Protestantism becomes clear. Droysen came from a clerical family. Gehrke emphasizes his "deeply anchored personal-Protestant . . . religiosity."[13] His scientific goal was "inquiring understanding," the "interpretation of ideas."[14] The individual elements to this end derive from the critical investigation of the sources. But this leads to an overall picture of events. As recently as Jörn Rüsen,

---

9. Baruch de Spinoza, *Theologisch-Politischer Traktat* (Philosophische Bibliothek 93; Hamburg, 1984) 95.

10. Ibid.

11. Ibid., 106.

12. Hans-Joachim Gehrke, *Johann Gustav Droysen* (ed. Michael Erbe; Berlinische Lebensbilder, Geisteswissenschaftler; Berlin, 1989) 127ff.

13. Ibid., 127.

14. Ibid., 138.

we find Droysen's statement quoted: "Our faith gives us the conviction that we are led by a hand of God, that it guides fate. . . . And the science of history has no higher task than confirming these beliefs; that is why it is science."[15] A second great name in the flowering of history as an independent science is Leopold von Ranke. [[12]] Committed to objectivity, he intended, in an equally well-known quotation, "simply to describe things as they really were" [["bloß zeigen, wie es eigentlich gewesen"]].[16]

We said that the striving for objectivity, the development of historical criticism within the general science of history, and the insistence on "things as they really were" intensified the pressure for self-justification on the part of historically-oriented Old Testament theology. But now quite another question must be considered: Has not the striving for an overview brought entirely different, rationally uncontrollable, esthetic, philosophical, or theological elements into the methodical-rational procedures of source criticism? Modern historical science concedes this without beating around the bush.[17] But did not this also create for the theologians the possibility that, following individual critical analysis, there could be a pious, edifying overview or "interpretation" that would in the end be no longer subject to question?

I would like to offer two examples of the consequences and possibilities of historical research for the Old Testament that bear on our topic. The first example comes from the work of Hartmut Gese, who until last year [[1995]] taught Old Testament at the University of Tübingen. As early as his collection *Zur biblischen Theologie* [['On Biblical Theology']] of 1977, he published an essay, "Das biblische Schriftverständnis" [["The Biblical Understanding of Scripture"]], in which he expounded the basic concepts of revelation-history as tradition-history. None of the individual classical theories, such as the assumption of various layers in the Pentateuch or the assumption of the centuries-long development of the components of the prophetic books or the assumption of pseudepigraphy, is rejected. All of these individual theories, however, are "raised up" into a superordinate whole in a veritable Hegelian sense. For Gese, it is a matter of "the actual, the essential, the truth that lies behind what is seen."[18] Despite contradictory, historically uncertain events or even recognizably nonhistorical reports and individual events, the implacable stream of tradition fights its way to ever-deeper insights and correlations. The fact, for example, that the Decalogue was certainly not revealed on Sinai does nothing to alter

---

15. Quoted in J. Rüsen, *Für eine erneuerte Historik* (Stuttgart, 1976) 32.
16. Cf. idem, *Historische Orientierung* (Cologne, 1964) 196.
17. Cf. idem, *Für eine erneuerte Historik*, 33.
18. H. Gese, "Das biblische Schriftverständnis," *Zur biblischen Theologie: Alttestamentliche Vorträge* (2d ed.; Tübingen, 1983) 24.

the theological truth that it belongs to the Sinai revelation. "Only a flat, superficial, supposedly objective conception of reality might offer the criticism that this Decalogue in fact (on Sinai!) was not revealed at all."[19] One
must recognize "in the lived life," that is, in [[13]] the living process of tradition, its "truth."[20] It concerns the "development of truth" on processual
levels, for which Gese continually invokes the "true essence."[21] Its counterpart is the "discoverable superficiality," the "superficial thinking."[22] What
is historically ascertainable belongs overwhelmingly to the latter: "When
in the Pentateuch it says 'Moses said,' a truth is expressed to which our objection (arising from superficial thinking) that it is not historical is inappropriate."[23] According to Gese, as firm historical basis, the basic fact
suffices that a divine revelation happened at Sinai.[24] This impressive view
of Old Testament history thus develops from a necessary diastasis between
reality and truth, from the necessary crossing over the historically-real toward the intentionally-truthful. False facts can nonetheless make true interpretations possible.

As a second, quite different example I will take Herbert Donner and
his *Geschichte des Volkes Israel und seiner Nachbarn in Grundzügen* [['Outline
of the History of the People of Israel and Their Neighbors']], the two volumes of which appeared in 1984 and 1986. Donner insists first of all that,
as a result of the history of theology over the last century, "the rigorous
deconstruction of the traditional picture of history conveyed by the Pentateuch, Joshua, and Judges" has occurred.[25] He sees no way, however, to
undo this deconstruction. On the contrary. The very "possibility that
something could have taken place as described" is rejected as a "methodologically impermissible assumption."[26] The burden of proof, then, lies
on the researcher who investigates the Old Testament historically. Thus
emerges the danger of "microhistory" of which Rüsen spoke.[27] All that remains of Moses is that he was born in Egypt and probably was a Semite.[28]
Again with Donner we encounter the diastasis between truth and reality,
but now in such a way that the historically-verifiable reality in many places

---

19. Ibid., 14–15.
20. Ibid., 15.
21. Ibid., 16, 24, 29.
22. Ibid., 16, 20.
23. Ibid., 20.
24. Ibid., 23.
25. H. Donner, *Geschichte des Volkes Israel und seiner Nachbarn in Grundzügen* (2 vols;
Göttingen 1984–1986) 1.25.
26. Ibid., 26.
27. Cf. Rüsen, *Zeit und Sein*, 70.
28. Donner, *Geschichte des Volkes Israel*, 1.109–10.

contradicts the "truth," that is, the orienting nexus of meaning that the Old Testament texts mean to convey. [[14]]

The Current Discussion of the Possibility of Theological Interpretation in the Science of History

Surprisingly, the current discussion of the possibility of theological interpretation in the science of history is neither so diffident nor so rare as theologians of the twentieth century might expect.

For decades, the modern science of history has been based on a three-step method: heuristics, criticism, interpretation.[29] Heuristics refers to the detection/observation [[*Wahrnehmung*]] of sources, criticism the critical investigation of these sources, and interpretation the deliberative presentation in chronological sequence. The second of these steps, source criticism, is most susceptible to the development of a methodology. This is where the development and evaluation of sources takes place, by means of a method called either the "historical-critical method"[30] or simply the "historical method."[31] Source criticism is then divided into three areas: external source criticism, internal source criticism, and a third called either "ideology criticism"[32] or more recently "construction of more highly aggregated facts."[33] External source criticism examines the authenticity of a text (for example, regarding authorship or date of composition or wording).[34] Internal source criticism, occasionally also called "historical criticism,"[35] examines the received "facts" and "events" with attention to their reality.[36] "Ideological criticism," finally, is understood by Peter Borowsky, in his introduction to historical science, among other things, as the "question concerning the political, 'worldview' standpoint of the author of a text" and also the question "concerning the standpoint of the historian as agent of investigation."[37]

---

29. Cf. Peter Borowsky, Barbara Vogel, and Heide Wunder, *Einführung in die Geschichtswissenschaft, I: Grundprobleme, Arbeitsorganisation, Hilfsmittel* (2d ed.; Opladen, 1976); and Rüsen, *Historische Orientierung*, 104.

30. As in Borowsky, Vogel, and Wunder, *Einführung in die Geschichtswissenschaft*, 157, for instance.

31. As in J. Schmidt, *Studium der Geschichte* (Munich, 1975) 54.

32. As in Borowsky, Vogel, and Wunder, *Einführung in die Geschichtswissenschaft*, 157–58.

33. As in Rüsen, *Historische Orientierung*, 109.

34. Cf. Borowsky, Vogel, and Wunder, *Einführung in die Geschichtswissenschaft*, 157, where "methodological doubt concerning the 'authenticity' of the text" is demanded as point of departure.

35. As in Borowsky et al., ibid., 158.

36. Ibid.

37. Ibid.

For our purposes, what interests us most here is "internal source criticism" or "historical criticism." What role do *facts*, or what I refer to with the key word *reality*, play in it? For the science of history in general, it is clear that there can only be "probability judgments."[38] Donner's polemic against the well-founded "assumption of the possibility that something could [[15]] have taken place exactly as described"[39] is unknown, it seems to me, to the *communis opinio* [['shared opinion']] of the general science of history. But how is the judgment of probability to be arrived at? Jörn Rüsen provides an answer to this question in his *Historische Orientierung* [['Historical Orientation']] of 1994: "Of course, sources can be imprinted with an entirely different understanding of reality from that of the historians who work with them. Decisive for the plausibility of what a source reports as fact is in doubtful cases not the source's statement, but the historian's understanding of reality."[40] He thus reiterates the typical position of the modern science of history. But it must be noted that this priority of the modern historian's understanding of reality represents an a priori position for which justification is no longer offered. It is clear that a problem immediately arises when we are dealing with religious texts whose own understanding of reality is provided with a higher religious authority, as is the case for the documents of Islam or Christianity.

Internal source criticism again invites our attention when it comes to determining the causes of particular events. According to Karl-Georg Faber, whose *Theorie der Geschichtswissenschaft* [['Theory of the Science of History']] is held in high regard, the historian makes two presuppositions: "1. All history is under the control of causal relationships. 2. All history is chance."[41] Concerning both presuppositions, Faber notes that the historian cannot prove them.[42] Reinhart Koselleck, another leading contemporary historian, stresses that we cannot do without chance, since otherwise we surrender to ideology.[43] For Faber, one of the typical problems of the science of history lies in the fact that it often has too many causes and cannot decide which cause(s) was (were) decisive.[44] The complexity of history defends itself against any monocausality. Moreover, within the science of history the principle of causality is doubted on various grounds: unpredictability in history (Wittram), or recent developments in natural history (Huizinga), or because the internal connection of events is differ-

38. Cf. e.g. Rüsen, *Historische Orientierung*, 109.
39. Cf. n. 26 above.
40. Rüsen, *Historische Orientierung*, 109.
41. Karl-Georg Faber, *Theorie der Geschichtswissenschaft* (3d ed.; Munich, 1974) 66.
42. Ibid.
43. R. Koselleck, *Vergangene Zukunft* (Frankfurt, 1989) 158ff.
44. Faber, *Theorie der Geschichtswissenschaft*, 71.

ent from the causal nexus in nature (Gadamer).[45] On balance: there are "no more in history than in the natural sciences absolutely certain laws of causality" and "for historical reality as chance there is no explanation."[46] Any ever-valid [[16]] principle of causality, such as Troeltsch once maintained for historical method in theology, thus fails. On the other hand, already at the level of internal source criticism the possibility of a theistic explanation presents itself, to the extent that the concept *chance* is interpreted through the concept *God*. But this naturally depends on the viewpoint of the historian.

As already noted, only source criticism is indisputably susceptible to the development of a methodology. But what about interpretation? It is after all the ultimate goal of the entire investigative procedure. From the outset we must realize that it is not susceptible to rules. Interpretation remains "as to methodological regulation (so far) an open problem."[47] Neither is the end stage of interpretation—as it were, the writing of history (historiography)—susceptible to the development of a methodology, even though it represents one of the principal tasks of the historian.[48] This even makes it look as though it is "unclear whether there is in fact such a thing as 'the' historical method."[49] Paradoxically, there is at the same time an overarching agreement that in interpretation the most varied ideological impressions vie for expression. For historians, history is "in no wise an assumptionless science."[50] I have already referred to the example of Droysen, the father of modern traditional history. A further example is Karl-Georg Faber, who could say: we need "insight into the extra-historical dimension of the problem of evaluation" that arises in historical interpretation.[51] Should one lay claim to [[historical]] truth as having [[contemporary]] validity, then the problem becomes an obvious dilemma. For at that moment the historian claims to establish meaning that carries normative weight. But can historical science as such accomplish this? As Rüsen writes: "If, on the one hand, it claims as science that its knowledge is universally valid, it can, on the other hand, only with difficulty conceal the fact that in achieving just this knowledge evaluations are unavoidable, for which the same universal validity cannot be claimed."[52] The science of history thus faces the double challenge of being "both objective and biased

---

45. Cf. further ibid., 68.
46. Ibid., 77, 86.
47. Rüsen, *Historische Orientierung*, 113.
48. Ibid.
49. Ibid., 101. Cf. idem, *Für eine erneuerte Historik*, 11, 20, 23–24.
50. Faber, *Theorie der Geschichtswissenschaft*, 204.
51. Ibid., 182.
52. Rüsen, *Zeit und Sinn*, 79.

at the same time."[53] To frame the issue positively, following Golo Mann: every historian has a philosophy![54] This is the place [[17]] where the Christian interpretation of the meaning of history and of history in general finds expression. That the possibility of such a Christian interpretation exists is beyond question. Quite recently Reinhart Koselleck has spoken in a thoroughly appreciative fashion of the fact that "Judeo-Christian interpretations import standards that at the same time indirectly indicate historical structures, as they hitherto and elsewhere had not been formulated."[55] Right at the start of his ground-breaking monograph on *Zeit und Sinn* [['Time and Sense']], Jörn Rüsen offers the possibility for such an interpretation: "Within the horizon of Christian salvation history, the experience that life is coming apart at the seams can be interpreted as an indication of future salvation, the return of Christ, and the introduction of a new and better world."[56] Toynbee saw the historian as standing fundamentally before the question of God and noted: "It is beyond human understanding . . . to prove or disprove the existence of a higher spiritual being."[57] Consequently, within the general science of history the possibility exists of a Christian interpretation of history, as long as it announces its own presuppositions and in a controlled way brings them to bear.

I shall attempt to set down a number of conclusions from the contemporary discussion of the science of history:

1. Every text is to be interrogated as to the reality or facts described in it. An "occurrence in the past" can have no sense or meaning if it does not allow its own "factuality" to be declared (the fundamental principle of empirical correspondence).[58]

2. For the science of history, there is no fact without an interpretation. It is even questionable whether the "historical charts of a Doctor Ploetz," which Golo Mann facetiously offers as an exception,[59] actually represents such an exception.

3. With regard to judgments of probability about reported facts, the modern historian's sense of plausibility is decisive; that is, his own understanding of reality is the determining factor.

53. Ibid., 78, 11ff.

54. Golo Mann in Leonhard Reinisch, *Der Sinn der Geschichte* (Munich, 1961) 11. Cf. Rüsen, *Für eine erneuerte Historik*, 13.

55. Koselleck, *Vergangene Zukunft*, 138.

56. Rüsen, *Für eine erneuerte Historik*, 11.

57. In Reinisch, *Der Sinn der Geschichte*, 89.

58. Cf. Rüsen, *Für eine erneuerte Historik*, 94.

59. Golo Mann in Reinisch, *Der Sinn der Geschichte*, 11–12. Cf. Rüsen, *Historische Orientierung*, 196.

4. Causes are not simply to be understood according to the principle of causality but often are due to so-called "chance." This "chance" theory also leaves room for theistic explanations.

5. On the level of interpretation, a Christian interpretation is also possible, so long as it is offered in a considered and discussable manner. Every [[18]] historian is obligated to give account of his own philosophical, ideological, and religious presuppositions. But since every historian shares such presuppositions, a "confession of faith" also has a legitimate place.[60]

The Connection of Truth and Reality in the Old Testament Narrative Passages

We have now reached the point in our reflections where the texts themselves must be considered. We shall proceed in keeping with what Gese called the "fundamental postulate of hermeneutics": "A text is to be understood as it chooses to be understood—that is, as it understands itself."[61]

Nonetheless, let me begin with a preliminary remark that indicates a somewhat broader path. This preliminary remark can be formulated as follows: ancient Jewish and New Testament exegesis knows no diastasis of truth and reality in the Old Testament texts. It does indeed distinguish between the two, as can be seen especially in typological and allegorical exegeses.[62] But it brooks no doubt that Old Testament history took place in the very sequence and form of the events that are portrayed for us in the Old Testament. This recognition, as far as I can judge, is also not challenged by modern exegesis. But it is greatly minimized.

The great extent to which *Jewish thought was attached to the external observability of events—that is, their "reality"*—is clear, for instance, in 1 Cor 1:22. Whereas the Greeks were satisfied with *sophia* (that is, with the internal coherence and persuasiveness of a proclamation), the Jews sought 'signs' (*semeia*). That is, Jewish people want to discern God's activities in external, physical actions. That is why the Messiah hanging on the cross and dying there is such a great challenge (cf. 1 Cor 1:18–2:16).

To what extent is this Jewish way of thinking something special and characteristic? This question must be asked, because surely questioning the past and the meaning of history is simply part of being human.[63]

---

60. Cf. once more Rüsen, *Für eine erneuerte Historik*, 13. For the older, divergent opinion, cf. Theodor Litt in Reinisch, *Der Sinn der Geschichte*, 71ff., and Karl R. Popper, in ibid., 102–3.

61. H. Gese, *Alttestamentliche Studien* (Tübingen, 1991) 249.

62. Cf. in the New Testament 1 Cor 10:1ff., Gal 4:22ff.

63. So Reinisch, correctly, in the foreword to his collected essays, *Der Sinn der Geschichte*, 7.

Leopold von Ranke is not the only one who wants to know "how it [[19]] really happened." On the contrary, everyone inquires regarding his/her origin and history and thus regarding "how it really happened." Traces of this question can be observed in many places in the history of the ancient Near East. They range from the scarab in the Vatican's Egyptian Museum that portrays the story of the installation of an artificial lake, and from the statue that Ramses II had erected of his mother, to the Assyrian reliefs of the ninth and eighth centuries that portray the conquering of a city with ladders or the execution of prisoners. They include the baked bricks that were used in the foundations of a temple in northern Syria and already as early as the beginning of the second millennium B.C.E. tell of military campaigns and the fortification of a riverbank. They lead us to the Persian royal inscriptions and meet us finally in the form of annals that the kings of the Persian period caused to be proclaimed (Esth 2:23, 6:1ff.), just as Vespasian later did in Octavian's Gate at Sant'Angelo in Pescheria in Rome.

In this connection we come upon the term *remembrance*, or *memory*. While all of the Near Eastern examples that we have mentioned alike serve *remembrance* and *memory*, in the context of Old Testament and Jewish tradition two peculiarities make themselves felt. The first is the fact that throughout all the centuries it is repeatedly the acts of *one God* that are recalled, and not the acts of great men or multiple gods. This thread remains constant all the way through to Acts 2:11. The second peculiarity is that the Hebrew root word *zākar* [['remember']] expresses a spiritual-personal bond that includes an active component—for example, the obedience of the thinking man.[64] This bond arises from the historically experienced care of God. Therefore H. Eising is right to say that here "Israel's history with its God plays a highly significant role."[65] But this is a history in which reality and truth do not have a confrontational encounter but where truth is discovered in reality. To this extent one can invoke W. Schottroff's notion of salvation history, when he notes that *zākar* is often concerned with an "actualization of particular salvation-historical traditions."[66]

We inquired into the special character of the Jewish understanding of history and recognized in the discussion of the key word *zākar* 'remember' that the Jewish and Old Testament *understanding of history* cannot be clarified *without including their relationship with God*. [[20]] These thoughts now need to be set in a wider context. We do observe that Yahweh is not a "god per se." Rather, the God of the Old Testament is defined by history. It is

---

64. Cf. H. Eising, *TWAT* 2.575ff.
65. Ibid., 591.
66. W. Schottroff, *THAT* 1.517.

the God who led Israel out of Egypt (Exod 20:2; Deut 5:6).[67] It is the God "who summoned the Patriarchs and promised them the land."[68] It is the God who brought Israel into the Promised Land. This historicized definition of God can be seen especially clearly in the so-called Credo of Deut 26:5–9, where the Israelite making an offering first speaks of his father, "a wandering Aramean," and his history. But then the narrator concentrates on what Yahweh did and how he was experienced: "Yahweh listened to us and saw our sorrow, our tribulation and oppression. And Yahweh led us out of Egypt with a strong hand and an outstretched arm and great horrors, with signs and wonders, and brought us to this place."[69] Here Gerhard von Rad speaks of a "concentration on the objective facts of history."[70] It is obvious that one cannot speak of a "truth" of this presentation of history, if God did not actually bring about the history spoken of here.

It is not possible to object that this is a matter of professions of faith or "confessional summaries of salvation history."[71] Naturally history is told with kerygmatic and pedagogical intent here. *Nowhere are facts simply narrated without interpretation.* The only question is, which is the "correct" interpretation. What, then, is to be expected but that the Old Testament offers its own interpretation, complete with the claim that this is the "rightly" interpreted history? In any case the Old Testament cannot speak of God without telling of the history brought about by him, nor can it speak of history without bringing it into relation with God.

The close connection between an understanding of history and a relationship with God consistently yields the particular *teaching of history* that Israel experienced in the course of its life. The so-called Holiness Code in Leviticus is shot through with the constantly repeated refrain "I am Yahweh, your God."[72] This refrain aims at the remembrance of God, who revealed himself in Israel's history as the active and holy God. When children ask about the origin of certain customs, as at Passover, Israel's history [[21]] and God's revelations during it are supposed to be recounted (cf. Exod 12:26–27, 13:14–15; Deut 6:20ff.; Josh 4:6–7, 21ff.). The great penitential prayers of the Old Testament, such as Ezra 9, Nehemiah 9, and Daniel 9, are inconceivable without reviews of history. One sees the effect

---

67. Cf. G. von Rad, *Theologie des Alten Testaments* (4th ed.; Munich, 1962) 1.135ff. [[Eng. trans.: *Old Testament Theology* (2 vols.; trans. D. M. G. Stalker; London: SCM, 1975) 1.121–22]].

68. Ibid., 135 [[Eng., 1.121]].

69. Translated following von Rad, *Theologie des Alten Testaments*, 1.135–36 [[Eng., 1.121–22]].

70. Ibid., 136 [[Eng., 1.122]].

71. Ibid., 135 [[Eng., 1.121]].

72. Cf. esp. chap. 19!

this education in history had not least in the prophets, who could refer—as it were, in passing—to the history of Israel, without further explanation. A few examples from Amos, Hosea, and Micah, eighth-century B.C.E. prophets from the end of the eighth century B.C.E. Amos 5:25 considers it entirely self-evident that the forty years' sojourn *bammidbār* [['in the desert']] is known to every listener. Mic 6:3ff. runs very briefly through the Exodus from Egypt, Moses, Aaron, Miriam, Balak, Balaam, Shittim, and Gilgal—in the chronological sequence found in the Pentateuch, incidentally—and speaks of God's action encountered by Israel at each of these stages in its history, without needing to clarify any elements of this history. In the short space of Hosea 8–12, brief remembrances are included about the gift of the Torah, the earlier sojourn in Egypt, the Exodus, the wilderness, the Baal-peor of Numbers 25, the story of Jacob, Moses as prophet, and the scandal at Gibeah,[73] where the extent of the descriptions of or allusions to the events corresponds strikingly to how familiar they presumably are to listeners. The question whether what is reported in the tradition "really" happened is not asked. Here again we discover the inseparable connection between "truth" and "reality." Admittedly the "truth" that is proclaimed in connection with a historical event can transcend reality just as God's glory is far greater than is realized in punctiliar historical events.

Let us emphasize: Israel is more nurtured in history than other peoples of the Near East. Is it any surprise, then, that later generations guarded both the historical memory and the exactitude of that memory? Take the examples in the "Praise of the Ancestors" in Ben Sira (chaps. 44ff.) or 1 Maccabees, probably datable before the end of the second century B.C.E.[74] Later on, Josephus saw the uniqueness of Jewish historiography as its 'speaking the truth' (*talēthē legein*) and offering unadulterated 'facts'. Although the concepts 'facts' (*pragmata*) and 'truth' (*alēthēs*) were already held in high esteem by the Greeks,[75] Josephus explicitly distinguishes himself from Greek [[22]] historiography in that he intends to convey 'the exact historical picture' (*to d'akribēs tēs historias*), the facts "exactly and completely"—in a word, "the genuine [or: true] history" (*J.W.* 1.1ff.; *Ant.* 1.1ff.). Now and then in these historiographical reflections he even includes the famous formula in Deut 4:2: "neither add nor diminish."[76] Here it is clear as day that both are stressed: "reality" and "truth." Whatever is not based on unadulterated facts has no significance, is in fact not

73. Cf. Hos 8:1, 12, 13; 9:3, 9, 10; 11:1; 12:4[3], 10[9], 13[12], 14[13].

74. Klaus-Dietrich Schunck dates it "around 120 B.C." (*JSHRZ* 1/4 [1980] 292).

75. Cf. K. Löwith in Reinisch, *Der Sinn der Geschichte*, 42; W. F. Otto in Herodotus, *Historien* (4th ed.; Stuttgart, 1971) xxiff.

76. *Ant.* 1.17: *ouden prostheis oud'an paralipōn.*

"true." The 'facts' (*pragmata*), however, must be organized (*meta pollou ponou syllegein* 'collected with much care', *J.W.* 1.16), so that a comprehensive overview and a comprehensive judgment, in fact the "truth," results. Truth without facts is not to be had.

Let us note one further interesting aspect. Where Josephus sets forth his historiographic principles, he sees himself in a line with the authors of the Old Testament. He does nothing other than what those Jewish authors of the Old Testament did, who 'wrote the history of the ancestors with care' (*ta tōn progonōn synetaxanto met' akribeias*), while 'some Greeks who translated that work into their mother tongue [Septuagint?] did not essentially misrepresent the truth' [[*ou polu tēs alētheias diēmarton, J.W.* 1.17]]. Something similar appears in *Ag. Ap.* 1.37ff. One will not go far wrong in taking these reflections as the legitimate fruit of Israel's historical education. Furthermore, there is no reason to doubt that Jewish interpretation from the second century B.C.E. to the first century C.E. is a continuation of the Old Testament authors' understanding of history.

The findings we have arrived at are summarized as follows:

1. The Old Testament narrative texts do not develop an abstract understanding of history but combine history with an understanding of God.
2. They tell of a God who "does history" that is outwardly observable—that is, brings about real changes. Without real changes one cannot speak of the Old Testament God.
3. Within this notion of change there appears a noteworthy affinity of the Old Testament understanding of history to the modern science of history, which also only speaks of "meaning" and "truth" when real facts are at hand.
4. Affinity to the modern science of history similarly emerges from the fact that *fact* is always found in association with an *interpretation*. The [[23]] observation that we have a "kerygmatic" text before us says nothing about the reality that confronts us and can never be used as an objection to "historicity." One can only ask *which* interpretation is the *right* one.
5. Thus the modern science of history (as we have shown above) fully allows theistic or faith-based interpretation, though only as one possibility alongside another, at least equally entitled, possibility.
6. Truth and reality in the Old Testament narrative texts are so bound up together that one cannot have one without the other. To be sure, "truth," as we meet it in the history-laden texts of the Old Testament, transcends "reality," as we have noted several times. But this "truth" needs the base of "reality." This makes the "truth" of the history-laden

proclamation of the Old Testament vulnerable—should it be demonstrated that the facts have been falsified.

7. Like no other people in the Near East or perhaps in the entire history of the world, Israel was nurtured in the understanding of history. To inquire into the understanding of history and in particular into the relation between truth and reality is thus not a question inappropriate to the Old Testament texts but an inquiry that emerges directly from and is most consistent with the Old Testament itself.

History as Confession of Faith— History as Object of Scholarly Research

On One of the Basic Problems of the History of Israel

J. ALBERTO SOGGIN

1. [[161]] Already in the first edition of his *Theology*, Gerhard von Rad fittingly formulated the problem before us with the following words:[1] "The fact that these two views of Israel's history are so divergent is one of the most serious burdens imposed today on Biblical scholarship" [[trans. D. M. G. Stalker]]. He has in mind the picture constructed by "modern critical scholarship," on the one hand, and that "which the faith of Israel has erected" (namely, the kerygmatic picture), on the other. As far as I can see, this assertion has not encountered any fundamental criticism on the European mainland: it was predominantly in the United States in the circle of W. F. Albright that there was talk of "nihilism" and the like.[2]

Translated and reprinted with permission from "Geschichte als Glaubensbekenntnis—Geschichte als Gegenstand wissenschaftlicher Forschung: Zu einem der Grundprobleme der Geschichte Israels," *Theologische Literaturzeitung* 110 (1985) cols. 161–72. Translated by V. Philips Long. (An earlier version of this essay subsequently appeared in *Isac Seeligmann Volume: Essays on the Bible and the Ancient World* [ed. A. Rofé and Y. Zakovitch; Jerusalem: Rubinstein, 1983] 3.1–14.)

1. Gerhard von Rad, *Theologie des Alten Testaments* (Munich, 1957) 1.113ff. (4th ed. 1963) 1.119ff. [[English: *Old Testament Theology* (2 vols.; New York: Harper, 1962–65) 1.108]]. Cf. also "Offene Fragen im Umkreis einer Theologie des Alten Testaments," *ThLZ* 88 (1963) cols. 401–16 = *GS* 2 (1973) 289–321.

2. Only J. Hempel ("Mitteilungen," *ZAW* 70 [1958] 165–73; specifically p. 169) speaks of M. Noth's "nihilism." Perhaps a printing error?

[[162]] Even Walther Eichrodt,[3] who complained of the "vehemence" with
which Gerhard von Rad had stated the problem, nevertheless found that
the "discrepancy" between the two historical pictures had "become ever
more pronounced in the research of the last century." Indeed, von Rad's
statement is becoming virtually an Archimedean point for those (for example, Franz Hesse) who would like to unhinge his theology of the Old
Testament on methodological grounds.

Now, one could of course avoid the problem by claiming that on close
inspection there are [[163]] not *two* pictures, especially of the early history
of Israel: for the so-called kerygmatic picture is one of the chief components of Israel's faith and so belongs to the history of Israelite religion and
to the theology of the Old Testament. It would then have to be treated
within the framework of Israel's history, which comprises precisely the object of historical-critical research.[4] This is indeed an important observation. It appears to me, however, that with this approach the problem
simply shifts to a different level but is not resolved. Sooner or later we
shall have to ask the question how it could be that Israel testified to its
faith in divine acts of salvation, acts that were revealed precisely in source
materials that, especially for the earlier time periods, are often utterly unverifiable historically and sometimes even incorrect. Is it then possible
that Israel had no access to additional, verifiable source materials, as is often the case? Or was Israel not at all interested in this sort of verifiability,
as is the case, for example, in 1 and 2 Chronicles? If so, then the oft-
stressed and highly praised historical sense of Israel is in a bad way, and
one would surely have to say, with my Italian colleague Giovanni Garbini,[5]
that Israel's theologians and history writers have transposed nature-myth
onto the events of their own people and presented a "history" that has
abolutely no correspondence to reality.

One could evade the question by following R. de Vaux[6] in his view

---

3. Walther Eichrodt, *Theologie des Alten Testaments* (4th ed.; Berlin, 1961) vol. 2/3, p. vii
[[English: *Theology of the Old Testament* (2 vols.; Philadelphia: Westminster, 1961); German
"Vorwort" not translated; but cf. the Excursus in ibid., 1.512–20]].

4. So already M. Noth, *Überlieferungsgeschichte des Pentateuch* (Stuttgart, 1948) 272 [[En-
glish: *A History of Pentateuchal Traditions* (Englewood Cliffs, N.J.: Prentice-Hall, 1972) 252]]:
"The transmission history of the Pentateuch is itself a part of the history of Israel." Cf. also
R. Rendtorff, "Hermeneutik des Alten Testaments als Frage der Geschichte," *ZThK* 57 (1960)
26–50; and "Geschichte und Überlieferung," in *Studien zur Theologie der alttestamentlichen
Überlieferungen: Festschrift Gerhard von Rad zum 60. Geburtstag* (Neukirchen, 1961) 81–94, both
in *GS* (1975) 11–24 and 25–38.

5. G. Garbini, Review, *AION* 35 (1975) 287–88.

6. R. de Vaux, "Peut-on écrire une 'Théologie de l'Ancien Testament'?" in *Mélanges
M.-D. Chenu* (Paris, 1967) 439–49 = *Bible et Orient* (Paris, 1967) 59–71 [[English: *The Bible and
the Ancient Near East* (Garden City, N.Y.: Doubleday, 1971) 49–62]].

that both pictures, though each on its own level, are "alike true," for "l'interpretation divine échappe au jugement de l'historien" [['the divine interpretation escapes the judgment of the historian']]. As true as this may be from a theological-philosophical perspective, it is not exactly satisfying to the historian!

In this short essay I would like to concern myself briefly with this problem. The essay is dedicated to the memory of I. L. Seeligmann, respected teacher in Jerusalem and friend, who made so many important contributions on these issues.

2. Several years ago I myself wrestled with the aforementioned problem in two essays.[7] Since then, various things have happened that have prompted me to reinvestigate the issues and fundamentally to revise and correct my earlier theses. I would like to summarize those theses in the following three points.

(a) Over against the historical-critical picture of the early history of Israel, which was developed mainly in the German-speaking world but also elsewhere on the European continent, there stood an alternative, which was formulated primarily in the United States. It derived from the group of archaeologists, philologists, and theologians grouped around William Foxwell Albright,[8] even though Albright himself was neither theologian not philosopher. As is well known, this view judged the traditional picture of the early history of Israel, as it emerges from the biblical sources, very positively. One can well say that, despite all of the individual criticisms of the tradition, an important portion of it was deemed reliable. Here there was no "divergence" but, rather, a convergence of the two pictures, even though the American researchers often admitted that a large proportion of the tradition was not verifiable by their methods. Still, with the help of what John Bright called the *balance of probability*,

---

7. J. A. Soggin, "Alttestamentliche Glaubenszeugnisse und geschichtliche Wirklichkeit," *ThZ* 17 (1961) 285–98; and "Geschichte, Historie und Heilsgeschichte im Alten Testament," *ThLZ* 89 (1964) cols. 721–36.

8. I hope I demonstrated while he was alive that the scientific presuppositions of both pictures are the same; see my "Ancient Biblical Traditions and Modern Archaeological Discoveries," *BA* 23 (1960) 95–100 = *Old Testament and Oriental Studies* (Rome, 1975) 3–10. Arriving at a similar conclusion were M. Weippert, *Die Landnahme der israelitischen Stämme* (FRLANT 92; Göttingen, 1967) 59; T. L. Thompson, *The Historicity of the Patriarchal Narratives* (BZAW 133; Berlin, 1974) 5; and C. H. J. de Geus, *The Tribes of Israel* (Assen, 1976) 50. The latter rightly emphasized that the divergent results that the two schools achieved are only a question of evaluation. Sadly, we cannot here get into the theses of G. E. Mendenhall, "The Hebrew Conquest of Palestine," *BA* 25 (1962) 66–87; and *The Tenth Generation* (Baltimore, 1973) chap. 7; cf. also N. K. Gottwald, *The Tribes of Yahweh* (Maryknoll, N.Y., 1979) passim. Certainly one may infer from this complex picture that it need not necessarily have to do with a dispute between "Europeans" and "Americans."

one could apparently offset this difficulty somewhat.[9] Stated differently: if one must make a conjecture, then one should at least choose the most probable among the conjectures, which means in cases of doubt to prefer the tradition. Back then I claimed that it was impossible to speak of *one* historical-critical picture: one had to consider at least two possibilities, since the American research also proceeded scientifically and was certainly not to be confused with precritical "fundamentalism."[10] [[164]]

(b) On the basis of this principle of probability, to which I at that time subscribed, it appeared to me possible to grasp, at least in outline, the chief features of the early history of Israel and, in fact, in the following traditional sequence: patriarchs, Egyptian sojourn, exodus and wilderness wandering, conquest (*Landnahme*)—irrespective of the problems of how things may have related to one another in detail, of which of the patriarchs may have been involved in each episode, and of how the various elements stand chronologically, relative to one another.

(c) I claimed further that such problems arise not only in the case of Israel: one encounters them with every people, especially with respect to their prehistory, but also elsewhere. So how does it stand today with these claims?

Regarding (a): It remains puzzling that hardly any scientific discussion has developed between American and European colleagues, despite their mutual respect. To be sure, M. Noth[11] at various times took a position on these issues and often rejected certain pronouncements that were correctly felt to be inappropriate and sometimes even offensive. But still it never came to a true debate of the fundamental questions. Much was written by both groups, but for the most part their writings passed each other by. Admittedly, as I believed myself to have demonstrated at that time,[12] the theses of the two groups diverged far less than one might suppose from a first impression. Indeed, I spoke of a "convergence" of the two in principle. All the same, there can be no doubt that at the time of Gerhard von Rad and for many years there were *two* scientific historical reconstructions of ancient Israel and not just one.

9. J. Bright, *Early Israel in Recent History Writing: A Study in Method* (SBTh 1/19; London, 1956) passim. I probably do not need to stress that I have in the meantime distanced myself from the *balance of probability*.

10. I have always been rather reserved with respect to the American school, despite the worthiness of its method and its results (cf. my review, *ThZ* 15 [1959] 299–301) and already early on I expressed a certain sympathy with the theses of A. Alt and M. Noth.

11. M. Noth, "Grundsätzliches zur geschichtlichen Deutung archäologischer Befunde auf dem Boden Palästinas," *PJb* 34 (1938) 7–22; and "Der Beitrag der Archäologie zur Geschichte Israels," VTSup 7 (1960) 262–82; both essays now available in *Aufsätze* . . . (1971) 1.3–16 and 34–51. The sentence to be discussed in the following lines is found in "Der Beitrag," 263 n. 1 = *Aufsätze*, 1.35 n. 2.

12. See my essay cited in n. 8 above.

Regarding (b): Recent studies, since the 1960s, have profoundly altered the question.[13] And the process still continues. Indeed, as far as I can see, the results of the "German" school are also now largely obsolete, which has led to a convergence in a negative sense. Thus I can today no longer defend the assertions I formulated back then.

Regarding (c): As I shall attempt to show below, I hope that this point still retains its validity and that it is worthwhile to continue researching in precisely this direction. I wish to commit the remainder of this essay to this task.

3. History-writing, as is well known, has never been a simple matter, and this is particularly true today. Objectivity, impartiality, nonpartisanship, and the like have quite rightly been suspect for a long time. Today, on the basis of many decades of critical scholarship, we know enough about backgrounds, preconditions, and preconceptions not to go looking immediately for objectivity and the like. The author of a source is as important as the source itself. Furthermore, one can no longer uncritically accept, if at all, the view (regarded near the end of the last century as a great discovery) that the God of Israel, and indeed only he, had revealed himself in the history of his people, so that they for theological reasons produced one of the oldest forms of history-writing, if not *the* oldest. First, the notion of a deity revealing himself in history does not apply so exclusively to Israel, as was claimed not so long ago and remains a widespread viewpoint today.[14] Second, the concept *history* is today not so unequivocal as it appeared to be earlier. Depending on the context in which it is used, its meaning varies. For instance, it is not the same whether I employ it in a general or a narrow sense; nor is it one and the same whether I use the word in a day-to-day or in a philosophical context and, in the latter case,

---

13. I refer to the important works by J. Van Seters, *Abraham in History and Tradition* (New Haven, 1975); and *In Search of History* (New Haven, 1983 [[repr. Winona Lake, Ind., 1997]]). Years ago I grappled with the problem in a similar way; cf. "Gerico, anatomia d'una conquista," *Protestantesimo* 29 (1974) 193–213; now in French, *RHPhR* 57 (1977) 1–17.

14. See B. Albrektson, *History and the Gods* (Lund, 1967) esp. p. 114 n. 52: "Israelite historiography is quantitatively [and probably also qualitatively, if I understand him correctly] superior to that of its neighbors." See further the introduction by B. W. Anderson to M. Noth, *A History of Pentateuchal Traditions* (Englewood Cliffs, N.J., 1972 [English translation of *Überlieferungsgeschichte des Pentateuch*]) xii–xxxii; on p. xxiii n. 25, he refers to an essay (not available to me) by W. Herberg, "Five Meanings of the Word 'Historical,'" in *The Christian Scholar* 47 (1964) 327–30. See also H. Cancik, *Grundzüge der hethitischen und alttestamentlichen Geschichtsschreibung* (Wiesbaden, 1976) esp. p. 88 and n. 180 to part 1. Instructive is the short work by R. Zoepffel, *Historia und Geschichte bei Aristoteles* (Heidelberg, 1975). I should also mention reference works. I myself considered this problem some years ago: "Iddio e la storia nel pensiero biblico," *Protestantesimo* 25 (1970) 129–37 (English, *Old Testament and Oriental Studies* [Rome, 1975] 59–66). What I believed in 1961 and 1964 to be capable of establishing rather conclusively would now have to be formulated in a much more qualified fashion, if at all.

whether it is used by an idealist, an existentialist, or a Marxist. We can certainly not go into this problem in detail here, and I am afraid that I must of necessity limit myself to what is important to our present concern.

4. It is now time to draw attention to a widespread but almost unrecognized phenomenon: It is not [[165]] only in Israel that somethng like two pictures of history exist, a "kerygmatic" and a historical-critical. This kind of duality is attested elsewhere—in fact, it occurs so frequently that it forms the rule. Normally, this kind of picture comprises the following elements: The first is a historical picture that is meant to teach, to train, sometimes to edify, or even to engender commitment in the hearer. This I would call, for just these reasons, the "kerygmatic" history, even if it has nothing to do with religion or theology. What is important, rather, is that it presents itself to the person(s) concerned as a confession that demands a personal response. This, by the way, is the kind of history most frequently encountered by the majority of people, for it meets us in the classroom and in the religious community. A second, entirely different picture of history exists as the object of scientific research, as *Historie*, and is therefore limited to a modest number of researchers. In theory at least this history should lack kerygmatic content for, as G. von Rad rightly emphasized, it strives for objectivity and for "a critically assured minimum."[15] In practice, however, it is always difficult, if not impossible, to draw a precise distinction between the two pictures, for the researcher also lives in a particular time and partakes of its philosophical categories.

5. History as "confession" comes to us, as stated, mainly in teaching and, wherever it is still common, in the tradition. With all its external distinctions of theme and situation, the fundamental content of such narration changes very little, and the reader repeatedly receives the impression that such history (the English use the word *story* for this type of history, not *history*) constantly moves toward the same purpose: to teach, to train, to engage. The *dramatis personae* and the situations are often amazingly similar, sometimes even interchangeable, for they are meant to work as examples, to lead to the reader's psychological identification with the main character: the virgin who offers herself for her virtue, for freedom, or for her land; the political or military leader who appears courageous, honest, unselfish, humble, who is magnanimous in victory, steadfast in crisis,

---

15. Von Rad, *Theologie*, 1.114, [[4th German ed. =]] 120 [[English: *Theology*, 1.108]]. The problem becomes all the more complex by virtue of the fact that the Old Testament sometimes describes the same event *in both forms*, without the editing apparently giving any special thought to this fact. I. L. Seeligmann himself once commented on this noteworthy circumstance; cf. I. L. Seeligmann, "Menschliches Heldentum und göttliche Hilfe: Die doppelte Kausalität im alttestamentlichen Geschichtsdenken," *ThZ* 19 (1963) 385–411. I begin with similar presuppositions, though I come to different conclusions; without Seeligmann's essay, however, I would have developed my ideas differently, if at all.

whose word is ever reliable. Seldom if ever does the idea that such figures move in a political or economic arena appear to play any role. They are mostly unpolitical, while naturally belonging to the political orientation of the author or tradent. Often they receive virtually hagiographic characteristics. As a result, their personal power of decision, their heroism, and their initiative appear all the stronger. And yet the enemy has no understanding of their virtues; indeed he sometimes even despises them. And should the enemy ever succeed, he rarely does so through bravery or ability but through nefarious means: coercion, trickery, betrayal, as if it were a sport. The enemy, where he is present, is normally evil, cowardly—in a word, ignoble. And even when he is presented as brave, this is generally done only to glorify the actual hero. To oppose such an enemy with virtues is to cast pearls before swine, but the hero, in his nobility, does not shy away from doing just that. When there is a problematic issue in these histories, it is the inner life of the hero—his doubt, his discouragement, the thoughts of his unworthiness—all of course repeatedly overcome through strong internal struggling. Such things as political-economic analyses, statistics, and the like have no place; at most, one hears of poverty, oppression, or both. Thus our genre [[*Gattung*]] resembles epic, though we cannot indentify the two without qualification, for an epic can also speak of the honorable, brave, and loyal enemy.

In recognizing such things, we are all the more in a position to determine something more specific about the Sitz im Leben [['life-setting']] of this kind of history. A few things have already been said.

Every society, whether already existing or still in the process of emerging, needs certain values and human models in order to arrive at its societal [[166]] contours and self-understanding. The models serve to make these values visible, to concretize them. The society in question can refer to them, appeal to them, and from them create its exemplars for rational-ethical, logically consistent behavior. In authoritarian societies of the recent past the "heroic" per se was often held up as a model, both in the individual and in the collective sphere. In nonauthoritarian societies, such models are admittedly harder to create. For the most part they are drawn from the past or present at those junctures where the connections to both are unbroken. In this regard, note the following:

a. Such models arise through a glorifying, often hagiographic, history-writing that cannot stand up to critical scrutiny. Thus they better qualify as propaganda than as true history-writing.

b. No matter how unpolitical they may be, they almost always are indirectly or directly tied to the political power—with the groups in power or with those striving for power, who therefore oppose the reigning models with "alternative" models.

6. Admittedly, it is today no longer possible to determine the origin of this highly simplified written genre: it simply exists, ever since teaching has been done in schools and elsewhere. It is misleading, however, to seek the origin in the genre *Idealbiographie*, which probably arose in the Near East. In this regard, in the West Semitic and Akkadian realm, I think of the autobiography of Idrimi, the king of Alalakh (beginning of the 15th century B.C.; *ANET*[3] 557ff.), which is so far probably the best-known and oldest writing in which a "confessional" view of history is prominent and a propagandistic purpose is unequivocal.[16] The protagonist is a hero who distinguishes himself through steadfastness and endurance, through bravery and skill, and through these virtues he succeeds in reconquering his paternal inheritance, the kingdom. Whether Idrimi was actually, as he claims, the rightful heir of the kingdom remains an open question. There are sufficient grounds for doubting that he was, however, so that on a closer look the narrative actually constitutes the legitimation of a usurper. A similar thought process can be found in the writings of the Hittites, though here it has to do not with autobiographies but with state treaties. Such materials are certainly to be handled with great caution by historians for the following reason: often a historical-critical spirit is ascribed to them, which in itself would make them precursors of the second kind of history-writing, the historical-critical. But a closer examination of the Hittite texts (especially of the "historical" prologues of the treaties) shows certain characteristic elements, such as structural symmetry and tendentious purpose, that are sufficient to emphasize both their distance from a direct reproduction of the event and their fundamental, intentional tendentiousness. The partner to the treaty, whether equal or inferior, was meant to be "convinced" that the Hittite Great King was fully in the right, which by the way, in most cases could easily have been achieved by other means! This too we cannot explore in detail; but see the latest literature.[17]

The *Idealbiographie*, to which a recent treatise is dedicated,[18] is also well attested in the Old Testament. One need only think of the Joseph story (whether we follow G. von Rad's or D. B. Redford's interpretation) or various reports about the judges of Israel, especially Gideon, or the figure of David, and perhaps also (in a postulated original edition as hero story)

---

16. On Idrimi, see Cancik, *Grundzüge der hethitischen und alttestamentlichen Geschichtsschreibung* (n. 14, unfortunately insufficient); and the important treatise by M. Liverani, "Partire col carro, per il deserto," *AION* 32 (1972) 403–15.

17. H. Cancik would like to attribute such a critical sense to Hittite literature from the Testament of Hattusili I (first half of the 16th century B.C.) to the end of the empire. Against such a view, decisive and convincing, see M. Liverani, "Storiografia politica hittita—I," *OA* 12 (1973) 267–97; further, "Memorandum on the Approach to Historiographical Texts," *Or* 42 (1973) 178–94. It appears to me that Cancik is unfamiliar with Liverani's works.

18. K. Baltzer, *Die Biographie der Propheten* (Neukirchen-Vluyn, 1975).

of Saul. Further, we could think of various prophet stories. The Deuteronomistic History (DtrG) in fact offers no *Idealbiographie* but does intend, as a "unique, monstrous *vaticinium ex eventu* [['a prophecy after the event']]"[19] "to interpret . . . theologically the ruins of two kingdoms."[20] This sufficiently indicates its didactic function—the reader or hearer is intended to learn not to imitate the mistakes of the fathers but to manage the good things received [[from God]] in a better way. [[167]] A modern history writer would certainly discover better reasons for the catastrophe of 587 or 586; however, within the frame of the Deuteronomistic Historian's goal, his presentation accomplishes its purpose splendidly, indeed better than the modern, historical presentation, which would hardly call its hearers or readers to repentance and a change of behavior.

But such approaches are found not just in Israel, even though Israel's theological orientation lends them a distinctive form. For instance, such approaches are well known also in classical antiquity, although at a later stage and without theological background. All "serious history writers of [classical] antiquity" evidently set themselves pedagogical goals: to study the past is useful, because the future can look the same or similar (Thucydides) or, as the Latin saying goes, *historia magistra vitae* [['history is the instructor of life']].[21] Sometimes, such a historical presentation has a special relationship to an earlier period of history that is regarded as normative or particularly noteworthy for the time of the tradent. For example, among Roman and Hellenistic writers whose object of investigation was ancient Roman history, especially Titus Livius, the ideal character of the early republican time was especially emphasized. It was then that customs and morality in public and private life were simple and strict, sometimes raw, but virtuous, honest, and heroic. The time in which the authors lived, by contrast, was one of decadence and moral decline, even if Livius and some of his contemporaries cherished the hope that Augustus would succeed in reviving the ancient Roman religion and *pietas* and the good, old morality. Thus the model of the Roman woman was impressively conveyed through figures such as Lucretia and Cornelia; that of Roman higher officials through men such as Cincinnatus and M. Atilius Regulus; that of fighters through heroes such as Mucius Scaevola.[22] This picture of ancient

---

19. Cancik, *Grundzüge der hethitischen und alttestamentlichen Geschichtsschreibung*, 40: "einziges, monströses *vaticinium ex eventu.*"

20. L. Perlitt, *Bundestheologie im Alten Testament* (WMANT 36; Neukirchen-Vluyn, 1969) 7ff.: "die Trümmer zweier Reiche theologisch . . . deuten."

21. On this topic, see the detailed study by M. Adinolfi, "Storiografia biblica e storiografia classica," *RiBib* 9 (1961) 42–58; further documentation there.

22. This is not the place, as I have already said, to pursue this theme in detail. See the reference works. Seeligmann also worked extensively in this area, though with a different approach and thus also with different results; I. L. Seeligmann, "Aetiological Elements in Biblical Historiography," *Ṣion* 26 (1960–61) 141–69 [Hebrew, with English summary].

Roman history has remained alive even in Western schoolteaching to this very day, which confirms my earlier claim that this is the level on which many people encounter history.

Approaching the matter from a different angle, we find in the Deuteronomistic History the presentation of the league of twelve tribes. Here one observes clearly that this is the form of government that a portion of the redaction advocates and holds up as an alternative to kingship. Thus it is not surprising that King Josiah attempted to revive elements of the old tribal league. The starting point was already different with Hosea and Jeremiah: it was the time in the wilderness that served as normative antecedent history for them, despite their relationship with the Deuteronomistic History. It is difficult to escape the impression that the other prophets also derived behavioral norms for the people from a prior history regarded as normative. It seems fairly clear, therefore, that despite all its theological distinctiveness the Old Testament operates with just such a conception of history as noted above. This only supports the appropriateness of applying the aforementioned distinction between different kinds of history-writing to the Old Testament.

In this manner, readers or hearers of the Old Testament were offered examples worthy of imitation or just the opposite, that is, examples with whom they were meant to identify psychologically or not. It is also interesting that these examples, just as in the classical world, often do not have the same meaning for the history writer as they appear to have for the pedagogue. Indeed, they often seem insignificant when viewed historically. But still, just as in the classical histories, they repeatedly appear in the foreground.

The situation is no different if we leave the biblical and classical world and approach our own times. Noble figures confront us in patriotic portrayals in school and in religious instruction. From the ancient church and the Middle Ages we have [[168]] legends of saints; from the later poetic recastings [[*Nachdichtungen*]] in Switzerland we have figures like William Tell and Winkelried; in old England there is Robin Hood, who stole from the rich to give to the poor; during the Reformation there circulated many a story about Martin Luther; and later also about the Puritans in the United States. Such stories were also woven around Frederick II of Prussia. In the German-speaking world, figures such as Michael Kohlhaas and Schillers Räuber meet us and provide the welcome occasion for later poetic recastings, without which we might not even remember them. In the American Revolution there is the figure of Paul Revere on horseback, of whom we would know next to nothing were it not for Longfellow's poem. Anyone who has attended school in Italy thinks immediately of course about Garibaldi, high atop his steed, while it is fitting for Austrians to feel the greatest spite. Even in our own century, which is certainly neither romantic nor sentimental, there are corresponding examples.

Now I am not at all claiming that such figures are fundamentally unhistorical, born out of a delight in creating fables or the like.[23] Depending on what story it is, it is entirely possible that historically valuable materials have been retained within it, about which we would otherwise know little or nothing. On the other hand, as already noted, we are dealing here with undeserved accentuation and emphasis, with painting in black and white that lacks any shading or complexity. Virtue, justice, the good cause, and nobility stand on the one side and provide the decisive conditions for certain victory, while vice, injustice, loathsomeness, and oppression stand on the other and are almost certain to lead to defeat—that is, to just punishment. The behavior of the individual repeatedly appears conclusive or decisive. For this reason, one happily hears of deeds that are seldom historically verifiable, but the possibility of verification is hardly the purpose of the respective narratives!

7. It is certainly tempting to explore from this perspective many traditions from the history of Israel, especially from its prehistory, but also from the time when people were already thinking in historically mature categories. But here an important observation must be made: insofar as ancient Israel lauds the redemptive acts of God as the decisive factor far more than the heroic acts of its ancestors, it allows little room for the heroic (a fact, incidentally, that was often cited by more-or-less antisemitic authors as a reproach).[24] Moreover, it seldom made a secret of the weaknesses of its main characters, at least in its older traditions. And as for virtues and the like to be imitated, these come to expression mainly in the relevant person's fulfilling specific divine commands or in obedience to the Torah in general. The subjects—for example, the patriarchs—often appear more like "anti-heroes": they fight little if at all;[25] they seldom come into consideration as examples of virtues to be emulated, as the three-times-recurring motif of the endangerment of the ancestress shows [[Genesis 12, 20, 26]]. When there is something in the patriarchs worthy of emulation, it has to do with, for example, faith. In the case of Abraham, see Gen 15:6 ("J"? or perhaps more likely a later redaction, close to Deuteronomy), where "faith" appears simply to mean (as in Isa 7:9b) that Abraham adopted the

---

23. See in this regard, however, the essay by D. Grimm, which takes an entirely different approach: "Geschichtliche Erinnerungen im Glauben Israels," *ThZ* 32 (1976) 257–68. At the same time, he shows how complicated the situation can be in individual cases.

24. One need only consider statements like those made by Friedrich Delitzsch, *Die große Täuschung* (Stuttgart, 1920) 93ff.

25. This point was emphasized by M. Rose, "Entmilitarisierung des Kriegs?" *BZ* n.s. 20 (1976) 196–211.

stance in respect to God that was required of him. An opposite example is provided by Ahaz (Isaiah 7). In "E" as well Abraham is known as a man of faith (see Gen 22:1–18). It appears, however, that J also pursued rather clear and decisive political goals: for example, the legitimation of the Davidic–Solomonic kingdom, as is evident in various texts.[26] But in both cases, the didactic function of the texts is hardly neglected, even if it occurs on a different level. It is no different with Moses: here the sources do indeed give ample indication of his giftedness and moral greatness, but the tradition is also well aware of his [[169]] obvious hesitancy—Exod 4:10ff. indicates that it was only through God's intervention that he became what he was. Indeed, in the wider context, he did not exactly distinguish himself as a man of faith: Num 20:12; 27:12–14; Deut 1:37; 3:24; compare Deut 34:4. It is thus not surprising that Deuteronomy and the Deuteronomistic History developed a principle of retribution whereby faith and obedience became conditions for well-being, while unbelief and disobedience became conditions for judgment. Such thinking eventually becomes the axis around which the Chronicler's history turns. Only much later, in Hellenistic time, did human heroism begin to play a role in Israel and stories such as 2 Macc 6:18ff. and 7:1ff. become ever more prominent. In other words, when it has to do with heroes and heroic deeds in ancient Israel, it is God and not man who is the hero. Thus one sings of the *ṣidqôt yhwh* [['righteous/saving acts of Yahweh']] (see Judg 5:1ff. and 2 Sam 1:19ff.), even though human heroism is given greater scope in these texts than elsewhere (these are, after all, epics).

8. To summarize: It appears to me that the prehistory of Israel, as it is now presented in the older sources of the Pentateuch and in the Former Prophets (but also in many parts of the later history of the people), belongs to that kind of history-writing that I have provisionally called "confessional history." To this very day it continues to accomplish its purpose. This kind of history is attested, as I have indicated, among all peoples and societies right up to the present, and it will not cease to exist. Indeed, it will continue even where history-writing has long since achieved a historical-critical stage. Thus it has nothing to do with an alleged "primitive" cultural stage in a people's political, intellectual, and economic development, for its purpose, as we have seen, is education within a particular community.

---

26. For specific references, see my *Introduzione all'Antico Testamento* (3d ed.; Brescia, 1979) 154ff. (English translation, 2d ed.; Philadelphia [1980] 101ff.). Incidentally, it is not uninteresting that Umberto Cassuto, who always rejected the Documentary Hypothesis, himself placed his "maestro di altissimo genio" [['master of greatest genius']], allegedly responsible for the redaction of the Pentateuch, in the final period of David's kingdom; and he did so, in fact, on the basis of texts that are regularly assigned to "J"; see *La questione della Genesi* (Florence, 1934) 394–95.

The Old Testament seems well aware of this as it now and then announces its catechetical intentions—one thinks for instance of the "children's questions" regarding etiologies.[27]

If we accept this, then the "divergence" between the confessional and historical-critical pictures of history, as formulated by Gerhard von Rad at the end of the 1950s, presents not a problem but the rule, provided that it is possible to draw strict boundaries between the two.

---

27. I have for some time assumed catechetical intentions behind the so-called "children's questions"; cf. "Kultätiologische Sagen und Katechese im Hexateuch," *VT* 10 (1960) 341–47.

Historie and *Geschichte*

[[207]] The Old Testament has no concept of history, in the sense that history is only *history* that can be documented and that follows a verifiable course governed by causal laws. While the Old Testament does contain historical writing in approximately this sense, it does not recognize the sharp distinction of this kind of *history* from all unverifiable events which cannot be rationally documented in dates and facts—a distinction which grows out of Enlightenment thinking. In approaching the question of history in the Old Testament, then, one cannot proceed from an understanding of history which selects from all other events only those that are *historically* documented as authentic and which makes the contrast *historical–unhistorical* an absolute criterion equivalent to authentic–inauthentic.[1]

History in this sense, which grows out of the Enlightenment, is limited to the time and to the form of nationhood. Outside this definition re-

Reprinted with permission from *Understanding the Word: Essays in Honor of Bernhard W. Anderson* (ed. James T. Butler, Edgar W. Conrad, and Ben C. Ollenburger; Journal for the Study of the Old Testament Supplement Series 37; Sheffield: JSOT Press, 1985) 207–19.

Author's note: To my colleague, B. W. Anderson, in grateful memory of our encounters in Heidelberg, and the semester during which we taught together at Drew.

[*Translator's note*: The two German words, *Historie* and *Geschichte*, are both rendered by the English 'history'. In this essay when 'history' translates *Historie*, or its derivatives, it will be italicized. Otherwise, it is to be understood as a translation of *Geschichte*.]

1. The designation "the *historical* Jesus" is problematic, because the New Testament contains no *historical* reports. Likewise problematic is the designation of a method of interpretation as *historical*-critical, if it deals with non-*historical* texts.

main pre-history and primitive history, in which there are no documents. This definition of *history* presupposes the invention of writing. According to this definition, pre-literate communities can have no history in the strict sense. The early stages of the later civilizations, and primitive nations as well, remain excluded from history. That is a problematic demarcation which can no longer be maintained.[2]

Just as problematic is that *history* in this sense, limited to the time and to the form of nationhood, actually makes this one form of community absolute: the subject of *history* is only the nation, or nations. All other forms are subordinated to this one. A politically constituted nation [*Volk*] is usually composed of tribes; a tribe is composed of clans (families). They are henceforth recognized only as integrated into or subordinated under the state; the tribe and the family are reduced to the categories of the "provincial" and the "private." They are no longer independent subjects of history.[3]

For the Enlightenment concept of history, beginning and end are [[208]] *eo ipso* [['by definition']] excluded from history. All conceptions of the course of events which lead from a beginning to an end are thus *unhistorical* from the outset, and are relegated to the realm of philosophy or religion. But then, at the same time, the history of humankind is excluded from *history*, because the subject of the primeval and final events in myths and religions is humankind. What is said of humankind can in no case be historical. A further limitation of the Enlightenment's understanding of history follows from the reduction of events to that which is verifiable through documentary evidence. What can be authenticated from the distant past through documents are primarily events fixed in names and dates: kings and the years of their reign, battles and treaties, names of defeated foes, conquered lands and vanquished cities. What cannot be comprehended in names and dates, however, are cycles of growth and decline and, in general, the part played by natural processes in historical development. What goes on silently between documented events can often be more important than the cardinal events themselves.

Historical occurrence is bi-polar: it comes to pass in events and in fixed processes, which are given in human phenomena. Historical-critical methods cannot comprehend these processes and events in the same way. Therein lies a further limitation of the concept of history formed in the eighteenth and nineteenth centuries.

---

2. In place of the framework of *historical* dates, e.g., the dates of kings, primitive peoples have genealogies, which exercise the same function.

3. The absolute priority of the political is demonstrated also in a present tendency to broaden the concept of the political excessively.

History in the Old Testament

'History' (Historie) and the History of Israel

If the Old Testament deals with the history of Israel, the term "history" here involves several levels of meaning, only one of which is equivalent to *history* in the strict sense. The growth of the Pentateuch is toward the goal of Israel's development as a nation in a settled and politically constituted way of life. Prior to this goal, however, is a series of stages, none of which can be called strictly *history*, and whose form of linguistic expression is thus not historical writing. Let us assume that somewhere in the world discoveries were made which brought to light texts that corresponded to the patriarchal history. One would expect them to be studied not by historians but by ethnologists or sociologists. There are no *historical* texts which, despite all the energy expended on them by exegetes, would show the patriarchal history to have a *historical* "core." We have in the Pentateuch a work of history only in the sense that it intends to [[209]] present the prehistory of the nation Israel. It is not, however, a *historical* work in the sense of the nineteenth century's understanding of history. For its fundamental linguistic unit is the narrative: the patriarchal history has grown up out of narratives. But narrative is not a form of *historical* presentation. "Israel's history" has a broader meaning than the "*history* of Israel."

The movement beyond the pre-*historical* into the *historical* is shown in exemplary fashion in Genesis 36, the final chapter of the patriarchal history proper. In this chapter the descendants (*tôlᵉdôt* = history) of Esau are presented in three sections, which correspond to three stages of the history of Esau (= Edom). The chapter enumerates the sons of Esau in the first section (vv. 1–14); in the second (vv. 15–19) the princes of Esau (paralleled by the sons of the Horite Seir and the princes of the Horites, the previous inhabitants, in vv. 20–30); and in the third section the kings of Edom (vv. 31–39). The history of the family, the tribe and the nation follow on one another, each in its own linguistic form. It would not be appropriate to apply to this chapter the criterion *historical–unhistorical*, according to which only the material contained in the royal chronicles would be *historical*, while the other two sections would be *unhistorical*. Both of the first two sections are considered by the author to belong as much as the third to the history of Edom. All three sections participate in reality. All three sections speak of actual events—of the three successive stages of one and the same community. It is only that these three stages are presented in different forms of speech. The understanding of history which underlies this chapter is broader than that of the nineteenth century.

In addition to the pre-political, the Old Testament also recognizes a post-political stage in Israel's history. Israel continues to exist after its political collapse. In political significance it is reduced to a province, the province of an empire, and from that point forward continues to have political significance in the strict sense only as a component of an empire. It is registered and appraised in the central offices of the empire, in the edicts of this province's administration, in the succession of its administrators, in the case of revolts, of religious conflicts, etc.

But even in these circumstances the history of Israel continues underground in the province of Judah. It perseveres in a historical consciousness which continues to know itself as Israel and which understands its present situation as a stage in the history of the [[210]] nation on the basis of the nation's past, including its political catastrophe. This is demonstrated in the historical works which arose during this period, the Deuteronomistic and Chronicler's histories. It is also evident in Lamentations and in Israel's future expectation. There corresponds, then, to the pre-*historical* phase of Israel's history, a post-*historical* phase. This post-*historical* phase is made possible in that the nation preserves its identity as a nation in its religion, and in that the communal form of the family continues to uphold its function as the bearer of the religious tradition—a function which it had in the pre-political stage of Israel's history—and at the same time preserves the historical traditions as well.

The historical works of this post-political phase have a strongly "*unhistorical*" character; their *historical* worth is, in part, questionable. Nor does their significance lie in their historical-critical verifiability, but in their preservation of the identity of Israel in the post-political phase of the nation's history. This significance attaches in even greater measure to the emergence, in this late period, of the Old Testament as canon, the Bible of the nation Israel, which was nothing less than decisive for the preservation of Israel's identity. Precisely from this post-political situation it is understandable that all three phases of the history reported in the Bible belong to the historical understanding of those who formed the canon: the pre-*historical*, the *historical* and the post-*historical*. It is these three phases together that constitute the history of Israel. Thus the historical understanding of the Enlightenment is, in this respect, inadequate.

That which forms these three components of Israel's history into a coherent history in three phases in the action of God on Israel's behalf and the response of Israel to this divine action. This reciprocal relation between God and Israel is not confined to the middle phase but encompasses all three. That is possible because the action of God is not restricted to the social form of the nation but comprehends also the prepolitical and post-political forms of community: the family, the tribe, the religious community and individuals as a part of humankind. This comprehensive divine action is governed by two poles. In the Old Testament

God's saving and judging activity is differentiated from his acts of blessing; the one is accomplished through events, the other in the fixed processes of growth and decline, of vitality and decay. He acts not only in a history of salvation, governed by the "mighty acts of God," which reach from [[211]] the deliverance from Egypt to the judgment on Jerusalem, but also in the pre-historical period of the patriarchs, and in the post-historical as well. Moreover, both in the latter and in the former, he works through families and small groups.

The Relationship of Historical to Non-historical Forms of Community and Forms of Speech

Forms of Community.   The Old Testament's understanding of history is shown with particular clarity in the history of the succession to David's throne because in it the new form of life represented by the nation-state is a completely new discovery. It is a discovery of the political as an autonomous sphere of life, with its own laws of historical causality, in particular contrast to the histories of the patriarchs and the judges. Precisely because the political is here discovered for the first time, the struggle to understand and to master the new form on the basis of the old can be recognized in the Throne Succession Narrative. The struggle is that of trying to make the experience of reality characteristic of the old era fruitful for the new. In the case of the monarchy there is the possibility that familial experiences can be exploited for their political significance. Actually, the Throne Succession Narrative deals in large part with family conflicts, beginning with the adultery of David in 2 Samuel 12. But here, in contrast with the treatment of the same motif in the patriarchal history, the political effect is made clear. Gerhard von Rad saw in this a "marked deficiency, in that political conflicts are anchored so exclusively in the personal and family spheres."[4] At the basis of this critique is the assumption that familial affairs have no place in *historical*-political events, which have to do instead with the nation, not with the family.

To the contrary, the author of the Throne Succession Narrative consciously presents the succession to the throne as a complex combination of familial and political events. One encounters here the same motifs as in the patriarchal history: the childlessness of Michal; David's adultery (the temptation of the powerful to break into the family and take for himself whatever he wants; cf. Gen 6:1–4; Genesis 12); the death of the favorite wife's son; Ammon's violation of Tamar; Absalom's desertion of his

---

4. Gerhard von Rad, "Die Anfänge der Geschichtsschreibung im alten Israel," *TBü* 8 (1958) 148–88 (ET: "The Beginnings of Historical Writing in Ancient Israel," *The Problem of the Hexateuch and Other Essays* [Edinburgh: Oliver & Boyd, 1966] 166–204).

father's house and his return; rebellion against the father; rivalry between brothers. The only way in which the operation of the new form of government, the dynasty, can be presented is in terms of familial events.

[[212]] The contrast reaches its climax in the death of Absalom and David's lament over his death. The author shows the two lines which merge in his work and which have led to this contrast when Joab, the army commander, must compel David to attend to what is politically necessary. The conclusion with Solomon's succession to the throne thus contains its dark side. Leading up to it is a broken continuity, which thus brings into the history of the monarchy a critical aspect. All that glimmers in the kingdom of Solomon is not gold.[5]

Another example of reflection aimed at reconciling two different forms of community is the Joseph narrative. It presents an encounter between the form and understanding of life characteristic of families following their herds, and that of a royal court. The monarchical form of government is sharply rejected by the brothers of Joseph at the beginning; at the conclusion it is the monarchy with its surplus economy which saves the family threatened by famine. This narrative is connected to the controversy over kingship as a form of government early in the monarchical period, during which some were friendly and others hostile toward the monarchy. The editor of the Joseph story wants to point out to its opponents the positive economic aspects of this form of government; in doing so, however, he lets its dangers and temptations appear as well. But above all he wants to show them that the essential elements of family-centered life can be taken up into the new monarchical form of government.

Both of these examples show that very serious consideration was given in Israel to the relation between the two forms of community. In both cases this consideration took place in the passage of unsettled family groups to the sedentary, national form of life in the monarchy. Since this passage signified a threatening break with tradition, it is perfectly understandable that the monarchy would be rejected precisely by the conservatives. For them acceptance of the monarchy was only possible to the extent that earlier forms of community were integrated into the new.

These two examples also make clear that it is not possible in the Old Testament understanding of history to isolate the national-political form of life from all others and to ascribe to it an absolute value.

Forms of Speech. The Old Testament understanding of history is also differentiated from that of the nineteenth century by forms of speech. The form of speech characteristic of a purely rational understanding of

---

5. I have shown this in more detail in my essay, "Zum Geschichtsverständnis des Alten Testament," *Probleme Biblischer Theologie. Festschrift Gerhard von Rad* (ed. H. W. Wolff; Göttingen: Vandenhoeck & Ruprecht, 1971) 611–19.

history in terms of causal determination is that of [[213]] the report, or that of historical writing based on documents, which are themselves dependent upon reports. It is concerned with facts, with dates and with causal connections. The report form is appropriate to it; that is universally granted. The Old Testament also knows and uses this report form for the *historical* phase from the beginning of the monarchy until the exile.[6] But because the history of Israel encompasses, for the Old Testament, both a pre-political and a post-political phase, history can also be presented in narratives. The pre-political period of Israel's history has grown up out of narratives, the passage from the pre-political to the political phase is depicted in narrative, and narratives can appear in the midst of a historical report (e.g., 1 Kings 9).[7] In addition to narrative, the primeval history and the patriarchal history contain genealogy, and the patriarchal history also contains itineraries (a narrative and enumerative form of speech).[8] While in the narratives the concern is with events and their consequences, the genealogies preserve the continuity of events in the sequence of generations. Both are pre-*historical* and pre-national forms of historical presentation which emerge from the family setting. While both were earlier seen as secondary constructions, as by Wellhausen and Gunkel, they are now recognized, particularly through ethnological studies, in terms of their own original significance. The way in which genealogy passes into royal chronology is shown in Genesis 36 (see above).

There is a whole series of other forms of speech for the transmission of pre-*historical* events. A characteristic example is provided by the tribal speeches (Genesis 49; Deuteronomy 33) about the history of the tribes prior to the emergence of the nation. The etiological motifs in the narratives should also be included here, in particular the naming of a place after an event. These etiological narratives were formerly seen without exception as *unhistorical*; their original significance has since been recognized (see the discussion between M. Noth and J. Bright).

The Problem of the Exclusion of Religion from "History"

In his essay on the throne succession of David, Gerhard von Rad refers to the judgment of the historian, Eduard Meyer, on this story. Meyer is dis-

---

6. The New Testament, on the other hand, contains no *historical* reports. This is one of the reasons why Old Testament and New Testament studies are so estranged from each other.

7. In our understanding of history that would be impossible, because we tend to feel that the historical novel (Felix Dahn, Gustav Freitag) and historical drama (Shakespeare, Schiller) must be sharply separated from a *historical* report.

8. See C. Westermann, *Genesis* (BKAT 1/1, 2; Neukirchen-Vluyn: Neukirchener Verlag, 1966–81) 1.8–23; 2.46–51.

turbed "that these thoroughly profane texts serve Jews and Christians as holy Scripture." Von Rad objects to the contrary that these stories mention God in three important places (2 Sam 11:27, 12:24, 17:14).[9] In addition to this we need to reflect on the context out of which the history is transmitted to us.

[[214]] It was already pointed out that the Old Testament does contain historical writing in the specific sense of the term; this is limited essentially to the four books of Samuel and Kings and to the time of the nations Israel and Judah. But the demarcation of *historical* texts in the Old Testament is possible only to a very limited extent. This is true in the first place because the texts to be recognized as *historical* in Samuel and Kings are embedded in the redaction of the Deuteronomistic History, which as a whole has a thoroughly religious orientation. Thus the distinction of the political from the religious elements is extremely difficult, if not impossible. That the author of the Deuteronomistic History wants to speak of what has happened between God and his people is shown most clearly in the early history of prophecy, which has been incorporated into his work.[10] But also the traditions which lie behind this work, such as the Throne Succession Narrative or the History of David's Rise, speak self-evidently of the action of God in history (in more places than the three listed by von Rad); the authors do not want, nor are they able, to abstract this history from its connection with God.

In addition, a delineation of those texts which are *historical* is only possible to a limited extent, because the historical books in the canon of the Old Testament belong to a totality which consists of three parts: history–word–answer.[11] Against the reproach of Eduard Meyer it must be said that Scripture is the Old Testament in its totality. To the history of Israel in all of its phases there belongs first the word of God issued into history, and in addition the answer of the people in word and deed. Corresponding to this, the history of Israel is an essential part of both the other divisions of the canon, the Prophets as well as the Psalms.

Those elements of the Prophets and the Psalms in which we can recognize the emergence of a historical consciousness in Israel show, on the

---

9. 11:27, "But the thing that David had done displeased Yahweh." 12:24, ". . . and Yahweh loved him (Solomon)." 17:14, "For Yahweh had ordained to defeat the good counsel of Ahithophel."

10. The author of this historical work understands the speech and action of the prophets, and the reaction of the kings and the people, as a component of the history of the monarchical period.

11. For a more detailed treatment, see my *Elements of Old Testament Theology* (Atlanta: John Knox, 1982).

other hand, that the sphere of the *historical*-political in the Old Testament is not to be dissociated from the relation of the people of Israel to God.

In the Psalms. In the laments of the people there is the motif of contrast: the people cry out of their distress, urging God to remember his earlier acts of salvation and holding up this contrast before him. Why? Past history is actualized in the prayer of the people, which demonstrates an explicit historical consciousness. In the Psalms of praise the redeemed, in their joy directed to God, narrate his saving acts as a sequence of events: their distress–their entreaty–God's [[215]] attention–God's intervention. They have experienced a history with God. It can then be understood that out of this grow entire historical Psalms. Without this historical consciousness which arises in experiences with God there would never have emerged the great historical works of the Old Testament.

In the Prophets. The relation of word and history is so explicit in the prophets that one needs only to refer to a few points. The prophecy of salvation, or promise, accompanied Israel in its entire history. We should not separate the promise of the land in the patriarchal history, or the promise of deliverance from Egypt, from the events which then took place. These promises had an eminently historical significance, even if they cannot be regarded as '*historical*' according to the stringent criteria of *historical* criticism. They have set events in motion. In the tension which arose between promise and fulfillment the Israelites and their ancestors learned to understand history as a journey, as duration, as continuity. The prophets' announcements of judgment, to which the same remarks apply, have in addition the *historically* evident significance that they were able, as particularly Deutero-Isaiah demonstrates, to bridge the abyss of national collapse, which brought with it the termination of the kingdom and the end of the temple. Apart from prophecy, the emergence of the Deuteronomistic History is inconceivable. But apart from prophecy, the emergence of the historical conception in the three other phases mentioned is just as inconceivable.

The founders of the Enlightenment concept of history could draw a line of demarcation between *history* and religion in a phase of human history which began with the first movements toward enlightenment in antiquity. In these movements the separation of politics from religion was made possible by leaving to individual citizens the choice of belonging to a religious community, leaving the citizenry as a whole without a religious affiliation. But this separation cannot be applied to a phase in which being a part of the state is identical to being a part of the national religion. It makes a fundamental difference whether the religion is sustained by the nation as a whole constituted as a state, or whether it is sustained by one religious group among others with the same nation.

Beginning and End, the History of Nations
and the History of Humankind

For the *historian* there is no such thing as beginning and end, because [[216]] neither is *historically* verifiable. Since for the *historian* history is identical to the history of a politically constituted nation, or nations, there can be no history of humankind. One can speak of world empires, but there has never been a world empire in the sense that humankind has been united in *one* nation.[12] But this does not accord with our natural way of thinking. Rather, it would seem, if a person has a beginning and an end this would apply as well to humankind as a whole. For that reason people all over the world have been speaking for millennia of the beginning and the end, and also of the history of humankind; one has only to think of the doctrine of world epochs.

The concept of a history of humankind has been taken up in philosophy of history. A typical idealistic example is Karl Jaspers in *The Origin and Goal of History*.[13] He sees in the midst of world history what he calls the "axial period," between 800 and 200, but especially around 500 B.C. In this period the age of myth has come to an end, and the step into the universal and spiritual has been made. At the beginning it is limited to one general locale but then it is spread over the world. The axial period assimilated all others, and from it world history receives a single structure which penetrates everywhere. The axial period signifies the joining together of humankind in the action of world history.

To this could be added the example of materialism. The Marxist-Leninist understanding of history speaks of a determinism of history in five phases. First is the epoch of the primitive community, then the epochs of slavery, feudalism, capitalism and finally socialism, in its two phases of socialization and the classless society.

The Bible too has a conception of the history of humankind, but in it the world and humanity are bound inseparably together. Both are God's creation. As God's creation they have a beginning, and to the beginning there corresponds the end. Only the creator is eternal, not the world. The history of humankind in the Bible is consistently conceived in terms of beginning and end. This is shown already in the primeval history in which the creation of humankind corresponds to the judgment of annihilation in the deluge. In this the Bible is not in agreement with *history*, because the latter does not recognize the beginning or the end of humankind. The

---

12. To speak of "world history" means to speak of the history of the nations of the world, but not of the history of humankind.

13. New Haven: Yale University, 1953.

Bible does, perhaps, coincide with the natural sciences for which the human race has a beginning and is proceeding toward an end.[14]

The biblical primeval history clearly distinguishes between the beginning of humankind and the beginning of nations and states. In [[217]] Genesis 1–9 it speaks of the creation of the world and of human beings, and of the origin of all humankind. Only then, in Genesis 10 and 11, does it go on to speak of the division of humankind into nations. Things are quite different in the near eastern empires, Assyria–Babylon and Egypt, in which humankind originates together with the monarchy and the state: "When kingship was lowered from heaven." In this respect the historical understanding of the nineteenth century is closer to the ancient near eastern conception than it is to that of the Bible.

The distinction between the creation of humankind and the origin of the state corresponds to a fact that has not yet been properly explained: the motifs of creation and of the primeval period found all over the world are in striking agreement with one another.[15] With reference to this primeval event one can speak of a form of human culture which is decidedly prior to that of the state. Corresponding to this, in the Bible the family-oriented form of community is coordinated with creation, but not with the state.[16]

There is also a correspondence between what the Bible says about the beginning and what it says about the end, especially insofar as the subject of the final events, as of the primeval events, is humankind. Beginning and end correspond to each other in a whole series of motifs, especially in Revelation, as has often been observed.

It is particularly characteristic of biblical apocalyptic, which is indeed common to both Testaments, that what is said in it about final events is connected with the Old Testament understanding of history. With the end of history, the history of the nations and also the particular history of God's people come to an end and flow again into the history of humankind. From the perspective of history's end, the history of humankind is fitted into a sequence of periods. Thus, the great empires have a particular significance for the apocalyptic drama, particularly in the book of Daniel—the image composed of four elements in chap. 2, and the sequence of four beasts in chap. 7. It is this apocalyptic view which first makes possible a conception of world history: the history of the nations

---

14. This agreement of the Bible with the natural sciences, over against history, is of the greatest significance. The concept of 'progress' must be thought through anew from this perspective.

15. The same applies to pre-*historical* forms of speech, such as the narrative.

16. The family will exist so long as humankind exists. The same cannot be said of the state.

moving toward its end becomes the history of humankind. Such a conception is only possible as a product of the Old Testament understanding of history which looked on the totality of events as a whole.

It is certainly no accident that this conception of the events of the end in terms of the history of humankind has its locus in the third phase of Israel's history, when Israel was merely a province within an [[218]] empire. This demonstrates again the Old Testament's comprehensive understanding of history as a totality.

History and Fiction
What Is History?

V. PHILIPS LONG

[[58]] "History . . . is all fictionalized, and yet history."[1] It may come as a surprise to readers unfamiliar with recent debates in biblical studies to discover the frequency with which the term *fiction* has begun to appear in discussions of biblical narrative. Robert Alter, for example, in a provocative essay entitled "Sacred History and the Beginnings of Prose Fiction," emphasizes the vital role of fiction in biblical historiography. He even goes so far as to claim that "prose fiction is the best general rubric for describing biblical narrative."[2] It will be my aim in this chapter to argue that the concept of fiction, *if it can be properly defined and guarded against misunderstanding*, may be fruitfully employed in discussions of biblical historiography, but that it is in practice often applied in inappropriate and confusing ways, perhaps not least by Alter himself.[3] I shall suggest further that the confusion over fictionality derives in part from ambiguities within the term *fiction* itself. To complicate matters further, the term *history* is also ambiguous, being understood even by nonspecialists in at least two distinct senses.

Confusion over the role played by fictionality in history is [[59]] apparent since some are proclaiming fictionality as lying at the heart of history-

Reprinted with permission and excerpted from *The Art of Biblical History* (Foundations of Contemporary Interpretation 5; Grand Rapids: Zondervan, 1994) 58–86.

1. B. Halpern, *The First Historians: The Hebrew Bible and History* (San Francisco: Harper & Row, 1988) 68.

2. The essay constitutes chap. 2 of *The Art of Biblical Narrative* (New York: Basic Books, 1981), and the quotation is from p. 24.

3. See M. Sternberg, *The Poetics of Biblical Narrative: Ideological Literature and the Drama of Reading* (Bloomington: Indiana University Press, 1985) 23–30.

writing, while others are declaiming fiction as the very opposite of history. Craig Blomberg insists, for example, that "a historical narrative recounts that which actually happened; it is the opposite of fiction."[4] Similarly, Colin Hemer observes that "it is no good raising the question of historicity if we are dealing with avowed fairy-tale or fiction."[5] But Alter seems to have in mind some other concept of fiction, for he insists that fictionality and historicity are not antithetical. He writes:

> In giving such weight to fictionality, I do not mean to discount the historical impulse that informs the Hebrew Bible. The God of Israel, as so often has been observed, is above all the God of history: the working out of his purposes in history is a process that compels the attention of the Hebrew imagination, which is thus led to the most vital interest in the concrete and differential character of historical events. The point is that fiction was the principal means which the biblical authors had at their disposal for realizing history.[6]

A first step in coming to terms with the apparent, disagreement is to clarify what the terms history and fiction can mean. History, for example, as the term is commonly employed, can refer either to the past or to the study of the past; or, to put it another way, history can denote both events in the past and verbal accounts of these events. Consider the following illustration provided by David Bebbington.

> A visitor to the Tower of London may well buy a copy of its history. When 'history' is used in this way it means something different from 'history' in the claim that history repeats itself. A history of the Tower of London is its written history, a record of the past. The history that may or may not repeat itself, on the other hand, is the past itself, not a record but what really took place. In the English language the word history can mean either what people write about time gone by, that is historiography; or else it can mean what people have done and suffered, that is the historical process.[7]

No doubt many disputes could be settled if the various terms of discussion were consistently defined and applied. If, for example, as Philip Davies suggests, the term *history* were reserved for "the events of the past as a *continuum*" and the term *historiography* for "the selective telling of

4. C. L. Blomberg, *The Historical Reliability of the Gospels* (Leicester: Inter-Varsity, 1987) xviii n. 2.

5. C. J. Hemer, *The Book of Acts in the Setting of Hellenistic History* (Tübingen: J.C.B. Mohr, 1989 / Winona Lake, Ind.: Eisenbrauns, 1990) 34.

6. *Art of Biblical Narrative*, 32.

7. *Patterns in History: A Christian Perspective on Historical Thought*, new ed. (Leicester: Apollos, 1990) 1.

those events," much confusion could be avoided.[8] But since such terminological consistency is frequently lacking in academic discussion,[9] about all one can do is to recognize that *history is* used in two quite distinct senses—to refer to the past itself and to interpretive verbal accounts of the past—and to discern in each context which is intended.[10] (It is perhaps also worth mentioning that much confusion and misunderstanding could be avoided if specialists would bear in mind that laypersons often have little understanding of the way *history* and *historical* are used as technical terms in professional discussions and, not surprisingly, are baffled when confronted by statements that both deny that some event is *historical* and at the same time insist that this does not mean it didn't happen.[11] To the layperson, history is what happened in the past.)

What about the term *fiction?* To the average person, who [[60]] tends to regard history and fiction as virtual opposites, a statement like the one by Alter quoted above—"fiction was the principal means which the biblical authors had at their disposal for realizing history"—will seem like nonsense. But Alter explains:

> The essential and ineluctable fact is that most of the narrative portions of the Hebrew Bible are organized on literary principles, however intent the authors may have been in conveying an account of national origins and cosmic beginnings and a vision of what the Lord God requires of man. We are repeatedly confronted, that is, with shrewdly defined characters, artfully staged scenes, subtle arrangements of dialogue, artifices of significant analogy among episodes, recurrent images and motifs and

---

8. J. Rogerson and P. R. Davies, *The Old Testament World* (Englewood Cliffs: Prentice-Hall, 1989) 218.

9. E.g., with respect to Old Testament studies, J. Van Seters (*In Search of History: Historiography in the Ancient World and the Origins of Biblical History* [New Haven: Yale University Press, 1983] [[reprinted, Winona Lake, Ind.: Eisenbrauns, 1997]] 209) comments: "the subject of Israelite historiography has become highly diversified and the terminology increasingly ambiguous and confusing, [so that] the same terms are used in quite different ways."

10. This discussion of *history* might easily be extended to cover such terms as *historic* and *historical, Historie* and *Geschichte,* and so forth, but what is important for our present purposes is the basic distinction between history-as-event and history-as-account. On the former pair, see G. B. Caird, *The Language and Imagery of the Bible* (London: Duckworth, 1980) 202; on the latter, see R. N. Soulen, *Handbook of Biblical Criticism* (Atlanta: John Knox, 1976), s.v. "Historie"; F. S. Leahy, "The Gospel and History," *Reformed Theological Journal* (Nov. 1985) 52–54.

11. Cf. J. Barr, *The Scope and Authority of the Bible,* Explorations in Theology 7 (London: SCM, 1980) 9: "Again, it may be argued that the view just expressed assumes that God does not act in history and does not affect it. It assumes nothing of the sort. It simply observes that we do not apply the term 'history' to a form of investigation which resorts to divine agency as a mode of explanation."

other aspects of narrative that are formally identical with the means of prose fiction as a general mode of verbal art.[12]

What Alter seems to be saying, in essence, is that literary shaping and artistry play no less significant a role in biblical historiography than in fiction. Halpern puts it succinctly when he states that "history [by which he means history as account] is fictional and employs the devices of all narrative presentation."[13]

The point in all this is that the word *fiction*, like the term *history*, may be used in two senses. Unfortunately, the two senses of fiction are not always clearly distinguished in discussions of narrative historiography. Alter, for example, sometimes speaks of "historicized fiction" and other times of "fictionalized history," without ever offering a clear articulation of the rather fundamental difference between the two.[14] The crucial term in each of these expressions, however, is the last one. In "historicized fiction," the weight of emphasis falls on *fiction*, suggesting that whatever bits of [[62]] factual information may be included the story itself is nonfactual (as, for example, in a historical novel). In "fictionalized history" on the other hand, the weight falls on *history*, the claim being that the story is a representation of a real event in the past, whatever fictionalizing may be involved in the crafting of the narrative.[15] Only when this double sense of the term fiction is understood—fiction as *genre* and fiction as *artistry*, or *craft*—does it become possible to agree with Blomberg that history "is the opposite of fiction" and at the same time to agree with Halpern that "all history . . . is fictionalized, and yet history."[16] Blomberg's focus is on history and fiction as distinct literary genres, whereas Halpern's point seems to be that any representation of the past, inasmuch as it is not (literally) the past, involves a "fictionalizing" aspect.[17] Halpern has in mind *form*

12. "How Convention Helps Us Read: The Case of the Bible's Annunciation Type-Scene," *Proof* 3 (1983) 116.

13. *First Historians*, 269.

14. He does show awareness of the distinction on occasion; see, e.g., *Art of Biblical Narrative*, 25, 33–34, 41. But his lack of clarity on this important point still leaves him open to criticism; e.g., D. Patrick and A. Scult (*Rhetoric and Biblical Interpretation*, JSOTS 82 [Sheffield: Almond, 1990] 50) write: "Alter has done much to open the Bible to serious reading by a wider audience, but by limiting himself to aesthetic judgments, he still does not integrate the Bible's truth-claims, as they are spoken, into his interpretative approach. He essentially reads the text as realistic fiction."

15. For a similar distinction, cf. F. F. Bruce ("Myth and History," in *History, Criticism and Faith*, ed. Colin Brown [Leicester: IVP, 1979] 84), where he favors mythologization of history" to "historicization of myth," but prefers "theological interpretation of history" to both.

16. Both quotations occur at the beginning of this essay.

17. Cf. M. A. Powell, *What is Narrative Criticism?* (Minneapolis: Fortress, 1990) 100: "The real world is never identical with the world of a story, even if that story is regarded as portraying life in the real world quite accurately."

(i.e., the way the story is told), while Blomberg is apparently thinking of *function* (i.e., for what purpose the story is told).

So long as we bear in mind this important distinction, between form and function we may speak of a certain fictionality involved in all narrative discourse while still maintaining the common-sense differentiation between *historical* narratives, which "claim to tell us what really happened," and *fictional* narratives, which "portray events that of course by definition never happened, [though] they are often said to be true-to-life."[18] The point is simply that fictionality of a certain sort is as likely to be found in the historian's toolbox as in the fiction writer's.[19]

[[63]] Still, given the potential for (and indeed the presence of) much confusion resulting from the use of an ambiguous (bivalent) term like *fiction*, it would be far better, at least with respect to the perceptions of the average person, to substitute a term like *artistry* to describe the historian's literary technique, and reserve the term fiction for the nonfactual genre of that name. Since this is not likely to happen, however, it will be necessary when reading this or that scholar to discover how the term *fiction* is being used.

The issues raised so far can be elucidated by comparing historiography, which might be fairly described as a kind of a verbal representational art, with a visual type of representational art such as painting.[20]

---

18. D. Carr, "Narrative and the Real World: An Argument for Continuity," *HTh* 25 (1986) 117.

19. Sternberg (*Poetics of Biblical Narrative*, 28) illustrates this point well by citing an evaluation of historian Garret Mattingly's *The Defeat of the Spanish Armada* (1959) by a fellow professional historian and observing "how many of [Robert] Alter's *measures of fictionality* are invoked to define Mattingly's professional *excellence as a historian*" (insertion and italics mine).

20. The analogy between historiography and art has a venerable history and continues to evoke interest today; see, e.g., F. R. Ankersmit, "Historical Representation," *HTh* 27 (1988) 205–28. No analogy is perfect, of course, and a criticism that could be made of this one is that a text should not be treated "as a static spatial form, like a painting, a sculpture, or a piece of architecture" (so R. M. Fowler, *Let the Reader Understand: Reader-Response Criticism and the Gospel of Mark* [Minneapolis: Fortress, 1991] 42), since reading is a "dynamic, concrete, temporal experience, instead of the abstract perception of a spatial form" (ibid., 25). I would argue, however, that the distinction between reading texts and viewing paintings should not be overpressed. While countless tourists may spend a few hours in the Louvre casting a glance this way and that to see the paintings, it can hardly be said that many of them have properly *viewed* the paintings. Time and dynamic interplay are as involved in giving a painting a "close viewing" as they are in giving a text a "close reading." If anything, the distinction between viewing a painting and reading a text is in the sequence of perception: with a painting, one generally begins with an impression of the whole, then proceeds to study individual *passages* of the painting, and finally returns to a greater appreciation of the whole in the light of its parts; with an unfamiliar narrative, one must generally begin by reading the individual passages in sequence, which leads eventually to an impression of the whole, and then finally to a greater appreciation of the parts in the light of the whole.

History-Writing as Representational Art

In his oil painting classes in Chicago, my former teacher Karl Steele would occasionally reflect on a criticism that he, as an impressionist painter, sometimes received from those more attracted [[64]] by what is commonly called abstract or expressionist art. The basic criticism was that since his paintings were *representational*, or at least *realistic* (primarily landscapes and seascapes), there was less *artfulness* in his craft—he simply *copied* nature. Steele's response was to challenge his critics to inspect at very close range any two-inch square of one of his canvases. Should the critics agree to the challenge, what they would find would not be nature, or even an exact copy of the appearance of nature, but a tiny abstract painting! In other words, each of Steele's *realistic*[21] paintings consisted of a series of abstractions, which taken together and viewed from the proper vantage point gave a convincing and indeed realistic impression of the scene depicted. In one sense, then, Steele's paintings were *fictions* and not *literal* renderings of reality. There could be no question of counting blades of grass or leaves on trees; each brush stroke was an abstraction, just paint on canvas. In another sense, however, his paintings were very much representations of reality, imparting to receptive viewers a truer sense and appreciation of the scene, as Steele perceived it, than even the best color photography could have done.

The above illustration relates to the issue of historiography in the following manner. Common sense suggests that it would be a *reductio ad absurdum* to argue that since Steele's paintings at one level make use of techniques indistinguishable from those employed by abstract or expressionist painters, they therefore cannot be representational, or make reference to a reality outside themselves. One can find, however, among the writings of those who challenge the representational capacity of narrative discourse, statements that seem similarly reductionistic. Roland Barthes, for example, in drawing attention to what he calls "the fallacy of referentiality," writes:

> [[65]] Claims concerning the "realism" of narrative are therefore to be discounted. . . . The function of narrative is not to "represent," it is to constitute a spectacle. . . . Narrative does not show, does not imitate. . . . "What takes place" in a narrative is from the referential (reality) point of

---

21. I am using the term in a general, not a technical sense, as a virtual synonym for *naturalistic*—i.e., concerned with depicting the world more or less as it appears. For a more technical description of these two terms, see, e.g., K. Reynolds with R. Seddon, *Illustrated Dictionary of Art Terms: A Handbook for the Artist and Art Lover* (London: Ebury Press, 1981) ad loc.

view literally *nothing*; "what happens" is language alone, the adventure of language, the unceasing celebration of its coming.[22]

This sounds very much like saying that "what happens" in one of Steele's paintings is *paint alone*. Barthes's statement may be true of some narratives, but surely not all. If paintings can be broadly divided into representational and nonrepresentational varieties, into those that attempt to depict some aspect of the world outside and those that simply celebrate the potentialities of paint as a medium, then is it possible that narratives can be similarly classified? Of course, even representational (referential) painters enjoy considerable freedom in terms of how they choose to depict their subject—compositional and stylistic decisions have to be made.[23] But this does not mean that a generic distinction cannot and should not be made between paintings that are representational and those that are not. By the same token, I would contend that a distinction can and should be made between narratives that are essentially representational (historiographical) and those that are not.

On what basis then are narratives to be classified? Form alone is not a sufficient criterion: "there are simply no universals of historical vs. fictive form. Nothing on the surface, that is, [[66]] infallibly marks off the two genres. As modes of discourse, history and fiction make *functional* categories that may remain constant under the most assorted *formal* variations and are distinguishable only by their overall sense of purpose.[24] In other words, "there are no formal features, no textual properties that identify a given text as a work of fiction,"[25] yet history and fiction can still be distinguished on the basis of their overall purpose. Aristotle, writing more than two thousand years ago, came close to saying the same thing: "The difference between a historian and a poet is not that one writes in prose and the

---

22. "Introduction to the Structural Analysis of Narratives," (1966) 124; quoted by Hayden White ("The Question of Narrative in Contemporary Historical Theory," *HTh* 23 [1984] 14), which see for an extended critique of Barthes's position (pp. 12–15).

23. E. H. Gombrich ("The Mask and the Face: Perception of Physiognomic Likeness in Life and in Art," in *Art, Perception, and Reality*, ed. Maurice Mandelbaum [Baltimore: The Johns Hopkins University Press, 1972] 1–46) offers an extreme example of this in his description of a portrait painted by Picasso in which the subject's head is given a perfectly oblong shape, but then, in "a balancing of compensatory moves . . . to compensate for her face not being really oblong but narrow, Picasso paints it blue—maybe the pallor is here felt to be an equivalent to the impression of slimness" (p. 30). The interesting point is that despite the abstractions, the painting retains a referential function.

24. Sternberg, *Poetics of Biblical Narrative*, 30.

25. So K. J. Vanhoozer "The Semantics of Biblical Literature: Truth and Scripture's Diverse Literary Forms," in *Hermeneutics, Authority, and Canon* (ed. D. A. Carson and John D. Woodbridge; Grand Rapids: Zondervan, 1986) 68, summarizing the view of J. R. Searle, "The Logical Status of Fictional Discourse," *New Literary History* 6 (1975) 319–32.

other in verse. . . . The real difference is this, that one tells what happened and the other what might happen."[26] This general point can be illustrated by observing the chiastic structure of the last four chapters of 2 Samuel.

21:1–14	A	Famine resulting from Saul's sin is stopped
21:15–22	B	Short list of Davidic champions
22:1–51	C	Long poetic composition: David's song of praise
23:1–7	C'	Short poetic composition: David's last words
23:8–39	B'	Long list of Davidic champions
24:1–25	A'	Plague resulting from David's sin is stopped

As Sternberg points out, chiasm is now widely recognized as "one of the indisputable literary devices" found in the Old Testament, and yet the chief goal of the epilogue to 2 Samuel "remains informational and memorial." The conclusion to be drawn from this is that while "form can produce or imply an artistic function, it still cannot enthrone one regardless of context."[27]

If, then, historical literature and fictional literature are "distinguishable only by their overall sense of purpose," *context* becomes one of the primary means of discovering this purpose. [[67]] We are reminded of one of the fundamental principles of discourse introduced in the preceding chapter [[not reproduced here]]—viz., that "each successively higher level of textual organization influences all of the lower levels of which it is composed." The question to be asked then is this: What is the apparent function of a particular narrative within its broader context? A sense of the purpose of a narrative is, as Sternberg puts it, "a matter of inference from clues planted in and around the writing."[28] Again let me illustrate with an example from the visual arts.

Imagine that we are viewing a painting of an old railroad depot. Imagine also that for the moment we are not allowed to look around to gain our bearings and to discover where the painting is hung. Without some knowledge of the painting's setting, we may be unable to decide whether the painting's primary function is a *historical* one—to be a lasting reminder of the appearance of an old landmark—or an *aesthetic* one—simply to be a pleasing work of art. Imagine that we are now allowed to look around. If we find that the painting is prominently displayed (with a bronze plaque beneath it) in the foyer of a brand new railroad terminal, we shall likely

26. *Poetics*, Loeb Classical Library (Cambridge, Mass.: Harvard University Press, 1982) chap. 9 (1451b).
27. *Poetics of Biblical Narrative*, 40–41.
28. Ibid., 30.

conclude that some *historical* function is being served (perhaps this was the old terminal that was demolished to make room for the new one). If, on the other hand, we find that the painting is displayed in an art gallery along with other paintings depicting various subjects, we shall be more inclined to assume that the aesthetic function is primary. Now, of course, the historical (or referential) purpose implicit in the first scenario does not exclude a concern with artistic quality. It is the greater aesthetic appeal of a painting over a photograph that will have prompted the railroad company to choose the more expensive option. The first scenario does imply, however, that the artist will have worked under some *referential constraints*. He will have been constrained by the actualities of the subject, at least to the point of making the subject recognizable. In the second scenario, though the artist may in fact fairly represent the appearance of the old depot, he will have been under no obligation to do so.[29]

[[68]] What is true of visual art (paintings) is true also of verbal art (narratives). The difference between a narrative whose primary purpose is representational (or referential) and one whose primary purpose is aesthetic is the degree to which the artist is constrained by the actualities of the subject matter. As Matt Oja puts it, "historians are constrained by the need to discover and work with a set of facts which already exist and which they look upon from without. Writers of fiction are not so constrained. . . . A fictional narrative does not have objective reality until the author creates it."[30] In some instances external evidence—material remains, eyewitness reports—may offer clues as to a narrative's purpose and its degree of adherence to the "facts,"[31] but in all instances our quest to discover a narrative's overall sense of purpose should begin with attention to clues in and around the narrative. If both the subject matter of the narrative itself and the nature of the surrounding context suggest a representational purpose, then we may assume that the writer has been in some measure constrained by the facts. I say "in some measure," because neither representational artists nor historians simply reproduce their subjects.

---

29. Illustrations of the continuum between referential and aesthetic interests might easily be multiplied: an architectural blueprint is referential, while an architectural rendering of the planned construction combines representational and aesthetic interests in almost equal measure; a "mug shot" is referential, while a portrait combines representational and aesthetic interests, etc.

30. "Fictional History and Historical Fiction: Solzhenitsyn and Kiš as Exemplars," *HTh* 27 (1988) 120; similarly, Sternberg, *Poetics of Biblical Narrative*, 29.

31. For nuanced discussions of the slippery concept of "facts," see M. Stanford, *The Nature of Historical Knowledge* (Oxford: Basil Blackwell, 1986) 71–74; R. H. Nash, *Christian Faith and Historical Understanding* (Grand Rapids: Zondervan, 1984) 93–109.

History-Writing as a Creative Enterprise

I have argued that the chief difference between writers of history and writers of fiction is that the former are constrained by the facts of the past, while the latter are not. Does this disallow any creative input from the historian in the writing of history? Not at all, for as we have just noted, historians do not simply reproduce the past. Rather, they must contribute to the work they produce in at least a couple of ways. First, they must study all available [[69]] evidence pertinent to their subject and develop their own vision of the past. Second, this vision must be encoded in a verbal medium in such a way that it can be shared with others. The first task, "the historian's construction of the past," is described by Stanford as "the pivot of historical knowledge" that stands between "history-as-event and history-as-record." The second task, the transposition of this construction into "written or spoken form," is equally important, since it "stands between the historian's mental construction and those of the audience."[32]

Few historians or philosophers would dispute the notion that writers of history make significant contributions in the ways mentioned above. What is hotly disputed, however, is the *nature* and *extent* of the historian's contribution. One of the major points of debate is whether *narrative form* as such is an aspect of reality itself or is a product solely of the historian's imagination. A narrative is characterized by having a plot, for example, with a beginning, a middle, and an end. Are such features aspects of reality itself or constructions created solely in the mind of the historian? Does the past present itself in narrative form, as a meaningful sequence, or is it a meaningless chaos, upon which the historian must impose a narrative structure?

Some historians and literary theorists today assume that "real events simply do not hang together in a narrative way, and if we treat them as if they did we are being *un*true to life."[33] Others, however, disagree. David Carr, for example, strongly challenges the view that meaningful sequence is merely an invention of historians.[34] He sets the stage by quoting such notables as Louis Mink ("Life has no beginnings, middles and ends. . . . Narrative qualities are transferred from art to life") and Hayden White ("Does the world really present itself to perception in the form of [[70]] well-made stories? Or does it present itself more in the way that the annals

---

32. *Nature*, 143–44. Similarly, J. Axtell ("History as Imagination," *The Historian: A Journal of History* 49 [1987] 458) writes: "Since history at its best is shared discovery, the historian's final and most important task is to *translate* his vision, his 'achieved awareness' and understanding, of the past for the modern reader."

33. Carr ("Narrative and the Real World," 117), who goes on to contest this view.

34. Both in the article mentioned in the preceding note and in a book entitled *Time, Narrative, and History* (Bloomington: Indiana University Press, 1986).

and chronicles suggest, either as a mere sequence without beginning or end or as sequences of beginnings that only terminate and never conclude?").[35] Carr himself maintains that "narrative is not merely a possibly successful way of describing events; its structure inheres in the events themselves."[36]

If Carr is correct, does this mean that the historian simply finds historical narratives rather than constructs them? I would contend that the answer lies somewhere in the middle; and that two extremes should be avoided: (1) that which denies the importance of the historian's vision and creative imagination and (2) that which denies to the past any inherent/coherent structure whatsoever. Historians, as verbal representational artists, find themselves in a position analogous to that of visual representational artists. The latter can paint a number of different pictures of a single subject, no two of which are alike, but this does not mean that the subject itself lacks inherent structure or that the artists are unconstrained by the facts. The production of a representational painting involves a coordination of creativity and constraint, the creativity of the artist under the constraint of the subject. The subject matter does not simply present itself to the artist as a painting waiting to be painted. The artist must make various kinds of choices. First, a subject must be chosen from among the multitude of possible subjects in the world around. Second, a vantage point must be chosen from which to view the subject. Third, compositional decisions must be made: what are to be the boundaries or limits of the painting? Do these boundaries result in an overall sense of balance? Depending on the purpose of the painting, the artist may have some freedom to arrange or rearrange elements of his subject. The portrait artist, for example, enjoys considerable freedom to rearrange objects in the setting but is rather constrained when it comes to rearranging the subject's face! Fourth, a paint medium must be chosen (oil, acrylic, watercolor, etc.), the palette of colors selected (will it include a limited or a full range of colors?), the style decided (will the painting be rendered [[71]] in intricate detail with small brushes or will it be executed boldly and rapidly with a palette knife?), and so forth.

Just as the physical world does not present itself in such a way that no creative choices are required of artists who would depict some aspect of it, so the past does not present itself in such a way that historians need make no creative choices in the construction of a historical account of some aspect of it. But if the past does have some inherent structure (as I believe it does), then the first task of historians is to seek to discern that

---

35. "Narrative and the Real World," 118.
36. Ibid., 117.

structure. Beyond this, they must also choose a point of view—the most appropriate perspective from which to depict the subject and the "best light" in which to see it. And they must make aesthetic choices—how shall the work be composed, what degree of detail shall be included, what shall be the boundaries of their "picture" of the past, and so forth.

Constraint by the subject matter, point of view, aesthetic choices—our painting analogy can help us begin to understand how the three impulses mentioned in the preceding chapter might be coordinated in the biblical literature, not only its narratives but also in other genres (such as poetry) that may include historical reference. The *historiographical* impulse implies constraint by the subject, the *theological* implies point of view, and the *literary* implies aesthetic choices. But the fruitfulness of the painting analogy does not end here. So far, the creative choices required of painter and historian alike are but preliminaries to the actual execution of the work. When it comes to the latter, there are again a number of helpful parallels between the requirements of visual and of verbal representation.

Characteristics of Successful Representation

Of the numerous points of advice that Karl Steele would customarily offer his painting classes, several stand out as particularly important. First, he would often instruct students at work on their paintings to blur their vision occasionally by half-closing their eyes; the effect of this was to eliminate the distraction of too much detail and to facilitate perception of the major contours and tonal relationships of the subject. Second, and as a corollary to this first point of advice, he would stress the importance of standing back from the canvas, or even walking backward, in order to view the subject and the canvas from a distance. Close proximity to the canvas, he would say, does not guarantee more accurate results but quite often the opposite, since the painter sometimes gets lost among the trees and loses sight of the overall shape of the forest. Third, he would contend that the most effective paintings are those that exploit the suggestiveness of visual ambiguities—lost edges, mysterious shadows, etc. He would point out that a common mistake of beginners is to attempt to record the great mass of detail exhibited by the subject, whereas the best way to achieve a realistic representation is to be very selective, limiting the depiction of details to a suggestive few so as to allow the mind of the viewers to fill in the rest.

These procedures of the visual artist—what we might call, *creative means* to *representational ends*—find ready analogues in the work of the verbal artists we call historians. Since the "Ideal Chronicler"—viz., one who records everything that happens as it happens—does not exist, it is obvious that all historians must, to some extent at least, simplify their presentations of their subjects.[37] As Peter Ackroyd rightly observes, "the recounting of what happened, even a few moments later, inevitably introduces simplifications, selections, interpretations."[38] Indeed, one of the main tasks of historians, Axtell reminds us, is to discern and represent "the larger patterns, structures and meanings behind particular events and facts which contemporaries were not able to see."[39]

How do historians accomplish this? Where data are plentiful, [[73]] historians must seek to discern the major contours of the subject by, as it were, half-closing their eyes so as to perceive the big picture. Alternatively, or additionally, they may enjoy the advantage of being able to view the subject from a distance, from across the room of time. As important as empirical evidence and eyewitness testimony are, historians standing at some remove from the subject are often in a favorable position to discern the major shapes and relations of the past. We often say of prominent contemporaries (presidents or prime ministers) that "it will be interesting to see how history treats them." Again, Ackroyd makes the point well: "the historian who writes at some distance from the events may be in a better position to give a true appraisal than one who is so involved as to see only a part of what makes up the whole."[40] One reason that the historian writing some time after the event may be at an advantage is that "the significance of a historical phenomenon is often recognized by its sequences or consequences, i.e., its posthistory."[41] Finally, historians, like painters, must avoid the temptation to include too much detail in their depiction. There must be an economy to their craft; if carefully selected, only a few suggestive details may be necessary to capture their subject (Esau's hairiness, Ehud's left-handedness, Eli's heaviness, etc.). "What matters most in history . . . is the great outline and the significant detail; what must be avoided is [a] deadly morass of irrelevant narrative in between."[42]

---

37. For a critical evaluation of the concept of the "Ideal Chronicler," see P. A Roth, "Narrative Explanations: The Case of History," *HTh* 27 (1988) 1–13; also L. O. Mink, "Narrative Form as a Cognitive Instrument," in *The Writing of History: Literary Form and Historical Understanding*, ed. R. H. Canary and H. Kozicki (Madison: University of Wisconsin Press, 1978) 140. Even if an exhaustive "Ideal Chronicler" existed, the resulting history would be so massive as to be useless.

38. "Historians and Prophets," *Svensk Exegetisk Årsbok* 33 (1968) 21.

39. "History as Imagination," 457.

40. "Historians and Prophets," 21.

41. M. Tsevat, "Israelite History and the Historical Books of the Old Testament," in *The Meaning of the Book of Job and Other Biblical Essays* (New York: Ktav, 1980) 181; note also Tsevat's important qualification that "the significance is not bestowed by the latter upon the former; the consequences are indicators and not generators" (ibid.).

42. Axtell, "History as Imagination," 459; quoting Lewis Namier.

The Adequacy and Authority of Representation

Simplification, selectivity, suggestive detail—these hallmarks of effective historiography are reminiscent of the kinds of features often highlighted in discussions of the *literary* artistry of [[74]] biblical narrative. I hope that by now enough has been said to make the point that literary artistry and reliable historiography should not be set in opposition. But still the challenge might be raised: "In making a case that the Bible presents us with 'representational paintings,' have you not reduced our confidence in what the Bible can tell us about the past? Wouldn't photographs serve us better?" The answer to this question is that it very much depends on the artist! Admittedly, painting often involves a greater interpretive component than does photography (though even the latter requires that creative choices be made), but this is not necessarily a bad thing. As Carl F. H. Henry asserts, "Christian faith requires not simply the redemptive historical act but its meaning or significance as well; historical research alone is impotent either to guarantee any past event or to adduce its meaning or theological import."[43]

"But I'm just interested in the bare facts," the challenge might continue. Such a statement is both wrong-headed and a bit naive. Since the past is *past* and unrepeatable, it will never be possible to recover the "bare facts" pure and simple, at least not all of them; we are inevitably dependent on witnesses and evidences. As Caird explains, "History has a factual content, but it comes to the historian not as fact but as evidence, emanating from persons with whom he must engage in conversation."[44] Even if we could return to the past and record it on videotape, this would still not guarantee us an adequate understanding of the past. In the aftermath of the Persian Gulf War, I remember hearing a commentator on National Public Radio express a frustration he had felt while the war was in progress. It went something like this: "They kept sending us videotapes, but they didn't tell us what they meant. We had the video images, but no interpretation."

It is the greater interpretive capacity of painting over photography that makes it the generally preferred medium for portraiture (visual historiography). And it is the greater interpretive (explanatory) capacity of literary narrative over bare chronicle that makes it the preferred medium of biblical historiography. [[75]] These preferences are only justified, of course, to the extent that the narrators or painters are skillful and competent in their craft, and they have adequate access to their subject. No one

---

43. *God, Revelation and Authority* (Waco: Word, 1976) 2.330.
44. *Language and Imagery*, 202.

would dispute that a portrait by an artist who is incompetent or who has no clear notion of the character and appearance of the subject will be inferior (on either artistic or referential grounds, or both) to even a simple photograph of the subject. But recent studies are increasingly demonstrating that the biblical narrators were consummate literary artists. And for those willing to accept it, their claim to have written under divine inspiration more than adequately guarantees their access to their subject.[45]

There are, of course, many in today's world who dismiss any notion of divine inspiration. In so doing, however, they find themselves in a rather perplexing position. As Mink explains in "Narrative Form as a Cognitive Instrument," many moderns continue to embrace (consciously or unconsciously) a concept of Universal History—the notion that "the ensemble of human events belongs to a single story"—but they have no notion as to "who devises or tells this story. In its original theological form, as with Augustine, Universal History was the work of divine Providence; but as the idea became secularized by the eighteenth century, God the Author retreated, leaving the idea of a story which is simply *there*, devised by no one . . . but waiting to be told by someone" (pp. 136–37). Mink's proposed solution to this rather unstable state of affairs brought about by modernism's elimination of the Author but retention of the Story is, in the end, to abandon altogether the residual belief that the past contains an "untold story to which narrative histories approximate" and to assert that only "individual statements of fact" are "determinate." But since "the significance of past occurrences" cannot be grasped except insofar as they find a place within a narrative, Mink concludes that a story must yet be told, and it is *we* who must tell [[76]] the story; *we* must "make the past determinate in that respect" (p. 148). Having shown "God the Author" the door, modernism is left to tell the story itself. And though Mink does not address the issue, it would seem that since "we" denotes a plurality of persons, none of whom possesses more than a relative authority, the inevitable result of Mink's "solution" will be a thoroughgoing historical relativism.

The alternative to modernism's dilemma, is to embrace a concept of biblical inspiration such that the authority of the Bible's pictures of the past (whatever may be the differences between them, and however incorrectly we may at times view them) is as secure as the authority of the One who inspired them.

---

45. As Henry aptly puts it (*God, Revelation and Authority,* 2.330): "Empirical probability can indeed be combined with inner certainty when the meaning of specific happenings is transcendently vouchsafed, that is, when that meaning is objectively given by divine revelation." Cf. also Sternberg, *Poetics of Biblical Narrative,* 32–35.

An Example: Samuel–Kings and Chronicles

In the preceding paragraph, mention was made of differences that sometimes exist among the Bible's pictures of the past. Indeed, even biblical accounts of the same events often differ in various ways. Some might wish that these differences did not exist, but the fact of the matter is that our having different presentations of the same subject often puts us at an advantage! Multiple presentations enable us to view the subject from different angles and under various lights, and to benefit from the narrative artists' own interpretive contributions. However brilliantly a biography may be written, or however masterfully a portrait may be painted, our knowledge of the life and visage of a given individual is surely enhanced if we have access to more than one biography or portrait. When approaching the New Testament's four gospels, for example, or the Old Testament's two histories of the monarchy (Samuel–Kings and Chronicles), we do well to keep this perspective in mind.[46] [[77]]

To investigate how we might go about negotiating differences among biblical accounts purporting to cover similar historical terrain, let us look more closely at the synoptic histories of the Old Testament. As Roddy Braun has observed, a comparative reading of Israel's synoptic histories affords an opportunity "to learn much about both the nature of historical writing in Israel and the manner in which God used His inspired writers to speak a message to their own day."[47] Even a quick reading discovers that Samuel–Kings and Chronicles paint rather different pictures, not only in points of detail but even in terms of their overall shape. The Chronicler's history, for instance, has little or nothing to say on matters that were of great concern in the earlier history of Samuel–Kings: reference to King Saul (whose election, rejection, and decline occupy much of 1 Samuel) is limited to a brief summary of his death and its cause in 1 Chronicles 10;[48]

---

46. The real question, of course, for those who are perplexed by differences among accounts of the same event(s) is whether or not these constitute *irreconcilable* differences—that is, contradictions—that would force us to call in question the narrative artists' competence, motives, control of the subject matter, or the like. While it would be obscurantist to deny that the Bible presents vexing difficulties for which solutions are not readily forthcoming, I would maintain (1) that a properly nuanced understanding of the nature and purpose of the biblical literature greatly lessens the number of perceived difficulties and (2) that the remainder of stubborn cases should be held in abeyance or, preferably, made the object of special study by those whose technical training and theological orientation might place them in a position to find, not strained harmonizations, but true solutions.

47. "The Message of Chronicles: Rally 'Round the Temple," *Concordia Theological Monthly* 42 (1971) 502.

48. For a recent discussion of the significance of the brief treatment of Saul in Chronicles, see Saul Zalewski, "The purpose of the story of the death of Saul in I Chronicles X," *VT* 39 (1989) 449–67; cf. also Ackroyd, "The Chronicler as Exegete," *JSOT* 2 (1977) 2–32.

nothing is said of the Saulide opposition to David's rise to power (though this opposition is a focus of interest in the second half of 1 Samuel and the early chapters of 2 Samuel); no mention is made of David's adultery with Bathsheba and his arranged murder of Uriah, nor of the disastrous political and domestic consequences of these actions (though 2 Samuel 11–20 are largely taken up with these matters); no mention is made of Adonijah's threat to Solomon, or of Solomon's palace, or of his apostasy (though these figure prominently in 1 Kings 1–11); no mention is made of the prophetic ministries of Elijah and Elisha that occupy center stage in 1 Kings 17–2 Kings 8, save the report of a letter of judgment from Elijah to Jehoram of Judah in 2 Chronicles 21:11–17 (which letter, [[78]] curiously, is not mentioned in Kings);[49] no mention is made of the fall of the Northern Kingdom (an event of signal importance recounted in 2 Kings 17). The list could continue and be presented in much greater detail, but enough has been indicated to show that by virtue of its omissions the Chronicler's presentation of Israel's past is given a quite different shape than that of Samuel–Kings.

Not only does the Chronicler's picture omit much that is found in Samuel–Kings, it also includes much that is not found in the earlier corpus: extensive genealogical lists stretching back to Adam (1 Chronicles 1–9); additional lists of David's mighty men (chap. 12); reports of David's levitical appointments (chaps. 15–16); descriptions of his preparations for temple building and temple worship (chaps. 22–29); much additional material relating to the Kingdom of Judah (various additions in the stretch of text from 2 Chronicles 11–32); and Cyrus's decree marking the end of the exile (36:22–23).

From this very general overview, we can see that the Old Testament's two histories of the monarchy present different pictures in terms of overall shape and composition. But the differences between them are not limited to such large-scale matters. The two histories often differ significantly even in the way they render the same event or in the way they portray the same person. As an example, we might compare the two accounts of God's dynastic promise to David as presented in 2 Samuel 7 and 1 Chronicles 17.[50] That "there is a clear literary relationship [[79]] between the

---

49. For discussion, see R. Dillard, 2 *Chronicles*, WBC (Waco: Word, 1988) 167–69.

50. Other instructive examples would include, e.g., the Chronicler's depiction of King Abijah, which is comparatively more positive than that found in Kings (cf. 2 Chronicles 13 and 1 Kings 15; for discussion see D. G. Deboys, "History and Theology in the Chronicler's Portrayal of Abijah," *Biblica* 71 [1990] 48–62); the Chronicler's presentation of David's census as compared to the Samuel account of the same episode (1 Chronicles 21 and 2 Samuel 24; see Dillard, "David's Census: Perspectives on 2 Samuel 24 and 1 Chronicles 21," in *Through Christ's Word: A Festschrift for Dr. Philip E. Hughes*, ed. W. R. Godfrey and J. L. Boyd

two" is beyond dispute.[51] But when we compare the two passages, we discover a number of differences between them. The chart on the next two pages basically follows the NIV, but with some adjustments to reflect more closely the Hebrew texts. In the chart, some (though not all) differences have been highlighted: material peculiar to one passage only is placed in italics and the location of this material is indicated by a [[single underline]] in both texts; [[double]] underlining identifies noticeable differences in phraseology; alternation of the divine names *God* and *Lord* (Yahweh) are in bold type. (See chart now [[pp. 250–251]].)

A side-by-side reading of these parallel texts discovers numerous divergences—some minor, others more major. What are we to make of them? In the present context we must limit ourselves to a few brief comments on some of the apparently more significant differences. But first a word of caution: it should not be assumed that all differences represent motivated changes by the Chronicler.[52] Some may simply reflect the Chronicler's freedom to paraphrase or generalize, as he does often in his composition.[53] Other differences seem to result from stylistic or lexical preferences.[54] In still other instances, the Chronicler may simply be repeating what he finds in his *Vorlage* (the text of Samuel with which he was familiar).[55]

[[82]] There are, however, some differences between the two renditions that may require explanation on other grounds. Particularly striking are the Chronicler's omission in v. 13 of any reference to the chastisement

---

[Phillipsburg, NJ: Presbyterian and Reformed, 1985] 94–107; J. H. Sailhamer, "1 Chronicles 21:1–A Study in Inter-Biblical Interpretation," *TrinJ* 10 [1989] 33–48); the depiction of Josiah and his reforms in Chronicles as compared to the presentation in Kings (see, on 2 Chr 34:4–7 and 2 Kgs 23:4–14, D. L. Washburn, "Perspective and Purpose: Understanding the Josiah Story," *TrinJ* 12 [1991] 59–78); and many more.

51. So H. G. M. Williamson, "Eschatology in Chronicles," *TynB* 28 (1977) 134.

52. See Dillard, "David's Census," 94–96; Williamson, "History," in *It is Written: Scripture Citing Scripture. Essays in Honour of Barnabas Lindars*, ed. D. A. Carson and H. G. M. Williamson (Cambridge: Cambridge University Press, 1988) 31–32.

53. This may be all that is involved in the Chronicler's "You are not the one . . ." (v. 4) instead of 2 Samuel's "Are you the one . . ." (v. 5).

54. An example would be the Chronicler's preference for the shorter form of the first person singular pronoun (*'anî*) over the longer form (*'ānōkî*) that is prevalent in Samuel–Kings. Whereas in Samuel–Kings the ratio of shorter to longer is something like 3 to 2, in Chronicles it is more like 25 to 1.

55. For example, 2 Sam 7:7 has "tribes" (*šibṭê*), while 1 Chr 17:6 has "leaders" (*šōpṭê*). Since the latter is contextually more appropriate and is attested also in 2 Sam 7:11, it appears that the Chronicler's *Vorlage* may preserve the better reading. On this and other matters discussed in this paragraph, see R. L. Braun, *1 Chronicles*, WBC (Waco: Word, 1986) 198. For speculation on the character of the Chronicler's Hebrew *Vorlage*, see Dillard, "David's Census," 94–95.

2 Samuel 7:1–17

[[80]]After the king was settled in his palace *and the LORD had given him rest from all his enemies around him*, [2] the king said to Nathan the prophet, "Here I am, living in a palace of cedar, while the ark _____ _____ of **God** remains in a tent." [3] Nathan replied to the king, "Whatever you have in mind, *go ahead and* do it, for the **LORD** is with you." [4] That night the word of the **LORD** came to Nathan, saying: [5] "Go and tell my servant David, 'This is what the LORD says: "Are you the one to build me a house to dwell in? [6] I have not dwelt in a house from the day I brought the Israelites up *out of Egypt* to this day. I have been moving from place to place with a tent as my dwelling.

[7] Wherever I have moved with all the Israelites, did I ever say to any of their tribes whom I commanded to shepherd my people *Israel*, 'Why have you not built me a house of cedar?' " ' [8] Now then, tell my servant David, 'This is what the LORD Almighty says: "I took you from the pasture and from following the flock to be ruler over my people Israel. [9] I have been with you wherever you have gone, and I have cut off all your enemies from before you. Now I will make your name *great*, like the names of the greatest men of the earth. [10] And I will provide a place for my people Israel and will plant them so that they can have a home of their own and no longer be disturbed. Wicked people will not wipe them out anymore, as they did at the beginning [11] and have done ever since the time I appointed leaders over my people Israel. I will also give you rest from all your enemies. The LORD declares to you that the LORD will establish a house for you: [12] When your days are over and you rest with your fathers, I will raise up your offspring to succeed you, who will come from your own body, and I will establish his kingdom. [13] He is the one who will build a house for my Name, and I will establish the throne *of his kingdom* forever. [14] I will be his father, and he will be my son. *When he does wrong, I will punish him with the rod of men, with floggings inflicted by men.* [15] But my love will never be taken away from him, as I took it away from Saul, *whom I removed from before you.* [16] Your house and your kingdom will endure forever *before me*; your throne will be established forever." ' " [17] Nathan reported to David all the words of this entire revelation.

---

of David's royal descendant, should he sin (contrast 2 Sam 7:14), and his alteration of pronouns in the succeeding verse from "your house and your kingdom" to "my house and my kingdom." What are we to make of changes such as these?

1 Chronicles 17:1–15

⟦81⟧After <u>David</u> was settled in his palace, _____
_____ <u>David</u> said to Nathan the
prophet, "Here I am, living in a palace of cedar, while the ark *of the cove-*
nant of the **LORD** <u>is under</u> a tent." ²Nathan replied to <u>David</u>, "Whatever
you have in mind, _____ do it, for **God** <u>is with</u> you." ³That
night the word of **God** came to Nathan, saying: 4 "Go and tell my servant David, 'This is what the LORD says: "<u>You are not</u> the one to build me
a house to dwell in. ⁵I have not dwelt in a house from the day I brought
Israel up _____ to this day. I have moved from <u>one tent site</u>
<u>to another, from one dwelling place to another.</u>
⁶Wherever I have moved with all the Israelites, did I ever say to any of
their <u>leaders</u> whom I commanded to shepherd my people ____, 'Why have
you <u>not built</u> me a house of cedar?' " ' ⁷Now then, tell my servant David,
'This is what the LORD Almighty says: "I took you from the pasture and
from following the flock to be ruler over my people Israel. ⁸I have been
with you wherever you have gone, and I have cut off all your enemies from
before you. Now I will make your name ____ like the names of the greatest men of the earth. ⁹And I will provide a place for my people Israel and
will plant them so that they can have a home of their own and no longer
be disturbed. Wicked people will not <u>oppress</u> them anymore, as they did
at the beginning ¹⁰and have done ever since the time I appointed
leaders over my people Israel. I will also <u>subdue</u> all your enemies. I declare to you that the LORD will <u>build</u> a house for you:
¹¹When your days are over and you <u>go to be</u> with your fathers, I will raise
up your offspring to succeed you, <u>one of your own sons,</u> _____ and
I will establish his kingdom. ¹²He is the one who will build a house for <u>me</u>,
_____ and I will establish <u>his</u> throne _____ forever. ¹³I will be <u>his</u>
father, and he will be my <u>son</u>. _____
_____ I will never take my
love away from him, as I took it away from <u>your predecessor</u> _____
_____ ¹⁴<u>I will set him over my</u> house and <u>my</u> kingdom forever _____,
<u>his</u> throne will be established forever." ' " ¹⁵Nathan reported to David all the
words of this entire revelation.

(Return to p. 249, second paragraph.)

Perhaps the way to begin is to recognize that the Chronicler presents
a *second* painting of Israel's monarchical history, not an *over*painting of
Samuel–Kings. It is now widely acknowledged that both the Chronicler
and his audience were well familiar with the Samuel–Kings material, and

that the Chronicler's aim was to recast and supplement, not repress or supplant, the earlier history.[56] Thus, the Chronicler could feel free, for example, without pang of historical conscience, to omit the warning of 2 Sam 7:14 as of little interest to his particular purpose for writing. After all, those who had experienced the Babylonian captivity and could look back on the checkered history of the divided monarchy did not need reminding that wrongdoing leads to "floggings inflicted by men." Moreover, in keeping with his overall purpose, the Chronicler wished to highlight Solomon's obedience, not his disobedience.

What then was the Chronicler's overall purpose for writing? To answer this question adequately would require not only a thorough study of the entirety of the Chronicler's work but also a [[83]] consideration of the Chronicler's intended audience. The former is, of course, out of the question here.[57] As regards the Chronicler's audience, 2 Chr 36:22–23 (along with the evidence of the genealogies in 1 Chronicles 3) makes it clear that the Chronicler is addressing the postexilic, restoration community in Jerusalem. We must ask, then, in assessing the Chronicler's rendition of the dynastic promise, "What must have been the pressing theological concerns of those who had returned out of exile in Babylon, or their descendants?" The unthinkable had happened—Judah had fallen and God's elect people had been swept away into exile. The question as to why this calamity had befallen God's people had been answered already for the exiles by Samuel–Kings. But for those now back in the land of Israel the pressing

---

56. B. S. Childs insists that "it is a basic error of interpretation to infer . . . that the Chr's purpose lies in suppressing or replacing the earlier tradition with his own account" (*Introduction to the Old Testament as Scripture* [Philadelphia: Fortress] 646, which see for Childs's reasoning). Similarly, Dillard points out that "the numerous points at which he [the Chronicler] assumes the reader's familiarity with the account in Samuel/Kings shows that he is using the Deuteronomic history as a 'control' to an audience well familiar with that account" ("The Reign of Asa [2 Chronicles 14–16]: An Example of the Chronicler's Theological Method," *JETS* 23 [1980] 214). On the Chronicler's many allusions to the earlier history, see also Ackroyd, "The Chronicler as Exegete."

57. If we were to attempt such an investigation, we might take our initial cues from the overall structure of Chronicles. It appears, for instance, that the Chronicler wishes to stress the continuity of Yahweh's dealings with (and interest in) his chosen people, as this is most strikingly expressed in the covenant with David. The Davidic kingdom is at a fundamental level the kingdom of Yahweh. And since this is so, events pertaining to the kingdom of Judah, where Davidic descendants once reigned, take on significance for "all Israel." Moreover, since in the Chronicler's day there is no Davidic king on an earthly throne, greater emphasis falls on the temple as the locus of Yahweh's continued rule. For more adequate appraisals, see the literature; e.g., Ackroyd, "Chronicler as Exegete"; Braun, "Message of Chronicles"; J. Goldingay, "The Chronicler as Theologian," *BTB* 5 (1975) 99–126; M. A. Throntveit, *When Kings Speak: Royal Speech and Royal Prayer in Chronicles*, SBLDS 93 (Atlanta: Scholars Press, 1987) 77–88; Williamson, *Israel in the Book of Chronicles* (Cambridge: Cambridge University Press, 1977).

questions must surely be not "Why the exile?" but, rather, "Is God still interested in us? Are the covenants still in force?"[58] The Chronicler's answer to these questions is affirmative: God still cares for his people and is bound to them in covenant.

In his rendering of the promise to David, the Chronicler seeks to underscore these truths by bringing into the light what could only be dimly perceived in the shadows of the earlier rendering. That is to say, the Chronicler draws forth and makes explicit what was only implicit in 2 Samuel 7.[59] Perhaps it is this [[84]] practice of making the implicit *explicit* that best explains the Chronicler's alteration of the pronouns in v. 14. At the time of the Chronicler's writing, there is no longer a Davidic kingdom, literally speaking, but the kingdom of God, of course, remains. Thus "your house and your kingdom will endure forever before me" of 2 Sam 7:16 becomes "I will set him over my house and my kingdom forever." In underscoring the theocratic character of the Davidic throne, the Chronicler is simply making explicit what is already implicit in the promise of 2 Sam 7:14: "I will be his father, and he will be my son."

In other ways as well, the Chronicler renders the dynastic promise so as to drive home its pertinence to his audience. Perhaps his replacement of "the king" with the more personal "David" in vv. 1 and 2 is meant to evoke the thought that, though Israel no longer has a human king on the throne, the Davidic line has not vanished and neither has God's promise, which after all was made *personally* to David. His addition of a reference to the "covenant" in v. 1 may serve to remind his hearers that they are still bound to God in covenant. His omission of "out of Egypt" in v. 5 tends to generalize the statement and make it perhaps more immediately relevant to those who themselves have been delivered out of bondage, though in a different land. A similar dynamic may be involved in the Chronicler's replacement of "Saul" with "your predecessor" in v. 13. Even his rephrasing of the reference to God's dwelling in a tent may serve to take the focus away from the tabernacle per se and to suggest the more general point that God's presence is not confined to any particular locale or structure. Could it also be that the change in terminology from "who will come from your own body" (which recalls the promise to Abraham in Gen 15:4 and seems to suggest an immediate descendant) to "one of your sons" (which allows reference to future descendants; compare 2 Kgs 20:18) is meant to hearten the Chronicler's hearers with the thought that the Lord may yet

58. Cf. Dillard, "David's Census," 99–101.
59. This is fully in keeping with the Chronicler's general practice; so, e.g., Childs: "Often the Chronicler spelled out in detail what was already partially implied in his source" (*Introduction,* 652; cf. p. 648). Cf. also Dillard, "Reward and Punishment in Chronicles: the Theology of Immediate Retribution," *WTJ* 46 (1984) 164–72.

raise up a Davidic scion? In context, of course, the literal referent remains Solomon (v. 12: "He is the one who will build a house for [[85]] me"). But a future son of David is not thereby excluded, at least not if the significance of the "house for me" is allowed to extend beyond the physical temple of Solomon.

To the above considerations, more could be added,[60] but perhaps we had better stop and hear Williamson's caution that the Chronicler's "handling of the dynastic oracle in 1 Chronicles 17 is but one element of this larger whole [i.e., the 'larger narrative structure' of Chronicles], and rash conclusions concerning his *Tendenz* should thus not be drawn hastily from a single text without further ado."[61] For our immediate, purpose, however, it does not so much matter that we discover the precise nature of the Chronicler's *Tendenz* as that we recognize that he had a *Tendenz*—a desire to present Israel's history in a certain light and for a certain purpose—and that this has influenced his depiction of the dynastic promise.

What then have we learned from this brief comparison of Israel's synoptic histories? Does the fact that 2 Samuel and 1 Chronicles present the dynastic promise to David in distinctive ways present a problem for those who wish to take seriously the historiographical character of each? If both texts are given a flat reading, as if they were verbatim transcripts of the event, then the answer would have to be yes. But as we have tried to show in this chapter, historical reportage is often more akin to painting than photography. That the Chronicler should explicitly present what is implicitly present in his source is entirely acceptable. After all, we do this sort of thing everyday. Imagine that in response to an invitation, we are told, "I'm afraid that we shall be busy that evening." If we then bring home the report, "They said they couldn't come," we will not be accused of fabrication—we have only made explicit what is implicit in the literal reply. The Chronicler's more interpretive presentation, focusing as it does on the inner significance of the promise, is all the more justified inasmuch as he seems to assume knowledge of the Samuel version [[86]] on the part of his audience. In short, what the comparison of the two renderings of the dynastic promise illustrates is the extent to which historians may be creative in their presentations, while at the same time remaining constrained by the facts.

---

60. We have not discussed, e.g., the Chronicler's avoidance of the term *rest* in his parallels to 2 Sam 7:1, 11–12; see Dillard, "The Chronicler's Solomon," *WTJ* 43 (1980) 294.

61. "Eschatology in Chronicles," 136.

Narrative Art in Joshua–Judges–Samuel–Kings

L. ALONSO SCHÖKEL

[[145]] Were I writing a chapter for a "History of Narrative Literature," I would dive directly into the subject, and I think readers would appreciate it. But I am aiming in the first instance to reach professional exegetes, who are accustomed to studying the Bible from a different perspective. Thus I have no other choice but to find a legitimate place for the study of narrative literature next to the study of history and historiography.

History, Historiography, Literature

History

[[146]] History, historiography, and narrative art are three interwoven themes. Reflecting on them, we observe that we can trace them in the shape of a well-measured, mobile triangle. One can take any of the three sides as its base.

The historian's interest is to reconstruct the events: how did they happen to come about? To do this, the historian consults monuments and documents, among which antecedent works of historiography may also be included. The modern historian takes his place in a tradition.

The historian of Greece will endeavor to reconstruct what happened in the wars against Persia or the Peloponnesus; to this end he will judiciously use, among other documents, the accounts of Herodotus and Thucydides, that is to say, ancient works of historiography, works by historians who aspired to narrate events that occurred. A modern historian will

Translated and reprinted with permission from "Arte narrativa en Josue–Jueces–Samuel–Reyes," *Estudios Bíblicos* 48 (1990) 145–69. Translated from Spanish by Daniel Legters.

apply himself to reconstruct what happened in the conquest of the Aztec
and Inca Empires. Among other sources, he will use the chronicles and accounts of contemporaries, those called the "Indian historians," led by the
brilliant Bernal Díaz del Castillo.

In the same manner, a historian of ancient Israelite history will want
to reconstruct events as they actually happened. For this he will use archaeological material as stammering (not eloquent) evidence; he will also
make use of ancient works of historiography that are preserved as an integral part of the Bible.

The historian is interested in the works of Thucydides, of Díaz del
Castillo, and of the books of Samuel and Kings in order to reconstruct a
history or prehistory. The historian will not pretend to do a commentary
on the Bible; he will inquire into and expose what happened, which may
not be precisely what the Bible says or how it says it. The result of his investigation will have as its generic title "History of Israel," unto which will
be added small specifics such as "from . . . to. . . ."

Historiography

A second look at historiographical works of the past will cause us to realize
that they are works belonging to the history of the culture. How was history written in Greece: Herodotus, Thucydides, Polybius? How was history
[[147]] written in Rome: Titus Livius, Tacitus, Suetonius? How was history
written in the Middle Ages: *Gesta Dei per francos*, *Grande e general estoria*
[[*The Deeds of God through the Franks*, by Guibert de Nogent (1053–1124);
The Grand and General History, by Alfonso X of Castile (1221–1284)]]? How
is modern history written: Mommsen, von Ranke? And also how was history written in Israel: Joshua, Judges, Samuel, Kings? The student will concentrate on such works, not to reconstruct the past they narrate, but to
comprehend and reconstruct the mentality and habits of those writing for
their contemporaries or perhaps for those in the future (*ktēma eis aei* [['a
possession forever']]). The romantic ballad of Bernardo del Carpio will
not be very useful for reconstructing medieval history, but it is a witness of
the culture that produced and read with interest such history. We take
little out of the song "Mio Cid" for understanding our political and military history but much for knowing one moment in our historiographical
culture.

Narrative Art

The last two examples move me to the third point of view, which is to read
and enjoy and study these accounts as literary works. Apart from their
value as documents of actual events, these songs and ballads are literary

monuments that should be conserved and studied as part of our literary culture. Their literary value does not come down to just a few techniques or extrinsic artifacts and ornaments; rather, they transcend the events they narrate—actual or invented: they transcend the historical moment in which they were born and began to live. To literary history, by all rights, belong Herodotus and Thucydides, Titus Livius and Tacitus, Bernal Díaz del Castillo and Father Mariana—and, of course, many biblical reports. (We should remember that Mommsen and Churchill received the Nobel prize for historical works.)

Mutual Involvement

I have mentioned three ways of considering the biblical text; or, as the scholastics said, three formal objects out of one material object. Now then, these three perspectives can hardly be isolated in practice, because the aspects are intertwined or tied together in a tenacious triangle. In effect, whoever wants to reconstruct history must first examine and define the nature and value of the testimonies being handled: from historiography to history. Without knowing the individual method that the author used to write history, a historian cannot [[148]] use an ancient report. That is why the question of history provokes and carries with it the question of historiography.

What type of documents are the biblical books that used to be called historical but would be better called narratives? We call them historical because their authors wanted to tell of events that happened, not invent them; we call them narratives so as not to prejudge their value as historical documents.

Yet we cannot understand the nature or the historical value of such documents if we do not take into account the literary conventions that the narrators worked under or used. When we can compare the account with the events as they happened, it becomes clear that the literary conventions make themselves evident and stand out. Literary appreciation, prior to distinguishing between history and fiction, is relatively easy. Those who say that the pure historicity and objectivity of an account is not a literary category are correct. We can read an account as a fascinating piece of fiction and then discover that it is rigorously historical. On the other hand, I have known someone who could not enjoy an account if he knew that it was not historical.

To the literary category belongs the true manifestation of human experience in its plurality and complexity, which does not become exhausted in pure historicity. Historicity is one form of truth, not the only form.

A Verification

History, historiography, literature—to reiterate the distinctioni between the three aspects as well as their mutual interconnectedness, I want to remind us briefly of a few things about our tradition.

The "historical" books—Joshua, Judges, Samuel, and Kings—were for centuries read as transparent historical chronicles. It was thought that there were no filters or transformations between the events as they happened and as they are recorded in the Bible. It is not that the ancients totally lacked a critical sense. They did distinguish the epic genre of the *Iliad* and the *Odyssey*. They did recognize literary artifacts in the works of Thucydides and Titus Livius. But they did not think of transferring such judgments to the biblical books. They assumed that divine inspiration had guaranteed their full historicity. Furthermore, premodern man had little trouble accepting the narrated events as plausible. And, if that were not enough, he could always appeal to miracles, which made anything plausible, in view of divine power.

Ancient commentators did not try to reconstruct history apart from the narratives found in the biblical texts because they did not ask themselves [[149]] the question. On the other hand, even though they knew how to appreciate the literary value of the biblical accounts in a spontaneous manner, they did not elevate their perceptions to a reflective plane, because the canons of their times imposed the Greco-Latin authors as models.

Critical study of biblical historiography was impeded because ancient scholars thought of historiography in purely theological terms. And when pioneers, such as Spinoza and Richard Simon, presented the problem, we know what the authorities did with them. More occurred when historical criticism started extending and imposing itself on the biblical texts. The conservatives kept thinking that the only form of truth in an account, if nothing was said to the contrary (parable), was pure historicity. They identified fiction with lies and falsehood.

Narrative art was the one thing that did not hold the attention of the investigators, either because they were afraid of falling into estheticism, or because they thought that art was not suited to rigorous scientific analysis.

Before moving on, I propose a brief but important bibliographical list [[in ascending order by date]].

Schulte, H. *Die Entstehung der Geschichtsschreibung im Alten Israel.* BZAW 128. Berlin, 1972.

Weippert, M. "Fragen der israelitischen Geschichtsbewusstein." *VT* 23 (1973) 415–42.

Miller, J. M. *The Old Testament and the Historian.* Philadelphia, 1976.

Ramsay, G. W. *The Quest for the Historical Israel.* Atlanta, 1981.
Friedman, R. (ed.) *The Poet and the Historian.* Chico, Calif., 1983.
Van Seters, J. *In Search of History: Historiography in the Ancient World and the Origins of Biblical History.* New Haven, 1983. [[Reprinted, Winona Lake, Ind., 1997]]

Narrative Art

Times have changed in the last few decades, as you will see in the succint bibliography that I give at the end. The linear or angular approach is becoming more and more triangular.

A Retrospective

To study and to expose the literary aspect of a biblical account is, curiously, only a recent development. Standard introductions still neglect the literary aspect of a work if it is not classified as roughly literary in genre.

Let us look at J. A. Soggin's *Old Testament Introduction*, the second edition of which appeared in 1976. He distinguishes between textual or "lower" criticism and [[150]] historical or "higher" criticism. He has no place for literary criticism dedicated to the artistic values of the Old Testament. He tells us that overall the Bible is a "book of history" and, above all, "the Word of God." He does not tell us about its being a literary work. Chapters 5 and 6 of the book address biblical literature but only to describe and classify its genres: among its narratives, namely, myths, legends, sagas, fables, and stories. Chapter 6, following Eissfeldt's organization (3d ed., 1964), assigns the literary genres to the "preliterary," that is, the oral, stage of the Old Testament.

Gottwald's *Introduction* (1985) represents an innovation, calling itself "literary and sociological." Besides the introductions of the normal scientific kind, space is increasingly given to articles and monographs formally dedicated to studying the biblical account as literature. The pages that follow are an added contribution of a synthetic nature. As indicated at the beginning, they can be seen as a chapter in a history of narrative literature.

When one starts to discourse about narrative art in the Bible, one is tempted to side with those who say that art should be appreciated and enjoyed, not analyzed or explained. On second thought, one reevaluates his position and then either resigns himself to the job or becomes inflamed with the study. I will not let myself be guided by analytical anxiety because, among other reasons, in my commentaries on Joshua, Judges, Samuel, and Kings in the Libros Sagrados series (1973), literary criticism abounds. I believe that in this respect the 833 pages in these commentaries still stand out among other exegetical commentaries preceding and even following (I am not referring to monographs).

The Deuteronomist contains stupendous narrative pages that belong to universal literature and have become implicit or explicit models for occidental narrators. In the literary panorama of the ancient Near East, two narrative complexes stand out: the Sumerian and Akkadian Gilgamesh, and the accounts of the Old Testament.

Abimelech's usurpation and fall, Jephthah's choice, the Samson cycle, Saul's visit to the witch at En-dor, Absalom's rebellion and defeat, the Jehu cycle, the scene of the woman of Tekoah, the Elijah cycle, and so on, comprise masterful pages. Is it possible to characterize or describe the art in these accounts?

What Biblical Narratives Are Not

I will begin the characterization of the above-mentioned accounts through negation. To do so, I have put myself in an elevated observatory, where I take up other forms of story-telling. It is only through comparison that I can discover what is not there. [[151]]

(1) The biblical narrator is not interested in the landscape or in the scenery. He is so interested in his characters and their actions that he does not take into account where they are or where the action takes place, except on extraordinary occasions, such as:

> On each side of the pass that Jonathan intended to cross to reach the Philistine outpost was a cliff. (1 Sam 14:4)

> As she (Abigail) came riding her donkey into a mountain ravine, there were David and his men descending towards her, and she met them. (1 Sam 25:20)

> There was Saul, lying asleep inside the camp with his spear stuck in the ground near his head. . . . Then David crossed over to the other side and stood on top of the hill some distance away; there was a wide space between them. (1 Sam 26:7, 13)

Every once in awhile, when the action deems it necessary, the narrator introduces summary indications of this sort. He leaves the rest to the reader's imagination or to the imagination of those hearing the reports who know the landscape. He does not begin his account with a description of the landscape that would help orient the reader. When detailing an ambush, a military maneuver, or a battle, his narrative technique proves inadequate. Look at the battle at Ai in Joshua 8, or the war against the Ephraimites in Judges 20–21; compare these pages with the narrative technique found in 1 Maccabees (which incorporates Greek learning).

In reading the biblical text, we cannot tell what cities, homes, roads, fields, and mountains were like. Nor does the author provide us much detail about clothing and instruments, though Goliath's armor in 1 Samuel 17 is a notable exception, albeit somewhat imprecise. In contrast, we do get a precise description of the priestly garments, either because of liturgical preoccupation (Exodus 28) or uninhibited enthusiasm.

To illustrate this contrast we can look at Jesus Ben Sira. In 45:6–12, he enumerates Aaron's ornaments without describing them (without forgetting the sound of the bells on his belt). In 50:5–11, he replaces the counting of the ornaments with a series of comparisons.

(2) The narrator does not delve into the minds of the characters to reveal their internal life to us—what they think and feel—as though the omniscient narrator did not have access to the inside of his characters. He could cite the proverb, "As the heavens are high and the earth is deep, so the hearts of king are unsearchable" (Prov 25:3). Shaded and changing thoughts and feelings, articulately expressed, are used in the lyrics of the Psalms, but they do not interfere with the biblical account. The narrator lets his characters speak and act. If the reader wants to know more about their motives, their internal [[152]] tensions, their capacity to think things over, then let him deduce these things from their actions, let him figure it out through analogy.

A young man feels an impassioned yet impossible love toward his half-sister. Would not this be the time to penetrate into his innermost being, to where so many love songs have inspired our literature? The biblical narrator has little to say. He focuses on the external aspect, as seen from another character (another point of view).

> Amnon became frustrated to the point of illness on account of his sister Tamar, for she was a virgin, and it seemed impossible for him to do anything to her. Now Amnon had a friend named Jonadab. . . . He asked Amnon, "Why do you, the King's son, look so haggard morning after morning?" (2 Sam 13:2–4)

This passage can be compared with a later, autobiographical text. Nehemiah is offering a cup to King Artaxerxes:

> So the king asked me: "Why does your face look so sad when you are not ill? This can be nothing but sadness of the heart." I was very much afraid, but I said to the king. . . . (Neh 2:2–3)

Even here the point of view is one of an interlocutor of the account, though he is immersed in the autobiographical narrator's point of view.

Saul, the envious and suspicious king, exalts himself and then gets depressed. What an occasion to analyze the character's contradictions! Do not look for it in the biblical account. To avenge the death of his brother, Joab betrays and murders Abner. King David forces his nephew Joab to take part in the burial of and mourning for Abner. The murderer also has to listen to the dirge the king sings and repeats:

> Should Abner have died as the lawless die? . . . You fell as one falls before wicked men. (2 Sam 3:33–34)

What is Joab feeling? What is his internal reaction? What a lost occasion to study the character's spirit. It is not the custom of the biblical narrator to do so.

(3) Furthermore, we do not find the great narrators' generalized reflections, which give profundity and transcendency to the individual act they are narrating. Using this technique, a text tries to enter into a wider human context, or it opens a door to shared human experience. The biblical account transcends individual humanity and is accessible to many, but not through the bridge of general reflection. I am referring here to the accounts as such. By contrast, theological generalizations dominate in the superposed scheme of the historiographer. [[153]] The book of Judges and the reflective and retrospective breaks taken in 2 Kings 17 belong in this area. In addition, even some interspersed lyrics can fulfill such functions as, for example, 2 Sam 23:6–7 (David's poetic last words).

Essence

I will now leave behind negation as a way to characterize the accounts and instead ask, in positive terms, what the biblical accounts have to recommend themselves. Answer: essence and immediacy. The narrator makes magnificent and varied plots. The poetic: a father who to keep his vow must sacrifice his daughter (great theme of tragedy). The comical: David behaving like a fool in Achish's court, drooling and scrawling on the walls. The heroic: Saul advancing to his announced death. The mysterious: Elijah on Mount Horeb and the final rapture; the ghost of the defunct Samuel being called back by a witch. The novelesque: the hidden spies in the well, a blanket spread over the edge and grain spread over the blanket. The fantastic: the chariots of fire and the whirlwind that take Elijah away. The miraculous: well supplied in the Elisha cycle. The dramatic: the great judgment on Mt. Carmel.

(1) *Action.* When we recall some of the accounts of these books in their totality, we have the impression of having attended an endless, grand, age-old parade. But when we return to look at one account in particular, we are surprised by its extreme brevity. Less than a page for Jephthah's episode, less then two for David's adultery and murder. A page and a half for Saul's visit to the witch, one page for the crime of Gibeah, two pages for the defeat and death of Sisera. How is it possible?

It is possible due to concentration on the essentials. The supreme talent of the narrator, who in picking out the essentials can sacrifice the rest, triumphs. "Leaping upon the mountains, skipping upon the hills," says the beloved of the lover. I would apply it to the biblical narrator who, inspired by an infallible instinct, sets his foot, his attention, on the summits of the action.

Chapter 9 of Judges, taking up three pages, is one of the most complex of these narratives. What happens in it? All this: Abimelech kills his brothers and proclaims himself king in Shechem (vv. 1–6); a survivor, Jotham, issues an accusation and a challenge to his kinsmen and then flees (7–21, with a fable included); the relationship between the citizens and their king becomes estranged (22–25); Gaal takes advantage of the situation to incite a revolt (26–29); there is an armed encounter between Abimelech and the leader of the revolt and with the population, victory (30–45); the rebels' last resistance [[154]] in the tower of Shechem, siege and usurper's death (46–57). The quantity of the narrative material is large, and the "tempo" of the narrative is quick. The account stops and concentrates on four or five climactic points of action. In the end, we have a clear and substantial vision; but let no one ask us about complementary details.

Increasing the scale, I could repeat the exercise, for example, with the Jehu cycle: it takes up two large chapters and concentrates on five or six events that stand out.

In the classic accounts of the Bible, the lengthy story of Joseph and his brothers is an exception to the rule. When we reach the age of Hellenism, we find narrations such as the books of Judith and Tobit. Judith, the heroine, does not enter the scene until chap. 9 of the book. I would classify as brief accounts the biblical accounts of Ruth and Jonah.

(2) Another aspect involved is *dialogue*. In general, there is an equilibrium between dialogue and action. The dialogues, in fact, are even more essential than the action. They involve two interlocutors. If there is a third or a fourth interlocutor, another round begins, without mixing together three or four in the same conversation. Even in deliberations, two voices are enough: Ahithophel and Hushai present to Absalom their opposing advice and know how to measure their words without taking away the rhetorical force behind them (2 Samuel 17). Rehoboam consults about the politics he should follow in order to respond to the demands of the people: he could have convoked different groups to reach a general deliberation. Two autonomous groups meet to give their advice to Rehoboam: the old men and the young men. If the separation has any special function, it is in response to the habit of limiting the interlocutors to two. If there is an exception, it would be the episode of Micaiah son of Imlah (1 Kings 22),

which presents a quick-moving scene, with two kings, two prophets, and several counselors.

When a character gives a speech, a large crowd may gather to listen, but the crowd is never presented as differentiated interlocutors (for example, in the speeches given by Jotham and Gaal in the above-mentioned Judges 9 passage). 1 Samuel 12 mentions the choral response of the people; something similar is the shout of independence of the Northern tribes. It is a unanimous response given by a collective interlocutor.

Interlocutors often take care of business in just a few exchanges. Many times it only takes them three rounds. Five or six exchanges turn it into a medium dialogue. Eight or ten exchanges are considered a large dialogue by biblical standards. If the dialogue of Samuel with Jesse (1 Samuel 16) seems large to us, it is because it contains a triad schematic enumeration.

In just a few exchanges, the interlocutors say the essentials. Of course, the essentials involve a play of ambiguities, as in the verbal [[155]] exchanges between David and Uriah. Let us look closely at a chapter rich in dramatic incidents, 1 Samuel 14.

> So both of them showed themselves to the Philistine outpost. "Look," said the Philistines, "the Hebrews are crawling out of the hole they were hiding in." (v. 11)
>
> The men at the outpost shouted to Jonathan and his armor-bearer, "Come up to us and we will teach you a lesson."
>
> So Jonathan said to his armor-bearer, "Climb up after me; the Lord has given them into the hand of Israel." (v. 12)

Three unadorned exchanges with a change in interlocutors: Philistines to themselves, Philistines to Jonathan, and Jonathan to his armor-bearer. The attitudes are revealed and contrasted in three lines. The scene could be transposed perfectly into cinematographic language (dramatic dialogue). In the same chapter, when chance reveals Jonathan's guilt, a dramatic dialogue takes place between father and son; it is dramatic because of its emotive intensity, not because of the dialogue's development.

> Then Saul said to Jonathan, "Tell me what you have done." (v. 43)
>
> So Jonathan told him, "I merely tasted a little honey with the end of my staff. And now I must die?"
>
> Saul said, "May God deal with me, be it ever so severely, if you do not die, Jonathan." (v. 44)

The narrative skills are so frequent and they seem so obvious that the reader continues reading without appreciating them. Lacking is a focused reading, a sensible analysis, a recitation shaded with accents and pauses (I know of no systematic study of dialogue in biblical narrative).

In later writings, tradition is maintained and new usages appear. The dialogue of Tobit with Raphael (Tobit 5) includes thirteen exchanges. In Raguel's house (Tobit 7), we have a glimpse into a family scene, with three or four interlocutors taking part. In Judith's dialogues with Holofornes, brevity loaded with ironic ambiguities prevails.

(3) *Described action.* The character's action can be spoken or described. The descriptive technique can vary. I will look specifically at two particular types: capturing the action in a single brushstroke and articulating the action in a sequence of movements.

The modern reader is accustomed to watching movies. He has easily assimilated the capacity of an image to represent a totality: a character walks away with his back turned to us, a door closes slowly or quickly, a light is turned off behind a window, [[156]] two hands are separated by force. . . . We remember the crime of Gibeah: the woman who was raped in the square by the neighbors. I am now going to underscore the data that interests me.

> When her master got up in the morning and opened the door of the house and stepped out to continue on his way, there lay his concubine, fallen in the doorway of the house, with her hands on the threshold. He said to her, "Get up, let's go." But there was no answer. (Judg 19:27–28)

How easy it would be for a movie director to translate this into an image. There is a quick and articulated action, with some supporting material: "he got up, opened the door, went out, found, said," a chilling vision of the hands (close up), ultimate silence—to which the ignorance of the husband and the knowledge of the reader are added.

By order of the usurper Jehu, some eunuchs of the guard throw Jezebel from the balcony.

> "Throw her down!" Jehu said. So they threw her down, and some of her blood splattered the wall and the horses as they trampled her underfoot. Jehu went in and ate and drank. "Take care of that cursed woman," he said, "and bury her, for she was a king's daughter." (2 Kgs 9:33–34)

Naturally, we ought to read these lines as the outcome of a larger story. We need to bear in mind Jezebel's merciless cynicism, her crime. Then we must see her getting dressed up with seductive intent—Jehu, the triumphant, winning over Jezebeel, the beautiful one who is offering herself—now superimpose blood splattering, horses' hooves trampling everything in sight!

I am going to focus on the technique of articulating an action in several pithy moments. Let us look at two violent deaths (I am using the term *look* in the imaginative sense). I will indicate with slashes the segments of action:

> As the king rose from his seat, / Ehud reached with his left hand, / drew the sword from his right thigh / and plunged it into the king's belly. / Even the handle sank in after the blade which came out his back / and the fat closed over it. (Judg 3:21)

> But Jael, Heber's wife, picked up a tent peg / and a hammer / and went quietly to him while he lay fast asleep, exhausted. / She drove the peg through his temple / into the ground, and he died. (Judg 4:21)

The density in the verbs describing the action is typical of this technique. Everything happens at once. The narrator does not beat around the bush or dress the action in curious or entertaining details. He lets others do the paraphrasing and lets the cooperating fantasy of the reader contemplate the scene.

Linear Movement

[[157]] The narration of the Deuteronomist is ordinarily linear and chronological. Because the narrator is omniscient and has a good command of the whole action, in presenting it he generally allows it to unfold naturally.

(1) The *delaying* or *accelerating* of narrative time, however, is a right that is reserved and exercised regularly. I am referring to the now classical distinction between narrated time and narrative time (or *tempo*). Since the narrator concentrates on essential moments and segments, he logically gives them more verbal space, while he sums up a large amount of time in a couple of phrases. In this regard, the biblical account is indistinguishable from other ancient or modern accounts. Judging the tempo is a typical talent of a good narrator rather than necessarily a procedure consciously applied.

The technique that in classical rhetoric we call *suspense* is not common in the biblical account, even though at some points it could have been used. Take, for example, the episode in which the spies find refuge in Rahab's inn, are sought in the city and on the roads, hide on the roof, are let down the wall with ropes. Instead of giving us a satisfying, suspenseful espionage story, the narrator offers a theological reflection out of Rahab's mouth (Judges 2). When Samson's countrymen tie him with ropes (Judges 15) and bring him out to give him to the Philistines, and the Philistines come, exhilarated at the opportunity to get Samson, the story line could have been cleverly delayed in order to slow down the action, increasing the sense of danger. But the narrator does nothing of the sort. Rather, he resorts without further ado to the "spirit" who infuses superhuman strength to the hero.

Judith's exploit, with its time-frame of five days, could belong to the category of suspense, but it belongs to another narrative school.

(2) Linear narrative also means that the narrator does not resort to *simultaneous* action; he does not arrange and tie two parallel actions together, nor does he bring two linear narratives to a final point of convergence. It cannot be said that the histories of the Northern and Southern Kingdoms comprise a linear account told in parallel. Rather, it has to do with the insertion of notices at the beginning or end of a reign. When Jehoshaphat of Judah and the king of Israel undertake a common campaign, there is no double action or parallel, only a single action (1 Kings 22).

But simultaneity can function within the frame defined by a narrative. In the story of Ehud and Eglon, it produces a burlesque effect at the expense of the obese king.

> After he had gone, the servants came and found the doors of the upper room locked. [[158]] They said, "He must be relieving himself in the inner room of the house." They waited to the point of embarrassment. . . . While they waited, Ehud got away. (Judg 3:24–26)

In the following example, simultaneity works to transpose the action from the wide scene of battle to the narrow space of a Bedouin tent, where the general will meet his death:

> But Barak pursued the chariots and army. . . . Sisera, however, fled on foot to the tent of Jael. (Judg 4:16–17)

After the death of Absalom, there is a sort of challenge to see who will be the one to take the news of his death to David. Ahimaaz wants the mission, but Joab refuses and instead dispatches a Cushite. While the Cushite is running to take the message, Ahimaaz continues to debate with Joab until he is allowed to run with the news also. "Too late," the reader may think.

> Then Ahimaaz ran by way of the plain and outran the Cushite. (2 Sam 18:23)

A similar, more refined example is the incident involving Gehazi, Elisha's servant, and Naaman. The storyteller simultaneously narrates Naaman's traveling and the mental calculations of the servant (an extraordinary case of psychological information).

> After Naaman had traveled some distance, Gehazi said to himself, "My master was too easy on Naaman, this Aramean, by not accepting from him what he brought. As surely as the Lord lives, I will run after him and get something from him." So Gehazi hurried after Naaman. When

Naaman saw him running toward him, he got down from his chariot to meet him. (2 Kgs 5:20–21)

(3) Lineality also suggests that there is neither anticipation nor delay of information. However, the narrator of the biblical historical books has no objection to breaking the linear movement with common literary techniques.

Delays seem to be frequent, as when a fact is not mentioned at the time it is executed but instead when the narrator needs it the most, when it is the most effective. Then the narrator resorts to what we call the pluperfect. There are times when this occurs for narrative convenience. The narrator does not preview or present up front all the facts that will influence the outcome. He preserves them in memory or produces them at the moment they are needed.

The opposite of delay is to anticipate information before the deed is done. This can occur when the narrator drops a hint, or it can be a narrative parenthesis, as in a confidential relationship between the omniscient narrator and the curious reader.

[[159]] In biblical narratives—and not just in later elaborations—one encounters transcendent anticipation in the form of predictive prophecy, whether a promise, a threat, or a simple announcement. The narrator accompanies human action with the divine word, mediated in turn by the prophet. To look ahead at the result or the outcome could kill or at least dull curiosity and interest. But interest remains to see how everything is going to turn out, and it is compensated with another type of interest that is born from the event's new dimensions. I am now going to focus on some examples of anticipation and delay.

When Absalom dies, the author adds some news in the pluperfect.

> During his lifetime Absalom had taken a pillar and erected it in the King's Valley as a monument to himself, for he thought, "I have no son to carry on the memory of my name." (2 Sam 18:18)

The news, communicated at this time, is as pathetic as it is plain. It sounds like a melancholic epitaph—the place, the reference to an ephemeral reign—it denies a hereditary succession, but the mausoleum will perpetuate the name of the rebellious, ill-fated son.

The slaughter of those faithful to Baal at the hand of Jehu's soldiers is told in 2 Kings 10. In one section, the author communicates some information, sharpening the reader's curiosity (10:19, Jehu acted craftily in order to eliminate those faithful to Baal). Furthermore, the account delays some information that, strictly speaking, belonged to the preparation (10:24: "Jehu had posted eighty men outside . . .").

The account of the siege and hunger in Samaria found in 2 Kings 7 is a bit more complex and elaborate. It begins with Elisha's prediction to the king that the siege would be lifted and food would become available (7:1). Because the king's officer does not want to believe, Elisha adds another prediction for him: "you will see it, but you won't eat it" (7:2). The account continues and is transferred to another zone and to other characters—insignificant characters, one would say. At the entrance of the city there is a group of lepers (people affected by a grave and contagious skin disease). Desperate enough to take a chance, they march to the enemy's camp and discover that the perpetrators have left: "When they reached the edge of the camp, not a man was there" (7:5). At that moment, the narrator interposes a retrospective parenthesis to tell of another miracle in the prophetic cycle: "For the Lord had done . . ." (7:6). The succession of events continues until it reaches the outcome in which Elisha's first prediction becomes true: "Then the people went out and plundered the camp of the Arameans" (7:16). Elisha's second prediction is left hanging, so the narrator turns back: "Now the king had put the officer on whose arm he leaned in charge of the gate, and the people trampled him in the gateway and he died, just as the man of God had said to the king" (7:17).

Human presentiment and supernatural announcement are conjoined in one of the most suggestive accounts of the whole work, 1 Samuel 28 (Saul and the witch of En-dor). By contrast, [[160]] in 2 Kings 5 the prophetic vision is communicated somewhat delayed, after the event, after Naaman's healing.

> When Gehazi came to the hill, he took the things from the servants and put them away in the house. He sent the men away and they left. Then he went in and stood before his master Elisha. "Where have you been, Gehazi?" Elisha asked. "Your servant didn't go anywhere," Gehazi answered. But Elisha said to him, "Was not my spirit with you when the man got down from his chariot to meet you?" (2 Kgs 5:24–26)

The delay is a narrative achievement. The news is more effective at this point than at any other point in the story. The reader already knows that the servant is lying but does not know that Elisha was watching from a distance. Greed and lies are denounced at a single point, justifying the sentence against him.

The premonitions of Saul, Jonathan, and Abigail regarding the future reign of David seem to be based on the subsequent elaboration that idolizes the national hero. Such premonitions are a virtual *Leitmotiv* of the history: 1 Sam 20:13–16; 23:17; 25:30–31; 26:25.

Characters

Many characters traverse the pages of the Deuteronomistic History. The impression of humanity the reader gets is rich and varied. When he re-reads the book, paying attention to the different characters, he discovers that well-rounded, well-developed characters are rare. In [[E. M.]] Forster's distinction, the characters are "flat," not "round."

What do we know of Ehud? He was left-handed. What do we know of Eglon? He was overweight. And Barak? He was a coward and indecisive. And Jael? She was crafty and decisive. Just a feature or two. It might be objected that a character cannot be manifested or developed in just a page or two. Well, look at Gideon, who takes up three beautiful chapters. Can we describe his character? Samson may be a little more defined, though he may deceive us with the attractive contrast of strength and weakness, courage and seduction.

(1) The *external appearance* of the characters is seldom described. But on a few occasions the narrator notes a feature that he judges important. Of Saul he tells us, "he was a head taller than any of the others" (1 Sam 10:23)—an aspect that contrasts with the preceding gesture of one who was hiding among the baggage. David, Israel's favorite, "was ruddy, with a fine appearance and handsome features" (1 Sam 16:12). It was this that motivated the giant Goliath to despise him, who "looked David over and saw that he was only a boy, ruddy and [[161]] handsome, and he despised him" (1 Sam 17:42). Absalom's beauty is pondered: "in all Israel there was not a man so highly praised for his handsome appearance as Absalom," and about his hair: "whenever he cut the hair of his head . . . he would weigh it, and its weight was two hundred shekels by the royal standard" (2 Sam 14:26. His hair seems to play a role in the outcome of the narration.

If external appearance is only seldom described for the male characters, the same is true of the women. Abigail stands out for her common sense, not her beauty. The woman at Tekoah is skillful. Nothing is mentioned about the physical aspects of Jezebel or Athaliah. The modern reader, accustomed to cinema, notices the biblical silence. What was Jael's voice like when she whispered her invitation *sûrâ ădōnî sûrâ 'ēlay 'al-tîrā'* [['turn in, my lord, turn in to me; fear not']]? Was Tamar as beautiful as her brother Absalom? The value of feminine beauty is attested to in Canticles, but the historical narrator seems not to be interested in it. The author of Judith is also esthetically different from our narrator in this regard.

(2) Furthermore, the narrator does not characterize his characters with a *spiritual profile*: temperament, sensitivity, attitudes, values. When Ahithophel is about to enter the scene to act out his brief part (2 Samuel 16–17), the narrator does not stop to explain to us that "he was a counse-

lor without scruples, clever in appreciating the entirety of a situation, quick to make decisions, but pathologically sensitive in regard to his reputation." This is what a modern commentator would say, someone trained in the reading of novels who would draw inferences from the biblical text.

The narrator puts his characters on stage and lets them speak and act, as Deut 8:2 says, "to test you in order to know what was in your heart." Put in various situations, they will reveal who they really are. Words are frequently the most significant aspect of a character. Gideon, as another Moses, intersperses his objections to the divine messenger:

> But sir, if the Lord is with us, why has all this happened to us? . . .
>
> But Lord, how can I save Israel?
>
> Give me a sign. (Judg 6:13, 15, 17)

Later on, he will ask the Lord for the sign of the fleece and the dew (6:34–40). To the Ephraimites, who reproach his manner of action, he responds with flattering words, "what have I accomplished compared to you?" (8:2). In contrast, he threatens the neighbors of Peniel sharply, "when I return in triumph, I will tear down this tower" (8:9).

(3) I have said that the biblical characters manifest themselves through action. It follows that if we were to give them more pages and more action, they would have more space to mature narratively. Among the numerous biblical [[162]] characters in the Deuteronomistic History, I think that the most successful ones are Joab, David's nephew, and Jehu, the Northern usurper. Some prefer David, to whom the narrator assigns some 38 chapters that involve a variety of situations. Solomon is an idealized and schematic figure. Neither Hezekiah nor Josiah is set as an interesting character, even though Hezekiah has a good role and has some happy moments.

(4) What shall we say about the *collective character*? It is only on rare occasions that it assumes a decisive or important role in the account. I look for times when the community takes the initiative and is not content with just following orders.

The community takes the initiative when the Israelites want to change their status and establish a monarchy. 1 Sam 8:4: "So all the elders of Israel gathered together and came to Samuel at Ramah." Even the later schism between North and South is provoked by a community being lead by Jeroboam (1 Kings 12). Their cry for independence is collective; all together they stone to death the chief of forced labor.

I consider 1 Sam 14:45 to be one of the most significant cases. The troops rebel against the general's decision to condemn to death the hero of the day, his son, a victim of both ignorance and censure.

But the men said to Saul, "Should Jonathan die—he who has brought about this great deliverance in Israel? Never! As surely as the Lord lives, not a hair of his head will fall to the ground."

(As an aside—what a missed opportunity to scrutinize Saul's interior, torn by paternal love and sacred vows, political and military authority being threatened, yet with the wish to yield.)

(5) Last, even *God* (or his presence as "Angel of the Lord") can enter into the narrative account as a narrative character. This occurs at the beginning of the Gideon and Samson cycles (Judges 6 and 13). In these cases, the author does not speak of God immediately but through an intermediary, a narrative character. In Samuel and Kings, God no longer enters directly into the scene; rather, he delegates representatives, to whom he gives direct orders and instructions.

Point of View

Point of view is a concept that has begun to be emphasized in modern studies of narrative (which has begun to be called narratology). The expression is not to be taken in a physical sense, but rather in a spiritual sense. It is obvious that Jehu's chariot driving and Ahimaaz's race with the Cushite were seen by the respective sentinels, and that Bathsheba was seen and reseen by David. Here we are talking about the point of view that the [[163]] narrator adopts or introduces. Does he narrate in the first person, in the third person? Does he interpose another character as narrator? In general, the accounts of the Deuteronomist are presented from the point of view of an omniscient narrator, who has a transcendent gaze, who is interested yet tendentious. Let us try to sharpen the focus.

(1) If the Deuteronomistic History really begins in Deuteronomy 1, then it begins with Moses' point of view, who is narrating the preceding history as autobiography. The narrator does not make his presence felt immediately. His point of view slowly becomes clear. From the beginning, Moses mentally transfers himself to Sinai/Horeb, and he attributes the initiative to the Lord, while he is a mediator with a limited field of action. The Lord controls and directs him from above; the people below are stubborn interlocutors and reluctant executors. The text does not advance as a circle that rolls smoothly but as a triangle or square that bumps along: the Lord told me—then I said to them—they answered me—we did.

In Judges, those who speak or sing are anonymous narrators of heroic accounts—a specie of epic poems. Their accounts are trapped within the net or frame of a conventional scheme, almost cyclical, and the book ends with an appendix containing a refrain that defines the time as "premonarchic." Judg 21:25: "In those days Israel had no king; everyone did as he saw fit." Whoever speaks in such a manner betrays his point of view. What is notable and worthy is that he has not manipulated the preceding accounts, with the result that his point of view sounds restrained, like an a posteriori verdict.

In the first book of Samuel, the point of view is defined by its favorable stance toward David as opposed to Saul. These preferences do not stop the author from also recounting the weaknesses and even the crimes of his hero. In the Elisha cycle we have the impression that a member of a prophetic community has interposed his point of view, that of a hagiographer fond of miracles. It is a common and frequent opinion that the author of the Josianic redaction and the last author (from the time of exile) superimposed their points of view, not only narrating, but also explicating and evaluating.

Sometimes there is a point of view that can be called liturgical, as if the narrator takes his particulars from a liturgical ritual or stylizes them in the form of a celebration. The most notable cases are the crossing of the Jordan (Joshua 3–4), the conquest of Jericho (Joshua 6), and the death or transporting of Elijah (2 Kings 2).

(2) Despite their national solidarity and religious conviction, the accounts in these books sound to us totally objective, almost cold and a little [[164]] distant. Does the narrator approve or condemn Jehu's brutalities? Is it enough for him that through Jehu's actions God's word and purpose are being accomplished? It is as if someone says: Jehu is the divinely appointed executor and I am not one to discuss his procedures.

Even so, there is no lack of places, either in the original or in the elaboration, where the reader is invited to choose a particular point of view. David's double crime (adultery and premeditated murder) is terrible, horrifying. Regardless, the narrator speaks of it without shame, leaving the reader to feel the shame. At the end he does add an unadorned epilogue: "But the thing David had done displeased the Lord" (2 Sam 11:27). This is true; later will come Nathan's denunciation, Absalom's and Sheba's rebellions, a dialectic of tragic consequences, some of them underscored in later elaboration.

For the reader who shares a system of values with the author, a precise legal code, a feeling for humanity, the cool report can be more impressive than explicit, effusive emotion. Test your own reactions by comparing 2 Samuel 11 with any chapter in 2 Maccabees, which in narrative style is just the opposite. To present naked acts with a disparaging look can be, beside the duty to inform, an act of denunciation and an ethical or religious lesson. Consider, for instance, proverbs of simple observation, lacking in explicit commentary:

The sluggard buries his hand in the dish; he is too lazy to bring it back to his mouth. (Prov 26:15)

Those whose teeth are swords and whose jaws are set with knives to devour the poor from the earth, the needy from among mankind. (Prov 30:14)

Narrators shape their readers. Or do they take them for granted? Those who received the biblical historical accounts, hearers at first but later readers, were all members of Israel. This fact alone assumes many things, since the narrator shares definite traditions and convictions with his audience. To shape a reader was always part of the plan. The modern reader, however, is another story. Since he does not share all of the narrator's presuppositions, it is possible that instead of allowing himself to be shaped, he may react in a dialectic game with the point of view of the narrator. Secular and cultural distance can add richness to the reading, if the fundamental human values are shared.

If the Deuteronomistic body of literature begins with Deuteronomy, then the decalogue (Deuteronomy 5) is a solemn ethical and religious frame of reference. Because the Decalogue hangs at the front, in a visible place, there will be no need to evaluate every episode. [[165]]

(3) *Ambiguity.* The differing degrees to which an author identifies with or dissociates from his characters, in addition to affecting the reader, can give the text moments of tension and ambiguity. The reader can share them and resolve them to his liking. Ambiguity is today a positive concept in the art of narration.

Take, for example, Jephthah. A bastard who is expelled by his brothers, he becomes the leader of a group of adventurers. He later accepts his brothers' offer of leadership as a means of vengeance and in saving his countrymen he thinks he is justified. He takes an unfortunate vow and then he has to keep it. The reader's reaction is ambiguous: if he is not in agreement with the choices of the character, he at least shares his pain: "I have made a vow . . . I cannot break it" (Judg 11:35).

On a much greater scale, something similar occurs with Saul. From initial astonishment and admiration for Saul's first exploits, the reader turns to contemplating the psychological depravity of the character, then to gathering hope from a few noble and ephemeral reactions, but in the end participating in his tragically noble death in battle.

Samson is continually breaking his nazirite vow. But . . . he is one of us. He challenges the enemy, he defeats him, he wins. We tolerate his weakness with women. In the end, we respectfully support his tragic victory: killing as he dies!

Am I choosing tragic figures on purpose? Then let us read the present rendering of Judges 19–21: a somber and horrifying beginning, a disproportionate and appalling civil war, rounded off with a victory in which the losers and winners both lose. Then comes the reconciliation and the abduction of the maidens of Shiloh from a dance: a happy and hopeful ending with some touches of humor.

We call this type of story-telling narrative tension or ambiguity. The accounts of the Deuteronomist do not degenerate into the sentimental, the schmaltzy, or the corny. Throughout the centuries, "from generation to generation," they retain their elemental vigor, their mysterious attraction. The biblical God does not nullify man; instead, he exalts him, and the narrator knows it.

Notes on Style

Throughout my 1973 commentary I made some specific observations about style in the biblical text. I will mention only a few of those observations at this point.

(1) We cannot say that *sonorous material* [[e.g., assonance]] in narrative prose has attracted the same attention as in literary verse. I can point out, however, an alliteration of six words beginning with ʾ*alep*, a kind of murmur of love, spoken by Amnon: [[166]]

> ʾ*et tāmār,* ʾ*ăḥôt* ʾ*abšālōm* ʾ*āḥî* ʾ*ănî* ʾ*ōhēb.* (2 Sam 13:4)
> [['I love Tamar, the sister of my brother Absalom.']]

I have already mentioned Jael's flattering invitation to Sisera:

> *sûrâ* ʾ*ădōnî sûrâ* ʾ*ēlay* ʾ*al-tîrā*ʾ. (Judg 4:18)
> [['Turn in, my lord, turn in to me; fear not']]

I remember the mocking reproach of Elijah to those who 'limp with crutches'.

> *pōsĕḥîm ʿal-štê hassĕ ʿippîm.* (1 Kgs 18:21)
> [['go limping with two different opinions']]

The sound of a name being exploited in order to get narrative meaning out of it is conspicuous in the case of Solomon: *šĕlōmōh* [[Solomon]] is a *môšēl* [['ruler']] (1 Kgs 5:1[4:21]), author of sayings in the *māšāl* [['proverb']] genre (1 Kgs 5:2[4:22]), *šālam* = 'finishes' his tasks (1 Kgs 7:51; 9:25), offers 'sacrifice' *šĕlāmîm* (1 Kgs 8:63–64), enjoys *šālôm* (1 Kgs 5:4[4:24]; 5:26[5:12]), offers a splendid 'table' *šûlḥān* (1 Kgs 5:7[4:27]; 10:5). Elijah ʾ*ēliyāhû* [['my God is Yahweh']] rises to proclaim that *Yhwh* is God. With Absalom's name (ʾ*ab-šālôm* [['father of peace']]), one can play a pathetic game (2 Sam 18:28–29).

(2) The *rhythm* of narrative prose is made up of brief phrases in a sequence that is almost always paratactic. More than a regular rhythm (as in

epic poems or romances), the narrator can look for special effects, for example: a tight sequence of verbs, the staccato of an enumeration, the tightening or stretching of phrases. A phrase with five accents appears to be preferred for action. The spoken sections have a tendency to be regular in rhythm, so much so that some dialogues or exchanges can be read easily as verse (as in the frequent octosyllables in our [[Spanish]] prose or the hendecasyllables in the prose of Valle Inclán). These factors do not, however, confirm the theory that the accounts once existed in verse.

(3) *Repetition* is one of the most important techniques of biblical narrative prose. Given the reduced vocabulary and the compact nature of the accounts, the narrator has to add weight to some words by repeating terms or roots at strategic points and in a perceptible way. It is reasonable to suppose that the ancients who recited accounts knew how to emphasize such repetitions in an expressive manner. The modern reader is not used to paying attention to such techniques. It is the task of the exegete to draw the reader's attention to them. Occurrences of repetition are not always translatable, given the polysemy of Hebrew words and the major differences in our vocabulary.

The word *hand* is very ordinary. Yet when planted at the beginning of an account, it may prepare us for its expressive reappearance at the outcome: Ehud and Eglon, Judges 3; Jael, Judges 4. Elijah, tired of battle and of life, asks God to 'take [him] away' *lqḥ* (1 Kgs 18:4); in the end, God will take him away (*lqḥ*) in a chariot of fire (2 Kgs 2:11). Gideon's stealthy, nocturnal descent to the enemy camp with his armor-bearer will widen into the three tribes' grand, crushing descent against the enemy (Judg 7:9–11, 24). [[167]]

(4) An important variation consists in the *numeric repetition* of a word or word-stem in order to convert it into a *Leitmotiv*. As an illustration, the verb 'to serve' (*ʿbd*) is repeated 14 times (7 × 2) when the covenant is renewed in Joshua 24. During the conquest of Jericho, the number 7 dominates: 7 days, 7 times around the city on the last day. The word *trumpet* is repeated 14 times. Joshua 7 is the account of Achan's crime perpetrated against the 'devoted things'. The root *ḥrm* is repeated 8 times in different forms. Seven times it is repeated in 1 Samuel 15 in the account of Saul's crime. In Joshua 8 the stratagem of the ambush against the city of Ai dominates: the root *ʾrb* 'to lie in wait' is repeated 8 times. In the account of David's succession (1 Kings 1), the problem of the son is primary: a variation of the phrase 'my/a son will succeed me to the throne' is repeated 7 times. The story of Elijah's confrontation of Baal's priests repeats the key word *ʿnh* 'to respond, pay attention' 8 times. In 2 Kings 1, *yrd* 'to go down, to fall' is the *Leitmotiv*, repeated 12 times.

(5) A variant or inversion of repetition is *contrast*: of words, situations, or characters. Contrast can lend significance to the laconic and serve the

internal tension. There is a type of contrast that uses semantic repetition more than verbal repetition. 1 Kings 18–19 plays with the nuanced contrast of silence and voice. In the story of Elijah, eating twice and reclining twice (1 Kings 19) marks the change in Elijah's spiritual route: from escape to ascension. Observe the two springs [[i.e., Rogel and Gihon]] and two banquets in 1 Kings 1.

Perhaps the accounts of the three executions in 1 Kings 2 are told with a little dramatic irony based on the characters' ignorance or on the unforeseeable plot. Adonijah, in asking to take one of his dead father's concubines as wife, unwittingly brings death upon himself. Joab, taking refuge at the altar, stains the Temple asylum with his guilty blood and dies next to the altar as a guilty victim, expiating and purifying the monarchy. Shimei, in capturing his two fugitive slaves, signs his own death sentence. Confined at home, he would have saved his life. By enslaving his servants once more, he loses his life.

The biblical account is linear, though undulating and oscillating with contrasts. One must read and reread it carefully. One must even step back in order to see the big picture and to put together the pieces that are distant from each other: the mutilated and humiliated king of Judg 1:6ff. and the reestablished king of 2 Kgs 25:27–30; the frustrated maternity of Jephthah's daughter (Judges 11) and the deflowered virginity of Tamar (2 Samuel 13); Michal saving the life of the fugitive David and then despising her husband's festive dance (1 Sam 19:11–17 and 2 Sam 6:20–23); Abigail, affectionate and conciliatory with David; Jezebel, perverse and domineering with Ahab (1 Samuel 25 and 1 Kings 21). [[168]]

(6) *Symbolic values.* The symbolic meaning of scenes or situations is not usually deposited in one word or phrase. Rather, it is spread throughout the semantic tissue of the episode. The symbolic sense becomes charged, crystalizes through accumulation, then detaches itself and communicates in a manner clear or almost sublime. Symbolic profundity in many cases compensates or counteracts the immediacy and obviousness of the scenes. The analysis of narrative symbols requires more coaching to catch it, more delicacy, so as not to exaggerate.

Let us take, for example, the famous battle of David and Goliath (1 Samuel 17). The contrast of pastoral and military traits compares two figures more than two names: the shepherd and the soldier. During the unfolding of the account, a suggestive association emerges: Goliath is like one of those lions or bears that the shepherd has taken on and destroyed. David will be the shepherd of his people.

David wants to build a "house" to the Lord: a temple, enclosure, space. The Lord wants to build a "house" for David: descendants, time, space (2 Samuel 7). The statue of the god Dagon lies face down, beheaded, hands cut off, before the ark of the Lord (1 Sam 5:4). The cows instinctively recognize the power of the load they are carrying, the ark of the Lord; they abandon their calves, accept the yoke, and pull the cart without turning to the left or to the right, someone mysteriously guiding them (1 Samuel 6).

Saul's spear is the opposite of David's harp: it is driven into the wall of the palace (1 Sam 19:10), it presides over the unjust trial of the priests of Nob (1 Sam 22:6), it is impotent while assisting the king's sleep (1 Sam 26:7); the Amalekite (according to his own version) finds Saul mortally wounded, "leaning on his spear" (2 Sam 1:6).

Bibliographical Note

The publication of a manual on biblical narrative, entitled *Our Fathers Have Told Us*, by J. L. Ska, is anticipated for the fall of 1990 [[now *"Our Fathers Have Told Us": Introduction to the Analysis of Hebrew Narratives* (Subsidia Biblica 13; Rome: Pontifical Biblical Institute, 1990)]]. As a manual for study and analysis, it explains all the concepts (with listings in several languages) and offers an abundant and up-to-date bibliography. Having mentioned this study, I can content myself here with a recent bibliography [[in ascending order by date]].

Conroy, C. *Absalom, Absalom!* Rome, 1978.

Crenshaw, J. L. *Samson.* Atlanta, 1978.

Gunn, D. M. *The Story of King David: Genre and Interpretation.* Sheffield, 1978.

Licht, J. *Storytelling in the Bible.* Jerusalem, 1978.

Polzin, R. *Moses and the Deuteronomist.* New York, 1980.

Fokkelman, J. *Narrative Art and Poetry in the Books of Samuel.* Assen, 1981.

Alter, R. *The Art of Biblical Narrative.* New York, 1981.

Clines, D. J. A., D. M. Gunn, and A. J. Hauser. *Art and Meaning: Rhetoric in Biblical Literature.* Sheffield, 1982.

Gros Louis, K. R., and J. S. Ackerman (eds.). *Literary Interpretations of Biblical Narratives.* Nashville, 1975, 1982.

Gottwald, N. K. *A Socio-literary Introduction to the Bible.* Philadelphia, 1985.

Sternberg, M. *The Poetics of Biblical Narrative.* Bloomington, Indiana, 1985.

Liptzin, S. *Biblical Themes in World Literature.* Hoboken, New Jersey, 1985.

Jobling, D. *The Sense of Biblical Narrative: Structural Analysis in the Hebrew Bible.* Sheffield, 1978, 1986.

Preminger, A., and E. L. Greenstein. *The Hebrew Bible in Literary Criticism.* New York, 1986.

Alonso Schökel, L. Pp. 359–81 in *Arte narrativa en el libro de los Jueces*, vol. 2 of *Hermenéutica de la palabra.* Madrid, 1987.

Alter, R., and F. Kermode. *The Literary Guide of the Bible.* Cambridge, Massachusetts, 1987.

Part 4

Writing Israel's History: The Methodological Challenge

Introduction

Having considered in part 3 the multiplex character of ancient Israel's history writing, in part 4 we shall consider the methodological challenge of writing ancient Israel's history. There is, of course, hefty disagreement about whether it is in fact possible to write a history of ancient Israel.[1] Some scholars are of the opinion that "ancient Israel" is nothing more than a "scholarly construct."[2] According to such scholars, whatever histories of "historical" Israel might yet be written, they must bear little resemblance to histories written heretofore. Other scholars are of the opinion that the more traditional histories of Israel, despite the considerable differences among them, are moving in the right direction, so that future work can build on them. Still other scholars find previous histories convincing only insofar as they are compatible with the broad outline of Israelite history as presented in the pages of the Hebrew Bible. This state of affairs raises the question why there is such wide divergence in scholarly opinion? Individual preference for different methodological approaches is part of the answer. But, as I have argued elsewhere, methodological preferences are at some level and to some degree prompted by the metaphysical commitments of practising scholars, whether acknowledged or not.[3]

So how then is true progress to be made in addressing the methodological challenge of writing Israel's history? Baruch Halpern suggests that, while one would be ill advised to jettison the biblical text, one should at least keep *theology* to the side: "The task of the coming century will be to discard these vestiges of a promising youth: keeping theology to the side, yet without ceasing to be a Biblical historian, the scholar must become an Israelite and Canaanite historian" (Halpern 1987: 132). Given the *aspectual* (and especially theological) character of the biblical narratives discussed

1. See, e.g., L L. Grabbe (ed.), *Can a "History of Israel" Be Written?* (Sheffield: Sheffield Academic Press, 1997).

2. So, e.g., P. R. Davies, *In Search of "Ancient Israel"* (Sheffield: Sheffield Academic Press, 1992).

3. See V. P. Long, *The Art of Biblical History* (Foundations of Contemporary Interpretation 5; Grand Rapids: Zondervan, 1994) 171–76 and passim.

above in part 3, it is difficult to see how a scholar can both be a *biblical* historian and keep *theology* to the side. Moreover, if Halpern has in mind that the scholar should neutralize his own fundamental beliefs and don the robes of the "objective" scholar, one would have to query whether this is ever truly possible. As K. L. Younger remarks: "The historical work is always the historian's interpretation of the events, being filtered through vested interest, never in disinterested purity" (p. 313 below).

Bearing in mind, then, that a scholar's choice of methods and the use he or she makes of them is invariably to some extent a reflection of his or her deeply held beliefs about fundamental reality, we are in a position to assay various approaches to the task of writing Israel's history. The first section below contains general discussions of what is involved in "doing history in biblical studies"—the title of Diana Edelman's essay, with which we begin (pp. 292–303). Edelman offers a lucid, brief treatment of how the Bible, along with other literary and also material/artifactual remains, can be used as historical sources. Her treatment of the "main steps" in "historical-critical investigation"—namely, "familiarization, conceptual invention, and inductive verification" (p. 302), generally followed by the writing of a history (cf. p. 295)—is sensible enough (compare my own independently conceived four steps in doing historical research: amass the evidence, assess the evidence, attempt a reconstruction, advocate the reconstruction [Long 1997]). Of interest also is Edelman's caveat that "the causal links they [that is, historians] 'discover' are never all those operative and influential at the time" (p. 294). Edelman does not tease out the implications of this insight, but it would seem important to do so. For instance, judging from the pages of scripture, the ancient Israelites appear to have seen in certain turns of events the hand of God at work. Modern historical criticism, however, eliminates such an explanation on the basis of an a priori methodological principle. But the point is this: unless the faith expressed in the Hebrew Bible is entirely misplaced (which modern theists should be reticent to assume), then Edelman's caveat leaves open the possibility that the actually operative causal link has been methodologically excluded. Unfortunately, this arbitrary exclusion is often not acknowledged, with the result that alternate causal explanations are inserted that may not actually relate at all to historical reality, to what "actually happened."

Edelman's caution against the social-science quest for "laws" of history is well targeted (p. 298 below), and she is correct to stress the fact that human conciousness is at the heart of history and historical process (p. 303). Her contention that the biblical texts are to be evaluated in a manner identical to all literary evidence (p. 300) oversimplifies the issue of the Bible's macro-genre, it seems to me. And while her methodological pluralism and her comment that historians must in some measure rely on the expertise of others are sensible (p. 300), she does not address the important question of "which others" are to be relied upon. Again, I would contend that one must inspect the "control beliefs" of the experts before simply relying on their judgments.

It is just in this latter regard that our second essay, an excerpt from Younger's *Ancient Conquest Accounts* entitled "The Underpinnings" offers assistance (pp. 304–45). Beginning with a clear acknowledgement that, as M. I. Finley has written, "the historian is no mere chronicler, and he cannot do his work at all without assumptions and judgments,"[4] Younger seeks to bring these (sometimes hidden) assumptions and judgments to light. In so doing he focuses on three important issues: (1) how the idea of *history* should be conceived (here he first removes "old roots" and then nurtures "new shoots"); (2) in what sense the term *ideology* is best understood (that is, in the *narrow* sense as "false conciousness," in the *restrictive* sense as selective distortion, or in the *neutral* sense as "a pattern of beliefs and concepts [both factual and normative] which purport to explain complex social phenomena"—Younger prefers the latter); and (3) what a coherent historical approach to biblical texts might look like (Younger commends an approach that uses "semiotics in conjunction with a contextual method" [p. 338]).

Both Edelman and Younger agree that the Bible can and should be used as a historical source in the reconstruction of ancient Israelite history, but anyone conversant in current scholarly discussion will know that this is not a universally held opinion. In our third essay below (pp. 346–55), Siegfried Herrmann offers a brief, insightful survey of the place of the scripture in the historical study of ancient Israel and underscores the wrong-headedness of simply dismissing the Bible from the process of historical reconstruction. He surveys the contributions of Astruc, Wellhausen, Gunkel, Alt, Weber, Noth, Albright, Mendenhall, de Geus, Gottwald, Lemche, Thompson, and others, and notes that, whatever differences existed between them, scholars up to Albright agreed at least that the Bible was middle and measure of the enterprise. In the 1960s, however, Mendenhall introduced a perspective that swept away such hitherto accepted assumptions as that the twelve tribes of Israel entered Canaan from the outside, were (semi)nomads before settling, were bound together ethnically and thus distinct from the Canaanites. After Mendenhall's work, de Geus, Gottwald, and Lemche adopted antitext assumptions that opened the way to their own creative reconstructions. Herrmann does not welcome this development, and he fears two potentially dire consequences. First, he fears that, if very

---

4. M. I. Finley, *The Use and Abuse of History* (London: Chatto and Windus, 1975) 61.

many accept T. L. Thompson's contention that the crisis in biblical scholarship can be relieved by divorcing historical and exegetical studies from one another, then the crisis will truly begin, because the relation of the Bible to history cannot be so easily dismissed. Second, he fears that, once the biblical picture has been dismissed, there will emerge purely personalized renditions of Israel's (?) history based on subjective readings of the archaeological evidence—itself, of course, open to various interpretations.

As previously noted, there is a sense in which every hisorical reconstruction is a personal vision. As Max Miller observes in the fourth essay below ("Reading the Bible Historically: The Historian's Approach," pp. 356–72), "historians seek objectivity" but must recognize that "complete objectivity is a goal never reached." Since "the historian's own presuppositions, ideology, and attitudes inevitably influence his or her research and reporting," it is fair to say that "any history book reveals as much about its author as it does about the period of time being treated" (p. 357). In keeping with this view, Miller is commendably candid about his own stance: he positions himself in the "middle ground" between biblical literalists, on the one hand, and extreme skeptics, on the other. He is convinced that "the Bible preserves authentic historical memory" but regards it as the historian's task "to separate the authentic historical memory from its highly theological and often legendary context" (p. 361). In setting "historical" and "theological" in opposition, Miller evidences his allegiance to the historical critical method in which "God-talk" is methodologically eliminated (p. 358). He is keenly aware of the tension between the "dynamic" worldview of the Bible and the exclusively naturalistic assumptions of the historical critical method, but he shows little inclination to question the latter. As a representative of the "middle ground" position taken by perhaps a majority of working biblical scholars and as one of the most prolific American writers on the history of Israel, Miller is well placed to comment on (1) history and historical methodology, (2) the Bible as history, and (3) biblical scholarship and the study of ancient Israelite history, which form the three sections of his essay.

In the fifth essay below, entitled "Contingency, Continuity, and Integrity in Historical Understanding: An Old Testament Perspective" (pp. 373–90), F. E. Deist begins with an assessment of historicism's emphasis on *contingency*—the notion that historical change comes about essentially by accident—and concludes that it ultimately undercuts historical explanation. He then moves to a consideration of nomological approaches' emphasis on *continuity*. Model oriented and seeking to pattern themselves after the human sciences such as sociology, psychology, and anthropology, the nomological (or "law" governed) approaches fall short in a number of respects, according to Deist: they tend to be reductionistic, they often in-

volve over-generalization, which can prevent true understanding of *people*
in the past by people in the present, and there is always the question of
whether the model imposed upon Israel's past is in fact appropriate—that
is to say, whether there is conceptual *continuity* between ancient Israelite
society and the society on which the model is based. Dissatisfied with both
historicist and nomological approaches, Deist proposes an approach that
he regards as having more integrity with respect to its object of study. Essential to Deist's proposal is his definition of "history" as "an explanation
of the meaningful connectedness of a sequence of past events in the form
of an interested and focussed narrative" (p. 380). Deist unpacks this definition in a way that merits careful scrutiny. In the end, Deist recognizes, as
others we have cited, that "human involvement in any process of interpretation is accompanied by interests" (p. 386). For this reason, Deist insists
that integrity in historical explanation requires that

> the perspective from which a historian selects and combines, interrelates
> and connects events, that is, the perspective from which s/he assigns
> meaning to the whole should be explicated. This allows fellow historians
> as well as the "average intelligent person" to evaluate the argument from
> the correct perspective, and to criticize the perspective itself. The integ-
> rity of historical narration has very much to do with the question whether
> the perspective giving explanations for series of events of the past is
> stated in such a way that it can be discussed and criticized by those for
> whom (and/or about whom!) the history has been written. (p. 386)

Common to all five of the essays in the first section of part 4 is the belief that Israel's history writing (contained in the Hebrew Bible) has some
role to play in the writing of Israel's history. But, of course, not all others
are agreed. Keith W. Whitelam, for instance, dismisses the Bible as "a danger and a distraction," at least for those interested in the "real people" of
ancient Palestine, whom he defines not as the (largely male) group of individuals who figure in the pages of the Bible but rather as "the vast
majority of people who inhabited ancient Palestine" and whose "living
conditions" he assumes to be the proper object of historical study (Whitelam 1991: 70–71; cf. also idem 1986). P. R. Davies insists that the task of
the historian of Israel "will be increasingly divorced from literary criticism" of the Bible and must focus on "the (combined) methods of the social sciences: sociology, anthropology and archaeology" (Davies 1987: 4).
T. L. Thompson (1995) contends that as historians we must first develop
a history of Israel independent of the biblical witness, in order then to see,
in relation to the history of Israel that we have made, whether and to what
extent the biblical materials may be relevant. In the current volume, this
general view, sometimes characterized as "minimalist," is represented by

the sixth essay below, N. P. Lemche's "Is It Still Possible to Write a History of Ancient Israel?" (pp. 391–414).

A central question for Lemche is whether it would not "be preferable if the modern historian simply skipped over the biblical historical construction and made his own reconsruction of what he thought to be the history of ancient Palestine." For Lemche the answer is clearly yes, though unlike some other "minimalists" he does allow that the Hebrew Bible might remain "one source of knowledge (albeit a rather comprehesive one) among others." His main contention is that "there should be no reason to pay special attention to the Old Testament version in contrast to other information" (p. 396). In practice, Lemche does not put much stock in the Hebrew Bible as a source of *historical* information, for he believes it to be "unrelated to any objective reality" (Lemche 1984: 114). Lemche appears to draw this conclusion on three grounds relating to (1) worldview, (2) late datings of biblical texts, and (3) archaeological evidence: (1) "there exists an almost absolute contrast between our idea of history and of the world and the one common among ancient peoples" (Lemche 1984: 120); (2) "the lapse of time between the assumed 'historical' events in the premonarchical era and the written narratives dealing with them in the Old Testament is so conclusive that it must be considered absolutely wrong to think that the Old Testament narratives form a point of departure for the historical study of Palestine during the later half of the 2.mill.B.C. *The Old Testament narratives are, perforce, secondary historical sources*" (Lemche 1984: 121); (3) "the Old Testament model—or account—of early Israelite history is . . . disproved by the archaeological sources to such a degree that I consider it better to leave it out of consideration" (Lemche 1984: 122).

The issues of dating texts of the Hebrew Bible and of interpreting archaeological evidence are far more open than Lemche's statements imply, and it needs to be asked what Lemche means by "our idea of history and of the world"—surely current scholars are not undifferentiated in regard to their "idea of history and of the world," and many share at least the theistic aspect of the worldview "common among ancient peoples." Something of the magnitude and the emotion of the disagreement among current scholars is evidenced by the seventh essay below, Baruch Halpern's "Erasing History: The Minimalist Assault on Ancient Israel" (pp. 415–26). Halpern offers a stinging critique of "minimalist" writers who would late-date virtually all biblical material to the Persian period and deny even the existence of kings such as David and Solomon. He shows how the minimalist approach must simply sweep aside much archaeological and inscriptional evidence that would support the picture painted by, for example, the book of Kings—though he himself dismisses "much of the Pentateuch" as "legend presented as though it were historical fact"

(p. 424). Halpern laments the fact that "uncritical allegiance to the biblical text is . . . common among students and a signficant slice of scholars" (p. 426), but he makes no comment on the possibility of a "critical allegiance" to the biblical text. Placing himself between the extremes, Halpern predicts that the "best scholars" in the field will "continue to resist the 'minimalist' overtures" (p. 426). What Halpern finds particularly curious and vexing is the fact that "the views of these critics would seem to be an expression of despair over the supposed impossibility of recovering the past from works written in a more recent present—except, of course, that they pretend to provide access to a 'real' past in their own works written in the contemporary present" (p. 418). (In his own essay, Lemche seems both to deny and to admit to a similar charge by Herrmann that he has "created nothing but my own personal version of the history of Israel"—"unrightfully accused," protests Lemche, but then he adds, "but at least it is *my* version, not just a new paraphrase of the Deuteronomistic one" [396 n. 13]). As to what motivates the minimalists, Halpern suggests that this differs from scholar to scholar. And whatever one makes of Halpern's conjectures, they at least underscore once again the notion that one's historical reconstructions are highly reflective of one's worldview—one's epistemological and ontological commitments.[5]

In the third and final section below, we move to a consideration of how recent trends in literary criticism might bear upon the historical study of ancient Israel. In the first essay in this section, "Historical Criticism and Literary Interpretation" (pp. 427–38), John Barton argues that historical study and literary criticism are more interrelated than many scholars seem to recognize. For instance, if "biblical criticism proper depends on contemplating the possibility that texts are incoherent" and concludes in many instances that they are, and if modern literary criticism, contrariwise, is able to "show the possibility of reading texts as unitary," thereby weakening "the foundation for a source criticism based on the detection of inconsistencies," then surely literary study, "far from being irrelevant to historical issues, has much to contribute *at the historical level*" (pp. 433–34). The final essay, Herbert Klement's "Modern Literary-Critical Methods and the Historicity of the Old Testament" (pp. 439–59), offers a brief survey of the rise of modern literary approaches and of their significance for historical study of the Bible and includes a number of illustrative examples.

---

5. For T. L. Thompson's own characterizations of himself, P. R. Davies, N. P. Lemche, and G. Ahlström, see T. L. Thompson, "A Neo-Albrightean School in History and Biblical Scholarship?" *JBL* 114 (1995) 696.

At the beginning of this introduction to part 4, I drew attention to the high level of scholarly disagreement about how the methodological challenge of writing Israel's history is to be met. There is little reason to hope that scholarly disagreement will soon subside. With respect to the just-mentioned advances in the literary understanding of biblical narratives, for example, some regard the demonstration of greater literary coherence than previous historical criticism had assumed as grounds for greater confidence in the texts' testimony (including their testimony about the past). Keith Whitelam, by contrast, believes that "recent changes in perspective regarding the biblical text mean that the biblical historian is forced to proceed with ever greater caution. New literary studies have, above all else, illustrated the artistry and coherence of many biblical narratives . . ." (Whitelam 1986: 51). On the issue of presence or absence of literary coherence, Barton remarks that sometimes "one interpreter's chaos is another's rich tapestry" (below, p. 434). It would now seem, further, that even where there is agreement that a rich tapestry is present, one interpreter's cause for confidence is another's cause for caution.

Additional Reading

General Discussions of Method

Abraham, W. J.
  1982 *Divine Revelation and the Limits of Historical Criticism*. Oxford: Oxford University Press.
Ackroyd, P. R.
  1985 The Historical Literature. Pp. 297–323 in *The Hebrew Bible and Its Modern Interpreters*. Edited by D. Knight and G. Tucker. Atlanta: Scholars Press.
Halpern, B.
  1987 Biblical or Israelite History? Pp. 103–39 in *The Future of Biblical Studies: The Hebrew Bible*. Edited by R. E. Friedman and H. G. M. Williamson. Atlanta: Scholars Press.
Hayes, J. H.
  1987 On Reconstructing Israelite History. *Journal for the Study of the Old Testament* 39: 5–9.
Long, V. P.
  1997 Old Testament History: A Hermeneutical Perspective. Pp. 73–89 in vol. 1 of *The New International Dictionary of Old Testament Theology and Exegesis*. Edited by W. VanGemeren. Grand Rapids: Zondervan.
Miller, J. M.
  1992 Reflections on the Study of Israelite History. Pp. 60–74 in *What Has Archaeology to Do with Faith?* Edited by J. H. Charlesworth and W. P. Weaver. Philadelphia: Trinity Press International.

Murphy, R. E.
1991   Reflections upon Historical Methodology in Biblical Studies. Pp. 19–25 in *The Land of Carmel: Essays in Honor of Joachim Smet, O. Carm.* Edited by P. Chandler and K. J. Egan. Rome: Institutum Carmelitanum.
Noort, E.
1991   Klio und die Welt des Alten Testaments: Überlegungen zur Benutzung literarischer und feldarchäologischer Quellen bei der Darstellung einer Geschichte Israels. Pp. 533–60 in *Ernten was man sät: Festschrift für Klaus Koch zu seinem 65. Geburtstag.* Edited by D. R. Daniels et al. Neukirchen-Vluyn: Neukirchener Verlag.
Roux, J. H. le
1990   Biblical and Modern Historiography: The Widest Horizon. *Old Testament Essays: Journal of the Old Testament Society of South Africa* 3: 23–42.
Sasson, J.
1981   On Choosing Models for Recreating Israelite Pre-monarchic History. *Journal for the Study of the Old Testament* 21: 3–24.
Scheffler, E.
1988   Op weg na 'n komprehensiewe geskiedenis van Ou-Israel. *Hervormde Teologiese Studies* 44: 665–83.
1993   Oor die metodiek van 'n holistiese geskiedenis van Oud-Israel. *Hervormde Teologiese Studies* 49: 908–33.
Smelik, K. A. D.
1992   The Use of the Hebrew Bible as a Historical Source. Pp. 1–34 in *Converting the Past: Studies in Ancient Israelite and Moabite Historiography.* Edited by A. S. Van der Woude. Oudtestamentische Studiën 28. Leiden: Brill.

Social Science and the Battle over the Bible

Ahlström, G. W.
1991   The Role of Archaeological and Literary Remains in Reconstructing Israel's History. Pp. 116–41 in *The Fabric of History.* Edited by D. Edelman. Journal for the Study of the Old Testament Supplement Series 127. Sheffield: JSOT Press.
Brandfon, F.
1987   The Limits of Evidence: Archaeology and Objectivity. *Maarav* 4: 5–43.
Clements, R. E.
1989   *The World of Ancient Israel: Sociological, Anthropological and Political Perspectives.* Cambridge: Cambridge University Press.
Davies, P. R.
1987   The History of Ancient Israel and Judah. *Journal for the Study of the Old Testament* 39: 3–4.
Dever, W. G.
1995a   "Will the Real Israel Please Stand Up?" Part I: Archaeology and Israelite Historiography. *Bulletin of the American Schools of Oriental Research* 297: 61–80.

1995b   "Will the Real Israel Please Stand Up?" Part II: Archaeology and the Religions of Ancient Israel. *Bulletin of the American Schools of Oriental Research* 298: 37–58.

Finkelstein, I.
1989   The Emergence of Monarchy in Israel: The Environmental and Socio-Economic Aspects. *Journal for the Study of the Old Testament* 44: 43–74.

Frevel, C.
1989   "Dies ist der Ort, von dem geschrieben steht . . .": Zum Verhältnis von Bibelwissenschaft und Palästinaarchäologie. *Biblische Notizen* 47: 35–89.

Gates, M.-H.
1988   Dialogues between Ancient Near Eastern Texts and the Archaeological Record: Test Cases from Bronze Age Syria. *Bulletin of the American Schools of Oriental Research* 270: 63–91.

Hauer, C., Jr.
1987   Anthropology in Historiography. *Journal for the Study of the Old Testament* 39: 15–21.

Herion, G. A.
1986   The Impact of Modern and Social Science Assumptions on the Reconstruction of Israelite History. *Journal for the Study of the Old Testament* 34: 3–33.

Knapp, P.
1984   Can Social Theory Escape from History? Views of History in Social Science. *History and Theory* 23: 34–52.

Lemche, N. P.
1984   On the Problem of Studying Israelite History: Apropos Abraham Malamat's View of Historical Research. *Biblische Notizen* 24: 94–124.

Mendenhall, G. E.
1983   Ancient Israel's Hyphenated History. Pp. 91–103 in *Palestine in Transition: The Emergence of Ancient Israel*. Edited by D. N. Freedman and D. F. Graf. Sheffield: Almond.

1987   *Biblical Interpretation and the Albright School: Archaeology and Biblical Interpretation*. Edited by L. G. Perdue, L. E. Toombs, and G. L. Johnson. Atlanta: John Knox.

Miller, J. M.
1987   Old Testament History and Archaeology. *Biblical Archaeologist* 50: 55–63.

Norin, S.
1994   Respons zu Lemche, "Ist es noch möglich die Geschichte des alten Israels zu schreiben?" *Scandinavian Journal of the Old Testament* 8: 191–97.

Osiek, C.
1989   The New Handmaid: The Bible and the Social Sciences. *Theological Studies* 50: 260–78.

Otto, E.
1984   Sozialhistorische Grundsatz- und Einzelprobleme in der Geschichtsschreibung des Israel: Eine Antwort auf N. Lemche. *Biblische Notizen* 23: 63–80.

Rodd, C. S.
1981 On Applying a Sociological Theory to Biblical Studies. *Journal for the Study of the Old Testament* 19: 95–106.

Rogerson, J.
1986 Anthropology and the Old Testament. *Proceedings of the Irish Biblical Association* 10: 90–102.

Rose, D. G.
1987 The Bible and Archaeology: The State of the Art. Pp. 53–64 in *Archaeology and Biblical Interpretation*. Edited by L. G. Perdue, L. E. Toombs, and G. L. Johnson. Atlanta: John Knox.

Thompson, T. L.
1995 Gösta Ahlström's History of Palestine. Pp. 420–34 in *The Pitcher is Broken: Memorial Essays for Gösta W. Ahlström*. Edited by S. W. Holloway and L. K. Handy. Journal for the Study of the Old Testament Supplement Series 190. Sheffield: Sheffield Academic Press.

Whitelam, K. W.
1986 Recreating the History of Israel. *Journal for the Study of the Old Testament* 35: 45–70.

1991 Between History and Literature: The Social Production of Israel's Traditions of Origin. *Scandinavian Journal for the Old Testament* 5/2: 60–74.

1995 Sociology or History: Towards a (Human) History of Ancient Palestine? Pp. 149–66 in *Words Remembered, Texts Renewed*. Edited by J. Davies, G. Harvey, and W. G. E. Watson. Journal for the Study of the Old Testament Supplement Series 195. Sheffield: Sheffield Academic Press.

Literary Study and Historical Reconstruction

Alter, R.
1987 Introduction to the Old Testament. Pp. 11–35 in *The Literary Guide to the Bible*. Edited by R. Alter and F. Kermode. Cambridge: The Belknap Press of Harvard University Press.

Campbell, E. F.
1992 Relishing the Bible as Literature and History. *Christian Century* 109: 812–15.

Geller, S. A.
1983 Through Windows and Mirrors into the Bible: History, Literature and Language in the Study of Text. Pp. 3–40 in *A Sense of Text: The Art of Language in the Study of Biblical Literature (Papers from a Symposium at The Dropsie College for Hebrew and Cognate Learning, May 11, 1982)*. A Jewish Quarterly Review Supplement: 1982. Winona Lake, Ind.: Eisenbrauns.

Long, V. P.
1994 How Did Saul Become King? Literary Reading and Historical Reconstruction. Pp. 271–84 in *Faith, Tradition, and History*. Edited by A. R. Millard, J. K. Hoffmeier, and D. W. Baker. Winona Lake, Ind.: Eisenbrauns.

Polak, F.
  1986   Literary Study and 'Higher Criticism' According to the Tale of David's Beginning. Pp. 27–32 in *Proceedings of the Ninth World Congress of Jewish Studies: Jerusalem, August 4–12, 1985*. Jerusalem: World Union of Jewish Studies.
Polzin, R.
  1980   Criticism and Crisis within Biblical Studies. Pp. 1–24 in *Moses and the Deuteronomist: A Literary Study of the Deuteronomistic History*. New York: Seabury.
Prickett, S.
  1989   The Status of Biblical Narrative. *Pacifica* 2: 26–46.
Provan, I. W.
  1995   Ideologies, Literary and Critical: Reflections on Recent Writing on the History of Israel. *Journal of Biblical Literature* 114: 586–606.
Rendtorff, R.
  1988   Between Historical Criticism and Holistic Interpretation. Pp. 289–303 in *Congress Volume: Jerusalem, 1986*. Supplements to Vetus Testamentum 40. Leiden: Brill.
Younger, K. L., Jr.
  1990   The Figurative Aspect and the Contextual Method in the Evaluation of the Solomonic Empire (1 Kings 1–11). Pp. 157–75 in *The Bible in Three Dimensions: Essays in Celebration of Forty Years of Biblical Studies in the University of Sheffield*. Edited by D. J. A. Clines, S. E. Fowl, and S. E. Porter. Sheffield: JSOT Press.

Doing History in Biblical Studies

DIANA EDELMAN

Introduction

[[13]] Although we are all familiar with the term "history," we do not always stop to think about its dimensions and the processes associated with "doing history" as an investigative discipline. History can designate actual events that transpired in the past, the recoverable traces of actual events that transpired, and the interpretation of past events through the creation of cause-and-effect chains to relate the recoverable traces of those events.[1] The following presentation will focus upon the method associated with the third definition, that involving the discipline devoted to the study of events, changes, and the particularities of our human past through present traces of that past and how historical method is to be applied in biblical studies.

A historical investigation of the events described in the Bible properly belongs to the subdivision of history known as ancient Syro-Palestinian history and within that subdivision, the history of ancient Israel and Judah. Although the term "biblical history" is often used as a synonym for ancient Near Eastern history or the history of ancient Israel and Judah, strictly speaking, biblical history would be an investigation of the process that led to the formation of the Bible. It would include the drawing of interconnections between particular events over time relating to the writing of individual biblical texts, their joining into larger coherent blocks of material, their organization into books, and the ordering of books to form a com-

Reprinted with permission from *The Fabric of History: Text, Artifact and Israel's Past* (ed. D. V. Edelman; Sheffield: JSOT Press, 1991) 13–25.

1. G. R. Elton, *The Practice of History* (New York: Thomas Y. Crowell, 1967) 10.

prehensive, canonical piece of sacred literature. By contrast, ancient Syro-Palestinian history is the branch of the study of particular events and changes that took place within the geographical region of ancient Syria–Palestine [[14]] or affected population groups associated with these regions, while the history of ancient Israel and Judah focuses more narrowly on the study of events and changes within the region and among groups associated with the states of Israel and Judah.

Time parameters for the adjective "ancient" in the term "ancient Syro-Palestinian history" are determined by consensus rather than by logic or self-evident demands of history itself. The beginning date would be the earliest period from which traces of past human events have been or will be found. The closing date is less easily established; since history is a continuum, the fixing of all subdivisional points within it is arbitrary to some degree and becomes a matter of convention. Generally, events that took place during the time span when Rome controlled most of the ancient Near East are considered to qualify as "ancient"; the Byzantine era usually falls outside the "ancient" classification. Any human events dating through the end of the 2nd century C.E. that took place within the geographical region of ancient Syria–Palestine should therefore qualify as potential topics of historical inquiry within the field of ancient Syro-Palestinian history. All events described within the Bible are within the domain of the ancient Syro-Palestinian or ancient Israelite historian. The ancient Israelite historian is free to pursue additional events that impacted on Israel or Judah but which were not mentioned in the Bible; a myriad of additional events not related to those few preserved in the Bible and not restricted to the states of Israel and Judah alone are equally valid topics of investigation for the ancient Syro-Palestinian historian.

The Historical Process

Studies conducted within the discipline of history are accomplished through a standard multistep process,[2] with the exact set of methods to be employed being multidisciplinary and determined by the nature of the available evidence. Historical investigations begin when historians choose general topics or problems for study. They then immerse themselves in all the potentially relevant source material, making initial evaluations concerning the genuineness of the available evidence. The immersion step is commonly referred to as familiarization [[15]] and forms the basis for the next step, conceptual invention. As G. R. Elton has noted,

2. So, e.g., Elton, *Practice*, 63–67; P. Conkin and R. Stromberg, *The Heritage and Challenge of History* (New York: Dodd and Mead, 1971) 216–17.

historical research does not consist, as beginners in particular often suppose, in the pursuit of some particular evidence which will answer a particular question; it consists of an exhaustive, and exhausting, review of everything that may conceivably be germane to a given investigation.[3]

The crucial step of conceptual invention involves the interpretation of the data. The historian, now intimately familiar with the culture and thought habits of the people in the chronological era and geographical region under investigation, uses instinctive understanding and imagination to create a formal construct such as a schema, a convincing pattern or theme, or a crucial causal hypothesis that will link together pieces of evidence to form a coherent pattern of meaning.

> In the last analysis, whether consciously or no, it is always by borrowing from our daily experiences and by shading them, when necessary, with new tints that we derive the elements which help us to restore the past. For here in the present, is immediately perceptible that vibrance of human life which only a great effort of the imagination can restore to the old text.[4]

Historians are aware that they cannot compose a complete or fully sufficient account of the past events they are studying; they know and accept that the causal links they "discover" are never all those operative and influential at the time.[5] Nevertheless, they are content to be able to make sense of some portion of the complex of past events they are studying by interconnecting the disjointed remains of those events. The interpretive stage is "the outlet for historical genius, for the man who can meet an age in diverse, fragmentary surviving artifacts, and quickly see a unifying pattern and likely connections."[6] "Meaningful interconnection in the particular, illuminating generalization beyond the individual case—these are the marks that distinguish the inspired and inspiring historian from the hack."[7]

[[16]] The next step in a historical investigation involves the inductive verification of the formal interpretive construct. The historian actively seeks to "flesh out" the unifying pattern with the appropriate evidence. The selected evidence now must be carefully analyzed to establish its genuineness. Questions and problems raised by the formal construct must be answered and solved convincingly. At times, these questions and answers will force the modification of the unifying pattern, as will the analysis of

---

3. Elton, *Practice*, 66–67.
4. M. Bloch, *The Historian's Craft* (trans. P. Putnam; New York: Alfred Knopf, 1953) 44.
5. For types of causal judgments, see Conkin and Stromberg, *Heritage*, 187–88, 192, 197, 202–3.
6. Conkin and Stromberg, *Heritage*, 217.
7. Elton, *Practice*, 98.

selected evidence. The interpretive process is one that involves fine-tuning through continued examination and consideration of the evidence. The final step, which is not always undertaken, is the communication of the knowledge acquired in the previous steps to others through writing, that is, historiography.

When attempting to understand the past, all disciplines that deal with investigations of past human events must rely on the same body of evidence, the surviving records or artifacts that have been recovered. Historians, archaeologists, social anthropologists, social psychologists, sociologists, economists, and political scientists must all engage in the identical task of critically analyzing the known body of texts and artifacts to establish their forms and to examine the social and individual psychological factors that determine their quality and credibility. Regardless of one's discipline, one must distinguish between the witness of a participant in the events and testimony of others and weigh each type of report accordingly. One must distinguish between evidence that is deliberately transmitted (annals, chronicles, inscriptions, diaries, memoirs, genealogies, ballads, tales, sagas, certain art works) and that which is unconsciously transmitted (human remains, business and administrative records, language, customs and instructions, certain artifacts). One must distinguish between forgeries and genuine documents, in order to assess the usefulness of each item for the investigation at hand. Judgments as to the neutrality and intentionally biased or deceptive nature of records and remains must be made before any text or artifact can be considered to be acceptable evidence for the events under investigation, regardless of one's particular discipline. The date of texts and artifacts must be established in order to evaluate their appropriateness to the investigation at hand.

History and the Social Sciences

[[17]] All disciplines investigating past human events will share the same set of methods for evaluating potential evidence for a given set of events, and those methods will vary, depending upon the nature of the recovered remains. In practice, not every investigator will be able to master the requisite methods for evaluating every type of evidence that will be recovered. Different disciplines train their members to analyse materials that are frequently encountered as forms of primary evidence within their areas of concern, but since the recovered material often takes a range of forms that cuts across the particular concerns of many disciplines, few will have the trained expertise necessary to evaluate all available evidence personally. In the case of human, faunal, and botanical remains, investigators in all disciplines studying the past will need to rely on the expertise of trained specialists who can identify types and date remains through radiocarbon dating, established pottery sequences, and other special processes. In the case of documents, all disciplines will be dependent upon the evaluations of linguists, those trained in paleography, and in some cases, literary critics.

How then does one distinguish a historical investigation of a past event or cluster of events from those conducted in connection with the same set of events within social scientific disciplines such as cultural anthropology, archaeology, or sociology? What are the boundaries of a historical investigation, when there is a shared pool of available evidence and the need to use the same set of multidisciplinary methods to evaluate that evidence among the historical, social scientific and literary disciplines? Simply put, history attempts to understand a given problem from the inside; it is ideographic, that is, it particularizes, while social scientific disciplines generally attempt to explain a problem by linking it to the operation of a law or a more complex, multivariable system; they are nomothetic, that is, designed to establish general laws or models.[8]

> History remains essentially a way of looking at data, and asking and answering the question "Why?" in relation to specific occurrences. It seems generally less concerned to establish and test generalizations about [[18]] the properties of social institutions than to trace trains of events over time in terms of chains of cause and effect.[9]

Social scientific investigations, on the other hand, have often been designed to put into the background the particulars of actual events that make them unique and to focus instead on those aspects that allow them to be identified with other entities or events of a similar kind and so provide the basis for abstracting behavioral or physical laws or systems governing behavior or reactions. In practice then, there will be a certain degree of overlap in the pieces of the available pool of evidence that will be selected for inclusion in a historical reconstruction and a social scientific one, but inevitably there will also be differences. A historical reconstruction will usually include many more event-specific details.

Within recent decades there has been a visible shift within the focus of many social scientific investigations away from establishing generalizations in the form of laws that tend to establish a single cause-and-effect chain to explain observable phenomena toward the formulation and de-

---

8. Elton, *Practice*, 18, 26–27.

9. I. M. Lewis, "Introduction," in *History and Social Anthropology* (ed. I. M. Lewis; ASA Monographs, 7; New York: Tavistock, 1968).

scription of systemic models that recognize the simultaneous operation of a number of variables and cause-and-effect relationships. This has led in turn to a focus on the study of the particulars of a specific society within a delimited time frame. While the shift in emphasis still often maintains the testing and modifications of systemic models as a primary goal, it also seems to reflect the recognition that the idiosyncrasies of different societies are as important as their commonly shared traits. Studies undertaken within the framework of new archaeology are to be included within the more recent type of social scientific investigation on one of two premises. The artifactual remains recovered through excavation either are to be used "to discover laws through the testing of their implication," or "to describe the inner workings of extinct cultural systems in terms of multiple causality and mutual effect."[10]

Should a social scientist and/or a political scientist decide to investigate Jehu's coup in Judah, for example, their evaluation of available sources would be made using the identical set of methods that a [[19]] historian of Judah would employ. They might even select the same pieces of evidence to include in their reconstructions, so that the final products might seem to be alternative solutions to the same issue, arrived at by using the same methodology. It is likely, however, that each professional's background field would be able to be discerned from the larger context within which the specific investigation was undertaken, the particular set of related problems that are defined and examined, the nature of the cause-and-effect chains or system created to link together the pieces of evidence, and the relative use of theory or generalized law to inform the reconstruction. Investigators coming from a discipline that regularly uses models and theories that have been abstracted from a number of specific case studies will tend to analyze data with such constructs in mind, whether consciously or not.

By contrast, a person undertaking a historical investigation will select and arrange evidence on the basis of the imagination and instinctive judgment of one who, through immersion in the evidence, lives in a past age "as a contemporary equipped with immunity, hindsight, and arrogant superiority"[11] and so is able to use personal judgment to discern one or more patterns of interrelations, of cause and effect, among as much of the body of evidence as possible. The historian will not have a set of models and theories designed to explain laws of behavior or nature as part of the tools of the historical trade. While individuals will inevitably draw on their

---

10. F. Hole and R. F. Heizer, *An Introduction to Prehistoric Archeology* (3rd edn.; Chicago: Holt, Rinehart & Winston, 1973) 31–37.

11. Elton, *Practice*, 17.

entire range of personal experience to select data and link it into causal patterns and so may unconsciously be swayed by knowledge of social scientific models and theories, there will be no conscious and systematic application of a specific theory or model to the evidence. Instead, there will be a tendency to use analogies drawn from personal knowledge or experience that are both consciously and subconsciously perceived to share similarities with specific situations or details under investigation.

At times, the historian may not be able to arrive at a cause-and-effect chain to interrelate the evidence; "very often he finds that no strategy whatsoever can wring from the fragments that have survived answers to the questions it purports to deal with."[12] In this case, the historian will abandon the investigation or shift to another topic that [[20]] might be more conducive to the body of available data. By contrast, social scientists faced with such a situation might employ an established model or theory from their particular field of inquiry to bridge the evidentiary gaps and provide plausible explanations for missing steps in logical causation. In so doing, they would be appealing to an underlying body of analogous events from disparate time periods and cultures whose particulars have been played down or eliminated from consideration in the interest of the establishment of a generalized scientific law. Such a use of theory or model does not invalidate a proposed bridging effort, but neither does it strengthen its results. The lack of essential data cannot be overcome until the data themselves become available, if ever.

Many people presume that a social-scientific approach to humanity's past is somehow "better" or "truer" than a historical one because it can relate events to established models of behavior that can be independently tested and verified. However, such an attitude rests on the false premise that there are empirical "laws" or models governing the march of history, similar to the "laws" or models of behavior or physical science that are studied within the sciences. There are no such historical "laws" to be used to explain or deduce the chain of events in an individual case under study. We no longer need to follow in the footsteps of past generations who were

> mesmerized by the Comtian conception of physical science. This hypnotic *schema*, extending to every province of the intellect, seemed to them to prove that no authentic discipline could exist which did not lead, by its immediate and irrefutable demonstrations, to the formulation of absolute certainties in the form of sovereign and universal laws.[13]

12. J. H. Hexter, *Doing History* (Bloomington, IN: Indiana University Press, 1971) 109.
13. Bloch, *Historian's Craft*, 14.

In the light of continuing intellectual development, "we no longer feel obliged to impose upon every subject of knowledge a uniform intellectual pattern, borrowed from natural science, since, even there, that pattern has ceased to be entirely applicable."[14]

This is not to deny, however, that historians can and often regularly do employ closed generalizations, which consist of time-conditioned, culturally relative but enduring regularities in human behavior. Although they are not concerned with their verification as a social scientist would be, they are very much concerned with their veracity. [[21]] Many social scientists use such closed generalizations for predictive purposes; when they do, they should "acknowledge a historical rather than a truly 'lawful' backdrop for them."[15]

Since there are no empirical "laws" governing the historical process, the historian is content to be able to discover some sort of pattern among a chosen set of events through creative reason. Some may object that irrationality can play a role in the fashioning of events so that the creation of causal chains through rational insight is not always legitimate. In reply, one can simply note (as does G. R. Elton) that

> reason does in measure work in men's lives, and on balance actions and motives are much more commonly explained correctly on assumption that some form of thinking has taken place, rather than that they welled up out of some unconscious which defies analysis.[16]

Even if one accepts reason as a legitimate operational tool in a historical enterprise,

> it is easy for a logician to demonstrate the tenuous chain of arguments that mark almost any complex historical judgment. In this sense, much of history is a stab into partial darkness, a matter of informed but inconclusive conjecture. The available evidence rarely necessitates our judgments but is at least consistent with them. Obviously, in such areas of interpretation, there is no one demonstrably correct "explanation," but very often competing, equally unfalsifiable, theories.[17]

Historians are content to accept the tentativeness of their insights and the need to modify, adjust, or abandon their interpretations of the evidence in light of new evidence or a better interpretive framework.

---

14. Bloch, *Historian's Craft*, 17.
15. Conkin and Stromberg, *Heritage*, 165.
16. Elton, *Practice*, 98.
17. Conkin and Stromberg, *Heritage*, 219.

The Task of the Ancient Israelite Historian

The ancient Syro-Palestinian or ancient Israelite historian who chooses to study an event described in the Bible will need to utilize the following range of methods associated with different disciplines, intersecting partially or sometimes totally with the other disciplines' concerns. After choosing a general topic for investigation, he or she must set about establishing a pool of potentially relevant evidence. The easiest place to begin is with the pertinent biblical account(s) and then [[22]] to move on to any extant extrabiblical texts deemed potentially relevant to the chosen topic. The process of evaluation will be identical for all literary evidence.

After reading the texts, the historian must establish what parts of the narrative are reliable evidence and what parts are fictional embellishment and ideological rhetoric. To do this, one must employ a number of methods developed by the discipline of literary studies: text criticism, to establish the definitive text to be used; literary criticism, to establish the structural and literary devices used to create the final form of the narrative, to spot any internal inconsistencies that might indicate later reworking, to understand authorial intentions, and to deduce a possible date of composition; form criticism, to understand the genres of literature found within the narrative as possible clues to the author's life-setting or the life-setting of possible sources used to create the narrative; and finally, source criticism, to move behind the final form of the text and discover what possible types of sources could have been available to the author, what kinds were likely to have existed, their date, which ones were likely to have been used and why.

Historians must either personally master all of the skills necessary to perform all of the above methods of evaluation or must rely upon the expertise of literary scholars for whatever methods they are unable to employ with confidence themselves. While a text-critical, literary-critical, form-critical, or source-critical analysis can stand on its own within the field of literary studies, for the historian, each is a necessary, initial, and incomplete step in the sorting of fact from fiction in the quest to judge the genuineness of details in the selected group of texts. Historians will have completed a literary analysis of all of the potentially pertinent texts, but their communication of findings, their historiographic reconstructions of the chosen events, will not necessarily describe in detail the stages of literary analysis. Instead, they will build upon the results of the literary evaluation by employing what has been judged to be genuine evidence, possibly placing limited analytical arguments in footnotes.

In addition to literary evidence, ancient Syro-Palestinian and ancient Israelite historians usually have at their disposal potentially relevant artifactual evidence that has been gathered through surface surveys and site excavations. After deciding on the appropriate chronological and geographical frames, historians must sift through the available [[23]] remains. If not themselves experts in pottery forms or chronology, or in faunal and floral identification, they will have to rely upon the judgments of experts within these areas and their published findings in initial and final archaeological excavation and survey reports. Nevertheless, it is crucial for every historian to read such reports critically to be sure that all judgments of date and identification have been made on the basis of appropriate criteria—context, and comparative stratigraphy and morphology. Historians also need to be familiar enough with the goals and limitations of archaeological methods that they can judge the relative strengths and weaknesses of artifactual evidence and assign appropriate weight to the evidence for their own investigations.

At times, an archaeologist will use the Bible or other textual materials inappropriately to date or identify remains, confusing the initial task of reporting finds and identifying levels of occupation with the final task of undertaking a reconstruction of the history of the excavated site—whether in terms of describing its workings as a system or of testing the implication of laws, premises, or systems through recovered data. It is only here, in the final step involving the reconstruction of the past—however that reconstruction is framed—that a synthesis of artifacts and occupational remains with relevant textual evidence, itself fully criticized by the investigator or literary experts, is to take place. The archaeologist must now employ historical methodology, or defer to a historian able to do so, immersing himself or herself fully in the evidence, linking it through creative reason, and fleshing out the resulting pattern with appropriate details. It is particularly crucial that the archaeologist should not fall into the trap of importing a social scientific model or system to explain the data and create cause-and-effect relationships when his goal is historical reconstruction. This is an easy and safe way out for one not trained in the use of creative reason, but the results will be disastrous, eliminating the particulars that make history history.

Having evaluated the potential pool of evidence, the historian is now ready for familiarization, conceptual invention, and inductive verification. Some scholars may prefer to delay their reading of other secondary discussions and proposed solutions to the problem until after they have worked through the primary evidence and arrived at their own tentative solutions. Others may prefer to have read the secondary discussions prior to launching their personal investigation. At [[24]] times, dissatisfaction with existing explanations will prompt historians to undertake a new investigation of a topic. Secondary discussions by other historians, literary scholars and social scientists can often serve as invaluable aids to focus one's attention or improve one's grasp of the full breadth of the problem. Subtle relationships that the historian might not have personally considered in the familiarization process may have been noted by others and can now be incorporated into his or her own interpretive framework or in the inductive verification process, with due credit given in footnote citations. At other times, observations made by others will challenge the historian's own tentative conclusions and force the modification of the initial interpretive scheme.

At whatever point historians decide to evaluate secondary reconstructions by colleagues in their own and related fields, it is essential that such an enterprise be undertaken before they reach their final interpretation of the evidence and any historiographic presentation of their findings. The secondary reconstructions themselves form a secondary pool of "evidence" for the crucial interpretive stage of the historical process, the stage that is based on creative invention. While there is always the danger that a historian will unconsciously impose a pattern on the artifactual and textual evidence that has been primarily influenced by other interpretations of the evidence rather than by the evidence itself, the results will speak for themselves. If the proposed interpretation is able to integrate as much of the evidence as possible into a coherent and plausible cause-and-effect pattern, then the proposed solution will be deemed successful, whatever the source of its inspiration. In theory, the evidence should be the primary source for inspiration and the interpretive insights of others a secondary source for further refinement of insights initially formulated from an encounter with the evidence.

Conclusion

What then are the boundaries of historical method within biblical studies? Any topic dealing with events, changes and the particulars of the human past that are mentioned within the Bible, one source providing potential traces of the past within the subdiscipline of ancient Syro-Palestinian history, is fair game. The topic will usually focus on an attempt to answer the question "why" in relationship to a constellation [[25]] of circumstances involving who, what, when and where, all of which must also be established. A historical-critical investigation will need to include the main steps of familiarization, conceptual invention, and inductive verification of the formal interpretive construct through the use of the evidence, not through an appeal to generalized "laws." The specific set of methods used as evaluative tools will be determined by the nature of the potentially relevant evidence available and so will vary from topic to topic. Always included will be text criticism, literary criticism, form criticism, and source criticism, because the Bible will be one, if not the main, source of literary evidence. Should artifactual evidence be available, which it generally is, then methods for identifying and processing artifacts within the fields of archaeology and related scientific disciplines such as paleobotany and zooarchaeology will also be necessary.

"In the last analysis, it is human consciousness which is the subject matter of history. The interrelations, confusions and infections of human consciousness are, for the historian, reality itself."[18]

18. Bloch, *Historian's Craft*, 151.

The Underpinnings

K. LAWSON YOUNGER, JR.

Historia est proxima poetis et quodammodo carmen solutum[1]
—Quintilianus

Part I
History: Cultivating an Idea

[[25]] While the number of articles and books devoted to the subject of Old Testament historiography has increased exponentially, there is seldom within these works any discussion of what history is.[2] One rarely finds any kind of definition given, and usually writers work with the assumption that there is a unified view of what history is: i.e., "modern scientific."[3] Biblical scholars have generally ignored recent developments in the philosophy of history, developments which have clarified numerous aspects of "narrative history." And since most history writing in the Old Testament is "narrative history," an investigation into these developments promises to yield positive results.

Reprinted with permission from *Ancient Conquest Accounts: A Study in Ancient Near Eastern and Biblical History Writing* (JSOTS 98; Sheffield: Sheffield Academic Press, 1990) 25–58 (plus notes).

1. "History is akin to the poets and is, so to speak, *a prose poem* [emphasis mine]" (*Institutio Oratoria* X.i.31) (in this context *solutum* means free of metrical restrictions).

2. One notable exception is the work of B. Halpern in which he devotes two chapters to this topic and makes a real contribution to its understanding (*The First Historians*, 3–35). For him "history is the undertaking of rendering an account of a particular, significant, and coherent sequence of past human events . . . histories purport to be true, or probable, representations of events and relationships in the past . . . a selective approximation. History, in sum, is a literally false but scientifically more or less useful coherence imposed by reason on reality" (pp. 6–7).

3. E.g., G. Garbini, *History and Ideology in Ancient Israel*.

Many may object to the inclusion of theoretical discussions from the realm of the "philosophy of history." But the words of M. I. Finley easily counter such objections:

> Historians, one hears all the time, should get on with their proper business, the investigation of the concrete experiences of the past, and leave the "philosophy of history" (which is a barren, abstract and pretty useless activity anyway) to the philosophers. Unfortunately the historian is no mere chronicler, and he cannot do his work at all without assumptions and judgments.[4]

Removing "Old Roots"

[[26]] So completely is modern biblical scholarship the grateful recipient of the gifts of the German historiographic tradition that the general tenets of that tradition are immediately assumed to be one and the same with what any right-minded student of the religion of Israel would do almost intuitively.[5] But perhaps a caution should be penned: "beware of Germans bearing historiographic gifts"![6]

Two biblical scholars' definitions of history will demonstrate this: John Van Seters and George Coats.[7] Van Seters has recently assumed a definition of history proposed by the Dutch historian Johan Huizinga:

> History is the intellectual form in which a civilization renders account to itself of its past.[8]

He uses this definition "because I regard the question of genre as the key issue in the discussion, whether we are dealing with the biblical writers or

4. M. I. Finley, *The Use and Abuse of History*, 61. H. White correctly points out that "those historians who draw a firm line between history and philosophy of history fail to recognize that every historical discourse contains within it a full-blown, if only implicit, philosophy of history" (*Tropics of Discourse*, 126–27).

5. See in this regard, R. A. Oden, Jr., "Intellectual History and the Study of the Bible," in *The Future of Biblical Studies*, 1–18.

6. Obviously, the German historiographic tradition had its impact on German Old Testament scholars (for the German tradition itself, see: G. Iggers, *The German Conception of History*; for its impact on German OT scholarship, see: R. A. Oden, Jr., "Hermeneutics and Historiography: Germany and America," in *Seminar Papers of the SBL*, 135–57).

7. John Van Seters, *In Search of History*; and George Coats, *Genesis*. We have chosen to examine these two scholars basically for two reasons: (1) because they offer detailed definitions which require interaction, and (2) because they are representative of opinions concerning history writing which make up a large segment of Old Testament scholarship.

8. Van Seters, *In Search of History*, 1. He is quoting J. Huizinga, "A Definition of the Concept of History," in *Philosophy and History: Essays Presented to Ernst Cassirer*, 9. For Huizinga's concept of history, see: R. L. Colie, "Huizinga and the Task of Cultural History," *AHR* 69 (1963–64) 607–30.

the Greek and Near Eastern materials."[9] Moreover, he feels that "in conformity with Huizinga's definition, this work examines the development of national histories and the history of the Israelites in particular." Thus he associates history writing with national identity. "Only when the nation itself took precedence over the king, as happened in Israel, could history writing be achieved." After a long survey of ancient Near Eastern material he argues that the "historiographical genres" of the Egyptians, Hittites, and Mesopotamians (e.g., annals, chronicles, king lists) "did not lead to true history writing." He subsumes all historical texts under the term "historiography" as a "more inclusive category than the particular genre of history writing."[10]

If one consults Huizinga's essay, the following arguments appear:

> The idea of history only emerges with the search for certain connexions, the essence of which is determined by the value which we attach to them. It makes no difference whether we think of a history which is the result of researches strictly critical in method, or of sagas and epics belonging to former phases of civilization. . . . We can speak in the same breath of historiography and historical research . . . of the local annalist and the designer of an historical cosmology.
>
> [[27]] Every civilization creates its own form of history . . . If a civilization coincides with a people, a state, a tribe, its history will be correspondingly simple. If a general civilization is differentiated into distinct nations, and these again into groups, classes, parties, the corresponding differentiation in the historical form follows of itself. The historical interests of every sectional civilization must hold its own history to be the true one, and is entitled to do so, provided that it constructs this history in accordance with the critical requirements imposed by its conscience as a civilization, and not according to the craving for power in the interests of which it imposes silence upon this conscience.[11]

It appears that Van Seters has misunderstood Huizinga's definition and invested it with a quite different meaning.[12]

---

9. Van Seters, *In Search of History*, 354.

10. He states: "most historical texts of the ancient Near East do not really fit this nationalistic sense of history writing, . . . For the sake of discussion, all historical texts may be subsumed under the term *historiography* as a more inclusive category than the particular genre of history writing" (pp. 1–2). There is also a transformation between these two: "One must pay close attention to the matter of the genre and function of historical texts, for it is in *the transformation of such limited forms of historiography into a particular form of literature* that the origin of history is to be found" (p. 6). So Van Seters's genre analysis becomes a hunt for the point of transformation into the nationalistic form.

11. Huizinga, "A Definition of the Concept of History," 5–7.

12. See our review of Van Seters in *JSOT* 40 (1988) 110–17. Huizinga was a "cultural historian," a fact of which Van Seters seems to be unaware. See: Colie, *AHR* 69 (1963–64)

For Huizinga, history writing is not necessarily "nationalistic." Van Seters never defines what he means by "nation," and there are serious doubts whether by any definition of "nation" history writing is so restricted, especially to "when the nation itself took precedence over the king."

In this emphasis on the nation, Van Seters (whether he is aware of it or not) shows a dependence on the German historiographic concept that the political history of the state is primary.[13] Of all the historians for Van Seters to choose, Huizinga is certainly one of the least likely to have been in sympathy with this notion since he saw cultural history as a deeper and more important pursuit than political history.[14]

While for many late 19th century and early 20th century historians (especially in Germany), there was an inseparable connection between "history" and "political" or "national history," modern historians have long ago abandoned such a notion. And yet it persists in biblical studies!

But the argument becomes circular. For Van Seters the question of genre is the key issue. Genre determines what is history, but the definition of history determines what is history's genre.

Biblical scholars have often maintained that a rigid, essentialist genre analysis alone is sufficient to identify (and hence define) history writing.[15] They believe the matter of genre to be all important because they think that genre is a determinate category with fixed constituents. These scholars seem to conclude that if one can simply understand correctly which [[28]] genre is being employed, then the correct interpretation will necessarily follow. In this way genre functions as a type of magic wand for

---

608; and also B. Halpern, *JBL* 104/3 (1985) 507. For a more accurate reading of Huizinga, see W. W. Hallo, "Biblical History in Its Near Eastern Setting: The Contextual Approach," in *Scripture in Context: Essays on the Comparative Method*, 6 [[reprinted in this volume, p. 83]].

13. Emphasis on the political history of the nation was an emphasis common throughout the period of German historicism. German historians from Johann Herder on lay emphasis on the nation/state (howbeit with variations) (Iggers, *The German Conception of History*, 35ff.). For example, Hegel stated: "It is the state which first presents a subject-matter that is not only adapted to the prose of History, but involves the production of such History in the very progress of its own being" (*Vorlesungen über die Philosophie der Geschichte*, 83). In the opinion of F. Meinecke, historicism found its highest achievement in Ranke (*Entstehung des Historismus*, 642).

14. "De Taak van Cultuurgeschiedenis [The Task of Cultural History]," in *Verzamelde Werken*, Vol. 7, 46. See also Colie, *AHR* 69 (1963–64) 614–22.

15. E.g., H. Gunkel maintained that genre analysis alone could differentiate history from legend or saga ("Die Grundprobleme der israelitischen Literaturgeschichte," in *Reden und Aufsätze*, 29–38; and "Die israelitische Literatur," in *Die Kultur der Gegenwart: Die orientalischen Literaturen*, 52. Gunkel felt genre was the key data because it gives one access to history's general process. So, the origin of any genre was to be sought in the people's overall social life (Oden, "Hermeneutics and Historiography," 146).

interpretation. This essentialist or classificationist view of genre (the classical view of genre) has been thoroughly debunked.[16]

The essentialist believes that there are inherent traits belonging to the genre itself which are part of the genre's very nature. There are three reasons to question an essentialist position: the very notion that texts compose classes has been questioned; the assumption that members of a genre share a common trait or traits has been questioned; and the function of a genre as an interpretative guide has been questioned. Fredric Jameson has gone so far as to conclude that genre criticism has been "thoroughly discredited by modern literary theory and practice."[17] J. Derrida argues that no generic trait completely or absolutely confines a text to a genre or class because such belonging falsifies the constituents of a text:

> If . . . such a [generic] trait is remarkable, that is, noticeable, in every aesthetic, poetic, or literary corpus, then consider this paradox, consider the irony . . . this supplementary and distinctive trait, a mark of belonging or inclusion, does not belong. It belongs without belonging. . . .[18]

While questioning the essentialist position, Ralph Cohen does not feel that genre criticism has been totally "discredited." Instead, he advances a new approach to genre theory. Cohen argues that genre concepts in theory and practice, arise, change, and decline for socio-historical reasons. And since each genre is composed of texts that accrue, the grouping is a process, not a determinate category. He adds:

> Genres are open categories. Each member alters the genre by adding, contradicting or changing constituents, especially those of members most closely related to it. Since the purposes of critics who establish genres vary, it is self-evident that the same texts can belong to different groupings or genres and serve different generic purposes.[19]

16. Either by assimilating classification within other more essential functions of genre (Hirsch—determination of meaning; Todorov—relation of single texts to others), or by going beneath classification to some larger or more fundamental dimension of the task of defining genre (Gadamer—genre history; Ricoeur—production of text). See: Mary Gerhart, "Generic Studies: Their Renewed Importance in Religious and Literary Interpretation," *JAAR* 45 (1977) 309–25.

17. Jameson, *The Political Unconscious*, 105. See also G. N. G. Orsini, "Genres," in *Princeton Encyclopedia of Poetry and Poetics*, 307–9.

18. J. Derrida, "The Law of Genre," *Critical Inquiry* 7 (1980) 64–65.

19. Ralph Cohen, "History and Genre," *New Literary History* 17 (1986) 204. Along these same lines Hans-Georg Gadamer has argued that genres can no longer be regarded as timeless a priori categories since they are history-bound (much more than literary critics usually acknowledge). Thus their rise and decline are intrinsic to text-interpretations (*Truth and Method*, 250ff.).

Furthermore, classifications are empirical, not logical. They are historical assumptions constructed by authors, audiences and critics in order to serve communicative and aesthetic purposes. [[29]] Genres are open systems; they are groupings of texts by critics to fulfill certain ends.[20]

Cohen argues that genre theory does not have to be dependent on essentialist assumptions. Rather, because of the fluidity of genre, "a process theory of genre" is the best explanation of "the constituents of texts."[21] He also points out that there is a relationship between genre and ideology. D. LaCapra notes in this regard:

> One obvious point is that the defense or critique of generic definitions typically involves a defense or critique of discursive and social arrangements, since genres are in one way or another inserted into sociocultural and political practices. This point is frequently not made explicit because it would impair the seeming neutrality of classifications and the way they function in scholarship.[22]

Thus there cannot be a neutral, objective classification of texts along the lines advocated by the essentialist approach. And certainly such classifications cannot function as "interpretive keys."

Van Seters's discussion of the genre of the Apology of Hattušili illustrates this.[23] He argues that the text is not an apology, but "comes close to the mark" of an "endowment document" (p. 120). Because it is a "special defense of an interested party in a quasi-legal context," and since ". . . one cannot thereby include all texts recording legal judgments under the rubric of historiography" the text cannot be historiographic (p. 121). He asserts that it is not an apology because one thinks of an apology as:

> implying a legal context with a fairly clearly defined "jury" and one's status or life at stake. But this work is not directed to such a body as the senate or to any other political organ for a judgment. (p. 119)

I have absolutely no idea where Van Seters obtained such a restrictive definition of an apology! Obviously, the most famous apology of all time is Plato's dialogue in defense of Socrates before the tribunal that sentenced Socrates to death. But certainly apologies are not restricted only to the courtroom and to life-threatening circumstances. J. A. Cuddon defines an apology as "a work written to defend a writer's opinions or to elaborate [[30]] and clarify a problem";[24] and Harry Shaw offers: "a defense and

---

20. Ibid., 210, 212.
21. Ibid., 217.
22. D. LaCapra, "Comment," *New Literary History* 17/2 (1986) 221.
23. For another example of misuse, see: our article in *JSOT* 40 (1988) 116.
24. J. A. Cuddon, *A Dictionary of Literary Terms*, 52.

justification for some doctrine, piece of writing, cause or action."[25] But let one apply the magic wand and one can remove the text from the genre of apology and argue that it is not history writing.

This becomes even harder to accept when one considers Van Seters's argument. He claims that an apology implies a "legal context" and the text of Hattušili is, therefore, not an apology. But on Van Seters's own admission, the Hattušili text is very similar to a legal document (an endowment document), and this becomes even more clear if one compares it to the *Proclamation of Telipinu*. He argues that an edict (specifically the Telipinu text) is a legal text and not a history. Thus, the Hattušili text, since it is a quasi-legal text, is not history writing. What are we to conclude from such a discussion? Is an apology not history writing because it has a legal context? Must a historical text not include an edict because that is legal material? Can a quasi-legal text never be history writing? Such loosely controlled hairsplitting tends to the absurd!

It is ironic in light of Van Seters's definition of apology that in the *Proclamation of Telipinu* the two Hittite words for "political assembly" (*panku-* and *tuliya-*) occur.[26] On the basis of this and other arguments, H. A. Hoffner concludes in his analysis of this work that it is an apology!

> The two clearest examples of apologies among the official texts in the Hittite archives are the Telepinu Proclamation and the Apology of Hattušili III.[27]

Thus, the very evidence, which distinguishes a work as an apology according to Van Seters, can be used to support an argument to identify the Telipinu text as an apology. And this is the text which Van Seters wants to compare to the Hattušili text to prove that that text is not an apology! "This is the form-critic shaking an impotent fist at the refractory ancient who wrote to suit his own selfish ends."[28]

To sum up: essentialist generic approaches fail because they see genre as a determinate category made up of fixed constituents. Many scholars who follow this type of approach feel that they can distinguish historiography from fiction simply by form. But this is very fallacious because of

---

25. Harry Shaw, *Dictionary of Literary Terms*, 27.

26. Hoffmann, *Der Erlass Telipinus*, 76ff.; concerning these two terms see G. Beckman, "The Hittite Assembly," *JAOS* 102 (1982) 435–42). But obviously, the text does not have to be addressed to the *panku-* or a specific political assembly in order to be an apology. On the propagandistic and apologetic character of the Hattusili text see A. Archi, "The Propaganda of Hattusili III," *Studi Micenei ed Egeo-Anatolici* 14 (1971) 185–216; and H. M. Wolf, *The Apology of Hattusilis Compared with Other Political Self-Justifications of the Ancient Near East*.

27. H. A. Hoffner, "Propaganda and Political Justification in Hittite Historiography," in *Unity and Diversity*, 51.

28. Halpern, *JBL* 104 (1985) 508.

the variability of [[31]] literary conventions employed in both.[29] Such approaches to genre cannot succeed in helping to solve the difficulties confronted in the study of ancient Near Eastern and biblical historiography.

Finally, Van Seters views history as secular, unbiased, scientific, and antithetical to religion. Moreover, he implies that true history writing is non-pragmatic and non-didactic. Thus, he argues:

> The Hittites were more interested in using the past than in recording it, and they used it for a variety of purposes. In the Old Kingdom . . . there was the strong tendency . . . to use the past for didactic purposes. The past could be used to justify exceptional political actions and behavior or it could provide a precedent to support a continuity of royal rights and privileges. . . . The Hittites' use of the past here as elsewhere is too pragmatic to give rise to actual history writing.[30]

This view is difficult to accept. Many works of history are didactic or pragmatic. They are designed to teach future generations (so that mistakes of the past will not be repeated!) or to influence present public opinion through propaganda. In her work on Islamic historiography, M. Waldman devotes an entire chapter to the didactic character of that historiography.[31] It seems, therefore, that Van Seters's understanding is totally inadequate for an investigation of ancient Near Eastern or biblical history writing.[32]

Another recent attempt to define history, which in many ways is representative of OT scholarship, is that of George Coats. He states:

> History as a genre of literature represents that kind of writing designed to record the events of the past *as they actually occurred* [emphasis mine]. Its structure is controlled, then, not by the concerns of aesthetics, nor by the symbolic nature of a plot, but by the chronological stages or cause-effect sequences of events as the author(s) understood them. It is not structured to maintain interest or to provoke anticipation for a resolution

---

29. M. Sternberg puts it this way: "Equally fallacious, because unmindful of convention and its variability, are the attempts to distinguish fictional from historiographic writing by their form . . . one simply cannot tell fictional from historical narrative—still less, fiction from history within narrative—since they may be equally present in both, equally absent, equally present and absent in varying combinations. So, to the possible disappointment of shortcut seekers, . . . there are simply no universals of historical vs. fictive form" (*The Poetics of Biblical Narrative*, 26, 29–30).

30. Van Seters, 122–23.

31. M. Waldman, *Toward A Theory of Historical Narrative: A Case Study in Perso-Islamicate Historiography*, chap. 3. G. W. Trompf points out the didactic character of the Hebrew concept of historical recurrence ("Notions of Historical Recurrence in Classical Hebrew Historiography," *Studies in the Historical Books of the Old Testament*, 213–29).

32. Rogerson points out that Van Seters's definition of history has to be stretched in order to sustain his thesis (*JTS* 37/2 [1986] 451–54).

of tension. It is designed simply to record. . . . History writing marks a movement away from the contexts of the family or tribe, with their story-telling concerns, to the record-keeping responsibilities of the nation. History writing would thus be identified in some manner with the affairs of the royal court, with its archives. It derives from the concern [[32]] to document the past of the people in order to validate the present administration.[33]

Coats's definition is problematic. First, he equates history writing with the nation and its politics:

> History writing marks a movement away from the contexts of the family or tribe, with their storytelling concerns, to the record-keeping responsibilities of the nation.[34]

Second, his idea of recording events "as they actually occurred" is a recent echo of a notion which is usually attributed to Ranke's influential phrase, "wie es eigentlich gewesen."[35] Inspired by the search for the past as it really was, many scholars assumed that an objective knowledge of the past was not only possible but mandatory. Anything less than a complete and impartial account of some event or series of events in the past was bad history (the more the "objective" detail, the better the history).

This concept (that history writing is rooted in objectivity) has prevailed in biblical studies. For example H. Gunkel concluded:

---

33. Coats, *Genesis*, 9.

34. Coats, 9. Note the influence of the German "historicist" view. Historicism is a widely used term. See the discussion of Lee and Beck, "The Meaning of 'Historicism,'" *AHR* 59 (1954) 568–77. We are following Iggers's discussion (*The German Conception of History*, 4–10, 29, 270, 287–90).

35. This phrase was used by Ranke in the preface to his *Geschichten der romanischen und germanischen Völker von 1494 bis 1514* (1824) vii. Iggers and von Moltke note: "Indeed Ranke's oft quoted dictum, 'wie es eigentlich gewesen,' has generally been misunderstood as asking the historian to be satisfied with a purely factual recreation of the past. Ranke's writings make it clear that he did not mean this. In fact the word 'eigentlich' which is the key to the phrase just quoted has been poorly translated into English. In the nineteenth century this word was ambiguous in a way in which it no longer is. It certainly had the modern meaning of 'actually' already, but it also meant 'characteristic, essential,' and the latter is the form in which Ranke most frequently uses this term. This gives the phrase an entirely different meaning, and one much more in keeping with Ranke's philosophical ideas. It is not factuality, but the emphasis on the essential that makes an account historical" ("introduction," in Leopold von Ranke, *The Theory and Practice of History*, ed. Iggers and von Moltke, xix–xx). Thus Ranke's emphasis on understanding of the uniqueness of historical characters and situations led him to reject speculation. To understand the unique individuality in history required a reconstruction of the past "wie es eigentlich gewesen," beginning with a strict dedication to the relevant facts. Hence, his insistence on strict method (p. xlii). Our point is that Coats' definition reflects Ranke's phrase although embedded now with some of its popular misconceptions.

Only at a certain stage of civilisation has objectivity so grown that the interest in transmitting national experiences to posterity so increased that the writing of history becomes possible . . . ["history" is prosaic and aims] to inform us of what has actually happened.[36]

Thus for Gunkel objectivity was one of the major criteria for the development of history writing in a civilization.

Likewise, H. Gressmann believed that "history" portrays what actually happened, and shows a remarkable moral objectivity toward its subjects.[37] R. A. Oden comments:

Just as the tradition founded by Herder and Humboldt claimed to be free of ideology, so too Gressmann proclaimed that alone an investigation which pursues "nur die geschichtlichen Tatsachen als solche" [['only the historical facts as such']] can be free of dogma.[38]

E. H. Carr sarcastically criticized this idea, wrongly attributed to Ranke ("wie es eigentlich gewesen" [['as it really happened']]), stating:

Three generations of German, British, and even French historians marched into battle intoning the magic words "wie es eigentlich gewesen" like an incantation—designed, like most incantations, to save them from the tiresome obligation to [[33]] think for themselves. . . . [According to this view] the facts are available to the historian in documents, inscriptions and so on, like fish on the fishmonger's slab. The historian collects them, takes them home, and cooks and serves them in whatever style appeals to him. . . . The facts are really not at all like fish on the fishmonger's slab. They are like fish swimming about in a vast and sometimes inaccessible ocean; and what the historian catches will depend, partly on chance, but mainly on what part of the ocean he chooses to fish in and what tackle he chooses to use.[39]

Carr's caution must be heeded.

The historical work is always the historian's interpretation of the events, being filtered through vested interest, never in disinterested purity.[40] Thus, Oden argues:

---

36. *Legends of Genesis*, 1–2. Along similar lines, see: I. Guidi, "L'historiographie chez les Sémites," *RB* 15 (1906) 509–19.

37. Gressmann, *Die älteste Geschichtsschreibung und Prophetie Israels*, XIII–XV.

38. R. A. Oden, "Hermeneutics and Historiography," 143.

39. E. H. Carr, *What is History?*, 9 and 23. See also F. Braudel, "The Situation of History in 1950," in *On History*, 11.

40. Jürgen Habermas has shown how all knowledge is related to matters of interest, and that any imagined objectivity is likely to be an exercise in self-deception (*Knowledge and Human Interests*). See, however, R. Nash's balanced critique, *Christian Faith and Historical Understanding*, 82ff.

. . . it is undeniable that the role of the German historiographic tradition, and hence that tradition's manifestations in biblical study, is great, and probably greater than many have been willing to allow. Barry Barnes has recently reminded us that "those general beliefs which we are most convinced deserve the status of objective knowledge—scientific beliefs—are readily shown to be overwhelmingly theoretical in character." If this is true of scientific beliefs, it is true as well of the concepts with which biblical scholarship has operated for most of this century. The occasional reminder of how thoroughly theory dependent is biblical criticism can only aid us in our attempt to direct further research.[41]

While the facts/events must be interpreted in light of the significance they have won through their effects so that coherence and continuity are maintained, there is not necessarily a "logical bond of implication between the cause and effect";[42] and one must remain conscious that it is "our understanding . . . [not the objective facts] as the first sources saw them" which superintends our writing of history. Consequently, R. Nash argues:

> It hardly seems necessary to waste any time critiquing hard objectivism. Why beat a horse that has been dead for several generations? Whatever the value of their own theories may have been, idealists like Dilthey, Croce, and Collingwood unveiled the folly of any quest for history as it really was. The nineteenth-century model of a scientific history was an oversimplified distortion of the historian's enterprise.[43]

Thus a document does not have to be objective or unbiased in order to be in the category of history writing. Let us consider [[34]] a specific text: the Babylonian Chronicle. Some have argued that this text is an objective, unbiased historical document.[44]

But L. D. Levine has questioned this:

> whatever its record for accuracy, the Chronicle is fully as biased a source as any other. Its particular bias can probably best be described as Babylocentric.[45]

---

41. Oden, "Hermeneutics and Historiography," 148. He is quoting Barry Barnes, *Scientific Knowledge and Sociological Theory*, 10. See also the comments of Keith Whitelam, *JSOT* 35 (1986) 54.

42. P. Ricoeur, "Explanation and Understanding: On Some Remarkable Connections Among the Theory of the Text, Theory of Action, and Theory of History," in *The Philosophy of Paul Ricoeur*, 156.

43. Ronald Nash, *Christian Faith and Historical Understanding*, 82.

44. A. K. Grayson, *ABC*, 11–14; "Problematical Battles in Mesopotamian History," in *Studies in Honor of Benno Landsberger on His Seventy-Fifth Birthday*, 342; and Van Seters, *In Search of History*, 80–85.

45. L. D. Levine, *JCS* 34 (1982) 50.

For example, in the case of the battle of Halule, the result was, from the Babylonian point of view, a retreat by the Assyrian army. The Assyrians had, up to the battle, been marching to Babylon. After the battle, the Assyrians were no longer so marching. Thus while the Babylonian Chronicle could not record an Assyrian defeat, it could record a retreat. Apparently, "retreat, like beauty, is in the eye of the beholder."[46] Thus an outcome can be viewed by different spectators to mean different things, and neither is necessarily right or wrong. This is what is often called "objectivity relative to a point of view." Thus, Millard correctly remarks:

> Undoubted bias need not provoke the modern reader to a totally adverse attitude to a document, nor give rise to allegations that the accounts are untrue or imaginary. Recognition of the unconcealed standpoints of many ancient documents has resulted in fuller understanding of their contents, without any recourse to a devaluation or discrediting of them. The fact that the modern interpreter does not share the beliefs and aims of the writers does not prevent him from respecting them and giving them their due weight.[47]

A third problem with Coats's definition is that it advocates a chronological, sequential approach to history. History writing is linear and developmental. Such an approach to history cannot be maintained in light of the many examples which can be cited from many different civilizations of other ways of recording the past. What of certain historical poems, cross-sectional histories, or histories of particular technologies? What of presentations of history which are non-developmental or employ cyclic patterns?

The fourth problem with Coats's definition is that he believes that the structure of the historical narrative is simply to record. It is "controlled not by the concerns of aesthetics, nor by [[35]] the symbolic nature of a plot, but by the chronological stages or cause-effect sequences of events." Hayden White has recently argued that one of the primary ways of presenting a coherent history is in the form of a narrative:

> I treat the historical work as what it most manifestly is: a verbal structure in the form of a narrative prose discourse. Histories. . . . combine a certain amount of "data," theoretical concepts for "explaining" these data, and a narrative structure for their presentation. . . . The same event can serve as a different kind of element of many different historical stories. . . . In the chronicle, this event is simply "there" as an element of a series; it does not "function" as a story element. The historian arranges the events in the chronicle into a hierarchy of significance. . . . Providing the

46. Ibid., 50.
47. A. R. Millard, "The Old Testament and History: Some Considerations," *FT* 110 (1983) 41.

"meaning" of a story by identifying the *kind of story* that has been told is
called explanation by emplotment. . . . I identify at least four different
modes of emplotment: Romance, Tragedy, Comedy and Satire. . . . For
example, Michelet cast all his histories in the Romantic mode, Ranke cast
his in the Comic mode, Tocqueville used the Tragic mode, and Burkhardt
used Satire. . . . With the exception of Tocqueville, none of these historians thrust the formal explanatory argument into the foreground of the
narrative . . . the weight of explanatory effect is thrown upon the mode
of emplotment. And, in fact, that "historism" of which Michelet, Ranke,
Tocqueville, and Burkhardt are now recognized to have been equally representative can be characterized in one way as simply substitution of emplotment for argument as an explanatory strategy.[48]

Let us recapitulate. History writing is not nationalistic or based on an
unbiased objectivity. In the formulation of a definition of history, these in-
valid criteria must be repudiated. Moreover, history is artistically constructed and does not necessarily follow a strict chronological format of
presentation.

Nurturing "New Shoots"

Thus far we have investigated what history is not via two definitions which
Old Testament scholars have put forth. In this next section we will investigate what history is.

Numerous philosophers of history have pointed out that historical
narrative is differentiated from fictional by means of its commitment
to its subject-matter ("real" rather than "imaginary" events) rather than
by form.[49]

[[36]] It is, however, important that this "real" or "true" (rather than
"imaginary") narrative be understood culturally. For instance, the mentioning of a deity or deities may be the result of cultural or religious
encoding, and should not, therefore, be taken as evidence per se that the
narrative deals with "imaginary" or fabricated events. One must allow for
the possibility of cultural encoding of the narrative. This is especially true
in ancient Near Eastern history writing.

Two examples will perhaps illustrate this point. If I related this historical narrative:

> when my daughter was two months old, she suffered a tachycardia and
> was on the verge of death. My wife and I prayed to the Lord and by his
> grace she survived, and to this day is a healthy little girl,

48. White, *Metahistory: The Historical Imagination in Nineteenth Century Europe*, ix, 7–8,
142–43.
49. E.g., H. White, *History and Theory* 23 (1984) 21.

it would be improper to conclude that since prayer and a deity's activity are mentioned in the narrative that this is imaginary and not historical. Another example comes from a passage from prism A of Tiglath-Pileser I:

> The land of Adauš was terrified by my strong belligerent attack, and they abandoned their territory. They flew like birds to ledges on high mountains. But the splendor of Aššur, my lord, overwhelmed them, and they came back down and submitted to me.[50]

Again, it would not be wise to conclude that on the basis of the use of a divine name or figurative language that this text is not historical. Cultural and religious encoding of the story must be taken into consideration.

Another point must be made concerning "real" as opposed to "imaginary" events. While the use of direct speech is not acceptable in today's modern canon of history writing unless it is a quote, in ancient history writing direct speech was quite common.

Whybray sees the abundance of direct speech in the Succession Narrative as a problem. He accepts that ancient historians artistically reconstructed *public* speeches. For him the question is:

> whether in the reports of *secret* conversations and scenes the author can be said in any sense at all to have recorded historical events . . . it is almost entirely by means of these private [[37]] scenes that he gives his interpretation of the characters and motives of the principal personages and of the chain of cause and effect . . . [thus the Succession Narrative] is not a history either in intention or in fact.[51]

Whybray's sentiments can be compared with another author who has discussed the use of direct speech by Thucydides. At the beginning of his work, Thucydides describes his method of dealing with the two elements that compose his work—the speeches and the deeds. Concerning the speeches, he states:

> in so far as each of the speakers seemed to me to have said the things most relevant to the ever-current issues—I have presented their words, keeping as close as possible to the general sense of what was actually said.[52]

D. Rokeah points out that Thucydides's aim was to present material which would further his description of the Peloponnesian War, and because of

---

50. Prism A. Col. III lines 66–71.

51. R. N. Whybray, *The Succession Narrative*, 16, 19.

52. Thucydides: *Peloponnesian War*, Book I.22.1–3. The translation is that of D. Rokeah, "Speeches in Thucydides: Factual Reporting or Creative Writing?" *Athenaeum* 60 (1982) 386–401, esp. 395. Cp. A. W. Gomme, *A Historical Commentary on Thucydides*, Vol. 1, 140.

this he censored those parts of the speeches (just as he also censored the accounts of the actions) which were not useful for the understanding of matters on his agenda.[53] Furthermore, the style and literary art of the speeches is Thucydides' own.[54] Kieran Egan argues that Thucydides' speeches function in a similar way to the speeches in Greek drama: they "point up the moral," "alert our expectations" and "echo irony and prophecy."[55] But while many of the speeches were so structured, their content was what Thucydides "knew or thought he knew from the reports of others, had in fact been used on those occasions; e.g., 'my information is that the Athenians did use those arguments at Melos.'"[56]

Thus, direct speeches in a document must be read carefully; and their inclusion in a work—public or secret speeches—does not prejudice the work so that one can conclude that the work is not history writing.[57]

Systematic methods and categories of analysis through which questions of the validity of referents in a historical narrative could be approached are virtually nonexistent.[58] The whole issue of the veracity of the narrative naturally leads into the question of "story."

"Story" embraces both historical and fictional narratives.[59] A number of scholars use the term "story" to describe the OT historical narratives. For example, J. Barr states:

> [[38]] the long narrative corpus of the Old Testament seems to me, as a body of literature, to merit the title of story rather than that of history.[60]

Barr enumerates some of the ways in which this material possesses the characteristics of history and yet must be differentiated from it. For ex-

---

53. Ibid., 388–89.

54. Gomme, *A Historical Commentary on Thucydides*, Vol. 1, 160.

55. Kieran Egan, "Thucydides, Tragedian," in *The Writing of History: Literary Form and Historical Understanding*, 78, 82.

56. Gomme, 145. Cp. Egan's opinion on this passage (p. 82). But also see: Rokeah's arguments (*Athenaeum* 60 [1982] 386–401).

57. Otherwise, the majority of Egyptian historical texts, as well as Hittite historical texts, are not examples of history writing. For instance, the secret dialogue between Thutmose III and his captains concerning the particular route to take to Megiddo in Thutmose's Annals—according to Whybray's position—prejudices the work so that it is not history writing in the modern sense. The whole issue of the place and understanding of direct speech in ancient history writing is in much need of investigation.

58. Waldman laments this same situation in Islamic historiographic studies (*Toward A Theory of Historical Narrative: A Case Study in Perso-Islamicate Historiography*, 3).

59. E.g., Ricoeur uses "story" to mean "historical text," in particular, narrative discourse (Reagan, *The Philosophy of P. Ricoeur*, 152 and 161).

60. James Barr, "Story and History in Biblical Theology," in *Scope and Authority of the Bible*, 5. Also see: R. J. Coggins, "History and Story in Old Testament Study," *JSOT* 11 (1979) 36–46; and Hans Frei, *The Eclipse of Biblical Narrative*, 10 and passim.

ample, the Old Testament does not make the distinction essential for a modern historian between the legendary elements of stories and those parts which might have a more solid historical foundation. Divine and human actions are inextricably bound together without any sense of impropriety—which may be an admirable thing, but is clearly not history. In short, the narrative portions of the Old Testament are of primary importance, yet they are not history but "history-like." Thus for Barr history writing is a secular enterprise.[61]

Such a view is not very helpful. As White has pointed out, there is no difference *in form* between an imaginary story and a historical narrative. And Barr's problem with divine action in the midst of human events is the result of a misunderstanding of the cultural encoding nature of ancient Near Eastern and biblical narrative. If one were to adopt Barr's view, then there would be virtually no history writing in the ancient world (not to mention the medieval world or the Far East) for there are very few ancient historians who do not intermingle divine intervention with human events. They reported occurrences which they could only express in terms of divine intervention (as a considerable number of examples from Assyrian, Egyptian, and Hittite sources demonstrates).[62]

Ronald Clements follows a similar line of argument to that of Barr, although he seems to prefer "theological or religious narrative" instead of "story." To him, history is objective, impartial, political, non-religious, non-pragmatic and non-didactic.[63] Hence, he feels that the purpose of the stories of David's rise was not

> simply to report events in an impartial and objective fashion, such as the critical historian would do. On the contrary, it becomes abundantly plain that the events have been recounted in such a fashion as to justify and legitimate the usurping [[39]] of Israel's throne by David and the subsequent succession of Solomon to this office.[64]

Moreover, what we have is:

---

61. Von Rad felt that the way God's activity was depicted distinguished "history writing" from saga. In saga, the activity of God is "confined to sensational events." In history writing, the historian "depicts a succession of occurrences in which the chain of inherent cause and effect is firmly knit up—so firmly indeed that [the] human eye discerns no point at which God could have put in his hand. Yet secretly it is he who has brought all to pass" (G. von Rad, *The Problem of the Hexateuch and Other Essays*, 166–204).

62. See: Weinfeld, "Divine Intervention in War in Ancient Israel and in the Ancient Near East," in *HHI*, 121–47; and Millard, *FT* 110 (1983) 34–53.

63. Ronald Clements, "History and Theology in Biblical Narrative," *Horizons in Biblical Theology* 4–5 (1982–83) 51–55.

64. Ibid., 54.

a kind of narrative-theology, rather history-writing in the true sense . . .
what we are faced with here are first and foremost ancient religious narratives which possess a distinctive historical form.[65]

Like Barr, it is primarily divine activity in human affairs within the narrative which is the problem for Clements. God has divinely elected David
and his dynasty to rule and has rejected Saul.

Again, this kind of view of history is deficient. History is not objective,
impartial reporting. Simply because there is justification and legitimation
of the Davidic dynasty's seizure of power in the narrative, does not exclude the text from the category of history writing. H. Tadmor has shown
that through a comparison with the apologies of Esarhaddon and Aššur-
banipal one can come to a better understanding of Davidic material as
royal apology[66] (which is certainly within the category of history writing).
In the Assyrian texts, divine election plays a major role in the argument of
justification and legitimation. Thus, Clements' understanding of history
writing is incorrect since many of what he considers unique theological issues in the biblical texts are regularly encountered within the ANE historical texts.

What underlies many views concerning the biblical narrative is the
conviction that the Bible's storytelling is partly or wholly fictional. For instance, Robert Alter concludes:

> As odd as it may sound at first, I would contend that *prose fiction* [empha-
> sis mine] is the best general rubric for describing biblical narrative. Or,
> to be more precise, and to borrow a key term from Herbert Schneidau's
> speculative, sometimes questionable, often suggestive study, *Sacred Dis-
> content*, we can speak of the Bible as *historicized* prose fiction.[67]

Alter feels that the Bible is different from modern historiography since
there is no "sense of being bound to documentable facts that characterizes history in its modern acceptation."[68]

Earlier Robert Pfeiffer argued that the bulk of the Old Testament narratives were fictional since it was:

---

65. Ibid., 55.

66. H. Tadmor, "The Autobiographical Apology in the Royal Assyrian Literature," in
HHI, 36–57. One wonders how Clements treats any historical text which seeks to justify or
legitimate (e.g., The Apology of Hattušili or the inscription of Bar-Rakib, etc.).

67. Robert Alter, *The Art of Biblical Narrative*, 24. Alter quotes H. Schneidau, *Sacred Discontent*, 215. A. Cook has recently complained that "attention to this element [fiction] runs
the risk of implicitly slighting the predominantly historiographic thrust of these writings"
("'Fiction' and History in Samuel and Kings," *JSOT* 36 [1986] 27).

68. Ibid., 24. Cp. Sternberg, *The Poetics of Biblical Narrative*, 32.

only in the recital of events on the part of an eyewitness (unless he be lying as in I Sam. 22:10a and II Sam. 1:7–10) may exact historicity be expected in the Old Testament narratives. Their credibility decreases in the ratio of their distance in time from the narrator . . .

these are . . . popular traditions and tales long transmitted orally. . . . What holds a simple audience of Bedouins, shepherds, or peasants spellbound in listening to a tale is interest in the plot, curiosity as to the denouement, romantic atmosphere, conscious or unconscious art (as in the Andersen and Grimm fairy tales, respectively), but not in the least the historical accuracy. . . .

tales that are the product of either some scanty memories of actual events or out of the storehouse of a vivid Oriental imagination. . . .[69]

Clearly one of the major concerns of both Pfeiffer and Alter is the issue of the eyewitness. According to their view, the most powerful argument for the historicity of a particular text is its dependence on eyewitness accounts. A. Danto has addressed this problem in his discussion of the "Ideal Chronicler."[70] The "Ideal Chronicler" would be an individual who had knowledge of everything that happens, as it happens, the way it happens. He would also record accurate, full descriptions of everything as it occurred. This Chronicler's account would hence be an "Ideal Chronicle," a cumulative record of "what really happened." Danto then poses the question: "what will be left for the historian to do?" The obvious answer would be "Nothing." This "Ideal Chronicle" is complete and the past, as it is often maintained, is "fixed, *fait accompli*, and dead" so it cannot change.

But Danto answers differently. He argues that the historian's task is not done. While the "Ideal Chronicle" is complete in the way in which an ideal witness might describe it, "this is not enough."

For there is a class of descriptions of any event under which the event cannot be witnessed, and these descriptions are necessarily and systematically excluded from the I.C. ["Ideal Chronicle"]. [[41]] The whole truth concerning an event can only be known after, and sometimes only *long* after the event itself has taken place, and this part of the story historians alone can tell. It is something even the best sort of witness cannot know.[71]

Hence, without referring to the future, without going beyond what can be said of what happens, as it happens, the way it happens, the historian could not write in 1618, argues Danto, "the Thirty Years War begins now." To this the "Ideal Witness" is blind. So even if we could witness certain

69. R. Pfeiffer, *Introduction to the Old Testament*, 27–29.
70. A. Danto, *Analytical Philosophy of History*, 149ff.
71. Ibid., 151.

events, we could not verify them under *these* descriptions. "Cut away the future and the present collapses, emptied of its proper content."[72] Thus, "any account of the past is *essentially* incomplete" because "a complete account of the past would presuppose a complete account of the future."[73]

Two obvious implications to be drawn from his discussion are: (1) a "full description" cannot adequately meet the needs of historians, and so fails to represent the ideal by which we should judge accounts; (2) not being witness to the event is not such a bad thing if our interests are historical. Thus, whether the author of the biblical text was an eyewitness or not need not effect our decision concerning whether it is history or not. So, the credibility of the biblical accounts does not necessarily decrease "in the ratio of their distance in time from the narrator."

What hinders many biblical scholars is a misunderstanding that historians use the same techniques as any literary artist to *arrange* or *fashion* their materials.[74] There seem to be two reasons for the failure of many to realize this. One reason is that what the historian says about his ostensible topic and how he says it are really indistinguishable. D. Levin puts it this way:

> I discovered that some fallacies persist as stubbornly today as if the work of Benedetto Croce, R. G. Collingwood, Carl Becker, and others had not shown them to be indefensible. The notion that none but the romantic histories are "literary" thrives as vigorously as the discredited conviction that the facts of history can speak for themselves. Too many historians and teachers of literature accept also the dubious corollary that good literature—whether history or fiction—always takes liberties with "the facts."[75]

Levin then concludes that "there is no necessary conflict between historical fidelity and literary merit, no easy division of the historian's work into two distinct parts, the one essential and the other ornamental."[76]

Another reason for the failure to understand that historians employ the same devices as any literary artist to *arrange* or *fashion* their works is the assumption that historical actuality itself has narrative form which the historian does not create but discovers, or attempts to discover. History-as-it-was-lived, that is, is an untold story. The task of the historian is to find that untold story, or part of it, and to retell it even though in abridged or edited form.[77] While fiction writers fabricate their stories any way they

---

72. A. N. Whitehead, *Adventures of Ideas*, 246.

73. Danto, 17.

74. H. White, *History and Theory* Beiheft 14 (1975) 60.

75. D. Levin, *In Defense of Historical Literature*, viii.

76. Ibid., 14.

77. L. Mink, "Narrative Form as a Cognitive Instrument," in *Literary Form and Historical Understanding*, 137.

wish, historians discover the story hidden in the data. Thus history needs only to be communicated, not constructed. It is because of this presupposition that some historians have not emphasized literary skill—like my 8th grade history textbook!—or found it instructive or accurate to compare the historian with the novelist. Louis Mink believes that while no one consciously asserts that past actuality is an untold story, many implicitly hold this presupposition. He argues that this assumption is the legacy of the idea of Universal History—"the idea that there is a determinate historical actuality, the complex referent for all our narratives of 'what actually happened,' the untold story to which narrative histories approximate." He contends that this presupposition should be "abandoned" because:[78]

1. If past actuality is a single and determinate realm then narrative histories should aggregate because they each tell a part of that untold story. But in practice they do not. In fact, histories are more like fiction in that they have their own beginnings, middles and ends. Historical narratives can and do displace each other.

2. If past actuality is a single and determinate realm then the truth value of the historical narrative should simply be a logical function of the truth or falsity of its individual assertions taken separately: the conjunction is true if and only if each of the individual propositions is true. But while this may be true of chronicle it is not true of history. Historical narratives, like fictional narratives, contain indefinitely many ordering relations, and indefinitely many ways of *combining* these relations. It is such combination which we mean when we speak of the coherence of a narrative, or lack of it. Historical narrative claims truth not only for each of its statements, but for the complex form of the narrative itself.

3. If past actuality is a single and determinate realm then the term "event" should presuppose "both an already existing division of complex processes into further irreducible elements, and some *standard* description of each putative event." But hardly any concept is less clear than that of "event." Uncertainty sets in as soon as we attempt to consider the limits of the application of the concept.[79]

Consequently, the function of narrative form is not just to relate a succession of events but to present an ensemble of interrelationships of many different kinds as a single whole. Historical understanding converts congeries of events into concatenations.[80] While in fictional narrative the coherence of the whole may provide aesthetic or emotional satisfaction,

---

78. Ibid., 135–41, 148.
79. Ibid., 146.
80. This is one of the things which differentiates history from science. See: Louis O. Mink, "The Autonomy of Historical Understanding," in *Philosophical Analysis and History*, 160–92.

in historical narrative it additionally claims truth. Sternberg elaborates on this point:

> The difference between truth value and truth claim is fundamental. If the title to history writing hinged on the correspondence to the truth—the historicity of the things written about—then a historical text would automatically forfeit or change its status on the discovery that it contained errors or imbalances or guesses and fabrications passed off as verities.[81]

> For history writing is not a record of fact—of what "really happened"—but a discourse that claims to be a record of fact. Nor is fiction-writing a tissue of free inventions but a discourse that claims freedom of invention. The antithesis lies not in the presence or absence of truth value but of the commitment to truth value.[82]

But this is where the problem arises. On the one hand, the analysis and evaluation of historical evidence may in principle resolve disputes about facts or to some extent about the relations among facts; but on the other hand, such procedures cannot resolve disputes about the possible combination of kinds of relations. The same event, under the same description or different descriptions, may belong to different stories (historical or fictional). And its particular significance will vary with its [[44]] place in these often very different narratives. Also, just as "evidence" does not dictate which story is to be constructed, so it does not always bear on the preference of one narrative over another. When it comes to the narrative treatment of an ensemble of relationships we credit the imagination or the sensibility or the insight of the individual historian. And we cannot do otherwise. There are no rules for the construction of a narrative as there are for the analysis and evaluation of evidence.[83] Consequently, bad historiography does not yet make fiction; *bad* historiography is bad *historiography*: no more, no less.[84] Because of this and because no past is ever given, history is *always* the imposition of form upon the past. Even mere narration is already the communication of a meaning. Thus

---

81. Sternberg, *The Poetics of Biblical Narrative*, 24–25.

82. Ibid., 25. Intentionality is the issue. Halpern recognizes this and roots the intentionality in the *author*: "As readers, we identify what is historiography and what is not based on our perception of the author's *relationship to the evidence*" (*The First Historians*, 8). On the other hand, Alan Cooper argues for a *reader* based understanding of history: "history is nothing but our relation to the work through time or, more concretely, the work mediated through the history of its interpretation" ("Reading the Bible Critically and Otherwise," in *The Future of Biblical Studies*, 66). We would prefer grounding intentionality in the text itself!

83. L. Mink, "Narrative Form as a Cognitive Instrument," 145.

84. Sternberg, *The Poetics of Biblical Narrative*, 25.

history is imaginatively constructed and is always constructed from a particular point of view.[85]

But such an acknowledgement, White argues, need not lead to historical skepticism:

> This fashioning process need not—be it stressed—entail violations of the so-called "rules of evidence" or the criteria of "factual accuracy" resulting from simple ignorance of the record or the misinformation that might be contained in it.[86]

Hence, it is evident that all historical accounts are artistically constructed and there is no necessary conflict between rigorous historical method and literary construction.

Thus if history writing is the imposing of an interpretive form on the past, then it is, in a sense, artificial. The form itself is not reality; it is only one figurative way of re-figuring, or better, re-presenting reality. It is always the writer's selective arrangement or presentation of the events. Obviously, different modes may be employed to accomplish this task. Whether "narrative" is the best way to impose form on the past is moot here since we are not discussing the writing of a history of Israel (i.e., our own reconstruction of Israelite history), but the interpretation and understanding of already extant narratives which have imposed form on the past.[87]

Thus narrativization in historiography always produces figurative accounts. H. White explains this in his typically eloquent style:

> [[45]] To present the question of narrativization in historiography is to raise the more general question of "truth" of literature itself. On the whole, this question has been ignored by the analytical philosophers concerned to analyze the logic of narrative explanations in historiography. And this because, it seems to me at least, the notion of explanation which they brought to their investigation ruled out the consideration of *figurative discourse* as productive of genuine knowledge. Since historical narratives refer to "real" rather than "imaginary" events, it was assumed that

---

85. White argues that this is the key to historical interpretation; namely, "to recognize that there is no such thing as a single correct view of any object under study but that there are many correct views, each requiring its own style of representation. This would allow us to entertain seriously those creative distortions offered by minds capable of looking at the past with the same seriousness as ourselves but with different affective and intellectual orientations" (*Tropics of Discourse*, 47).

86. H. White, *History and Theory* Beiheft 14 (1975) 60.

87. Concerning the fact that narratives are prominent, although not universal, ways of history writing, see: W. H. Dray, "On the Nature and Role of Narrative in Historiography," *History and Theory* 10 (1971) 157; M. Mandelbaum, "A Note on History as Narrative," *History and Theory* 6 (1967) 417; and idem, *Anatomy of Historical Knowledge*, 25–26.

their "truth-value" resided either in the literal statements of facts contained within them or in a combination of these and a literalist paraphrase of statements made in figurative language. It being generally given that figurative expressions are either false, ambiguous, or logically inconsistent (consisting as they do of what some philosophers call "category mistakes"), it followed that whatever explanations might be contained in an historical narrative should be expressible only in *literal language*. . . .

. . . If there is any "category mistake" involved in this literalizing procedure, it is that of mistaking a narrative account of real events for a literal account thereof. A *narrative account is always a figurative account, an allegory*. To leave this figurative element out of consideration in the analysis of a narrative is not only to miss its aspect as allegory; it is to miss the performance in language by which *a chronicle is transformed into a narrative*. And it is only a modern prejudice against allegory or, what amounts to the same thing, a scientistic prejudice in favor of literalism, that obscures this fact to many modern analysts of historical narrative.[88]

Thus the historical narrative is always figurative. Obviously, there are varying degrees in the use of figurative language. But all historical narratives can be analyzed in terms of the modes of figurative language use that they variously favor. Thus figures of speech are the "very marrow of the historian's individual style." Remove them from his discourse, and you destroy much of its impact as an "explanation" in the form of an "idiographic" description. The theory of figures of speech permits us "to track the historian in his encodation of his message." This means that the clue to the meaning of a given historical discourse is contained "as much in the rhetoric of the description of the field as it is in the logic of whatever argument may be offered as its explanation."[89] This, however, as White argues, does not mean that the figurative discourse of [[46]] the historical narrative is not productive of genuine knowledge and "truth." It simply means that the interpreter of the historical text must work that much harder at the interpretive process.

Hence, when we say that a historical narrative is figurative, we are speaking primarily of this impositional nature of the account. This nature manifests itself in three ways:[90] (1) the structural and ideological codes

---

88. H. White, *History and Theory* 23 (1984) 24–25. In no way, in affirming this poetic feature of history writing, are we denying the factual nature of narrative emplotment in history (see in this regard, W. H. Dray, *History and Theory* 27 [1988] 286).

89. H. White, *History and Theory* Beiheft 14 (1975) 53–54.

90. P. Stambovsky delineates the three fundamental ways that metaphor functions in historiography (corresponding to Mandelbaum's historiographic forms: explanatory, sequential, and interpretive). Thus he sees in the following three categories: (1) *heuristic imagery*

underlying the text's production, (2) the themes or motifs that the text utilizes,[91] and (3) the usage of rhetorical figures in the accounts. The second and third can very often be understood in terms of the old-time standard type of ANE and OT parallels. The first is a different concept for biblical studies: that the biblical narratives are the structures which communicate the historical image. Both of these are utilized as ideological communicators. Obviously, while, at times, it is possible to isolate these aspects, they generally overlap so that a rhetorical figure communicates the ideological codes of the text and vice versa. Consequently, we will not always attempt to differentiate and demarcate these aspects, since to do so would impair the reader.

In conclusion, history might be defined as "a committedly true account which imposes form on the actions of men in the past." It must be stressed that a literary mode of cultural production is connected with the rise of history writing.[92] So while it is possible to have an oral account of the past, the fact that in oral cultures there is "the unobtrusive adaptation of past tradition to present needs" means that "myth and history merge into one."[93] In the ancient Near East history writing included such literary categories as king's lists, chronicles, annals, royal apologies, memorial inscriptions, historical poems, narratives, etc. Finally, from a technical standpoint, historiography is "the principles, theory, and history of historical writing."[94] Thus historiography, as F. J. Levy comments, "is inter-

---

which advances deliberative, analytic understanding and falls within the domain of explanatory discourse; (2) *depictive imagery* which presentationally facilitates the (phenomenological) apprehension of meanings and occurrences, and which is a component of sequential discourse; and (3) *cognitive imagery* which is operative on the meta-historical plane and orchestrates interpretive discourse ("Metaphor and Historical Understanding," *History and Theory* 27 [1988] 125–34). Our interest is primarily in number 2, *depictive imagery*.

91. Concerning the figurative nature of the biblical motifs, S. Talmon argues: "In its literary setting, which by definition is secondary, a motif constitutes a concentrated expression of the essence which inheres in the original situation. . . . A motif stands for the essential meaning of a situation or an event, not for the facts themselves" ("*Har* and *Midbar*: An Antithetical Pair of Biblical Motifs," in *Figurative Language in the Ancient Near East*, 122).

92. M. Brett, "Literacy and Domination: G. A. Herion's Sociology of History Writing," *JSOT* 37 (1987) 20–24. And also, Goody and Watt, "The Consequence of Literacy," *CSSH* 5 (1963) 304–45.

93. Goody, *Literacy in Traditional Societies*, 34, 48. See also along these lines, M. Noth, "Geschichtsschreibung im A.T.," *RGG*[3], 2, 1498–1504; J. J. M. Roberts, *CBQ* 38 (1976) 3, n. 15; and Van Seters, *In Search of History*, 209–27. For the implications of this for those who assume a great degree of reliability in oral tradition, see: M. Brett, *JSOT* 37 (1987) 37, n. 9.

94. *Webster's 3rd New International Dictionary*, Vol. 1, 1073. Here we are attempting to maintain a distinction which will help clarify our discussion. For two examples of this use of the term, see: W. W. Hallo, "Sumerian Historiography," in *HHI*, 1–12; and M. Lichtheim, "Ancient Egypt: A Survey of Current Historiography," *AHR* 69 (1963–64) 30–46.

ested primarily in the methods previous historians have used to attain
their results."[95]

Part II
Ideology: Unmasking the Concept

[[47]] Few concepts play a larger part in present-day discussions of ancient
Near Eastern and biblical historical topics than does that of ideology;[96]
and yet, it is not always clear what meaning is applied to the term by those
who employ it. It is important to remember what David Apter has correctly noted:

> Ideology is not quite like other subjects. It reflects the presuppositions of
> its observers.[97]

There are at least three different meanings for the notion of ideology:[98]

First, ideology can be defined in the narrow sense as "false consciousness." Karl Marx gave prominence to the term "ideology," and used it for
distorted or selected ideas in defense of the *status quo* of a social system
(i.e., "a capitalist ideology").[99] Ideology was the distortion of reality because of a society's "false consciousness." This concept of ideology as
"false consciousness" leads back to the problem of establishing the true
consciousness which will enable men to understand their role. The reason
that they do not possess true consciousness is because "social being . . .
determines consciousness"; hence, the truth about man is one and the
same for all stages of history, but every stage produces its own illusions.
And this has been the state of affairs in history, but is due to disappear
when a rational order has been created. Thus the concept of ideology
demonstrates that men are not in possession of true consciousness
which—if they had it—would enable them to understand the totality of the
world and their own place in it.[100]

Second, ideology can be defined in a restrictive sense. In other words,
it is only those aspects which are distorted or unduly selective.

> Ideology consists of selected or distorted ideas about a social system or a
> class of social systems when these ideas purport to be factual, and also
> carry a more or less explicit evaluation of the "facts."[101]

95. Levy, "Editor's Foreword" to *The Theory and Practice of History*, vi.
96. E.g., G. Garbini, *History and Ideology in Ancient Israel.*
97. D. Apter, "Ideology and Discontent," in *Ideology and Discontent*, 16.
98. Harry M. Johnson, "Ideology and the Social System," in *International Encyclopedia of the Social Sciences*, 76–77.
99. Cf. G. Lichtheim, "The Concept of Ideology," *History and Theory* 4 (1965) 173.
100. Ibid., 174–77.
101. Johnson, "Ideology and the Social System," 77.

Thus ideology consists *only* of those parts or aspects of a system of social ideas which are distorted or unduly selective from a scientific viewpoint. This definition does not restrict ideology to the conservative type.

Third, ideology can be defined in a "neutral sense." Thus Geertz defines ideology as "a schematic image of social order."[102] He argues that it is hardly scientific to define ideology as distortion and selectivity because distortion and selectivity are secondary and an empirical question in each case. In this view, ideology embraces both normative and allegedly factual elements; and these elements are not *necessarily* distorted.[103]

In many ways it is the issue of "distortion" that distinguishes these definitions from one another. Consequently, we will attempt to investigate this issue more fully.

While Marx was the first to emphasize the concept of "false consciousness" and subsequent "distortion," he has influenced many (especially Georg Lukács and Karl Mannheim who developed the tradition of the sociology of knowledge). This approach, represented in the Frankfurt School of German sociology, has concentrated mostly on understanding the ideological basis of all forms of social knowledge including the natural sciences.[104] The tradition's most recent advocate is Jürgen Habermas.[105]

Mannheim distinguished between utopias and ideologies. The proponents of utopias contend for the realization of an "ideal" which they allege has never existed previously within a society; while on the other hand, ideologies work for the realization of an "ideal" which existed in the past but no longer exists. According to Johnson, Mannheim also used the term "ideology" to refer to conservative ideas as distortions (although he was not consistent on this point).[106] Thus,

> ideology is by its nature untruthful, since it entails a "masking" or "veiling" of unavowed and unperceived motives or "interests." . . . [It] is a manifestation of a "false consciousness."[107]

102. Clifford Geertz, "Ideology as a Cultural System," in *Ideology and Discontent*, 63.

103. Cf. J. Gould, "Ideology," in *A Dictionary of the Social Sciences*, 315–17.

104. See: J. Friedman, "Ideology," in *The Social Science Encyclopedia*, 375–76.

105. Georg Lukács, *Geschichte und Klassenbewusstsein: Studien über marxistische Dialektik*; Karl Mannheim, *Ideology and Utopia*; Jürgen Habermas, *Theorie und Praxis: Sozialphilosophische Studien*; and *Knowledge and Human Interests*. On Mannheim's derivation from Weber and dependence on the early Lukács, see: G. Lichtheim, "The Concept of Ideology," 186–92.

106. Johnson, 77. It must be stressed that not everyone who assumes the Marxist definition of "false consciousness" applies it only to the Right. E.g., U. Eco, *A Theory of Semiotics*, 290–97.

107. Shils, "Ideology: The Concept and Function of Ideology," in *International Encyclopedia of the Social Sciences*, Vol. 7, 73. The concept of ideology as a mask is rooted back in Nietzsche's thought of "unmasking." For him all thought is ideological and must be "unmasked" (see G. Lichtheim, "The Concept of Ideology," 183).

Werner Stark, a follower of Mannheim, puts it this way:

> ideological thought is . . . something shady, something that ought to be
> overcome and banished from our mind. . . . Both [lying and ideology]
> are concerned with untruth, but whereas the liar tries to falsify the
> thought of others while his own private thought is correct, while he him-
> self knows well what the truth is, a person who falls for an ideology is
> himself deluded in his private thought, and if he misleads others, does so
> unwillingly and unwittingly.[108]

[[49]] Putting it more on a linguistic level, Eco argues that ideological
manipulation endeavors to conceal the various present options, and must
therefore involve a rhetorical labor of code shifting and overcoding (via
what he calls "inventio" and "dispositio"). Ideology is "a partial and dis-
connected world vision." By disregarding the multiple interconnections of
the semantic universe, it also conceals the pragmatic reasons for which
certain signs (with all their various interpretations) were produced. This
oblivion produces a "false conscience."[109]

Thus ideology has the unfortunate quality of being psychologically
"deformed" ("warped," "contaminated," "falsified," "distorted," "clouded")
by the pressure of personal emotions like hate, desire, anxiety, or fear. Ideology is a dirty river such that if one drinks from it, he will be poisoned.[110]

According to this view in which vested interest plays a vital role, ideology is a mask and a weapon; its pronouncements are seen against the
background of a universal struggle for advantage; men pursue power and
control often in the midst of class conflict. This view that social action is
fundamentally an unending struggle for power leads to an unduly Machia-
vellian view of ideology as a form of higher cunning and, consequently, to
a neglect of its broader, less dramatic social functions.[111]

Shils points out the incorrectness of this view. Ideologies, like all complex cognitive patterns, contain many propositions; even though ideolo-
gists strive for, and claim to possess, systematic integration, they are never
completely successful in this regard. Hence, true propositions can coexist

---

108. W. Stark, *The Sociology of Knowledge*, 48.
109. Eco, *A Theory of Semiotics*, 297 and 312, n. 54. Garbini clearly sees ideology in the
sense of false consciousness and distortion (*History and Ideology in Ancient Israel*, xvi).
110. Stark, 90–91. See also, Mannheim, *Ideology and Utopia*, 55–59.
111. Cf. Geertz, "Ideology as a Cultural System," 52–54. This view is evident among recent structural Marxists (e.g., Althusser, "Ideology and Ideological State Apparatuses," in *Lenin and Philosophy*, 35–51), within their extreme functionalism where ideological *apparatuses*
are conceived as instruments that exist to maintain the coherence of a mode of production,
a system of economic exploitation that generates its own self-maintenance by way of the production of appropriate mentalities, political structures and socialized subjects who are only
mere agents of the system (see: Friedman, "Ideology," in *The Social Science Encyclopedia*, 375).

alongside false ones.[112] It follows, therefore, that to understand "ideology" simply as "a distortion of reality"[113] is not adequate. There is distortion, but not every element in the ideology is necessarily distorted.

Moreover, because many sociologists have failed to recognize the usage of figurative language within ideological discourse, they have often confused this usage with "distortion." Geertz has observed that:

> It is the absence of such a theory [of symbolic language] and in particular the absence of any analytical framework within which to deal with figurative language that have reduced sociologists to viewing ideologies as elaborate cries of pain. [[50]] With no notion of how metaphor, analogy, irony, ambiguity, pun, paradox, hyperbole, rhythm, and all the other elements of what we lamely call "style" operate—even, in a majority of cases, with no recognition that these devices are of any importance in casting personal attitudes into public form, sociologists lack the symbolic resources out of which to construct a more incisive formulation.[114]

He points out that although very few social scientists seem to have read much of the literature on metaphor, an understanding of it is quite useful in the discussion of ideology. In figurative language there is, of course, a stratification of meaning, in which an incongruity of sense on one level produces an influx of significance on another. The feature of metaphor that has most troubled philosophers (and, for that matter, scientists) is that it is "wrong":

> It asserts of one thing that it is something else. And, worse yet, it tends to be most effective when most "wrong."[115]

The power of a metaphor derives precisely from the interplay between the discordant meanings it symbolically coerces into a unitary conceptual framework and from the degree to which that coercion is successful in overcoming the psychic resistance such semantic tension inevitably generates in anyone in a position to perceive it. When it works, a metaphor transforms a false identification into an apt analogy; when it misfires it is mere extravagance.

Obviously, a metaphor (in the strict sense of that term) is not the only stylistic resource upon which ideology draws. Geertz notes:

112. Shils, 73.
113. If we level ideology to only distortion of reality/false consciousness, are we not then faced ultimately with a type of Nietzsche's nihilism?
114. Geertz, "Ideology as a Cultural System," 57.
115. W. Percy, "Metaphor as Mistake," *The Sewanee Review* 66 (1958) 79–99. Cf. U. Eco's discussion of metaphor. Although Eco, himself, follows the Marxist notion of ideology as "false consciousness," he also recognizes its "rhetorical labor" (*A Theory of Semiotics*, 290–97).

Metonymy ("All I have to offer is blood, sweat and tears"), hyperbole ("The thousand-year Reich"), meiosis ("I shall return"), synecdoche ("Wall Street"), oxymoron ("Iron Curtain"), personification ("The hand that held the dagger has plunged it into the back of its neighbor"), and all the other figures the classical rhetoricians so painstakingly collected and so carefully classified are utilized over and over again, as are such syntactical devices as antithesis, inversion, and repetition; such prosodic ones as rhyme, rhythm, and alliteration; such literary ones as irony, eulogy, and sarcasm.[116]

Moreover, not all ideological expression is figurative. The bulk of it consists of quite literal, flat-footed assertions, which, a [[51]] certain tendency toward *prima facie* implausibility aside, are difficult to distinguish from properly scientific statements: "The history of all hitherto existing society is the history of class struggles"; "the whole of the morality of Europe is based upon the values which are useful to the herd"; and so forth. As a cultural system, an ideology that has developed beyond the stage of mere sloganeering consists of an intricate structure of interrelated meanings—interrelated in terms of the semantic mechanisms that formulate them—of which the two-level organization of an isolated metaphor is but a feeble representation.[117]

Thus there exists an ideological language a subtle interplay of which concepts like "distortion," "selectivity," or "oversimplification" are simply incompetent to formulate. Not only is the semantic structure of the figure a good deal more complex than it appears on the surface, but an analysis of that structure forces one into tracing a multiplicity of referential connections between it and social reality, so that the final picture is one of a configuration of dissimilar meanings out of whose interworking both the expressive power and the rhetorical force of the final symbol derive. This interworking is itself a social process, an occurrence not "in the head" but in that public world where "people talk together, name things, make assertions, and to a degree understand each other."[118]

Hence, it would seem best to advocate a neutral sense for the understanding of the concept of ideology so that:

> ideology is a "schematic image of social order," "a pattern of beliefs and concepts (both factual and normative) which purport to explain complex social phenomena" in which there may be simplification by means of symbolic figurative language, code shifting and/or overcoding.

116. Geertz, "Ideology as a Cultural System," 74, n. 30.
117. Ibid., 74, n. 30.
118. Ibid., 60.

While ideology is often equated with rationalization in the psychological sense because it is assumed to be essentially a defense of vested interests (which is partly true), many people may have ideological ideas that are even contrary to their interests or that are related to their interests in so complex a way that experts would hesitate to attempt to calculate the net effect.[119] So,

> [[52]] the likelihood that groups and individuals who have vested interests will defend them by means of distorted arguments is too well known to require extended comment. If anything, many people *exaggerate* the relative importance of concern for vested interests as a source of ideology.
>
> Those who stand to gain from a proposed social change are also, of course, likely to be less than objective in their appraisal of the *status quo* and of the general merit of the proposed change.[120]

Part III
Method: Obtaining Comprehension

Establishing the Framework

In the interpretive endeavor, it seems important to employ what W. W. Hallo has called the "contextual approach":[121] in other words, a "comparative/contrastive" investigation of "the literary context itself, broadly interpreted as including the entire Near Eastern literary milieu to the extent that it can be argued to have had any conceivable impact on the biblical formulation."[122] For instance, if one compares the conquest account in the book of Joshua with other ancient Near Eastern conquest accounts, one will gain a better understanding of the biblical narrative. Such a method offers controls on the data. It is exactly a lack of controls which has contributed—at least in part—to some of the interpretive problems in Old Testament studies.

119. One example that we can cite: While the "New Right" was gaining power in the U.S. during the election of 1980, many older, very conservative southerners refused to vote Republican because of ideological hangovers from the days of Reconstruction. One old Texan remarked, "I would rather vote for a dead dog than a Republican!" Yet through the election of the Republican candidate, Ronald Reagan, that man stood to gain much more because of his social position than if the Democratic candidate Jimmy Carter had been elected.

120. Johnson, 80.

121. W. W. Hallo, "Biblical History in Its Near Eastern Setting: The Contextual Approach," in *Scripture in Context: Essays on the Comparative Method*, 2 [[reprinted in this volume, p. 78]]. Also K. A. Kitchen, *Ancient Orient and the Old Testament*.

122. Hallo, "Biblical History in Its Near Eastern Setting, 2 [[reprinted in this volume, p. 78]].

Some scholars have voiced the belief that the ancient Near East, while it produced many historical texts, did not produce works of history. Von Rad, for example, felt that only in Israel and Greece did a "historical sense" arise that could apply causal thinking to sequences of political events.[123]

A similar type of objection is expounded by R. J. Thompson. He argues that because Israel was unique in the ancient Near East (Israel alone developed real historiography), the relevance of the comparative material is questionable.[124] He cites Mowinckel for support of this claim:

> It is a well known fact that Israel is the only people in the whole ancient Near East where annalistic writing developed into real historiography . . . neither the Babylonians nor the Assyrians took it beyond short chronicles in annalistic form; . . . From Egypt we know some historical legends, but no historiography, [[53]] where the historical events are seen in the larger context. Something more of a historical view is found among the Hittites, but even here in fragmentary form, as tendencies, not as realizations. The only exception is Israel.[125]

It is very interesting that the comparative method can be dismissed by a comparative argument! Mowinckel has made an assessment of Israelite historiography by comparing it to ancient Near Eastern historiographies (an assessment which is highly debatable).[126] Thompson has accepted this judgment (uncritically) and turned it into an argument against the comparative method. Such an objection (unfortunately common among OT scholars) is groundless.[127]

Another form of this objection is that the influence on Israel during the OT period was minimal; Israel developed its own culture and traditions without a great degree of foreign influence. While the degree of influence varied at different periods, this is again a case of using a com-

---

123. Von Rad, *The Problem of the Hexateuch and Other Essays*, 166–204. See also: M. Noth, "Geschichtsschreibung im A.T.," *RGG³*, 1500. But Van Seters correctly points out one of the errors in such thinking: "there is an implied comparison here on the level of "historical thinking" between a Near Eastern mythological perspective and an Israelite "historical" perspective that at least prejudices any comparative approach on the literary level" (Van Seters, *In Search of History*, 209–48, esp. 218, n. 33).

124. R. J. Thompson, *Moses and the Law in a Century of Criticism since Graf*, 118–20.

125. Mowinckel, "Israelite Historiography," *ASTI*, 2, 8. See also B. Maisler [[Mazar]], "Ancient Israelite Historiography," *IEJ* 2 (1952) 82–88; U. Cassuto, "The Rise of Historiography in Israel," in *EI* 1, 85–88 [Hebrew]; idem, *Biblical and Oriental Studies*, Vol. 1, 7–16.

126. E.g., his judgment concerning Egyptian history writing is quite wrong.

127. See: B. Albrektson, *History and the Gods*; and Van Seters, *In Search of History*, esp. p. 59. While Albrektson overstates the case, he nevertheless does undermine the argument against the comparative approach.

parative argument to dismiss the need of a comparative method. This objection should be spurned. There is no question that there are differences between the Hebrew histories and their ancient Near Eastern counterparts, just as there are differences between each ancient Near Eastern culture's history writing. Moreover, it is only through comparison that these differences can be discerned. But there are also many similarities that argue in favor of "real" history writing among these ancient Near Eastern cultures, and cry out for comparison with the Israelite material as Hallo, Tadmor, Roberts, and others have pointed out.[128]

One area of the ancient world which will not be included in this contextual investigation is Greece. One might wonder—especially in light of Van Seters's recent work—why this area will not be included for he contends:

> it would appear to be self-evident and entirely natural for biblical scholars who treat the subject of the origins of history writing in ancient Israel to give some attention to the corresponding rise of history writing in Greece and to the work of Herodotus in particular. (p. 8)

[[54]] Is it really "self-evident and entirely natural"? Most biblical scholars believe that there was some contact and subsequent influence between the Hebrews and the Greeks, but that it was minimal in the early biblical period. Van Seters argues that the issue of date cannot be used to avoid such a comparison, but he does so by redating the biblical material by means of such a comparison.[129] This is highly circular argumentation! But going further, he asks the reader to take a "leap of faith":

> The question of the origin of other shared features, such as the paratactic style of early prose and the anecdotal digressions within chronologies, is hard to answer on the basis of the *extant material* from Phoenicia. But it would appear *most reasonable* that these features clearly shared by Greek and Hebrew historiography also belonged to the Phoenicians, who were the close contact with both regions. It is, of course, doubtful that there was much direct cultural contact between the Greeks and the Hebrews before the fourth century B.C. Once we *admit* that Phoenicia could serve as a bridge between Israel and the Aegean as well as a center for the dissemination of culture in both directions, *nothing stands in the*

---

128. Hallo, "Scripture in Context," 1–24; Tadmor, "The Autobiographical Apology . . . ," in *HHI*, 56; J. J. M. Roberts, *CBQ* 38 (1976) 13. Thus Millard concludes: "where comparisons are possible they should be made, otherwise the Hebrew writings have to be treated in a vacuum, and the results of that can be, in fact often have been, extremely misleading" (*TB* 36 [1985] 75).

129. Van Seters, 8. We agree with his debunking of the idea that Greek and Hebrew thought were entirely in contrast.

way of an intensive comparative study of the Bible and early Greek historiography. [emphasis mine][130]

If there were some extant evidence, then perhaps this might be "reasonable," but by taking the theory and making it fact, Van Seters not only can argue for the legitimacy of his comparison of Greek and Hebrew historiography, but can also argue for the later dating of the biblical material. He has not proved that there was a definite "conceivable impact on the biblical formulation."

Moreover, Van Seters uses the same argumentation concerning the extant material to contest H. Cancik's claim that the Hittite texts explain the rise of historiography in both ancient Greece and ancient Israel. He argues against Cancik that "to see the agent of cultural mediation through 'Canaan' is hardly justified. No evidence for this kind of cultural influence is evident at Ugarit or in any extant Canaanite-Phoenician inscriptions" (p. 103). So on the one hand, Van Seters can use the absence of extant material to argue (probably rightly) against Cancik's thesis; while on the other hand, he can choose [[55]] to ignore the same absence of extant material to advance his own theory.

Performing the Reading

Another important aspect in the interpretation of historical texts is the method of analysis. In other words, how should one read historical texts? Gene Wise has suggested that in the initial stage of analysis the critic must practice "a willing suspension of disbelief" in order to conduct an "intricate textual analysis." He must ascertain the structure of the text and its mode of communication.[131]

It is important to consider the "willing suspension of disbelief." The reader of a historical text must curb his skepticism in order not to misconstrue the obvious. This is not an endorsement of a naive approach which

130. Ibid., 53–54. Parataxis can be found on different levels in many different languages and in many different periods. Thus it does not follow that because one finds parataxis in Greek and Hebrew history writing there is a necessary link between the two. While the existence of parataxis might explain certain problems, one cannot use parataxis to argue for dating as Van Seters does. Van Seters has not delineated exactly what he sees as the demarcations of parataxis in Greek and/or Hebrew literature B. Long has attempted to define the parameters of parataxis in the Hebrew historical narrative (*I Kings*, 19–30). Even so, exact relationships and dating remain very moot.

131. Gene Wise, *American Historical Explanations*, 171. Wise is advocating a "New Critic" reading. In this connection, Karel van der Toorn insists that we practice "self-restraint" when dealing with ancient cultures in order to sweep away the generalizations and mis- (or pre-)conceptions we invariably bring to our disciplines (*Sin and Sanction in Israel and Mesopotamia: A Comparative Study*, 9ff.).

has repudiated criticism. Rather, it is a warning that the modern reader must not dismiss something in the text simply because he finds it unbelievable. He must willingly suspend his disbelief in order to "participate" in the world of the text. The following will exemplify Wise's point.

Due to overt skepticism, H. Cancik dismisses the "staff meeting" by Thutmose III before the battle of Megiddo as a fictitious element from the so-called *Königsnovelle* [['royal novella']].[132] But how many kings, rulers, or generals down through the ages have taken counsel or held a "staff meeting" before a major battle? To even consider a "meeting" of this type as fictitious, one must have some very strong reason beyond a simple suspicion of the presence of a Königsnovelle motif. But, on the contrary, A. J. Spalinger has recently shown that this war council at Yhm prior to the battle of Megiddo originated from war dairy accounts so that the account is, in all likelihood, historical.[133]

To accomplish this "intricate textual analysis" of which Wise speaks, semiotics appears to offer a viable method. Hence, one seeks to discern and understand the *transmission code(s)* which are used to convey the "message" of the text.[134] As a text, a piece of writing is understood as "the product of a person or persons, at a given point in human history, in a given form of discourse, taking its meanings from the interpretative gestures [[56]] of individual readers using the grammatical, semantic, and cultural codes available to them."[135] The narrative form of the discourse is a medium for the message, having no more truth-value or informational content than any other formal structure, such as a logical syllogism, a metaphorical figure, or a mathematical equation. The narrative is a vehicle, apparatus, or trellis for the transmission of the message. The strength of this method is that it does not confuse "literary" questions with "referential" or "historicity" questions. The historical writing must be analyzed primarily as a kind of prose discourse before its claims to objectivity and truthfulness can be tested.[136] Thus the dilemma of whether and to what

132. H. Cancik, *Grundzüge der hethitischen und alttestamentlichen Geschichtsschreibung*, 130.

133. Spalinger, *Aspects of the Military Documents of the Ancient Egyptians*, 107, 116, 134–41.

134. It must be kept in mind that every narrative discourse consists, not of one single code monolithically utilized, but rather of a complex set of codes, the interweaving of which by the author—for the production of a story infinitely rich in suggestion and variety of affect, not to mention attitude toward and subliminal evaluation of its subject matter—attests to his talents as an artist, as master rather than as the servant of a single code available for his use. This explains the "density" of the various ANE and biblical historical texts (see further: White, *History and Theory* 23 [1984] 18ff.).

135. Robert Scholes, *Semiotics and Interpretation*, 16. With reference to biblical studies, see A. Cooper, "The Life and Times of King David According to the Book of Psalms," in *The Poet and the Historian: Essays in Literary and Historical Biblical Criticism*, 117–31.

136. H. White, "Historicism, History, and the Figurative Imagination," *History and Theory* Beiheft 14 (1975) 52.

extent the events of a text correspond to the "truth"[137] (i.e., the question
of the veracity or reliability of the text) can be put aside (at least temporarily) in order to shift one's attention to the texts themselves.[138]

So while it is perfectly valid, important and necessary to ask questions
concerning *which* events were narrated, it is equally valid, important and
necessary to ask questions concerning *the way* in which the events were
narrated. In fact, it is the latter questions which reveal the text's ultimate
meaning and purpose. F. M. Fales puts it this way:

> the utilization of the document as source of information on the narrated
> events must be preceded by an analytical breakdown of the document it-
> self into its ideological and compositional foundations, i.e. into *the com-
> plex of ideas* (as indicated by lexical items) and into the *literary structures*
> (as indicated by the organisation of words into syntagms, etc.). . . .[139]

Since reading a text entails "expanding [étoiler] upon the text rather
than gathering it together,"[140] R. Barthes proposed anthrology—"the science of the components"[141]—to account for the interweaving of code and
message in the system of a text. Thus it is important to distinguish the
components of a text in order to understand its meaning.[142]

Robert Scholes has suggested that "we can generate meaning by situ-
ating a text among the actual and possible texts to which it can be related."[143] Consequently, it is our assertion that by using semiotics in
conjunction with a contextual method, it will be possible to achieve a better understanding of the biblical historical narrative. It must be emphasized that [[57]] we are not arguing that the semiotic approach will give us
"the final, definite, and authoritative interpretation" of any historical text.
We are only suggesting that it will reveal certain aspects of the text's make-
up which will further the interpretive endeavor. It permits finer distinctions to be maintained in the analyses.

Obviously this type of approach is very different from the common
diachronic method with its concerns for correctly dating various stages in

---

137. R. Barthes, *La Plaisir de Text*, 49. Hence, one can overcome the "fallacy of referentiality." See also: U. Eco, *A Theory of Semiotics*, 65.

138. H. White's criticism at this point is valid. He argues that a discourse should be regarded "as an apparatus for the *production* of meaning, rather than as only a vehicle for the
transmission of information about an extrinsic referent" (*History and Theory* 23 [1984] 19).
However, semiotics remains a practical means of analysis, especially in light of the overemphasis in biblical studies on referentiality. So our utilization is in many ways pragmatic.

139. F. M. Fales, "A Literary Code in Assyrian Royal Inscriptions: The Case of Ashurbanipal's Egyptian Campaigns," in *ARINH*, 170.

140. R. Barthes, *S/Z*, 20.

141. R. Barthes, *Eléments de Sémiologie*, 130.

142. H. White, *History and Theory* 23 (1984) 20.

143. Scholes, 30.

a tradition's development, for separating early traditions from redactional elements, and so forth. Because the inheritance of the nineteenth century has been so powerful for such a long time in biblical study, research has been dominated by these diachronic concerns. Hence this approach has come to be seen as self-evidently correct and as particularly appropriate to the alleged character of the biblical texts. So much is this the case that an initial response to some methods of understanding which accent rather a synchronic analysis has been that these latter methods looked suspiciously a priori and theoretical.

But Oden points out that this response is fundamentally mistaken:

> The clash of the traditional, historical approach with newer methods of analysis is not, as the partisans of the former might wish to assert, a clash between an objective, scientific approach on the one hand, and a subjective, theoretical approach on the other. The conflict is rather a conflict between two equally theoretical methods of understanding, neither of which can claim to be working in the first instance from a direct confrontation with the text itself. The pressing question for us is therefore that of which theory is the more coherent.[144]

Consequently we are not arguing that the combination of the contextual method and semiotics is the only method to understand historical texts. We are offering it as a possibly more coherent method to analyze these texts.

Therefore, in line with the contextual method, a thorough examination of ancient Near Eastern conquest accounts will be necessary.[145] In the first stage of the study, conquest accounts from the Assyrians, Hittites and

144. Oden, "Hermeneutics and Historiography," 149.

145. Two areas with which this book will not deal are: (1) the idea of history in the ANE and the Bible. Numerous scholars have written on this subject [e.g., E. A. Speiser, "Ancient Mesopotamia," in *The Idea of History in the Ancient Near East*, 35–76; and "The Biblical Idea of History in its Common Near Eastern Setting," *Biblical and Oriental Studies*, 187–210. M. Burrows, "Ancient Israel," in *The Idea of History in the Ancient Near East*, 99–131. H. Gese, *ZThK* 55 (1958) 127–45. J. Krecher and H.-P. Müller, *Saeculum* 26 (1975) 13–44. B. Albrektson, *History and the Gods*. N. Wyatt, *UF* 11 (1979) 825–32].

But Van Seters points out that these studies are often flawed by the notion of a uniform idea of history in a particular culture (*In Search of History*, 57–58). Cf. Hoffner's important comment: "What we may learn, therefore, is not a single uniform "view" of history writing held by the Hittites, but many individual viewpoints held by some of the Hittites who undertook to write down portions of their past as they conceived it" (*Or* 49 [1980] 288). So also it appears to be the case with other nations.

Moreover, these studies are flawed by their selectivity (see: Van Seters, 57 and 238; and note G. A. Press's remarks, *The Development of the Idea of History in Antiquity*, 142). [A vivid example of this problem is Gese's study in which the selectivity of the ANE and biblical materials does not present an accurate picture of any of the cultures' ideas of history]. Often similarities are oversimplified (e.g., A. Malamat, *VT* 5 [1955] 1–12).

Egyptians will be investigated.[146] In the next stage, there will be an examination of the conquest [[58]] account in Joshua. Throughout a semiotic approach will be employed. Lastly, these two stages of the inquiry will be integrated and an evaluation of the evidence offered.

---

and (2) a reconstruction of Israelite History. Since a thorough investigation of the ANE and biblical accounts must be completed before the issue of a reconstruction of Israelite history can be addressed, the main concern must be with how to read and interpret these texts. Thus, in our discussion of the Joshua conquest account, we will offer no reconstruction; not only because of the pragmatics of space, but also because a historiographic inquiry is primarily a literary study, while a reconstruction is, of necessity, concerned with questions of historicity.

146. The kinds of ANE texts that we will be investigating are ANE conquest accounts— obviously including many literary genres (e.g., Annalistic texts, Display/Summary inscriptions, Letters to the God, etc.). Our primary concern is with texts that contain more than one episode or campaign, although we will not neglect scrutiny of single campaign texts (like the Kadesh Inscription of Ramesses II). By investigating this broad category (genre?!) we will be better able to understand Joshua's main conquest account (chaps. 9–12).

Works Cited

Albrektson, B. *History and the Gods: An Essay on the Idea of Historical Events as Divine Manifestations in the Ancient Near East and in Israel.* Lund, 1967.

Alter, Robert. *The Art of Biblical Narrative.* London and Sydney, 1981.

Althusser, L. "Ideology and Ideological State Apparatuses." In *Lenin and Philosophy.* New York, 1971.

Apter, David L. "Ideology and Discontent." In *Ideology and Discontent.* Ed. David L. Apter, pp. 1–17. New York, 1964.

Archi, A. "The Propaganda of Hattusili III." *Studi Micenei ed Egeo Anatolici* 14 (1971) 185–216.

Barnes, Barry. *Scientific Knowledge and Sociological Theory.* London and Boston, 1974.

Barr, J. "Story and History in Biblical Theology." In *Scope and Authority of the Bible*, pp. 1–12. = *JR* 56/1 (1976) 5.

Barthes, R. *Eléments de Sémiologie.* Paris, 1964.

———. *La Plaiser de Text.* Paris, 1971.

———. *S/Z.* Paris, 1970.

Beckman, G. "The Hittite Assembly." *JAOS* 102 (1982) 435–42.

Braudel, F. "The Situation of History in 1950." In *On History.* Trans. S. Matthews. Chicago, 1980.

Brett, M. "Literacy and Domination: G. A. Herion's Sociology of History Writing." *JSOT* 37 (1987) 20–24.

Burrows, M. "Ancient Israel." In *The Idea of History in the Ancient Near East*, ed. R. C. Dentan, pp. 99–131. New Haven and London, 1955.

Cancik, H. *Grundzüge der hethitischen und alttestamentlichen Geschichtsschreibung.* Wiesbaden, 1976.

Carr, E. H. *What is History?* 1961.

Cassuto, U. "The Rise of Historiography in Israel." In *Eretz-Israel* 1, pp. 85–88 [Hebrew].

_____. "The Beginning of Historiography among the Israelites." In *Biblical and Oriental Studies*, ed. U. Cassuto, Vol. 1, pp. 7–16. Jerusalem, 1973.

Clements, R. "History and Theology in Biblical Narrative." *Horizons in Biblical Theology* 4–5 (1982–83) 51–55.

Coats, G. W. *Genesis.* [FOTL, 1]. Grand Rapids, 1982.

Coggins, R. J. "History and Story in Old Testament Study." *JSOT* 11 (1979) 36–46.

Cohen, Ralph. "History and Genre." *New Literary History* 17 (1986) 204.

Colie, R. L. "Johan Huizinga and the Task of Cultural History." *AHR* 69 (1963–64) 607–30.

Cook, Albert. "'Fiction' and History in Samuel and Kings." *JSOT* 36 (1986) 21–35.

Cooper, Alan. "The Life and Times of King David According to the Book of Psalms." In *The Poet and the Historian: Essays in Literary and Historical Biblical Criticism* [HSS, 26]. Ed. R. E. Friedman, pp. 117–32. Chico, California, 1983.

_____. "On Reading the Bible Critically and Otherwise." In *The Future of Biblical Studies*, ed. R. E. Friedman and H. G. M. Williamson, pp. 61–79. Atlanta, 1987.

Cuddon, J. A. *A Dictionary of Literary Terms.* Revised Edition, Oxford and Cambridge, Mass., 1979.

Danto, A. *Analytical Philosophy of History.* Cambridge, 1965.

Derrida, Jacques. "The Law of Genre." *Critical Inquiry* 7/1 (1980) 64–65.

Dray, W. H. "On the Nature and Role of Narrative in Historiography." *History and Theory* 10 (1971) 153–71.

Eco, Umberto. *A Theory of Semiotics.* Bloomington, 1976.

Egan, Kieran. "Thucydides, Tragedian." In *The Writing of History: Literary Form and Historical Understanding*, ed. R. H. Canary et al., pp. 78–82. Madison, 1978.

Fales, F. M. "A Literary Code in Assyrian Royal Inscriptions: The Case of Ashurbanipal's Egyptian Campaigns." In *ARINH*, ed. F. M. Fales, pp. 169–202. Rome, 1981.

Finley, M. I. *The Use and Abuse of History.* New York, 1975.

Frei, Hans. *The Eclipse of Biblical Narrative.* New Haven, 1974.

Friedman, Jonathan. "Ideology." In *The Social Science Encyclopedia*, ed. Adam Kuper and Jessica Kuper, pp. 375–76. London, Boston, and Henley, 1985.

Gadamer, Hans-Georg. *Truth and Method.* New York, 1978.

Garbini, G. *History and Ideology in Ancient Israel.* New York, 1988.

Geertz, Clifford. "Ideology as a Cultural System." In *Ideology and Discontent*, ed. David E. Apter, pp. 47–76. New York, 1964.

Gerhart, M. "Generic Studies: Their Renewed Importance in Religious and Literary Interpretation." *JAAR* 45/3 (1977) 309–25.

Gese, H. "Geschichtliches Denken im Alten Orient und im Alten Testament." *ZThK* 55 (1958) 127–45. Translated by J. F. Ross as "The Idea of History in the Ancient Near East and the Old Testament." *Journal for Theology and the Church*[2] (1965) 49–64.

[[Gomme, A. W. *A Historical Commentary on Thucydides.* 5 Volumes. Oxford, 1945–81.]]

Goody, J. R., and Watt, I. "The Consequence of Literacy." *Comparative Studies in Society and History* 5/3 (1963) 304–45.

_____. "The Consequences of Literacy." In *Literacy in Traditional Societies,* ed. J. R. Goody, pp. 27–68. Cambridge, 1968.

Gould, Julius. "Ideology." In *A Dictionary of the Social Sciences,* pp. 315–17, ed. Julius Gould and William L. Kolb. New York, 1964.

Grayson, A. K. "Problematical Battles in Mesopotamian History." In *Studies in Honor of Berno Landsberger on His Seventy-Fifth Birthday.* [Assyriological Studies, 16]. Chicago, 1965.

Gressmann, H. *Die älteste Geschichtsschreibung und Prophetie Israels.* SAT 2/1. Göttingen, 1910; 2nd ed., 1921.

Guidi, Ignazio. "L'historiographie chez les Semites." *RB* 15 (1906) 509–19.

Gunkel, H. "Die israelitische Literatur." In *Die Kultur der Gegenwart: Die orientalischen Literaturen.*

_____. *The Legends of Genesis.* Translated by W. H. Carruth. Chicago, 1901. Reprinted with a new introduction by W. F. Albright. New York, 1964.

_____. "Die Grundprobleme der israelitischen Literaturgeschichte." In *Reden und Aufsätze,* pp. 29–38.

Habermas, Jürgen. *Knowledge and Human Interests.* Boston, 1971.

_____. *Theorie und Praxis: Sozialphilosophie Studien.* Neuwied, 1963.

Hallo, W. W. "Sumerian Historiography." In *History, Historiography and Interpretation,* ed. H. Tadmor and M. Weinfeld, pp. 1–12. Jerusalem, 1983.

_____. "Biblical History in its Near Eastern Setting: The Contextual Approach." In *Scripture in Context: Essays on the Comparative Method,* ed. Carl D. Evans, W. W. Hallo, and John B. White, pp. 1–12. Pittsburgh, 1980.

Halpern, B. *JBL* 104/3 (1985) 506–9.

_____. *The First Historians, The Hebrew Bible and History.* San Francisco, 1988.

Hegel, G. *Vorlesungen über die Philosophie der Geschichte.* Frankfurt am Main, 1970.

Hoffman, I. *Der Erlass Telipinus.* Heidelberg, 1984.

Hoffner, H. A., Jr. "Histories and Historians of the Ancient Near East: The Hittites." *Or* 49 (1980) 283–332.

_____. "Propaganda and Political Justification in Hittite Historiography." In *Unity and Diversity: Essays in the History, Literature, and Religion of the Ancient Near East,* ed. H. Goedicke and J. J. M. Roberts, pp. 49–62. Baltimore and London, 1975.

Huizinga, J. "De Taak van Cultuurgeschiedenis." In *Verzamelde Werken,* ed. Leendert Brummel et al. Vol. 7, pp. 45ff. Haarlem, 1948–53. 9 Volumes.

_____. "A Definition of the Concept of History." In *Philosophy and History: Essays Presented to Ernst Cassirer,* ed. R. Klibansky and H. J. Paton, pp. 1–10. (Dutch original 1928; translated by D. R. Cousin in 1936.) Cambridge, 1936.

Iggers, Georg G. *The German Conception of History: The National Tradition of Historical Thought from Herder to the Present.* Middletown, Connecticut, 1968.

Jameson, Fredric. *The Political Unconscious.* Ithaca, 1981.

Johnson, Harry M. "Ideology and the Social System." In *International Encyclopedia of the Social Sciences*. Vol. 7, pp. 76–85, ed. David L. Sills. New York, 1968.

Kitchen, K. A. *Ancient Orient and the Old Testament*. Downers Grove, Illinois, 1966.

Krecher, J., and Müller, H.-P. "Vergangenheitsinteresse in Mesopotamien und Israel." *Saeculum* 26 (1975) 13–44.

LaCapra, Dominick. "Comment." *New Literary History* 17/2 (1986) 221.

Lee, Dwight E., and Beck, Robert N. "The Meaning of 'Historicism.'" *American Historical Review* 59 (1954) 568–77.

Levin, D. *Defense of Historical Literature*. New York, 1967.

Levine, L. D. "Sennacherib's Southern Front: 704–689 B.C." *JCS* 34 (1982) 49–51.

Levy, F. J. "Editor's Foreword." In *The Theory and Practice of History*, p. vi.

Lichtheim, George. "The Concept of Ideology." *History and Theory* 4/2 (1965) 164–95.

Long, B. O. *I Kings with an Introduction to Historical Literature*. [FOTL, 9]. Grand Rapids, 1984.

Lukács, G. *Geschichte und Klassenbewusstsein: Studien über marxistische Dialektik*. Berlin, 1923.

Maisler [Mazar], B. "Ancient Israelite Historiography." *IEJ* 2 (1952) 82–88.

Malamat, A. "Doctrines of Casuality in Hittite and Biblical Historiography: A Parallel." *VT* 5 (1955) 1–12.

Mandelbaum, M. "A Note on History as Narrative." *History and Theory* 6 (1967) 414–19.

[[Mandelbaum, M. *The Anatomy of Historical Knowledge*. Baltimore, 1977.]]

Mannheim, K. *Ideology and Utopia*. London, 1936. 2nd Edition, 1960.

[[Meinecke, F. *Die Enstehung des Historismus*. Munich, 1959.]]

Millard, A. R. "The Old Testament and History: Some Considerations." *FT* 110 (1983) 34–53.

_____. "Sennacherib's Attack on Hezekiah." *TB* 36 (1977) 61–77.

Mink, Louis O. "The Autonomy of Historical Understanding." In *Philosophical Analysis and History*, ed. William H. Dray, pp. 160–92. New York and London, 1966.

_____. "Narrative Form as a Cognitive Instrument." In *Literary Form and Historical Understanding*, ed. R. H. Canary and H. Kozicki. Madison, 1978.

Mowinckel, S. "Israelite Historiography." *ASTI* 2 (1963) 4–26.

Nash, Ronald H. *Christian Faith and Historical Understanding*. Grand Rapids, 1984.

Noth, M. "Geschichtsschreibung im A.T." In *Die Religion in Geschichte und Gegenwart*. 3rd ed. Vol. 2, pp. 1498–1504, ed. K. Galling. Berlin, 1957–62.

Oden, R. A., Jr. "Hermeneutics and Historiography: Germany and America." In *Seminar Papers of the SBL*. 1980.

_____. "Intellectual History and the Study of the Bible." In *The Future of Biblical Studies*, ed. R. E. Friedman and H. G. M. Williamson, pp. 1–18. Atlanta, 1987.

Orsini, G. N. G. "Genres." In *Princeton Encyclopedia of Poetry and Poetics*, ed. A. Preminger, pp. 307–9. Princeton, 1967.

Percy, W. "Metaphor as Mistake." *The Sewanee Review* 66 (1958) 79–99.

Pfeiffer, Robert H. *Introduction to the Old Testament*.[2] New York, 1948.

Press, Gerald A. *The Development of the Idea of History in Antiquity.* Kingston and Montreal, 1982.

Rad, G. von. "The Beginnings of Historical Writing in Ancient Israel." In *The Problem of the Hexateuch*, pp. 166–204. 1944.

[[Ranke, L. von. *Geschichten der romanischen und germanischen Völker von 1494 bis 1514.* Leipzig, 1824.]]

[[Ranke, L. von. *The Theory and Practice of History*, ed. G. G. Iggers and K. von Moltke. Indianapolis, 1973.]]

[[Reagan, C. E. *The Philosophy of Paul Ricoeur*, ed. D. Stewart. Boston, 1978.]]

Ricoeur, P. "Explanation and Understanding: On Some Remarkable Connections Among the Theory of the Text, Theory of Action, and Theory of History." In *The Philosophy of Paul Ricoeur*, ed. C. E. Reagan and D. Stewart. Boston, 1978.

Roberts, J. J. M. "Myth versus History: Relaying the Comparative Foundations." *CBQ* 38 (1976) 1–13.

Rogerson, J. W. *JTS* 37/2 (1986) 451–54.

Rokeah, D. "Speeches in Thucydides: Factual Reporting or Creative Writing?" *Athenaeum* 60 (1982) 386–401.

Schneidau, Herbert. *Sacred Discontent.* Baton Rouge, La., 1977.

Scholes, Robert. *Semiotics and Interpretation.* New Haven, 1985.

Shaw, Harry. *Dictionary of Literary Terms.* 1972.

Shils, Edward. "The Concept and Function of Ideology." In *International Encyclopedia of the Social Sciences*, ed. David L. Sills. Vol. 7, pp. 66–76. New York, 1968. 17 Volumes.

Spalinger, A. J. *Aspects of the Military Documents of the Ancient Egyptians.* [Yale Near Eastern Researches, 9.] New Haven and London, 1983.

Speiser, E. A. "Ancient Mesopotamia." In *The Idea of History in the Ancient Near East*, ed. R. C. Dentan, pp. 35–76. New Haven, 1955.

_____. "The Biblical Idea of History in Its Common Near Eastern Setting." In *Biblical and Oriental Studies*, ed. J. J. Finkelstein and M. Greenberg, pp. 187–210. Philadelphia, 1967.

Stambovsky, P. "Metaphor and Historical Understanding," *History and Theory* 27 (1988) 125–34.

Stark, Werner. *The Sociology of Knowledge.* London, 1958.

Sternberg, Meir. *The Poetics of Biblical Narrative: Ideological Literature and the Drama of Reading.* Bloomington, Indiana, 1985.

Tadmor, H. "The Autobiographical Apology in the Royal Assyrian Literature." In *History, Historiography and Interpretation*, ed. H. Tadmor and M. Weinfeld, pp. 36–57. Jerusalem, 1983.

Talmon, S. "*Har and Midbar*: An Antithetical Pair of Biblical Motifs." In *Figurative Language in the Ancient Near East*, ed. M. Mindell, M. J. Geller, and J. E. Wansbrough, pp. 120–40. London, 1987.

Thompson, R. J. *Moses and the Law in a Century of Criticism Since Graf.* Leiden, 1972.

Trompf, G. W. "Notions of Historical Recurrence in Classical Hebrew Historiography." *Studies in the Historical Books of the Old Testament.* [VTS, 30.] Ed. J. A. Emerton, pp. 213–29. Leiden, 1979.

van der Toorn, Karel. *Sin and Sanction in Israel and Mesopotamia: A Comparative Study.* [Studia Semitica Neerlandica, 22.] Assen/Maastricht: Van Gorcum, 1985.

Van Seters, John. *In Search of History: Historiography in the Ancient World and the Origins of Biblical History.* New Haven and London, 1983. [[Repr. Winona Lake, Ind.: Eisenbrauns, 1997.]]

Waldman, M. *Toward a Theory of Historical Narrative: A Case Study in Perso-Islamicate Historiography.* Columbus, Ohio: Ohio State University Press, 1980.

Webster's 3rd New International Dictionary. Vol. 1. s.v. "historiography," p. 1073.

Weinfeld, M. "Divine Intervention in War in Ancient Israel and in the Ancient Near East." In *History, Historiography, and Interpretation,* ed. H. Tadmor and M. Weinfeld, pp. 121–47. Jerusalem, 1983.

White, H. *Tropics of Discourse.* Baltimore and London, 1978.

_____. *Metahistory, The Historical Imagination in Nineteenth-Century Europe.* Baltimore and London, 1973.

_____. "The Question of Narrative in Contemporary Historical Theory." *History and Theory* 23 (1984) 2–42.

_____. "Historicism, History, and the Figurative Imagination." *History and Theory* Beiheft 14 (1975) 48–67.

Whitehead, A. N. *Adventures of Ideas.* New York, 1971.

Whitelam, K. W. "Recreating the History of Israel." *JSOT* 35 (1986) 45–70.

Whybray, R. N. *The Succession Narrative.* [SBT, 2/9.] London, 1968.

Wise, Gene. *American Historical Explanations.* Homewood, Ill., 1973.

Wolf, H. M. "The Apology of Hattušiliš Compared with Other Political Self-Justifications of the Ancient Near East." Dissertation, Brandeis University, 1967.

Wyatt, N. "Some Observations on the Idea of History among the West Semitic Peoples." *UF* 11 (1979) 825–32.

Younger, K. L., Jr. "A Critical Review of John Van Seters, *In Search of History.*" *JSOT* 40 (1987) 110–17.

The Devaluation of the Old Testament as a Historical Source

Notes on a Problem in the History of Ideas

SIEGFRIED HERRMANN

[[156]] Let no one suppose or expect that this is going to be a "counter-lecture" to the congress theme, *sola scriptura* [['scripture only']]. The stimulus for my reflections is found instead in the current state of research on the history of Israel—not just with regard to hypotheses about the early history of Israel from Mendenhall to Lemche[1] but also with regard to the later stages of the development of Israel, consideration of which threatens to be pulled into the vortex of the investigation of early Israel. Israel itself sought the roots of its power and convictions in its early history. Thus if one disputes Israel's understanding of its early history, the consequences are inevitable for understanding the Old Testament overall, not just the historical books, but the Prophets and Writings as well.

Reprinted and translated with permission from "Die Abwertung des Alten Testaments als Geschichtsquelle: Bermerkungen zu einem geistesgeschichtlichen Problem," in *Sola Scriptura, VII: Europäischer Theologen-Kongreß, Dresden, 1990* (ed. H. H. Schmid and J. Mehlhausen; Gütersloh: Mohn, 1993) 156–65. Translation by Peter T. Daniels.

Author's note: The original lecture style has generally been retained to facilitate the recollection of those who participated in the seminar.

1. At the present time these two names mark out a specific, albeit very complex, research program, on which more will be said in the course of this lecture.

Now the following exposition is not intended in the least to present the latest state-of-the-question in early Israel research or to critique it in detail; least of all is there any intent to offer a new model alongside the existing ones. What concerns us here are the presuppositions and assumptions that have led to the current state of affairs and that, as has occasionally already been claimed, might lead to a crisis in Old Testament study, if this has not already set in, here and there.

A critical evaluation of the present cannot be accomplished without looking back on the past. In the short time available to me today, it must suffice to mention the stages and results of earlier research with a few comments.

I

That we have no "original sources" of the Old Testament, only edited material, is an oft-lamented fact. Even Jean Astruc believed, however, that we had the "mémoires originaux, dont il paroit que Moyse s'est servi pour composer le Livre de la Genèse" [[original notes that Moses seems to have used in compiling the book of Genesis]].[2] But it was Astruc who began the division into [[157]] sources, and with that we are immediately faced with literary problems, with questions of composition and redaction of the books of the Bible, not with the reconstruction of the history of events.

Division into sources, which a hundred years ago was in full bloom, was inspired by the search for the great source documents, to the extent that the extant text allowed the recognition of their shape. Scripture in its extant form remained the immoveable basis of all endeavors, whereby however the question about the supposed *mémoires originaux* [['original memoirs']] generally receded or appeared in a different light—I am thinking, say, of Wellhausen's reversal in assessment of the literary sequence, bestowing on the Prophets, contrary to the canon, a place ahead of the "Law."

From the form of scripture Gunkel inferred oral tradition—the oral precursors of what came to be written down. The *mémoires originaux* suddenly seemed very near, yet at the same time so very far away, for the discovery of form-criticism [[*Formgeschichte*]] and its predilection for rules clouded the direct view of history, which one would have preferred to see attested in original documents rather than in artifical literary creations. But now another door opened: oral tradition and form-criticism led away

---

2. The complete title of Astruc's anonymously published work begins "Conjectures sur les mémoires originaux . . ." (Brussels, 1753); for the details, cf. R. de Vaux, "A propos du second centenaire d'Astruc: Réflexions sur l'état actuel de la critique du Pentateuque," *Congress Volume, Copenhagen 1953* (VTSup 1; Leiden: Brill, 1953) 182–98.

from the rather academic differentiation of sources and toward bounteous life. Where people spoke and wrote and how people spoke and wrote—these are sociological questions. Literary differentiation made possible the sociological localization of tradition as well.

It is no overstatement when I say that the first to draw consistent, noteworthy consequences for the history of Israel from these various starting points and their methodological outworkings was Albrecht Alt. For Alt did not thrive on source differentiation, the principles of which he therefore did not question, but on Gunkel and form-criticism; and without saying it loudly, let alone stressing it, he trod close to the pathways of thought laid out by Max Weber. Not just the topography of the oldest and later scenes, but also the organization of early Israel and the constitutional history of later Israel interested him. To be sure, he did take leave of the notion of an Israelite "confederation" [[*Eidgenossenschaft*]][3] and argued instead for an amphictyony.[4]

But when Martin Noth defended the "Old Israelite amphictyony" as the bearer of the pre-state form of organization of Israel and attributed to it a narrowly circumscribed historical function, Alt kept his distance. For him the supposition that Israel could be understood as an amphictyonic union was little more than an explanation [[158]] for how and why Israel could be described as a people of twelve tribes. He deduced from this no further consequences as regards the *historical* organization of early Israel and its modes of operation.[5] In this respect Noth was more bold than his teacher. He drew out the historical consequences of the amphictyonic concept and transposed the origin of Israel as a people of twelve tribes out of the wilderness and into civilized territory. Israel in its delimitation as twelve tribes originated in Canaan. This was Noth's idea. What preceded it in time were, in his opinion, "traditions of the amphictyony."

Let us pause a moment: The trains of thought just presented are so familiar to us that I have not noted that we have come no small distance from the *mémoires originaux*, whose existence is always presupposed. The "amphictyony," as applied to Israel, is a hypothesis (and that is how Noth understood it explicitly in his 1930 book), not an institution that can be

---

3. M. Weber, *Gesammelte Aufsätze zur Religionssoziologie*, volume 3: *Das antike Judentum* (1920) 1–280.

4. For the history of the hypothesis, see O. Bächli, *Amphiktyonie im Alten Testament: Forschungsgeschichtliche Studie zur Hypothese von Martin Noth* (1977).

5. Of course it must be remembered that Alt had already completed his works on "Landnahme" (1925) and "Staatenbildung" (1930) by the time Noth published his book on "Das System der zwölf Stämme Israels." But Alt also declined to follow Noth's path later on, even when the opportunity presented itself, in his "Erwägungen über die Landnahme der Israeliten in Palästina" (1939). These articles of Alt's may be found in his *Kleine Schriften* 1 and 2.

read with certainty from the documentation, not an institution to which one would have referred in the Old Testament.

Inadequate textual contact and grounding must also be ascribed to another hypothesis, oft repeated in reconstructions of Israel's early history and to which high probability was and is attributed. This is Alt's concept of "peaceful acquisition of land" [[*friedlichen Landnahme*]]. It strongly contradicts the biblical presentation. The transhumance theory[6] represents a problem within Alt's overall view right from the start. It was a hypothesis emerging less from the texts than from observation of modern Bedouin practice, behind which Oppenheim's book on the Bedouin was in many ways the driving force.[7]

Alt's view of "acquisition of land"—an only apparently neutral concept introduced by him—has been almost exclusively associated with the idea of a peaceful event, especially in the English-language literature, where Alt stood for "peaceful infiltration." But Alt had warlike events following the peaceful ones, particularly in the context of the so-called "land expansion," that is, the period of increasing consolidation of the Israelite tribes in the land.

[[159]] At this point a further factor, so far unmentioned, must be introduced: archaeology. In combination with historical-topographical information about the land (which since the nineteenth century has been growing ever more detailed), archaeology has attempted to rediscover and confirm the earliest traces of Israel in ancient Palestine. We have known for a long time that determining the relationship between archaeological evidence and history always represents a problem. This is particularly true in the matter of dating but also in the evaluation of individual finds as over against historical facts attested in documents. At this point, the controversy between Noth and Albright only needs to be mentioned briefly: Albright accused Alt and Noth of "nihilism" because they threatened to snatch the textual foundation that he considered secure and that he used as support for his archaeological results away from him on literary grounds. While Albright branded Alt and Noth with "nihilism," others called him a "fundamentalist."

---

6. Alt esp. in ibid., vol. 1 (1953) 139–53. [[The transhumance theory proposed that the Israelites were peoples that migrated with their flocks to whatever green pastures they could find, eventually settling down peacefully in the land.]]

7. M. Frhr. von Oppenheim, *Die Beduinen* 1 (1939), 2 (1943). I should note that in Alt, *Kleine Schriften,* 1.141, in the reference to Oppenheim there is a note that Oppenheim's first volume was not available to Alt when his article was published in 1939. He referred to other works but later found confirmation in Oppenheim and frequently referred to him in class lectures.

But these peculiarly judgmental categories (which Noth sharply repudiated) still centered on the biblical text as mean and measure: the text's historical value was either denied or apparently denied ("nihilism") or overvalued ("fundamentalism"). In debate with Albright, Noth called his activity a "scientific method" that "has a scientific basis" and that should not be dismissed with an ideological-political slogan.[8]

To this point, despite many variations in detail, we have been able to follow what is in essence a well-defined and well-founded line in the history of research. In this line, the biblical text was explored in relation to different models of interpretation, be they more exegetical-literary or historical-archaeological in nature—leaving aside for the moment theological considerations.

II

But since the 1960s, a consciously different perspective that has shown no desire to attach itself to previous procedures has opened up. I am referring to the mindset associated with the name of George Mendenhall, a way of thinking that he began to present, if not to a large extent to originate, in his 1962 article "The Hebrew Conquest of Palestine."[9] With one stroke he brushed aside a number of presuppositions that hitherto had been considered constitutive and irrefutable:

a. the twelve tribes came from outside the civilized land; they entered it at the time of or shortly before the "conquest"; [[160]]
b. the Israelites were nomads or seminomads who became sedentary in the land;
c. the connection of the tribes was ethnic in nature, and kinship connections were the basis for the contrast between Israelites and Canaanites.

Once all of these presuppositions are abandoned, virtually nothing of the biblical presentation remains, for wilderness, land acquisition, and opposition to the Canaanites are quite truly the constitutive components of the Old Testament's presentation of the early history of Israel. They characterize the development of Israel not only in the sense of the external historical passage from wilderness to civilized land but also as directly and indirectly detectable in the spiritual and religious growth process that Israel itself experienced and strove to preserve in its traditions. The experi-

---

8. M. Noth, "Der Beitrag der Archäologie zur Geschichte Israels" (VTSup 7; Leiden: Brill, 1960) 263 n. 1; repr. *Aufsätze zur biblischen Landes- und Altertumskunde* 1 (1971) 35 n. 2.
9. G. E. Mendenhall, "The Hebrew Conquest of Palestine," *BA* 25 (1962) 66–87.

ences at God's mountain, however they appeared (and we'll set aside Kadesh!), established a form of belief contradictory to the nature religion of Canaan. Mendenhall must have felt this, for he allowed a certain status to the Exodus tradition. In his opinion, what it comprised and what it radiated had a stimulating effect on the other tribes. Its history, however, he sought not in the wilderness; the entire emphasis of his argumentation lay on developments within Canaan, on what he assumed to be an opposition between city and country, on the liberation of oppressed strata from dependence on the cities. We know the slogan: *peasant's revolt.*

There is little point in expounding on the details and modifications of these starting points in the way that, say, de Geus and Gottwald did.[10] Mendenhall himself leveled harsh reproaches at Gottwald, who considered the Yahweh religion to be an ideological superstructure built on populist political events. The reproaches peaked with sharp attacks of an ideological nature. For instance, in his chapter in the volume *Palestine in Transition,* Mendenhall said: "And now we have a large work [that is, Gottwald's] that systematically attempts to force the ancient historical data into the Procrustes' Bed of nineteenth-century Marxist sociology."[11]

Niels Peter Lemche's endeavors to see Israel's development as an evolutionary process that had begun in the social upheavals in Canaan at the end of the Late Bronze age were free of the revolutionary model and of ideological premises, however.[12] From the declining [[161]] Canaanite cities and their obsolescent city-state structures the vital elements would have decamped, then regrouped in the mountainous hinterlands, there to construct Israel. Israel was thus the result, not of an east–west movement, but of a west–east movement. The conclusion that follows is inescapable. Yahweh-religion is an offshoot of Canaanite religion. What we are accustomed to call specifically Israelite or Jewish is a manifestation of this religion that did not arise before 500 B.C.E.

One may ask: how are opinions so contradictory to the biblical version possible? Are they justified? What is the stimulating factor? Lemche is convinced that the Old Testament contains scarcely any sources older than the seventh century B.C.E. The Moses tradition, he claims, has long been recognized as unhistorical. We do not know how it happened that

---

10. Their main works: C. H. J. de Geus, *The Tribes of Israel: An Investigation into Some of the Presuppositions of Martin Noth's Amphictyony Hypothesis* (1976); N. K. Gottwald, *The Tribes of Yahweh: A Sociology of the Religion of Liberated Israel, 1250–1050 B.C.E.* (1979).

11. D. N. Freedman and D. F. Graf (eds.), *Palestine in Transition: The Emergence of Ancient Israel* (1983) 91.

12. N. P. Lemche, *Early Israel: Anthropological and Historical Studies on the Israelite Society before the Monarchy* (VTSup 37; Leiden: Brill, 1985); idem, *Ancient Israel: A New History of Israelite Society* (1988).

later traditions felt obliged to make him into the founder of a religion but if there was no Moses, he had to be invented, and with Mario Liverani we must say "that they did in fact invent him"![13] In this way Lemche clears the way for presenting the early history of Israel without any longer being excessively burdened with biblical assertions.

What we need, in Lemche's view, is a history of Israel based on archaeology, on tangible results of research carried out independently of the Bible. The biblical traditions contain no obligatory material for historical evaluation. Israel, as a whole, as we know it and as it is represented in scripture, is for Lemche the product of a late period, which gradually developed out of Canaanite predecessors, out of a Canaanite milieu. It differed neither in its state organization nor in its religion from its surroundings. At least in the royal period there was nothing to distinguish the worship of Yahweh from other types of West Asiatic religion. What later promoted Yahweh to paramount significance can only be explained by Israel's experiences in the Exile.

Let us leave Lemche for a moment: What he touched on and what appeared to be radical is not so unusual in our time. The shaping of monotheism since the seventh century and especially since the Exile; the combination of earlier traditions in late works, most clearly in the Deuteronomistic History, later also in the Priestly writings; the doubt about the early dating of the Yahwist and the Elohist; the late dating of collections of prophetic texts and the concept of what is called the "projection" [[*Fortschreibung*]]—these are without exception well known terms in modern research and are liable [[162]] to grant (more or less) legitimacy to Lemche's idea or at least to make it difficult to find counterevidence for some of his theses. Perhaps we are only at the beginnning of a really bewildering process of argumentation, in which older and newer methodological approaches will combine.

Two things, however, need to be avoided. Thomas L. Thompson puts it trenchantly, as is his wont, in his book *The Origin Tradition of Ancient Israel*:[14] "No less than Syro-Palestinian archaeology, Israelite history must proceed as a discipline independent of biblical exegesis. So too, biblical exegesis needs to be understood as an historical-critical discipline with its own autonomy apart from historical and archaeological research." He is convinced of the necessity "of separating biblical interpretation from modern historiography. This, once achieved, ends the crisis in biblical scholarship." I, however, would say that this is when the crisis really be-

---

13. Ibid., 256.
14. T. L. Thompson, *The Origin Tradition of Ancient Israel*, vol. 1: *The Literary Formation of Genesis and Exodus 1–23* (JSOTSup 55; Sheffield: JSOT Press, 1987) 40.

gins! Let no one think that finding relationships between the biblical text and history will come to an end and that, through the separation of their methods, their drama will be lost.

The second thing to avoid is what must appear as a result of such methodological duality and already does appear in Lemche. He builds up a picture of history that he means to reconstruct from archaeology, without any reference to the biblical picture of history. This Lemchean picture, however, is *his* picture, and it remains to be asked whether all in all the biblical picture isn't better and more relevant than Lemche's construction based on extrabiblical evidence that can be interpreted in various ways. In debate with Lemche, Frederick H. Cryer has put it memorably: "He [Lemche] proffers a model based on modern sociological studies of nomadism, ethnicity, and the like. In so doing, Lemche is in reality composing a new 'source,' . . . that is, he proposes for our consideration a narrative of his own devising."[15]

Here lies the true upheaval in the history of the discipline, and it is where we find ourselves at this point in time. While, hitherto, biblical tradition has been queried for its historical background, and to a large extent felicitous correspondence with archaeology and extrabiblical evidence has been discovered, for Lemche and others using a similar approach, a theoretical concept independent of textual interpretation dominates; the biblical texts are set aside as useless for an accurate historical judgment, because they do not correspond to the preconceived theories. The devaluation of the Old Testament as a historical source is thus based very fundamentally on a constructed incongruence between source statement and theoretical postulate. Older [[163]] research sought to establish a close relationship between Bible and history; newer research does not, but, as we have seen, at the cost of ignoring the Old Testament as a historical source or dismissing it as a late construct.

III

In view of this development, what in the subtitle of this lecture is called the "problem in the history of ideas" becomes urgent. For historicism, the key issue regarding the text was the question of historical verification. In the meantime, various methodological approaches to text analysis have attained predominance, and this has lead to experimentation with texts and a crippling of historical interest.

---

15. F. H. Cryer, "Divination in Ancient Israel and Her Near Eastern Environment: A Socio-Historical Investigation" (Ph.D. diss., Aarhus 1989) 15–16.

A pertinent issue of another sort should not be overlooked here. In his article "Toward the Establishment of a Scientific History of Israel," Tatsu-hito Koizumi presented some general considerations.[16] On the "so-called Alt–Noth school," he says: "These scholars seem to maintain that their dependence on the stories in the Bible is based on scholarly reasons, but to me it seems more likely that their judgements are based on their implicit belief in the Bible as the Word of God. And this kind of approach appears to me more warmly accepted in their society than Noth's."[17]

Koizumi then goes into more detail about how the state of things is different in Japan—a non-Christian society, in which the Bible generally has no theological authority at all. Koizumi has admittedly not worked out the consequences of this notion. They would have to include the general observation that where the Bible has lost normative value, passionate interest in the unconditional validity of all of its statements naturally subsides. This also leads to an indifferent position regarding historical statements and their substance. One is freed, as it were, from canonical viewpoints and is satisfied with proof or demonstration of other possibilities of understanding.

Who would deny that this is correct? This holds primarily for parts of the Christian camp that consider themselves to represent the tradition of the Enlightenment. For Judaism the facts are quite different. There the Old Testament is at once a firm component both of popular and national history and of religious consciousness. Thus historical interest is also more strongly developed and present as an ingredient of social culture.

[[164]] But, we must ask, is it then necessary at all to take into account such interests? Shouldn't historical-critical work gradually unearth what to a large degree or entirely corresponds to historical truth or optimally approaches it?

The following might be said: the theory of two paths, one an autonomous exegetical science, the other an autonomous contemplation of history on archaeological foundations, would be deprived of the extant possibilities of yielding a credible overall picture. Both paths must be trodden with determination and not independently of each other. The Old Testament cannot be excluded as a historical source or regarded as the pure product of independent, non-history-dependent traditions, for their roots are within history itself and are still universally interrogable "sources." Even a supposed "late" statement or source that refers to ear-

16. T. Koizumi, "Toward the Establishment of a Scientific History of Israel: From the Nomadic Period to the Organization of the Four Leading Tribes," *Annual of the Japanese Biblical Institute* 12 (1986) 29–76, esp. pp. 29–31.

17. Here Noth stands for the extreme critical position. Koizumi has not yet engaged the recent American investigations since Mendenhall or the ideas put forth by Lemche.

lier times has a claim to be interrogated regarding the factuality of its statements about older or earlier things. It must always be kept in mind that supposed editorial items may come closer to historical facts than we might perhaps believe.

What is so frightening about this so-called "modern historiography" is the often bold leapfrogging over very sound observations of older research, particularly from the first half of this century, when excellent foundations were laid for understanding Israel as a component of the ancient Near Eastern world and as embedded in it—not with the intention of submerging Israel into that world but of recognizing and defining its particular character, its particular development. These are old insights to which Martin Noth has already given clear expression, not inventing them out of underlying dogmatic conceptions, as a sort of credo, but because the texts themselves invited such asessments.[18]

Surely one does not become master of things when one sets aside every spark of religious insight and subjective experience and only admits the more-or-less random material legacy yielded by the ground as the standard for reconstructing history according to "modern" understanding.

I would call Lemche's model neopositivistic, in all ways eclectic and thus in many respects speculative. This is not intended as a casual label. It is intended, rather, above all to indicate that by this approach one will never do justice to the special development of Israel, which doubtless exists.

What the Old Testament divulges about the development of Israel as a people and about the formative process of its thought and belief is an adequate and serviceable model, especially with an appropriately critical reading of the texts; and [[165]] archaeology does not contradict it, if one draws the biblical text into commentary on it.

Thus we have a guideline that remains with us beyond all doubt and which the Old Testament itself in relation to the neighboring cultures reveals to us. Likewise, with respect to the material remains unearthed nowadays by archaeological excavation, the decisive judgment regarding their historical import belongs to *sola scriptura* [['scripture only']].

18. M. Noth, *Geschichte Israels* (6th ed.) 11.

Reading the Bible Historically

The Historian's Approach

J. MAXWELL MILLER

History and Historical Methodology

[[11]] Although "history" is a much-used term, it is not easily defined. Is history the sum total of past people and events? Or does it include only those people and events whose memory is preserved in written records? The available written evidence from ancient times is uneven in coverage, with some peoples and periods better represented than others. Moreover, the ancient documents provide very selective kinds of information. This information often is ambivalent, and sometimes the ancient sources make unbelievable or conflicting claims. Would it be more accurate, then, to say that history is the past as understood by historians, based on their analysis and interpretation of the available evidence but not necessarily identical with the claims made by ancient documents? What if the historians disagree? And does history belong to the professional historians anyhow? Perhaps history should be equated instead with the common consensus notions about the past held by the general public. These notions might be influenced by what professional historians say as well as by other factors, such as prevailing political, social, and religious attitudes. For that matter, are not professional historians themselves deeply influenced by prevailing attitudes?

Reprinted with permission from *To Each Its Own Meaning: An Introduction to Biblical Criticisms and Their Application* (ed. S. R. Haynes and S. L. McKenzie; Louisville: Westminster/ John Knox, 1993) 11–26.

It may be said, in any case, that historians seek to understand the human past and that they depend heavily on written sources for their information. Heavy reliance on written evidence is perhaps the main distinguishing characteristic of historical research as compared with other disciplines that also seek to understand the human past. This does not mean, of course, that contemporary historians concentrate solely on written evidence or that historical research is conducted independently of other disciplines. Contemporary scholars exploring the history of ancient Israel find themselves necessarily involved, for example, in Palestinian archaeology and sociology.

[[12]] Historians seek objectivity. They are interested in discovering and reporting what really happened in the past, as opposed to collecting and passing on fanciful stories, writing "docudramas," or producing "revisionist" accounts of the past for propagandistic or ideological purposes. However, complete objectivity is a goal never reached. The historian's own presuppositions, ideology, and attitudes inevitably influence his or her research and reporting. Perhaps it is not an overstatement to say that any history book reveals as much about its author as it does about the period of time treated. If so, then a proper definition of history would suggest that it consists neither of the totality of past people and events on the one hand, nor of what we contemporaries know (or think we know) about the past on the other, but of an ongoing conversation between the past and the present. As we humans, individually and collectively, seek to understand the present, we naturally look to the past for bearings. At the same time, we constantly revise our understanding of the past in light of current developments, understandings, and attitudes.

Basic to modern historiography is the principle of "analogy." Historians assume, consciously or unconsciously, that the past is analogous to the present and that one human society is analogous to another. Thus a historian's understanding of present reality serves as an overriding guide for evaluating evidence and interpreting the past, and the cultural patterns of a better-known society may be used as a guide for clarifying those of a lesser-known society. As an example of how this works in modern treatments of ancient Israelite history, note that the Bible presupposes a dynamic natural world into which God intrudes overtly upon human affairs from time to time. It is a world with waters rolling back so that the Israelites can escape Pharaoh's army, a world of burning bushes and floating ax heads. God hands down laws on Mount Sinai and sends angels to defend Jerusalem against the massive Assyrian army. Modern Western historians tend to perceive the world as being more orderly, however, and one of the standard tenets of modern historiography is that a natural explanation for a given historical phenomenon or event is preferable to an explanation that involves overt divine intervention. When speculating about the "actual historical events" behind the biblical account of Israel's past, therefore, what historians often do, in effect, is bring the biblical story into line with reality as we moderns perceive it. Surely the Assyrian army was not routed by angels, because angels, if they exist at all, do not play this sort of role in the world as we experience it. What other "more reasonable" explanation might there be for the rout of the Assyrians—"more reasonable" in the sense that it is more in keeping with our modern Western perception of reality? Possibly a plague broke out among the Assyrian troops, or maybe the narrator of the biblical account embellished the report. Either of these possibilities would be analogous to the world as we perceive it. But angels are not. In effect, then, the modern [[13]] historian offers explanations that do not involve miracles or "God talk" for historical developments reported in the Bible.

The analogy principle also is at work when historians draw upon knowledge of other societies, ancient and modern, in attempts to clarify aspects of Israelite and early Christian history. The Bible reports the names of court officials who served under David and Solomon, for example, but does not describe the duties of these various officials. Historians, assuming that the royal court in Jerusalem would have been similar to other royal courts of the day, search the records of neighboring kingdoms for information regarding the duties and responsibilities of such officials.

Another example pertains to the chronological data provided in the Bible for each of the Israelite and Judean kings following Solomon. Specifically, each king's accession to the throne is dated relative to the reign of his contemporary on the other throne; and also the length of each king's reign is recorded. The following verses are typical.

> In the twentieth year of King Jeroboam of Israel Asa began to reign over Judah; he reigned forty-one years in Jerusalem. (1 Kgs 15:9)

> Nadab son of Jeroboam began to reign over Israel in the second year of King Asa of Judah; he reigned over Israel two years. (1 Kgs 15:25)

> In the third year of King Asa of Judah, Baasha son of Ahijah began to reign over all Israel at Tirzah; he reigned twenty-four years. (1 Kgs 15:33)

However, the figures provided do not always "add up." This may be due in part to copyist's mistakes in the transmission of the ancient manuscripts. But there are also other factors to be considered in view of the records of other ancient Middle Eastern kingdoms. It is known, for example, that some of these records presuppose a fall-to-fall calendar year while others presuppose a spring-to-spring calendar year. Some designate as the first year of a king's reign the year during which he ascended to the throne; others count only his first full year (i.e., the first full fall-to-fall or spring-to-spring year, depending on the calendar used). The possibility arises, therefore, on analogy with the practices of neighboring peoples, that the two Hebrew kingdoms, Israel and Judah, used separate and different calendars, employed different methods of reckoning their respective kings' reigns, and may even have changed calendars or methods of reckoning at one time or another. One or more of these factors may explain why the biblical figures seem to be internally inconsistent. It is hardly surprising, moreover, in view of the confusing biblical figures and the various factors to be taken into account, that historians rarely agree on exact dates for the Israelite and Judean kings.

[[14]] Other than this principle of analogy, which is basic also to the other approaches treated in this volume, there is no specific methodology for historical research. Rather, the historian might be compared to an investigative lawyer who searches out and examines whatever evidence is available and relevant to a particular case, employs whatever techniques and methods of analysis apply to the evidence (often relying on the opinion of specialists), constructs a hypothetical scenario as to what probably happened, and then presents the case for this scenario to other historians and the public. The last step is as important as the first. The leading historians who have been able to influence academic and public opinion regarding the past have not only been outstanding scholars who demonstrated amazing coverage, competence, and creativity in research, but have also been able to present their ideas in an understandable and convincing fashion. Thus history is a search for "what really happened," but it is also what the historians can convince us really happened.

The Bible as History

The opening books of the Hebrew Bible, Genesis through 2 Kings, present a narrative account of people and events that extends from creation to the end of the Judean monarchy. Another sequence of books, 1–2 Chronicles, Ezra, and Nehemiah, presents an overlapping account that begins with Adam and concludes with Nehemiah's activities in Jerusalem under Persian rule. The so-called prophetical books (Isaiah, Jeremiah, Ezekiel, Hoea, etc.) make numerous references to national and international circumstances. The first part of the book of Daniel (chaps. 1–6) describes events that supposedly occurred in the Babylonian court while Daniel and other Jews were exiled there. The latter part (chaps. 7–12) reports a dream-vision that organizes world history into a sequence of four great empires and anticipates the culmination of history during the fourth. The Gospel of Luke dates Jesus' birth in relation to Roman history (Luke 2:1), and all four of the Gospels narrate episodes in Jesus' ministry in what the reader is left to suppose is an essentially chronological sequence. The book of Acts describes the emergence of Christianity from the immediate aftermath of Jesus' crucifixion to Paul's arrival in Rome for trial. Finally, the book of Revelation reports dream-visions similar to those of the book of Daniel and also presupposing a schematic view of history.

In short, the biblical writers were very conscious of history, and the Bible itself may be looked upon as largely historical in format and content. It is not history written for the sake of history, of course, and not history of the sort one would read in a modern history book. One might argue, in fact, that the biblical writers were more akin to contemporary theologians than to historians. Nevertheless, the theological messages that the biblical writers sought to convey are so thoroughly intermeshed with their perceptions of history that it is [[15]] difficult to separate one from the other. The Bible itself, in other words, confronts us with history and raises historical questions that are difficult to ignore. It is only natural, therefore, that biblical scholarship through the ages has involved attention to historical matters.

Reflected to some degree in earlier biblical research, but becoming especially intense during the twentieth century, are differences of opinion regarding the trustworthiness and accuracy of the Bible as a source of historical information. At one extreme are those who, usually on theological grounds, insist that the Bible is literally accurate in all historical details, including the chronological data provided in Genesis–2 Kings that place the creation of the world approximately 6000 years ago. Historical research for those who hold this extreme position involves harmonizing the information provided in different parts of the Bible—for example, the overlapping accounts of Genesis–2 Kings and 1 Chronicles–Nehemiah—and interpreting evidence from extrabiblical sources (other ancient documents and archaeology) to fit. Apparent contradictions within the Bible are viewed as being only "apparent," usually the result of the modern reader's failure to understand all of the surrounding circumstances. Conflicts between the Bible and extrabiblical sources also are explained away in one way or another.

At the opposite extreme are those who regard the biblical accounts as being so theologically and nationalistically tendentious and composed of such a hodgepodge of literary genera (myths, legends, etc.) that, except where extrabiblical sources shed some light, any attempt to reconstruct the history of ancient Israel is fruitless. This extreme is sometimes stated or implied by scholars who take essentially ahistorical approaches to the text, such as structuralist, narrative, or reader-response criticisms.

However, it is very difficult to hold consistently to either of these extreme positions. The first, that of unwavering confidence in the historical accuracy of the biblical materials, is difficult to maintain in view of (1) the obvious tension between the dynamic and theocentric view of nature and history presupposed by the biblical writers and the more "scientific" or positivistic approach to reality that characterizes modern Western thought, (2) the mental gymnastics required to harmonize some of the apparent contradictions within the biblical narratives and to bring extrabiblical evidence into line, and (3) the results of close analysis of the biblical materials in accordance with source criticism, form criticism, tradition history, and other historical-critical methods.

As for the second position, that of extreme skepticism, it can hardly be doubted that there was an ancient Israel, that Israel had a history, or that the Bible is somehow relevant for understanding that history. Indeed, the very existence of the Bible, regardless of what one makes of its historical claims, is an undeniable item of historical evidence pointing to ancient Israel. It is difficult, [[16]] moreover, regardless of the theory behind one's methodology, to approach an ancient document totally free of the influence of notions regarding the historical context from which it emerged. This is especially true with the Bible, which, as indicated above, is overtly attentive to history and makes such forceful historical claims. Close attention to the wording of their comments, therefore, often reveals that scholars who seem to take totally ahistorical approaches to the biblical materials nevertheless work with presuppositions regarding the history of ancient Israel that influence their overall understanding of the Bible if not their individual research.

Most biblical scholars, therefore, fall somewhere between the two extremes described above. On the one hand, they proceed in confidence that the Bible preserves authentic historical memory. On the other hand, they recognize that the Bible is not a monolithic document, that its different voices reflect different perceptions of ancient Israel's history, that these perceptions usually are heavily influenced by theological and nationalistic interests, and that some of the biblical materials were not intended to be read as literal history in the first place. The historian's task, therefore, is to separate the authentic historical memory from its highly theological and often legendary context.

Naturally, there is a wide range of views even within this middle ground between the extreme positions, with some scholars tending to place greater confidence in the historical accuracy of the biblical materials regardless of the theological, nationalistic, or legendary overtones and others tending to place less confidence in them. To see how this works out on a passage-by-passage basis, one might compare the *NIV Study Bible* (1985) with *The New Oxford Annotated Bible* (1991). The commentary and explanatory notes of the former were prepared by scholars who, although not biblical literalists, tend to take the biblical accounts of Israel's past as essentially historically accurate. Those of the latter were prepared by scholars who tend to be much more cautious on the matter.

Biblical Scholarship and the
Study of Ancient Israelite History

Biblical scholarship and the study of ancient Israelite history are integrally related. On the one hand, most of our information about the history of ancient Israel prior to Roman times comes from the Bible. There are, to be sure, certain other ancient written sources and an ever-increasing amount of archaeological data to take into account. As will become apparent below, however, these extrabiblical sources are useful primarily in that they shed light on the general cultural, social, and international circumstances of biblical times. Usually they tell us very little specifically about the people and events of Israelite history, except when interpreted in light of the biblical record. On the other hand, as observed above, analysis of biblical literature generally involves some [[17]] knowledge of (or at least some notions about) the history of ancient Israel. This is particularly true insofar as the analysis is historical-critical in approach. Historical-critical analysis (including such specialized approaches as source criticism, form criticism, tradition-historical criticism and redaction criticism) seeks to determine the historical contexts out of which the various biblical materials emerged, and what changes occurred in these materials as they were transmitted from ancient times to the present. Even to speculate on such matters presupposes some knowledge of the history of biblical times.

It is not surprising, therefore, that modern histories of ancient Israel typically have been written by scholars also deeply involved in biblical research, and that their application of historical-critical methodology to the biblical materials has significantly influenced their treatments of Israelite history. This is noticeable especially when one compare histories of Israel written during the nineteenth century. H. H. Milman's *History of the Jews* (1829) represents the emerging spirit of critical biblical scholarship during the first half of the century. H. G. A. Ewald's *Geschichte des Volkes Israel bis Christus* (1843–1855)[1] was based on a systematic source analysis of the Pentateuch, although not yet the classical "documentary hypothesis." While recognizing that the biblical traditions derive from a much later

---

1. English edition, *The History of Israel*, 3rd ed. (London: Longmans, Green & Co., 1871–1876).

time than the period they describe and include imaginative elements, Ewald went to great lengths to explain that these traditions nevertheless preserve historical memory. He never clearly committed himself on what, if any, historical memory is preserved in the opening chapters of Genesis (which describe creation, the great flood, and the spread of population following the Tower of Babel episode), but he regarded the patriarchs (Abraham, Isaac, Jacob) as personifications of tribal groups. Ewald was also noncommittal regarding the specific circumstances of the exodus but believed that it was a historical event in connection with which Moses inaugurated a Hebrew monotheistic theocracy that set the direction for the future of Israelite history.

Julius Wellhausen, so closely identified with the documentary hypothesis in its classical form, spelled out the radical implications of this and other late nineteenth-century historical-critical developments in his compelling *Prolegomena zur Geschichte Israels* (1878).[2] Since, according to the documentary hypothesis, none of the four sources that compose the Pentateuch predates the Israelite monarchy, neither these individual sources nor the Pentateuch as a whole is trustworthy for reconstructing history prior to that time. According to the hypothesis, moreover, the "Priestly" source, which accounts for the bulk of the narrative and legal instructions associated with Moses, actually reflects circumstances at the end of Judah's history, the time of the Babylonian exile and following. In Wellhausen's treatment of Israel's history, therefore, Moses becomes a very shadowy and virtually unknown figure, and the characteristic features of the Mosaic era as presented in the Pentateuch (monotheism, a [[18]] highly developed priesthood, elaborate legal and cultic practices, etc.) are seen instead as characteristic of exilic and postexilic times.

During the present century, as other historical-critical methodologies (especially form criticism, tradition history, and redaction criticism) have added their voices to source criticism, usually it has not been a question of whether treatments of Israelite history should presuppose a historical-critical approach to the Bible but of how much emphasis to place on the results of the analysis of the biblical literature itself as opposed to those of Palestinian archaeology or sociological models. This is illustrated by two widely used histories of Israel that were written during the 1950s and became very influential during the 1960s and 1970s—Martin Noth's *Geschichte Israels* (1950)[3] and John Bright's *A History of Israel* (1959).

2. English edition, *Prolegomena to the History of Ancient Israel* (Gloucester, Mass.: Peter Smith, 1973).

3. English edition, *History of Israel*, trans. Peter Ackroyd (New York: Harper & Row, 1960).

Noth was one of the pioneers of tradition history, published comprehensive studies of the Pentateuch and the Deuteronomistic History,[4] and agreed with Wellhausen's conclusion that the Pentateuchal account of Israel's origins is an artificial literary construct composed largely of legendary materials. Thus Noth's history of Israel does not treat the patriarchs as historical figures, nor does he regard the exodus from Egypt or the conquest of Canaan as historical events. Drawing instead upon the sociological theories of Max Weber, the creative ideas of his teacher Albrecht Alt, clues from his own extensive tradition-historical studies of the Pentateuch, and what he thought were close parallels between early Israelite society and that of ancient Greek and Italian tribal leagues (known as amphictyonies), Noth argued that the ancestors of Israel probably were seminomads who ranged between the desert fringe and Canaan in search of pasture until they gradually settled down and took up agriculture. In stages, for which Noth believed there are clues in the Pentateuchal traditions, these tribal settlers formed an amphictyonic cultic league. Finally, under Saul and David, there emerged the Israelite monarchy, and it was only with the expansion of this monarchy under David that it is appropriate to speak of an Israelite conquest of Canaan.

Bright, while not ignoring the implications of historical-critical analysis, was inclined to give the biblical presentation of Israel's origins the benefit of the doubt except where it seemed to be in serious conflict with extrabiblical evidence. Also, he was much influenced by the ideas of his teacher W. F. Albright, who had been one of the pioneers in Palestinian archaeology and had advanced some rather appealing correlations between the biblical account of Israel's origin and archaeology. Thus Bright's *History* began with the patriarchs and followed the biblical outline fairly closely from that point on. Following Albright, he saw these as historical figures who lived approximately 2000 B.C.E. and probably were associated with Amorite movements that were believed to have been underway at the time. The exodus from Egypt occurred during the reign of Ramses II (ca. 1304–1237 B.C.E.), and the Israelite conquest [[19]] of Canaan, which occurred near the close of the thirteenth century, was reflected in the pattern of city destructions that brought the Late Bronze Age to an end in Palestine.

While Noth's and Bright's histories of Israel still are widely read, the 1970s witnessed a decided shift in the discussion. This is reflected, for example, in a series of essays by an international team of scholars published

---

4. The Deuteronomistic History is a term for the books of Deuteronomy, Joshua, Judges, 1–2 Samuel, and 1–2 Kings, which scholars generally regard as originally a single work.

under the title *Israelite and Judean History*.[5] Before turning our attention to recent developments in this discussion, however, some observations are in order regarding epigraphy, archaeology, and sociology.

Epigraphical Evidence

In its broadest sense, epigraphy is the study of written documents recovered from ancient times. Over the past two centuries, thousands of such documents have been recovered and numerous languages of the peoples of the ancient Middle East deciphered. Among the major developments are the decipherment, beginning in 1822, of Egyptian hieroglyphic writing; the decipherment, beginning in 1846, of the cuneiform scripts of several Mesopotamian languages; the discovery in 1887, in the el-Amarna district of Egypt, of correspondence between Egypt and various Syro-Palestinian rulers during the late fifteenth–early fourteenth centuries B.C.E.; the decipherment in 1915 of royal Hittite archives discovered at Boghazköy (ancient Hattusas) in central Turkey; the discovery in 1929 at Ras Shamra (ancient Ugarit) on the Syrian coast of a mid-fourteenth- to early twelfth-century B.C.E. archive of Canaanite documents, including mythical texts concerning the Canaanite god, Baal; the discovery, beginning in 1947, in caves along the northwest shore of the Dead Sea, of Hebrew documents from the first centuries B.C.E. and C.E., including manuscript fragments of most of the books of the Hebrew Bible; and finally, in 1975, the discovery of Tell Mardikh in Syria of royal archives of the ancient city of Ebla.

The recovery and decipherment of extrabiblical documents from the ancient Middle East understandably has had a major impact on biblical studies. The Israelites are not mentioned very often in these documents, however, which probably is to be explained on two grounds. First, epigraphical evidence from ancient Palestine is meager compared to the extensive archives that have been discovered in Egypt, Mesopotamia, Syria, and Asia Minor. Second, the Israelites rarely played a significant role in international affairs outside of Palestine, so that there was little occasion for them to be mentioned in the documents from ancient Egypt, Mesopotamia, and so forth.

---

5. [[J. H. Hayes and J. M. Miller (eds.), *Israelite and Judean History* (Philadelphia: Westminster, 1977; reprinted London/Philadelphia: SCM/Trinity Press International, 1990). Essays by an international group of scholars that signaled a move away from the Albright-Bright and Alt-Noth approaches to Israelite history. Especially useful is the opening chapter by Hayes, which surveys approaches and trends in the study of Israelite history from ancient to modern times. See reprint, pp. 7–42 in this volume.]]

A hieroglyphic inscription from the reign of Merneptah, an Egyptian pharaoh of dynasty XIX (thirteenth century B.C.E.), provides the earliest epigraphical reference to "Israel." Unfortunately, we learn very little about Israel from this inscription, and no other such references turn up in the epigraphical [[20]] sources for the next three and a half centuries, until the time of Omri and Ahab in the ninth century B.C.E. This means that none of the characters or events that appear earlier than Omri and Ahab in the biblical narrative (Abraham, Isaac, Jacob, Joseph, Moses, the exodus from Egypt, Joshua, the conquest of Canaan, Saul, David, Solomon, etc.) are mentioned in any ancient sources outside the Bible. Another Egyptian inscription from the tenth century reports Pharaoh Sheshonk's military campaign into Palestine, an event that is mentioned also in 1 Kgs 14:25–28 (where he is called Shishak). But while Sheshonk claims to have conquered some cities in Palestine, some of which presumably belonged at that time to the separate kingdoms of Israel and Judah, his inscription is conspicuously silent regarding these kingdoms.

Israel (the northern kingdom) seems to have enjoyed a brief period of national strength during the reigns of Omri and Ahab in the ninth century. But Assyria was beginning to expand westward during the same century and continued to grow in strength and to dominate much of the ancient Middle East for the next two centuries. Thus several kings of Israel and Judah are mentioned in the records of the Assyrian kings as having been subjugated by them or having paid tribute to them. Since these Assyrian rulers can be dated fairly securely, the points of contact between their records and the biblical account serve as valuable benchmarks for working out the chronology of the Israelite and Judean kings. With the collapse of Assyria and the rise of Babylon, the Palestinian kingdoms (including Judah) that had survived Assyrian domination fell into Babylonian hands. One of the Babylonian Chronicles reports Nebuchadrezzar's conquest of Jerusalem in March of 597 B.C.E., and King Jehoiachin of Judah is mentioned in Babylonian lists of exiles in Babylon during Nebuchadrezzar's reign (604–561).

Of the epigraphical evidence from Palestine that pertains to the time of the Israelite and Judean monarchies, the following items are especially noteworthy. The *Mesha Inscription* reports the accomplishments of Mesha, king of Moab in the ninth century B.C.E. Mesha boasts that he rid Moab of Israelite domination and identifies Omri as the Israelite king who subjugated Moab in the first place. Mesha himself figures in the narrative of 2 Kgs 3:4–28. The *Siloam Inscription* commemorates the completion of a tunnel hewed out of solid rock for the purpose of transferring water from the Gihon Spring to the Siloam Pool in Jerusalem. Most scholars associate it with Hezekiah (cf. 2 Kgs 20:20; 2 Chr 32:30), although no king is mentioned by name on the surviving, legible portion of the inscription. Groups of *ostraca* (inscribed pottery fragments) from the ruins of several ancient cities in Israel and Judah contain administrative records and military correspondence.

There are no specific references to either the province of Samaria or Judah in surviving records of the Persian rulers (who succeeded the Babylonians as masters of Syria–Palestine in 539 B.C.E.) or of the Ptolemaic and Seleucid [[21]] rulers who dominated Syria–Palestine following Alexander the Great's conquest of the East. For the period following Alexander, the writings of Josephus, a Jewish historian in the latter half of the first century C.E., become our chief source of information for Samaritan and Judean affairs. Other Greek and Roman writers add further details and perspectives on the history of Palestine following Alexander. Also, occasional papyrus and manuscript discoveries from this time are useful for historical research. Included among these are the Dead Sea Scrolls, which provide insight into a Jewish sect around the time of the emergence of Christianity in the first centuries B.C.E. and C.E.

Archaeological Evidence

Artifactual evidence—that is, material remains of the sort usually associated with archaeology (city and village ruins, architectural remains, remnants of tools, potsherds, etc.)—is to be distinguished from epigraphical evidence, even though artifacts occasionally bear written messages (ostraca, scarabs, seal impressions, etc.), and many of the epigraphical texts discussed above were discovered in the course of archaeological excavations. With systematic analysis of the artifactual evidence surviving in a given area, archaeologists can learn a great deal about the settlement patterns and life-styles of the people who lived there in times past. Since artifactual evidence typically is nonverbal, however, it usually is neither ethnic-specific nor very useful for clarifying matters of historical detail. If the people who lived in the cities, used the tools, and produced the pottery are to be identified in terms of their ethnic identity, in other words, or if any details are to be known about specific individuals and events of their history, the artifactual record must be coordinated with and interpreted in the light of written sources. The following is an example of how this works in the case of Palestinian archaeology and Israelite history.

Palestinian archaeologists recognize the end of the thirteenth century as a time of transition between two major cultural phases—that is, the end of the Late Bronze Age (ca. 1550–1200 B.C.E.) and the beginning of the Iron Age (ca. 1200–332 B.C.E.). Among the changes that marked the transition was the appearance of numerous Early Iron Age villages in the central Palestinian hill country, an area that had been only sparsely settled during the Late Bronze Age. Nothing has been discovered in any of the Early Iron Age village ruins that identifies the settlers by name. Taking into account Merneptah's Inscription, however, which places Israel on the scene in Palestine at the end of the thirteenth century, and also the biblical narratives that associate the Israelite tribes specifically with the central hill country, it makes sense to suppose that the Israelites and the Early Iron Age settlements were connected in some way.

It is not always a simple task to locate the archaeological ruins of particular cities and villages mentioned in the Bible, or, from the other direction, to identify archaeological sites in terms of their ancient names. Places like Jerusalem, [[22]] which have been occupied continuously since ancient times, pose no problem. But for many abandoned sites whose ancient names have long since been forgotten, archaeologists must turn to the Bible and epigraphical sources for clues as to which ruins represent which ancient cities. The following are some of the cities that figure prominently in the biblical narratives and, in parentheses, the modern Arabic names of their respective ruins: Jericho (Tell es-Sultan), Ai (et-Tell), Gibeon (el-Jib), Samaria (Sebastiyeh), and Megiddo-Armageddon (Tell el-Mutesellim). When the ruins of biblical cities are excavated, naturally it is of interest to archaeologists and biblical scholars alike whether the archaeological findings corroborate the biblical record. In some cases, there seems to be a confirming fit. In other cases, there is obvious conflict. Often it is a matter of interpretation and debate. Research pertaining to the interface between biblical studies and archaeology sometimes is referred to as biblical archaeology.

Sociology

Historians necessarily work with conceptual models—hypothetical notions about how human society functions and what patterns of change tend to occur and under what circumstances. The Bible presents some very pronounced conceptual models and notions—for example, the idea that ethnic groups (Israelites, Moabites, Edomites, etc.) are extended families descended from individual male ancestors, that the direction of human history is guided by divine intervention, that Yahweh selected the Israelites as his special people and gave them the land of Canaan, and that the course of Israelite history was determined by Israel's fidelity or infidelity to Yahweh. These notions undergird the Genesis–2 Kings narrative, which in turn has provided the basic outline for postbiblical treatments of Israel's history throughout the centuries, all the way from Josephus to Bright.

As mentioned above, the Alt-Noth reconstruction of Israel's origins and early history relied heavily on the sociological theories of Max Weber. Specifically, Weber distinguished four basic social structures in ancient Palestine (nomadic bedouin, seminomadic herders, peasant farmers, and city dwellers) and three basic types of societal authority (legal, traditional, and charismatic). The conceptual models undergirding the Alt-Noth scenario have been seriously challenged in recent years. Several studies have suggested that seminomadic herding normally exists in symbiotic relationship with a village farming economy rather than in competition with it and that seminomadic herding is more likely to have derived from sedentary agriculture in ancient Palestine than to have intruded from the desert fringe.

The most aggressive challenge to Alt and Noth argued that the early Israelite tribes did not enter Palestine from elsewhere but emerged from a revolt within the indigenous Canaanite population. This would have been a peasant [[23]] uprising against the oppressive Canaanite city-states that resulted in an egalitarian tribal society. This notion of a peasant revolt also is influenced by a sociological model, specifically Marxism. The peasant revolt model was very influential from the late 1960s through the 1970s but receives little attention now. But two aspects of this model remain influential—the idea that the early Israelite tribes emerged from the Canaanite population rather than entering the land from elsewhere and the recognition that any satisfactory explanation as to how this occurred must be well grounded in sociological research.

Recent Developments

Three major histories of Israel were published during the last decade, all of them appearing about the same time. H. Donner's *Geschichte des Volkes Israel und seiner Nachbarn in Grundzügen* (1984–1985) falls well within the Alt-Noth tradition. J. A. Soggin, in his *A History of Ancient Israel* (1984), finds the biblical presentation of Israel's history prior to the time of David as untrustworthy for the historian's purposes. Beginning with David, however, he places considerable confidence in the biblical narrative and follows it fairly closely. *A History of Ancient Israel and Judah* (1986) by J. M. Miller and J. H. Hayes also declines any attempt to reconstruct events prior to the establishment of the monarchy. Miller and Hayes are neither as reluctant as Soggin to speculate on the sociopolitical circumstances of the Israelite tribes from which the monarchy emerged nor as trusting of the biblical materials pertaining to monarchical times. Specifically, Miller and Hayes argue that

1. The clan was probably the basic sociopolitical unit among the early Israelite tribes, with the tribes themselves being essentially territorial

    groupings of clans whose sense of identity and mutual kinship developed in Palestine over a period of time.

2. The name "Israel" in premonarchical times probably referred specifically to the tribe of Ephraim and certain neighboring clans/tribes, such as Benjamin and Gilead, which Ephraim dominated.

3. This Ephraim-Israel tribal domain became the core of Saul's "kingdom," which itself remained essentially tribal in character.

4. Both Saul and David began their careers as military adventurers of a sort that may not have been typical of Ephraim-Israel but for which there was precedent nevertheless—that is, Saul and David followed in the tradition of Abimelech and Jephthah, who also had organized private armies with which they provided protection to their kinfolk in return for material support and engaged in raids on surrounding peoples. [[24]]

5. David succeeded in carving out a territorial state that included as its core a southern grouping of tribes dominated by Judah, the city-state of Jerusalem, and the Ephraim-Israel tribes.

6. The biblical presentation of Solomon's "empire" is largely a literary fiction. Actually, his territorial domain probably was not any larger than David's, which did not even include some parts of Palestine (such as Philistia), much less all the lands between Egypt and the Euphrates.

7. Of the two kingdoms that resulted from the split at Solomon's death, the northern kingdom—which included the old Ephraim-Israel tribal domain and took the name Israel—emerged as the more powerful. Under the Omride dynasty, in fact, Israel achieved a level of commercial strength and international prestige superior to that achieved by either David or Solomon.

8. Beginning with the Omride period, moreover, and until Israel's defeat and annexation by the Assyrians, Judah often was little more than an Israelite vassal.

    In yet more recent discussions about Israel's history the following positions have emerged. Some conservative biblical scholars continue to correlate an essentially literal reading of the biblical account of the Israelite conquest of Canaan with the available epigraphical and archaeological evidence. However, Albright's solution, which called for a thirteenth-century conquest, has been largely abandoned in favor of a conquest at the end of the fifteenth century. An opposite perspective is represented by scholars who regard the biblical materials as products almost entirely of exilic and postexilic Judaism and thus irrelevant for reconstructing the history of earlier periods. This means that we can know little about the history of earlier Israel beyond whatever information can be derived from epigraphy and archaeology and that, for all practical purposes, therefore, the history of Israel begins in the ninth century B.C.E.

Certain archaeologists have raised hopes that data from recent archaeological surveys and excavations will clarify such questions as whether the Israelites entered Palestine from elsewhere or emerged from the indigenous population, whether they were agriculturalists or pastoralists when they first settled in the hill country, and by what stages they spread throughout the land. Obviously, these new data are extremely important, but they are still inconclusive. For one thing, these archaeologists treat all of the Early Iron Age hill country settlements as Israelite and thus beg the question of what would have been meant by "Israelite" during premonarchical times and why the biblical narratives pertaining to this period distinguish between Israelite and non-Israelite villages in the hill country (cf. Judg 19:12). Also, the chief proponents of this [[25]] approach have not yet reached agreement on their interpretation of the new data with respect to Israel's origins.

Yet other scholars are calling for a highly multidisciplinary approach to ancient Israelite history, involving close attention to the geographical features of Palestine, its various ecological zones, long-range settlement patterns as indicated by archaeological surveys, agricultural techniques and potentials, international trade patterns, and so on. Informed by the most up-to-date anthropological and sociological theories and models, archaeologists utilize all of these various data to explain the process by which Israel came into being and gradually was transformed from tribal society into monarchy. One can only affirm the theoretical appropriateness of this approach; certainly all of the factors that these studies bring into consideration are relevant for understanding the history of ancient Israel. Perhaps their main contribution to this point, however, is that they raise new kinds of questions and warn against oversimplified answers. Thus far, in other words, it can hardly be said that this multidisciplinary approach has produced any notable breakthroughs or compelling clarifications—at least none that does not depend as much on the researcher's methodological presuppositions and working models as upon the various data compiled. An unfortunate characteristic of these studies is that they tend to use very jargonistic language—sometimes, it seems, belaboring the obvious. Also, they discuss such a wide range of factors at such an abstract and theoretical level that it is often difficult to understand what it all means with respect to the specific people and events of ancient Israel. The proponents of this approach tend to be deterministic in their social philosophy—that is, history unfolds in predictable fashion as determined largely by environmental circumstances; individual initiative plays a minor role in the course of human affairs, and specific events are incidental items in the broad sweep of social change.

Finally, the charge is being heard from several quarters that biblical studies in general, including historical-critical methodologies and treatments of ancient Israelite history, are biased to the core and should be approached from totally different perspectives. This bias begins, so the argument goes, with the ancient written sources, which tend to be male and elitist—that is, written records normally were produced by and for the powerful in ancient times (kings, priests, etc.). Even archaeology tends to present an elitist picture, since the substantial structures of the politically powerful naturally survive in greater proportion than the humble dwellings of the lower classes. This bias in the ancient sources has only been exacerbated by religious leaders in the Judeo-Christian tradition, it is charged, who usually have been men. Moreover, contemporary biblical scholarship in Western universities is decidedly Eurocentric—that is, culturally biased—in approach.

An increasing number of studies are appearing that attempt to redress the situation. Some attempt to do this by uncovering and correcting the old biases. [[26]] Others, apparently liberated by the recognition of modern historians that complete objectivity is an unattainable goal anyhow, put aside even any effort in that direction and write essays on historical topics that unabashedly replace the old biases and ideologies with new ones.

Contingency, Continuity and Integrity in Historical Understanding
An Old Testament Perspective

FERDINAND DEIST

[[99]] The picture W. H. Walsh (1966: 58) painted of his colleagues in Oxford is to a large extent applicable to historical research in biblical studies,

> To most of my historical colleagues in Oxford . . . history is a specialist activity, an affair of greater and greater detail, subtle, exacting, in a real sense esoteric; it is emphatically not an attempt to tell the story of mankind to the average intelligent man.

There is, of course, nothing wrong with specialization. What is wrong in biblical research, is this: the more we research the history of Israel, early Christianity and the Bible, the less we seem to be able to contribute to the context in which we live, that is, to theology as a discipline (cf. Whybray 1989) and to common people's understanding of themselves, their world and their faith, and the more the Bible becomes a dead book of the distant past. Fletcher (1987) rightly observes that this state of affairs leads among ordinary people to "the sharing of ignorance by well-intentioned but ill-informed people" (cf. Patterson 1990; Thiselton 1990).

To suggest a way out it is necessary to inquire into the reasons for this state of affairs.

Historicism and Contingency

Romantic and Historicist Explanation

The romantic era of historiography, commencing with Herder, Burke and Rousseau, probably reached its summit with Leopold von Ranke, who

Reprinted with permission from *Scriptura* S11 (1993) 99–115.

initiated the quest for "what really happened." This phrase is often misunderstood as an effort to establish whether a particular incident "really happened," for instance, whether Jonah had really been in the belly of a big fish. However, Ranke's quest for "what really happened" has to be understood against the background of two approaches to historiography of his time.

[[100]] On the one hand there was the classicist approach which used examples from the classical period as models for the interpretation of later times. The history of an emperor like Napoleon would, for instance, be described using Alexander the Great as model. Ranke suggested that researchers immerse themselves into the documents of the relevant period in an effort to understand that time in itself. Only in that way, he argued, would we ever be in a position to say "what really happened" as compared to what ideally happened.

On the other hand Ranke reacted against the rationalist, or rather mechanistic, approach to historiography, according to which universal, and therefore absolute, laws could be abstracted from the sequence of historical events to serve as historical explanations for events. Over against this trend Ranke insisted on the *lokalkolorit* [['local coloring']] or individuality of every historical event. Every event had to be understood with reference to its own context and values, and not with reference to an overarching historical process or underlying historical law.

The Concept of Contingency

Much can, no doubt, be said in favour of the romanticist movement. A critical evaluation of contemporary documents and artefacts and their empathetic interpretation remain prerequisites for sound historiography. Romanticism's deep respect for cultural and temporal differences between people (*jede Epoche ist unmittelbar zu Gott* [['every epoch is immediate to God']] prevented individual prejudgments from producing prejudiced labels such as "the dark ages," "dark Africa" or "primitive people." Its emphasis on human decisions as causes for historical change by and large thwarted mechanistic determinism. But it also had negative consequences.[1] For the present purpose I shall only briefly comment on one aspect of historicism, namely its view of the individuality of historical events.

---

1. In view of my theme I am not commenting on Ranke's conservative political stance or his view of God in history. Compare the harsh criticism by Gay [[1974:]] 91, which, although it is factually correct, seems to lack historical perspective in its judgment. "Ranke blandly affirmed the powers that be; he adroitly fitted treaty breaking, illegal invasions, economic warfare into God's scheme for man; he threw the mantle of respectability over terrible men and terrible deeds . . . Behind the screen of scientific objectivity, Ranke made definite political choices."

The emphasis on past events as products of a set of individual or unique historical circumstances led to the notion of historical relativism, that is, the incomparability of any event with previous or subsequent events. It was Bury's concept of contingency that took the idea of historical relativism to its logical consequences. Oakeshott (1966: 200) explains,

> The historian is to explain the course of events not by referring to general causes, but by seeing it as the product of accident. Change in history is the result of accident, not specific cause.

[[101]] The application of this concept not only terminates historical inquiry at certain points. It also destroys historical explanation itself.

Firstly, by ascribing the occurrence of an event to mere chance, the principle of contingency invokes a *deus ex machina*, which precludes any further inquiry, for nobody can read the minds of the gods. Secondly, where the gods enter the scene the past becomes incomprehensible and the future unpredictable. That is why contingency undermines historical understanding. The principle of contingency is, thirdly, illogical, for if the merging of two or more causal sequences produces a new series of events that would not have taken place had they not flowed together, the reasons for their merging should be accounted for. One therefore has to agree with Oakeshott (1966: 203–6) that

> such a principle is not to be found in history unless we have first put it there. No course of historical events exists until it has been constructed by historical thought, and it cannot be constructed without some presupposition about the character of the relation between events . . . In short, chance or accident is a mask which is the precise duty of the historian to tear away.

The romanticist principle of uniqueness, formulated to counter mechanistic and rationalist tendencies in historiography, therefore not only led to historical relativism in general, but also to the destruction of historical understanding as such.

Nomological Approaches and the Search for Continuity

In an effort to escape from rationalist and mechanistic explanations for events as well as from the deadlock caused by historical relativism historiographers from the nomological (or New History) school turned to other human sciences for assistance[2] and applied theoretical insights gained

---

2. For an explanation of this line of thought, see Hempel 1966, and for a rebuttal Donagan 1966.

from psychological, sociological and anthropological research to explain why particular events of the past led to particular consequences.

On the one hand such model oriented approaches link up with older rationalistic and mechanistic studies in that they try to find (contrary to the notion of contingency) more universal explanations for particular historical events. On the other hand they join forces with the older historicist approach in that they include as legitimate historical explanations for events factors such as physical, economic and social conditions. That this approach enhanced insight into historical processes as products of human actions seems to be beyond dispute.[3] [[102]] However, whether the application of this approach to ancient Israelite history (a) really leads to historical understanding and (b) restores historical continuity depends entirely on the way in which scholars employ such social theoretical models in the process of historical explanation. Two tendencies in present nomological oriented studies seem to limit the contribution of such studies to historical understanding and to the restoration of historical continuity. The first tendency is of a more theoretical nature and has to do with historical understanding as such while the second is of a more practical nature and has to do with historical continuity.

Models and Historical Understanding

There are at least four areas of concern regarding the use of models in "biblical" historiography. The first concerns the applicability of such models to the culture concerned, the second the establishment of the facts to be fed into a model's theoretical framework, the third has to do with reductionism, and the fourth with over-generalization.

The Applicability of Models. One of the bones of contention in present Old Testament studies is which model to pick from the larger number of possibilities. Some sociological models have a positivist, others a relativist or deterministic or reductionist basis (Mayes 1988b), while some anthropological models have an "emic" and others an "etic" approach to culture (Rogerson 1986b).[4] Of particular interest to us in Africa is the opinion that anthropological models derived from the study of African cultures were more appropriate for the reconstruction of at least early Israelite history than models developed from the study of other cultures (cf. Frick 1986; Wernhardt 1992), even though this assumption as well as the reliability of the existing "African" models themselves have been seriously questioned (see Rogerson 1986b; Fiensy 1987).

---

3. For an overview of such studies in the field of biblical studies, see Clements 1989; Mayes 1989.

4. See, for instance, Gnuse (1991) for a description of some of the models employed in the reconstruction of "early Israel."

The present difference of opinion on the most appropriate model does not argue against the usefulness of such models in historical research. It is, however, necessary to determine which, if any, of these models can reflect or do justice to the assumptions on which ancient Israelite communities had been based,[5] because if their underlying assumptions of a model run counter to the [[103]] self-understanding of Israelite society it will not only thwart empathetic historical understanding but also lead to a complete distortion of history itself.

Establishing the Facts. Even though it is a serious problem in the case of ancient Near Eastern, and therefore also of Old Testament, documents,[6] I leave aside the problem whether something that is said by historical records to have occurred really happened. Of greater concern for the present discussion is another, more philosophical problem.

The establishment of the facts that have to be fed into any chosen model is very problematic, because facts do not present themselves to researchers. Facts are discovered. Theories discover them. A historical fact is a statement about a phenomenon that assigns value and significance to that phenomenon in terms of the historical process conjectured to be at work. The historical process conjectured to be at work is, in its turn, suggested by the model employed, while the selection of the model itself is very often determined by the training (Yitzhaki 1987) or personal bias of the researcher (Mosala 1986). Whatever the reasons for the choice of a model, it is the model that recognizes phenomena as facts and colligates them[7] to form meaningful parts of the story. As a result the application of models from the social sciences to historiography may result in a fairly distorted picture of the past and may suggest a continuity in history that never was.

Reductionism. The consistent application of any one model leads to the same answers irrespective of the era to which it is applied. For instance, applying a conflict model as explanatory framework in writing a history of Israel will inevitably elevate (socio-economic) class conflict as

5. Horsley (1991), for instance, questions the applicability of modern economic theories to the description of ancient societies.

6. See, for instance, the debate between Carroll (1990), Overholt (1990) and Auld (1990) on the issue of the probable existence of a particular prophet. While Overholt accepts his existence because his applied model makes this assumption appear reasonable, Carroll warns against such a procedure. See also Jobling's (1991) criticism of Carroll's position, and for a more general discussion of the problematic nature of establishing facts from Old Testament literature, see Flanagan (1987); McNutt (1987); Knauff (1991) and Thompson (1991).

7. Walsh (1967: 59–63) pays special attention to colligation in history and defines it as "explaining an event by tracing its intrinsic relations to other events and locating its historical context." The problem is that "intrinsic value" of an event is only recognized once its significance has been recognized, while this recognition—let alone the historical context—depends on the overall theory of what was going on.

the major force of historical continuity in Israel's history and (because the model determines the facts) show this to have been the case. Examples of such an approach may be the reconstruction of the rise of the Israelite monarchy by Gottwald (1986) and Chaney (1986). While Gottwald's explanation clearly tends towards economic reductionism, Chaney, even though he is aware that the reconstruction should reveal [[104]] a dynamic social process reverberating through all dimensions of Israel's life, still provides little more than an economic explanation for the change.

Such explanations are grossly reductionist.[8] Sir Isaiah Berlin's (1966: 24) remark on nomological historical explanations remains valid. The application of general theories to historical data, he contended, leads to

> distortions, and the accounts that result, even when they contain illuminating ideas . . . , are liable to be rejected as being over-schematized, that is exaggerating and omitting too much, as too unfaithful to human life as we know it.

Thiel (1988), for instance, rightly refers to at least two formative factors seldom accounted for in model based histories of early Israel, namely religious convictions and outside forces, while Ben-Yoseph (1985) warns against climatic reductionism in some studies. In an effort to escape from reductionism Finkelstein (1989) attempts a reconstruction of the rise of the Israelite monarchy on the basis of ecological, social, economic and demographic factors.

Over-Generalization. The last theoretical problem with the nomological approach to historiography concerns its tendency to explain human actions with sole reference to some or other covering law from the social sciences, and therefore to over-generalize. Humans, who are the main actors in history, are not robots, and sociological generalizations about human behavior [[are]] not universal laws ascribing planetary orbits to them.[9] History is about people, real people who lived under particular circumstances and who might have been driven by motivations which fall outside the scope of the generalizations of sociological models, as Lemche (1990) rightly observes. Insofar as a model approach does indeed lead to over-generalizations it may even prevent true historical understanding.

---

8. M. Brodbeck (1966: 305) would say, "The possibility of 'reduction' is the issue raised by asking whether the phenomena of one field, say chemistry or psychology, can be explained in terms of the phenomena of another, say physics or physiology respectively."

9. A. Donagan (1966: 148) is certainly right when he says, "Historians do not, indeed, deny that an agent's intentions can often be explained, by deriving them from some more general intention or intentions he has and his estimate of the situation. . . . But most historians would be sceptical of a proffered explanation in which it was assumed that all agents of the same psychological type, or the same sociological position, when confronted with a situation of the same kind, will act in a certain kind of way."

Perhaps one of the major disadvantages of the nomological approach has been that it has all but eliminated human beings from the scene of history. The causes suggested for historical events by these theories have to do with rainfall patterns, social conflicts among classes, social specialization, economic specialization, etc., all of which are general, impersonal forces providing the mere conditions of human actions and decisions. History is, however, not about generalities, but exactly about the human factor in the course of events, as Hart and Honoré (1966) forcefully argue. In this respect history writing has [[105]] much in common with the procedures in a court of law, they say. When in a court of law the cause of a victim's death has to be established, medical causes (e.g., suffocation) play a secondary role. The court is looking for a human cause: who killed this person and what were the murderer's motives?[10] Similarly, a person reading an ordinary history is not interested in economic of social "laws" or in rainfall per se, but in what people did under those circumstances and why they acted in that way. The answer to such questions calls for specifics, not generalities. It is the explanations for specific human decisions and actions in specific conditions that link specific people of the past with specific people living now.

Applied Models and Historical Continuity

Biblical scholars applying sociological or anthropological models to historical research tend to get stuck in the study of a particular period. It takes so much effort to get into the intricacies of any model and then to collect the data to be ordered by that model that scholars rarely attempt its application to another era to see whether that model really works as a model for historical explanation, that is, to account for continuity between eras. The practical situation thus is that we have bits the pieces of information on this or that era based on this or that model, but few complete histories of Israel based on a particular model. Apart from the fact that models can thus only rarely be evaluated on the basis of their explanatory power, their possible contribution to the restoration of Israelite history as a continuous whole is frustrated.

Moreover, at the moment most of the nomological studies in the field of Israelite history are based on traditional demarcations of historical periods in that history. Historical "periods" are artificial constructions based on turns of events that seem significant from the point of view of the explanatory framework. For example, the traditional periodization of Israelite

---

10. "When the question is how far back a cause shall be traced through a number of intervening causes, such a voluntary act very often is regarded as both a limit and also as still the cause even though later abnormal occurrences are recognized as causes" (Hart and Honoré 1966: 236).

history rests on the historicist view that kings, governmental decisions and wars (politics) make history. Contrary to this view most of the social models employed at the moment are based on the description of interaction between ordinary people and their various environments. Such theories, if applied consistently, may therefore suggest a kind of historical continuity quite different from the traditional view on which so many theological constructions have been and are still being based.

Summary

The foregoing description of some of the problem areas in the nomological approach would have made it clear why I concurred with Walsh that our historical [[106]] work is a specialist activity, an affair of greater and greater detail, subtle, exacting, in a real sense esoteric, but emphatically not an attempt to tell the story of humankind to the average intelligent person. It would also have made it clear that we shall have to find a way out if our work should have any meaning for our context.

Historical Inquiry and Continuity

In order to suggest a way out of this dilemma I shall first present a short, preliminary working definition of historiography[11] and then proceed to explain a few concepts in that definition. History, I would say, is an explanation of the meaningful connectedness of a sequence of past events in the form of an interested and focused narrative.

History as an Explanation of the Meaningful Connectedness of a Sequence of Past Events

Sequence.   History has as its "raw material" reports on or material remains of events that occurred in sequence. History writing is not about mere sequence in time, though. Had it been, it would have produced mere chronicles of contingencies. History writing is about ascribing logical relations to sequences of events. These relations are not entailed by the linear sequence of the events, but established by acts of interpretation.

Explanation.   Since every explanation or interpretation of things unknown occurs in relation to things known there is no way in which any series of events can be explained "in themselves" as romanticists believed.

---

11. In formulating this definition I acknowledge the influence of the views expressed by Henri-Irénée Morrou, namely that history is supposed to supply people with material that may assist them in exercising their faculties of judgment and will. For a short review of his thoughts, see van Jaarsveld (1980: 89–93) and Mohan (1970: 158–60).

Even the father of phenomenology, Edmund Husserl, was forced to accept the necessary existence of (individual) "horizons of understanding." In historical explanation this horizon of understanding consists, first of all, of the interpreter's (more or less informed) personal experience. Since individual experience supplies the first "grasp" on the logical connectedness of past events it immediately links the past with the present and establishes at least a sense of historical continuity. The past is, as it were, "relived" in the present.[12] Whether this first "grasp" on the past is of a sophisticated or unsophisticated nature is immaterial to the [[107]] principle at work. It is this "grasp" that links the historical understanding of nonspecialists (Walsh's "average intelligent" person) with that of specialists.

However, ordinary experience may (and for the sake of sound historiography should) be assisted, affirmed, corrected, enriched and refined by all sorts of relevant historical information as well as by accepted theories of human experience and behavior. This is where psychological, anthropological, sociological, economic, ecological and other theories may become very fruitful for the purpose of historical inquiry.[13] Knowledge of these theories may serve as heuristic devices, that is, as a "fertile source of suggestions" or as regulative ideas that are "suggestively, rather than deductively fertile" (Mink 1966: 174).[14] Or to put it in the words of Scriven (1966: 250), they may serve as "possibilities rather than regularities."[15]

Any theory dealing with human actions and reactions may suggest particular conditions or motives for human action in particular circumstances and therefore supply historical insights around which facts may colligate.[16] Some of these theories may be more fertile for the study of a particular culture or era than others, but all of them may in principle contribute towards our understanding of a particular series of events. However, even

12. The procedure involved is thus not, as romanticists believed, the "transference" of the researcher to the past (which is impossible), but of reliving the past as if it were the present.

13. Historians are not clairvoyants who can read other people's minds, like Collingwood (1946: 214) seemed to have thought when he said that historians look "through" events "to discern the thought within them." Historians, as Walsh (1967: 57) correctly argues, need experience, first or secondhand, of the ways in which people commonly react to the situations in which they find themselves.

14. Mayes (1989: 2) may be expecting too much from such theories when he says that they are perspectives through which information may be given comprehensible order. Mayes' statement seems to imply a deductive procedure, which may lead to one or more of the deficiencies of the nomological approach as described before.

15. This approach thus contrasts with the nomological approach according to which such theories are employed as covering laws from which historical continuity may be deduced.

16. This is also the view of Herion. For a criticism of his views, see Brett 1987.

though such theories may inform historical judgment they can never replace it, as sometimes happens in nomothetic studies. Where social theories serve as the sole explanatory framework for historical occurrences
one inevitably ends up with generalizations, which is the express purpose
for which these theories have been constructed. But history is not about
generalities. History seeks to understand not only the general causes, but
also the meaning of a particular turn of events in relation to particular human decisions. This goal of historical research distinguishing it from the
research goals of the social sciences does, however, not minimize the contribution of social scientific theories to historical judgment. Moreover, the
mere fact that such theories, developed from observations of present human behavior, may serve as fertile heuristic devices for understanding human actions of the past underlines the similarity and therefore continuity
between the past and the present.

The integrity of historical research partly depends on the insight it
provides into human actions and decisions in particular circumstances of
the past. If [[108]] historical research ends up with mere generalities about
extra-human historical conditions influencing or even dictating events its
integrity is risked.

Meaningful Connectedness.   All acts of understanding have to do with
finding (i.e., assigning) meaning. One of the major reasons for historical
research lies exactly in our desire to assign meaning to our existence. This
is achieved, firstly, by history's assisting us to understand who we are and
where we came from, and secondly, by its enabling us to venture informed
guesses about possible future developments in our history. To put it differently, history assists us in obtaining hindsight, insight and foresight.[17] To
function in this way history has to provide us with at least two things.
Firstly, it should provide us with a picture of the whole (hindsight, insight).
Secondly, it should provide us with examples of human actions and their
consequences (insight, foresight).

A View of the Whole.   Understanding the past has much in common
with understanding a sentence or a text (Mink 1966: 182). Just as no single
social theory suffices as a tool for historical interpretation there is no single gateway to understanding a sentence. To interpret a sentence one
needs knowledge of the interplay between the vocabulary, morphosyntax,
syntax, and phonetic layers of the sentence as well as a lot of pragmatic
information. The interpretation of texts requires even more complex
skills. To interpret events of the past one needs, what Mink (1966: 182)
calls, the ability of recognizing "the grammar of events." Interpretation

---

17. Logically there is no difference between explanation and prediction, as Mink
(1966: 170–71) convincingly argues.

means to, through a synoptic judgment, see things together (Mink 1966: 184–87).[18] This judgment is comparable to that exercised by a literary critic or psychology. Both of them have access to and employ theories in order to understand their "objects." But, as Mink (1966: 187) argues, "it is not theory which elucidates the poem [or] cures the patient. Success in any of these enterprises depends at least as much on the ability to make synoptic judgments as on the correctness of theory." It is only after we have succeeded in seeing (that is, constructing) historical events (of a period, a particular community or world history) together as a whole that makes sense to us that we say we have understood what happened.[19] This "seeing things together as [[109]] a whole in a manner that makes sense to us," which is a definition of "insight," links the past with the present.

These remarks should not be misconstrued as a plea for a return to the idealist notion of determining "the" (metaphysical) meaning of the whole or as the restoration of the hermeneutical rule of understanding the whole in relation to its parts and the parts in relation to the whole. Just as the meaning assigned to a text is the result of the interplay between a whole series of intertexts (including the interpreter's experience, knowledge and memory) and therefore implies a reinscription of that text, the meaning assigned to the "whole" in the case of historical understanding is by definition relative to a number of factors contributing to understanding. Moreover, "seeing" or "observing" something, so theoretical physicists have come to learn, disturbs the observed object as a matter of principle. The point here is rather that assigning meaning requires a conscious act of constructing a picture of the whole. Just as there is no contingency in history unless we see things as contingent and just as there is no relativism unless we declare things relative, there will be no continuity in history unless we put it there. My argument is that we need that constructed continuity in order to make sense of our existence, that is, to provide us with insight into human decisions, their conditions and

18. Without viewing logic and judgment as mutually exclusive, Sir Isaiah Berlin (1966: 29) describes judgment as "a form of thinking dependent on wide experience, memory, imagination, on the sense of 'reality,' of what goes with, which may need constant control by, but is not at all identical with, the capacity for logical reasoning and the construction of laws and scientific models—the capacity for perceiving the relations of particular case to law, instance to general rule, theorems to axioms, not of parts to wholes or fragments to completed pattern."

19. The reference to a "meaningful whole" should here not be confused with the realistic notion of the (intrinsic) meaning of history. As will become clear in the ensuing argument, this "meaning of the whole" is a deliberate construction, and therefore always partial and relative. The argument is that understanding of parts of an historical process occurs in relation to a sense of what the whole means, even if that knowledge is limited and only preliminary.

consequences. A refusal to do this may put the integrity of historiography as a humanistic discipline at risk.

Examples of Human Actions. Since understanding foreign things or concepts entails the activation of existing knowledge and experience, one of the ways in which we manage to understand a particular turn of events of the past is by recognizing resemblances ("analogies") between those and other (similar) human actions. It is important to understand what is meant by resemblance. Firstly, resemblance is not identity, that is, resemblance between two historical events does not entail historical repetition (as cyclicists believe). Recognizing historical resemblance is like suddenly becoming aware that Ms. Johnson, whom we have just met, resembles Betty, whom we already know, an awareness that does not imply that Ms. Johnson is a replica of Betty. Every sequence of events remains an individual sequence. But if such a sequence of events bore no resemblance whatsoever with other series of events, that is, if it were genuinely unique, it would have been very difficult, if not impossible, to make sense of it. It is, among other things, similarities between sequences of events that assist us in understanding individual sequences.

Secondly, a recognition of resemblance seldom, if ever, is the product of prior analysis. It rather is the product of an intuitive grasp, the fertility and power of which depend upon the experience and historical informedness of [[110]] the individual imagination. One of the problems with the concept of contingency is precisely that it is based on an analysis of the particular rather than on intuitive judgment that "sees things together."

Thirdly, recognizing resemblances is perspectivist and partial. It is perspectivist, because the validity of recognized resemblances often depends on the particular angle of observation. Someone observing Ms. Johnson from another angle may, therefore, not see the resemblance with Betty as we see it from our angle. It is partial, because resemblance does not entail repetition. Our seeing a resemblance between Ms. Johnson and Betty may be founded on her way of walking, her smile, something in her voice. But even though seeing resemblances is perspectivist and partial the recognition of its role in historical understanding is of the utmost importance if we are to escape from the prison of relativism and contingency.

Of course, intuition may be shown by analysis to have been under a faulty or even false impression. Seeing resemblances (as part of the process of assigning meaning) is not and has never been the result of mere analysis. The best interpreter of a text is precisely that reader who does not have to get stuck in the analysis of grammatical forms, but has the ability (and experience) to see intra-, inter-, and extra-textual relations. It is only after a reader has grasped the meaning through an intuitive grasp of these relations that s/he is able to analyze the text and justify that reading with reference to the interplay of parts as s/he sees it. Analysis is an *ex post facto* [['after the fact']] procedure with a view to arguing for or against the validity of an initial insight.

Our present problem of discontinuity in history has, among other things, been created by our "scientific" analyses which led to relativism in the case of historicism and to generalities in the case of nomothetic approaches, both of which are destroyers of the meaning of particularities. It is only "seeing things together" that enables us to recognize resemblances and that puts us in a position to speak of the meaningful connectedness of particular events. The integrity of historical research has much to do with its assisting us in exercising our ability to form historical judgments on the meaningful connectedness of series of events, while constructing such a meaningful connectedness of events is greatly enhanced by spotting resemblances between series of events or between general social theories and particular series of events.

Explanation in the Form of an Interested and Focused Narrative

History is a Narrative.   Reception aesthetics and some deconstructionist approaches to literature have shown that finding, or rather assigning, meaning is always the product of a creative process involving reinscription. Writing a history is also to reinscribe historical texts and phenomena. There is no way in which we can tell in a logocentric manner "how things really were," that is, what the real meaning of [[111]] past events are. What we do, is telling a story about the past. That is why I refer to history as a narrative. This analogy may assist us in saying a few things about history.

A narrative is constituted, among other things, by the selection and combination of events, the two major factors involved in redescription. But both selection and combination are guided by the perspective of the narrator, which is the instance assigning meaning to the narrated events. Such a perspective inevitably flows from a view of the whole and results in a number of generalizations about human behavior. The validity of that perspective depends on two factors, namely the correctness of the information provided[20] and the success or otherwise of the narrator to relate or connect the narrated events in such a way that their functions in the

---

20. To ensure the accuracy of facts presented is the duty, but not the task of the historian. His/her task is to establish relations among such facts. The more distant and foreign the investigated era or community becomes, the more difficult it becomes to establish the correctness of facts. This difficulty does not detract from the main concern of history, though.

narrative are intelligible as necessary conditions for the meaning assigned to the whole.

Such a narrative will be judged "meaningful" if it provides insight not into social or economic processes—for which purpose a sociological or economic study would have been more appropriate—but into historical processes which center mainly around human decisions (Walsh 1967: 48–70) as pro-actions or reactions to social, economic and other environmental changes (Ben-Yoseph 1985). Such human decisions might have been influenced by a number of factors among which—in the case of ancient Israel—religious convictions might have played a significant role.

It is precisely because the validity of an historical narrative is relative to the way in which it interrelates events and thereby assigns meaning to the whole that historiography cannot produce detachable conclusions (Mink 1966: 179–83). While a natural scientist may publish the results of an experiment in the form of a formula that can be detached from the research itself, historians have to read each other's books. The conclusion is the argument.

History is an Interested/Focused Narrative. In view of developments in the theory of knowledge and literary theory it is to articulate the obvious to say that there is no such thing as objectivity. Historical narratives are also by nature perspectivist. The perspectivist nature of historical research is one of the reasons why history is not an accumulative science. Every historian has to redo the whole thing for his/her own context, that is, from his/her perspective. That is why there presently is a very legitimate cry against "Eurocentred" and "white-centered" histories of South Africa. Choosing a meaning-assigning perspective foreign to the relevant society more than risks historical integrity.

[[112]] But ideology criticism has taught us that human involvement in any process of interpretation is accompanied by interests. That is why the perspective from which a historian selects and combines, interrelates and connects events, that is, the perspective from which s/he assigns meaning to the whole should be explicated. This allows fellow historians as well as the "average intelligent person" to evaluate the argument from the correct perspective, and to criticize the perspective itself. The integrity of historical narration has very much to do with the question whether the perspective giving explanations for series of events of the past is stated in such a way that it can be discussed and criticized by those for whom (and/or about whom!) the history has been written.

Finally, since history is a perspectivist and interested affair is not possible to write a true to life history. In real life the physical environment, climate, economics, social circumstances, political occurrences and a dozen other things operate simultaneously with human decisions in the process of the "making of history." That is why many historians opt for a diffusionist approach and choose to focus their investigations on this or that area of human experience, e.g., economics, social history, and the like. Such studies are, of course, necessary, but they do not constitute history. History has to do with insight into the whole process involved in human decisions. But even if a historian should opt for such a diffusionist approach it remains important that s/he does not reduce human beings to mere economic commodities or to slaves of any so-called social law. Even if a history is focused, it should try to relate that focus to as many sides of human experience as possible (cf. Walsh 1967: 64–65), while the "human experience" should be recognizable as such from the perspective of the society for which the history has been written.

Conclusion

Cancik (1970; see also Kremer 1987) said of tradition that, if people experience it as relevant for their value system and orientation in life, it functions as a source of insight for individuals to ascertain their position within the cosmos, society or a particular institution (e.g., the family), and induces in them a subjective reassurance, which supports and affirms them as people, and assists them in accepting their relevant roles and their acceptance by the community, and thereby in experiencing their identity.

If all the knowledge we have and all the techniques we are capable of handling could produce a history that could fulfill in our time with integrity the function tradition fulfilled in pre-modern times we would have rendered society a great service. [[113]]

Bibliography

Auld, A. G.
    1990   Prophecy in Books: A Rejoinder. *JSOT* 48: 31–32.
Ben-Yoseph, J.
    1985   The Climate in Eretz Israel during Biblical Times. *Hebrew Studies* 26: 225–39.
Berlin, I.
    1966   The Concept of Scientific History, in Dray (ed.) 1966 [[below]] 5–53.
Brett, M. G.
    1987   Literacy and Domination: G. A. Herion's Sociology of History Writing. *JSOT* 37: 15–40.
[[Brodbeck, M.
    1966   Bibliographic information omitted by author—*editor*.]]

Cancik, H.
1970   *Mythische und historische Wahrheit.* Stuttgart: Verlag Katholisches Bibelwerk.
Carroll, R. P.
1990   Whose Prophet? Whose History? Whose Social Reality? Troubling the Interpretative Community Again: Notes towards a Response to T. W. Overholt's Critique. *JSOT* 48: 33–49.
Chaney, M. L.
1986   Systemic Study of the Israelite Monarchy. *Semeia* 37: 53–76.
Clements, R. E. (ed.)
1989   *The World of Ancient Israel: Sociological, Anthropological and Political Perspectives.* Cambridge: University Press.
Collingwood, R. G.
1946   *The Idea of History.* Oxford: University Press.
Donagan, A.
1966   The Popper-Hempel Theory Reconsidered, in Dray (ed.) 1966, 125–59.
Dray, W. H. (ed.)
1966   *Philosophical Analysis and History.* New York: Harper & Row.
Fiensy, D.
1987   Using the Nuer Culture of Africa in Understanding the Old Testament:
An Evaluation. *JSOT* 38: 73–83.
Finkelstein, I.
1989   The Emergence of the Monarchy in Israel: The Environmental and Socio-
economic Aspects. *JSOT* 44: 43–74.
Flanagan, J. W.
1987   Beyond Space-Time Systemics. *JSOT* 39: 22–29.
Fletcher, J. D.
1987   Bible Study for Adults: Let's Stop Cheating God's People. *The Living Light*
23: 236–42.
Fokkema, D., and Ibsch, E.
1979   *Theories of Literature in the Twentieth Century: Structuralism, Marxism, Aes-
thetics of Reception, Semiotics.* London: C. Hurst.
Frick, F. S.
1986   Social Science Methods and Theories of Significance for the Study of the
Israelite Monarchy. *Semeia* 37: 9–52.
[[Gay, P.
1974   *Style in History.* New York: Basic Books.]]
Gnuse, R.
1991   BTB Review of Current Scholarship: Israelite Settlement of Canaan: A
Peaceful International Process. Part 2. *BTB* 21: 109–17. [[114]]
Gottwald, N.
1986   The Participation of Free Agrarians in the Introduction of Monarchy to
Ancient Israel: An Application of H. A. Landsberger's Framework for the
Analysis of Peasant Movements. *Semeia* 37: 77–106.
Hart, H. L. A., and Honoré, A. M.
1966   Causal Judgment in History and in the Law, in Dray (ed.) 1966, 213–37.

Hauer, C.
1986   From Alt to Anthropology: The Rise of the Israelite State. *JSOT* 36, 3–15.
Hempel, C. G.
1966   Explanation in Science and History, in Dray (ed.) 1966, 95–126.
Horsley, R. A.
1991   Empire, Temple and Community—But No Bourgeoisie! in Davies, P. R. (ed.). *Second Temple Studies I: Persian Period* (JSOTS 117): 163–74. Sheffield: JSOT Press.
van Jaarsveld, F. A.
1980   *Westerse historiografie en geskiedenisfilosofie.* Pretoria: HAUM.
Jobling, D.
1991   Texts and the World—An Unbridgeable Gap? A Response to Carroll, Hoglund and Smith, in Davies, P. R. (ed.). *Second Temple Studies I: Persian Period* (JSOTS 117): 175–82. Sheffield: JSOT Press.
Knauff, E. A.
1991   From History to Interpretation, in Edelman, D. V. (ed.). *The Fabric of History* (JSOTS 127): 26–64. Sheffield: JSOT Press.
Kremer, J.
1987   Mythos, Wissenschaft und Bibel. *Stimmen der Zeit* 205: 195–203.
Lemche, N. P.
1990   On the Use of "System Theory," "Macro Theories" and "Evolutionistic Thinking" in Modern OT Research and Biblical Archaeology. *SJOT* 2: 73–88.
Licht, J.
1989   The Hebrew Bible Contains the Oldest Surviving History. *BRev* 5/6: 22–25, 28.
Mayes, A. D. H.
1988a   Idealism and Materialism in Weber and Gottwald. *Proceedings of the Irish Biblical Association* 11: 44–58.
1988b   Sociology and the Study of the Old Testament. Some Recent Writings. *Irish Biblical Studies* 10: 178–91.
1989   *The Old Testament in Sociological Perspective.* London: Marshall Pickering.
McNutt, P.
1987   Interpreting Israel's "Folk Traditions." *JSOT* 39: 44–52.
Mink, L. O.
1966   The Autonomy of Historical Understanding, in Dray (ed.) 1966, 160–92.
Mohan, P. M.
1970   *Philosophy of History. An Introduction.* New York: The Bruce Publishing House.
Mosala, I. J.
1986   Social Scientific Approaches to the Bible: One Step Forward, Two Steps Backwards. *JTSA* 55: 15–30. [[115]]
Moye, R. H.
1990   In the Beginning: Myth and History in Genesis and Exodus. *JBL* 109, 577–98.

Oakeshott, M.
1966   Historical Continuity and Causal Analysis, in Dray (ed.) 1966, 193–212.
Overholt, T. W.
1990   It Is Difficult to Read. *JSOT* 48: 51–54.
Passmore, J. A.
1966   The Objectivity of History, in Dray (ed.) 1966, 75–94.
Patterson, S. J.
1990   Bridging the Gulf between Bible Scholarship and Religious Faith. *BRev* 6/6: 16, 44.
Rogerson, J. W.
1986a   Was Israel a Fragmentary Society? *JSOT* 36, 17–26.
1986b   Anthropology and the Old Testament. *Proceedings of the Irish Biblical Association* 11: 90–102.
Scriven, M.
1996   Causes, Connections and Conditions in History, in Dray (ed.) 1966, 238–64.
Thiel, W.
1988   Von revolutionären zum evolutionären Israel? Zu einem neuen Modell der Entstehung Israels. *TLZ* 113: 401–10.
Thiselton, A. C.
1990   On Models and Methods. A Conversation with Robert Morgan, in Clines, D. J. A., *The Bible in Three Dimensions* (JSOTS 87): 337–56. Sheffield: JSOT Press.
Thompson, T. L.
1991   Text, Context and Referent in Israelite Historiography, in Edelman, D. V. (ed.), *The Fabric of History* (JSOTS 127): 65–92. Sheffield: JSOT Press.
Walsh, W. H.
1966   The Limits of Scientific History, in Dray (ed.) 1966, 54–74.
1967   *An Introduction to Philosophy of History.* London: Hutchinson.
Wernhardt
1992   Altes Testament und Schwarzafrika, in S. Kreuzer and K. Lüthi (eds.), *Zur Aktualität des Alten Testaments: Festschrift für Georg Sauer zum 65. Geburtstag,* 219–26. Frankfurt: Lang.
Whitelam, K. M.
1986   Recreating the History of Israel. *JSOT* 35, 45–70.
Whybray, R. N.
1989   Today and Tomorrow in Biblical Studies. II: The Old Testament. *ExpTim* 100: 364–68.
Yitzhaki, M.
1987   The Relationship between Biblical Studies and Ancient Near Eastern Studies. A Bibliometric Approach. *ZAW* 99: 232–48.

Is It Still Possible to Write a History of Ancient Israel?

NIELS PETER LEMCHE

[[165]] A few months ago, I lectured at a symposium in Bern in Switzerland on the theme "Kann von einer 'israelitischen Religion' noch weiterhin die Rede sein?" ("Is it still possible to speak of an 'Israelite religion'?") The subtitle of the lecture was "Aus der perspektive eines Historikers" ("From an historian's point of view").[1] My answer was "yes and no" at the same time. Yes, it is still possible to speak of an Israelite religion, although the only place this religion should be sought is in the Old Testament. No, Israelite religion, as it is described by the authors of the Old Testament, should be considered quite different from the types of religion present in Palestine during the so-called Old Testament period. The Old Testament does not describe a religion that could be found in Palestine in ancient times; rather, Israelite religion should be studied in the light of later Jewish religious sentiments. One could also put it in the following manner: in the field covered by OT scholars, two religions are likely to exist side by side. On the one hand there is the biblical religion, a literary form of religion which is usually considered to be a true expression of ancient Israelite religion, and on the other we find a variety of West Asian religion, which the OT writers hardly ever allow to speak for itself; instead it is mostly described in desultory terms and heavily criticized as religious abuse.

It should be recognized that scholars have generally used the term "Israelite Religion" in an absolutely questionable way. First of all it is obvious that most scholars have formed their opinion of Israelite religion almost solely on the basis of the description to be found in the OT. Secondly, it is

Reprinted with permission from *Scandinavian Journal of the Old Testament* 8 (1994) 165–90.

1. [[Now]] published in W. Dietrich [[and M. A. Klopfenstein]] (eds.), [[*Ein Gott allein? JHWH-Verehrung und biblischer Monotheismus im Kontext der israelitischen und altorientalischen Religionsgeschichte*]], OBO [[139]], Freiburg and Göttingen, 1994 [[pp. 59–75]].

equally obvious that these scholars work at the mercy of the OT authors, and that their understanding of religious matters derives almost entirely from the Bible. It follows that the [[166]] religious standards of the biblical writers still survive and form the basis of a modern religio-historical analysis of ancient Israelite religion. Thus scholars working with the biblical description of Israelite religion have often paid insufficient attention to questions that may arise because of the dating of OT texts, and they have certainly been rather evasive when they have had to face the fact that the greater part of biblical literature belongs to the so-called exilic or post-exilic periods.[2]

Now, I am not going to discuss Israelite religion here. Instead the theme of this paper will be the history of ancient Israel, and I intend to present some ideas of how I think we should in future continue our study of this history, whether or not it is in any sense legitimate to speak of such a history.

In order to introduce my subject today, I shall briefly mention some of the important new elements that have changed the course of the study of ancient Israel. It cannot be ignored that most of the changes have occurred at the beginning of this history, that is, before 1000 B.C.E., while the following periods have until recently been left almost untouched by modern developments. There is, however, reason to believe that the period after 1000 B.C.E. will in future be the focus of our interest, and that dramatic changes are also about to take place in this field. Be this as it may, when discussing historical matters I shall beg our indulgence for starting this section by referring to my study, *Early Israel*,[3] although I still believe that this step can be justified because the idea of the history of ancient Israel presented here seems to have played an essential role and [[to have]] helped [[in]] promoting the present situation characterized by the rapidly changing views of biblical scholars on historical matters.

It could, of course, be maintained—and it should not be forgotten—that already George Mendenhall (since 1962[4]) and Norman Gottwald [[167]]

---

2. "So-called" because the term "the Exilic Period" presupposes that it ended, some day, that is in 538 B.C.E. This was, however, only partially true as most "exiled" Jews remained in Babylonia for the rest of their lives. I sometimes maintain that the real end to the Babylonian exile only came in 1948 C.E., when the proclamation of the modern state of Israel trickered off [[*sic*; read triggered(?)]] the second *Alia* [['emigration']], the one from modern Iraq to Palestine/Israel, leaving only a tiny remnant of Jews back in their age-old home in Mesopotamia. This is of course intended to be understood as a joke, however a joke that has some reality behind it. The presuppositions for speaking about an exile certainly did not end in 538 B.C.E.

3. *SVT* 37 (Leiden 1985).

4. The year of publication of his "The Hebrew Conquest of Palestine," in *BA* 25 (1962) 66–87.

(since 1974[5]) started their deconstructions of OT history, and that they certainly contributed to the change of paradigm that has taken place in OT studies. It should at the same time not be forgotten that their theories also have their fair share of problems, since Mendenhall's and Gottwald's major contributions are idiosyncratic and their results often misleading. Thus Mendenhall seems prepared to sacrifice the history of Israel to preserve the history of Israelite religion, whereas Gottwald is only "revolutionary" in the sense that he is applying a *revolutionary model* to the study of Israel's origins. Aside from this, Gottwald's methodology is rather conventional, and the number of new ideas presented by him is limited. If anyone should be in doubt on this issue, he should consult Gottwald's introduction to the OT,[6] which makes it obvious that, apart from a certain "sociological" flavor imposed on the textual analysis, the main view of scripture to be found in this volume is most traditional and not very inspiring.

The main reason for quoting my own study is the "maxims" which are formulated at the end of that book; these are the propositions that (1) our most important duty is to acknowledge our ignorance, and (2) once we have acknowledged the state of our ignorance we are in a position to acknowledge what we really do know. These sentences could be understood as the motto underlying many studies that have appeared since their publication, not least the recent one by Thomas L. Thompson.[7]

When I finished writing *Early Israel* (now more than ten years ago), it seemed all too clear to me that a literary theory was missing which might provide an answer to the all too obvious discrepancies between the OT description of the early history of Israel and the history of Palestine at the transition from the Late Bronze Age to the Early Iron Age. This writer, like most of his contemporaries, was at that time still entangled in the historical network laid out by the OT writers, according to whom the history of Israel is divisible into fixed periods such as the settlement, the time of the Judges, the united monarchy, [[168]] the divided monarchy, and the exilic and post-exilic periods. In the middle 1980s we were only prepared to make a few scratches to the picture painted by the OT narrators.

In his *Who Were the Israelites*, the late Gösta W. Ahlström in many ways went further,[8] as he correctly questioned the identity of the so-called early Israelites. Very few really understood what Ahlström's intention was—this writer had to write two more books before he saw what was going on and

---

5. See his lecture at the IOSOT meeting in Edinburgh, 1974, "Domain Assumptions and Societal Models in the Study of Pre-Monarchic Israel," *VTS* 28 (1975) 89–100.

6. N. K. Gottwald, *The Hebrew Bible. A Socio-Literary Introduction*, Philadelphia 1985.

7. *Early History of the Israelite People* (Studies in the History of the Ancient Near East 4; Leiden, 1992).

8. Winona Lake (1986).

when he told Gösta Ahlström that he must be slow-witted, Ahlström of course replied: Yes, since you say so yourself!

As a matter of fact, Ahlström preceded Philip R. Davies in demonstrating that the ancient Israelites represented no more than a phenomenon invented by the OT historians; the Israelites were never themselves an historical reality. Philip Davies has, however, discussed these matters in a very pointed way in his recent polemical contribution to the discussion, *In Search of 'Ancient Israel.'*[9] According to Davies, OT scholars have for more than two hundred years tried to grasp the historical truth behind the OT narratives, as if this truth were the holy grail itself, and the modern knights of the grail, that is the biblical scholars, have in no way been more successful than were their colleagues gathered about King Arthur's round table.

Ahlström and Davies are certainly right in maintaining that the ancient Israelites were invented by the OT writers. They play the role of "the good guys" (who don't need to be particularly good, if only they happen to be better than their opponents). On the other hand, once we have succeeded in identifying the heroes of the tale, we also need to find some bad guys, for without the conflict between the good and the bad there would hardly be any narrative at all. "The bad guys" of the OT narratives can surely be identified as the Canaanites. Here Davies was able to build on the results presented in my *The Canaanites and Their Land*[10] that the biblical Canaanites hardly reflect any historical or ethnic reality; rather, they owe their existence to a construction made by the biblical historians. As I put it in my study, the first Canaanites who understood themselves to be Canaanites were Punic peasants living in Northern Africa in the days of Augustine,[11] and no person from the ancient Near East has ever—as [[169]] far as the preserved documentation says—called himself a "Canaanite." Transferred from the literary to the historical level this tells us that without bad guys there will be no good guys. If the Canaanites owed their existence to the creative mind of the OT writers, these writers may also have invented their counterpart, the Israelite nation.

This does not mean that there was never an "Israel" in ancient times. To maintain this would be foolish, as the name itself, "Israel" is well represented in ancient documents, including documents that have nothing to do with the OT. We need only refer to the stela of Merneptah mentioning an "Israel" in Palestine at the end of the 13th cent. B.C.E., or to the "Israel" found in King Mesha's Moabite inscription, or the "Israel" (spelled

---

9. JSOTSup 148 (Sheffield 1992).
10. *The Tradition of the Canaanites* (JSOTSup 110; Sheffield 1991).
11. Cf. *The Canaanites*, 56–57.

Sirla'a[12]) that, according to Assyrian sources, was governed by King Ahab. Thus there is absolutely no reason to doubt that the Israel mentioned by King Mesha or by the Assyrian documents was the same Israel which, according to the OT, was to be sought in the highlands of central Palestine. It is, however, in the first place not evident that this Israel of the 9th century is necessarily the same as Merneptah's Israel, and in the second, even if it were permissible to speak of an ethnic continuity between Merneptah's Israel and Ahab's Israel, we cannot be sure that the real history of this Israel has much—if anything—to do with the history of the Israel to be found in the pages of the OT—apart, that is, from the commonplace conclusion that there once existed a Palestinian state called "Israel" that was destroyed by the Assyrians at the end of the 8th cent. B.C.E. It is, for example, evident that in the OT the name of "Israel" is a national name attached to a special Israelite people having a peculiar status and history. This is, on the other hand, the only conclusion we can safely reach, as we have no information about the ethnicity of this so-called nation of "Israel," nor much knowledge about its pre-history. The national identity of the Israelites was certainly not strong enough to prevent that fact that all traces of the deportees from Samaria in 722 disappeared just a few years after their deportation, a fact which makes it likely that the deportees may have "forgotten" their Israelite identity after only a few years of captivity in Mesopotamia. Thus not even West Semitic names that could be connected with the Israelite deportees have been found in the remains from the Neo-Assyrian kingdom.

Then again, when discussing the "Israel" of Merneptah, it should not [[170]] be overlooked that we have no assured idea as to what this concept really covers or whether there ever existed any political or ethnical continuity between *this* Israel and the Israel of the OT. The only thing the two entities may have had in common is the *name*. However, even the modern state to be found in this area is called "Israel," although the relations of this modern Israel to ancient Israel, that is, the Northern Kingdom, is mainly a matter of ideology. Whether the inhabitants of Central Palestine during the time of Omri and Ahab ever understood themselves to be "Israelites" in the ethnic and national sense is unknown to modern scholars; they may merely have seen themselves as human beings who happened to pay taxes to a king of a state called "Israel"—although it was equally possible at the time also to call it "Samaria" or "the House of Omri" (*Bît Khumriya*). The only thing we can safely assume is that the *OT writers* considered this population to be Israelite in the ethnic sense of the word.

---

12. In Shalmanaser III's version of the battle at Qarqar in 853 B.C.E., *ANET*[3], 279.

At the center of the debate stands the question as to whether we should follow the OT historians here. Should modern historians tamely allow these writers to decide the course of research? Would it not be preferable if the modern historian simply skipped over the biblical historical construction and made his own reconstruction of what he thought to be the history of ancient Palestine?[13] Here the OT would be but one source of knowledge (albeit a rather comprehensive one) among others, and there should be no reason to pay special attention to the OT version in contrast to other information.

In this connection I must draw attention to a number of related questions that should also be discussed. Thus we have questions of definition, the most important of these being the use of the name "Israel." The importance of this as well as other matters of definition becomes obvious when reading the contributions to the volume published by Diana Edelman, *The Fabric of History.*[14] In this volume [[171]] there are studies that from a terminological point are undistinctive and evasive—for example the one by William B. [[*sic*; read G.]] Devers [[*sic*; read Dever]][15] —as well as other studies that present some relevant comments on the problem of terminology—especially the one by J. Maxwell Miller[16] —or contributions that seem already to have overcome this problem—especially the ones by Thomas L. Thompson[17] and Ernst Axel Knauff.[18] On the other hand, it should be obvious that in the event that the problems of definition and terminology are not solved, then the discussion will end up in a terminological morass and the issues will become blurred.

Another matter to be discussed has to do with the question of the kind of historical interest likely to be present in ancient times. Did the OT

---

13. Allowing for the fact that any reconstruction of history can only be a *reconstruction*. It is certainly not to be mistaken as *the history*. I have sometimes been unrightfully accused of having—like the ancient deuteronomists—created nothing but my own personal version of the history of Israel (cf., e.g., S. Herrmann, "Die Abwertung des Alten Testaments als Geschichtsquelle. Bemerkungen zu einem geistesgeschichtliches Problem," in H. H. Schmid and J. Mehlhausen [eds.], *Sola Scriptura* [VII. Europäischer Theologen-Kongreß, Dresden 1980; Gütersloh 1993] 156–65 [[reprinted in this volume, pp. 346–355]]). This may be true, but at least it is *my* version, not just a new paraphrase of the Deuteronomistic one.

14. D. V. Edelman (ed.), *The Fabric of History. Text, Artifact and Israel's Past* (JSOTSup 127; Sheffield 1991).

15. "Archaeology, Material Culture and the Early Monarchical Period," in Edelman, *The Fabric of History,* 103–15.

16. "Is it possible to Write a History of Israel Without Relying on the Hebrew Bible?," in Edelman, *The Fabric,* 93–102.

17. "Text, Context and Referent in Israelite Historiography," in Edelman, *The Fabric,* 65–92.

18. "From History to Interpretation," in Edelman, *The Fabric,* 26–64.

historians really want to write *history?* How would they have understood the modern concept of history? During the last decade several scholars including this writer have offered these problems considerable attention, and it now seems clear that a history writing which has anything in common with the modern concept of history should not be expected from the hands of the OT "historians"; this kind of writing was certainly not on their agenda when they presented their version of a history of Israel. Although Baruch Halpern tried to argue a few years ago that the OT historians were true historians,[19] it would be misleading to maintain that he has presented a strong argument in favor of his thesis. I have only to refer to his very extensive discussion of Ehud's killing of Eglon, which obviously goes against his own interests.[20]

The third question to be discussed in this connection will concern the problem of the survival of historical information in the OT historical literature. Excluded from this discussion will be the clearly historical information about Sennacherib's siege of Jerusalem in 701 and that pertaining to Nebuchadnezzar's conquest of the same city in 597. The fact that the authors of the stories about Sennacherib's siege have embellished their narrative by introducing legendary means does not [[172]] imply that this siege must be considered unhistorical; instead, it merely tells us something about the methods used by the OT history writers when they constructed their histories.

Now I have finally reached the theme of this paper, to discuss the possibility that there may—after all—be some historical information contained in the OT writings, even in those parts that concern the early history of Israel. However, although it cannot be excluded that such information may be present, it is far from a safe assumption that they are placed in a context that from an historian's point of view is the correct one.

It is my intention here to present three examples of the way possibly historical information has been handled by the OT historians. My first example is related to the sojourn of the Israelites in Egypt; the second will deal with the Benjaminite immigration into Palestine; and the third concerns the relations between David and Omri. It goes without saying that as far as the early history of Israel is concerned, the discussion can only be called preliminary; it certainly does not intend to provide the final truth about these matters. I cannot present anything but proposals and ideas that may (or may not) some day become part of a more comprehensive discussion.

19. *The First Historians. The Hebrew Bible and History* (San Francisco 1988).
20. *The First Historians,* 39–75.

Pithom and Ramses

The note in Exod 1:11 that the Israelites in Egypt were forced to build the
storage cities of Pharaoh, Pithom and Ramses, has often been considered
proof that there was an historical background to the Exodus narrative. In
this connection scholars usually refer to the mention in an Egyptian document of *'apiru* who, in the days of Ramses II (1279–1212), participated in
the construction of the great pylon–gate tower—namely Ramses Mia-
mon.[21] Thus the note in Exod 1:11 is assumed to be historically correct,
as, at least from a linguistic point of view, the *'apiru* of the Egyptian documents are supposed to be identical with the biblical Hebrews, and it has
certainly not escaped the attention of modern scholars that in the Joseph
and Exodus narratives the Israelites are often referred to as "Hebrews."

Both Pithom and Ramses are place names known from the history of
Egypt. The city of Ramses should beyond doubt be identified with the ruins of *Khatana-Qantir* in northeastern Egypt. During the late New Kingdom, this site was called Pi-Ramesse (taking its name from the famous
Ramses II, the great builder of this city) and here the residence [[173]] of
the Pharaohs of the 19th and 20th dynasty could be found. After that period the place was forsaken by its inhabitants and the residence moved to
nearby Tanis, the *Zo'an* of the OT, the city that was to become the new capital of Egypt in the days of the 21st dynasty. In light of this fact, it would
be reasonable to consider the information of Exod 1:11 to be historical
and to be connected to conditions which obtained in Egypt at the end of
the 2nd millennium B.C.E., and only then. Although this may seem un-
problematical and beyond doubt, some problems will arise as soon as we
turn our attention to the identity of the second storage city, that is,
Pithom.

According to Exod 1:11, Pithom should be regarded as a city comparable to Ramses. This is, however, historically impossible, as "Pithom" was
only used as the name of a city in the Saite period, from the 7th century
onwards. Pithom means "the House of (the god) Atum," and was also
known prior to the Saite period as the name of temples and temple estates
belonging to this god (or better: the priests of Atum). The name was, however, never connected with cities. Moreover, archaeologists working at *tell
el-Maskhuta* in northeastern Egypt have found clear evidence that this was
the ancient city of Pithom and that it was founded by Pharaoh Necho II
between 609 and 606 B.C.E.[22] Hence, the information that the Israelites
should have worked before the Exodus as forced laborers at the site of

---

21. J. Bottéro, *Le probleme des ḫabiru* (Paris 1954) n. 188, pp. 169–70.
22. Cf. J. S. Holladay, *The Wadi Tumilat Project. The Excavations of Tell el-Makhuta* (Mal-
ibu, CA, 1982).

Pithom is simply anachronistic. On the other hand, it cannot be excluded that prisoners of war from the territory of the former state of Israel—or from Judah—may have been employed by Necho for his building activities in northern Egypt. These prisoners may have been transported to Egypt by Necho following his 609 campaign during which King Josiah of Judah lost his life at Megiddo. It is also possible that immigrants from Palestine who already in those days lived in Egypt were conscripted for building purposes.

It may not be possible to point to a moment in the history of Egypt when both cities mentioned in Exod 1:11 existed simultaneously, and it may be difficult to say anything about the time when the Israelites are supposed to have worked at the storage cities of Pharaoh. One part of the content of Exod 1:11 seemingly belongs in the 2nd millennium, another in the middle of the 1st millennium. It may, nevertheless, be possible to create some coherence if the Egyptologist Edward F. Wente should happen to be right in maintaining that the [[174]] name of "Ramses" in Exod 1:11 need not be directly connected to the city of Ramses, going back to Ramses II; Ramses may in Exod 1:11 refer to Tanis, which had by and large been built by recycling stones from nearby Ramses. Also the colossal statues of Ramses II were moved from Ramses to Tanis, and until the Hellenistic Period traces of a cult of Ramses II can be found at Tanis. Wente accordingly maintains that the OT writers have simply transferred the name of Ramses (which was never lost to the Egyptian traditionalists) to another place—that is Tanis—which was still in existence when they wrote their history, while they at the same time transferred their information about the building activities of the "Israelites" that may have happened in the days of Pharaoh Necho back to the assumed stay of Israel in Egypt in ancient times.[23]

If this explanation is plausible, the main argument in favor of the *historical* content of the Exodus narrative has lost its foundation. Instead of being able to prove that the Israelites once upon a time were in Egypt, Exod 1:11 can be taken as evidence of the ways and manners of OT historians who, in this case, have obviously manipulated their sources in order to create the impression of Israelites working as slaves in Egypt at an early point in the history of Israel. Thus the note in Exod 1:11 about the building of Pithom and Ramses may after all be historical, but this history has nothing to do with the old history of Israel; instead, it should be understood in relation to later conditions that were used by the authors to create their own fictitious picture of the sojourn of the Israelites in Egypt. However, in its present context the note is absolutely anachronistic.

23. Cf. E. Wente, "Rameses," *ABD* (1992) Vol. 5, 617–18.

This example may seem obvious. The next case, which deals with the settlement tradition in the book of Joshua, will demand more patience from the reader.

The Settlement of the Benjaminites

When it was first formulated, the classic German explanation of the settlement of the Israelites was hailed as an important breakthrough in the history of scholarship, because the two main characters who are associated with this explanation, Albrecht Alt and Martin Noth, preferred to disregard the information contained in the book of Joshua as far as an Israelite *conquest* of Canaan was concerned. In this place there is no reason to review Alt's and Noth's research, nor to deal with the alternative ideas about the conquest prevailing in [[175]] other quarters of biblical scholarship.[24] Here only one among a number of interesting observations made by these scholars will be in the focus of interest. This is their observation that all of the specific conquest narratives in Joshua concern localities which are to be found in the territory of the tribe of Benjamin (although the hero of the conquest, Joshua, was himself from Ephraim).

Alt and Noth considered these conquest narratives to depend on Benjaminite local traditions and legends which the Deuteronomistic authors of Joshua had remolded into pan-Israelite traditions that should be seen in conjunction with the immigration of the Israelite tribes led by Joshua.[25] The historical content of the narratives was, however, not in the focus of attention except from the fact that it was mostly believed to refer to the second phase of the settlement, to the so-called phase of the *Landübernahme* [['occupation of the land']], that is, to the time when the growing Israelite tribes had to confront opposition from the original Canaanite population of Palestine—a thing that, on the other hand, only occurred many years after the immigration had taken place. The fact that no comparable conquest traditions have survived from other parts of the Israelite territory was believed to be the result of a traditio-historical coincidence.

In light of the present almost predominant view of the origin of the historical Israel (however understood), these Benjaminite legends and sagas seem to have lost their historical basis. It should, however, still be a matter of interest to know more about the origins of the legends themselves. Where did they arise and what do they intend to say? If we assume that the Israelites were originally Canaanites (and I have to say that I per-

---

24. My review of these theses can be found in my *Early Israel*, 35–48.

25. A. Alt, in his article "Josua" (1936), *Kleine Schriften zur Geschichte Israels I* (1953) 176–92; M. Noth, thus in his introduction to his commentary on Joshua, *Das Buch Josua* (2. Aufl.; *HAT* 17; Tübingen 1953) 11–13.

sonally abstain from using this terminology any more), why should legends and sagas have survived from one particular part of Palestine that inform us about a military conquest of this region? Is it really a tradition-historical coincidence, or may we assume that other reasons may lie behind this state of affairs.

Besides, who were the Benjaminites who were suspected of having conquered their territory by military means? According to some traditions they used their left hands, and some scholars have assumed that this was due to some kind of secret weapon employed by such Benjaminites as Ehud in connection with his killing of the Moabite [[176]] king Eglon.[26] It is, however, preferable to speak of a joke, the Hebrew word Benjamin meaning "the son of the right (hand)," who was actually left-handed. There is certainly no reason to believe that this was a special physical mark indigenous to the tribe of Benjamin. It is therefore still necessary to find a plausible explanation for their tribal name, "the son of the right (hand)." One solution is to say that this could also be translated as "the son of the south"—the way of geographical orientation (the right hand pointing to the south) in the ancient world taken into consideration—and since Benjamin was the tribe that lived to the south of the other Israelite tribes, this name will naturally have accrued to the Benjaminites. The historical reasoning for this state of affairs is, however, not easy to reconstruct, as we have no information that Benjamin was considered the southernmost of the Israelite tribes before the time of the divided monarchy, and even thereafter only partially, because a part of Benjamin belonged to the kingdom of Judah. Moreover, this proposal presupposes that a tribal name should depend on the formation of a state, which from a socio-anthropological point of view would be something of a sensation.

The name "Benjamin" is also unusual because it is the only Israelite tribal name that contains the element *ben* 'son'. This part of the name is, on the other hand, well known from other tribal groups of the Near East in antiquity as well as in later periods, and tribal names of this type can be found both in Mesopotamian documents and among Arab tribes of the present days. The other Israelite tribal names are, as M. Noth as excellently explained, either,[27] (1) names for people having a specific "occupation" (so Issakar), (2) names of landscapes (so Ephraim, Judah), or (3) tribes which may have been named after gods (so Gad). Only Benjamin seems in this connection to be a genuine tribal name.

---

26. Cf. Judg 3:15, 17, 21, and esp. 20:16. Cf. among the more recent, B. Halpern, *The First Historians*, 41.

27. M. Noth, *Geschichte Israels* (Göttingen 1950) 56–67.

It should in this connection not be forgotten that the biblical Benjaminites may not have been the only Benjaminites in the ancient world. According to the documents from ancient Mari, a tribal group were in existence in Upper Mesopotamia around 1800 B.C.E. who were most likely called the *binu jamina*. Scholars formerly doubted that the name of the Benjaminites was related to the Marian Benjaminites since, in the cuneiform writing employed by the scribes of Mari, the [[177]] first name of the Mesopotamian Benjaminites was always rendered as DUMU^MEŠ *jamina*, with a sumerogram instead of the proper Akkadian transcription. According to Hayim Tadmor, this tells us that there were no Benjaminites around Mari, because the scribes of Mari never used sumerograms to render West-Semitic words; in the Marian texts sumerograms are invariably used to render Akkadian names and concepts, and the proper Akkadian rendering would not be *banu* or *binu jamina* but *maru jamina*.[28] Such a compound that is made up of an Akkadian word as well as a West-Semitic one (*jamina* is doubtless West-Semitic. In proper Akkadian its counterpart would be *imnu[m]*) is certainly very uncommon and most scholars have therefore considered the sumerogram DUMU^MEŠ here to be used with a general meaning to indicate members of a tribal group that was only known as *jamina*. It has accordingly been normal not to speak about Benjaminites but about "jaminites" living in the province of Mari. The situation may now have changed as also the first component of the name has now turned up in a document from Mari, written syllabically—however, surprisingly as *binu* and not, as was to be expected, as *banu*, making it likely that the name DUMU^MEŠ *jamina* was always intended to be rendered as *binu jamina*.[29]

At Mari the name "the son of the south" makes excellent sense, because there also are traces of another tribal group called the DUMU^MEŠ *sim'al*, that is, "the sons of the north." We are badly informed about the whereabouts of this second group. This is not very important here; important is only the fact that "the sons of the south" seem to carry their name in opposition to "the sons of the north," somehow in the same fashion as the Ostrogoths (the eastern Goths) who were so called because also the Visigoths (the western Goths) were around at the same time, although not always living to the west of the Ostrogoths.

28. H. Tadmor, "Historical Implications of the Correct Rendering of Akkadian 'dâku'," *JNES* 17 (1958) 129–41.

29. Cf. *ARM* XXII: 328:111. Cf. on this A. Malamat, *Mari and the Early Israelite Experience* (The Schweich Lectures 1984; Oxford 1989) 31 and 35 n. 29. Since the syllabically written name has so far only occurred as a personal name, Malamat is still of the conviction that we should speak about *jaminites*, the first part to be a kind of semantic indicator. However, this will not change much, as all later examples of tribal names of this type could also be said to contain the word "sons of" as "semantic indicators," including the biblical Ben-jaminites.

The question remains whether the Benjaminites from Mari have anything to do with the Benjaminites of Palestine. Such a connection [[178]]
has been proposed, by, among others, M. Astour in his characteristically
fanciful fashion.[30] In this connection Astour refers to religious ties which,
on his view, should have existed between the two areas. The Benjaminites
of Upper Mesopotamia lived—at least seasonally—in an area where the
dominant deity is supposed to have been the moon-god Sin, whereas in
the OT a city name that also implies worship of the moon, that is Jericho,
is actually to be located inside the tribal area of Benjamin. If no additional
arguments could be provided, the most generous thing to say would probably be that this theory should simply be forgotten. However, although
they are hardly to be considered conclusive, such arguments may eventually be found, and here the "reference" preserved in Gen 35:23–26 may be
of interest, that Benjamin like the other sons of Jacob was born in Paddan-
Aram (the anachronistic term applied by P for Upper Mesopotamia in the
days of the Patriarchs).

This information demands attention because it clearly contradicts the
narrative about the birth of Benjamin just before the note in Gen 35:23–
26. According to the main narrative, Benjamin is supposed to have been
born in the land of Canaan near the city of Bethlehem after the return of
Jacob to his own country; Benjamin is therefore said to be the only one
among the sons of Jacob who originated in Palestine, whereas his eleven
brothers were all born in Mesopotamia. We must therefore ask how it can
be that the conflicting note in Gen 35:23–26 has survived. Maybe the person who included the note may have "nodded off" or forgotten that we
have just been told about the birth of Benjamin and the death of Rachel
in Canaan? However, this does not seem to be a reasonable explanation—
after all, how should he be able to forget such an obvious contradiction?
It is more likely that the note in Gen 35:23–26 owes its existence to a special tradition that runs counter to the official version of Benjamin's birth
and thus has to be evaluated as an independent piece of information.

One may pay as much attention as one wishes to such a special tradition; it should on the other hand not be forgotten that it has always been
characteristic of classic historical research to focus on information that
does not conform with, but which rather *contradicts* the mainstream information to be found in the available documentation. Historians are generally trained to grasp such contradictions in order to show whether they
derive from a special source or have something to say which the authors
of the main traditions never intended to pass [[179]] on to posterity. Such
"fossilized traces of tradition" may provide the historian with an opportunity to get behind his main source and to evaluate its content not only on

---

30. M. Astour, "Benê-iamina et Jéricho," *Semitica* 9 (1959) 5–20.

the basis of what the main tradition says, but also on the basis of what it does not say, but which has, all the same, filtered through the official screen laid out by the author of the main document.

Even though historians of the present time may have found other methods and rather prefer to focus on totalities and *la longue durée* [['the long duration']], it should nevertheless be maintained that it is appropriate from the standpoint of source criticism not to disregard any nonnormal piece of information that may be present in a given corpus of documents, as such pieces may give us information about matters not included in the main narrative, and which were not intended to become publicly known. And when we return to the question of Gen 35:23–26, it will be possible to maintain that, in contrast to the main narrative, which maintains that Benjamin originated in Canaan, another less elaborated tradition simply says that Benjamin, like his brothers, came from Mesopotamia. The implications of the place where Benjamin was born, Paddan-Aram, should in this connection be kept in mind.

In order to cut the discussion short, I would like to argue that it still remains a possibility that the biblical Benjaminites came from Mesopotamia, and were formerly members of the comprehensive tribal group known to the scribes of ancient Mari as the *binu jamina*. How the two parts of the Benjaminites are related is totally unknown, but the following scenario may be possible: the documents from Mari make it evident that a serious conflict existed between the authorities of the kingdom of Mari and the tribal society of the Benjaminites, a conflict that mostly arose from the fact that the Benjaminites only temporarily visited the territory of Mari, and soon had to leave it again by crossing the Euphrates at a point close to the city of Mari in order to reach their winter grazing areas to the east of the Euphrates. During the summer period, the Benjaminites seem to have been visiting the area around *Djebel Bishri* in the central part of Syria, to the west of Mari. Although they often tried, the kings of Mari never succeeded in halting the migrations of the Benjaminites, but it cannot be excluded—although it can only be a theory—that when king Hammurabi conquered Mari and included it in his empire, he may have gained sufficient strength to impede the free migrations of the Benjaminites to such a degree that at least a fraction of this tribal group decided to move, not from the west to the east, from *Djebel Bishri* [[180]] to Upper Mesopotamia, but from the north to the south, from *Djebel Bishri* down to Transjordan and Palestine, an area in those days not occupied by as strongly centralized states as those which we think were present in Mesopotamia in the first half of the 2nd millennium.

The distance from *Djebel Bishri* to, e.g., Jericho, is about the same as the distance from *Djebel Bishri* to Upper Mesopotamia. So the distance could hardly have prevented a change of the Benjaminite migratory route towards the south (although the terrain may have been more difficult along this route than along the usual one to Mesopotamia). The distance in time between the references to the Benjaminites in the Marian archive and the OT narratives about the Benjaminites is, on the other hand, formidable, and is generally considered the main reason for not accepting a straightforward identification between the two tribal entities.

The last-mentioned problem can, however, be compared to a hydra with many heads. One of these concerns the literary aspects. How old are the OT historical books? From the beginning, the middle or the end of the 1st mill. B.C.E.? The importance of the chronological gap between the Mari letters mentioning the Benjaminites and the biblical sources for the history of Benjamin will increase or decrease depending on decisions made in this area. Another issue is related to the main historical problem: when did the Benjaminites arrive in Palestine? Ca. 1200 B.C.E., which would be the natural consequence of an immigration theory like the one proposed by Alt and Noth? or later or earlier than this? It can hardly have happened after 1200 B.C.E., as nothing indicates a large-scale nomadic immigration into Palestine after 1200 B.C.E., at least not before the Roman and Arab Periods.[31] The date 1200 B.C.E. derives from the general Israelite immigration hypothesis, which, on the other hand, draws little support from recent discussion.[32] If anything like a nomadic migration happened in those [[181]] days, the scale of action must have been so small that nobody ever noticed it, and certainly not the archaeologists of the present time. Such a small-scale migration would, on the other hand, also seem inadequate to explain why we still possess a conquest tradition. Reductions like the one proposed seem more unlikely than ever.

It would, on the other hand, be possible to propose a date for the immigration of the Benjaminites before the "magical" year of 1200 B.C.E., and to connect this migration with the destructions that occurred at the end of the Middle Bronze Age. Conservatives and evangelicals alike would properly—or so I assume—be only too happy with such a theory, because here they would then have found the explanation for the destruction of

---

31. I, accordingly, have problems considering the proposal of G. A. Rendsburg, "The Date of the Exodus and the Conquest/Settlement: the Case for the 1100s," *VT* 42 (1992) 510–27, to be seriously meant. It is rather like a desperate wish that at least a tiny part of the settlement tradition should be preserved, and at all costs!

32. There is really no reason to discuss this subject any further—at least not in light of our present knowledge of the situation in Palestine at the end of the 2nd mill. B.C.E. The two studies by the late Gösta W. Ahlström, *The History of Ancient Palestine from the Palaeolithic Period to Alexander's Conquest* (JSOTSup 146; Sheffield 1993), and Thomas L. Thompson, *Early History of the Israelite People* (1992) seem more to stand at the end of this discussion than at the beginning of a renewed one.

Jericho around 1550 B.C.E.[33] To accept such a connection would, however, be premature, since it does not solve the problem of Ai, which in the
16th cent. B.C.E. would have been in ruins for more than 700 years,[34] and
the Benjaminites of the 16th cent. would still have to wait for another 400
years before they could negotiate with the inhabitants of Gibeon, as no
settlement was found on this spot before the Iron Age.[35]

One thing speaks in favor of an early date—apart from the fact that we
possess no precise information about this period (which is always an advantage when historical conjectures are involved)—the demographic
changes that occurred in the Central Highlands, which were almost completely devoid of village settlements in the Late Bronze Age, leaving only
a small number of insignificant townships in that part of Palestine.[36] It is
not before the beginning of the Iron Age that we should expect to see villages reappearing in Central Palestine.[37] An important argument against
such a theory of an early Benjaminite [[182]] migration is the fact that they
are not mentioned in any document from the Late Bronze Age, although
it should at the same time not be forgotten that in spite of the fact that
nomads were a well-known and established feature of LBA society, they
were known to the Egyptians solely as the *Shasu,* and to people writing in
cuneiform Akkadian as the *Sutu.* Neither the term *Shasu* nor the term
Sutu should be considered names of individual tribal groups. In the
Amarna Age they were used by the Egyptian as well as the Akkadian
scribes of Western Asia as general designations for "nomads." Thus human beings who, according to the Egyptians, should be considered members of the *Shasu* group, would in an Akkadian letter most likely turn up
as *Sutu.* Be this as it may, both Akkadian and Egyptian texts of the Late
Bronze Age provide information about nomadic groups living in Palestine
itself, or in its neighboring countries.[38]

---

33. The date, 1550 B.C.E., for the destruction of MB Jericho, is generally accepted; cf.
recently, T. A. Holland, *ABD* (1992) Vol. 3, 735–36. This destruction could, however, with
some reason be explained as the work of marauding Egyptian troops.

34. The former results of the French expedition under the direction of J. Marquet-
Krause (1933–35), have been reconfirmed by J. Callaway's more recent excavations (1964–
76), as Callaway himself has observed in several publications, the most recent being his article "Ai" in the *ABD* 1 (1992) 125–30.

35. This is the outcome of J. B. Pritchard's excavations, as maintained by himself in a
number of publications, for example in his article "Gibeon," *EAEHL* 2 (1976) 446–50.

36. Cf. T. L. Thompson, *The Settlement of Palestine in the Bronze Age* (TAVO Beihefte B
34; Tübingen 1979).

37. Cf. on this, above all, I. Finkelstein, *The Archaeology of the Israelite Settlement* (Jerusalem 1988).

38. On the *Sutu,* cf. among others, M. Heltzer, *The Suteans* (Naples 1981), and on the
Shasu, R. Giveon, *Les Bédouins Shosu des documents égyptiens* (Leiden 1971).

I have no intention to say that this proposal should be considered a well-founded one, and it would be difficult to object if colleagues would prefer to dismiss it without further discussion. However, even if the theory should be accepted as a kind of working hypothesis, it certainly does not prove the Bible to be true. The conquest narratives in the book of Joshua do not prove that the Benjaminites conquered Central Palestine or even migrated to this area at some time between, say 1800 B.C.E. and 1500 B.C.E. The only conclusion we can safely draw is that the inhabitants of Central Palestine may, at a later date, have preserved the general idea that they were not themselves indigenous, and that they may have maintained that their origins should not be sought in the area where they lived. Such an idea would not be remarkable, either among the inhabitants of the territory of Benjamin or among other comparable groups. It is certainly a coincidence, though an interesting one, that the social anthropologist Abdul Lutfiyya in his study of modern *Beitin* (Bethel) mentions that the inhabitants of this small Palestinian town consider themselves to be descendants of migrants from the Arabian Peninsula, although this claim seems to have little basis in the real world.[39] Thus the inhabitants of the former tribal territory of the Benjaminites in Palestine may never have been descendants of the ancient Benjaminites who once may [[183]] have migrated from Syria to Palestine—it is enough that they may have *considered* themselves to be descendants of former nomadic tribal groups, irrespective of the fact that this claim may from an historical angle not be true.

To conclude this section, it may be argued that, if any attention is to be paid to a theory like this, it may be used to illustrate my point that the OT historians had no idea of history as we see it. On the contrary, the example of the Benjaminite migration and conquest narratives may illustrate the ways and manners of these "historians." The writers who composed the book of Joshua were not forced to "invent" the idea of a conquest; they already possessed immigration traditions that circulated among the inhabitants of the territory north of Jerusalem. These writers, however, had no idea of the historical background of these legends and traditions, but it is obvious that this did not worry them. The inclusion of the Ephraimite hero of the conquest, i.e., Joshua, should, on the other hand, be regarded as a redactional way to change the outlook of the conquest traditions from a local to a pan-Israelite perspective.

I have often maintained that little of historical value has been preserved in the OT historical books. On the other hand, nobody ever forbade the OT historians to present something that may eventually turn out to be historical. The writers who created the book of Joshua will most

39. A. M. Lutfiyya, *Beytīn. A Jordanian Village* (The Hague 1966).

likely have been in possession of migration traditions. The concrete content of these traditions is impossible to recover today. The only thing we can safely argue is that the writers had no concrete idea of what may have happened or when it happened. They only turned a popular tradition into a piece of literary invention, part of a much larger description of *their* early history of Israel.

David and Omri

The above example will not prove my case. Perhaps the next can provide my argument with the necessary strength. My next example concerns the relations between David and Omri—in tradition and history. Both were kings of great importance and both were founders of great kingdoms. Or, at least this is what the OT has to say about David, while the importance of Omri has, at the same time, been reduced considerably by the OT historians. Omri's greatness can only be deduced from other documents from the ancient Near East that mention him or the members of his dynasty as important West-Semitic monarchs. The similarity between the two kings, however, [[184]] goes further. Just like David, who was succeeded by his brilliant son. Solomon, Omri was succeeded by his son, the no less important Ahab, the mightiest king the kingdom of Israel was ever to see. We could also provide more similarities like the one that says that both David and Omri were originally professional soldiers in the service of the previous king, whom they were to succeed, not because they personally murdered their masters, but because they removed the usurpers who were supposed to be the real scoundrels. It is a well-known fact that the author of "David's Rise" (1 Samuel 16–2 Samuel 7) has invested considerable interest in clearing his hero of accusations for having liquidated most, if not all of the dynasty of King Saul. Omri's case is more clear; he had only to remove and execute the usurper Zimri, who had rebelled against his and Omri's master, King Elah of Israel.

It is, however, a remarkable fact that from the ancient Near East there are plenty of references to the two Israelite kings, Omri and Ahab, while nothing has survived that has anything to say about David and Solomon, except for the narratives of the OT.[40] This could be a coincidence, and would perhaps not be very important if it was the only argument that could be called upon when questioning the historicity of David and Solo-

---

40. This is valid as far as the moment of writing is concerned, although non-confirmed rumors say that a new inscription has been found in an archaeological dump at Tell Dan, mentioning King Asah of the Beth-David as well as Ben (Bar?) Hadad. However, before its proper publication, it is hard to say anything conclusive based on this inscription. [[See now the essay by B. Halpern, below, pp. 415–426—*editor*.]]

mon. Much more attention should, however, be paid to the growing conviction that no United Monarchy and no Israelite empire ever existed in
the 10th cent. B.C.E., which had just a vague resemblance to the greatness
of Omri's kingdom. It is unnecessary to present the details in this place;
more will be said in an article of mine that will be published in early
1994.[41] Nevertheless, it may be enough to point to the size of the Jerusalem of David, the capital of a putative great empire which the biblical authors believed extended from the Egyptian border to the Euphrates. This
"great" city of Jerusalem in the days of David covered an area of no more
than four hectares allowing—by a very generous calculation—for ca. 2000
inhabitants (men, women and children) to live there. If we reckon with an
estimated average size of the family of about six persons this would mean
that ca. 300 grown-up males (between, say 17–18 years and 45 years) living
in Jerusalem would have been [[185]] present inside the walls of this truly
impressive "city."[42]

The kingdom of David was based on the tribal population of Judah,
and the Judaean population of course numbered more persons than
merely the inhabitants of Jerusalem. However, if we apply the same
method of calculation for the other sites of Judah in the 10th century, the
total population of this area will not have superceded [[*sic*; read ex-
ceeded]] 10–15,000 individuals, which allows for a male force of about
2000 persons.

These conclusions are based on the recently produced statistical material to be found in David Jamieson-Drake's study of the kingdom of
Judah, and his conclusions are absolutely worth mentioning. First of all,
he maintains that there was never an empire in the 10th cent. B.C.E., the
capital of which is supposed to have been Jerusalem, and secondly, that
the only thing that may have existed in this area may have been a small
and non-centralized chiefdom, ruled by the local chief, David. On the basis of this embryonic political assembly a small state or kingdom was to
arise in another 200 years, the shirt-lived kingdom of Judah, known from
the OT. In the future the results of Jamieson-Drake's study will certainly be
questioned, and archaeologists may object to the value of his evidence or
his way of presenting his material (although to date no challenge of importance has appeared from that quarter). It should in this connection not be

---

41. Cf. n. 1 above.
42. Based on a calculation system explained by S. Parpola, in J. M. Sasson, *Jonah* (AB
24B; New York 1990) 311–12, allowing for 358 persons per hectare (= 2.5 acres). That this
calcule is generous to ancient Jerusalem can be seen from the fact that according to the same
system, Hazor in the Bronze Age contained at least 25,000 persons, which is more than is
usually assumed today—although Y. Yadin himself believed that the population of Hazor may
have been even bigger than that.

overlooked that the only legitimate way to depart from Jamieson-Drake's conclusions will be to make it certain that his statistics are totally wrong or grossly misleading; they cannot be refuted by referring to the evidence of the OT. Furthermore, it seems to be a safe assumption that it will not be possible to present any archaeological material, that will make it likely that a great Judean kingdom of the 10th cent. B.C.E. ever existed.[43]

[[186]] It is a deplorable fact that no comparable statistically arranged analysis is available of the remains from the Northern Kingdom in the 10th cent. B.C.E. It is, on the other hand, possible to draw some conclusions based on the present material. To prove the greatness of David and especially Solomon, many scholars have referred to the similarity between public buildings to be found in many Palestinian sites dating back to the 10th cent. B.C.E. Such buildings may include the so-called "stables" present at Megiddo, Hazor and Beersheba, or the city gates of Megiddo, Hazor, Gezer and elsewhere, and they are understood to be evidence of Solomon's building activities as described in 1 Kgs 9:15–19. Strangely enough, this building activity seems not to have made its imprint on conditions in the capital—at least not in the parts of Jerusalem that are available for archaeological exploitation.[44]

To the best of my knowledge, no archaeologist is able to date anything from between, say the end of the 10th cent. and the beginning of the 9th cent. B.C.E. without allowing for a margin of error of about fifty years. This is not just another theory, but seems to be confirmed, for example by the age-old discussion between Yigael Yadin and Yohannan Aharoni concerning the date of the public building at Hazor and Megiddo—whether these should be Solomonic or only derive from the days of Omri and Ahab—a discussion that has yet to be terminated.[45] These buildings can

43. D. W. Jamieson-Drake, *Scribes and Schools in Monarchic Judah* (JSOTSup 109; Sheffield 1991). Now his results seem to be confirmed by the independent analysis of H. M. Niemann, *Herrschaft, Königtum und Staat. Skizzen zur soziokulturellen Entwicklung im monarchischen Israel (Forschungen zum Alten Testament* 6; Tübingen 1993). As a matter of fact, Niemann's results almost echo Jamieson-Drake's, although Niemann at the time of writing did not know Jamison-Drake's buch [[read book]], nor used the same method and material as his North American colleague.

44. Even if we allow for some historical reality behind the description of Solomon's building activities in Jerusalem, especially his construction of a palace complex and a small temple, this would hardly have changed the general conditions of the town, nor provided the town with a major increase of its population. The public area that consisted of the temple and the palace complex will not have been densely populated, but would mostly have consisted of workshops, archives (if necessary), ceremonial buildings and housing for the royal family, some retainers, and perhaps the highest officials and priests.

45. Cf. recently on Y. Aharoni's criticism of Yadin's Solomonic datings, Y. Aharoni, *The Archaeology of the Land of Israel* (Philadelphia 1982) 192–239. Cf. also the evaluation of this discussion in A. Mazar, *Archaeology of the Land of the Bible ca. 10,000–586 B.C.E.* (New York 1990) 381–82. Mazar favors Yadin's datings as do H. Weippert, *Palästina in vorhellenistischer*

hardly go back to Solomon, but it is still a matter of debate whether they were constructed in the 9th cent. B.C.E. or already at the end of the previous century, i.e., by King [[187]] Jeroboam and his successors.

In contrast to the so-called great kings of Judah, some evidence of an early Northern Kingdom may be available, and especially its first king, Jeroboam Ben Nebat, may be a historical ruler of this kingdom. I am referring to the presence of the famous lion seal, that was found at Megiddo early in this century, and which can be seen on the front page of every issue of the journal *JSOT*. The inscription on this seal reads "belongs to Shema, the servant of Jeroboam." The general opinion has been that this Jeroboam must be the second one who reigned over Israel, that is, in the 8th century, although the archaeological context of the finding may point to an earlier date which makes it a reasonable assumption that it really belongs to a person that was employed by Jeroboam I.[46] The seal was found in connection with the remains of public buildings that predate the "stables" at Megiddo, and it cannot, accordingly, be excluded that already before the days of Omri a centralized kingdom was in existence in Northern Palestine, on the basis of which Omri and Ahab were able to create a small empire which, in its own time, belonged among the important states of Western Asia.

If this is true, then we certainly have to discuss the background of the stories about David and Solomon in the books of Samuel and Kings. From a Judaean angle, it seems impossible to talk about an empire. However, the ancient world was rich in empires and great states, so it may be that the tradition of David's and Solomon's greatness simply derives from some other part of the Near East. Hence, it is possible that traditions which had originally nothing to do with Judah or conditions in Jerusalem in the 10th century B.C.E. were simply transformed into Judaean traditions. This can only be a qualified guess; the only safe thing to say is that in case we are looking for an old background for the stories about David and Solomon, this has nothing to do with Judah; instead of this it cannot be excluded that the idea of a great *Palestinian* kingdom simply derives from the tradition of the Omride kingdom, a tradition that was at a later date transferred to Judah and Jerusalem in order to become the new founding legend of the Judean kingdom (for my purpose here it is immaterial whether this happened in the pre- or post-exilic period). According

Zeit (*Handbuch der Archäologie. Vorderasien* 2/1; München 1988) 431. Among other scholars who have criticized Yadin's interpretation, we should mention K. M. Kenyon, "Megiddo, Hazor, Samaria and Chronology," *Bulletin of the Institute of Archaeology* 4 (1964) 143–56, and D. Ussishkin, "Was the 'Solomonic' City Gate at Megiddo Built by King Solomon?" *BASOR* 239 (1980) 1–18.

46. Cf. G. W. Ahlström, "The Seal of Shema᷉," *SJOT* 7 (1993) 208–15.

to the reworked tradition of former greatness, the two important Israelite kings were no longer Omri and Ahab, but David and Solomon, who—if they were at all historical personages—will [[188]] only have ruled over an uncoordinated chiefdom in the backyard of ancient Palestine.

This may be another example of OT writers who have included an old tradition without paying attention to its historical content. The outlook of these writers was certainly a Judaean one, and they accordingly transformed David and Solomon, the ancestors of the Judaean royal family, the House of David, into great kings, kings of all Israel and creators of great empires. It is, however, an interesting fact that nobody else seems to have known or been interested in these two "important" figures of the Israelite history, not even the Moabite king, Mesha, who only few years after the time of Solomon describes how he liberated his country from the yoke of Israel, a yoke which king Omri had imposed on his land. His inscription includes not a single reference to David who was supposed to be the "Israelite" king who subdued Moab (and who killed a great number of its male population: 2 Sam 8:2) [[But see the essay by B. Halpern that follows in this volume (esp. n. 9)—*Editor*]], nor does it say that Mesha's father, who according to Mesha himself reigned for "thirty years," had recovered Moab by fighting off the Israelite armies of Solomon.

I have already in an article published many years ago demonstrated what a cunning work the story of David's Rise really is.[47] It is also clear that external parallels to this narrative can be found in the documents from Western Asia, and here especially the inscription of King Idrimi of Alalach should be consulted (16 cent. B.C.E.).[48] There is accordingly no reason to continue along these lines. On the other hand, if it is correct to assume that the authors of David's Rise as well as the Succession Narrative have their ideas of the greatness of their [[189]] heroes from the tradition of the great Israelite kings, Omri and Ahab, this will be another example of how the OT historians felt free to manipulate traditions to serve their own

---

47. In my "David's Rise," *JSOT* 10 (1978) 2–25. Other authors have since then dealt more extensively with these matters. However, one important point should be noted, that the so-called "negative evidence," i.e., the stories of David's seemingly criminal acts, as well as the obvious cover-up in connection with the killings of respectively Abner, Ishba'al and Saul, which are often considered proofs of the basic historicity of "David's Rise," can just as well be seen as literary means to describe the hero as the clever "trickster." As a matter of fact, these matters make it more likely that "David's Rise" and "the Succession Narrative" are products of literary inventions as only the hero of the political propaganda (for example Idrimi) is blameless. I owe my thanks to Cand. theol. Pernille Carstens of Aarhus for presenting me with these insights into the nature of "the hero as trickster."

48. Cf. my *Ancient Israel* (Sheffield 1988) 53–54. The honor of having pointed at this connection should, however, be bestowed on G. Buccellati, cf. his "La 'Carriera' di David e quella di Idrimi, re di Alalac," *Bibbia e Oriente* 4 (1962) 95–99.

purposes irrespective of the original historical content of these traditions. They were also allowed to elaborate on these traditions by adducing literary patterns, fairytale style or whatever stylistic means suited their purpose.

Conclusions

The results based on these examples, which could be multiplied, if necessary—especially if we should direct our attention to the traditions of the Pentateuch—may lead us behind the present shape of the OT narratives, not only in order to show whether or not these are proper historical narratives connected with the real world or "only" brilliant fictions, but also to study the "minds" of the writers who employed such means—including historical traditions freed of their proper historical contexts—in order to create a "history of Israel" that conformed with the intentions of the writers and lived up to the expectations of their audience. In this they were seemingly not bothered by questions of historical correctness, and they hardly possessed the means and methods to distinguish between what was historically correct and what was only invention. In spite of this, it should be maintained that their enterprise was crowned with success, since these narratives have survived to the present time and have always been able to make their impression on the mind of the human race.

But let us stop here by returning to the beginning of this paper. The important issue was whether it is still possible to write a history of ancient Israel. In this connection it is important to notice that my three examples are different in the sense that they show three different ways of manipulating the "history." The first example quoted above shows how late information is referred back to the earliest times in order to create a picture of the Israelite sojourn in Egypt. The second example may demonstrate the opposite, that old traditions were at a later date employed to create a story of the Israelite conquest. The third example clearly exposes an author who has reshaped two great figures of Israelite history in order to create a new entity, the Judaean empire of David and Solomon, although this Judaean realm may never have existed.

To compose a history of Israel based on the information of the OT would be the same as to make a bargain with the authors who manipulated [[190]] this history in their own interest, that it, it would be to continue in the tradition of these authors and to make their viewpoints one's own. This is certainly a legitimate procedure as far as dealing with the *literary* content of such stories is concerned, but it is hardly advisable for the historian who may be interested in reaching the historical "truth" (whatever this means). It is certainly best to proceed with historical studies in such a way as not to confound literary intervention with historical events.[49]

Thus it would be correct to maintain that we are in possession of two "histories": on the one hand we have the history of Palestine, that is the history of the real world, and on the other the history of Israel, that is the *literary* history which is found in the OT. Sometimes these two histories overlap, as, for example, in the description of Sennacherib *ante muros* [['before the city walls']]; but more often the two histories have little or nothing in common. The situation of the modern historian can be summed up in the way of the late Gösta Ahlström who once explained to me: "If I were to write a history of Israel in the Iron Age, it would hardly cover more than a few pages, but if I were to write a history of Palestine in the same period, it would take a thousand pages." As is well known, he actually wrote those thousand pages.[50]

---

49. J. A. Soggin's three "histories" of Israel (*A History of Israel* [London 1984]; *Einführung in die Geschichte Israels und Judas* [Darmstadt 1991]; and *An Introduction to the History of Israel and Judah* [London 1993]) show an increasing understanding of the problems involved. They are, on the other hand, also examples of the kinds of problems that may appear when biblical and extra-biblical sources are believed to speak about the same thing, the history of biblical Israel. *Extra-biblical sources do not speak about biblical Israel.*

50. *The History of Ancient Palestine from the Palaeolithic Period to Alexander's Conquest.*

Erasing History
The Minimalist Assault on
Ancient Israel

BARUCH HALPERN

[[26]] The recent discovery at Tel Dan of a ninth-century B.C.E. inscription—the first extra-biblical reference to the House of David—is causing extraordinary contortions among scholars who have maintained that the Bible's history of the early Israelite monarchy is simply fiction. According to these scholars, the history of the Israelite monarchy was made up after the Jews went into exile following the Babylonian destruction of Jerusalem in 586 B.C.E.

What, then, is this embarrassing reference to the *dynasty* of David doing in a ninth-century B.C.E. Aramaic stela? One scholar has gone so far as to suggest that the inscription may be a fake, presumably salted in the tell by some desperate biblical literalist.[1] Other scholars in this camp have advanced arguments no less far-fetched in an attempt somehow to eliminate the reference to David—arguing, for example, that the three Semitic letters forming David's name should really be read as "uncle" or "kettle."[2]

How insubstantial these arguments are has been demonstrated elsewhere.[3] But this high-decibel dispute has focused attention once again on

Reprinted with permission from *Bible Review* 11/6 (1995) 26–35, 47.

1. F. H. Cryer, "On the Recently-Discovered 'House of David' Inscription," *Scandinavian Journal of the Old Testament* 8 (1994) 14–15. After defending the suggestion at length, Cryer concludes, "For the record, I doubt that the inscription is a forgery," citing Joseph Naveh's expertise in epigraphy and the "nuance . . . surrounding the language of the inscription." Cryer, however, also attempts to downdate the inscription to the eighth or seventh century B.C.E.

2. Philip R. Davies, "'House of David' Built on Sand," *Biblical Archaeology Review*, July/August 1994.

3. See David Noel Freedman and Jeffrey C. Geoghegan, "'House of David' Is There!" *Biblical Archaeology Review*, March/April 1995.

the reliability—or unreliability—of the Bible's account of the Israelite monarchy, from its origins to its demise.

In the last few years, numerous books have appeared that question the existence of David and Solomon.[4] These works have been written from literary, archaeological, anthropological and philosophical perspectives. What they share is a sharply "minimalist" approach to Israelite history. Their authors deny the existence of an Israelite state, or a [[28]] kingship in Jerusalem, until its attestation in external inscriptions—the earliest of which is in annals of the Assyrian king Shalmaneser III, which record events from 853 B.C.E. The first mention of Judah is a reference to King Ahaz in the annals of Tiglath-Pileser III, dated to 734 B.C.E.

A historian confronted with such "minimalist" contentions is tempted to adopt a dismissive posture. After all, these "minimalists" are not *real* historians. Biblical scholars such as Philip Davies, John Van Seters, Niels Lemche and their ilk have typically been trained in either theological seminaries or departments of Near Eastern studies or religion. Their exposure to history as it is practiced with respect to other times and other places is almost always marginal. Many years ago, my own graduate program in Near Eastern Languages refused my request for a minor field in the philosophy of history. What was important was acquiring philological skills and taking divinity-schoolish "exegesis" courses; history was perhaps a worthy end, but method—philological method, not historical method— was the centerpiece of the Albrightian tradition, indeed, of all professional biblical scholarship since the Middle Ages.

A good case can be made for learning philological method. And nothing is more repugnant to someone interested in truth than playing the "union card"—since so-and-so is not a "historian," his or her ideas can be dismissed a priori. The idea that one must have a doctorate in some field in order knowledgeably to discuss that field—whether history or comparative literature or whatever—is a chronic [[29]] affliction of academic discourse.[5] Credentialism in scholarship is much like used-car dealing: "Trust me: you wouldn't understand the reasons, but this is just the clunker, oops, vehicle, for you!"

---

4. Among the most recent and prominent are Thomas L. Thompson, *Early History of the Israelite People* (Brill, 1992); Philip R. Davies, *In Search of Ancient Israel* (Sheffield Academic Press, 1992); John Van Seters, *Prologue to History* (Yale University Press, 1992); and Gösta W. Ahlström, *History of Ancient Palestine* (Sheffield Academic Press, 1993).

5. This affliction originates in the insecurity of professionals who, like the American Bar Association, attempt to limit access to their professions. Like attorneys, professional scholars do this in two ways: by writing obscurely and by insisting on ticket-punching that has nothing to do with the issue at hand. The pretense is a maintenance of standards. The idea is to discourage competition—not so much from people who lack technical knowledge as from those who have it.

So the philological upbringing of recent entrants into the battle over the history of ancient Israel is not in itself an argument against their positions. Nevertheless, their exclusive reliance on philological method has led them to call into question various aspects of the biblical paradigm of Israelite history. "Call into question" is perhaps too mild a term. They reject, or ignore, the Bible's history *totus pro parte* [['the whole as the part']]—based on suspicion of some of its parts.

The difference between history and philology is simple. Philology is deterministic, deductive, mathematical; if we knew all the details, all the facts, then we could create a grand synthesis. The philological approach to history reduces the complexities of human interaction—the complexities of war, politics, society, economics, art and thought—to schemes of rules, laws and regulations. For a philological historian, things human can never be more than the sum of their parts, and their parts are few indeed.

Why is the United Monarchy, the Israel of David and Solomon, not "historical" according to the "minimalists"? Their argument is that there is a possibility that cannot be utterly excluded on the basis of the evidence that the whole construct is a lie. In other words, biblical descriptions especially in the books of Samuel and Kings—but also in other books—of a pan-Israelite state centered in Jerusalem in the tenth century are insufficient evidence on which to base a reconstruction of that period. Any reconstruction! For the biblical texts were brought to their final form only in the Persian era, in the sixth–fifth centuries B.C.E. In sum, Persian-era Judah schemed to create the myth of an earlier David and Davidic state.

This is a quintessentially philological, not a historical, argument. Its proponents attempt to isolate archaeological from textual data and to rely only, or at least overwhelmingly, on the former.[6] Such strategies are useful as heuristic devices: They answer the question, what is the minimum that we can know or reconstruct from one corpus of data? But precisely in discarding one sort of evidence, rather than simply setting it aside for the moment, the philological historians evince an overly mechanistic tendency concerning the construction of knowledge. The idea is that archaeological remains in themselves, without knowledge gleaned from other sources, place the interpreter in some superior [[31]] cognitive location.

The most extreme forms of this new historiography do not even engage the archaeology in an intellectually honest fashion. They appeal to archaeology, instead, to subvert the validity of the textual (biblical) presentation.

---

6. The main proponents are Thomas L. Thompson, J. W. Flanagan, D. W. Jamieson-Drake and Philip Davies. For a far better and actually constructive example of the method, see John S. Holladay, Jr., "Religion in Israel and Judah Under the Monarchy: An Explicitly Archaeological Approach," in *Ancient Israelite Religion. Essays in Honor of Frank Moore Cross*, eds. Patrick D. Miller, Paul D. Hanson and S. Dean McBride (Philadelphia: Fortress, 1987).

Individual passages in Samuel and Kings can be dated anywhere from the tenth to the fifth centuries B.C.E. The present edition of the books of Kings is no earlier than the mid-sixth century B.C.E. Individual sources of the Pentateuch are considerably older, although the present, combined narrative is no older than the sixth century and was possibly written as late as the fifth. Thomas Thompson and Davies, in particular, simply equate the content of the biblical books with the period of their literary completion, and deny any extensive use of earlier sources. John Van Seters is even more vehement: He dates the combination of J and E[7] (his J) in the Pentateuch quite late; in his view, no earlier sources were used in any Israelite writing about the past.

To quote Wolfgang Pauli, this "isn't even wrong."[8] The views of these critics would seem to be an expression of despair over the supposed impossibility of recovering the past from works written in a more recent present—except, of course, that they pretend to provide access to a "real" past in their own works written in the contemporary present.

Fortunately, we can test the validity of the "minimalist" contention by looking at the period of the Divided Monarchy recounted in the books of Kings, for which there happens to be abundant extra-biblical evidence. If the books of Kings were wholly, or even largely, a product of the Persian era and written without access to pre-exilic sources (as the "minimalists" claim with regard to the United Monarchy of David and Solomon), we should expect multiple errors both in chronology and in the names of major public figures, such as kings. Herodotus, writing at the very time Davies, Thompson and Van Seters posit the activity of our biblical authors, commits such errors with obstinate regularity, despite the fact that he traveled extensively in the lands on which he reports. He relied, it would seem, primarily on oral sources.

Yet the books of Kings *do* in fact preserve a very large assortment of accurate information on international affairs. In table 1, I briefly summarize some of this biblical history—biblical memory, really—for which we have extra-biblical confirmation. And these are far from being the only examples—for the books of Kings, with one exception arising from oral transmission, consistently get the names and dates of *foreign* kings right as well.

---

7. According to the documentary hypothesis, the first four books of the Pentateuch, or Torah, were created through a combination of three major narrative sources. The three sources are the J or Yahwist source (which starts with the Eden story in Genesis 2–3), the E or Elohist source (which includes the story of the binding of Isaac) and the P or Priestly source (which starts in Genesis 1, then resumes in Genesis 5). J and E were combined first; P was combined with J and E afterward, perhaps by the time of the Book of Deuteronomy. For a summary, see Richard Elliott Friedman, *Who Wrote the Bible?* (Summit, 1987).

8. See Jeremy Bernstein, "Julian. 1918–1994," *American Scholar* (Spring 1995).

Table 2. Israelite Kings in Non-biblical, Non-Israelite Inscriptions

Kings	Source	Text
United Monarchy		
David (ca. 1003–971 B.C.E.)	(1) Tel Dan stela (9th century B.C.E.)	(1) "house of David"
	(2) Stela of the Moabite king Mesha (ca. 849–820 B.C.E.)	(2) "house of David"
Northern Kingdom of Israel		
Omri (ca. 885–874 B.C.E.)	(1) Stela of the Moabite king Mesha (ca. 849–820 B.C.E.)	(1) "As for Omri, king of Israel, he humbled Moab many years . . . but I have triumphed over him and over his house, while Israel hath perished for ever."
	(2) Black Obelisk of the Assyrian king Shalmaneser III (ca. 858–824 B.C.E.)	(2) "In the 18th year of my rule . . . I received the tribute of the inhabitants of Tyre, Sidon, and of Jehu, son of Omri."
	(3) Annals of the Assyrian king Tiglath-Pileser III (ca. 744–727 B.C.E.)	(3) "The Land of Omri (Israel) . . . all its inhabitants and their possessions I led to Assyria."
	(4) Annals of the Assyrian king Sargon II (ca. 721–705 B.C.E.)	(4) "I conquered . . . all of the Land of Omri (Israel)."
Ahab (ca. 874–853 B.C.E.)	Kurkh Monolith of the Assyrian king Shalmaneser III (ca. 858–824 B.C.E.)	"[Karkara] brought along to help him . . . 10,000 foot soldiers of Ahab, the Israelite."
Jehoram (ca. 852–841 B.C.E.)*	Tel Dan stela (9th century B.C.E.)	"[Jeho]ram"
Jehu (ca. 841–814 B.C.E.)	Black Obelisk of the Assyrian king Shalmaneser III (ca. 858–824 B.C.E.)	"The tribute of Jehu, son of Omri; I received from him silver, gold . . . tin, a staff for a king."
Joash (ca. 805–790 B.C.E.)	Tell Al-Rimah stela of Adad-Nirari III (ca. 873–810 B.C.E.)	"Joash (*Ia-'a-su*) the Samarian"
Menahem (ca. 740 B.C.E.)	Annals of the Assyrian king Tiglath-Pileser III (ca. 744–727 B.C.E.)	"As for Menahem, I overwhelmed him like a snow-storm and he . . . fled like a bird."
Pekah (ca. 735 B.C.E.)	Annals of the Assyrian king Tiglath-Pileser III (ca. 744–727 B.C.E.)	"The Land of Omri . . . all its inhabitants and their possessions I led to Assyria. They overthrew their king Pekah and I placed Hoshea as king over them."
Hoshea (ca. 730–722 B.C.E.)	Annals of the Assyrian king Tiglath-Pileser III (ca. 744–727 B.C.E.)	"They overthrew their king Pekah and I placed Hoshea as king over them."
Southern Kingdom of Judah		
Ahaziah (ca. 841 B.C.E.)**	Tel Dan stela (9th century B.C.E.)	"[Ahaz]yahu"
Uzziah? (early 8th century B.C.E.)	Annals of the Assyrian king Tiglath-Pileser III (ca. 744–727 B.C.E.)	"[I received] the tribute of the kin[gs . . . A]zriau (Uzziah?) from Iuda (Judah)."
Ahaz (ca. 740–725 B.C.E.)	Annals of the Assyrian king Tiglath-Pileser III (ca. 744–727 B.C.E.)	"I received the tribute of . . . Ahaz (*Ia-u-ha-zi*) of Judah."
Hezekiah (ca. 725–696 B.C.E.)	(1) Taylor Prism of the Assyrian king Sennacherib (ca. 704–681 B.C.E.)	(1) "As to Hezekiah, the Jew, he did not submit to my yoke . . ."
	(2) Bull Inscription of Sennacherib	(2) "I laid waste the large district of Judah and made the overbearing and proud Hezekiah, its king, bow in submission."
	(3) Nebi Yebus Slab of Sennacherib	(3) "I . . . put the straps of my yoke upon Hezekiah, its (Judah's) king."
Manasseh (ca. 696–642 B.C.E.)	(1) Prism B of the Assyrian king Esarhaddon (ca. 680–669 B.C.E.)	(1) "I called upon the kings . . . on the other side of the Euphrates . . . Manasseh, king of Judah."
	(2) Rassam Cylinder of the Assyrian king Ashurbanipal (ca. 668–633 B.C.E.)	(2) "Manasseh, king of Judah"
Jehoiachin (ca. 597–560 B.C.E.)	Ration documents of the Babylonian king Nebuchadnezzar II (ca. 605–562 B.C.E.)	"10 (*sila* of oil) to Jehoiachin ([*Ia*]-'-*kin*), king of Judah (*Ia*[. . .])."

*The Jehoram referred to in the Tel Dan stela may have been the Judahite king of the same name, who ruled ca. 846–843 B.C.E.

**The Ahaziah referred to in the Tel Dan stela may have been the king of the northern kingdom of Israel who bore the same name and ruled ca. 852–851 B.C.E.

This litany is not meaningful to the biblical "minimalists" because they simply deny the historical content of the parts of Samuel and Kings that cannot be checked in external sources. In this way, the "minimalists" abdicate that primary responsibility of historians: to understand a source's purposes, and then to ascertain the received particulars on which its authors base their views and the thinking underlying their reconstructions or embellishments. And the minimalists also evade the evidence from the archaeological record.

There is not much doubt that the archaeological record of the eighth–sixth centuries comports in almost every particular with the general political picture we derive from the biblical record, critically regarded.

Here, however, I want to comment on the period about which there has been the most controversy, the period when Israel was forming as a nation, variously called the pre-monarchic period, the period of the Judges or the period of the settlement in Canaan. The "minimalist" technique is succinctly illustrated by this controversy—not only their [[32]] approach to the biblical text, but their way of dealing with the archaeological materials.

The population of the territory of Israel exploded in the period preceding the Israelite monarchy, in the 13th–11th centuries B.C.E. (what archaeologists call Iron Age I). The facts clearly indicate that the biblical tradition of a pre-monarchic period of settlement and expansion is perfectly reasonable. At the beginning of this population explosion comes the reference to Israel in hieroglyphics in the famous Merneptah Stela from Egypt.[9] This late-13th-century B.C.E. inscription contains the earliest reference to Israel; it conforms nicely with the picture supplied by the abundant archaeological evidence from the next century of Israel's presence in Canaan.[10]

The "minimalists," however, call our attention to the fact that Israelite material culture at this time was virtually identical with that of settlements in Transjordan that would later be incorporated into Ammon and Moab. Thus, they argue, Israel was an indigenous people, not a people formed outside who entered the land with their ethnic identity already formed, as the Bible claims. But the identity of Israelite and Ammonite or Moabite

---

9. For information on the Merneptah Stela (also called the Israel Stela), see the following articles in *Biblical Archaeology Review*: Frank J. Yurco, "3,200-Year-Old Picture of Israelites Found in Egypt," September/October 1990; and Anson F. Rainey, "Rainey's Challenge," November/December 1991. See also "Frank Moore Cross—An Interview, Part 2: The Development of Israelite Religion," *Bible Review*, October 1992.

10. See, for example, Baruch Halpern, "Settlement of Canaan," *Anchor Bible Dictionary* (New York: Doubleday, 1992), with bibliography. Interestingly, in the handful of sites where archaeologists have bothered to collect animal bones, pigs are notable for their almost complete absence from what we would normally identify as Israelite levels.

material culture in Iron Age I is hardly evidence of anything other than that the same influences were at work on each, as distinct from the different forces at work in the coasts and lowlands. In fact, much later biblical testimony claims that these cultures were of the same vintage, and indeed the same ancestry, as Israel's.

Another point of difference is the date of the origin of the Israelite state. Davies, Lemche, Thompson and D. W. Jamieson-Drake all downdate these events drastically. They move the beginning of the monarchy of the Davidic dynasty in Jerusalem down to the eighth century, instead of the tenth. One would have thought that the preservation of the memory of Shishak's campaign, just after Solomon's reign, was evidence that the Biblical testimony here was reliable—since there is epigraphic evidence of the reality of that campaign in the tenth century B.C.E.[11] That Judah was called the House of David, given references both in the Mesha stela and in the Tel Dan stela,[12] is not in doubt, except among "minimalists" fighting a rearguard action for their original denials of the historical value of 2 Samuel and 1 Kings 1–11.

[[33]] Moreover, the fact that Kings is so accurate about the history of the eighth–seventh centuries, *when the Temple still stood*, suggests that our authors had both continuity and records on their side in naming the Temple's builder.

And then there is the archaeology to consider: Similar tenth-century fortifications with nearly identical six-chamber gates have been found at Megiddo, Hazor and Gezer, three towns the Book of Kings says Solomon fortified (1 Kgs 9:15). One can argue about the attribution of the gates to Solomon (and archaeologists do). But since the upper gate at Gezer was very likely the one destroyed by Shishak, whose exploit is attested epigraphically, and since Megiddo fell in the same campaign, it seems probable that traditions of a national state in the tenth century are accurate.

What is more, as David Ussishkin has shown, the major palace at tenth-century Megiddo (strata VA–IVB), Palace 1723, matches the Bible's description of the Jerusalem palace in 1 Kings 6 to a tee.[13]

---

11. See Ronald S. Hendel, "Finding Historical Memories in the Patriarchal Narratives," *Biblical Archaeology Review*, July/August 1995.

12. For the Mesha Stela, see the following articles in the May/June 1994 issue of *Biblical Archaeology Review*; André Lemaire, "'House of David' Restored in Moabite Inscription"; "Translation of the Mesha Stela"; and "Can You See the Letters?" For the Tel Dan inscription, see the following articles in *Biblical Archaeology Review*, "'David' Found at Dan," March/April 1994; Davies, "'House of David' Built on Sand," July/August 1994; and Freedman and Geoghegan, "'House of David' Is There!" March/April 1995.

13. See David Ussishkin, "King Solomon's Palace and Building 1723 at Megiddo," *Israel Exploration Journal* 16 (1966).

Beginning in the tenth century, moreover, come various kinds of evidence suggesting that Israelite culture was characterized by large public works and social differentiation—as indicated by excavations at Izbet Sartah, Tel Far'ah North, Tel en-Nasbeth and elsewhere. The tenth century also saw a regularization of settlement in the central Negev, reflecting an order imposed on pastoral elements on the fringe of Judah (which was then undone by Shishak's raid). All this indicates a centralized governmental authority.

The "minimalists" remained unmoved by such evidence. They maintain instead that Jerusalem's population in the early Iron Age II was insufficient for it to be the center of a real state. But a town of 5,000 people was a large one in Iron Age Israel. Besides, new capital cities like Ottawa, Washington, D.C., or Brasilia tend to have medium to small populations: Part of the object of founding a capital on the border between rival groups, or away from traditional constituencies, is to free government from the influence exerted by surrounding populations.[14]

Israel of the United Monarchy in the territory of inland Canaan maintained a policy of distancing the domestic population from state centers. Megiddo strata VA–IVB and Hazor strata X–IX are both tenth-century state centers without domestic population: Only monumental architecture is present on top of the mounds.[15] This is strong archaeological evidence for the presence of a central state.

So the archaeology and the epigraphy and the critical assessment of biblical texts all land us in the same place. And that leaves us with the question, why are these revisionists so insistent?

The answer is complex.

As late as the 1970s, the standard histories of ancient Israel were nothing more than summaries of the biblical record, occasionally sprinkled with supposed archaeological illustrations. What the Book of Kings said was history. What Exodus said was history. Sometimes, what Genesis said was history. Figures such as William F. Albright, John Bright, George E. Mendenhall and Ephraim A. Speiser[16] were still holding the line on the

---

14. We find the same phenomenon for Nabonidus at Teima and various Assyrian kings, such as Sargon, at Dur-Sharrukin (Khorsabad).

15. The same might be true at Beth-Shean V, but special problems, including the ongoing presence of Egyptian elements, attach to the site.

16. See William F. Albright, *Archaeology and the Religion of Israel* (Baltimore: Johns Hopkins, 1942); idem, *The Archaeology of Palestine* (Baltimore: Penguin, 1961; originally published 1949); and idem, *From the Stone Age to Christianity* (Garden City, NY: Anchor/Doubleday, 2nd ed., 1957). John Bright, *A History of Israel* (Philadelphia: Westminster, 3rd edition, 1981). George E. Mendenhall, "Biblical History in Transition" in G. Ernest Wright, ed., *The Bible and the Ancient Near East* (Garden City, NY: Doubleday, 1961); see also Mendenhall, "Ancient Oriental and Biblical Law," *Biblical Archaeologist* 17 (1954), and idem, "Covenant Forms in Israelite

existence of a "patriarchal age." No one with a whiff of independence from the biblical worldview accepted this as reality. The evidence for the patriarchal age was, at best, evidence of the antiquity of some social practices possibly reflected in the narratives. That such practices might have survived after their early attestation was never taken into account by Albright et al. This defect was seized upon by Van Seters, and it forms the essence of his critique: Evidence of social practices that allegedly defined the patriarchal age could be found in later periods as well. As for some other social practices, Kenneth Kitchen argues the reverse—that the Bible sometimes accurately describes practices no longer current when the biblical narratives were written down—and there is a great deal to be said for his point of view.[17] But the fact remains that the "Albrightian" defense of the patriarchs as historical led to serious fissures in the field.

The biblical accounts of the Exodus and the conquest of the Promised Land occasioned similar problems. As early as the 1850s, critical scholars attempted to make historical sense of these narratives without according them unquestioned fidelity. The inevitable revolt against the tyranny of orthodoxy, led by some of the scholars now regarded as extremist revisionists—Van Seters, Thompson, Gösta Ahlström—had been presaged by continental scholars such as Martin Noth and Ivan Engnell, who were themselves heirs to 19th-century scholarship that had indicted the testimony of the conquests described in the Book of Joshua on the basis of materials in Judges. The modern representatives of this movement, such as Lemche and F. H. Cryer, have, however, gone much farther than the preceding generation ever meant to go.

[[34]] At the extremes, the reaction against tradition is emotional, not intellectual.

. If you want to understand the origin of these recent contentions, go back to the Deists, like Thomas Jefferson and Thomas Paine, who scoffed at the Bible's inconsistencies and contradictions. The defenders of the faith discovered source criticism and claimed that Moses and some subsequent figures relied on divergent sources. The Higher Criticism was in fact invented as a defense against attacks on the Church.

The Deist critique of the reliability of biblical narrative focused on the Pentateuch. The modern "minimalists" simply extend this rationalist critique to the books of Kings. But there is an enormous distinction between

---

Tradition," *Biblical Archaeologist* 17 (1954). Ephraim A. Speiser, *Genesis*, Anchor Bible Series (Garden City, NY: Doubleday, 1964).

17. Kenneth A. Kitchen, "The Patriarchal Age: Myth or History?" *Biblical Archaeology Review*, March/April 1995; see also Ronald S. Hendel, "Finding Historical Memories in the Patriarchal Narratives," *Biblical Archaeology Review*, July/August 1995.

legend presented as though it were historical fact (much of the Pentateuch) and history presented as such (the books of Samuel and Kings). Only a philologist could expect that an accurate written history must be devoid of untruth. The difference between history, which is one type of fiction, and romance, which is an altogether different type of fiction, is that the historian tries to avoid communicating what was not so. To this end, particularly [[35]] in antiquity, the historian might use vehicles of presentation—such as the made-up speeches by Thucydides and Josephus. Other vehicles of presentation used by ancient historians include psychologizing and the assignment of abstract causation—for example, economics, geopolitics, providence, luck. All this may be literally false but may still communicate a view of what the issues were at the time. This is true of much modern history as well, although it takes different forms.

Understanding history requires that the reader distinguish literal statements from the intent with which they are made. Even outdated works of history, works that were dead wrong, remain works of history after their reconstructions are discredited. In history, conscious intention is everything. Thompson's work is history, even if I thoroughly disagree with it. Amazing, then, that he does not accord the same courtesy to his ancient colleagues, in light of clear evidence that they were trying their best, in Samuel and Kings, to get things right.

The dialogue has deteriorated as well. A recent article by Lemche and Thompson accuses opponents of "the worst abuses of the biblical archaeological movement of the 1930s–1960s."[18] What had the opponents done? They had read the text *bytdwd* as house (*byt*) of David (*dwd*). These letters appear on the Tel Dan inscription, a public inscription of an Aramean king; the text also mentions "the king of Israel." The editors of the inscription very logically read "house of David"—the phrasing resembling expressions in Assyrian royal inscriptions, such as "son of Omri" and "house/son of Agusi"—and concluded that it referred to the kingdom of Judah. The "minimalists" focused on the fact that there was no word-divider between *byt* (house of) and *dwd* (David), arguing that the six Semitic letters really spell the name of a village otherwise unknown. That the presence or absence of a word-divider might determine this issue, pushed hard especially by Davies, is nonsense.[19]

---

18. Niels P. Lemche and Thomas L. Thompson, "Did Biran Kill David? The Bible in the Light of Archaeology," *Journal for the Study of the Old Testament* 64 (1994).

19. To put the matter simply, the two words are in construct—what T. O. Lambdin has called "close juncture": *byt* by itself, means 'house'; *byt* in front of *dwd*, means 'the house of [David]'. The determined noun, governed by the genitive proper noun, acquires considerable meaning in a construct relationship. This, and the fact that *byt* could not have stood alone, is the reason the word-divider is missing in the inscription (see Freedman and Geoghegan, "'House of David' Is There!").

The venom that has poured into print from the "minimalists" (they re-ject this soubriquet) and the traditionalists (ditto) is a matter of public record. Oxen have been gored all 'round, and yet "minimalists" complain about abuse—as though they have not been delivering it with regularity, in-sinuating that the objects of their scorn, for example, are [[47]] fundamen-talists.[20] Indeed, one member of the "minimalist" camp has even urged that Philip Davies adopt that peculiarly American form of intellectual vin-dication, the lawsuit. Why? Anson Rainey denied that Davies was an epig-raphist, a specialist in inscriptions such as that on the Tel Dan stela. Neither party to that sidebar looks altogether rosy: Which is better, a union card or an attorney?

To return to substance: What is particularly disturbing about the "minimalists" is their willful failure to distinguish between Kings, with its synchronistic chronologies and distinctive Israelite and Judahite regnal formularies, and the Pentateuch. They simply ignore the continuity of written documentation from Solomon's time to that of the writing of Kings, along with oral and written accounts that undoubtedly exaggerated the accomplishments of these kings.[21] The Tel Dan inscription unmistak-ably indicates the existence of a dynasty in the ninth century B.C.E. that traced its origin to David.

The recent contentiousness about David's existence, and, indeed, the periodic redating of all biblical narrative down to the Persian era, will prove to be essentially sterile. To know, after all, that David existed is to know very little indeed. To reason from biblical, archaeological and, now, epigraphic evidence that he founded a dynastic state says next to nothing about his methods or achievements. The best evidence for these remains the biblical record; and yet, that record is precisely the propaganda of his dynasty, and is extremely unreliable in its particulars.[22] Reasoned deconstruction of

20. In "Did Biran Kill David?" for example, Lemche and Thompson write: Avraham Bi-ran's and Joseph Naveh's *editio princeps* "distorted what could have been a discussion of the inscription . . . into an appeal for a fundamentalistic reading of the Bible." Of E. Puech's very competent treatment, they write: "Here is a very learned example of how not to proceed with inscriptions."

21. For information on Israelite kings, see the following articles in *Biblical Archaeology Review*: Ephraim Stern, "How Bad Was Ahab?" March/April 1993; Tammi Schneider, "Did King Jehu Kill His Own Family?" January/February 1995; André Lemaire, "Royal Signature: Name of Israel's Last King Surfaces in a Private Collection," November/December 1995; and Dan Gill, "How They Met: Geology Solves Mystery of Hezekiah's Tunnelers," July/August 1994.

22. In "Text and Artifact: Two Monologues?" (in a forthcoming volume of essays, ed. Larry Silberstein and David Small [New York University Press [[now published in *The Archae-ology of Israel: Constructing the Past, Interpreting the Present* (ed. N. A. Silberman and D. Small; JSOTSup 237; Sheffield: Sheffield Academic Press, 1997) 311–41]]), I argue that the main pur-pose of 2 Samuel is to acquit David of charges of serial murder, of which he was very likely guilty—which implies that the book stems from David's reign or the early part of Solomon's.

what are often exaggerated claims, typical of Near Eastern royal texts, is the only method by which some sort of historical reality can be approximated. Jettisoning the texts altogether will never generate positive results.

As minister responsible for Britain's re-armament, Winston Churchill was once asked, "Where will it all end?" "The gentleman reminds me," Churchill replied, "of the man who received a telegram from Brazil informing him that his mother-in-law had died, and asking for instructions. He answered, 'Embalm, cremate, bury at sea. Take no chances!'"

At the base of the extremism of contemporary "minimalism" lies a hysteria no less profound than that one. One may question the motives of the hysteria—they differ in different scholars. In one the motivation may be a hatred of the Catholic Church, in another of Christianity, in another of the Jews, in another of all religion, in another of authority.

This hysteria inheres in the nature of biblical debates. There is a tremendous emotional investment on the part of many scholars in the biblical presentation, and an equal and opposite reaction against that investment on the part of many others. Biblical archaeology has a nasty reputation for ideological polarization.

Where will it all end? Cacophony in scholarship is normal, and uncritical allegiance to the biblical text is, sad to say, common among students and a significant slice of scholars. So the reaction is nothing but normal. How should the scholars in the middle react? The answer is disappointing to those who assume that public discussion is the only discussion. In fact, competent scholars write more for one another than for any public forum, and content themselves with persuading colleagues they respect. In such an environment, only the best scholars have access to the most detailed treatments of the evidence. By and large, those scholars continue to resist the "minimalists'" overtures.

Historical Criticism and Literary Interpretation
Is There Any Common Ground?

JOHN BARTON

[[3]] There are of course many more than two positions among scholars about the way to interpret biblical texts. But my shorthand terms, "historical criticism" and "literary interpretation," point to a tendency to polarization in our field which would be widely acknowledged. Biblical studies at the moment well illustrate the phenomenon structuralists used to be so interested in, the binary opposition, and a few such pairs will be enough to identify the two trends involved: diachronic vs. synchronic; historical vs. literary; objectivist vs. subjectivist; empirical investigation vs. literary theory; what the text meant vs. what the text means (or what readers may mean by it).

Discussion between supporters of what might be called the right-hand or left-hand options in this list has become rather acrimonious, where it has not been broken off altogether, and there is considerable mutual suspicion and even mutual contempt. Occasionally a writer appears who tries to bridge the gap—one that comes to mind is Eep Talstra, whose monograph *Solomon's Prayer*[1] is a conscious attempt to combine a synchronic with a diachronic approach to 1 Kings 8. But they do not disturb the growing sense that our armies, like so many we read of in the Old Testament, are drawn up on opposite hills with a great valley between. The difference, of course, is that in our case each camp thinks it is the other that contains the Philistines.

Reprinted with permission from *Crossing the Boundaries: Essays in Biblical Studies in Honour of Michael D. Goulder* (ed. S. E. Porter, P. M. Joyce, and D. E. Orton; Leiden: Brill, 1994) 3–15.

1. E. Talstra, *Solomon's Prayer: Synchrony and Diachrony in the Composition of 1 Kings 8,14–61* (Contributions to Biblical Exegesis and Theology, 3; Kampen: Kok Pharos, 1993).

In asking whether there is any common ground I am not pretending to occupy a neutral position myself. Nor do I want to argue that there are really no fundamental differences between them, as if peace could be restored by a lazy eclecticism—treating contradictory critical theories as though they were simply alternative [[4]] items on a menu from which students of the Bible can choose whatever happens to appeal to them. The conflicts are not illusory or trivial, but reflect passionately held convictions about what it is to read a text. The extent of the disagreement, at a high theoretical level, can be gauged from the fact that the two sides never agree even in formulating just what the disagreement between them is. Typically, people committed to so-called "historical" criticism tend to be objectivists, and hence to argue in terms of what texts "really" or "actually" mean; whereas most literary interpretations regard it as obvious that texts have a plurality of possible meanings. The two positions thus do not clash head on, differing about what the text means; they slide past each other without real engagement. Whereas historical criticism has the goal of advancing our objective knowledge about a text, most literary critics think this is a hopeless quest. They talk not of where the evidence inexorably leads us but of the kinds of meanings that can be found now that we are working with a new, post-historical-critical paradigm.

"Paradigm"-language seems to have become embedded in our current discussions of method,[2] and it perfectly illustrates my point. For it is not as if everyone agrees that there is something called the "historical-critical paradigm," and that scholars committed to new methods attack this while traditionalists defend it. That *is* how it looks to those who attack historical criticism. But for historical critics themselves, to use "paradigm" language is already to have sold the pass. The "paradigm" paradigm, if I may call it that, *already presupposes* the relativism that traditional scholars rightly see, and (whether rightly or not) object to, in newer methods. "Paradigm" language implies that there are many valid ways of reading texts, and I choose this one, or that one. But what we have come to call "historical" criticism never saw the matter in those terms. Historical criticism was never meant to be one valid option among many: it was supposed to yield truth, and truth independent of the outlook of the investigator.

There is thus no way, at the theoretical level, in which older- and newer-style critics can even communicate their differences, let alone find agreement. They cannot even agree what it is they disagree about. On both sides there is an awareness of belonging [[5]] to irreconcilably opposed parties, which do not even enjoy a shared vocabulary for debate and are not, in fact, talking about the same things. A shared antipathy to "historical"

---

2. Compare the comments on this in my Oxford inaugural lecture, *The Future of Old Testament Study* (Oxford: Clarendon, 1993).

criticism unites such diverse critics as those committed to "close readings" of the Bible in a humanistic vein (Alter, Kermode, Josipovici, Sternberg), and more experimental interpreters who draw on post-structuralism, deconstruction, or various post-modernist modes of interpretation. And it is matched by the united front against a common enemy that can now be seen among the otherwise equally diverse proponents of traditional historical criticism. Very few envoys pass between these two opposing forces; at most the odd giant challenging opponents to single combat.

All this may make the question which forms my title seem pointless. There is no common ground unless we abandon the claims of both groups to intellectual seriousness, and trivialize the questions they ask. However, I want to suggest that there are more similarities between our two approaches than appears on the surface, and that it is possible to take their ultimate incompatibility seriously without thereby making *all* dialogue between them impossible or unfruitful. First of all I shall examine two (possibly unexpected) resemblances between so-called "historical" criticism and at least certain types of literary approach; then I shall try to point to two ways in which collaboration seems to be essential if interpretation is to make any progress.

I

There are two points of resemblance between these apparently so different approaches to criticism. First, I would argue that "historical" criticism has always been more like literary interpretation than it seems.

Traditional critics, when reviewing literary studies of the Bible, tend to use the distinction sometimes made by contrasting *ex*egesis—understood as exposition of what is actually said *in* the text—with *eis*egesis, pseudo-Greek for reading one's own ideas into a text that does not really contain them. Eisegesis of course is a term of abuse, but most current literary theory would regard the "reading in" of the reader's ideas into the text as unavoidable, and not just unavoidable but something it makes no sense to try to avoid: reader-response criticism only states explicitly what most other literary critics take for granted. Historical critics on the [[6]] other hand try to avoid "reading in" wherever possible. This apparently amounts to a complete contrast between the two styles of criticism.

However, once we move from theory to practice, the distinction becomes far more blurred, and it would be good if critics on both sides were to recognize this. It was acknowledged a long time ago in perhaps a surprising place, E. D. Hirsch's important book, *Validity in Interpretation*[3]—

---

3. E. D. Hirsch, *Validity in Interpretation* (New Haven and London: Yale University Press, 1967) 164–69.

surprising because Hirsch has come to be seen by many as the epitome of opposition to the more reader-oriented methods of recent years. Hirsch has a section called "The Self-Confirmability of Interpretation." This makes the point that all readings of texts are in some measure self-confirming. The reason for this is that any reading, however tentative, *orders* the text in at least a preliminary way, imposing structures of under-standing upon it. Hirsch's observation, made from a "historical" point of view, is in practice very close to what might be said by a "post-critical" literary interpreter.

The theoretical basis is different in the two cases. Proponents of "historical" and "literary" methods will argue about whether what is going on in reading is the recognition of a meaning already present in the text, or the attribution of meaning to the text (or indeed the discovery of meaning in dialogue with the text). Hirsch of course believes it is the first—recognition rather than attribution. So an irreconcilable theoretical difference remains. But the *mental processes* involved seem almost identical, and the reinforcement of the interpreter's initial intuition of meaning by the way the text is read in the light of it feels just the same for both sorts of interpreter. The psychological experience of exegetical work cannot itself adjudicate between the different modes of criticism, but is compatible with either: a point, I believe, that it would be valuable for both sides to recognize.

The same point might be made in a different way. Historical critics and their detractors sometimes seem to agree in thinking that historical criticism has about it a certain preference for "hard facts." Historical critics, so literary interpreters allege, are *not* interested in the finished form of a text as it lies before us, but only in the bits from which (perhaps) it was originally put together. Unable to see the wood for the trees, they have no [[7]] appreciation for the literary whole. Historical critics themselves nowadays often tend to endorse this way of looking at their own work, differing only in seeing it as perfectly correct. Both they and their opponents are thus apt to present the task of historical criticism in rather positivistic terms. If this were true, then the amount of common ground between historical and literary criticism would certainly be very small.

I am not at all convinced, however, that it is true. If we take the most obviously fragmentative branch of historical criticism, source analysis, still flourishing all over the world despite the supposed paradigm-shift away from it: there can be no doubt that the underlying perceptions that make such criticisms possible are essentially literary ones, related to the attempt to appropriate a text as a living whole, cohering in all its parts. Its German name, *Literarkritik* [['literary criticism']], is not the misnomer people sometimes think it. The difference between the different sorts of critic is a matter of how soon they give up this attempt in the face of a perception that they are dealing with recalcitrant material. Literary critics today, like other kinds of "final form" interpreters, generally see themselves as having a duty to persist with a holistic approach until the whole text is in focus as a unified entity, even if this involves suppressing intuitive suspicions that the text was not originally designed by anyone to have exactly its present form. Source critics on the other hand allow such suspicions to have full rein, and are content when they have divided the text into sections each of which in itself has a coherent shape. But in both cases the mental processes involved are literary. Both are concerned with the *Gestalt* of the text, with the attempt to grasp it as a comprehensible whole. Historical critics are much readier than modern literary interpreters to accept the possibility that the text is not such a whole. But the question ought to be discussible between them, not regarded as just a matter of incommensurable expectations.

Here, then, is one way in which so-called historical and so-called literary interpretations are close in practice, however different in theoretical aims and intentions. Both imply the quest for some unitary grasp of the text, an interest in its *Gestalt*. Both must engage with the text's discrete details; neither can rest content with describing the text as no more than these details.

A second resemblance between historical and literary method can be found by looking at an equal and opposite point. If historical criticism is more like literary interpretation than people think, so literary interpretation is seldom in practice completely [[8]] detached from historical interests. There are admittedly extreme (or ultra-consistent) forms of literary interpretation in our field where synchronic reading is treated as an absolute, and historical questions are simply not allowed. But in practice such cases are rare. Far more often a literary reading is one in which these questions are indeed not foregrounded, but are present nonetheless. This can produce what may correctly be criticized as inconsistency, but on the other hand may be seen as a sign that the lines of communication are still open.

The work of Robert Alter[4] presents interesting examples. On the one hand, it is obvious to any reader that Alter is cool towards any suggestion that we should treat biblical texts as collections of fragments or as composed from several sources. His criticism is an attempt to expound the biblical text as a unity. The unity extends even beyond the bounds of individual books: thus stories in the Former Prophets can be treated as alluding to stories in Genesis, for example, irrespective of any historical

---

4. See especially R. Alter, *The Art of Biblical Narrative* (London: George Allen & Unwin, 1981), and *The World of Biblical Literature* (London: SPCK, 1992).

questions of relative *date*. Such intertextuality is so intense as logically to imply that most of the books of the Bible are parts of a greater whole. Alter's assumptions seem not unlike those of canonical criticism, though of course without the theological implications.

But the conceptual basis for Alter's work seems to me often to shift in a puzzling way between historical and non-historical considerations. All we have, he argues in one mood, is the biblical text, and questions about what may underlie it are more or less unaskable, certainly unanswerable. Only a rather "unliterary" person would be interested in such "excavative" matters. Why should anyone want to know about the pre-history of such texts, instead of reading them in their finished form? This is a consistent literary-critical judgement: the pre-history of texts is irrelevant, we should read them as they now are.

In other places, however, Alter seems to argue in a different way. The reason why we should read the texts holistically is that they never were fragmentary or composite anyway. Source analysis and redaction criticism have been thoroughly misguided enterprises, not because they lack literary refinement, but because they are historically misinformed. You cannot study the redaction history of a text that was written all in one piece in the first place.

[[9]] Now at one level, Alter must be convicted of inconsistency here. Either questions about the origins of biblical texts can be asked, or they cannot; and if we know the answer to them, then it cannot at the same time be said that they are unaskable. Alter's literary proposals, if they are to be thoroughgoing, ought to be compatible with even the most extreme kind of source-critical theory. If only the finished whole is to be of interest to us, why should it matter if it is the result of thousands of sources being combined? The literary critic, qua literary critic, has neither interest nor competence in the realm of source analysis or redaction criticism. Thus we could say that Alter is trying to have his cake and eat it, despising historical criticism yet quite willing to meddle in it when it suits him.

Superficially I think there would be something in this: it certainly expresses some of the irritation Alter causes in old-style critics. But on another and more important level a more charitable account can be given of what is going on here, and one which recognizes Alter for the great critic that he is. Although Alter is interested in Hebrew literature from the viewpoint of a literary critic, he does not see it as a timeless body of writing, but as a corpus from a distinctive historical culture. Maybe the texts should be read synchronically, in the sense that they should be treated as existing in the same broad time-span as each other. But they are not, as on some post-modernist theories, to be read as synchronic with *us*, the readers. Alter's point then is that within their ancient context, of which he is fully aware, the discrepancies and developments within these texts can be shown, through literary methods of exposition, to be very much less than a historical but unliterary critic might think. In this Alter comes much closer to the agenda of traditional Biblical criticism than he acknowledges. Once again, the fundamental issue is how far one can grasp the text whole: and this literary question, far from being irrelevant to historical issues, has much to contribute *at the historical level*. Once Alter asserts that the historical unity or disunity of the text is not a matter of indifference, and that he knows the answer to it, then he cannot avoid engaging with historical critics. But (and this is my point here) it is literary perceptions that predispose him to think that he does know the answer to the historical question, and that the answer strongly favours the non-composite character of biblical texts; and these perceptions ought not to be indifferent to historical critics. To the extent that they show the possibility of reading texts as unitary, [[10]] they weaken the foundation for a source criticism based on the detection of inconsistencies.

Here again, therefore, so-called historical and so-called literary criticism are not in hermetically sealed compartments, but do have some opportunities for talking across the divide that appears to exist between them, and can even affect each other's conclusions. Once we recognize, on the one side, that a literary reading should not be anachronistic, or on the other that historical biblical criticism rests on the attempt to grasp the unity of a text even if that attempt is frustrated, then it becomes clear that there *is* common ground, and that both sets of critical and interpretative skills may be needed if justice is to be done to the texts.

II

So far my aim has been to suggest that historical critics and literary interpreters of the Old Testament already have more in common than they are prepared to acknowledge, and that there is considerable overlap between the questions they ask. Now I should like to draw attention to two aspects of biblical study where better progress could be made if critics of the two opposing schools collaborated more, because questions are being asked within one kind of criticism which cannot be answered without straying into the other.

Consistency

The first aspect is the question of inconsistency or incoherence in texts. It is not too much to say that the observation of inconsistency lies at the root of what we have come to call a critical attitude to the Bible. Or rather:

what is basic is the observation of inconsistency *together with a refusal* to think that it must be an illusion. Patristic, rabbinic, and mediaeval anticipations of critical insights differ from post-Enlightenment criticism because they are concerned to neutralize any inconsistencies they have noticed in the text, so that the road to any explanation in terms of the text's *actual* coherence, is effectively blocked. Biblical criticism proper depends on contemplating the possibility that texts really are incoherent, and seeking rational explanations for this: explaining the phenomenon, rather than explaining it away.

Some historical-critical scholars suspect that newer literary methods of detecting unity in texts previously thought incoherent [[11]] are a return to pre-critical solutions, and arise from a prior religious commitment to the unity of the text. The text is given the benefit of every doubt, because the interpreter already "knows," on religious grounds, that the text is a unified product of the mind of God. I believe this is sometimes what is happening. But it is certainly not always the reason why some interpreters see unity where others find only chaos. Sometimes the reason is that one interpreter's chaos is another's rich tapestry. And it seems to me that while interpreters will argue at length over whether or not a given text is incoherent, not much attention is paid to what counts as incoherence. Why should traditional historical critics and newer literary interpreters not engage together with the question of what we mean by calling a text incoherent or inconsistent?

This problem runs all the way from the divine names in the Pentateuch to the presence of double or multiple versions of a story, either interwoven (as traditionally supposed for the Flood Narrative) or found in different places in the text (as with the three "wife-sister" stories in Genesis). Historical critics face the problem that on their interpretation (a) only a theory of multiple sources will explain how the text can be so incoherent, but (b) it is then very hard to see why the editor, who was *ex hypothesi* [['hypothetically']] fully aware of the inconsistency, can have woven them into a finished text in which the inconsistency was allowed to remain. This is one of the great continuing problems in Pentateuchal criticism, but it is discussed by few writers on the Pentateuch.[5]

How can such a problem be handled? It is surely right to take the historical, empirical route pioneered by Jeffrey Tigay in his *Empirical Models for Biblical Criticism.*[6] This may be able to establish that composite works of the kind hypothesized did exist in the ancient world, and hence that the

5. An exception is R. N. Whybray, *The Making of the Pentateuch* (JSOTSup 53; Sheffield: JSOT, 1987).

6. J. Tigay (ed.), *Empirical Models for Biblical Criticism* (Philadelphia: University of Pennsylvania Press, 1985).

critics could be right to think that the Pentateuch is of that kind. But equally this is not the whole answer: for it gets us no further with the question how such (to us) incoherent works were read and understood. I believe that we are likely to get further only if modern literary critics are willing to join in the discussion, and offer us models from literature (either ancient or modern) where similar phenomena [[12]] occur *and where we know how they were or are handled interpretatively.* Robert Alter suggests that experience in reading James Joyce can help with the interpretation of the Pentateuch. Twenty years ago Frank Kermode was observing both the difference and the unexpected confluences between our own literary conventions and those not of the Bible but of the Middle Ages, where similar puzzles occur. In the *Chanson de Roland*, as he put it, "Roland dies three times, as if in a novel by M. Robbe-Grillet."[7] This hints at *common* problems in pre-modern and ultra- or post-modern literature, and suggests that a collaboration could be fruitful. Historical criticism may be able to tell us *how* the Pentateuch got put together; we may need help from literary critics if we are to understand *why.*

Theme

Commentators of every kind set out to answer the linked questions: what is this text about, and what does it say about what it is about? Such questions seem so obvious, and so unproblematic, that we hardly notice we are asking them. Literary theory is an essential reminder to the historical critic that on the contrary they are very complex indeed. The way that some biblical books have been read in the history of their reception and interpretation shows that people in the past did not necessarily ask what a book was "about" in the same way that we do: the idea that every book has a "theme" or "centre" would have been quite alien in some past cultures. Some critics would claim, of course, that literary works acquire themes only when the specific interpretative contexts in which the theme is not discovered but attributed. But those who regard this as an exaggeration should not therefore conclude that modern theory has nothing to contribute when it questions the assumption that themes reside in texts. Looking for themes or messages or overall thrusts in literary works might be a more time-bound and culture-bound preoccupation than we naively assume.

Two examples may illustrate this.[8]

7. F. Kermode, *Novel and Narrative* (Glasgow, 1972) 7.
8. I have used these examples before, though with some difference in the argument, in J. Barton, "Reading the Bible as Literature: Two Questions for Biblical Critics," *Journal of Literature and Theology* 1 (1987) 135–53.

(a) First, the book of Job. A modern reader is usually shocked by the discovery that for much of its history Job was interpreted by [[13]] both Jews and Christians as a tale about someone who suffered but was rewarded by God for his endurance (as in Jas 5:11). Such a reader usually argues, on the contrary, that the centre of the book lies in the dialogue, and that, accordingly, it is "about" the justice of God, or the comprehensibility of human suffering, or some similar theme. The speeches of Job, we take it for granted, are where the heart of the book lies. We wonder how past readers can have been so unintelligent as not to see this.

But an approach open to modern literary theory might remind us that books do not have to have a centre or a theme. When interpreters down the ages saw Job as a type of Christ, or as a hero who proved that God rewards the patient who endure, they were not necessarily saying that this was what the book was "about." For them, the book provided information about Job, and once we had the information, we were free to ask what God was teaching us through Job, not through the book as such. The book may have been seen, and conceivably may have been written, as a compendium of material about Job, a digest of the many Jobs that had probably existed for centuries before it was assembled. Such a book need not have a consistent theme at all. A literary critic used to reading plotless and themeless books written in the late twentieth century might, paradoxically, be more attuned to such a work than a traditional historical critic who tends to read Job as if it were a modern—not post-modern—novel, with plot, characterization, and theme.

(b) A second example could be the so-called Deuteronomistic History. Since Martin Noth's great redaction-critical study it has been usual to search for a theme, a plot, sometimes even a "kerygma" in this work. This is discovered by what is essentially a literary analysis, deciding which features to foreground, identifying the underlying structure of the work, spotting thematic connections running through it. It is seldom that any commentator questions the underlying literary model here, which is that of the realistic prose fiction we are familiar with from post-Enlightenment literature.[9]

9. Michael Goulder is one of the few to have questioned the idea that Old Testament books were written as literary art. "The completed D-corpus was never intended to be a literary work" (*The Evangelist's Calendar: A Lectionary Explanation of the Development of Scripture* [London: SPCK, 1978] 114); "A . . . remote possibility might be that the Chronicler was an artist. . . . Such a theory does not impress. Who wrote, who read works of art in the Jerusalem of 350 B.C.?" (*Midrash and Lection in Matthew* [London: SPCK, 1974] 218–19). It is a great pleasure to be able to dedicate this article to him, in gratitude for the many shafts of light he has thrown on biblical study. Perhaps I could suggest mischievously that his own work refutes his conclusions here: few people produce academic discursive prose which is so obviously also literary art!

[[14]] A more modern style of literary criticism might question whether this is really appropriate, and ask whether we might not see the Deuteronomistic History as altogether a more accidental piece of writing. Perhaps the author wrote some parts of it with deliberate skill, but in other places merely copied out what was before him in the form of sources and other previously existing documents. In that case, as with Job, searching for underlying themes or structures would be beside the point. The History would not be a work of "literature," as we now understand this—or as we understood it, until the self-undermining works of post-structuralism. The Deuteronomistic History may not be a work written to explore a theme. It may be a compilation of materials only loosely held together. And interpreting it may need different criteria for the meaning of texts from those historical redaction critics are accustomed to use.

But there is a paradox here; for to make suggestions like these is, in effect, to argue that *older* historical critics, practitioners of source criticism, may have been justified against their more recent redaction-critical successors, who practise a "close reading" in which exact verbal nuance is a central concern. The divide in biblical studies here runs, not so much between historical and literary criticism, but between redaction-critical investigation, on the one hand, and both source- and modern literary interpretation, on the other. Once we introduce the possibility of themelessness into biblical study, some of the old alignments start to look insecure.

This example may help to indicate why deliberate collaboration between historical critics and literary interpreters could be useful. The judgement—which of course may or may not be correct—that the Deuteronomistic History (or any other extended narrative in the Bible) is not a carefully planned work with intended structures and themes, but an uneven blend of original writing and mere transcription, is a historical judgement. Yet it is essentially recent literary criticism that has alerted us to the existence in modern writing, and hence potentially in ancient writing too, of apparently casual and unplanned works that are nevertheless not to be seen as accidental or meaningless, and [[15]] which offers resources for interpreting and making sense of such literary puzzles. The ultra-literary and the not-yet-literary seem to join hands, and both require interpretative skills somewhat more sophisticated than traditional historical biblical criticism can offer. At the same time, it is historical criticism that reveals the extent of the problem. At this point historical and literary criticism meet, even cross, and an ideal student of the Bible, it would seem, ought to be competent in both.

It is in the interests of all students of the Old Testament that historical and literary critics should somehow be brought to inhabit the same world, not to spend time staking out their own territory but to recognize that the whole land lies before them, and that most of the texts they interpret need *both* historical *and* literary skill if they are to be adequately interpreted. To suggest that historical criticism itself shows us features of texts that only literary interpretation can cope with, and vice versa, is probably to court unpopularity with both. Yet the Old Testament contains some very strange literature; perhaps it will not be surprising if it takes more than one kind of sensibility to understand it.

Modern Literary-Critical Methods and the Historicity of the Old Testament

HERBERT H. KLEMENT

[[81]] Those who inquire into the historicity of the events described in the Bible set themselves the task of suitably evaluating this literature as historiography. During extensive phases of Old Testament research—despite considerable variation in regard to detail—this has been carried out in dependence on literary-critical hypotheses formed at the turn of the century. It is only to be expected that the newer literary-critical exegesis carried out under the banner of synchronic methodology[1] appears unfamiliar. Both the historicity of the events reported in the Bible and the historical place and manner of origin of the Old Testament literature, up to its canonization,[2] can be considered from the point of view of literary observations and thus might provide the opportunity for new reflections. These are explored below.

Translated and reprinted with permission, from "Die neueren literaturwissenschaftlichen Methoden und die Historizität des Alten Testaments," in *Israel in Geschichte und Gegenwart* (ed. Gerhard Maier; Wuppertal: Brockhaus / Gießen: Brunnen, 1996) 81–101. Translation by Peter T. Daniels.

1. On the portrayal, see, inter alia, Paul R. House, "The Rise and Current Status of Literary Criticism of the Old Testament," in *Beyond Form Criticism: Essays in Old Testament Literary Criticism* (ed. P. R. House; Winona Lake, 1992) 3–22; cf. my "Beobachtungen zu literaturwissenschaftlichen Ansätzen in alttestamentlicher Exegese," *JETh* 7 (1993) 7–28. The present essay relates to the specific problematic of historicity.

2. For the closing of the canon in the second century B.C. at the latest, see, among others, R. T. Beckwith, *The Old Testament Canon of the New Testament Church and Its Background in Early Judaism* (London, 1985); idem, "A Modern Theory of the Old Testament Canon," *VT* 41 (1991) 385–95; Gerhard Maier, "Der Abschluß des jüdischen Kanons und das Lehrhaus von Jabne," *Der Kanon der Bibel* (ed. G. Maier; Gießen, 1990) 1–19.

Of course, as is well known, literary-critical approaches are far from uniform; they reflect the intellectual history of their time in all its breadth and cacophony. A complex picture must thus be reckoned with. The common idea that literary considerations necessarily imply fictionality or are not interested in historical investigation reduces the relationships in fundamental ways. Interest in and the value placed on historical questions in interpretation vary considerably, depending on the approach. Out of the multiplicity of possibilities, here I will discuss two contexts[3] as examples and will investigate them in relation to the topic.

"Literary Work of Art," Fictionality, and Traditional Historical-Critical Methodology

On the Emergence of Literary-Critical Exegesis

[[82]] In order to understand modern literary-critical approaches to exegesis, it is not insignificant to note that they began in the late 1960s.[4] The focal point marking the start may be considered the 1968 meeting of the Society of Biblical Literature. The Presidential Address on that occasion by James Muilenburg, "Form Criticism and Beyond,"[5] openly assaulted

---

3. The third topic discussed in the working group of the AfeT [[Arbeitskreis für evangelikale Theologie]] conference, history under the banner of the so-called "postmodern" approach, will be elaborated further and published elsewhere. Cf., inter alia, Fred W. Burnett, "Postmodern Biblical Exegesis: The Eve of Historical Criticism," *Semeia* 51 (1990) 51–80: "Historical discourse is still the horizon within which biblical critics must work. However, postmodern and poststructural ways of reading are requiring the historian to rethink the fundamental concepts of his or her discourse. . . . Far from being the threat many historians believe them to be, postmodern and poststructural ways of reading have provided the conditions of possibility for rethinking 'history' and how it should be written" (p. 51); Gary A. Philipps, "Exegesis as Critical Praxis: Reclaiming History from a Postmodern Perspective," *Semeia* 51 (1990) 7–50; Walter Brueggemann, *The Bible and Postmodern Imagination: Texts under Negotiation* (London, 1993); Terence J. Keegan, "Biblical Criticism and the Challenge of Postmodernism," *BibInt* 3 (1995) 1–14.

4. Criticism of prior theological scholarship in Germany in the same time-frame was also intense, although questions of New Testament hermeneutics and christological or soteriological significance clearly were at the forefront of discussion, in view of the foundation of the "No Other Gospel" movement (1966) and the conference of confessing communities (1969); cf., inter alia, Gerhard Bergmann, *Alarm um die Bibel: Warum die Bibelkritik der modernen Theologie falsch ist* (Gladbeck, 1963); Willi Marxen, *Der Streit um die Bibel* (Gladbeck, 1965); Klaus Bockmühl, *Atheismus in der Christenheit—Anfechtung und Überwindung: Die Unwirklichkeit Gottes in Theologie und Kirche* (Wuppertal, 1969); Gerhard Maier, *Das Ende der historisch-kritischen Methode* (Wuppertal, 1974). Overcoming the familiar difficulties was sought through alternative courses of training for theologians; we may recall the founding of the Staatsunabhängigen Theologischen Hochschule Basel [formerly FETA], the Theologischen Rüstzentrums Krelingen in northern Germany, and the Albrecht-Bengel-Haus in Tübingen, all in 1970.

5. James Muilenburg, "Form Criticism and Beyond," *JBL* 88 (1969) 1–18.

the assembled exegetes and triggered a lively echo.[6] The cautiously articulated uneasiness about the results of historical-critical exegesis, which
had little relevance for the affairs of the church or the parish, was obviously shared widely.[7] Building on form-critical findings [[83]] such as, for
example, the covenant formulary paralleling Hittite treaties,[8] Muilenburg
stimulated far-reaching observations. He argued that it was necessary not
to stop at the usual source- and form-critical considerations but to look
closely at the entirety of a text and especially to track down the rhetorical
features. The descriptions of forms and genres of the pericopes of the
biblical books should be supplemented by observations on structure and
construction of a composition. In the process, structural characteristics,
sequences, narrative technique, poetic construction, parallelism, repetition, chiastic structures, keywords (mottos), series, and so on must be clarified and evaluated.[9]

The adoption of literary inquiry soon followed on the broadest
planes.[10] After the first stages in individual departments, the inauguration
of the journal *Semeia* in the USA in 1974 and the *Journal for the Study of the
Old Testament* in England in 1976 made the concerns of literary text interpretation available to a broad international public. The publications of

---

6. So R. N. Whybray, "On Robert Alter's *The Art of Biblical Narrative*," *JSOT* 27 (1983)
76: "that the stimulus to the pursuit of this line of research came, notably from James Muilenburg, who . . . pointed out the limitations of current and earlier methods of biblical criticism and stimulated a whole generation of younger scholars by proposing a 'new' method
which he called 'rhetorical criticism.'" Tremper Longman, *Literary Approaches to Biblical Interpretation* (Grand Rapids, 1987) 16: "an event that has since become a touchstone for holistic and literary approaches."

7. House, "The Rise and Current Status," 3: "Besides the influence of interdisciplinary
trends, literary criticism arose at least in part because of impasses in older ways of explaining
Scripture. Many thinkers concluded that historical criticism, the standard means of biblical
analyses, had almost run its course. . . . These methodologies obscure the unity of large and
small texts alike. . . . An overemphasis on historical criticism subsumed textual issues."

8. Muilenburg, "Form Criticism and Beyond"; on p. 4, he refers to G. E. Mendenhall,
Law and Covenant in Israel and the Ancient Near East (Pittsburgh, 1955); and K. Baltzer, *Das
Bundesformular* (WMANT 4; Neukirchen-Vluyn, 1960).

9. Muilenburg, "Form Criticism and Beyond," 10–11. During the same period,
Brevard S. Childs was developing his alternative to the crisis in theology: *Biblical Theology in
Crisis* (Philadelphia, 1970). His program of canonical criticism was intended as an original
approach, further developed in idem, *Introduction to the Old Testament as Scripture* (London,
1979); idem, *Old Testament Theology in Canonical Context* (London, 1985); idem, *Biblical The-
ology of the Old and New Testament* (London, 1992). For summary and criticism, see, inter alia,
Eckhard Schnabel, "Die Entwürfe von B. S. Childs und H. Gese bezüglich des Kanons," *Der
Kanon der Bibel* (ed. G. Maier; Gießen and Wuppertal, 1990) 102–52.

10. House ("The Rise and Current Status," 3–22) describes three stages: "seeds of the
discipline," 1969–74; "roots of the discipline," 1974–81; and "flowering of the discipline,"
1981–89.

Luis Alonso Schökel, originally in Spanish,[11] should also be mentioned as significant for the development of the discipline. In Germany the stimuli of Erhard Güttgemanns[12] for the New Testament and Wolfgang Richter[13] for the Old Testament were also taken up, but with comparatively less resonance. In 1971 they initiated the journal *Linguistica Biblica*. The course of development in the Netherlands ran relatively independently; the direction known as the "Amsterdam School"[14] relied on the work of Martin Buber and [[84]] Franz Rosenzweig.[15] From the field of Jewish exegesis, further fundamental works of a literary-critical orientation may be listed.[16]

The publication of Robert Alter's *Art of Biblical Narrative*[17] at the beginning of the 1980s was the breakthrough for the acceptance of the approach. The book serves as both summary and introduction to the concerns of literary-critical work on the Bible. Its acceptance on an equal footing into the canon of established exegetical techniques underlies the exposition of John Barton, *Reading the Old Testament: Method in Biblical Study*.[18] Since that time a large number of books[19] and numerous articles

---

11. Luis Alonso Schökel, *Estudios de Poética Hebrea* (Barcelona, 1963); trans. *Das Alte Testament als literarisches Kunstwerk* (Cologne, 1971); idem, *A Manual of Hebrew Poetics* (Rome, 1988).

12. Erhard Güttgemanns, *Offene Fragen zur Formgeschichte des Evangeliums* (2d ed.; Munich, 1971).

13. Wolfgang Richter, *Exegese als Literaturwissenschaft* (Göttingen, 1971).

14. Already Karel Adriaan Deurloo, *Kaïn en Abel: Onderzoek naar exegetische methode inzake een 'kleine literaire eenheid' in de Tenakh* (Amsterdam, 1967). Cf. M. A. Beek, "Verzadigingspunten en onvoltooide lijnen in het onderzoek van de oudtestamentische literatuur," *Vox Theologica* 38 (1968) 2–14; K.-J. Illmann, *Leitwort-Tendenz-Synthese: Programm und Praxis in der Exegese Martin Bubers* (Åbo, 1975); K. A. Deurloo and R. Zuurmond, *De bijbel maakt school: Een Amsterdamse weg in de exegese* (Baarn, 1984); K. A. Deurloo, *Exegese naar Amsterdamse traditie, Inleiding tot de studie van het Oude Testament* (ed. A. S. van der Woude; Kampen, 1989) 188–98; R. Oost, *Omstreden bijbeluitleg: Aspecten en achtergronden van de hermeneutische discussie rondom de exegese van het Oude Testament in Nederland* (Kampen, 1986); Martin Kessler, *Voices from Amsterdam: A Modern Tradition of Reading Biblical Narrative* (Atlanta, 1994).

15. M. Buber and F. Rosenzweig, *Die Schrift und ihre Verdeutschung* (Berlin, 1936).

16. Cf., inter alia, Meir Weiss, "Die Methode der 'Total-Interpretation': Von der Notwendigkeit der Struktur-Analyse für das Verständnis der biblischen Dichtung," *VT* 21 (1972) 88–112; idem, *The Bible from Within: The Method of Total Interpretation* (Jerusalem, 1984); Shimon Bar-Efrat, *Narrative Art and the Bible* (JSOTS 70; Sheffield: Almond, 1989) [Hebrew, 1979].

17. Robert Alter, *The Art of Biblical Narrative* (New York, 1981).

18. John Barton, *Reading the Old Testament: Method in Biblical Study* (London, 1984) 5: "I try to argue . . . that all of the methods being examined have something in them but none of them is the 'correct' method which scholars are seeking."

19. Cf. Adele Berlin, *Poetics and Interpretation in Biblical Narrative* (Sheffield, 1983; [[repr., Winona Lake, 1994]]); Weiss, *The Bible from Within*; Bar-Efrat, *Narrative Art and the Bible*; Meir Sternberg, *The Poetics of Biblical Narrative: Ideological Literature and the Drama of Reading* (Bloomington, 1985); Longman, *Literary Approaches to Biblical Interpretation*.

have been published. "In a way, *The Literary Guide to the Bible* (1987), edited by Robert Alter and Frank Kermode, signaled an end to literary criticism's search for acceptance," noted Paul House in his short summary of its twenty-year history.[20]

What began at the end of the 1960s led to an alteration of the exegetical landscape that has often been described as a paradigm shift.[21] David Gunn notices a complete reversal of the standard method:[22] "So striking is the change, it has led me on more than one occasion to suggest that 'literary criticism' was becoming, has become perhaps, [[85]] the new orthodoxy in biblical studies." Even if this assessment is somewhat exaggerated, as a characterization of a trend it appears to be not without substance.

The Relationship of Historical-Critical Methodology to Literary Criticism

In his article "Classifying Biblical Criticism," John Barton[23] describes the context of a literary work as determined by three dimensions: historical frame, author's intention, and effect on the reader. To each dimension of the text correspond various inquiries and procedures. While earlier historical-critical investigation promised to enlighten the historical circumstances of the origin of the text, literary-critical inquiry attempts to view the text in isolation from the history of its origin. The change is carried out in the direction of questioning—from an author-oriented to a text-immanent search for meaning.

The traditional climate for research in Western culture is basically defined by the turning points of the Renaissance and the Enlightenment. The thought of this era was based in the conviction that what was original is good and pure and true, and change always brings some decay. The original is more valuable; the copy is of lesser quality, even when it is in better condition than the original. With respect to biblical exegesis, this presupposition fostered the search for the original forms of the biblical text. The idea had grown that the sort of text preferred for theological evaluation lay not in the canonical Bible text that needs to be verified text-critically but in the source writings from which the biblical authors took their information. Although such source writings themselves appear to be unavailable, the conviction that they could be satisfactorily extracted from

20. House, "The Rise and Current Status," 19; Robert Alter and Frank Kermode, *The Literary Guide to the Bible* (Cambridge, 1987).

21. Inter alia, Leland Ryken in the theological journal of the Dallas Theological Seminary, "The Bible as Literature," *BSac* 147 (1990) 3–15, 131–42, 259–69: "Evangelicals are witnessing a paradigm shift in how biblical scholars study and discuss the Bible" (p. 3).

22. David M. Gunn, "New Directions in the Study of Biblical Hebrew Narrative," *JSOT* 39 (1987) 65–75.

23. John Barton, "Classifying Biblical Criticism," *JSOT* 29 (1984) 19–35.

the extant texts was hardly challenged. Observation of changes in genre, repetitions, variations in usage of appellations for the same individual or the same fact, distinguishable biases, and so on counted as indexes with which theories about reconstruction of the forerunners of the available texts were equipped.

The theoretically derived forerunners of the existing texts were to be regarded as the real base-texts of scientific theology. Competence in scientific exegesis within this paradigm required good knowledge of the development of the theory in order to know which of the texts, portions of texts, and clauses that actually exist today [[86]] were assigned to which theoretical authors by whom and when and why. A major matter of concern was to compare and comprehend the actual biblical text in the light of the theories and then to develop, alter, rearrange, discard, and reformulate the latter, then to return to the tradition and draw out inferences. That was how the scientific nature and respectability of exegesis was demonstrated over the last two hundred years.[24]

The [[more recent]] decision to concentrate on the available literary form, without having to attend to a previously developed theoretical model of the genesis of the text, corresponds first of all to a different plane of investigation. While traditionally the search for origins had been the standard approach, this is by no means obligatory for interpretation that concentrates on the available text. In place of the origin, it is the available text that is decisive in the search for meaning. For David Robertson, the two approaches are clearly distinct:[25]

> The *paradigm* which has governed practically all modern research on the Bible is history. Scholars operating under this paradigm have either remarked on the literary quality of a text as an aside or have engaged in literary tasks for the purpose of answering historical questions. . . . The paradigm, or controlling idea, guiding the research of literary critics is, on the other hand, literature. Consideration of the Bible as literature is itself the beginning and end of scholarly endeavor. The Bible is taken first and finally as a literary object. [[punctuation corrected from p. 548 of the 1st ed., 1976]]

The diachronic, historical-critical search for the origin of the books and the synchronic interpretation of the texts are counterposed as alternatives that attempt to extract the meaning of the biblical text in different ways.

---

24. Cf. also my "Text-Recycling assyrisch und biblisch: Zur fälligen Revision der Literarkritik," *JETh* 9 (1995) 7–20.
25. David Robertson, "Literature, the Bible as," *IDBSup* (2d ed.), 547–51; idem, *The Old Testament and the Literary Critic* (Philadelphia 1977). Cf. Northrop Frye, *The Great Code: The Bible and Literature* (London, 1982).

The author-centered search for meaning, which is dedicated to the intention of the texts in the context of their location in history, and the search for the meaning inherent in a text mark distinct, paradigmatically different planes of interpretation.

Robert Morgan and John Barton, on the other hand, in their introduction to exegetical method make a plea for not treating the planes of inquiry as incompatible but for combining them. Although they consider the historical dimension irreplaceable, they hold that concentration on the literary quality of a text in a theological and religious dimension is productive, since historical inquiry [[87]] has fragmented the Bible too much:[26]

> Our third suggestion has been that a *literary* framework, which includes the results of historical and linguistic research, is today the more promising for the study of religion and for theology than the *historical* framework. . . . The main reason for this preference is that literary approaches offer more scope for making connections with a theory of religion. That is because they allow a large range of legitimate interpretations of the Bible. Historical study is a valuable control against the chaos of arbitrary interpretations, but its passion for a single correct answer, were it attainable, would leave the Bible looking more fragmented than ever.

This pragmatic approach, then, differing from David Robertson's, in no way springs from a fundamental disinterest in the author and his intention but, in addition to other concerns, from a degree of resignation with respect to the possibility of answers that traditional historical-critical work on the historical question was able to give.[27] It is only with difficulty that either the lasting theoretical character of its results or the imprecise and fragmented nature of the reconstructions from the atomistic material of preexisting textual contexts[28] can serve as the basis for a theological evaluation or meaningful acceptance in a pastoral [[*gemeindlich*, lit. 'parochial']] context.[29] For Morgan and Barton, this is the principal advantage of literary exegesis.

26. Robert Morgan and John Barton, *Biblical Interpretation* (Oxford, 1988) 286.

27. So also Gunn, "New Directions," 66: "It is no exaggeration to say that the truly assured results of historical critical scholarship concerning authorship, date and provenance would fill but a pamphlet."

28. Cf. Sternberg (*Poetics of Biblical Narrative*, 13) on Old Testament literary criticism, which he characterizes as "incredible abuse . . . for over two hundred years of frenzied digging into the Bible's genesis, so senseless as to elicit either laughter or tears. Rarely has there been such a futile expense of spirit in a noble cause; rarely have such grandiose theories of origination been built and revised and pitted against one another on the evidential equivalent of the head of a pin; rarely have so many worked so long and so hard with so little to show for their trouble."

29. Cf. among others Frank Crüsemann, "Anstöße, Befreiungstheologische Hermeneutik und die Exegese in Deutschland," *EvTh* 50 (1990) 535–45, who in his plea for taking

On the Relevance of Literary Analysis
for Historical Reconstruction

Fictionality or Non-fictionality

[[88]] The paradigm shift in methodology—refraining from discussion of the prior development of historical reconstruction on the basis of historical-critical theory in order to concentrate synchronically on a given text[30]— stands parallel to secular literary criticism schools of text-immanent interpretation such as "new criticism" or structuralism. Here the assessment of literature as art plays a significant role. The qualification of a text as art concentrates attention on the finished product in its non-time-bound significance. Considerations of text production and editorial reworking thus do not occupy a major portion of interest. The introduction to biblical texts of the notion of art evaluates them as timeless in meaning, which implies that they possess a pristine purity. The primary access for art is esthetic contemplation, not historic context. The notion of art, in all its plurality and lack of definiteness, makes available a multiplicity of approaches. Where biblical literature is treated as art, the historical question of authorial intent and contemporary meaning is often shaded out.

One advantage of this approach is to give methodological direction to a literary vision. The recognition of spoken forms seems more precise, and the text and its message move to the center of interest. Just as the physician's perspective can open up realms of understanding of dietary laws or the shepherd's perspective open up Psalm 23 or the sociologist's perspective Judges, so too can the approach of the literary critic enrich exegesis. Joannes Fokkelman, for example, defines a hierarchical sequence of "levels of interpretation" for his model of text interpretation, according to which he proposes to analyze a text, whether prose or poetry:[31]

---

liberation-theological exegesis seriously inter alia comes to the following judgments concerning the prevailing style of exegesis: "The triumphings of often frankly ridiculous literary critics who seriously believe they have the tools to uncover ten or more layers in a few verses, so that plausibility simply flies out the window, are one. The disconnecting of many investigations from any consideration of relevance, even from common sense, is the other; it is often nothing short of amazing"; or "the historical-critical method, which originally grew out of central theological concerns, not only threatens to ossify, it proves for many to be a variation of deadly Western science and technology that destroys what it investigates"; and "the supposed systematic indifference of exegesis corresponds to the fundamental disinterest in what such exegesis harms" (543), quoted in Eberhard Hahn, "Schriftauslegung im Spannungsfeld von Impetus und Skandalon," *KuD* 38 (1992) 72.

30. Robertson, "Literature," 548: "Literary critics in general do not believe it is necessary to use the traditional disciplines of biblical research (e.g., source, form, or tradition criticism) or to employ the findings of those disciplines."

31. J. P. Fokkelman, *Narrative Art and Poetry in the Books of Samuel* (Assen, 1986) 2.4.

Prose	*Poetry*
1. sounds	1. sounds
2. syllables	2. syllables
3. words	3. words
4. phrases	4. phrases
5. clauses	5. half verses/cola [[89]]
6. sentences	6. verses
7. sequences/speeches	7. strophes
8. scene-parts	8. stanzas
9. scenes	9. poems
10. acts	10. sections/groups of songs
11. sections/cycles	11. collection or book
12. book or composition	

The analytic ladder begins with the smallest unit, in order to push on to the next higher levels: "A powerful way of structuring is to divide up a text, an effort which should be carried out regularly from the 6th level onwards." This should be done very carefully, since "making the proper division has such great consequences because in this way we create frames of meaning."[32]

Robert Alter, one of the leading advocates of text-immanent synchronic interpretation, describes his concerns as follows:[33]

> By literary analyses I mean the manifold varieties of minutely discriminating attention to the artful use of language, to the shifting play of ideas, conventions, tone, sound, imagery, syntax, narrative viewpoint, compositional units, and much else; the kind of disciplined attention, in other words, which through a whole spectrum of critical approaches has illuminated, for example, the poetry of Dante, the plays of Shakespeare, the novels of Tolstoy.

Conscious emphasis on the esthetic, text-immanent search for meaning has the advantage that the interpretation does not have to be fed back permanently into diachronically determined results concerning text origins and nevertheless is able to make the claim that it analyzes texts in a scientific manner. The scientific character of the work is not defined by the historical-critical method; literary analysis that utilizes the procedures of literary criticism appears in this regard to have academic equal rights.

32. Ibid., 10–11: "By his own active intervention the interpreter discovers lines and connections which were applied at one time but are now latent in the text. No report on the origin of a text, no guide book as to figures and conventions has survived, so that the text must act on its own with its readers—and this conversely means that we must act on our own in handling the text by structuring it ourselves." To what extent Fokkelman's reasoning is circular will not be discussed here.

33. Alter, *Art of Biblical Narrative*, 12.

Despite the fact that the introduction of the notion of "literature as art" and the concomitant focus on the purity of methodological procedure in the school of "new criticism" or [[90]] "structuralism" predominantly led to renunciation of historical questions (sometimes postulated as necessary) for literary exegesis, yet by no means all who understand the value of literary-critical work agree on the categorical exclusion of any sort of historical dimension.[34] Robert Morgan and John Barton plead in their exegetical methodology[35] for a combination approach that in fact does proceed literarily but at the same time takes into account historic-diachronic inquiry. Meir Sternberg notes the following problems with the assumptions of literary-critical exegesis, from which he categorically wishes to distance himself:[36]

1. The exclusivity of text-immanent meaning-giving
2. That a text should always be treated as a supposed unity, as if there were no composite literature in the Bible
3. That the interest of exegetes should lie exclusively in structural form, not in historical inquiry
4. That literary-critical exegesis should be interested only in the literary reality of the biblical texts, not in a historical reality underlying the texts
5. That the Bible can be studied with the same methods as nonbiblical literature

Sternberg rejects all these assumptions for the literary exegesis of the Bible as he understands it. Literary forms, genres, and characteristics can be identified in any text, not just in those where fictionality of content is presupposed. For him there is no such distinction between history and fictionality in the Old Testament; instead, the statements about historical events are inseparably bound up with those about acts of God that are ordinarily not amenable to the judgment of a historian. It is exactly this combination of historical and ahistorical elements that constitutes the specific theological-ideological content of the biblical text, in which artificial literary form and historical reference play equally constitutive roles and must not be played off against each other:

> Herein lies one of the Bible's unique rules: under the aegis of ideology, convention transmutes even invention into the stuff of history, or rather obliterates the line [[91]] dividing fact from fancy in communication. So

---

34. E.g., Sternberg, *Poetics of Biblical Narrative*, 30–35; cf. F. C. Fensham, "Literary Observations on Historical Narratives in Sections of Judges," *Storia e Tradizioni di Israele* (J. A. Soggin Fs.; ed. D. Garrone and F. Israel; Brescia, 1991) 77–87.

35. Morgan and Barton, *Biblical Interpretation*.

36. Sternberg, *Poetics of Biblical Narrative*, 6–7.

every word is God's word. The product is neither fiction nor historicized fiction nor fictionalized history, but historiography pure and uncompromising.[37]

That observations of literary forms and conventions are not to be equated
with fictionality is clarified by a comparison, for example, of Judges 4 and
5. Both texts about the judge Deborah refer to the same events of a war,
a classic topos of historical inquiry. Each text provides information not
contained in the other. Recognition of the literary form of Judges 4 as
prose and Judges 5 as poetry is independent of the evaluation of the statements contained in them from the standpoint of history. An implicit connection is not provided by the literary description. If a connection is
claimed, it comes from some other motive than what is derived from the
literary analysis. The recognition of an artistic form as prose or poetry
does not transform an event or person celebrated therein into fiction.

This holds not only for texts from the ancient Near East but for modern forms as well. If a modern sports column is analyzed from a genre
viewpoint for its word choice, tone, mood, structure, emotional peaks of
rising enthusiasm and despairing groans, then recognition of the literary
genre (with its established repetitive verbal set-pieces, which can even be
virtually identical across different sports) alone cannot result in the inference that the event described is fictional. No one, based on the observation of sample sentences of the genre "sports reporting" or the analysis of
the structure and range of intensity found in such communications, would
come to the conclusion that the reported soccer game had not taken
place, even if every sentence in the commentary was already known, with
insignificant variations, from many other contexts. It must be considered
something between aberrant and bizarre to connect the observation of
features of literary form and structure with the assumption of fictionality.
The two occupy different planes of inquiry that should not be inter-
changed or confused.

That the exclusion of the historical dimension in literarily-oriented interpretations is commonly believed to be implicit in the approach is connected to two attitudes. On the one hand, there is a resigned discontent
with the results of the old historical-critical, [[92]] source-critical plowing
of the text. On the other hand, there is a growing interest in the specific
notion of art. Neither, however, can be taken as either self-evident or
necessary.

37. Ibid., 34–35: "For the biblical author also appeals to the privilege of omniscience—
so that he no more speaks in the writer's ordinary voice than Jane Austen does in hers, but
exactly as a persona raised high above him—with one crucial difference in convention. Omniscience in modern narrative attends and signals fictionality, while in the ancient tradition
it not only accommodates but also guarantees authenticity."

In a similar way, Leland Ryken and Tremper Longman have both come out in favor of the adoption of literary inquiry and methods by evangelical theologians.[38] That literary inquiry by no means implies fictionality has been demonstrated many times, precisely by conservative interpreters. Let us recall, among others, the work of Samuel Külling, *Zur Datierung der Genesis-P-Stücke.*[39] The diachronic fragmentation of Genesis 17, to which the main part of the work is dedicated, is contrasted with the synchronic unity of the text, which is justified on the basis of considerations of the genre of "covenant formula" by analogy to earlier Hittite vassal treaties. This kind of assignment of genre by recognizing and comparing conventions of textual forms by form-critical means are essentially literary-critical procedures.[40] For Külling, they are the starting point for the chronological delimitation and historical placement of the text under investigation.[41]

On the Relevance of Historical Inquiry to Macrostructural Interpretation

Example: Genesis 12:1–21:7. While comparisons with recognized ancient Near Eastern practices make it possible to draw conclusions on the basis of correspondences in the design of biblical texts or to find analogous forms,[42] it is still true that literary investigations arrive at their conclusions about structure primarily on the basis of internal textual evidence. The underlying criteria [[93]] are the procedures developed in the realm of literary-critical work. Despite the clarity that comes through acknowledging presuppositions, a strongly subjective element remains. Acknowledging this, however, cannot mean that the results are therefore fundamentally arbitrary; the observed structural principles must be present in the text and as such communicable and recognizable.[43]

---

38. Ryken, "The Bible as Literature"; Longman, *Literary Approaches to Biblical Interpretation*; L. Ryken and T. Longman, *A Complete Literary Guide to the Bible* (Grand Rapids, 1993).

39. Samuel Külling, *Zur Datierung der "Genesis P-Stücke": Namentlich des Kapitels Genesis 17* (Kampen, 1964).

40. Cf. the beginnings of recent literary-critical approaches from form criticism: Muilenburg, "Form Criticism and Beyond," a connection also recurring in the volume collecting twenty years of history: P. R. House (ed.), *Beyond Form Criticism*.

41. On the application of the ancient Near Eastern covenant or legal formulary to biblical texts, see, among others, Meredith G. Kline, *Treaty of the Great King* (Grand Rapids, 1963); J. Robert Vannoy, *Covenant Renewal at Gilgal: A Study of 1 Sam 11:14–12:25* (Cherry Hill, N.J., 1975). For a critical evaluation of the approach, cf. Kenneth A. Kitchen, "The Fall and Rise of Covenant, Law and Treaty," *TynB* 40 (1989) 118–35.

42. So Gordon J. Wenham, *The Structure and Date of Deuteronomy* (Ph.D. diss., London, 1970); on the basis of correspondences both to the conventions of the lawcodes and to the ancient Near Eastern vassal treaties, Wenham argues for an analogous but independent literary structuring of Deuteronomy.

43. Cf., e.g., J. Barton on drawing boundaries in the Creation story in Gen 1:1–2:1 in P. Beauchamp, *Création et séparation* (Paris, 1969), on the basis of observation of literary

The fact that, for example, repetitions in texts are not just to be inter-preted as markers of an unsuccessful blending of independent sources but can be understood as deliberately placed structural markers has been discussed many times as a literary device.[44] A classic example for source-critical sounding is the texts commonly labeled the "endangering of the ancestress."[45] As doublets, they are assigned to different source texts. The plausibility of this approach, however, is questionable. Just as the typical shaping and individual form of, for instance, a sports column do not go back to variations in the oral or literary transmission of an archetypal event but can be explained on the basis of innumerable events as a sort of model for the reportage, so from a literary point of view doublets are un-derstandable not so much as narrative variants of one single primeval event but rather as the stylized form of commonly-occurring events in a specifically circumscribed social space.[46]

[[94]] In a nomadic milieu, molestation and endangerment of women by the sedentary population when traversing rarely traveled regions can hardly be regarded an unusual occurrence. If, instead, the reverse is con-sidered, Alter's assessment of these texts as a *type-scene* is understand-

---

symmetry: "Of course for the historical critic such an answer is hopelessly circular: if the lim-its of the unit dictate our interpretation, but our interpretation itself is the only evidence for the limits of the unit. . . . But Beauchamp would no doubt retort that traditional source analysis suffers from just this same circularity; and we saw . . . that there is an uncomfortably large measure of truth in this."

44. Alter ("The Techniques of Repetition," *Art of Biblical Narrative*, 88–113) speaks of an "'Oriental' Sense of the intrinsic pleasingness of repetition in the underlying aesthetic of the Bible"; Sternberg, "The Structure of Repetition: Strategies of Informational Redundancy," *Poetics of Biblical Narrative*, 365–440; Kim Ian Parker, "Repetition as a Structuring Device in 1 Kings 1–11," *JSOT* 42 (1988) 19–27; Yehuda T. Radday, "Chiasmus in Hebrew Biblical Lit-erature," *Chiasmus in Antiquity* (ed. John W. Welch; Hildesheim, 1981) 50–117: "As to repeti-tions, they are the very essence and necessary material of a chiastic design, and may therefore have been intentionally inserted at their befitting places by the author or editor."

45. Gen 12:10–20, 20:1–18, 26:1–11.

46. So Alter, *Art of Biblical Narrative*, 47ff., "Biblical Type-Scenes and the Uses of Con-vention." He takes as his modern example the "Western" genre with its repeated typical ele-ments: sheriff, crook, cowboys, saloon, female beauty, Indians, horses, and so forth. The parallel traits are determined by the social milieu of a particular period, not by variations in the course of transmission of the story. Interestingly, Hans Jürgen Tertel, *Text and Transmis-sion: An Empirical Model for the Literary Development of OT-Narratives* (BZAW 221; Berlin, 1994), confirmed this interpretation in his empirical investigation of the transmission of the Assyrian royal annals text; he found that various incidents of war were increasingly assimi-lated in the course of the transmission process—that is, recorded in characteristic wording and forms: earlier versions appeared most rich in detail; later ones were schematized: "We cannot a priori assume that two similar narratives constitute alternative versions of one story. In the light of the literary development of Assyrian annals the assimilation of original-ity of different accounts with common features seems more probable" (p. 133).

able.[47] Stories of the nosiness, covetousness, and pushiness of city-dwellers, who contrast with the foreigners who live in tents and possess a markedly different culture, must have been compared by all who heard with their own experiences.

If we evaluate the parallel events of the endangerment of Sarah by King Abimelech and by the pharaoh as clues to structure, then an interesting macrostructural construct appears, in which the individual narrative fragments are grouped chiastically around a center, which can be represented as follows:

A	12:1–9	Promise: land, descendants, names, blessing
B	12:10–20	Endangerment of Sarah (pharaoh in Egypt)
C	13:1–14:24	Lot–Melchizedek and king of Sodom
D	15:1–21	Promise of a son for Abraham
E	16:1–16	Birth of Ishmael
E′	17:1–27	Covenantal promise: Isaac, not Ishmael
D′	18:1–15	Promise of a son from Sarah
C′	18:16–19:38	Lot–Sodom and Gomorrah
B′	20:1–18	Endangerment of Sarah (Abimelech)
A′	21:1–7	Birth of Isaac

The two texts of the endangerment of Sarah (B/B′) form a ring that encloses another pair of thematically-related texts (C/C′). Lot separates from Abram and chooses Sodom as his dwelling-place. His life is endangered by the kings from the East; Abraham fights for him and in the process also liberates the king of Sodom. In the binarily opposite text, Abraham, at Lot's request, in turn asks for Sodom to be delivered, but this time Lot alone is saved, while Sodom is destroyed.

The Lot–Sodom texts again comprise a frame around two texts (D/D′) in each of which Abraham is promised a son of his own. At the [[95]] center (E/E′) stands the birth of Ishmael as Abraham's firstborn and the conclusion of a covenant between El Shadday and Abraham in which not Ishmael but explicitly Isaac, Abraham's son by Sarah, is named as heir to the promise. The binding nature of this establishment by Yahweh is stressed as not springing from Abraham's desire and is sealed with the covenant sign of name-changing for Abram and Sarai, as well as circumcision. The acceptance of Isaac as heir to the promise in the center is made to correspond in the outer ring (A/A′) to the juxtaposed themes of the promise (land/descendants/name/blessing) and the birth of Isaac.

---

47. Alter, *Art of Biblical Narrative*, 50: "The variations in the parallels are not at all *random*, as a scrambling by oral transmission would imply, and the repetitions themselves are no more 'duplications' of a single *ur*-story than our eleven films about a fast-shooting sheriff were duplications of a single film."

When we look at the organization of the text in this way,[48] the themes appear to be ordered not by chance but rather by a sequence of points of view regarding the succession. After the promise is pronounced (text A), the dispatch of Sarah into Pharaoh's harem follows (text B), a first example of the total endangerment of the promise. A second such occurrence (text B') is reported directly before the promise's fulfillment with the birth of Isaac (text A').[49] The next ring (C/C') concerns the relationship of the promise to Lot, who as close kin of Abraham could be seen throughout, in view of Abraham's perpetual childlessness, as a potential sole heir. As further possible heir, the servant Eliezer is mentioned (text D); here follows, embedded in a covenant, the promise of an actual son for Abraham. The parallel text in the ring (D') contains the same promise, but the perspective of the narrative highlights the hearing and reaction of Sarah; thus she appears as the actual recipient of the message from the three visitors. Both texts include the promise of an actual son, the former accentuating [[96]] the fatherhood of Abraham, the second aiming rhetorically at Sarah's motherhood of this son.

The positioning of the birth of Ishmael at the center, parallel with and in contrast to the specific covenantal promises for Isaac, appears confusing. Such a concentric structuring of texts as is observed here can hardly be considered accidental but must be interpreted as intentional. This would respond to those who consciously were aware of the possible claim

---

48. A different chiastic organization of Gen 11:27–22:24 is recognized by Gary A. Rendsburg, *The Redaction of Genesis* (Winona Lake, 1986) 28–29; a discussion of the details would exceed the space available here:

11:27–32	a	Genealogy of Terah
12:1–9	b	Start of Abraham's spiritual odyssey
12:10–13:18	c	Sarai in foreign palace; Abraham + Lot part
14:1–24	d	Abram comes to rescue Sodom and Lot
15:1–16:16	e	Covenant with Abraham: Annunciation of Ishmael
17:1–18:15	e'	Covenant with Abraham: Annunciation of Isaac
18:16–19:38	d'	Abraham comes to rescue Sodom and Lot
20:1–21:34	c'	Sarah in foreign palace; Abraham + Ishmael part
22:1–9	b'	Climax of Abraham's spiritual odyssey
22:20–24	a'	Genealogy of Nahor

49. The recognition of such chiastic/thematic structuring suggests that the texts are not necessarily to be read in linear-chronological order. Sarah's attractiveness, described in 20:1–20, must not be thought of as temporally later than 18:12 but is chronologically detached from it. Also, the mention of Isaac in Genesis 17 before his birth in Genesis 21 represents an anachronism only in the context of Western expectation of a chronologically linear structure but not in the conventions as they can be recognized in chiastic formations. On the distinction between linear-chronological perspective in modern thought and aspectual perception in ancient Near Eastern cultures, cf. Emma Brunner-Traut, *Frühformen des Erkennens am Beispiel Ägyptens* (2d ed.; Darmstadt, 1992).

of Ishmael, as the firstborn of Abraham, to the inheritance. This, then, appears not only in a few sentences as subsidiary reminiscences (17:18, 21:11) but cannot be neglected as a fundamental feature of the structure of the whole. The fulfillment of the promise in Isaac, despite manifold dangers and competition, controls the organization of the text.

Chiastic organization of texts is common in ancient Near Eastern texts.[50] The context in chiastically-constructed macrostructures comprises not only nearby texts but also the binarily opposed units within the rings. The tension between periphery and center is also not without relevance, because in this arrangement the intention of the author is often recognizable: the central statement is clearly accentuated in comparison with the other texts.[51]

The mention of Ishmael in the center as someone who functions as a rival to Isaac for the inheritance promise is therefore to be regarded as especially emphasized above all other dangers and rivals.

When a ring-shaped structure of narrative units displays this kind of internally coherent thematic logic, which focuses attention on the danger to the promise from various potential rivals and other circumstances, it must be regarded as intentional. The question then arises as to when this thematization should be placed historically. If one accepts a late postexilic dating for it, after P, one would need to explain why an author would have positioned so centrally a potential claim by Ishmael on the legacy of Abraham in the postexilic Judaism of Jerusalem.

The literary observation of a logical structure for the text sequence, which follows conventions of ancient Near Eastern [[97]] chiastic text structure, leads to further considerations relating to the historical origin of such a text sequence, with no definitive positive statements being directly possible. It can hardly be denied, however, that a conclusion putting the text's origins in postexilic times is less understandable than other potential solutions.

The commonly observed similarity of the coloring of customs and mores in the patriarchal narratives to legal traditions from Nuzi,[52] which

---

50. See, among others, J. W. Welch (ed.), *Chiasmus in Antiquity: Structures, Analyses, Exegesis* (Hildesheim, 1981), especially the chapters by R. F. Smith, "Chiasm in Sumero-Akkadian," 17–35; J. W. Welch, "Chiasmus in Ugaritic," 36–49; idem, "Chiasmus in Ancient Greek and Latin Literatures," 250–68; Bezalel Porten, "Structure and Chiasm in Aramaic Contracts and Letters," 169–82; Y. T. Radday, "Chiasmus in Hebrew Biblical Literature," 50–117.

51. Angelico Di Marco, "Der Chiasmus in der Bibel: Ein Beitrag zur strukturellen Stilistik," *Linguistica Biblica* 36 (1975) 21–97; 37 (1976) 49–68; 39 (1976) 37–85; 44 (1979) 3–70. Translated from "Il chiasmo nella Biblia," Messina 1975 [unpub.].

52. See, among others, A. R. Millard and D. J. Wiseman (eds.), *Essays on the Patriarchal Narratives* (Leicester and Winona Lake, 1980), especially the chapters by A. R. Millard,

also are concerned especially with inheritances, opens the further possibility of taking into consideration this background as having parallel interest for the macrostructure as well. The sense of justice in the milieu of the stories and that of the logic in the organization of the texts obviously agree. This requires interpretation.

Example: The Book of Joshua. A detailed example of a literary analysis with implications for historical inquiry has been presented by Hendrik Koorevaar in his dissertation, *De Opbouw van het boek Jozua*.[53] The starting point of his structural investigation is his observation on the content, namely, that the train of events narrated in Joshua results each time from a direct instruction from Yahweh. Overall Koorevaar has found four such initiatives of Yahweh. The structure follows the model: (1) Yahweh orders, (2) the activity is carried out, and (3) the successful achievement is noted, with a summary, before the next activity ensues.

Beginning with such units, Koorevaar makes the further observation that the text-units included between the activity of Yahweh and the summary notice that appears when the activity is accomplished quantitatively stand in triple rhythm: in the first main part there are three units, then six, nine, and in the last, again three. The third main part exhibits a special characteristic in that here the text sequence exhibits a concentric ordering, with the focus on Josh 18:1–10, the text in which the erection of the central sanctuary at Shiloh is described. In front of this sanctuary of Yahweh, the casting of lots for the apportionment of the land inheritance among [[98]] the tribes of Israel is carried out (18:10). The cities and regions assigned to the individual groups are related in the preceding and following texts, which lie as pairs in rings around the central text [[see chart, p. 456 below]].

Just as Western readers by habit read and interpret texts in chronological order, so here other conventions appear to have guided the organization in chiastic structure. The structural architecture of the third main part appears not to be perfectly linear but almost dome shaped. A way of reading that treats the individual elements in isolation, rearranges them, or chips portions out also destroys the theological statement that underlies this organization. The careful structure, which must be considered deliberate, communicates the information that the distribution of the land

---

"Methods of Studying the Patriarchal Narratives as Ancient Texts," 43–58; M. J. Selman, "Comparative Customs and the Patriarchal Age," 93–138; D. J. Wiseman, "Abraham Reassessed," 139–56.

53. Hendrik Koorevaar, *De Opbouw van het boek Jozua* (Th.D. diss., Brussels University, 1990); cf. my "Josua und das Deuteronomistische Geschichtswerk: Zur Bedeutung von Hendrik J. Koorevaar, 'De Opbouw van het boek Jozua,'" *JETh* 5 (1991) 37–46.

A. *1:1–5:12*   *Keyword: Crossing (ʾābar)*

   ┌──── 1:1–19   1st Initiative of God: Cross the Jordan
   │   1:10–18   Joshua's Instructions to the Elders
   │   2:1–24   Reconnaissance of Jericho
   │   3:1–4:24   Crossing the Bed of the Jordan
   └──── 5:1–12   1st Conclusion: Circumcision + Passover in Gilgal

B. *5:13–12:24*   *Keyword: Taking (lākaḥ)*

   ┌──── 5:13–6:5   2d Initiative of God: Take Jericho
 │ ┌──── 6:6–27   Victory over a city: Jericho
 │ │   7:1–8:29   Victory over a city: Ai
 │ │ ┌── 8:30–35   Altar at Shechem: Reading the Torah
 │ │ └── 9:1–27   Covenant with Gibeon: Service in the House of God
 │ │   10:1–43   Victory over a league of cities: Jerusalem
 │ └──── 11:1–15   Victory over a league of cities: Hazor
 └──────── 11:16–12:24   2d Conclusion: Summary of the victories

C. *13–21*   *Keyword: Distributing (ḥālaq)*

   ┌──── 13:1–7   3d Initiative of God: Apportion Canaan
 │ ┌──── 13:8–33   Transjordan, inheritance portion: 2½ tribes
 │ │   14:1–5   Beginning of the allocation
 │ │
 │ │ ┌──── 14:6–15   Inheritance portion: Caleb (beginning)
 │ │ │ ┌─ 15:1–17:18   Inheritance portion: Judah and Joseph
 │ │ │ │ 18:1–10   Tent of Meeting in Shiloh, land division by lot
 │ │ │ └─ 18:11–19:48   Inheritance portion: The other 7 tribes
 │ │ └──── 19:49–51   Inheritance portion: Joshua (end)
 │ │
 │ │   20:1–6   4th Initiative from God: Cities of refuge
 │ └──── 20:7–21:42   Refuge and levitical cities
 └──────── 21:43–45   3d Conclusion: Summary

D. *22–24*   *Keyword: Serving (ʿābad)*

       22:1–34   Return of the 2½ tribes (altar at the Jordan)
       23:1–16   Joshua's farewell address
       24:1–28   Conclusion of covenant at Shechem
       24:29–33   4th Conclusion: Death + burial of Joshua

---

to Israel proceeds first and foremost from Yahweh and follows only after the erection of the Tabernacle in a worshipful setting.

In concentric structures, as is familiar by analogy from the conventions of ancient Near Eastern wall-painting, the principal thing stands at the center, with further particulars that are important enough to be in-

cluded being added on the flanks. The meaning of the center is thus enhanced by many side pictures. The picture of the people of Israel, who
camp with their new residential areas in rings around the sanctuary, manifests itself as a literary-structural formation: the dwelling of Yahweh in the
midst of his people.

In the second main part, it is clearly recognizable that the taking of
the land is told in three ways, with two examples of each: the conquering
of two individual cities (Jericho and Ai), two wars against coalitions of cities (Jerusalem and Hazor), and in between are two texts about living together with the native population (the Shechemites and the Gibeonites).
It is noteworthy that the last two groups stand in worshipful community
with Israel. Josh 8:33 explicitly mentions the sharing of the native Shechemites in the liturgical activities there; the Gibeonites are pledged to
unskilled labor in the central sanctuary.

Because the third main part, with its nine units on the division of the
land, contains the description of the book's goal, its center at the same
time emphasizes a principal concern of the book: the goal of the conquest
was achieved with the erection of the central sanctuary. That this is in
Shiloh is analyzed by Koorevaar with regard to the historical question of
the drafting of this literature. Shiloh is the place that Yahweh obviously
chose[54] and from which he blessed his people with land; in Joshua, Jerusalem has no theological significance. Instead, Jerusalem is the city of a
Canaanite king, a city that Israel was in no position to capture permanently.[55] This makes it quite unlikely, according to Koorevaar, that this
text, [[100]] which on the basis of its esthetically and theologically arranged
structure appears to be a carefully thought through unit, can have come
into existence after the end of the sanctuary in Shiloh or after the erection
of the Temple with the Ark of the Covenant in Jerusalem under Solomon.
This for Koorevaar is the termimus ad quem for the dating of the book.[56]

---

54. Cf. Deut 12:5 and often; Josh 9:27.

55. Josh 15:8, 63 name Jerusalem, not as part of the tribal territory of Judah, but as a
city in which the Jebusites live to this day.

56. According to Koorevaar (*De Opbouw van het boek Jozua*), breaks in the text such as
the fact that the legacies of Joshua and Caleb are not handled together are not the work of
subsequent redactors but the consequence of intentional structuring. He thinks that the theory that the familiar pentateuchal sources JEDP continue here is incompatible with his results. Concurrently, the book appears as a unified whole, not as part of a Deuteronomistic
History stretching all the way from Deuteronomy to 2 Kings: "Deze datering spreekt zowol
het model von 'het onstaan van het boek Jozua als onderteel van de Hexateuch' als het
model van 'het onstaan van het boek Jozua als onderteel van de Deuteronomistische Ge-
schiedschrijving' tegen" [[Ed.: "This dating speaks against both the model of 'the origin of
the book of Joshua as a unit within the Hexateuch' and the model of 'the origin of the book
of Joshua as a unit within the Deuteronomistic History.'"]] (p. 277).

The literary analysis of the macrostructure of the book of Joshua thus leads to various implications for the question of historicity. Not only are questions of authorship and dating of the text touched on; the possibility of the historical evaluation of the events reported in the texts is also accentuated. If one considers the structure of the book in the literary form analyzed by Koorevaar, then it becomes clear that the structure is not committed to a strictly linear-chronological interest. Literary sequencing and chronological order do not run parallel. The conflicts and cooperations with the Canaanite population obviously have a clearly exemplary character, each time occurring as a double example.[57] This must be kept in mind in any historical evaluation of this sort of historiography.

On the Operational Priority of Literary over Historical Analysis

While studies that concentrate synchronically on the extant text temporarily set aside the answers offered by historical-critical research regarding a text's origin, they nevertheless, after completion of their synchronic investigation, return anew to the questions of the text's origin and the historical relevance of its contents. The two examples discussed above make clear how far-reaching the implications of such studies can also be for the reevaluation of historicity.

Robert Polzin, who works almost exclusively in literary criticism, would in no way dispense with the historical dimension:[58] "A historical critical analysis of biblical material is necessary for an *adequate* scholarly understanding of what it means." However, he argues for a methodological priority of the literary over the historical [[101]] analysis. While recognizing the work of Robert Alter and David Robertson, he nevertheless is astonished "that at this late date there exists virtually no serious literary analysis of the Hebrew Bible." Here he sees a reason for the tense relationship to the historical-critical method:

> This literary lacuna is a primary reason why historical critical analyses of biblical material have so often produced disappointing and inadequate results. If adequate historical studies of literary texts operationally depend upon the existence of competent literary studies of such texts, we may have here a plausible reason for a good number of failures in historical critical understanding of biblical material.[59]

---

57. Cf. the relevance of corroborative testimony in juridical context; cf. Josh 13:1ff.

58. R. Polzin, *Moses and the Deuteronomist: A Literary Study in the Deuteronomistic History* (New York, 1980) 3.

59. Ibid., 5.

Polzin does not wish the priority of synchronic treatment to be understood as a matter of valuation [[as if literary issues were ultimately more important than historical ones]] but, rather, as a procedural matter suggested by the logic of a sensible step-by-step approach. He quotes Krystina Pomorska (1971) approvingly: "A literary work represents a complex phenomenon whose process is as significant as its ontological nature. But it seems impossible to study the process before knowing the nature of the product."[60] At the same time he refers to the methodology of the Russian literary theoretician Mikhail Bakhtin:

> In discussing why he does a literary critical analysis of Dostoevsky's work before tackling historical questions, he admits that such a preliminary literary investigation does need to be deepened by historical perspectives. Nevertheless, "without such preliminary orientation, historical investigation degenerates into a disconnected series of chance comparisons."[61]

It is by placing literary analysis prior to historical inquiry—not in setting the two in opposition—that progress can be made. The historical dimension must not be neglected. Where a literary analysis informed by the best insights of current research is allowed to precede historical assessment, the opportunity arises both to question and to surmount the sometimes spurious results of diachronic analyses of biblical texts emerging from the conceptual grid of the last century. Further works of this kind would be welcome.

60. Ibid., 6.
61. Ibid., 11.

Part 5

The Historical Impulse in the Hebrew Canon: A Sampling

Having briefly explored in part 2 of this volume the historical impulse among Israel's neighbors (and in pursuit of a loosely chiastic structure for the volume as a whole), we move in part 5 to a modest, selective sampling of the historical impulse within the Hebrew canon—a fully adequate sampling is impossible within the confines of this work. The four subdivisions below reflect basic divisions within the Hebrew canon: the Law, the Former Prophets, the Latter Prophets, and the Writings. Here, as elsewhere in the volume, my own preferences are evident in many if not all of the selections, but perhaps I may be forgiven, after all that we have seen so far, and perhaps even commended for not pretending that it is otherwise.

Unlike elsewhere in the volume, I have chosen in this part to break the "last twenty-five years" rule in order to include two older works. Roland de Vaux and Hans Walter Wolff have been highly influential in twentieth-century scholarship of the Hebrew Bible, and I believe that their voices need still to be heard. In the section below on the Law, the focus of the essays falls on the issue of the historicity of the Patriachal narratives. My intent in including de Vaux's "Hebrew Patriarchs in History" (pp. 470–79) is to acquaint the reader with the position that T. L. Thompson radically rejects in his oft-cited 1974 volume, *The Historicity of the Patriarchal Narratives*. Reprinted here are Thompson's concluding pages from that volume, in which he reflects on "Historical and Christian Faith" (pp. 480–84). Responding in turn to Thompson's general approach is an excerpt (pp. 485–91) from John Goldingay's 1980 essay, "The Patriarchs in Scripture and History." Taken together, these selections should give the reader a sense of how large the disagreements are among scholars on such matters as whether the "Patriarchs" ever existed or, for that matter, on whether "salvation history" ever happened (to borrow from Thompson's disavowal on p. 482). Along the way, the reader may also gain a sense of the integral relationship between what one thinks about the importance of historical issues and what one understands to be the essence of Christian faith.[1]

Moving from the Pentateuch to the Former Prophets (Joshua–Kings), we come to two quite different but significant essays. The first is R. S. Hess's "Early Israel in Canaan: A Survey of Recent Evidence and Interpretations" (pp. 492–518). In this wide-ranging essay, Hess offers a nice summary (and to some degree a synthesis) of the various views on Israel's emergence in Canaan. After rehearsing the four dominant views—two of which see Israel as coming from outside of Canaan (conquest model and peaceful infiltration model) and two from inside Canaan (peasant revolt and pastoral Canaanites)—Hess concludes that "aspects of each of the models may be attested in the biblical accounts of early Israel," that is, "aspects of each of them may well have been true in some measure" (p. 501). The fact that "the biblical evidence does not perfectly coincide with any of the models proposed" should not be surprising, since "the biblical material serves purposes other than those which the modern historian may seek" (p. 503). Hess then turns to consider further evidences that "may critically affect our understanding of early Israel" (p. 503). These include (1) Egyptian materials such as the Merneptah stele and the Karnak battle reliefs, (2) Zertal's discovery of a thirteenth-century structure on Mt. Ebal with possible relationship to the biblical story of Joshua, (3) the archaeology of Shiloh, which site may have served as an intertribal sanctuary for Israel, and (4) the evidence of animal bones and human diet that may suggest religious dietary restrictions among hill country inhabitants (Israelites?). In the light of these and other evidences, Hess finds the current skepticism of some scholars and their dismissal of the biblical text unwarranted. In the end, he urges "caution concerning all the attempts to 'prove' or 'disprove' the biblical accounts on the basis of extrabiblical evidence and of sociological models" (p. 512). In sum, Hess introduces readers to the more significant archaeological data relating to early Israel, illustrates how the various interpretations of the data are often affected by interpreters' own perspectives, and shows how a balanced view can perhaps gain something from each of the various theories, while still holding to the integrity of the biblical traditions.

The second essay relating to the Former Prophets is J. G. McConville's "Faces of Exile in Old Testament Historiography" (pp. 519–34). While Hess's focus was on extrabiblical evidences, McConville turns to the biblical texts themselves. He begins with the recognition that there are echoes

---

1. For further discussion of such matters, see chap. 3 of V. P. Long, *The Art of Biblical History* (Foundations of Contemporary Interpretation 5; Grand Rapids: Zondervan, 1994), esp. pp. 93–99, 116–19.

of the exile in Joshua–Kings (the corpus often called the Deuteronomistic History), so that in a sense these books must be read "from the end." But this leads him to ask an important question: are the books comprising the Deuteronomistic History to be regarded as nothing more than freely invented "history" that tells little about anything other than the exilic situation, or do they relate also to the actual past events that they purport to recount? To find an answer to this question, McConville traces several prominent themes in the DH—namely, exile, leadership, worship, and Israel—and notes within each that there are perspectives that seem clearly to antedate the exilic situation. As McConville observes, "this does not fit well with the proposal that the Hebrew Bible is the work of a systematizing bureaucracy with a self-serving agenda, nor that 'Israel' is a product of post-exilic imagination" (pp. 531–32). Instead, it is much more reasonable "to think of separate processes of composition for the different books, or at least blocks, of what is now DtH, all finally gathered under the umbrella of a broader horizon" (p. 533). As to the question, then, "how far, if at all, DtH was a record of an actual history," McConville answers affirmatively: "DtH consisted of a real dialogue between received material and the perspectives of the final composition" (p. 532).

Turning to the Latter Prophets, we come first to H. W. Wolff's "The Understanding of History in the Old Testament Prophets" (pp. 535–51). The SBTS series is already well served by a full volume on the prophets, entitled *"The Place Is Too Small for Us,"* and so the present volume, which also finds the "place too small" to cover its topic, can perhaps save a few pages in this section by including only two essays. But why include an older essay? While some may feel that Wolff's essay, originally delivered as his 1960 inaugural address in Mainz, is now, like the biblical theology movement that it reflects, outdated, I believe that Wolff's essay is in places profound and raises issues that still need to be discussed. Many of his observations—for example, that the prophetic word about the future naturally provoked in the prophets an interest in the past and the present, that the concept of "history" for the prophets was expressed simply as "the work of Yahweh," that the word *dābār* in Hebrew has a dual sense analogous to the dual sense of *history* in English (that is, as *event* and as *word* about the event), that in essence history was understood by the prophets as a *conversation*, or dialogue, between Yahweh and his human creatures—represent insights that merit consideration in the on-going debate over the Hebrew Bible's own philosophy of history.

The prophets' view, according to Wolff, is that "no hearer can understand their God if he does not at the same time understand reality as history determined by him and directed to him, as his conversation, first with Israel, but finally drawing in the whole world of the nations" (p. 546). P. R.

Davies, although writing in quite a different vein, puts the matter plainly: "The belief in a single transcendental being who can comprehend, indeed controls, all history is precisely a biblical belief: it is one of the major tenets of biblical historiography."[2] Davies makes it clear that he does not personally share this belief in a "transcendental observer" (God), with the result that for him "objective 'history'" is impossible. But he rightly acknowledges that his stance is a function of his worldview: "When I claim, then, that there is no 'objective' history I am implying a world-view incompatible with that of the biblical writings (except perhaps Qoheleth) for whom history was defined by divine deeds (or so they claimed in their writings; they may have thought differently). So a certain kind of religious belief *might* well dictate a certain definition of 'history.'"[3] Here Wolff's challenge to "our generation" still carries force: must we not recognize that certain worldviews are "founded in only a *portion* of reality" and thus endanger "the freedom of research into the *total* of actual events" (p. 548 below)?

If the first essay in the Latter Prophets section is unusual by virtue of its age, the second and final inclusion is unusual by virtue of its form—the only place in the volume that a review is republished. Recognizing the significance of Dwight R. Daniels's 1990 title, *Hosea and Salvation History: The Early Tradition of Israel in the Prophecy of Hosea*, I early decided that an excerpt should be included. In the end, Heinz-Dieter Neef's German review of Daniels's work in *Biblica* seemed to serve best both to summarize the work and to offer a few salient suggestions for further work. The review is published below (pp. 552–56) for the first time in English translation. Daniels's central thesis is that Hosea shows awareness of a preexisting, continuous history of Israel, to which he regularly refers in his own work, dividing the history into four major periods: Patriarchs, Exodus and wilderness wandering, Canaanization, and renewal. As Neef observes, such a thesis has significant implications for pentateuchal research and renders highly implausible the theory that Israel's history writing began first with an exilic "Yahwist."

Coming to the final division of the Hebrew canon, the Writings, we have room for but one essay, Gary Knoppers' "History and Historiography: The Royal Reforms" (pp. 557–78). In pursuit of the larger question regarding the historical value of the Chronicler's work, Knoppers attends in particular to the noncultic reforms recounted in Chronicles, noting the Chronicler's greater interest in matters administrative, judicial, and geopolitical, when contrasted with the Deuteronomist. Turning to historical

2. P. R. Davies, "Whose History? Whose Israel? Whose Bible?: Biblical Histories, Ancient and Modern," in *Can a "History of Israel" Be Written?* (ed. L. L. Grabbe; JSOTSup 245; Sheffield: Sheffield Academic Press, 1997) 116.

3. Ibid., 116–17.

considerations and archaeological evidences, Knoppers concludes that the Chronicles account is one-sided but not for that reason deficient. Chronicles reflects pre- as well as postexilic situations and is, in the final analysis, useful for those wishing to reconstruct Israel's history: "A discriminating understanding of Chronicles enables contemporary scholars to write more sophisticated, nuanced, and balanced histories of both ancient Judah and post-exilic Yehud" (p. 578). Knoppers demonstrates how literary and archaeological evidences may be responsibly brought together in the historical enterprise, and so his essay appropriately brings this volume toward its end.

Additional Reading

The Law

Greenstein, E. L.
1988   On the Genesis of Biblical Prose Narrative. *Prooftexts* 8: 347–63.
Hoffmeier, J. K.
1997   *Israel in Egypt: The Evidence for the Authenticity of the Exodus Tradition.* New York: Oxford University Press.
Kitchen, K. A.
1995   The Patriarchal Age: Myth or History? *Biblical Archaeology Review* 21: 48–57; 88–95.
Malamat, A.
1983   The Proto-History of Israel: A Study in Method. Pp. 303–13 in *The Word of the Lord Shall God Forth.* Edited by C. L. Meyers and M. O'Connor. Winona Lake, Ind.: Eisenbrauns.
Mendenhall, G. E.
1987   The Nature and Purpose of the Abraham Narratives. Pp. 337–56 in *Ancient Israelite Religion: Essays in Honor of Frank Moore Cross.* Edited by P. D. Miller Jr., P. D. Hanson, and S. D. McBride. Philadelphia: Fortress.
Millard, A.
1996   Evidence and Argument. *Buried History* 32: 71–73.
Pagolu, A.
1998   *The Religion of the Patriarchs.* Journal for Study of the Old Testament Supplement Series 277. Sheffield: Sheffield Academic Press.
Rendtorff, R.
1996   Welche Forgerungen hat der Wandel in der Pentateuchforschung für unsere Sicht der Geschichte Israels. Pp. 43–59 in *Israel in Geschichte und Gegenwart.* Edited by G. Maier. Wuppertal: Brockhaus / Basel: Brunnen.
Sarna, N.
1977   Abraham in History. *Biblical Archaeology Review* 3: 5–9.

Van Seters, J.
   1992   *Prologue to History: The Yahwist as Historian in Genesis.* Louisville: Westminster/John Knox.
Weinfeld, M.
   1988   The Promise to the Patriarchs and Its Realization: An Analysis of Foundation Stories. Pp. 353–69 in *Society and Economy in the Eastern Mediterranean (c. 1500–1000 B.C.).* Edited by M. Heltzer and E. Lipiński. Leuven: Peeters.

The Prophets (Former)

Bettenzoli, G.
   1986   Samuel und Saul in geschichtlicher und theologischer Auffassung. *Zeitschrift für die Alttestamentliche Wissenschaft* 98: 338–51.
Bimson, J. J.
   1991   Merenptah's Israel and Recent Theories of Israelite Origins. *Journal for Study of the Old Testament* 49: 3–29.
Cook, A.
   1986   "Fiction" and History in Samuel and Kings. *Journal for Study of the Old Testament* 36: 27–48.
Fritz, V., and P. R. Davies, eds.
   1996   *The Origins of the Ancient Israelite State.* Journal for Study of the Old Testament Supplement Series 228. Sheffield: Sheffield Academic Press.
Gooding, D. W.
   1982   The Compostion of the Book of Judges. *Eretz-Israel* 16 (Orlinsky Volume): 70–79.
Gordon, R. P.
   1980   David's Rise and Saul's Demise: Narrative Analogy in 1 Samuel 24–26. *Tyndale Bulletin* 31: 37–64.
McConville, J. G.
   1989   Narrative and Meaning in the Books of Kings. *Biblica* 70: 31–49.
Pyper, H. S.
   1993   Surviving Writing: The Anxiety of Historiography in the Former Prophets. Pp. 227–49 in *The New Literary Criticism of the Hebrew Bible.* Edited by J. C. Exum and D. J. A. Clines. Journal for the Study of the Old Testament Supplement Series 143. Sheffield: JSOT Press.
Revell, E. J.
   1985   The Battle with Benjamin (Judges XX 29–48) and Hebrew Narrative Technique. *Vetus Testamentum* 35: 417–33.
Stoebe, H. J.
   1989   Überlegungen zur Exegese historischer Texte — dargestellt an den Samuelisbüchern. *Theologische Zeitschrift* 45: 290–314.
Weippert, M., and H. Weippert
   1991   Die vorgeschichte Israels in neuem Licht. *Theologische Rundschau* 56: 341–90.

Younger, K. L., Jr.
  1995   The Configuring of Judicial Preliminaries: Judges 1.1.–2.5 and Its Depen-
         dence on the Book of Joshua. *Journal for the Study of the Old Testament* 68:
         75–92.

The Prophets (Latter)

Ackroyd, P. R.
  1968   Historians and Prophets. *Svensk Exegetisk Årsbok* 33: 18–54.
Delcor, M.
  1989   Storia e profezia nel mondo ebraico. *Fondamenti* 13: 3–33.
Krause, A. E.
  1988   Historical Selectivity: Prophetic Prerogative or Typological Imperative?
         Pp. 175–212 in *Israel's Apostasy and Restoration: Essays in Honor of Roland
         K. Harrison*. Edited by A. Gileadi. Grand Rapids, Mich.: Baker.
Laato, A.
  1994   History and Ideology in the Old Testament Prophetic Books. *Scandina-
         vian Journal of the Old Testament* 8: 267–97.
Nielsen, K.
  1994   History and Ideology in the Old Testament Prophetic Books. *Scandina-
         vian Journal of the Old Testament* 8: 298–301.
Overholt, T. W.
  1990   Prophecy in History: The Social Reality of Intermediation. *Journal for the
         Study of the Old Testament* 48: 3–29.

The Writings

Berg, S. B.
  1980   After the Exile: God and History in the Books of Chronicles and Esther.
         Pp. 107–27 in *The Divine Helmsman: Studies on God's Control of Human
         Events, Presented to Lou H. Silberman*. Edited by J. L. Crenshaw and S. Sand-
         mel. New York: KTAV.
Eissfeldt, O.
  1971   Die Psalmen als Geschichtsquelle. Pp. 97–112 in *Near Eastern Studies in
         Honor of William Foxwell Albright*. Edited by H. Goedicke. Baltimore:
         Johns Hopkins University Press.
Gordis, R.
  1981   Religion, Wisdom and History in the Book of Esther: A New Solution to
         an Ancient Crux. *Journal of Biblical Literature* 100: 359–88.
Graham, M. P., K. G. Hoglund, and S. L. McKenzie, eds.
  1997   *The Chronicler as Historian*. Journal for the Study of the Old Testament
         Supplement Series 238. Sheffield: JSOT Press.
Helberg, J. L.
  1995   The Determination of History According to the Book of Daniel: Against
         the Background of Deterministic Apocalyptic. *Zeitschrift für die Alttesta-
         mentliche Wissenschaft* 107: 273–87.

Japhet, S.
1991   "History" and "Literature" in the Persian Period: The Restoration of the Temple. Pp. 174–88 in *Ah, Assyria: Studies in Assyrian History and Ancient Near Eastern Historiography Presented to Hayim Tadmor.* Edited by M. Cogan and I. Ephꜥal. Scripta Hierosolymitana 33. Jerusalem: Magnes.

Peltonen, K.
1996   *History Debated: The Historical Reliability of Chronicles in Pre-critical and Critical Research.* Göttingen: Vandenhoeck & Rupprecht.

Sugimoto, T.
1990   The Chronicler's Techniques in Quoting Samuel–Kings. *Annual of the Japanese Biblical Institute* 16: 30–70.

Talmon, S.
1991   Esra und Nehemia: Historiographie oder Theologie? Pp. 329–56 in *Ernten was man sät: Festschrift für Klaus Koch zu seinem 65. Geburtstag.* Edited by D. R. Daniels, U. Glessmer, and M. Rösel. Neukirchen-Vluyn: Neukirchener Verlag.

Williamson, H. G. M.
1987   Post-exilic Historiography. Pp. 189–207 in *The Future of Biblical Studies: The Hebrew Bible.* Edited by R. E. Friedman and H. G. M. Williamson. Atlanta: Scholars Press.

1988   History. Pp. 25–38 in *It Is Written: Scripture Citing Scripture—Essays in Honour of Barnabas Lindars.* Edited by D. A. Carson and H. G. M. Williamson. Cambridge: Cambridge University Press.

The Hebrew Patriarchs and History

ROLAND DE VAUX

[[111]] This short article is clearly not intended as a discussion, even in a peripheral manner, of such a vast and difficult topic. It is concerned only to examine the way in which the problem is today presented, and to make a few remarks about methodology.

It is obvious that the history of the *people* of Israel can only be said to begin when Israel became a people. But when did this happen? There are two words in Hebrew which are not synonymous and which do not correspond exactly with the translations which are normally given to them in modern languages. They are *ʿam* and *gôy*. [1] The latter term denotes a human group which has political organization and is settled in a territory. It is usually translated, quite satisfactorily, as "nation." However, the common use of "people" as a translation of *ʿam* is inadequate since the original notion differs from what we understand by "people" in that it refers specifically to relationships of consanguinity. One speaks of a dead person as being "gathered to his people," Gen 25:8, 17, etc. A priest must not defile himself through contact with the corpse of any of his *ʿam*, except for his closest relatives, Lev 21:1–2, cf. v. 14 and elsewhere. There is no reason to propose two different words, as the dictionaries do, for *ʿam* means initially an immediate blood-relative but when employed collectively refers to kinship, and the "people" is an extension of the family. The marriages between the clan of Jacob and the inhabitants of Shechem would have

Reprinted with permission from *The Bible and the Ancient Near East* (transl. by Damian McHugh; London: Darton, Longman & Todd, 1972) 111–21.

Originally published in *Studii Biblici Franciscani Liber annuus*, 13, 1962–63, pp. 287–97.

1. For what follows, cf. L. Rost, "Die Bezeichnungen für Land und Volk im Alten Testament," in the *Festschrift Otto Proscksch*, 1934, pp. 125–48; E. A. Speiser, "ʿPeople' and ʿNation' of Israel," in *JBL* 79 (1960) 157–63.

made of the two groups, "one *ʿam*," Gen 34:16; the "people" of Israel are the sons of Israel," the descendants of the twelve sons of Jacob.

When Abraham left Haran with his wife, his nephew Lot, and all his household, the group already formed the kernel of an *ʿam*. God promised to make his descendants not a great *ʿam* but a great *gôy*, [[112]] Gen 12:2; cf. 17:5; 18:18, and this promise was linked with the promise that they would possess the Holy Land, Gen 12:7, cf. 17:8. The fulfillment of this promise, i.e., the evolution of the blood-related group (*ʿam*) into a nation (*gôy*) is affirmed in the confession of faith of Deut 26:5–9: "My father was a wandering Aramaean. He went down into Egypt to find refuge there, few in numbers; but there he became a nation (*gôy*), great, mighty and strong . . . Yahweh brought us out of Egypt . . . He brought us here and gave us this land." As far as the Israelites were concerned, their history as a "people" began with their ancestor Abraham. For the modern historian, however, the history of Israel can only be said to begin when the group acquired unity and stability by settling in Canaan and establishing the Federation of the Twelve Tribes, i.e., when Israel became a nation.

But the modern historian can very properly ask himself—and indeed he ought to—where this people came from, and from which larger group they had detached themselves, and in what way they had come together. Israel itself had answers to these questions, answers which it had received from tradition; some of them are concerned with the exodus from Egypt and the conquest of Canaan, while others go back to the very origins of the people, viz. the traditions relating to the Patriarchs, contained in Genesis 12–50. The problem is to know what use the historian may make of them.

At the end of the nineteenth century two extreme attitudes were current. For many the success with which documentary criticism had been applied to the Pentateuch and the relatively recent dates ascribed to the documents which made up Genesis proved that the traditions were devoid of any historical value. The classic expression of this opinion is Wellhausen's comment on the Genesis narratives that, "we attain to no historical knowledge of the patriarchs, but only of the time when the stories about them arose in the Israelite people; his later age is here unconsciously projected, in its inner and its outward features, into hoar antiquity, and is reflected there like a glorified mirage."[2] At the other extreme,

---

2. J. Wellhausen, *Prolegomena zur Geschichte Israels* 3, 1886, p. 331, = *Prolegomena to the History of Israel*, London, 1885, pp. 318–19. Cf. id., *Israelitische und jüdische Geschichte* (I quote the revised edition of 1958, p. 10): "The narratives about the patriarchs in Genesis are bound up with ethnological conditions and cultic institutions of the monarchic period, the origins of which they attribute to an ideal prehistory, though in fact that prehistory is simply the reflection of conditions in their own time."

those exegetes who [[113]] laid great stress on tradition and who would not accept the results of literary criticism interpreted the narratives about the Patriarchs as factual history and found justification for their standpoint in the Egyptian and Assyrian texts and monuments which at that time were beginning to provide a much broader understanding of the Ancient East. In the words of F. Vigouroux: "Through these comparative studies we shall be able to recognise easily the fidelity and scrupulous exactitude of Sacred History."[3]

No scholar nowadays would accept Wellhausen's position without modification, since it is generally agreed that even the most recent among the authors of the Pentateuch (and we can leave aside the question of the date of their final editing), could preserve, and did in fact preserve, some extremely ancient elements. Likewise no scholar would any longer wish to hold Vigouroux's position, since it is now an indisputable fact that both documents and traditions were used in the composition of the Pentateuch and that the process extended over several centuries.

Since the time of Wellhausen and Vigouroux two new factors have dominated the study of the origins of Israel. On the one hand the literary criticism of the text of the Pentateuch has advanced to a point where we are no longer exclusively concerned with the great "documents" in their final form (and there is a tendency to date these earlier and earlier), but we are caught up in the study of the pre-literary history of these documents and of the oral "traditions" from which they emerged. On the other hand, an enormous mass of texts and documents has been unearthed, and is still being unearthed, by excavations in the Near East. From these our knowledge of the ethnography, geography, and history of the Ancient East is being greatly extended, and precise parallels (onomastic and linguistic, juridical and social) with the patriarchal narratives have been discovered which date neither from the period when the "traditions" were finally established nor from the time when the "documents" were composed, but which can only belong to the period when the Patriarchs are supposed to have lived.

As a result of both these influences, the distance between opposing [[114]] camps has diminished, though as recently as fifteen years ago they stood far apart. By way of example we can take two scholars who are generally recognized to be of the very first rank and whose views command considerable influence. In Germany Martin Noth gave a new and different

---

3. F. Vigouroux, *La Bible et les découvertes modernes en Palestine en Egypte et en Assyrie* (5), 1889, vol. 1, p. 363. Cf. vol. 2, p. 212; "It is in fact ourselves, believing Catholics loyal to Tradition, who in attributing the composition of the Pentateuch to Moses provide the most simple, most satisfactory and indeed the only truly acceptable explanation of the peculiarly Egyptian quality of the story of Joseph."

impetus to Pentateuchal criticism by interesting himself particularly in the history of the traditions.[4] He is thoroughly acquainted with, and makes excellent use of, ancient Oriental texts, but he is less sensitive to the evidence of archaeology in its strict sense. In 1950 he published an authoritative *History of Israel.*[5] He begins this history with the establishment of the Federation of the Twelve Tribes, the Amphictyony, in Canaan. Every tribe had its own particular traditions about its ancestors and about events which took place before it settled in the land. These traditions were combined and contributed to the composition of the Pentateuch. He concludes: "If that is so, then we have no evidence, beyond what has been said already, for making any definite historical assertions about the time and place, presuppositions and circumstances of the lives of the patriarchs as human beings. Even the original tradition of the patriarchs was not, however, much concerned with their human personalities, but rather with the divine promises that had been made to them."[6] In America, however, there is W. F. Albright, a distinguished archaeologist who has done more than anyone else to place the findings of Palestinian archaeology and Oriental archaeology in general at the disposal of the historian;[7] he is also an outstanding linguist who has contributed enormously to the interpretation of numerous Oriental texts, but he is not so interested in specifically literary criticism. In a general work on the religious history of Israel, he expresses his views on the value of the patriarchal tradition: "So many corroborations of detail have been discovered in recent years that most competent scholars have given up the old critical theory according to which the stories of the Patriarchs are mostly retrojections from the time of the Dual Monarchy."[8] And again even more clearly, "As a whole, [[115]] the picture in Genesis is historical, and there is no reason to doubt the general accuracy of the biographical details and the sketches of personality which make the patriarchs come alive with a vividness unknown to a single extrabiblical character in the whole vast literature of the ancient Near East."[9]

These two contradictory judgments coming from the pens of two scholars who are equally well informed can be explained in terms of the

---

4. M. Noth, *Überlieferungsgeschichte des Pentateuch*, 1948; 2nd ed., 1960.

5. M. Noth, *Geschichte Israels*, 1950, several times revised and translated into several languages. Second English edition, Martin Noth, *The History of Israel*, London, 1960.

6. Loc cit., p. 108 = English translation, p. 123.

7. W. F. Albright, *The Archaeology of Palestine and the Bible*, 1932; *Archaeology and the Religion of Israel*, 1942; *The Archaeology of Palestine*, 1949.

8. W. F. Albright, *From the Stone Age to Christianity*, 1940, p. 183; several revised editions and translations; in the 2nd ed., 1946, p. 241.

9. *The Biblical Period*, 1950, p. 5 (repeated from *The Jews, Their History, Culture and Religion*, edited by L. Finkelstein).

different paths they follow. Noth takes as a starting point the biblical narratives, studies their literary genre and works back to the traditions on which they draw. He judges that the validity of these traditions is incapable of historical verification since there are no extrabiblical texts to confirm the "prehistory" of Israel; and in the absence of any proof he is skeptical. Albright, however, takes a general view of the many points of details on which the narratives in Genesis and the extrabiblical documents are in agreement. He recognizes also that the historical setting in which the extrabiblical texts originate is very similar to that which is presupposed by the stories of the Patriarchs; and consequently he is led to form a favorable opinion of the historical validity of these stories.

But things did not remain the same, and it is both interesting and instructive to follow the progress of research during the last ten years.[10] In 1956 John Bright, a pupil of Albright, in a general survey of recent historical essays on the origins of Israel,[11] strongly criticized the method and conclusions of Noth. In particular, he took him to task for his negative conclusions regarding the validity of the traditions, his refusal to consider archaeological evidence and his inability to give a sufficient explanation of the origins of Israel and the birth of its faith. Of course, Bright does not claim that archaeology (in its wider sense, including texts unearthed during excavations) "proves" the truth of the biblical stories, but he argues that it helps to set up a "balance of probabilities," which is inclined in their favor.[12] These principles are brought to bear by Bright [[116]] in his book *A History of Israel*, published in 1959. He accepts in general the conclusions of documentary criticism, but stresses that ancient Oriental texts recently discovered show that, "the patriarchal narratives, far from reflecting the circumstances of a later day, fit precisely in the age of which they purport to tell."[13] The traditions are therefore ancient but this is no guarantee that the information contained in them is true. Every item must be individually assessed for its historical value. We are also obliged to take into account the long period in which the traditions (both oral and written) were passed on, during which they were subject all the time to a process of reduction, accretion, and standardization which it would be impossible to reconstruct in detail. All this imposes very severe limits on the historian. As Bright says (p. 67),

---

10. This progress has already been noted by J. A. Soggin, "Ancient Biblical Tradition and Modern Archaeological Discoveries," in *The Biblical Archaeologist* 23 (1960) 95–100.

11. J. Bright, *Early Israel in Recent History Writing*, 1956.

12. Loc cit., especially pp. 83–89.

13. J. Bright, *A History of Israel*, 1959, p. 63.

It is, let it be admitted, impossible in the proper sense to write a *history* of Israel's origins, and that because of the limitations in the evidence both from archaeology and from the Bible itself. Even if we accept the Biblical account at face value, it is impossible to reconstruct the history of Israel's beginnings. Far too much is unknown. . . . In all the Genesis narrative no single historical figure is named who can, as yet, be otherwise identified. Nor has any mention of any Hebrew ancestor demonstrably turned up in any contemporary inscription. . . . It cannot be stressed too strongly that in spite of all the light it has cast upon the patriarchal age, in spite of all that it has done to vindicate the antiquity and authenticity of the tradition, archaeology has not proved that the stories of the patriarchs happened just as the Bible tells them. In the nature of the case, it cannot do so. At the same time—and this must be said with equal emphasis—no evidence has come to light contradicting any item in the tradition.

Archaeology restores the background to stories of Genesis and lends them "a flavor of probability" (p. 67). "Much must remain obscure. But enough can be said to make it certain that the patriarchal traditions are firmly anchored in history" (p. 69). This final statement is vaguer than Albright's, but we must not lose sight of Bright's initial reservations which are more explicit than in his first essay.

[[117]] A development in the opposite direction can be seen in the thought of Martin Noth. In 1957 the appearance of a popularizing work which had a resounding success[14] provided him with the opportunity to launch a quite justified attack on the misuse of archaeological discoveries to "prove" the Bible.[15] He makes a distinction between "mute" archaeology, i.e., monuments and other material remains, and "speaking" archaeology, i.e., ancient texts. Obviously the Patriarchs have left no traces which "mute" archaeology could uncover, and as for "speaking" archaeology it is surely asking too much of general Oriental history as known from texts to expect it to include a consideration of the Patriarchs. The most one could expect would be that some particular elements of the patriarchal narratives might be attested—for example, the names of the Patriarchs and certain aspects of their way of life to which one might be able to assign a context, either in time or space, in the history of the Ancient East. And such is indeed the case. But the onomastic evidence relates to long periods of time and to a population spread over a vast territory: "It is hardly possible to situate the Patriarchs in time and in space by using the evidence of nomenclature" (pp. 16–17). Juridical customs also were observed over

14. W. Keller, *Und die Bibel hat doch recht*, 1955; English translation *The Bible as History: Archaeology Confirms the Book of Books*, London, 1956.

15. M. Noth, "Hat die Bibel doch recht?" in *Festschrift für Gunther Dehn*, 1957, pp. 7–22.

long periods of time and in different places: "In these circumstances, how can one determine exactly when and where the Patriarchs may have come to know and to adopt them?" (p. 18). "The connections between biblical traditions and the findings of archaeology, cannot be determined for certain except by a thorough examination of each particular instance; and this presupposes not only a profound assessment of the archaeological material, but also a close familiarity with the biblical tradition and its problems." (This is his conclusion, p. 22.)

Two years later at the Old Testament Congress in Oxford,[16] Noth submitted a paper on the contribution of archaeology to the history of Israel. His remarks concerning the Patriarchs are as follows:

> It seems to me certain that the origins of Israel are rooted in [[118]] historical conditions which (so archaeological findings assure us) were verified in the middle of the second millennium B.C., and this is certainly important. But in the present state of our knowledge we cannot be more precise (pp. 269–70). . . . Extrabiblical testimony therefore sheds very little special light on the Patriarchs of the Old Testament. Certainly this light enables us to see in a way the background from which they came, but it does not enable us to date them, to give them a historical position or to interpret the stories. . . . Anyone who wants to say something about the Patriarchs must start from the tradition of the Old Testament, and therefore cannot escape the problems of the history of traditions and of literary criticism which go with this tradition. On this question, he cannot expect any substantial help from extrabiblical witnesses. (pp. 270–71)

Finally in 1961 Noth produced a study, "The origins of Ancient Israel in the light of new sources."[17] He begins by affirming that "the question of the origins of Ancient Israel is a historical question" (p. 9). The new sources which allow the question to be put in these terms are chiefly the Mari texts, in which there are evident parallels with the patriarchal narratives in various respects, including onomastics, language, social conditions, juridical traditions, and religious rites. All of these lead us to posit connections of kinship and history between the population of Mari and the ancestors of the Israelites. The inhabitants of Mari were the forerunners of the Aramaeans, i.e., "proto-Aramaeans," and the passages of the Bible which insist on the "Aramaean" descent of the Patriarchs thus appear to be verified. The Bible claims that these ancestors came from Upper Mesopotamia, from Aram Naharaïm, and, more specifically, from the Haran district. The extrabiblical texts provide no precise confirmation of

16. M. Noth, "Der Beitrag der Archäologie zur Geschichte Israels" in *Congress Volume Oxford, 1959* (*Suppl. to Vetus Testamentum*, 7), 1960, pp. 262–82.

17. M. Noth, *Der Ursprung des alten Israel im Lichte neuer Quellen* (*Arbeitsgemeinschaft für Forschung des Landes Nordrhein-Westfalen*, Heft, 94), 1961.

this, but the Mari texts do indicate that the region of the Middle Euphrates and its tributaries was the center of gravity of the proto-Aramaean movements: "thus the Old Testament tradition, which locates the original home of the Patriarchs in precisely this region, appears (to say the least) as not only historically possible in itself, but as probable" (p. 32). However Noth still has his reservations: "On the details of the origins of Israel, there is so far nothing but Israel's own tradition which can supply information, and it is scarcely to be expected that this will ever [[119]] be otherwise. On the other hand, it goes without saying that this tradition must always be considered in relation with what we know of the Oriental background of Israel" (p. 33).

We have now moved a long way from the pronounced skepticism of *The History of Israel* and even the positions held in 1957 and 1959 are themselves overtaken. In the end, it seems Noth accepts everything that Bright accepts with regard to the history of the Patriarchs. Here is Bright's conclusion on the matter:

> We conclude, then, that the patriarchs were historical figures, a part of that migration of semi-nomadic clans which brought a new population to Palestine in the early centuries of the second millennium B.C. . . . the tradition that Israel's ancestors had come from Mesopotamia cannot, in the light of the evidence, be gainsaid. We may assume that among these migrating clansmen, though no contemporary text observed them, there moved an Abraham, an Isaac and a Jacob, chieftains of sizeable clans, who remembered their origins in the "plain of Aram" near Haran.[18]

But there is still one difference in their points of view in that Noth stresses the limits of our knowledge, whereas Bright stresses the recent expansion of that knowledge. This difference stems from the fact that Noth begins by considering the biblical traditions and the problems they raise, while Bright takes as his starting point the Oriental background in which the traditions are most appropriately sited. At the risk of oversimplifying things, we might say that Noth views the problem of the historicity of the patriarchal traditions from the inside and that Bright (following Albright) views it from the outside. If we follow Noth's advice and make our starting point study of the text with constant reference to external evidence, it cannot be denied that this is the method which conforms most nearly to the accepted procedures of historical science. And it is gratifying to see that the consistent application of this method has led Noth to more and more positive results.

Recently the debate has shifted over to theological considerations. In 1957 and 1960 G. von Rad published the two volumes of his *Theology of*

---

18. J. Bright, *A History of Israel*, p. 86.

the Old Testament.[19] His basic theme is that "in principle Israel's faith is grounded in a theology of history. It regards [[120]] itself as based upon historical acts, and as shaped and reshaped by factors in which it saw the hand of Yahweh at work." But these facts of history are "those which the faith of Israel regarded as (divine acts)—that is, the call of the forefathers, the deliverance from Egypt, the bestowal of the land of Canaan, etc.—and not those established by modern critical scholarship, to which Israel's faith was unrelated" and these two constructs, i.e., scientific history and salvation history, or *Heilsgeschichte,* are different (vol. 1, pp. 112–13; ET, vol. 1, p. 106). After the publication of the first volume, the concept was contested by a number of people, who themselves had different points of view.[20] Von Rad defended his ideas in his preface to the second volume.[21] The debate, however, continued and was taken up both by his adversaries[22] and by some of his followers, though they were not always faithful to his ideas.[23]

These discussions are of particular importance for the traditions concerning the Patriarchs since it is here that the divergence between "true" history and "raw" history, i.e., between the events and the kerygma, is most marked. In his commentary on Genesis, Von Rad expressed the opinion that the historicity of the patriarchal narratives was not a matter of the reality of the events which they report (and which we are not in a position to verify), but in the authentic witness they bear concerning the religious experience of Israel.[24] This same position, which he developed in his *Theology of the Old Testament* has been criticized by G. E. Wright.[25] If

19. G. von Rad, *Theologie des Alten Testaments,* vol. 1, 1957; vol. 2, 1960; English translation [[*Old Testament Theology*]], vol. 1, Edinburgh, 1962; vol. 2, 1965.

20. Especially F. Hesse, "Die Erforschung der Geschichte Israels als theologische Aufgabe" in *Kerygma und Dogma* 4, 1958, pp. 1–19; J. Hempel, "Altestamentliche Theologie in protestantischer Sicht" in *Bibliotheca Orientalis* 15 (1958) 206–14; V. Maag, "Historische oder ausserhistorische Begründung alttestamentlicher Theologie?" in *Schweizer Theologische Umschau* 29 (1958) 6–18.

21. Vol. 2, pp. 8–11. [This passage is omitted in the English translation, Ed.]

22. Cf. especially J. Hempel, in his review of the second volume in *Bibliotheca Orientalis* 19 (1962) 267–73; F. Baumgartel, "Gerhard von Rad's 'Theologie des Alten Testaments'" in *Theologische Literaturzeitung* 86, 1961, cols. 806–16, 895–908.

23. Especially by R. Rendtorff and W. Pannenberg. For an account of the whole debate see M. Honecker, "Zum Verständnis der Geschichte in Gerhard von Rad's Theologie des Alten Testaments" in *Evangelische Theologie* 23 (1963) 143–68, and F. Hesse in the *Theologische Literaturzeitung* 88 (1963) cols. 752–54.

24. *Das erste Buch Mose* I (*Das Alte Testament Deutsch*), 1949, pp. 22–23, especially pp. 30–31; English translation, *Genesis,* in the Old Testament Library, London, 1961, pp. 30–42, especially pp. 39–40.

25. G. E. Wright, "History and the Patriarchs," in *The Expository Times* 71, 1959–60, pp. 292–96.

the Bible [[121]] presents the *Heilsgeschichte* as a series of events which man in the Bible believed to have actually happened and interpreted as the work of God, the master of human life and history, is it not of the utmost importance for theology that we should decide whether we are dealing with real history—interpreted by faith—or merely with cultic legends? Literary criticism and the history of traditions are poorly equipped to answer this question, and we have to look (though not exclusively) to archaeology, and in particular to the witness of extrabiblical texts. Von Rad has replied[26] by protesting that he is just as interested as Wright in the historical background to the narratives concerning the Patriarchs, but that these narratives represent the final flowering of religious experiences which had been part of people's lives from the most ancient times right up to the eventual date of their composition, and that these traditions only acquired their authority in the context of faith in Yahweh, which was not the faith of the Patriarchs. As far as theology is concerned, questions about the earlier forms of tradition and of their historical foundation can only be of secondary interest.

There must be some agreement. If we are concerned to decide what the Israelites believed, it is admittedly of secondary interest, though nonetheless worthwhile, to do some research into the extent to which this belief was founded on reality. If, however, we wish to establish a "theology" of the Old Testament, to study and present God's revelation to men, which was made in the first place to Israel, and through Israel to ourselves, and if we agree with Von Rad in admitting that the process of revelation took place in history and through history, then it becomes essential to know whether or not this "historical" revelation has any foundation in history. Von Rad regards as the fundamental confession of faith of Israel the "credo" of Deut 26:5–9, which was quoted at the beginning of this article: "My father was a wandering Aramaean." If this summary of "sacred history" is contradicted by "history," and if this confession of faith does not correspond to the facts, then the faith of Israel is void and so is our own. The place of the Hebrew Patriarchs in history is not just a problem for scholars.

---

26. G. von Rad, "History and the Patriarchs," ibid., 72 (1960–61) 213–16.

Historical and Christian Faith

THOMAS L. THOMPSON

> "Do not presume to say to yourselves, 'we have Abraham
> for our father.' I tell you that God can make children
> for Abraham out of these stones here." (Matt 3:9)

[[326]] More than forty years ago, Kurt Galling referred to this New Testament passage as an example to show that the theological significance of Israel's piety lies not in the history or the historicity of the Old Testament
phenomena, but in the traditions themselves, and in the understanding
which these traditions bring.[1]

Recently, however, many Old Testament scholars have been inclined
to believe that not only is history central to the message of Israel, but that
an acceptance of the historicity of Israel's early traditions, particularly
those about the biblical patriarchs, is essential to Christian faith, even,
that belief in the resurrection depends [[327]] directly on the historical
facticity of the promise to the patriarchs.[2] Roland de Vaux has asserted
several times that the task of scientifically establishing the historical foundations of these biblical traditions is of the utmost importance, "for if the
historical faith of Israel is not founded in history, such faith is erroneous,
and therefore, our faith is also."[3] De Vaux maintains that if faith is to

---

Reprinted with permission from *The Historicity of the Patriarchal Narratives* (Berlin: de Gruyter, 1974) 326–30.

1. K. Galling, "Die Erwählungstraditionen Israels," BZAW 48 (1928) 1f.

2. B. Vawter, *A Path through Genesis* (1965[2]) 8: "If God did not covenant with Israel, neither did the God of Abraham and Isaac and Jacob raise Jesus from the dead, for there is no
fulfillment without a promise."

3. English translation from: "The Hebrew Patriarchs and History," *ThD* 12 (1964) 22; cf.
"Les patriarches hébreux et l'histoire," *RB* 72 (1965) 7: "si la foi historique d'Israel n'est pas
fondée dans l'histoire, cette foi est erronée, et la notre aussi." See also, "Method in the Study
of Early Hebrew History," in *The Bible and Modern Scholarship* (ed. J. Ph. Hyatt, 1966) 16.

survive, the close relationship between "religious history" and "objective history" must be maintained.[4] He claims that to reject the historicity of Israel's "religious history" would be to question, in an ultimate way, the ground of faith itself.[5]

In a similar manner, George Ernest Wright believes that Christian faith depends ultimately on questions of historicity: "In biblical faith everything depends upon whether the central events actually occurred."[6] God is seen as one who acts in the events of Israel's history. Indeed, it soon becomes clear, it is not ultimately in the Bible that this "biblical faith" is grounded, but in the events of history, and in the Bible only insofar as the Bible retells historical events. This neo-orthodoxy is by no means a "biblicism" or a "fundamentalism" as it is often accused of being. In fact, there is very little room for any theology of the word. It is rather a deistic and positivistic historicism, which searches in its construction of a "biblical history"—to be found neither in the Bible nor in history—for the "real revelation" which could be learned if only the events which lie behind the biblical stories could be discovered.[7]

For those that are less agile than they, as indeed for those who do take history seriously, the neo-orthodox have set up an exceedingly [[328]] serious barrier to any acceptance of the biblical tradition as constitutive of faith; for not only has "archaeology" not proven a single event of the patriarchal traditions to be historical, it has not shown any of the traditions to be likely. On the basis of what we know of Palestinian history of the Second Millennium B.C., and of what we understand about the formation of the literary traditions of Genesis, it must be concluded that any such historicity as is commonly spoken of in both scholarly and popular works about the patriarchs of Genesis is hardly possible and totally improbable.

A serious evaluation of history—as well as of the literary forms used in the past—is essential for a clear elucidation of the theological significance of the Old Testament, for it is only in this way that we can understand the Old Testament as it was meant; but historical understanding, and, concomitantly, historical and archaeological research, is not the essential aspect of a Christian's commitment of faith. In respect to the commitment

4. Ibid.

5. Ibid.

6. *God Who Acts* (1962) 126, and: "To assume that it makes no difference whether they are facts or not is simply to destroy the whole basis of the faith" (ibid., 127). See also J. C. L. Gibson, "Light from Mari on the Patriarchs," *JSS* 7 (1962) 45, and R. de Vaux, *Method*, 16.

7. Wright speaks of history as the "primary data of faith" (ibid., 127) and that "history is the chief medium of revelation" (ibid., 13). The "biblical word is *not primarily a truth, but an event* . . . completely and entirely within history" and "The event brings into being . . . etc." (emphasis added): *History and Reality, The Old Testament and Christian Faith* (ed. B. W. Anderson; 1964) 186.

of faith, the question is not whether we take history seriously. The question of whether the Bible is a true source of faith will not be decided on the basis of the Bible's historical acceptability. Of far more importance is the question *whether we are prepared to see literary forms which are foreign to us, and philosophical presuppositions which are antagonistic to historical positivism, as media of truth; for it is only then that we can take the Bible seriously.* [8]

If we seriously affirm a "biblical faith," then it must be from the Bible that we begin to understand what that faith ought to be. And if it is true that the Bible does not speak about an historical Abraham, then a recognition of this leads us one step further towards an understanding of biblical faith. To learn that what we have believed is not what we should have believed is not to lose our faith.

Salvation history is not an historical account of saving events open to the study of the historian. Salvation history did not happen; it is a literary form which has its own historical context. In fact, [[329]] we can say that the faith of Israel is not an historical faith, in the sense of a faith based on historical event; it is rather a faith within history. It is a faith that is structured by the experience of Israel's history, and as such has the freedom and openness to the future which is characteristic of reflection on historical experience. It is a faith, however, which has its justification, not in the evidence of past events, for the traditions of the past serve only as the occasion of the expression of faith, but in the assertion of a future promise. The promise itself arises out of an understanding of the present which is attributed to the past and recreates it as meaningful. The expression of this faith finds its condensation in an historical form which sees the past as

---

8. Similarly, W. Stählin, *Auch darin hat die Bibel recht* (1964) 36: "Die Frage, ob die Bibel wirklich recht hat, entscheidet sich nicht an archäologischen Beweisen für die geschichtliche Zuverlässigkeit biblischer Berichte, sondern an der Frage, ob wir in der Lage und bereit sind, auch in Sage, Märchen, und Mythos als Denkformen, die der Bibel nicht fremd sind und die aus der Bibel nicht eliminiert werden können, die Stimme der Wahrheit zu vernehmen, die uns unbedingt angeht, weil darin die Grundstruktur unseres menschlichen Seins als Menschen und als Christen ihren Ausdruck gefunden hat. Und allein diese Freiheit, zu der ich damit aufrufe, gibt uns das gute Gewissen, die Bibel auch da ernst zu nehmen, wo alles rein historische Denken mit Notwendigkeit versagt, und ihr recht zu geben gerade darin, worin sie recht haben und recht behalten will." [['Whether the Bible is indeed correct is a question that must be answered not on the basis of archaeological proofs for the reliability of the biblical reports but, rather, in terms of whether we are ready and willing to hear the voice of truth also in modes of thinking such as saga, fairy tale, and myth, which are neither foreign to nor possible to eliminate from the Bible. This voice of truth addresses us directly, for it gives expression to the fundamental structure of our existence as humans and as Christians. Only this freedom, to which I now appeal, enables us in good conscience to take the Bible seriously, even in those places where pure historical thinking necessarily fails us, and to recognize the Bible's authority in just those areas in which it wants to have and hold authority.']]

promise. But this expression is not itself a writing of history, nor is it really about the past, but it is about the present hope. Out of the experience of the present, new possibilities of the past emerge, and these new possibilities are expressed typologically in terms of promise and fulfillment. Reflection on the present as fulfillment recreates the past as promise, which reflection itself becomes promise of a future hope. What is historical and therefore very much open to the historical-critical disciplines are the events and the historical situation in which Israel's past traditions achieve significance as promise, but prior to this new understanding, the traditions do not have significance for the understanding of faith.

Implicit in the writings of those theologians, who see revelation as the historical event itself, is that revelation is not in word or language, not in an existential experience of man reunderstanding his situation in history. Rather, for them there is little theology of the word; revelation is understood as a series of interventions in history by the divinity, which acts have been recorded and passed down through many generations. These acts of God are seen to culminate in the act of the resurrection. According to this view, the Old Testament has value according to its reportorial accuracy, and its theological significance is seen primarily as preparation. The acts of God recorded in the Old Law give confidence in the promise which is fulfilled in the New. It is not difficult to understand how questions of historicity must necessarily be of crucial significance in the authentication of such a faith; for, the argument goes: if these actions which have been reported did not happen, then there could not have been a real historical promise, and hence there could hardly be a fulfillment of what was not promised. The theological orientation is toward the past; for it is the events of the past which are seen as authentication of the present belief.

It is hardly accidental that this view of Christianity, while patterning itself on the biblical view of history, does not see the Bible itself as constitutive faith. Such a theological structure [[330]] creates serious difficulties for Christian faith, if only because it makes great demands on the credulity of Christians. Moreover, by presenting the faith of Israel as history, they demand for it a legitimation according to the norms of historical criticism. In maintaining that the history of Israel is the revelation to Israel, they have given to the historical disciplines the ultimate competence to decide what is and what is not revealed among the biblical traditions. The rejection of the historicity of large parts of the Old Testament, thought by them to be historical, is understood as a challenge to faith because it challenges their identification of revelation with event.

But the stories about the promise given to the patriarchs in Genesis are not historical, nor do they intend to be historical; they are rather historically determined expressions about Israel and Israel's relationship to its God, given in forms legitimate to their time, and their truth lies not in their facticity, nor in their historicity, but in their ability to express the reality that Israel experienced. To the extent that this experience can be communicated, it is a revelation of the faith that was Israel's. And it is through this communication in word that Israel's experience can become ours, and Israel's faith our faith; for it is through this revelation that we are enabled to see through to the reality and the truth of the human experience which transcends the historical forms in which this experience has been expressed.

The Patriarchs in Scripture and History

JOHN GOLDINGAY

[[35]] One of the aims of the attempt to interpret the patriarchal narratives above has been to see what kind of implied vested interest they may have in the historicity of the events they narrate. Are they the kind of stories that could be completely fictional but still be coherent and carry conviction? A parable is fictional, but nevertheless carries conviction on the basis of who it is that tells it and of the validity of his world-view as it expresses it. A gospel, however, invites commitment to the person portrayed in it, and in my view this implies that it cannot be both fictional and true. The kind of response it invites demands that the events it narrates bear a reasonably close relationship to events that took place at the time. Without this it cannot be coherent and carry conviction. In the absence of reference, it cannot even really have sense.

The patriarchal stories seem meaningful. Do they have to be fundamentally historical in order actually to be true? Are they more like a parable or a gospel?

Thomas L. Thompson closes his book *The Historicity of the Patriarchal Narratives*[1] by suggesting that they do not have to have any historical value in order to be true. He contrasts his own view with that expressed by scholars such as G. E. Wright,[2] who believe that the true locus of God's revelation to Israel is the events of her history, not the Bible itself. Logically,

Reprinted with permission and excerpted from "The Patriarchs in Scripture and History," in *Essays on the Patriarchal Narratives* (ed. A. R. Millard and D. J. Wiseman; Leicester: InterVarsity Press, 1980) 35–40 [[repr., Winona Lake, Ind.: Eisenbrauns, 1983, pp. 27–34]].

1. *BZAW* 133; Berlin and New York: de Gruyter (1974) 326–30.
2. E.g., *God Who Acts* (Chicago: Regnery and London: SCM, 1952) 126–27.

Wright then assumes, the factuality of Israel's account of these events is of key importance to the believer, and to establish it is a prime task of the historian. In opposition to this understanding, Thompson suggests that Israel's faith is rather a response of hope in God in some present situation, which expresses itself by drawing an imaginative picture of the past to embody its present hope. It is in this sense that salvation history is not something which actually happened but is a literary form arising out of a particular historical context (p. 328). The present is affirmed by creating a past of which it is the fulfillment. The believer therefore has no interest in the historical factuality of an Old Testament narrative. The Bible is a revelation of Israel's faith (embodied in an imaginative portrayal of the past) which makes it possible for us to share the experience of God that she had in the present and to respond with our own faith.

[[36]] As Thompson's historical views represent an extreme form of the current reaction against the Wright-Bright-Albright approach to biblical history, so his theological views represent an extreme form of the current reaction against the Wright-Cullmann approach to salvation history. This latter reaction is expressed in F. Hesse's desire to say goodbye to salvation history,[3] in the trenchant critique of the idea of salvation history in A. H. J. Gunneweg's *Understanding the Old Testament*,[4] and in R. E. Clements' scant attention to it in his *Old Testament Theology: A Fresh Approach*.[5] In various respects this reaction is quite justified, and in particular Thompson is correct that Wright's approach to history ignores the revelation in word or in language embodied in the Bible itself. Event and word are both part of revelation.

But Thompson's own position is as open to criticism on one flank as Wright's is on the other. The way in which the biblical testimonies to faith refer us to past historical events for their explanation and justification makes it difficult to believe that they imply no claim for their story's factuality.

Let us consider again some aspects of how the patriarchal traditions are set in a subsequent literary and historical context. First, Yahweh's words to the patriarchs constitute the divine undertaking fulfilled in exodus and conquest. They constitute Israel's charter for her possession of the land of Canaan. They explain how this was Yahweh's gift rather than the Israelites' desert. They set Israel's position in the land in the context of the sweep of a divine purpose concerned with the destiny of the na-

---

3. See his *Abschied von der Heilsgeschichte* (Zurich: TVZ, 1971); also J. L. McKenzie, *CBQ* 34 (1972) 504–5.
4. ET Philadelphia: Westminster and London: SCM, 1978.
5. London: Marshall and Atlanta: John Knox, 1978.

tions. If the patriarchal narrative is pure fiction (which Thompson suggests it may as well be), is anything lost? Surely much is, because the exodus-conquest narrative grounds its statements of faith in these events. If the events did not take place, the grounds of faith are removed.

We should note that Thompson is right that the mere factuality of certain patriarchal events would not in itself prove the validity of the faith perspective set up by the patriarchal narrative. We have seen that the narrative involves a perspective or an interpretation (the theme of blessing) as well as an account of events, and the historicity of the events does not prove the truth of the narrative. But while the historicity of the events is not a sufficient evidence of the truth of the narrative's interpretation, it is a necessary evidence of its truth. The narrative builds its interpretation on the factuality of the patriarchal events, so that without this factuality, faith in Yahweh as the giver of blessing, [[37]] the one who keeps his promises, the God of grace, and so on, may be true but is nevertheless groundless. If they are not fundamentally factual, the patriarchal narratives have sense but not reference.

Similar considerations apply to the patriarchal narrative in the context of the monarchy and—with more tragic force—in the context of the exile.

> Hearken to me, you who pursue deliverance,
> you who seek Yahweh,
> Look to the rock from which you were hewn,
> and to the quarry from which you were digged.
> Look to Abraham your father
> and to Sarah who bore you,
> for when he was but one I called him,
> and I blessed him and made him many. (Isa 51:1–2)

But on Thompson's thesis it does not matter that the call, the blessing, and the increase of Abraham are imaginative creations of faith! The prophet's position seems to be the opposite—not that faith creates Abraham, but that Abraham creates faith.

The debate in Old Testament scholarship in which Thompson sets his own position over against Wright's is by no means one confined to the United States. Indeed, much of the past two or three decades' discussion of the relationship between faith and history has taken place on the continent and refers back to Gerhard von Rad's exposition in his *Old Testament Theology*[6] of the problem of the "two histories"—one related by faith, in the Bible itself, the other related by the use of critical historical method. This exposition is anticipated in the Introduction to his commentary on

---

6. Volume 1 (ET Edinburgh: Oliver and Boyd and New York: Harper, 1962) 106–8.

Genesis[7] where von Rad describes the patriarchal stories as "saga." By the use of this term, he seeks to hold two convictions together. One is that a story in Genesis "narrates an actual event that occurred once for all in the realm of history." It is not "a product of poetic fantasy" (p. 31/[3]p. 32). But the other conviction is that saga is not concerned with history as mere this-worldly events of the past which are now dead and gone. It represents an intuitive response of faith that sees the activity of God in events, and portrays them accordingly. And it assumes that these events are thus relevant to and mirrored in the experience of later believers. "These narratives express everything that Israel had learnt from her association with Yahweh right down to the narrator's own time" ([3]p. 40). This does not mean "that these figures and the traditions about them are nothing more than subsequent projections of popular faith back into the primeval period. It means, [[38]] rather, that this material did not lie in the archives untouched but was moulded and substantially enlarged by being handed down for centuries" (p. 34/[3]p. 35). "At the beginning, the saga in most cases certainly contained a "historical" fact as its actual crystallizing point. But in addition it reflects an historical experience of the relevant community which extends into the present time of the narrator" (p. 33/[3]p. 34). Thus, for instance, the story of Jacob at the Jabbok (Gen 32:22–32) is "the witness of a past, and at the same time completely contemporary, act of God" (p. 34/[3]p. 35).

Von Rad's use of the word "saga" parallels Karl Barth's. For Barth, saga is "an intuitive and poetic picture of a pre-historical reality of history which is enacted once and for all within the confines of time and space."[8] Both von Rad and Barth can give the impression that they have abandoned the historical nature of biblical events. Yet Barth emphasizes their objective factuality, and in discussing the factuality of Christ's resurrection contrasts his own position with Rudolf Bultmann's.[9] Von Rad, similarly, responds to his critics on this point by affirming that the nature of Israel's faith is such that "there is little reason to fear . . . that in these descriptions of her early period Israel may have lost contact with actual history. They are rather utterances . . . of a people obsessed with its actual history."[10]

Barth and von Rad can give the impression that the event they discuss did not happen, because they recognize the limitations that, for good or ill, are imposed by modern assumptions regarding what can be described

---

7. London: SCM and Philadelphia: Westminster, 1961, [2]1963, [3]1972 (German original 1949).

8. *Church Dogmatics* 3, 1 (ET Edinburgh: Clark and New York: Scribner's, 1958) 81.

9. *Church Dogmatics* 3, 2 (ET Edinburgh: Clark and New York: Scribner's, 1960) 440–45.

10. *Old Testament Theology* 2 (ET Edinburgh: Oliver and Boyd and New York: Harper, 1965) 424.

as "historical." Such "history" cannot include events or statements that the historian cannot control, such as God calling Abraham from Mesopotamia or raising Jesus from the dead. So to say that these events are not historical is not to imply that they did not happen; it is only to imply that they cannot be investigated by the historical method. We can in principle investigate whether Abraham moved from Ur via Haran to Canaan or whether a body disappeared from a tomb belonging to Joseph of Arimathea; we cannot in the same way check the transcendent interpretation which the Bible gives to these events. Part of the difficulty of investigating the factuality of the Bible's history lies in the this-worldly assumptions of the historical method.

Yet this insight does not deal with all aspects of the question of the historicity of the patriarchs. Let us consider statements that are in fact capable of being checked by the historical method. Does the ancestry of the Israelites go back to certain pre-Israelite figures [[39]] who believed that God promised them many descendants and the possession of the land of Canaan, so that the Israelites' own possession of the land could be explained by a promise believed to have been given then? In principle this question can be investigated "historically" and indeed it has been so investigated, and the conclusion of many scholars is that the answer is "no." Does the faith that has based itself on these historical statements then collapse? To describe these stories as saga testifies to their background in some historical event, but if in the stories there is really more of the faith of the tellers than there is of actual events, we still seem to have faith creating Abraham rather than vice versa.

Von Rad himself hints at one resolution of this dilemma. Where did the material in the Genesis sagas that is not strictly "historical" come from? "It reflects an historical experience of the relevant community which extends into the present time of the narrator" (p. 33/³p. 44). One could say that the narrative of the jeopardizing of Sarah "is not 'historical,' but the experience that God miraculously preserves the promise beyond human failure was eminently historical (*geschichtlich*) for the community" (p. 39/³p. 41).

In contributions to the 1961 von Rad *Festschrift, Studien zur Theologie der alttestamentlichen Überlieferung*,[11] and in subsequent writings,[12] R. Rendtorff and W. Pannenberg have developed this point. The growth of Israel's traditions (in which Israel's faith is expressed) was itself part of her history. So the faith did arise out of the historical activity of Yahweh—his

11. Neukirchen: Neukirchener Verlag der Buchhandlung des Erziehungsvereins, 1961. ET of Pannenberg's essay in his *Basic Questions in Theology* 1 (London: SCM and Philadelphia: Fortress, 1970) 81–95.

12. E.g. Rendtorff's *Gesammelte Studien zum Alten Testament* (Munich: Kaiser, 1975).

activity in the development of her understanding of him. Indeed, Israel's national experience included Yahweh proving himself as her protector and provider, an historical experience that could then be seen as ret-rojected into the patriarchal narrative. Again, there is real historical experience here. From another perspective, Paul Ricoeur has pointed out that "fact" and "fiction" should not be distinguished by suggesting that only the former is historical. "History's reference and fiction's reference *intersect* upon the plane of the basic historicity of human experience."[13]

All these points are valid, but they actually reinforce rather than dis-solve the significance of the fact that large tracts of the Old Testament such as Genesis are put in the form of narrative about the factual past. Is-rael was capable of producing fictional parable and present testimony, but in the patriarchal stories she did not: she makes a point of telling a story about the factual past, [[40]] and refers to it (in a passage such as Isaiah 51) in such a way as to make it rather clear that she understands the story to be fundamentally factual.

The fashion of current Old Testament scholarship is to replace "his-tory" by "story" as the best category for Old Testament narrative, and my own approach will have made clear that I accept the validity of this insight. It is the story told in Genesis to which we are invited to listen and respond in faith, not whatever bare events of ancient near-eastern history lie be-hind it. And when (as is currently the case) it is difficult to be sure on his-torical grounds what actual events lie behind the Genesis narrative, this realization enables us still to interpret and profit from this story even when we have to be agnostic about at least some aspects of the history.

On the other hand, while (as R. J. Coggins puts it[14]) "we should laugh out of court anyone who approached *Hamlet* primarily with a view to im-proving his knowledge of Danish history, or *Henry V* as a source of knowl-edge of fifteenth-century England" and ought to query a parallel approach to Genesis, this does not mean that the investigation of the historical facts to which Genesis refers is irrelevant to the value of Genesis, as may be the case with Shakespeare's plays. In Genesis (and in cross-references to Gene-sis) the Bible appeals to factual history as the overt grounds of its faith statements, and it does therefore invite investigation by the historical method.[15]

13. "The Narrative Function," *Semeia* 13 (*The Poetics of Faith: Essays Offered to Amos Niven Wilder*, Part 2, ed. W. A. Beardslee; Missoula: SBL, 1978) 195.

14. "History and Story in Old Testament Study," *Journal for the Study of the OT* 11 (1979) 43.

15. Cf. A. Jepsen, "The Scientific Study of the Old Testament," *Essays on Old Testament Interpretation* (ed. C. Westermann; ET London: SCM; = *Essays on Old Testament Hermeneutics*, Richmond: John Knox, 1963) 267–71.

In his closing paragraphs, Thompson (pp. 329–30) notes that Wright's approach, which bases faith on history, thereby places a severe strain on faith when it is difficult (intellectually) to accept the factuality of the events that faith is supposed to be based on. The same observation applies to the position being defended here, that historical factuality is a necessary though not a sufficient basis for faith. It is not possible to have the advantages of history without its risks. But the pentateuchal narrative, like the preaching preserved in the book of Isaiah, invites us to take this risk.[16]

16. See further my paper "'That You May Know That Yahweh Is God': A Study in the Relationship between Theology and Historical Truth in the Old Testament," *Tyndale Bulletin* 23 (1972) 58–93. I hope shortly to publish a study of recent critical approaches to salvation history in a volume on "Interpreting the Old Testament" [[see now J. Goldingay, "The Old Testament as the Story of Salvation," chap. 3 in *Approaches to Old Testament Interpretation* (updated ed.; Leicester: Apollos, 1990 [orig. ed. 1981]) 66–96 and 1989 postscript 3 in ibid., 191–97]].

Early Israel in Canaan
A Survey of Recent Evidence and Interpretations

RICHARD S. HESS

[[125]] The purpose of this essay is to consider the present interpretations of the early period of Israel and to assess their likelihood in relation to the extrabiblical and biblical evidence. That a change has taken place concerning the evidence and its application is suggested by the opinions of two historians. The first reflects a view more than ten years old. The second represents a recent view.

> Our knowledge of the fortunes of Israel during the initial phase of her life in Palestine comes almost entirely from the book of Judges. Since this book presents us with a series of self-contained episodes, most of which cannot be related to external events with any precision, to write a continuous history of the period is impossible. Nevertheless, the impression one gains—of continual if intermittent fighting, with peaceful interludes alternating with times of crisis both external and internal—is a thoroughly authentic one. It tallies perfectly with the archaeological evidence, which shows that the twelfth and eleventh centuries were as disturbed as any in the history of Palestine. (Bright 1981: 176)

> The courts of the monarchic rulers of Israel produced documents now found in the Hebrew scriptures. David is the watershed because it was through him that, in a sense, the Egyptian and Philistine dream of an integrated Palestine was fulfilled and because it was in his court and cult that the documents that became the core of the Hebrew scriptures originated. For the reasons stated, it is doubtful that anything those documents could tell us about premonarchic Israel would be more valuable,

Reprinted with permission from *Palestinian Exploration Quarterly* 125 (1993) 125–42.

or even as valuable, as a schematic, generic picture of early Israel based on archaeology and analogy. . . . The agenda, I believe, for using such new evidence must pay close attention to these three issues: the Bible is to be critically discounted, Israel is to be defined politically, and the analytical standard for early Israel is to be a generic political history articulated in comparative terms. (Coote 1991: 43–44)

Is this change in the evaluation of the historical worth of the Biblical evidence legitimate? Does it reflect the development of theory or of evidence or the intrusion of other factors? Is it right that the Bible should now be discounted as a source for early Israel?

This essay will restrict itself to sketching some of the major trajectories which scholarship has taken and to highlighting some of the most significant historical sources which have had an impact on the interpretation and reconstruction of the period represented in the Bible especially in the books of Joshua and Judges. An interim assessment will conclude the study.

Israel's Formation as a Nation: The Interpretative Approaches

Archaeological and other social science disciplines have attempted to identify the origin of the Israelites once they settled in Canaan.[1] This has resulted in a number of theories, which can be broadly grouped into two categories, according to whether or not the Israelites originally came from outside Canaan or from within Canaan. According to [[the Conquest and Peaceful Infiltration theories]], they came from outside Canaan. According to [[the Peasant Revolt and Pastoral Canaanites theories]], they came from within Canaan.

Conquest

The first twelve chapters of the book of Joshua present the primary interpretation of Israel's appearance in Canaan as one involving the defeat and conquest of the Canaanite cities. Some of the archaeological evidence from major sites, such as the thirteenth century B.C. destruction layer at Hazor, does seem to point to such an interpretation (Yadin 1985). Nevertheless, there [[126]] are problems with this view. Many sites mentioned in Joshua have shown no archaeological evidence of having been destroyed

---

1. Lemche (1991a) has recently challenged the application of the terms "Canaan" and "Canaanite" to their traditional regions and peoples in the second millennium B.C. However one regards his interpretation of the biblical evidence, his conclusions require a particular interpretation of the references to Canaan in Egyptian sources and especially in the Amarna correspondence. Cf. my forthcoming review in *Themelios* [[(Jan., 1993) 24]].

during this period. Dever (1992: 548) notes 19 sites with possible identifications in Joshua. Of these, he finds only 2, Hazor and Bethel, to have evidence of destruction layers in the thirteenth century B.C. However, it may be that the accounts in Joshua describe the defeat of coalitions of kings but not necessarily the destruction of the cities they represent (11:13 and 12:7–24).

What about Jericho? This city has posed a problem for the Biblical account since Dame Kathleen Kenyon overturned the dates of John Garstang and established that there is virtually no evidence for habitation on the site during the time of Israel's entrance into Canaan, whether one accepts a fifteenth–fourteenth century B.C. date or a thirteenth–twelfth century B.C. date. Recent studies of the evidence from the excavations have not changed this opinion (Bienkowski 1986). Instead, they have confirmed the existence of a dwelling site and a few tombs.

The absence of walls in the Jericho of the time of Joshua is one example of the problems encountered in correlating the biblical and archaeological data. However, it should be noted that the absence of Late Bronze Age walls at major Canaanite sites is not limited to Jericho. For example, Gonen (1984: 69–70) has observed that, while both Megiddo and Hazor possessed monumental gates during this period, in neither case was the gate found to be attached to a wall. She suggests there may have been a fortified palace or the gate may have been ceremonial. Thus the last of discovery of Late Bronze Age walls at Jericho does not in itself say anything about the occupation of the site at that time, a fact which is noted by A. Mazar (1990: 331), "The archaeological data cannot serve as decisive evidence to deny a historical nucleus in the Book of Joshua concerning the conquest of this city."

The one other site to which a great deal of attention is given in Joshua is Ai. The absence of Middle or Late Bronze Age occupation has long been used to criticize the reliability of the conquest model of interpretation. Long ago Albright concluded that the account describing the destruction of Ai was originally based on a description of a military engagement with Bethel and later transferred to Ai, as an etiology to explain the meaning of the name, 'ruin'. Studies have challenged the traditional equation of an etiology with lack of historicity and called into question assumptions about the symbolic nature of etiologies in which the name must always precede the event (Childs 1974 and his review of research; van Dyk 1990). This provides opportunity to examine in a fresh light the suggestion that the ruin "Ai" might have been a ruin in the thirteenth century and the Early Bronze Age wall, still present, could have functioned as "a stronghold for villagers in the region if attackers came up from the Jordan Valley" (Millard 1985: 99).

This may be related to a problem which Dever (1991: 83) has noted for the Conquest Model. It has to do with the lack of fortifications in the small villages which appear in the hill country of Palestine in the twelfth century and which have been identified with early Israel (see below). Those that have been excavated reveal a lack of fortifications. This argues against a warlike conquest. It should be noted, though, that Khirbet ed-Dawwara and possibly Giloh do have fortifications, although, in the case of the former, they are not dated by Finkelstein (1990b: 197) before the mid–eleventh century. Finkelstein suggests a similar function for Khirbet ed-Dawwara as Millard does for Ai, a fort protecting the inhabitants of neighboring non-fortified sites in times of emergency. Future excavations may reveal the existence of additional fortifications of this sort.

Peaceful Infiltration

Earlier in this century Alt (1989) proposed a new interpretation of the evidence. He suggested that Israel's origin is to be found in wandering semi-nomadic clans who peacefully entered the [[127]] land and settled in the hilly country which was unoccupied. Brought together into a loosely knit association by a group of Yahweh worshippers from the desert, and perhaps ultimately from Egypt, this group populated the hill country and eventually grew strong enough to band together and to gain dominance in the rest of the land, during the period of the Monarchy.

This theory has certain advantages, given the existence of semi-nomadic groups attested in this area of the world throughout history and the fact that the earliest settlements of Israel probably were in the hill country. Nor is it without Biblical testimony. The Biblical text describes a "mixed multitude" which left Egypt (Exod 12:38). The possibility of foreign groups joining in with Israel on its journeys and after its entrance into the land might be remembered in the references to the Midianites (Numbers 22–25), the Kenites (Judg 4:11; 1 Sam 15:6), the Gibeonites (Joshua 9), and others. Further, there are records of areas of the hill country, such as the region around Shechem, which Israel is portrayed as occupying in the book of Joshua (8:30–35; 24:1, 32), but for which there is no account of conquest. This may attest to a peaceful settlement in such an area. Advocates of the peaceful infiltration hypothesis have recently emphasized the continuous presence of nomadic groups living in symbiotic relationship with the settled inhabitants throughout the Fertile Crescent. These groups could easily move into the hill country of Palestine and occupy it during the period in question.

There is increasing evidence to suggest that groups of settlers in the hill country came from the north, as well as from the east and south. At this time the Sea Peoples (including Philistines) and the Arameans were migrating. The collapse of the Hittites and the destruction of sites such as Ugarit may have stimulated northerners to migrate to the south, especially in the Jordan Valley, where archaeological and onomastic evidence suggests the presence of Northern influence (Hittite, Hurrian, and Indo-Aryan) for the fourteenth century (Hess 1989). The Bible preserves evidence of such "northerners" in Hivite Shechem (Judg 9:28), Luz/Bethel (Judg 1:22–26) in ethnic names ending in -zzi (e.g., Perizzites), and in the name of Araunah in Jerusalem (B. Mazar 1981). Burials in storage jars, reflecting customs from the last period of the Hittite empire, have been found on and near the coast (Tell Nami, Tel Zeror, Azor), in the Jezreel Valley (Kfar Yehoshua), at Tell el Farʿa (North) in the hill country, and at Tell es-Saʿidiyeh in the Jordan Valley (Gonen 1992: 22, 30, 142–44). It is possible that the bull figurine found in a cult site on a hilltop east of Dothan in the territory of Manasseh has origins to the north of Canaan (cf. Ahlström 1990b). All the evidence points to a presence in the hill country of other non-indigenous peoples, whether or not they were among those who subsequently became Israelites.

The migration of other groups at approximately the same time as Israel's appearance in Canaan has long been observed. Specifically these are the Philistines and the Arameans. This additional evidence for the presence of northern groups in the hill country suggests that Israel could have been one among many wandering peoples in the thirteenth century B.C. The argument that none of the hill country settlers could have migrated from the east or southeast because they were aware of technology for settlement in the hill country (i.e., storage pits and terracing, cf. Lemche 1992: 538–39) must answer the objections that (1) the knowledge of such techniques extended beyond the borders of Canaan and (2) such settlers did not live in isolation from native elements in the hill country (Finkelstein 1990a: 683–84).

There are problems with particular aspects of the peaceful infiltration theory, especially the view of a religious association of tribes, based on the number 12 and on a common sanctuary. This model, called an amphictyony, was imported from descriptions of tribal leagues of Classical Greece. It has been shown to be anachronistic and incompatible with the evidence from the Bible and from archaeology (see the critique of Gottwald 1979). However, this does not deny the presence of a federation of tribes and a common worship center, such as may be found [[129]] in Joshua 8 and 24 and in 1 Samuel. The theory of Alt continues to enjoy influence (cf., e.g., Fritz 1987 and Rainey 1991).

Peasant Revolt

Data. The impetus for this approach comes from the changing archaeological interpretation during the past two decades. Traditionally, when any new cultural element appeared in a land, the archaeological assumption was that this signaled the presence of a new people. For a long time, archaeologists identified the coming of Israel with the appearance of particular types of private houses, particular types of storage jars, and a particular means of storing water at the archaeological sites in the land of Canaan (Albright 1961). The house was the "four-roomed house," the jars was the collared-rim pithos, and the water storage method was the plaster-lined cistern. However, evidence for these types of cultural features has now been found in earlier strata of archaeological sites as well (Mazar 1990: 338–48).

For example, Schaar's survey (1991) of the evidence for the origins of the "four-room house" which appears ca. 1200 B.C. suggests that it has cultural antecedents in earlier Canaanite dwellings and in nomadic structures (cf. Dever 1991: 82). He argues it can no longer be considered a determinative means by which the appearance of Israel can be defined. However, this is not the view of Finkelstein (1988: 258–59) who would date all such houses after 1150 B.C. and assign this distinctive style of architecture to "the influx of settlers into the hilly regions of the Land of Israel at that time."

Recent studies of the data by Esse (1991; 1992) have confirmed that the collared-rim pithoi are determinative for the early Iron Age Canaanite/Israelite/other culture(s) of the Palestinian hill country and of the Transjordan hills. This may be compared with the distinctive ceramic culture usually attributed to the Philistines (and other Sea Peoples) which appears along the coastal plain and in the Western Jezreel Valley (though Raban [1991] notes that collared-rim pithoi are found here as well). The important point is that the material culture is distinctive to a particular region (i.e., the hill country), not necessarily to a particular ethnic group (e.g., Israelite rather than Canaanite).

Both terracing and cisterns of some sort were in use as early as the MB IIC, as evidenced by settlements in the western slopes of the hill country where both were needed (Finkelstein 1988–89: 144). Albright (1961: 341) had formerly attributed cisterns to the period of the coming of the Israelites. Instead, it is now necessary to look for evidence of a different sort.

Theory. Various theories of the social sciences have attempted to come to terms with the archaeological, biblical, and historical data. A significant representative of these theories is that which posits a peasant revolt which took place against the oppressive Canaanite aristocracy which maintained its cities at the cost of sizeable expenditures for defense in the forms of city walls, large buildings, and weapons, and for paying tribute to Pharaoh, who was maintaining an empire in this land. Such expenditures would come from the labor of the lower classes who may have been gradually dispossessed and turned into serfs and then into virtual slaves.

Whether the revolt was a more dramatic assault on the upper classes
(Gottwald 1979), or whether it simply involved the gradual movement of
individuals and groups of dissatisfied people into the hills (Mendenhall
1983, who emphatically denies the peasant revolt hypothesis), there was a
change and it brought about a change in living. In the hill country, where
the chariots and other weapons of the city-state armies could not reach
(Josh 17:14–18), it was possible to have simpler defenses and to live in
smaller communities without costly walls, palaces, and other large buildings. The impression created in the excavation of these villages is one of
an egalitarian society, certainly more so than one finds in the socially
stratified larger towns located in the lowlands. [[130]]

Evaluation. This new approach has caused the re-evaluation of much
archaeological and Biblical evidence. The Biblical texts also identify the
appearance of groups such as the Gibeonites who ally themselves with Israel although they are already in the land. In addition, we may suppose
that, as with the narratives concerning David who was joined by many
drifters and other dispossessed peoples when he fled from Saul, so early
Israel was joined by many who found here a more desirable community in
which to live. Finally, we should note that, as with the evidence from archaeological surveys, so the Bible records some of the earliest settlement
activities of the Israelites in Canaan as taking place in the central hill
country north of Jerusalem and south of the Jezreel Valley. However, the
reasons for the evidence of the society as egalitarian may be due as much
to the scarcity of food and natural resources as to any ideology. Indeed,
the application of Marxist models to explain a phenomenon about which
we know little may be anachronistic. It is this aspect of Gottwald's theory
which has come under the heaviest attack.

From an anthropological standpoint, Lemche (1985) has severely criticized Gottwald. He argues that nomads do not need to have an egalitarian system of rulership, that sedentarization is not necessarily an advance
on nomadism, and that farmers and urban dwellers are not necessarily opposed to one another. The use of a "heuristic model" to explain a society
is illegitimate because it implies that societies will behave in predictable
patterns, given the presence of certain phenomena (1992: 532–33). It is
not possible to rule out immigration or conquest models on the basis of
the little we know of early Israelite tribes. Although Lemche (1988: 110–
17; 1991b: 14–16) would deny value to any of the early Biblical traditions,
others would not agree. For example, Mayerson (1990: 271 n. 14) has suggested that early Biblical narratives "provide a fairly accurate tableau of
ancient nomadic and semi-nomadic lifestyles and attitudes."

From an archaeological perspective, the assumption that every ethnic
group must have a distinct, archaeologically observable culture is not well

founded. First, consider the example of the Philistines which is sometimes cited to demonstrate a distinct culture. The traditional evidence used to identify the Philistines, for example pottery, anthropoid coffins, and cultic assemblages, has been shown to not be distinctive to the Philistines. They are part of the coastal culture of all the peoples of lowland Palestine in Iron Age I (Bunimovitz 1990). Their use by the Egyptians in residence in Palestine (Bergoffen 1991) may explain their appearance in Jordan Valley sites of the twelfth and eleventh centuries, rather than the hypothesis of the presence of Sea Peoples in these places (Negbi 1991). Although some evidence exists for a distinct Philistine culture with origins in the Aegean, the exercise suggests it is premature to require that one be able to identify unique archaeological evidence for every ethnic group. In a wider context, Isserlin's (1983) comparison of early Iron Age Palestinian culture with a variety of other archaeological evidence from invading groups of different times and places leads him to conclude that the appearance of external groups does not require distinctive ceramic or other archaeological evidence.

Second, comparative studies of pottery and architecture in modern Cypriote village life have demonstrated that diversity in these features implies nothing about ethnicity. It only demonstrates that different lifestyles have requirements distinct to each community (London 1989, but cf. the critique of Finkelstein 1991 on some specific points).

Finally, in Israel's case, there are several factors which suggest that there would be little in the way of a distinctive archaeological assemblage. The Bible and archaeology attest to Israel's West Semitic origins, similar to all Canaanites in the land. Add to this the point of Rainey that a nomadic people would naturally adapt to the settled culture as they spent time in the same region. Thus the conclusion of Esse (1991; 1992: 103) that there is not a clear ceramic (pottery) [[131]] distinction between Canaanites and Israelites is not surprising. Additionally, Israel's tradition of an aniconic cult would leave little in the way of distinctive material evidence for religious identification.

Ecological/Economic Factors. Whether or not other theorists would classify their view as a variant on the peasant revolt model, some are similar insofar as they ascribe an economic motive to the appearance of Israel. Some views would find that political factors, such as the decline of the Egyptian empire in Palestine, are decisive, but all insist that the elements essential to early Israel's constitution are non-religious and unrelated to anything found in the biblical account. Coote and Whitelam (1986; cf. also Strange 1987) advocate this perspective. It is also found with Stiebing (1989: 186–87) who summarizes:

It was the growing frequency of drought—and the crop failures and hunger it brought with it—that set in motion the internal strife, warfare, plague, piracy, destruction of cities, decline in population, inflation, and population movements. . . . The widespread drought might very well have been largely responsible not only for the destruction of most of the Canaanite cities, but also for the creation in Canaan of detached groups of seminomads, refugee peasant farmers, and occasional bands of brigands who, together with a small contingent of escaped slaves from Egypt, would join to form the Israelite tribes.

The application of economic, ecological, and international political forces to understanding the history of population shifts in Palestine is important in understanding the changes in the political life of the societies there (Thompson 1992a; [[1992b]]). Thompson (1992a: 13) argues that the complexities of these forces renders doubtful the simple equation that drought produces nomadism while plentiful rain results in sedentarization.

Pastoral Canaanites

A dramatic change took place during the thirteenth and twelfth centuries B.C., the time when most scholars understand Israel to have appeared in the land of Canaan. This change is marked by the pattern of settlement throughout the land. In the period before Israel appeared in the land, Canaan was characterized by a few larger cities or city-states. In the period after Israel's appearance, the hill country of Canaan became occupied by many small villages. For example, in the area of the hill country allotted to the tribe of Ephraim, surveys have located 5 sites occupied in the Late Bronze Age, but 115 in Iron Age I (cf. Finkelstein 1988–89: 167). This change is the most distinctive alteration in what happened in the land. The evidence examined is quite dramatic. Such a change does not require the entrance of external peoples, for there is no new cultural form which must be traced from outside the land. Instead, this change may be simply a shift in the living patterns of inhabitants already in Canaan.

This view, now promulgated by Finkelstein, understands the Israelites as originally Canaanites. However, they did not come from the urban environment of the Canaanite city-states. Rather, they were the same peoples who lived in settlements in the hill country in the Middle Bronze Age. Internal factors caused them to abandon their settlements in the Late Bronze Age. They wandered about with flocks and herds from summer to winter pasturage and back again. Both regions of pasturage were located in the hill country west of the Jordan River. The presence of the nomads is attested by burials (esp. the large family tomb at Dothan) and cult centers (e.g., Shiloh), but they did not leave behind permanent settlements. At the end of the Late Bronze Age various circumstances, especially the

droughts already mentioned as well as the disruption of Egyptian hege-
mony in Canaan, led to the loss of the grain surplus which the (fewer) sedentary communities had been able to produce throughout the Late Bronze
Age (Finkelstein 1990a: 685). This required the settlement of the pastoralists in villages throughout the hill country.

[[132]] The settlement process, as observed by Finkelstein in the
southern hill country (i.e., that occupied by the tribe of Ephraim), was one
in which people settled in the eastern areas first. The eastern areas are the
best suited for cereals and pasturing, such as we would expect for a pastoral people. The western areas, which would sustain horticulture, were
settled later. Thompson (1992a: 12 n. 48) has challenged this interpretation as based on circular reasoning, although he does not provide details
as to the specific problems in Finkelstein's chronology. More significant is
his conclusion that the highland settlers were not re-sedentarized nomads
but lowland inhabitants who were dispersed eastward (1992a: 10–11).
This does not explain the evidence of the burial sites and cult centers
noted above, but it does suggest an additional source for the sudden increase in population in the hill country (though insufficient as the sole
source, cf. Stager 1985a: 83).

The settlement patterns may identify the presence of a group known
as Israel but they may also identify the presence of other newly settled
groups in the thirteenth and twelfth centuries B.C. Whether or not Zertal
(1991[[a]]) has found a pottery distinct to early Israel, both those who hold
to the Conquest model and those who affirm the peasant revolt approach
will agree that Israel could be expected to have a culture similar to that of
hill country Canaan. This is true whether or not the Israelites were direct
descendants of wandering groups in the hill country. Even if they entered
the land from outside, they came as a group ethnically related to the West
Semitic presence which dominated Palestine and the eastern Mediterranean throughout the second millennium B.C. (or at least before 1200 B.C.).

Conclusions

Aspects of each of the models may be attested in the biblical accounts of
early Israel (cf. Halpern 1983 on the first three models). Aspects of each
of them may well have been true in some measure.

1. Recent research has demonstrated that Joshua 9–12, in its form,
structure, and themes, is identical to other historical/ideological conquest
accounts found among the Hittites, Egyptians, and Assyrians (Younger
1990: 197–237). Thus it is not necessary to understand these chapters as
a theological interpretation of a class revolt (Brueggemann 1986), or as
modeled only on Neo-Assyrian accounts (and therefore necessarily late, so

Van Seters 1990). Instead, they could reflect the sorts of skirmishes which peoples who were beginning to settle in various areas might experience.

2. Other elements, both from outside and from within Canaan, became attached to any people who might be designated as Israel. In Joshua this is reflected in accounts concerning Rahab and concerning the Gibeonites. As already noted, the archaeological evidence in the hill country also attests to peoples from the north and from elsewhere.

However, there is no substantial evidence for an egalitarian origin to these texts (as argued by Gottwald 1979 and Brueggemann 1986). Indeed, Younger's careful comparison with other ancient Near Eastern sources leads him to conclude (1990: 255):

> The historical narrative in which Joshua 9–12 is cast utilizes a common transmission code observable in numerous ancient Near Eastern conquest accounts, employing the same ideology. Since the ideology which lies behind the text of Joshua is one like that underlying other ancient Near Eastern conquest accounts—namely, imperialistic—then "egalitarian, peasant" Israel is employing a transmission code (a "communicative mode") which is self-contradictory.

3. Thus to accept all the models to at least some degree is not simply to opt for a "middle of the road" position but to affirm the diversity of human motivations and social action involved in the [[133]] process of becoming a people. Israel's (re)appearance in the thirteenth century or earlier may have led to the establishment of a religious faith which brought together other "tribal" groups and so led to the formation of the people of Israel in Canaan.

4. Such an interpretation preserves an understanding of the Conquest. As already observed this has a strong tradition in the variety of literatures preserved in the Old Testament. This in itself raises a fundamental question as to the interpretation of biblical historical accounts. This question has been addressed by the Assyriologist W. W. Hallo in his 1989 presidential address to the American Oriental Society. He argues (1990: 193–94; cf. also the comments of A. Malamat [1983]):

> The Biblical record must be, for this purpose, scrutinized like other historiographical traditions of the ancient Near East, neither exempted from the standards demanded of those other traditions, nor subjected to severer ones than they are. . . . Unless one rearranges the Biblical evidence, like Séan Warner, or utilizes it eclectically as Norman K. Gottwald has essentially done with his reinterpretation, one can hardly deny the reality of a conquest from abroad, implying a previous period of wanderings, a dramatic escape from the prior place of residence and an oppression there that prompted the escape.

The conclusions which the evidence suggests is that the biblical evidence does not perfectly coincide with any of the models proposed. In itself this neither "proves" nor "disproves" these accounts. The biblical material serves purposes other than those which the modern historian may seek. Therefore, it is not surprising that coincidence is not perfect. An example of this difficulty in matching contemporary records and archaeological data may be found in R. Jacoby's comparison (1991) of the cities which Assyrians conquered and their depiction on reliefs. Although it is not a written source, what is distinctive and what is conventional is not obvious to the casual viewer of a relief with no training in Assyrian styles of representation. The same is true of the written records.

In addition to the site excavations and the survey data, there are several other pieces of evidence which need to be considered, as they may critically affect our understanding of early Israel.

Evidence from Egypt

The Merneptah Stele

The earliest mention of the name of Israel occurs on a victory stele erected by pharaoh Merneptah ca. 1207 B.C. It has been translated as follows (Wilson, in *ANET*, 378):

> The princes are prostrate, saying: "Mercy!" Not one raises his head among the Nine Bows. Desolation is for Tehenu; Hatti is pacified; plundered is the Canaan with every evil; carried off is Ashkelon; seized upon is Gezer; Yanoam is made as that which does not exist; Israel is laid waste, his seed is not; Hurru is become a widow for Egypt!

There are three groups of proper names which are divided by the determinatives associated with each name. There are the city-states Ashkelon, Gezer, and Yanoam. There are the lands or territories of Tehenu, Canaan, Hatti, and Hurru. A third type of determinative identifies a people or ethnic group. Only one name is associated with it, Israel.

In studying this passage, some have suggested that Israel is in parallel with one of the other place names in the inscription. This would be important for the interpretation of the text. Some have seen it in parallel with Canaan, arguing that it is another word for a place rather than a designation of a people (Ahlström and Edelman 1985). Others have related it to Tehenu and Hatti, as equivalent to these "superpowers" in terms of its military might (Bimson 1991). On the basis of its proximity in the text, Stiebing (1989: 51–52) has suggested that Hurru is a more [[134]] likely parallel. All of these proposals are inconclusive owing to the variety of possible ways to analyze the few lines of this poem, itself an addendum to a longer text.

However, no one has proved that "Israel" in the Merneptah stele should be regarded as a place name rather than an ethnic term. It is not enough to argue that patriarchal names were often place names or that the determinative for an ethnic group, which accompanies Israel on the stele, can sometimes be interpreted as a place name (Ahlström 1991: 27–31). One must explain why Israel is given a determinative distinct from that assigned to place names for lands and from that assigned to place names for towns or city-states. Kitchen (1966: 59 n. 12) refuted attempts to identify this name in Merneptah's stele with any population group other than Israel. More recently, Rainey (1991; 1992) has replied to the specific claims of Ahlström and Edelmn.

The Karnak Battle Reliefs

Related items regarding early Israel are some battle reliefs at Karnak. Formerly, these were assigned to Ramses II. However, Yurco (1990; cf. Stager 1985b) has re-analyzed them and concluded that they should be ascribed to the reign of Merneptah.

The reliefs contain four scenes. The lower right scene is clearly a scene of a battle with Ashkelon. The name of the city is provided. Two of the remaining scenes portray battles with cities. Their names are no longer visible. The upper right is mostly destroyed but it appears to be a battle scene in the open country. Yurco relates these reliefs to Merneptah's stele. If Ashkelon is one of the cities portrayed, he argues that the other two cities should be Gezer and Yanoam. The scene in open country would then be Israel. If so, the portrayal suggests that it possessed chariots and infantry to enable it to fight on the lowlands. It was not confined to the hill country.

Rainey (1991; 1992) has rejected this interpretation on the basis that a tribal Israel of this period would not have chariots and that the clothing of the people in the scene is that of Canaanites. As observed above, Rainey does not understand the Israelites as Canaanites, but as pastoralists from outside the country. He prefers to identify Shasu groups from adjacent scenes as Israelites, arguing that the Israelites were Shasu, i.e., pastoralists, with a distinctive type of clothing. Yurco (1991) has replied that the people in these scenes are explicitly called Shasu, never Israel (in the preserved fragmentary texts). Yurco does not believe that the Israelites came only from Canaan, but allows for elements external to the land. Whichever identification of the panels is correct, Israel does appear in the Metneptah stele as a foe whom Merneptah takes pride in claiming to have defeated.

Interpretations

Diachronic. The text of the Merneptah stele portrays Israel as strong and associated with other powers and with major city-states of Canaan. The events described by the book of Joshua suggest, as we have seen, a stronger unified people, involved in successful battles. However, in the Judges period, Israel is confined to the hill country with little military might. For example, Judges 5 describes Deborah's forces as a tribal confederation of pastoralists and farmers. In Judg 1:19 we read:

> The Lord was with Judah. He drove out the inhabitants of the mountains. But he could not drive out the inhabitants of the valley because they had chariots of iron.

Is the earlier, stronger Israel a reflection of the period of Joshua and the weaker Israel a reflection of its later weakness?

Zertal's survey work in the eastern hill country of the tribal territory of Manasseh has led him to conclude that a new culture with new settlements appeared in the thirteenth century. He [[135]] identifies this as the earliest Israelite settlement in Palestine. Further, he relates Josh 17:14–18 to this and concludes that originally the Josephite tribes (= Ephraim and Manasseh) as well as other tribes appeared here in Palestine and settled. This region became overpopulated and so Manasseh moved south and the other tribes began to move into their tribal allotments. The earlier more unified phase (with the religious center at Shechem) may have been the period of greater strength as suggested in Joshua and in the Merneptah stele. The later dispersal of the tribes may have led to a period of some weakness and vulnerability which led to oppression such as is suggested in the book of Judges. Indeed as Israel spread across Palestine and Transjordan they would begin to encounter more of the groups mentioned in Judges.

Synchronic. An alternative way of viewing the Biblical accounts in Joshua and (especially the first chapter of) Judges is to see them as reflecting two perspectives on similar events. Liverani (1990: 13–29) has analyzed Ancient Near Eastern documents of the contemporary period (1600–1100 B.C.) and has argued that they can be divided into two groups according to the ideological purpose which they serve. There are those whose purpose is to demonstrate how great the nation's leader, gods, and people are. These view all international events in terms of prestige. They emphasize the strengths of the particular nation concerned and serve to promote its policies through convincing its citizens of its inherent value. The second group of texts are those which are prepared for purposes of international diplomacy and correspondence. These are concerned to elicit the interest of other nations in supporting the particular nation concerned in trade, in peaceful relations, or in disputes with a third party. Liverani refers to these as serving purposes of interest rather than prestige. A nation can describe the same event from two different perspectives according to the purpose which the documents are to serve.

Perhaps Joshua and Judges can be viewed in a similar manner. So understood, Joshua reflects traditions of prestige in which there is a desire and concern to demonstrate the superiority of God's chosen leader and people against all enemies. Such a document could arise and find use in contexts concerned with persuading the nation to fight and with assuring them of divine support in their struggle against the enemy. On the other hand, Judges 1ff. may represent a view of the same and subsequent events from a tradition which was concerned with peaceful cohabitation (or, more accurately, mixing together) with a variety of groups, for example those northerners who shared the highlands with Israel. Its accounts are thus nuanced with both military failures and successes. This interpretation requires further development in its application to the books of Joshua and Judges. It may be suggested here as one means of relating these books and the events behind their records to the extrabiblical data and to the models which have been proposed to explain it.

Mount Ebal

The Site

Another item of extrabiblical evidence is a site which Zertal (1986–87) discovered on Mount Ebal. The identification of the purpose and use of this site could have some relation to early Israel. Mount Ebal contains three peaks. On the lowest peak, a site was found, which Zertal dated to the thirteenth and twelfth centuries B.C.

The site is on a stony hilltop which is crossed by a stone wall. No building was found in the outer court. There is an inner enclosure wall, encompassing the higher northern part. There are three steps at the entrance to this area. Although sites from the Persian, Roman, and later periods have been found at Mount Ebal, the mountain contains no other sites from the Late Bronze or Iron Ages. Two levels were found at the site. They are dated on the basis of Egyptianized scarabs, a small decorated limestone "seal," and the pottery which was found in [[136]] the excavations. The earlier level ends ca. 1200 B.C. and the later level terminates ca. 1150, when the site was abandoned and never resettled. The adjacent hill makes it possible for many people to gather and view what is happening.

Bones

Excavations revealed a central complex, a western wall with an entrance, and an outer enclosure wall. In the central complex were found two layers of ash with some 2,862 bones (Horwitz 1986–87). Ninety-six percent of the bones were those of sheep, goats, cattle, and fallow deer. West of what seems to be an altar were two courtyards. The major concentration of animal bones was found at the altar. One hundred and twenty-eight bones were burnt and 25 had cut marks. A large percentage of bones of fallow deer were found. Horwitz (1986–87: 187) concludes that we have here "a pastoral economy based primarily on caprovine herding and to a lesser extent cattle. In addition, the high proportion of hunted animals (fallow deer) supports the hypothesis of a nomadic or semi-nomadic society." The area was not a food producing place. No sickle blades were found, unlike all other contemporary sites.

There has been an attempt to interpret these remains in the context of the dietary regulations of early Israel. The sheep, goat and cattle bones found reflect animals whose consumption was in accord with the biblical dietary laws as found in Leviticus 11 and Deuteronomy 14. It is not clear whether the bones of the fallow deer should be associated with the species of "deer" mentioned in Deut 14:5, which are permitted for consumption. However, such evidence does not automatically identify a site as Israelite. The example of the Late Bronze Age Fosse temple at Lachish, should be kept in mind. Although no one suggests that this temple has anything to do with what becomes Israelite cult, a similarity with biblical dietary legislation is attested by the presence of sheep and goat bones only (Tufnell 1967: 301).

Altar?

The earlier, thirteenth-century, level included a round installation with ashes and animal bones, which was found at the center of the twelfth-century structure. About 1200 B.C., with no indication of a violent disruption or break, the larger structure was built. Zertal compares the first phase with what has been identified as a sacrificial altar in a contemporary installation at Tel Qasile. The second level of occupation lasted for about fifty years and then it was abandoned without any indication of what happened. No figurine was found, but jars, bowls, jugs, and cooking pots were found nearby in small installations. Zertal compares these with votive offerings known from other Syro-Palestinian sites about this time and with the biblical practice of bringing such offerings to a sacred site (1 Sam 1:24; 10:3). North of the courtyard Zertal identified a "ramp" going up to the structure. He also found a "veranda" around the top of the altar. He suggests that it could be used for cultic functions, such as sprinkling blood on the four corners of the altar.

Pottery

The dominant type of pottery changes between the two occupation levels. There is three times as much pottery in the later phase. However, the material culture does not otherwise appear different. Twenty percent of the pottery found is peculiar to the area occupied by the Israelite tribe of Manasseh. It appears at the beginning of the thirteenth century B.C. and disappears at the end of the twelfth century B.C. Its presence throughout this region is such that a movement from east to west has been detected. The abandonment could be related to the beginning of the Israelite settlement at Shiloh, where the Bible records the establishment of a sanctuary by Israel after entering the land.

Is This the Altar of Joshua?

[[137]] This interpretation has not gone unchallenged. A. Kempinski (1986) has sought to identify the site as a watchtower. The excavator, A. Zertal, disputes this interpretation, however. The rough stones for the "altar," the context of an area capable of handling a large public gathering, the type of animal bones found in the area, the lack of any sizeable wall which could be used for defense, the lack of sickle blades, and the position for the structure away from the peak, where it would be if it were a watchtower, may suggest something else. Indeed, both pattern of settlement and the lack of evidence of warfare at the Mount Ebal site attest to the absence of need for such a military structure. Of course, that is not the same thing as saying it is the altar of Joshua.

Thus the identification of the purpose for this site remains a matter of dispute. On the one hand, we can ask what would one expect to find at the site of an altar as it is described in Josh 8:30–35. On the other hand, we can ask why there is not more evidence for the presence of cultic activity at this site. A. Mazar (1990: 350) observes, "Zertal may be wrong in the details of his interpretation, but it is tempting to accept his view concerning the basic cultic nature of the site and its possible relationship to the biblical tradition." Such a site needs to be understood both in terms of a Palestinian context (e.g., the animal bones from the Fosse Temple at Lachish) and in terms of the biblical recollections.

Shiloh

Pre-Israelite Cult Center

The site identified with Shiloh has been excavated by I. Finkelstein (1985). A Middle Bronze Age shrine and a Late Bronze Age occupation with a pastoral population have been found. During the Late Bronze Age, Shiloh was a cult center without links to any permanent settlement. The animal bones found with the offering vessels are mainly those of sheep and goats, with a few cattle bones (the ratio of sheep/goats to cattle is 94 to 6). This is more suggestive of a nomadic pastoral economy than of a settled economy. As for the Shiloh of Iron Age I, Finkelstein (pp. 131–38, 169–70) did not find the cult center, but he did unearth stone-built pillared buildings containing storage vessels with an "exact north–south, east–west orientation." From this he concluded that the buildings formed part of a larger public building complex which may have included the sanctuary of 1 Samuel 1.

Local or Intertribal?

Noth suggested that Shiloh was an intertribal cult center during the period of the Judges. Orlinsky, de Geus, Mayes, and de Vaux have argued that it was local. The archaeological/settlement evidence suggests that in the first half of the eleventh century B.C., when occupation at Shiloh peaked, Israelite settlement was underway in Galilee (especially the tribal areas of Zebulun, Naphtali, and Ramat Issachar; Gal 1992: 84–92), but only beginning in the Beersheba Valley, and, to a certain extent, in the Judean hills (Finkelstein 1988: 37–52). Insofar as the Galilee settlements included Israelites, Shiloh could have been a center for such groups as well as those groups in the older settlements of the central hill country. Finkelstein (1985: 170) observes that "the high level of planning and construction at Shiloh" suggests a sphere of influence beyond Ephraim to Benjamin and Manasseh. On the basis of Gal's survey, parts of Galilee may also be included. Insofar as Israelite groups may be identified as tribal, Shiloh may have served as an intertribal sanctuary site.

Why Shiloh?

The region around Shiloh represented a dense Israelite settlement area with a sparse Canaanite population. Shiloh flourished from the second half of the twelfth century B.C. to the first half of [[138]] the eleventh century B.C., when it was destroyed, probably by the Philistines. Its size was comparable to larger villages such as Ai. Note that the cult site has not been found for the Middle Bronze, Late, Bronze, and Iron I occupations. It was probably on the summit and destroyed in subsequent occupations.

Animal Bones and Human Diet in the Hill Country

Given the predominance of sheep and goat bones at the sites of Ebal, Shiloh, and ed-Dawwara (northeast of Jerusalem; Finkelstein 1990b; Sadeh 1990) in the twelfth century B.C., the relationship of this diet to the Bible and its contrast to surrounding cultures is observed in a cogent paragraph by Ashkelon excavator Stager (1991: 31; cf. also Hesse 1986):

> Our staff zoo-archaeologists, Dr. Paula Wapnish and Professor Brian Hesse of the University of Alabama in Birmingham, have begun to document a rather dramatic shift in domesticated species at the end of the Late Bronze Age (13th century B.C.) and the beginning of the Iron Age (12th century B.C.). The shift is from sheep and goats to pigs and cattle. This shift occurred at Ashkelon and other coastal sites, but not in the central highland villages of the same period dominated by Israelites—settlements like Ai, Raddana and Ebal. From a strictly ecological perspective, this seems surprising. The oak-pine-and-terebinth woodlands that dominated the central hill country of Canaan, where the earliest Israelite settlements of about 1200 B.C. are to be found, are ideally suited for pig production, especially because of the shade and acorns. One reason why such a hog-acorn economy did not thrive in the early Israelite environment must ultimately be rooted in very early religious taboos that forbade the consumption of pork.

Stager goes on to point out how this evidence undermines various theories which require a later date for such dietary legislation among the Israelites as well as attempts to explain the prohibition of pork laws on the basis of ecological realities in the highlands. An understanding of these environmental factors further challenges theories that try to explain the absence of pig bones in the hill country as due to the dislike of these animals for "stony hills" (Ahlström 1990a: 92). Not only does this evidence provide a larger context for the animal bones from Zertal's altar on Mount Ebal, it also enables us to understand better the inhabitants of the hill country ca. 1200 B.C. and to relate them both to the "Israel" of the Merneptah stele and to the early Israel of the Bible.

Conclusion

Although provisional, a number of summary points can be made:

  1. In Canaan a people known as Israel is attested in the Bible and as early as the thirteenth century B.C. in the Merneptah stele. The usage of the ethnic determinative with "Israel" is unique in the proper names detailed for this particular campaign. The name should therefore be identified as an ethnic group. To say that there was no political entity named Israel before the late eleventh century (Finkelstein 1991: 56) is true insofar

as "political entity" is defined as an organized sedentary state such as may be found described in the biblical accounts of the kingdom(s) of Saul, David, and Solomon.

2. The Late Bronze Age and Iron Age I archaeological evidence in Palestine tells us little about the origins of Israel. The continuity of culture does not prove that Israel had its origins in Canaanites of the earlier periods (Gottwald 1979; Finkelstein 1988). Nor do the hints of Northern influence require assumptions about Israel's origins as being from the north, such as from Bashan (Coote 1990; de Moor 1990). In fact, the cultural remains from this time may or [[139]] may not be associated with Israel. However, the Merneptah stele and the archaeological evidence lead us to expect that at least some of the settlements in the hill country were identified by contemporaries as Israelite.

3. Aspects of the origins of Israel as suggested by the Bible are not disproven. This includes the following points: (a) that a group of slaves could have escaped from Egypt and made their way to Canaan; (b) that a group of nomadic tribal peoples could have entered and settled Canaan from east of the Jordan River; (c) that people in the hill country could have found themselves involved in competition for natural resources, in rivalry with other migrating groups and with existing Canaanite "city-states" and that this could have involved skirmishes and "wars"; and (d) that early Israel could have held to a faith in a deity known as Yahweh (cf. de Moor 1990).

4. Aspects of the origins of Israel as suggested by the interpretative models are not disproven. This includes the following points: (a) that early Israelites could have entered the land and been involved in the destruction of such sites as Hazor (Yadin; Frendo); (b) that nomadic and other peoples forced to flee for economic or political reasons, could have become Israelite at any time during its appearance and growth in Canaan (Alt); (c) that dissatisfied elements from Canaanite city-states could have become Israelites (Mendenhall and Gottwald); (d) that Egyptian "buffer groups" in Northern Palestine (Coote) or *hapiru* groups in Bashan, east of the Sea of Galilee (de Moor), could have become Israelite; and (e) that Middle Bronze Age hill country settlers who had taken on an "enclosed nomadic" existence during the Late Bronze Age (1550–1200 B.C.) could have "re-sedentarized" in the subsequent period and have become Israelites (Finkelstein).

5. Evidence for cult centers at Mount Ebal and at Shiloh, as well as details such as the diet of the hill country inhabitants, do correlate in a variety of points with the picture of early Israel's worship as suggested both by Biblical law codes and by the narratives of Joshua, Judges, and the books of Samuel.

6. Finally, a word should be said about the use of the biblical accounts. Because one can demonstrate that an account is ideologically biased or that it fits some Ancient Near Eastern literary form, one is not then entitled to argue conclusions about its "historicity." Again, if one could date a particular text early or late, this in itself would say nothing about its historical worth. Late texts may be of greater historical worth than early accounts, and authors may elect to portray historical events in literary form otherwise used to express fiction, or vice versa.

The analysis of ideological bias and literary form may be helpful in understanding the texts themselves, but they can say little about the date of the text or about its worth for reconstructing history. These depend more upon the nature of the interpreters themselves and the ideological, philosophical, and psychological dispositions which they bring to the study of the biblical texts and which they use to reconstruct Israelite history. Whether one understands the extrabiblical sources as little more than a commentary on the biblical text, whether one holds to notions of historical traditions embedded in later texts, or whether one discounts any historical value to the biblical account may have more to do with how and why one reads the Bible and with that community of readers where one has found or seeks to find acceptance. This observation is not intended to reduce the discussion of Israelite origins to a psychological or sociological determinism. Instead, it seeks to recognize how little we actually know about the world of ancient Israel (despite all the recent discoveries) and to urge caution concerning all the attempts to "prove" or to "disprove" the biblical accounts on the basis of extrabiblical evidence and of sociological models. [[140]]

Bibliography

Ahlström, G. W.
   1986   *Who Were the Israelites?* (Winona Lake, Ind.).
   1990a   "Diffusion in Iron Age Palestine: Some Aspects," *Scandinavian Journal of the Old Testament* 4/1: 81–105.
   1990b   "The Bull Figurine from Dhahrat et-Tawileh," *BASOR* 280: 77–82.
   1991   "The Origin of Israel in Palestine," *Scandinavian Journal of the Old Testament* 5/2: 19–34.
Ahlström, G. W., and Edelman, D.
   1985   "Merneptah's Israel," *JNES* 44: 59–61.
Albright, W. F.
   1935   "Archaeology and the Hebrew Conquest of Palestine," *BASOR* 58: 10–18.
   1961   "The Role of the Canaanites in the History of Civilisation," in G. E. Wright (ed.), *The Bible and the Ancient Near East. Essays in Honor of William Foxwell Albright* (reprinted, Winona Lake, Ind., 1979) 328–62.

Alt, A.
   1989   "The Settlement of the Israelites in Palestine," in A. Alt, *Essays on Old Testament History and Religion* (Repr. Sheffield) 133–69 (originally published as "Die Landnahme der Israeliten in Palästina," *Reformationsprogramm der Universität Leipzig*, 1925).
Bergoffen, C. J.
   1991   "Overland Trade in Northern Sinai: The Evidence of the Late Cypriote Pottery," *BASOR* 284: 59–76.
Bienkowski, P.
   1986   *Jericho in the Late Bronze Age* (Warminster).
Bimson, J. J.
   1991   "Merenptah's Israel and Recent Theories of Israelite Origins," *JSOT* 49: 3–29.
Biran, A. (ed.)
   1981   *Temples and High Places in Biblical Times. Proceedings of the Colloquium in Honor of the Centennial of Hebrew Union College–Jewish Institute of Religion. Jerusalem. 14–16 March 1977* (Jerusalem).
Bright, J.
   1981   *A History of Israel* (3rd edn, Philadelphia).
Brueggemann, W.
   1986   *Revelation and Violence: A Study in Contextualization.* The 1986 Père Marquette Theology Lecture (Milwaukee).
Bunimovitz, S.
   1990   "Problems in the 'Ethnic' Identification of the Philistine Culture," *Tel Aviv* 17: 210–22.
Childs, B. S.
   1974   "The Etiological Tale Re-Examined," *VT* 24: 287–97.
Coote, R. B.
   1990   *Early Israel: A New Horizon* (Philadelphia).
   1991   "Early Israel," *Scandinavian Journal of the Old Testament* 5/2: 35–46.
Coote, R. B., and Whitelam, K. W.
   1986   *The Emergence of Early Israel in Historical Perspective* (Sheffield).
Dever, W. G.
   1991   "Archaeological Data on the Israelite Settlement: A Review of Two Recent Works," *BASOR* 284: 77–90.
   1992   "Israel, History of (Archaeology and the 'Conquest')," *The Anchor Bible Dictionary* 3.545–58.
van Dyk, P. J.
   1990   "The Function of So-Called Etiological Elements in Narratives," *ZAW* 102: 19–33.
Esse, D. L.
   1991   "The Collared Store Jar: Scholarly Ideology and Ceramic Typology," *Scandinavian Journal of the Old Testament* 5/2: 99–116.
   1992   "The Collared Pithos at Megiddo: Ceramic Distribution and Ethnicity," *JNES* 51: 81–104.

Finkelstein, I.
1985	"Excavations at Shiloh: 1981–1984: Preliminary Report," *Tel Aviv* 12: 123–80.
1988	*The Archaeology of the Israelite Settlement* (Jerusalem).
1988–89	"The Land of Ephraim Survey 1980–1987: Preliminary Report," *Tel Aviv* 15–16: 117–83.
1990a	"The Emergence of Early Israel: Anthropology, Environment and Archaeology," *JAOS* 110: 677–86.
1990b	"Excavations at Khirbet ed-Dawwara: An Iron Age Site Northeast of Jerusalem," *Tel Aviv* 17: 163–208.
1991	"The Emergence of Israel in Canaan: Consensus, Mainstream and Dispute," *Scandinavian Journal of the Old Testament* 5/2: 47–59.

Freedman, D. N., and Graf, D. F. (eds.)
1983	*Palestine in Transition* (Sheffield).

Frendo, A. J.
1992	"Five Recent Books on the Emergence of Ancient Israel. Review Article," *PEQ* 124: 144–51.

Frick, F. S.
1985	*The Formation of the State in Ancient Israel* (Sheffield).

Fritz, V.
1987	"Conquest or Settlement? The Early Iron Age in Palestine," *BA* 50: 84–100.

Gal, Z.
1992	*Lower Galilee during the Iron Age* (ASOR Dissertation Series 8, Winona Lake, Ind.).

Gonen, R.
1984	"Urban Canaan in the Late Bronze Period," *BASOR* 253: 61–73.
1992	*Burial Patterns and Cultural Diversity in Late Bronze Age Canaan* (ASOR Dissertation Series 7, Winona Lake, Ind.).

Gottwald, N. K.
1979	*The Tribes of Yahweh. A Sociology of the Religion of Liberated Israel 1250–1050 B.C.E.* (Maryknoll, New York).
1989	"Israel's Emergence in Canaan—BR Interviews Norman Gottwald," *Bible Review* 5/3 (October, 1989) 26–34.

Hallo, W. W.
1990	"The Limits of Skepticism," *JAOS* 110: 187–99.

Halpern, B.
1983	*The Emergence of Israel in Canaan* (SBL Monograph Series 29, Chico).
1992	"Settlement of Canaan," *The Anchor Bible Dictionary* 5.1120–43.

Herzog, Z., Aharoni, M., and Rainey, A. F.
1987	"Arad. An Ancient Israelite Fortress with a Temple to Yahweh," *BAR* 13/2: 16–35. [[141]]

Hess, R. S.
1988	"Tribes, Territories of," in *International Standard Bible Encyclopedia. Volume 4, Q–Z* (Grand Rapids) 907–13.

1989   "Cultural Aspects of Onomastic Distribution in the Amarna Texts," *Ugarit-Forschungen* 21: 209–16.

Hesse, B.
1986   "Animal Use at Tel Miqne-Ekron in the Bronze Age and Iron Age," *BASOR* 264: 17–27.

Horwitz, L. H.
1986–87 "Faunal Remains from the Early Iron Age Site on Mount Ebal," *Tel Aviv* 13–14: 173–89.

Isserlin, B. S. J.
1983   "The Israelite Conquest of Canaan: A Comparative Review of the Arguments Applicable," *PEQ* 115: 85–94.

Jacoby, R.
1991   "The Representation and Identification of Cities on Assyrian Reliefs," *IEJ* 41: 112–31.

Kempinski, A.
1986   "Joshua's Altar—An Iron Age I Watchtower," *BAR* 12/1: 42, 44–46, 48–49.

Kitchen, K. A.
1966   *Ancient Orient and Old Testament* (London).

Laperrousaz, F.-M.
1987   "King Solomon's Wall Still Supports the Temple Mount," *BAR* 13/3: 34–44.

Lemche, N. P.
1985   *Early Israel. Anthropological and Historical Studies on the Israelite Society before the Monarchy* (SVT 37, Leiden).
1988   *Ancient Israel. A New History of Israelite Society* (Sheffield).
1991a   *The Canaanites and Their Land: The Tradition of the Canaanites.* (JSOT Supplement 110, Sheffield).
1991b   "Sociology, Text and Religion as Key Factors in Understanding the Emergence of Israel in Canaan," *Scandinavian Journal of the Old Testament* 5/2: 7–18.
1992   "Israel, History of (Pre-Monarchic Period)," *The Anchor Bible Dictionary* 3.526–45.

Leonard, A., Jr.
1989   "The Late Bronze Age," *BA* 52: 4–39.

Liverani, M.
1979   "The Ideology of the Assyrian Empire," in M. T. Larsen (ed.), *Power and Propaganda: A Symposium on Ancient Empires* (Mesopotamia: Studies in Assyriology 7, Copenhagen).
[[1990]] *Prestige and Interest: International Relations in the Near East ca. 1600–1100 B.C.* (History of the Ancient Near East/Studies 1, Padova).

London, G.
1989   "A Comparison of Two Contemporaneous Lifestyles of the Late Second Millennium B.C.," *BASOR* 273: 37–55.

Malamat, A.
1983   "The Proto-History of Israel: A Study in Method," in C. L. Meyers and M. O'Connor (eds.), *The Word of the Lord Shall Go Forth: Essays in Honor of*

David Noel Freedman in Celebration of His Sixtieth Birthday (Winona Lake, Ind.) 303–13.

Mayerson, P.
1990   "Towards a Comparative Study of a Frontier," *IEJ* 40: 267–79.

Mazar, A.
1990   *Archaeology of the Land of the Bible: 10,000–586 B.C.E.* (Garden City, New York).

Mazar, B.
1981   "The Early Israelite Settlement in the Hill Country," *BASOR* 241: 75–85.

Mendenhall, G. E.
1962   "The Hebrew Conquest of Palestine," *BA* 25: 66–77.
1983   "Ancient Israel's Hyphenated History," in D. N. Freedman and D. F. Graf (eds.), *Palestine in Transition: The Emergence of Ancient Israel* (The Social World of Biblical Antiquity Series 2, Sheffield) 91–103.

Millard, A. R.
1985   *Treasures from Bible Times* (Tring).

de Moor, J. C.
1990   *The Rise of Yahwism: The Roots of Israelite Monotheism* (BETL 91, Leuven).

Negbi, O.
1991   "Were There Sea Peoples in the Central Jordan Valley at the Transition from the Bronze Age to the Iron Age?" *Tel Aviv* 18: 205–43.

Noth, M.
1957   *Uberlieferungsgeschichtliche Studien* (2nd edition, Tübingen); pp. 1–110 trans. and reprinted as *The Deuteronomistic History* (JSOT Supplement 15, Sheffield, 1981).

Raban, A.
1991   "The Philistines in the Western Jezreel Valley," *BASOR* 284: 17–27.

Rainey, A. F.
1991   "Rainey's Challenge," *BAR* 17/6 (November/December) 56–60, 93.
1992   "Anson F. Rainey Replies," *BAR* 18/2 (March/April) 73–74.

Sadeh, M.
1990   "Animal Remains from Khirbet ed-Dawwara," *Tel Aviv* 17: 209.

Schaar, K. W.
1991   "An Architectural Theory for the Origin of the Four-Room House," *Scandinavian Journal of the Old Testament* 5/2: 75–98.

Schley, D. G.
1989   *Shiloh: A Biblical City in Tradition and History* (JSOT Supplement 63, Sheffield).

Shiloh, Y.
1984   "Past and Present in Archaeological Research on the City of David," in H. Shanks and B. Mazar (eds.), *Recent Archaeology in the Land of Israel* (Jerusalem) 149–57.

Stager, L. E.
1985a   "Session II: Archaeology, History and Bible. The Israelite Settlement in Canaan: A Case Study: Respondent," in J. Amitai (ed.), *Biblical Archaeology*

Today: Proceedings of the International Congress on Biblical Archaeology, Jerusalem, April 1984 (Jerusalem) 83–87.

1985b "Merenptah, Israel and Sea Peoples: New Light on an Old Relief," *Eretz-Israel* 18: 56*–64*.

1991 "When Canaanites and Philistines Ruled Ashkelon," *BAR* 17/2: 24–37, 40–43.

Stiebing, W. H., Jr.

1989 *Out of the Desert? Archaeology and the Exodus/Conquest Narratives* (Buffalo).

Strange, J.

1987 "The Transition from the Bronze Age to the Iron Age in the Eastern Mediterranean and the Emergence of the Israelite State," *Scandinavian Journal of the Old Testament* 1/1: 1–19.

Thompson, T. L.

1992a "Palestinian Pastoralism and Israel's Origins," *Scandinavian Journal of the Old Testament* 6/1: 1–13.

[[1992b]] *Early History of the Israelite People: From the Written and Archaeological Sources* (Studies in the History of the Ancient Near East 2, Leiden).

Tufnell, O.

1967 "Lachish," in D. Winston Thomas (ed.), *Archaeology and Old Testament Study* (Oxford) 296–308.

Van Seters, J.

1990 "Joshua's Campaign of Canaan and Near Eastern Historiography," *Scandinavian Journal of the Old Testament* 4/2: 1–12.

Weippert, H.

1988 *Palästina in vorhellenistischer Zeit* (Handbuch der Archäologie, Vorderasien, 2, 1, Munich).

Whitelam, K. W.

1991 "Between History and Literature: The Social Production of Israel's Traditions of Origin," *Scandinavian Journal of the Old Testament* 5/2: 60–74. [[142]]

Yadin, Y.

1985 "Biblical Archaeology Today: The Archaeological Aspect," in J. Amitai (ed.), *Biblical Archaeology Today: Proceedings of the International Congress on Biblical Archaeology, Jerusalem, April 1984* (Jerusalem) 21–27.

Younger, K. L., Jr.

1990 *Ancient Conquest Accounts: A Study in Ancient Near Eastern and Biblical History Writing* (JSOTS 98, Sheffield).

Yurco, F. J.

1990 "3,200-Year-Old Picture of Israelites Found in Egypt," *BAR* 16/5: 21–38.

1991 "Yurco's Response," *BAR* 17/6: 61.

Zertal, A.

1985 "Has Joshua's Altar Been Found on Mt. Ebal?" *BAR* 11/1: 26–43.

1986 "How Can Kempinski Be So Wrong!" *BAR* 12/1: 43, 47, 49–53.

1986–87 "An Early Iron Age Cult Site on Mount Ebal: Excavation Seasons 1982–1987," *Tel Aviv* 13–14: 105–65.

1991a "Israel Enters Canaan—Following the Pottery Trail," *BAR* 17/5 (September/October) 28–47.

1991b "The Trek of the Tribes as They Settled in Canaan," *BAR* 17/5 (September/October) 48–49, 75.

Faces of Exile in Old Testament Historiography

J. G. MCCONVILLE

The Exile in Old Testament Interpretation

[[27]] Arguably, critical study of the Old Testament has, at least since Wellhausen, been dominated by the Babylonian exile of Judah. The classical analysis of the Pentateuch saw it as taking its final form in or because of the exile, the Priestly document providing, as it were, the last word, and giving shape to the whole. The great history of the people in its God-given land ended with narratives about successive deportations of Judaeans, by now the sole remnants of the ancient people, to Babylon. The major prophetic books—Isaiah, Jeremiah, Ezekiel—all focussed in their own way on the same event. And the songs of the Old Testament (in many Psalms and in Lamentations) suggested that the exile had deeply affected the psyche of a people for whom the possession of land had marked its very identity. The trauma of this event has been well put by Rex Mason:

> It is difficult to exaggerate the profundity and far-reaching consequences of the change from a preexilic Yahwism which was the mortar binding the nation-state, so inextricably bound up with the Davidic dynasty and the city of Jerusalem, to a postexilic religion of a small, nonmonarchic, and remote province of a foreign world empire.[1]

Reprinted with permission from *After the Exile: Essays in Honor of Rex Mason* (ed. J. Barton and D. J. Reimer; Macon: Mercer University Press, 1996) 27–44.
    1. Rex Mason, *Preaching the Tradition* (Cambridge: Cambridge University Press, 1990) 131.

Generations of scholars, furthermore, have thought of the exile as decisive in the formation of the literature, for example, in the tradition of regarding the Pentateuch, rather than the Hexateuch, as the first main
division of the Old Testament.[2]

[[28]] What is true for the Old Testament in general is true of its history writing in particular. The Deuteronomic History's (DtH) domination
by the exile hardly needs demonstration. It is not merely that that is where
the story ends. (That circumstance on its own, indeed, has caused more
problems for interpreters than it has solved.) It is rather that a great deal
of the material is suggestive of exile, or at least can be read as having
something to do with it. How much this is a kind of wisdom after the
event is not immediately clear. That is, in the Old Testament's history writing (and we focus specifically on DtH) how much of what we read is really
saying something about the events that it purports to narrate, and how
much is it addressing the contemporary concerns of some later period?
These cannot be absolute alternatives, of course. Yet there is a real question about the nature of the text as a record of the past.

To take an example, 1 Kgs 9:1–9 has been thought to contain two
different perspectives. It is the narrative of an appearance of Yahweh to
Solomon following the dedication of the temple. As interpreted by R. E.
Friedman, 1 Kgs 9:3–5 betrays a Josianic outlook, full of confidence about
the future of both temple and Davidic dynasty. The sequel, however (vv. 6–
9), is said to reflect a quite different point of view, namely the chastened
perspective of the next generation, for whom destruction of temple and
exile of people have become all too real. In this way Friedman finds that
the passage confirms the double-redaction theory of the composition of
DtH advocated by F. M. Cross.[3] The method assumes, therefore, that the
passage has been formed entirely in the matrix of the period from Josiah
to the exile. This is similar to Rudolf Smend's analysis of DtH, in which
passages are interpreted for more and less confident views about the possibility of keeping the land secure, again in the latter days of Judah. His understanding of Josh 1:6–7 is very like Friedman's example.[4]

[[29]] A fundamental question is thus raised about the appropriate
way to read apparently historiographical texts in the Old Testament. It is
clear, at the outset, that there is some sense in which DtH is a composition

2. See James S. Sanders, *Torah and Canon* (Philadelphia: Fortress Press, 1972) 48 (on
the Pentateuch).

3. Richard E. Friedman, "From Egypt to Egypt," in *Traditions in Transformation*, ed.
B. Halpern and J. Levenson (Winona Lake, IN: Eisenbrauns, 1981) 167–92, 175.

4. Rudolf Smend, "Das Gesetz und die Völker," in *Probleme biblischer Theologie: G. von
Rad zum 70sten Geburtstag*, ed. H. W. Wolff (München: Kaiser, 1971) 494–509, citation on
495.

that must be read "from the end." All attempts to understand it assume that its meaning is bound up with the exile. And if the texts quoted above are at best ambiguous in their indication of an exilic setting, there are others which show clearly that the perspective of the narrative runs ahead of the events being narrated. A good example is the Song of Hannah (1 Sam 2:1–10). This forms an important part of the opening scenes of Samuel, helping to establish the themes of the book. The exaltation of the weak at the expense of the strong, for example, becomes concretized in the story of David in more than one way: David, the least of Jesse's sons, is preferred by God to his apparently more eligible brothers, 1 Samuel 16; David the youth overcomes Goliath the giant warrior, 1 Samuel 17; the obscure David excels and displaces King Saul. (Some of these themes are taken up again, furthermore, in the central poems of the "Appendix" to the Books of Samuel [2 Samuel 22; 23:1–7].) Most striking, however, is Hannah's anticipation of the theme of kingship, in terms reminiscent of certain Psalms of Zion:

> he will give strength to his king,
> and will exalt the horn of his anointed. (v. 10)

In this way an important issue, which awaits development in the complex action of the book, is presented beforehand as if it were already decided. It is clear, therefore, that a perspective "from the end" has shaped the narrative in some sense. The example in question is interesting, incidentally, because its "end" is not the end that is finally reached in the narrative of DtH, and that poses an intriguing question to which we shall return. At this point, however, we observe only that to recognize this influence of the "end" on the shape of the whole does not necessarily answer the question with which we opened, namely, how far the narrative here is concerned with telling what happened in the past.

That question has been answered in a number of ways. The older extension of the Pentateuchal sources into DtH has fallen from favor, displaced by tradition or transmission history, still perhaps the prevailing model in Old Testament studies. This approach to the material affords a way of accounting both for echoes within the material and a perspective "from the end." The method is still best illustrated by Noth's work on [[30]] DtH, with its postulate of a single mind applying a view of history to a mass of inherited sources.[5] The cogency of his synthesis was such that it has become the classical solution to the problem of the authorship of DtH. Even the influential variations of the theory, pioneered respectively

---

5. Martin Noth, *The Deuteronomistic History* (Sheffield: JSOT Press, 1981), ET of *Überlieferungsgeschichtliche Studien*, 2nd ed. (Tübingen: Max Niemeyer Verlag, 1957) 1–110.

by F. M. Cross and R. Smend, are compliments to Noth, because they share a basic methodology. That is, already extant literature is held to have undergone accretion and shaping, ultimately according to the perspective of a final hand.[6]

Yet the problems that follow from Noth's solution are well known. The underlying difficulty is that preexisting versions of the literature in question have to be hypothesized out of the form of it which actually exists. This means that criteria must be employed which have no firmer foothold than scholarly consensus. There is, however, no single consensus, but a list of available models. H. D. Preuss, in a review of scholarship on DtH, finds complete divergence in matters of detailed application. Historical-critical approaches to the material find results that are predetermined by the perspective of the school to which the scholar belongs. Theories about sources and editorial layers are *systemimmanent*.[7] They can also tax credulity, especially when they postulate several layers of editorial activity, constituting a kind of internal argument in the text, yet all from unknown hands working at the same time.[8]

[[31]] One response to this lack of certainty has been the newer literary criticism, which has forsworn historical enquiry and chosen instead to adhere to the text alone. This is in a sense a "pragmatic" answer, which simply lays aside questions that appear to be unanswerable.

Another kind of challenge is more direct. Two examples may be mentioned. First, John Van Seters has mounted a campaign against traditional thinking about the composition of the Pentateuch and DtH. He criticizes Noth and Gressmann, for example, challenging such important criteria of their approach as the belief that shorter fragments of tradition are older.[9] His general contention, which owes something to H. H. Schmid, is that "J" is not an ancient source document, but a historian from the exilic period, who already has access to DtH. J then models much of his own history on events and narratives from that earlier writing, using his imagination cre-

---

6. The essential similarity of the procedures adopted by Noth, Cross, Smend, and others has been well noted by Baruch Halpern. Having reviewed the methods of Noth, Smend, Cross, Richter, and others, he find that the differences between them consist in the adopting of different perspectives on the same subject, rather than conflicting methodologies, and concludes: "Basically there is no dispute!" *The First Historians: The Hebrew Bible and History* (San Francisco: Harper & Row, 1988) 110–18, 115.

7. H. D. Preuss, "Zum deuteronomistischen Geschichtswerk," *ThR* n.f. 58 (1993) 394.

8. I have made further comments on this approach, esp. in relation to T. Veijola, *Die Ewige Dynastie* (Helsinki: Suomalainen Tiedeakatemia, 1977), in *Grace in the End: A Study in Deuteronomic Theology* (Carlisle: Paternoster, 1993) 83–85.

9. John Van Seters, *The Life of Moses: The Yahwist as Historian in Exodus-Numbers* (Louisville, KY: Westminster/John Knox, 1994) 6.

atively where necessary. Pharaoh's Egypt in Exodus 1–2, for example, is modelled on Dtr's portrayal of Solomon's kingdom.[10] This method of explaining echoes across large reaches of the text, therefore, is somewhat minimalist when it comes to historicity.

In similar vein, Philip R. Davies has undertaken a critique of the idea of a "tradition" which underlies the methodology of tradition history. On the authorship of the books his essential break with the scholarly mainstream is in denying that there is a link between folklore memories and the text which has been preserved. That text is much more of a fiction than has been recognized hitherto by most scholars; it is itself a scholarly product, generated by and for the educated elite of the Jewish community in Palestine in the Persian period. Even the idea of the exile as the Old Testament's time of great creativity overstates, in Davies's view, the credibility of the biblical picture.[11] If the new literary approaches have sidelined the historical content of Old Testament historiography, the radical approach to Israel's history that is exemplified by Davies and Van Seters has attempted to abolish it.

[[32]] The fact that Van Seters and Davies (among others) can attempt such a critique of the prevailing view is indicative of the difficulties under which it labors. The "tradition" that is indispensable to it cannot be shown independently to have existed at all. Biblical scholars who have an interest in the history of texts have largely had to do without independent and empirical evidence of that history. And in that deficiency lies the danger of a certain subjectivity, and of hypotheses that are difficult to test.[12] (This point has been tackled recently from a quite different point of view, incidentally, by H. J. Tertel, who has pointed to the possibility of deducing scribal techniques in the Old Testament from those in Assyria, for which, he believes, greater controls exist.[13])

---

10. An example is his treatment of Exodus 1–2; ibid., 15–34.

11. Philip R. Davies, *In Search of "Ancient Israel"* (Sheffield: Sheffield Academic Press, repr. 1995) 90–97, 103–4, 110–15.

12. On this point, see the remarks of the Assyriologist A. Ungnad in "Gilgamesch-Epos und Odyssee," in K. Oberhuber, ed., *Das Gilgamesch-Epos*, WF 215 (Darmstadt: Wissenschaftliche Buchgesellschaft, 1977) 106–7.

13. Hans Jürgen Tertel, *Text and Transmission: an Empirical Model for the Development of OT Narratives*, BZAW 221 (Berlin/New York: de Gruyter, 1994). Tertel argues that Assyrian scribal methods follow completely different patterns from those which have been assumed by biblical scholars. Narratives which are retold are subject, e.g., to abbreviation and assimilation, not to expansion or proliferation of versions. By comparing Assyrian scribal methods, Tertel hopes to suggest new ways of understanding the redactional methods used by biblical authors. See the review of H. H. Klement, "Text Recycling assyrisch und biblisch: Zur fälligen Revision der Literaturkritik," *Jahrbuch für Evangelikale Theologie* 9 (1995) 7–20.

The Difficulty of Deciding Historicity

The above are all attempts to come to terms with a single basic issue, namely how to establish historical bedrock for texts, and the historical relationship between earlier and later forms.

The inherent difficulty of this task cannot be underestimated. In principle it is met in all parts of the Old Testament literature,[14] and many [[33]] individual Old Testament texts might, in principle, be found to have a wide variety of possible original settings. The narratives in the Old Testament do not escape the dilemma. In Smend's view, which we noticed above, the Joshua narrative has little to do with the original taking of the land of Canaan, but actually addresses issues that are contemporary with Dtr. Such a perspective on the character of the Deuteronomistic History is common. In many treatments of Deuteronomy and DtH, indeed, it is virtually axiomatic that a developed, or conditional, theology of land must arise from a time when the possession of it is threatened. On that view the whole history of occupation of land is a fiction; furthermore, texts which betray an interest in land are drawn inexorably into the Deuteronomistic net. Lothar Perlitt's treatment of Genesis 15 is a case in point.[15] And the point is made in passing by F. M. Cross:

> One may question, however, whether the alternating pattern of grace and judgment in the Deuteronomistic notices of the era of the Judges had as its original setting the Exilic situation. It is easier to understand it as exhortation to reform with the hope of national salvation.[16]

The issue in historiography, then, is whether texts may ever be held to relate to periods, incidents, events to which they purport to relate, or whether they are to be interpreted as commentaries on quite different times and circumstances. To the extent that the latter perspective prevails, the historical content found in a narrative will obviously diminish. All accounts, perhaps, which stress the work of the final author or redactor, leave open the possibility that a narrative bears very little on the events it

---

14. See H. G. M. Williamson's remarks on Isa 30:9, and his criticisms of a certain circularity in methods of dating: *The Book Called Isaiah: Deutero-Isaiah's Role in Composition and Redaction* (Oxford: Clarendon Press, 1994) 87. He opposes in particular, J. Vermeylen's contention that the verse is "deuteronomic" on the grounds of vocabulary: J. Vermeylen, *Du Prophète Isaie à l'apocalyptique: Isaie, I–XXXV, miroir d'un demi-millénaire d'expérience religieuse en Israel*, 2 vols., Ebib (Paris: J. Gabalda, 1977–1978).

15. Lothar Perlitt, *Bundestheologie im alten Testament*, WMANT 36 (Neukirchen: Neukirchener Verlag, 1969) 55–77.

16. Frank Moore Cross, *Canaanite Myth and Hebrew Epic* (Cambridge, MA: Harvard University Press, 1973) 278.

ostensibly narrates. Noth's model permits just this result.[17] At the other
[[34]] end of the scale, there are treatments which see texts very much in
terms of contemporary issues and concerns.[18]

A dilemma seems to be built into the study of the Old Testament's
narrative texts. There are two elements in it: first, the lack of external controls on the material; and second, the possibility of real analogies between
events and situations at different times. To take the case in question, does
the presence of "exilic" hints in the narrative have to be explained as a re-
flex of the Babylonian exile? Or might there have been real anticipations
of "exile" in Israel's earlier experience, which produced a kind of naturally occurring typology in the finished story? The problem is recognized
in principle by a number of scholars. Thus Van Seters:

> [I]t is not always so easy to decide where the author is merely attempting
> to reconstruct or report the past and where he is writing with an eye to
> addressing his own circumstances.[19]

Beyond this recognition, scholars simply vary in their evaluation of the
"historical" character of the texts. Baruch Halpern, for example, sees an
engagement between "antiquarian and factional factors,"[20] and insists on
the reality of the historian's antiquarian interest, distinguishing between
historiography and "romance," and even deploring the needless hostility
in some quarters to the historical motive.[21]

Beyond the Impasse: Themes in DtH

Is there a way in which some conclusion might be reached about the extent, if any, of historical reference in DtH? In principle, the thesis that the
work is predominantly a commentary on exilic, or postexilic, issues is
open to testing by asking how far it may be seen to address issues that
were current then. Admittedly our understanding of the period in question is formed in part by the way in which we read the books, and that
poses a methodological difficulty. Yet there is a degree of convergence in

---

17. H.-D. Hoffmann, *Reform und Reformen: Untersuchungen zu einem Grundthema der deuteronomistischen Geschichtsschreibung* (Zurich: Theologischer Verlag, 1980), is perhaps an extreme example of the application of the "Deuteronomistic" model in a way that diminishes
the historical value of the narrative.

18. E.g., Frank Crüsemann, *Der Widerstand gegen das Königtum* (Neukirchen: Neukirchener Verlag, 1978).

19. Van Seters, *The Life of Moses*, 16.

20. Baruch Halpern, *The First Historians: The Hebrew Bible and History* (San Francisco:
Harper & Row, 1988) 139.

21. Ibid., 138–40.

Old Testament literature which on most estimates allows a broad picture to [[35]] emerge (a fact that is surely underestimated by Davies, when he suggests a Persian origin even for the poems of Isaiah 40–55).[22]

A possible way forward is to observe the shape that is taken by the treatment of particular themes in DtH. This could in principle be a very extensive exercise, and there is no attempt here to exhaust the possibilities.[23] I have chosen a number of central themes of DtH, however which I hope will shed light on the present issue.

Exile. The natural place to begin is with that of exile itself, or to put it more broadly, nonpossession of land. The prominence of this topic in DtH hardly needs demonstration. The initial charge to Israel in Deuteronomy occurs outside the land, and this, together with the threat of land loss for covenant breach (Deut 28:64–68), makes a telling arc to the devastation of city, land and people at the end of Kings. With this beginning of DtH, exile becomes much more than a motif, but a profound dimension of the concept. The end of the story is matched by its beginning, and not in an accidental way, but in a framework whose power goes beyond the literal-historical plane, affording a platform for critique of Israel's institutions.[24] The death of Moses outside the land (Deuteronomy 34) adds an ominous twist to the possibilities that are held out to Israel.

In the interim, too, nonpossession always threatens. The well-known issue concerning the contrasting accounts of the entry to Canaan in Joshua and Judges illustrates the undercurrent of fundamental uncertainty on this crucial topic. Robert Polzin has shown that the contrast, as articulated in conventional criticism, is overdrawn, and that in fact an ambivalence about the possibility of ultimate possession hangs over both books.[25] Samuel seems to lay to rest the threat of loss, for the time being, yet precisely here there are moments in the narrative that might be read as metaphorical anticipations of the baneful outcome. The capture of the ark by the Philistines, albeit temporary, uncannily foreshadows its ultimate [[36]] loss, especially in the symbolic name of the grandson of Eli, Ichabod, and its explanation: "The glory has departed from Israel, for the ark of God has been captured" (1 Sam 4:22).[26] Samuel's speech to the

---

22. Davies, *Ancient Israel*, 95–96.

23. Richard Elliott Friedman, *The Exile and Biblical Narrative* (Chico, CA: Scholars Press, 1981) considers a number that we do not develop here (see below). Nor have we taken up the theme of Reform, identified by Hoffmann, n. 17.

24. See J. Halbe, "Gemeinschaft, die Welt unterbricht," in Norbert Lohfink, ed., *Das Deuteronomium: Entstehung, Gestalt und Botschaft* (Leuven: Leuven University Press, 1985) 55–75.

25. Robert Polzin, *Moses and the Deuteronomist* (New York: Seabury, 1980).

26. See Robert P. Gordon, "Samuel: Theology of," in *New International Dictionary of Old Testament Theology and Exegesis* [[ed. W. A. VanGemeren]] (Grand Rapids, MI: Zondervan, [[1997]]).

people in the aftermath of Saul's accession as king puts the matter in (Deuteronomic) terms which might have the outcome of the Books of Kings in mind:

> Only fear the LORD and serve him faithfully with all your heart; for consider what great things he has done for you. But if you still do wickedly, you shall be swept away, both you and your king. (1 Sam 12:24–25)

And David himself looks vulnerable both when he sojourns among the Philistines during his flight from Saul (1 Sam 21:10–15), and when in the same connection, he looks to Moab to find refuge for his family (1 Sam 22:3–4), the prophet Gad directing him back across the boundary of Judah (v. 5).[27]

Must these developments of the topic of loss of land be drawn into the vortex of the actual exile and the feverish scholarly activity that is hypothesized for it?

A first and obvious point is that there is comparatively little explicit reflection on the Babylonian exile as such. The end of the narrative (2 Kings 24–25), which reports the event of the exile, is silent both about possible outcomes of it, and about the true situation of the people who now find themselves in it. The account of the release of King Jehoiachin is notoriously ambivalent about that event's significance. Apart from that narrative, whose relevance to the exile is in the nature of the case, a case must be made for any other constituting an express reflection on it. Those which may be regarded as relevant are first and foremost reflections on taking or keeping the land. These "hope notes," however, as Cross rightly points out, need not be products of the exile.[28] Of a number of passages in DtH identified by H. Wolff as expressing hope, only 1 Kgs 8:46–53 [[37]] (outside Deuteronomy) relates expressly to the Babylonian exile.[29] Finally, Richard E. Friedman has rightly shown how much DtH (in his view both Dtr1 and Dtr2) is dominated by the idea of exodus from Egypt. It is a return to Egypt, rather than Babylon, that is feared in Deuteronomy (28:68).[30]

The tension between Egypt and Babylon in DtH is resolved by Friedman in the suggestion that DtH may have been brought to completion in

---

27. See Herbert H. Klement, "2 Samuel 21–24: Structure, Context, Meaning" (Ph.D. diss., Oxford, 1995) who sees a structural and thematic relationship between the prophecy of Gad here and that of Nathan in 2 Samuel 7.

28. Cross, *Canaanite Myth and Hebrew Epic*, 277–78.

29. H. W. Wolff, "Das Kerygma des deuteronomistischen Geschichtswerk," *ZAW* 73 (1961) 171–86; here 180–86.

30. Richard Elliott Friedman, *The Exile and Biblical Narrative*, 31–32; cf. idem, "From Egypt to Egypt."

the former.[31] This idea in itself is scarcely convincing in view of the actual end of the story in Babylon, and leans too much on information in Jeremiah. But Friedman has signalled an important point, namely the untidiness of the theme of exile in DtH. In Deuteronomy itself, the threat of a return to Egypt (Deut 28:68),[32] makes a satisfying contrast with the strong motif of exodus in that book. The vision of exile and return in 30:1–5 broadens the scope to "all the nations" (vv. 1, 3) to which Israel will be scattered, and even to "the ends of the heavens" (v. 4).

A further point has been made in the same connection by Jon Levenson, who observes that elsewhere in Deuteronomy, the threat of loss consequent upon breach of covenant is in terms of perishing from the land because of famine (Deut 11:13–17). A similar view occurs in Josh 23:13, 16. Levenson considers this to be in tension with Dtr1, because of the promise in the latter of an eternal dynasty for David.[33] Friedman offers in response his contention that the Davidic promise is never quite unconditional, and that the passage in Deuteronomy is in any case within the scheme of the Abrahamic promise, which is parallel to the Davidic.[34] This is a reasonable mitigation, but does not meet the point that the texts in question speak of a loss of land that is actually exile.

[[38]] The point may be developed further. In the Book of Joshua the theme of loss of land is suggested in terms of the dangers of the enemy within, in the form of Rahab (Joshua 2) and the Gibeonites (Joshua 9). In Judges, loss of land is also conceived of as an internal matter. The formulaic summary of Israel's experience in 2:11–23 speaks of defeat and invasion, of enemies no longer "driven out" in the language of Holy War (vv. 21–23). The worship of other gods also brings on a kind of inner collapse, an inhabiting of the land that is not real possession.[35]

Leadership.   It is not only in relation to exile that this diversity in DtH may be observed. A further important theme is that of leadership, or kingship, which obviously comes to an abrupt conclusion at the end of Kings, and here too variety reigns.

This topic occupies the foreground from an early stage, with the prominent position of Moses in Deuteronomy's portrayal of Israel at the

---

31. Ibid., 36.

32. The well-known difficulty of the phrase "in boats" adds to the impression of a rather independent view of exile.

33. Jon Levenson, "Who Inserted the Book of the Torah?" *HTR* 68 (1975) 203–33, esp. 223–31; cf. Matitiahu Tsevat, "Studies in the Book of Samuel, III," *HUCA* 34 (1963) 71–82; esp. 73.

34. Friedman, *The Exile and Biblical Narrative*, 27 and n.

35. The theme is developed by Barry Webb, *The Book of the Judges* (Sheffield: JSOT Press, 1987) e.g., 116; cf. Lillian R. Klein, *The Triumph of Irony in the Book of Judges* (Sheffield: JSOT Press, 1988) 23–24, 35–36.

beginning of its history, and the strong sense of Joshua's succession to him in the opening verses of the Book of Joshua. It continues in Judges and Samuel with the debate about the nature of leadership in Israel, and the establishment of the dynastic principle. This last then becomes one of the main springs of the action in the Books of Kings, where the performance of the kings themselves, in particular respects, is a key factor in weaving the fate of Israel. There is more than mere persistence, too, in the recurrence of this theme, for echoes have been observed between the books, suggestive of the conscious reflection of the one part upon the other. An example is the anticipation of the debate about monarchy—the domain of the Books of Samuel—in the stories of Gideon and Abimelech.[36]

As with exile, then, the theme of leadership runs throughout DtH. Yet here too it surfaces in a variety of ways. The issue turns on whether leadership in DtH is intended to be conceived throughout in terms of dynastic kingship. A number of scholars have argued just this. The material resists such a view, however, for neither Moses nor Joshua can [[39]] satisfactorily be turned into kings.[37] Rather an ideal of leadership emerges in close connection with the development of the topic of covenant, going back to Exodus 19. In this context dynastic kingship appears in its time, and the material (notably 1 Samuel 8–12) bears all the marks of a deep contention over it which, on a plain reading, echoes from a time before there were kings. Furthermore, with the theory of the Succession Narrative in retreat,[38] the prominence of David in the Books of Samuel looks increasingly like an issue that needs to be resolved first and foremost in those books. This may be the direction in which to look for a solution to the puzzling problem of how to assimilate the Davidic traditions to DtH. And finally, it has not yet been shown how a failed reforming king might be thought a model for an exilic community. Here, then, is an issue which

36. David Jobling, *The Sense of Biblical Narrative II* (Sheffield: JSOT Press, 1986) 66–84; and see Robert Polzin's review in *Biblica* 69 (1988) 123–25.

37. See C. Schäfer-Lichtenberger, *Josua und Salomo; Eine Studie zu Autorität und Legitimität des Nachfolgers im Alten Testament*, SVT 58 (Leiden: Brill, 1995), for an incisive critique of the view that Moses and Joshua are royal figures; as in Moshe Weinfeld, *Deuteronomy and the Deuteronomic School* (Oxford: Clarendon Press, 1972) esp. 167–71; G. E. Gerbrandt, *Kingship according to the Deuteronomistic History*, SBLDS 87 (Atlanta: Scholars Press, 1986); J. R. Porter, "The Succession of Joshua," in *Proclamation and Presence*, ed. J. I. Durham and J. R. Porter (London: SCM, 1970; new corr. ed. Macon, GA: Mercer University Press, 1983) 102–32; Van Seters, *The Life of Moses*, 3.

38. The theory of the Succession Narrative has suffered from the enhancement of the position of the so-called "Appendix" to Samuel (2 Samuel 21–24) in the structure of those books: see, e.g., R. A. Carlson, *David: The Chosen King* (Stockholm: Almqvist and Wikseel, 1964) 26; W. Brueggemann, "2 Samuel 21–24: an Appendix of Deconstruction?" *CBQ* 50 (1988) 383–97.

cannot easily be explained at the level of a Josianic, let alone an exilic, controversy.[39] The topic of kingship has left all the marks of a scarred and scarring history.

Worship. The them of worship bears directly upon the exile, because it is the sack of the temple in 587 B.C.E. that seems to mark the beginning of it. Interpretations of DtH that put it after the exile, furthermore, [[40]] make it at least in part an apologia for the religious apparatus that prevailed then.

The worship arc in DtH runs from Deuteronomy's legislation concerning "the place that the LORD your God will choose out of all your tribes as his habitation to put his name there" (Deut 12:5) to the fall of Jerusalem. The trajectory from "place" to Jerusalem, however, is not a simple one. As is well known, the tolerance in the area of worship that seems to have prevailed in monarchic times (e.g., 1 Sam 7:7–9; 9:12; 1 Kgs 18:30–38) called forth an explanation or apology from the author of 1 Kgs 3:2, who saw that the inherited material did not square easily with the ideal of a single chosen sanctuary. Levenson thought that these uncriticized accounts of sacrifices at various places of worship marked a discrepancy between Dtr1 and Dtr2.[40] Friedman, in contrast, attempts harmonization by noting that the ark, which identified the central sanctuary in Deuteronomistic thinking, was found at various places in the early period, and also that while it was at Kiriath-Jearim there could not have been a "place" in the strict sense. In his view, therefore, Dtr might have found ways of accommodating the awkward material.

It is not clear that Friedman has fully answered Levenson here. (There is no sign of a concern to confer legitimacy on Samuel's "high place" sacrifice in 1 Samuel 9, for example.) Rather, the material has left a legacy which the later authors can only accommodate and explain (as in 1 Kgs 3:2).

Even granted the coherence of the Deuteronomistic case in this respect, however, a further point arises even within the storyline that traces a succession of central sanctuaries. This goes off at more than one tangent, corresponding to the various places at which the ark is reported to have been more or less settled for considerable periods (e.g., Bethel, Judg 20:27). Deuteronomy itself highlights Shechem, and Joshua conducts two major ceremonies there (Deuteronomy 27; Joshua 24). The preeminent sanctuary before Jerusalem, however, is Shiloh, which features at important junctures in the Books of Joshua (Joshua 18), Judges (Judg 21:19) and Samuel (1 Samuel 1–3). Shiloh is dignified formally with the status of

39. The understanding of Josiah in DtH that is found in the Smend school is self-contradictory and open to serious criticism; see McConville, *Grace in the End*, 83–85, for remarks especially on Timo Veijola, *Die Ewige Dynastie*; and cf. above, n. 8.

40. Levenson, "Who Inserted the Book of the Torah?"

"chosen place," in Deuteronomic terms, in Jer 7:12. And it has entered the tradition so decisively that it holds its place well into [[41]] postbiblical interpretation of Old Testament, inviting explanation of its role in relation to that of Jerusalem.[41] The resultant picture is rational enough. But it is arguably not an ideal story in the context of an apologia for postexilic worship conditions.

Israel. A final theme that relates to the exile is that of Israel itself, or more precisely its election. In a sense the topic of election is central to Old Testament historiography. The idea of a united chosen people is a key component of Deuteronomy's theology, a justification for the command to take the land at the expense of other peoples. Yet the unity of the nation is problematical throughout the narrative. In Joshua the nature of the relationship between the Transjordanian tribes and the rest is aired (Joshua 22). In Judges, the celebrated Song of Deborah (Judges 5) raises the question of cohesion between the tribes in a fundamental way. The north-south split is heralded in the narratives of Samuel, both in the account of the war between David and the house of Saul and in its aftermath (e.g., 2 Sam 16:5–8; 20:1–2). Here too, the idea of election is given a new context in the matrix of dynastic kingship. And this is no straightforward birth, for the weakness of David brings the book to a close that hints at the possibility of loss.

In Kings, the question of election is at the core. The north–south split in Israel's history impinges on the narrative in Kings in an obvious way (that is, in the "separate development" of Israel and Judah that is built into the structure of the narrative). Yet this analytical method adopted in dealing with the problem posed by Jeroboam does not solve it. This is because of the ambiguity that now surrounds the very identity of Israel. The secession of the northern part of the kingdom occasions the problem, and the designation of the new entity, Jeroboam's kingdom, as "Israel," only sharpens the irony. Can this "Israel" be truly Israel? And yet the converse is inescapable too: can the rump Judah be Israel? The story of election turns out to be one of ambivalence and failure.[42] This doubleness in the constitution of Israel is inseparable from the story of its downfall.

[[42]] A study of this theme too, then, reveals a mass of diverse issues: the sense of vulnerability to traditional enemies, rivalries between tribes, and the running sore of the north-south division. This does not fit well with the proposal that the Old Testament is the work of a systematizing bureaucracy with a self-serving agenda, nor that "Israel" is a product of

41. See J. G. McConville and J. G. Millar, *Time and Place in Deuteronomy* (Sheffield: JSOT Press, 1994) 98–103, for an account.

42. Key texts on this topic are 1 Kings 20 and 2 Kings 3; see my "Narrative and Meaning in the Books of Kings," *Biblica* 70 (1989).

postexilic imagination. The sequence Israel-Judah-Jews certainly represents rather sophisticated reflection, but it is reflection on a real history.

Conclusions

We have considered the relationship between the unity and diversity of DtH. There is unquestionably a perspective "from the end," that inevitably affects the way in which the whole is read. This raised the question how far, if at all, DtH was a record of an actual history that corresponded in any sense to the period of time it purports to treat. If there were echoes of "exile" in the narratives of the earlier history, did it follow that this was purely theological reflection on the contemporary situation of the Babylonian exiles? Or were the issues that came to a head in that crisis already implicit in a rather extensive history of Israel? In the former case the author(s) are composing "history" rather freely; in the latter, they are perceiving patterns that derive from the history itself. The difficulty for the modern interpreter is in trying to decide between these two options.

One way to begin to solve the problem was to consider selected central themes of DtH: exile itself, leadership, worship and the concept of Israel. Our consideration of these topics showed that they were characterized by an unevenness which suggested actual trajectories in history. This in turn made it likely that DtH consisted of a real dialogue between received material and the perspectives of the final composition, rather than the artificial composition of the whole in a later period.

For this reason the theory of a double redaction of DtH may be thought preferable to that of a triple redaction within the exile, because the former reckons with the effect of real events in history upon the final form of the text. Friedman tried to combine that theory with a thematic approach that has elements in common with what I have offered here. I am not convinced that his thematic study finally supports the double-redaction theory, however. That study led him, in general, to a recognition that there are certain continuities in the material that transcend the postulated sources. We saw that he argued (against Levenson) that Dtr1 and [[43]] Dtr2 were in harmony on the matter of the conditions for keeping the land.[43] They agreed too on the possibility of chastisement for Israel: Josiah, after all, reacted in terror to whatever it was that he read in the Book of the Law (even if exile is not explicitly in view).[44] In these circumstances it becomes difficult to distinguish confidently between the two redactions. On the other hand, Friedman finds it impossible to decide

---

43. Friedman, *The Exile and Biblical Narrative*, 26–27.
44. Ibid., 30–31.

how far "the author/editor of Dtr1" consciously developed the theme of the experience of the divine presence, which he thinks undergoes a metamorphosis in the course of DtH from a greater to a lesser degree of miraculous intervention in the life of Israel. He concludes: "It is certainly due in part to the combination of varying genres of the sources, in part to the varying temporal distances between authors and their subjects, in part to what seems to be a common human feeling that ages of power stand behind us."[45] From two opposite directions, therefore (that is to say, certain agreements between the alleged sources on the one hand, and fundamental disparities on the other), the postulate of a double redaction comes under pressure from a thematic study.

The difficulty may belong to the concept of a DtH itself. Some of the themes discussed above are best understood within the context of the whole sweep of Genesis–Kings. For example, the themes of leadership and worship have origins, within the larger narrative, in the Sinai pericope (20:24–26; 24:13); and, as Friedman has shown, the exodus-exile nexus in DtH is given coherence by the focus on Egypt.

This centrality of the exodus in Genesis–Kings has recently been taken up by Claus Westermann, as part of his thesis that the various historical books have been independently edited.[46] In his thesis, the unity of the larger entity (Genesis–Kings) is retained, yet discrete redactional units are identified within it. Here is a different way of trying to account for unity and diversity. We may recall at this point our example of a perspective "from the end," namely the Song of Hannah. In this case the "end" [[44]] seemed to be the establishment of the royal dynasty. The perspective, therefore, was intelligible within the confines of the Books of Samuel, and we saw express connections between the Song and themes in those books. Yet there are obvious connections too between Samuel and Kings, especially in the development in Kings (though distinctively) of the dynastic promise. Probably therefore we have to think of separate processes of composition for the different books, or at least blocks, of what is now DtH, all finally gathered under the umbrella of a broader horizon.

This is not in itself a new proposal. It does have relevance, however, to the question with which we have been occupied, namely whether a perspective "from the end" makes it unlikely that our narratives have any connection with the historical events and issues to which they purport to relate. On the model proposed, it is not necessary, in the end, to select between polarized options. The history in this historiography has multiple

---

45. Ibid., 41.

46. C. Westermann, *Die Geschichtsbücher des Alten Testaments: Gab es ein deuteronomistisches Geschichtswerk?* TBü 87 (München/Gütersloh: Chr. Kaiser/GVH, 1994).

horizons. Thus the narrative of Gideon and Abimelech, for example, may well have thought-provoking echoes of that of Saul and David, and those echoes may even have been perceived by a final author of DtH. But that is not to preclude the intrinsic independence of either, nor the possibility that their mutuality is the result of a coming into focus that is not quite the work of any one author.

The Deuteronomistic mold, therefore, may not do justice to the full range of material in the histories. I have suggested, *en passant*, that it is somewhat exposed to the radical challenge of Van Seters and others. A model is needed instead that can do justice to a long history of writing and reflection, while allowing that a point of equilibrium and perspective is reached in the exile. I have tried to sketch here the lines that such a model might take.

The Understanding of History in the Old Testament Prophets

HANS WALTER WOLFF

[[336]] It is an alarming sign of our time that interest in history has become discredited.

To be sure, there is among us interest in past existence as a unique accomplishment of life. Also we are concerned in individual cases with the continuous pre-history of present relationships and tasks, as, for instance, in a problem in a scientific specialty. But who is still fired with an interest in universal history so as to inquire, after the manner of Friedrich Schiller's plan in his inaugural address in Jena, "Beginning with the latest state of the world back to the origin of things"?

However, wherever a passion for universal history is alive today, as in the Marxist historical science, questions concerning the present and the future dominate the field in such a manner that interest in past happenings exists only in as far as it refers to our own present and future. All attention is directed to the laws of evolution. Thus interest in past events, as simply things that happened, is extinguished, and with it the passion for research into the variants in analogies, for the individual and the contingent event.

Thus it is not surprising that among the great mass of our contemporaries interest in history is pushed into the background by interest in natural law and its application in technology. In this no one even dreams that

Reprinted with permission from *Essays on Old Testament Interpretation* (ed. C. Westermann; London: SCM, 1963) 336–55. Translated by Keith R. Crim.

Author's note: [[This paper was originally read as my]] Inaugural Address in Mainz, January 28, 1960.

by the schism between consciousness [[337]] of history and natural science *the* danger to life in our age arises, for indeed self-knowledge and responsibility are not to be separated from attention to history.

Therefore it is necessary that we inquire into the origins of the interest in the totality of past history as an elementary need of life. We must here assume as a result of research that these origins are to be sought in the Old Testament.[1] The Old Testament understanding of history received its particular expression in the prophecy of the 8th to the 6th centuries. Today we shall inquire into the distinctiveness of the prophetic understanding of history and its continuing significance.

I

1. The uniqueness of the prophetic understanding of history can be comprehended only in the light of the specific starting point of its message. The thought of the prophets is produced by a future event which they are to proclaim. Amos recognizes that "The end has come upon my people Israel" (8:2, RSV). In visionary and auditory experiences, Yahweh, the God of Israel, commissioned those who spoke for him to proclaim the future event. This word of the future evoked prophetic thought and speech about the past and the present of those who heard it. Thus the prophetic knowledge of history must first of all be understood as *knowledge of history from the point of view of the future.* How then does the future appear in prophecy?

(a) In prophecy the future appears throughout as the future of Yahweh, of the God of Israel himself. Yahweh appears personally before Israel in the superior Assyrian troops of Tiglath-Pileser III. "For I will be like a lion to Ephraim, and like a young lion to the house of Judah. I, even I, will rend and go away, I [[338]] will carry off, and none shall rescue" (Hos 5:14, RSV). As author of the future he is the absolute Lord of history. The appropriate expression for history in the prophetic books is, therefore, "the work of Yahweh." Isaiah uses it in this sense first of the future (5:19), in parallel to the "counsel of Yahweh" (28:29), but then by analogy, in the same manner of the past (28:21; 5:12), and of the whole course of history, which is called "all his (i.e., Yahweh's) work" (10:12). Significantly, the em-

---

1. Eduard Meyer, *Geschichte des Altertums*, II.2³ (1953) 285; Karl Löwith, *The Meaning of History* (1949) 18f.; Mircea Eliade, *The Myth of the Eternal Return* (1954) 160ff.; Gerhard von Rad, "Der Anfang der Geschichtsschreibung im alten Israel" (1944), reprinted in *Ges. Studien z. AT* (1958) 148ff.; Alfred Jepsen, *Die Quellen des Königebuchs* (1953) 106ff.; Hartmut Gese, "Geschichtliches Denken im Alten Orient und im Alten Testament," *ZThK* 55 (1958) 127ff.; Wolfhart Pannenberg, "Redemptive Event and History," [[in C. Westermann (ed.), *Essays on Old Testament Interpretation*]] 316ff.

phasis lies here again on the future, "When the Lord has finished all his work on Mount Zion and on Jerusalem he will punish the arrogant boasting of the king of Assyria and his haughty pride" (RSV). History is the whole work of the God who is coming.

(b) The future of God is anticipated in the prophetic word. "Surely the Lord GOD does nothing, without revealing his secret to his servants the prophets" (Amos 3:7, RSV). Consequently, a revealing of coming history takes place in the prophetic word. In this it must be noted that the Hebrew *dābār* denotes word as well as event; in this it can only be compared to our word "history," which we use for that which is spoken (recounted history) and for that which occurred (experienced history). Compare Jer 1:12, "For I am watching over my *dābār* to perform it"; and Ezek 12:25, 28, "the *dābār* which I speak will be performed," on which cf. Zimmerli, BK, 13, 274f., 277. History is imparted to the prophet in the word. According to Amos, there is no future which does not appear beforehand in the prophetic word.[2]

What follows from this? Since the future appears first in the historical event of the prophetic word, history is understood here [[339]] as a dialogue of Yahweh with Israel. This can be clarified by further observations. Amos saw that already in the past all kinds of catastrophes had broken in

---

2. Cf. Reinhold Schneider, "There is no catastrophe, unless it be preceded by a misunderstood prophet" (*Pfeiler im Strom* [1958] 55). That the word of the prophet anticipates history is particularly clear in the symbolic actions of the prophets. See H. W. Wolff, *Hosea*, BK 14, 72.

It is primarily in this light that the fact of the formation of tradition in prophecy must be seen. As a herald of history the word first awakens a waiting for history (Isa 8:17). The word which has gone forth and the facts which occur must be compared. If they do not correspond to one another, then one must wait under the "hidden face of God" while the word is carefully preserved for coming history (Isa 8:16), "as a witness for ever" Isa 30:8. Thus in prophecy the formation of tradition results from this objective necessity. And so, for the preservation of the prophetic words we are not "indebted, as in all history of tradition, to a chain of innumerable accidents" (Eduard Meyer, op. cit., 286) but above all to its peculiar nature, namely, that it is a word directed toward a future in history. This observation must be considered in the comparison of Old Testament prophecy with prophetic phenomena in the ancient East. See *EvTh* 15 (1955) 450.

Even the roots of the Old Testament *canon* must be understood in terms of such a comparison of the prophetic word which went forth, and the events which occurred. These roots are to be sought in the period of the Exile as prophetic words of judgment which had been fulfilled (Deut 18:22; Jer 28:9). The word of outsiders and opposers becomes canonical and at the same time determines what part of the literature of the pre-exilic period is to be handed on and what not. "Evaluation and revaluation took place in the burning light of the divine judgment" (Th. C. Vriezen, *Theologie des Alten Testaments in Grundzügen*, n.d., 39f.). So the correspondence of prophetic word and the course of history contributed greatly to the formation of tradition and of the canon. In relation to the course of tradition itself, cf. Antonius H. J. Gunneweg, "Mündliche und schriftliche Tradition der vorexilischen Prophetenbücher als Problem der Neueren Prophetenforschung," FRLANT 73 (1959).

on Israel: crop failures, plagues, earthquakes—in which, in the providence of Yahweh, his call to repentance went forth. Amos had to proclaim as Yahweh's word of accusation, "Yet you did not return to me" (Amos 4:6ff., RSV). The nature of history as dialogue is shown quite directly in that Yahweh's word for the future very often confronts the voice of the contemporaries in a quotation. "But you said, 'No! We will speed upon horses,' therefore you shall speed away; and, 'We will ride upon swift steeds,' therefore your pursuers shall be swift" (Isa 30:16, RSV).[3] In a great number of prophetic words, future history appears as Yahweh's judgment and its proclamation by the prophet as a court trial with occasionally a lively exchange of interrogation and defense, of accusation and pronouncement of sentence.[4] In this way first of all, in the prophetic word the character of history as conversation is disclosed.

By these observations a misunderstanding of history as the "work of Yahweh" is avoided, namely, in reference to the function of man in history. He is certainly not the antagonist of God, nor yet the prophet subject of history, but neither is he a simple object; he is to be understood as a partner in conversation with the God who creates history. [[340]]

(c) The future of God appears in the prophetic word mainly as a historical future, not as an end of history. It is comparable to past occurrences. A catastrophe will come over Ahaz that is comparable to the revolt of the ten tribes in the days of Rehoboam (Isa 7:17). A further future will follow the day that is coming. Assyria and Babylon are announced as Yahweh's implements of judgment against Israel "until the time of his own land comes" (Jer 27:6f., RSV; Isa 10:12f.). In the manifold character of the future actions of God, an intention can be recognized. "I will return again to my place, until they 'are laid waste' and seek my face. When they are in distress they will seek me" (Hos 5:15[5] ; cf. 3:4f.; 2:16f.[14f.]). Thus the prophet recognizes, with the future, the finality of history.[6]

---

3. Cf. H. W. Wolff, *Das Zitat im Prophetenspruch*, EvTh Beih., 4 (1937).

4. Cf. Isa 3:13–15; Hos 4:1–4; Mic 6:1ff.; Jer 2:5–13; also Hans Jochen Boecker, *Redeformen des israelitischen Rechtslebens*, Diss. Bonn (1959).

5. On the problem of the text, see H. W. Wolff, BK, 14 (1957) 147f.

6. There is an "alien work" of God in history (Isa 28:21b) that is related to his major work in a systematic way. Yahweh varies the methods and tools of his actions in history, as, in the life of the farmer, processes and tools vary with the respective seasons and fruits. This does not occur arbitrarily but in wisdom, in a freedom that corresponds to his saving plan. "He is wonderful in counsel, and excellent in wisdom" (Isa 28:23–29, RSV).

Thus far we have consciously avoided the catchword "eschatology." In this connection the reader should compare the recent works of Alfred Jepsen, *RGG*, 3rd ed., Vol. 2, 655ff., and Richard Hentschke, "Gesetz und Eschatologie in der Verkündigung der Propheten," *ZEE* (1960) 47. The prophetic proclamation of God's future is to be termed eschatological in the sense that the previous history of God with Israel reaches its end, an end in history, which

This decisive disclosure of the *finality*[7] of history has been already anticipated in the correspondence of prophetic word and history. It later becomes explicit in the transmission of the words of Jeremiah. That is, it is repeatedly stressed in the book of Jeremiah that the proclamation and transmission of the words of judgment took place with the aim that they should be heard, and awaken the spirit of repentance so that the threatened judgment might not occur (Jer 25:3ff.; 26:2f.; 36:2f.; Jonah 3:8ff.). The prophetic word is not here primarily directed toward its fulfillment in history, but is an instrument of history that is intended to bring about the conversion of those who hear it, and therewith the non-fulfillment of what was threatened. It shows in extreme clarity the character of history as dialogue, but at the same time its stirring finality.

Thus we hold as our first conclusion: *For the prophets, history is the goal-directed conversation of the Lord of the future with Israel.*

2. We inquire further, how the Old Testament prophets came to consider the whole course of history as seen from the announced future. To be sure, the decisive stimulus to prophetic thought is given by the prophecies that were to be announced. But the prophetic thought which resulted from this, and consequently the bulk of the oracles, does not deal with the future, but with the present and the past of the hearers. Phenomena from the whole course of history can appear in the prophetic word, for the God who is proclaimed as the Coming One is no other than he who has already dealt with Israel in past history and has spoken to it, and to whom the present Israel is therefore responsible. In this constancy of God the *unity of history* is established for the prophets. How is this second step of understanding arrived at?

(a) The future is always placed in relation to the observable course of history.

---

corresponds to the beginning in history. The sharpest threats express it as follows: Hosea, in the negation of the formula for the establishment of the covenant, "For you are not my people and I am not your God" (1:9, RSV); Amos, in the threat to drive the nation out of the land (4:3; 5:27; 6:7), which canceled the gift of the land in the early days (2:9f.); Isaiah, for example, in the return to the old holy war, in which Yahweh now fights against Israel instead of for her (28:21). In this end in history, history as such does not come to its end. Prophecy knows eschatology also in the other meaning, that there is to be beyond the end of the old salvation history a basically new meeting with God in the midst of judgment, with new divine ordinances.

7. The concept of finality is used in this paper to denote the purposive quality of God's historical actions as it appears in the witness given within concrete circumstances. It is not therefore to be interpreted in the sense of a teleological view of history which excludes contingency.

First of all, the many prophetic threats of judgment show by the accompanying accusations that the future is grounded in the present.[8] In this way, as elsewhere in the ancient Orient, a direct connection can be shown to exist between an action and its results. "Because you have plundered many nations, all the remnant of the peoples shall plunder you" (Hab 2:8, RSV). "Ephraim shall stumble in his guilt" (Hos 5:5, RSV). Here history appears above all as the consequence of human actions, as [[342]] if man were the subject of history. Prophecy takes up this view,[9] which, as the experience of wisdom, was widespread in the ancient Orient, in order to make clear the strict relations between events. It was, however, thoroughly permeated with the certainty that it is Yahweh who established the relationships. Thus Hosea proclaimed, "And I will requite them their doings" (4:9).[10]

In this way, man's deeds *can* return to him in the future, but it is not necessary that they do so. Casual thought became a secondary key to understanding, but not the absolutely dominant one. Yahweh is free. The words of promise appear always without any word of their being grounded in prior human conduct.[11] But even the connection between threat of punishment and the ground for punishment is not necessarily of itself definite. Rather, under the God to whom Israel has long been responsible, factors are regarded as guilt, which are related not to the future, but to prior acts of God and to the still valid covenant relationship. Thus the whole sweep of life can be observed, from the luxury of Samaria and Jerusalem to the misery of the widow; from the practice of rendering judgment to the priestly dereliction of office; from trade treaties with Assyria to war coalitions against Babylon.[12] In this manner the depth of history is disclosed; Hosea brings to light the revolution of Jehu of a hundred years before (1:4), many references are made to the time of David (Amos 9:11; Isa 29:1), or to the beginnings of the monarchy (Hos 9:15; 13:10f.), to the period of the judges (Isa 9:3[4]). The Exodus from Egypt and the possession of the land appear again and again (Jer 2:5ff.; Amos 2:9ff.; Hos 2:17[15]; 11:1ff.), as does the time in the desert (Amos 5:25, etc.). Hosea

---

8. Cf. H. W. Wolff, "Die Begründung der prophetischen Heils- und Unheilssprüche," *ZAW* 52 (1934) 1ff.

9. H. Gese, op. cit., 135ff.

10. For a critical development of the ideas by Klaus Koch, *ZThK* 52 (1955) 1ff. Cf. Friedrich Horst, *EvTh* 16 (1956) 72ff., and H. Gese, "Lehre und Wirklichkeit in der alten Weisheit" (1958) 45ff.

11. Cf. the exact presentation of R. Hentschke, op. cit., 50ff.

12. Prophecy does not distinguish "a sacred history" from "the profane as different in meaning" as Karl Jepsen erroneously assumes for Christian faith (*Von Ursprung und Ziel der Geschichte* [1955] 14). Neither Luther nor Melanchthon separated ecclesiastical and profane history. Cf. Reinhard Wittram, *Das Interesse an der Geschichte* (1958) 137.

can even trace the deceitful spirit of Israel back to Jacob in the patriarchal period (12:3ff.). As history under God, what has happened is not really [[343]] past, but a continuing fact. The unity of history in all areas and periods is contained in the constancy of the God of Israel.

Thus the course of history does not derive its continuity from man nor from an arbitrary, unchangeable divine will, but from the obligatory, continual, free conversation of God with Israel. In this way the structure of the conversation becomes even clearer. It has the continuity of an unbreakable covenant of life. Therefore Hosea can compare it to the story of love between a man and a maid (2:4–22[2–20]), or to the struggles of a father with a son who is hard to raise (11:1ff.; cf. Isa 1:2f.). For all its obligatory continuity the conversation retains the freedom of a partnership. Obedience occurs (Jer 2:1ff.; Hos 10:11) as well as the revolt of man (Jer 1:16; 2:5; Hos 9:10). God's righteous punishment as well as God's mercy (Hos 11:8f.). Thus continuity can be concealed in the concrete course of history by crass discontinuity; only through the prophetic word is it revealed and brought to light.

In such free, continuous conversation, reality is first disclosed as history. Now reality no longer mirrors mythical, cosmic events in such a way that all interest attaches to the cyclical return of things that are finally unalterable, nor to the synthetic world order of the context of an action and its result. Rather now it is the unforeseen fact which attracts interest, the change in history, the new in the irreversible progress of events. And yet—this must not be overlooked—history can be understood as a unity because of the constancy of God.

(b) The future is brought into relation to the historical beginning. The continuity of history is fully understood only when we see that in the prophetic eschatology an analogy to the beginnings of Israel's history occupies the foreground. The historical end defined by the prophets leads to a new beginning that corresponds to the historical beginning. It is truly a second word. In Hosea the threatened return to the wilderness contributes to the new, alluring conversation of God, who is Israel's constant lover despite all disappointments; he will then renew his gift of the civilized land to the faithless wife, and Israel will hear the echo of love, "as in the days of her youth, and as in the day when she came up out [[344]] of the land of Egypt" (Hos 2:15, KJV). Jeremiah (31:31–34) leads us a step further. In the coming days the new covenant will enter history. It will be the same as the old, in that all initiative proceeds from Yahweh, that its goal is Israel's freedom and its document a covenant agreement. But to the things that are the same, something new is added; no further external teaching of the law need take place, but each will know the will of his God in the new, intensive oneness of the people with their God; finally, the new covenant will be unbreakable because Yahweh will forgive guilt. So to the nuclei of the old and new covenants a new coefficient is added which means intensification and completion. Together with the faithfulness of God, his free, goal-directed will is recognized. This specific analogical relationship which is to be observed here and often elsewhere in the prophetic writings, and which presupposes historical continuity and shows therein intensification or fulfillment of specific and fundamental (typical) facts of history, we call typology.[13]

13. The Old Testament relationships which are so designated are of at least the same relevance for biblical hermeneutics as the Pauline typology (cf. especially E. Fuchs, *Hermeneutik* [1954] 200f.). If it is true "That the *comprehendere* starts from the Scripture and not from the exegete" (G. Ebeling, *ZThK* 48 [1951] 175), then it becomes of even greater importance to us how understanding occurs in the Scripture itself. We are faced with the task of clarifying typology as a hermeneutic aid. As a supplement to and a further development of what was said above [[here Wolff refers to pp. 160ff. of the volume from which this essay is reprinted]] I would like to present the following points:

1. The relation of prophetic eschatology to the themes of the salvation history as sketched above has been confirmed for me by the correctness of the criticism of W. Pannenberg (see above, pp. 326ff. [[in the original volume]]). Typology, in the prophetic writings as in the writings of Paul, presupposes the continuity of God's actions in history. The contents of the proclamations vary with the various relationships, but they stand nonetheless in a discoverable historical context. Because that variation and this context are to be seen in terms of the freedom and faithfulness of God, we remain free to see the correspondences as well as the differences and the contrasts.

2. In this way it becomes clear that typology, as it confronts us today, goes hand in hand with historical interpretation. In our theological and hermeneutic considerations we have paid too little attention to the meaning which typology gains in the present-day science of history, which has recognized the limits of the one-sided, individualized approach of historicism. Cf. Theodor Schieder, *Der Typus in der Geschichtswissenschaft*, Studium generale, 5 (1952) 228–34. He refers to Jacob Burckhardt and his concern "to seek to pursue the repetitive, the constant, the typical in history" (p. 229); he warns against "cryptotypes which enter in, where we are not conscious of the question concerning the true comparative types," and (p. 231) he distinguishes by way of clarification, structural, progressive, and form types (pp. 232–34). Cf. also R. Wittram, op. cit., Chap. 4, "Vergleich, Analogie, Typus," especially pp. 54–58. The stimulus given by J. Burckhardt has so far been worked out most fruitfully in the history of art; after that the question of historical types has especially promoted the disciplines of the history of constitutional law and jurisprudence. Basically no field of history is exempt from it. In that we have recently introduced it into biblical hermeneutics—where it found in prophecy and in the Pauline writings a use that was spiritual-historically, and also methodologically different, but nonetheless comparable, and, above all, relevant—we must carefully inquire into the "various fundamentals of historical occurrences," into the "astounding phenomena" in the chaos of events (Wittram, op. cit., 57). Therefore we by no means are inquiring into the "suprahistorical," but into the "limited number of patterns in history" (op. cit., 58).

3. Without this question concerning what is typical in the texts of the Old and New Testaments we will scarcely be able to find the narrow way between historical fragmentation and the leveling out of history through individualized investigation and an existential dissolving of history in historicity (cf., e.g., C. H. Ratschow, *Der angefochtene Glaube*, 150ff., 162f.). By

The relation of tension between beginning and goal can become such that it is possible to speak of discontinuity. This can be so strongly expressed that Second Isaiah can proclaim to the generation in exile that has lived through the judgment, "Remember not the former things, nor consider the things of old. [[345]] Behold, I am doing a new thing. . . . I will make a way in the wilderness and rivers in the desert" (Isa 43:18–19, RSV). He is moved by the incomparable nature of that which is coming— the new, which will eclipse not only the terrible time of judgment that has come upon their smug piety, but the old salvation history as well. And yet it is precisely in Second Isaiah that it is always recognizable in the presentation of the new that the earlier salvation history is being called to mind (48:20–22; 52:11f.; 55:12f.). Indeed, even the days of Noah are mentioned in 54:7–10, "For this is like the days of Noah to me: as I swore that the waters of Noah should no more go over the earth, so I have sworn that I will not be angry with you and will not rebuke you . . . and my covenant of peace shall not be removed" (RSV). The God of Israel ultimately remains true to himself and to his people. He remains the free God, free also not to be circumscribed by human defiance (Hos 11:9). To this extent, the continuity of history, which holds together all actual discontinuities, is not postulated on the basis of the oneness and constancy of the Lord of history, but makes itself known in the correspondence of beginning and end.

So we hold as a second conclusion: *Prophecy can perceive history to be a continuous unity because it recognizes in the coming actions of God the beginnings of the salvation history.* [[346]]

---

inquiring into the typical we overcome the non-obligatory comparison of partial phenomena, the capitulation before the "omnipotence of analogy" (Troeltsch). At the same time, in the light of this question, we will now be able, if at all, to evaluate the relevance of that which is always meaningful. In the present state of research we must particularly inquire into the typological building of traditions, into the typological structure of faith or exhortation, into the typological ways of speaking of God, into the typological relation of correspondence between word and event. However, above all, the types of testimonies of God's mighty deeds in history, which are the ground of faith, are to be recognized anew in the Old and New Testaments and in comparison with the surrounding world.

In this, typology helps to distinguish the variable from the constant, yet without making the constant absolute or the variants relative. Modern typology must no longer be permitted to succumb to a naïve objectification. In that it adopts as its own a recognition of existential interpretation. But, faith in Jesus of Nazareth finds its basis as the final Word of God in history because the types of the two Testaments help interpret each other and together stand in contrast to that which is typical in the surrounding world. God's dealings in Israel and in Jesus of Nazareth are witnessed to and known, and through them we are challenged to proclaim God's acts for ourselves and for our world, not in a way that is objectively of universal validity, nor, on the other hand, subjective and optional, but as a valid aid for each of the corresponding types of the kerygma for each corresponding hour.

3. The uniqueness of the prophetic understanding of history is not exhausted in the recognition of the finality and the continuity of history. Necessarily a view of universal history emerges.

(a) Already for Amos, reality as history is fully comprehended only when it is seen in the context of the history of the nations. He warns against misunderstanding Yahweh's dealings in the history of salvation as a sacral history without analogy: "'Are you not like the Ethiopians to me, O people of Israel?' says the LORD. 'Did I not bring up Israel from the land of Egypt, and the Philistines from Caphtor and the Syrians from Kir?'" (9:7; RSV). Beside the God of Israel there is no one else who initiates history in the world of the nations. Israel is distinguished only by the continuous address of Yahweh. This particular history, however, is inseparably intertwined with world history. Just as the superstate Egypt and the peoples of Palestine had to be mentioned immediately at the beginning of God's dealings with Israel, so in his new dealings Assyrian comes into the view of the prophets in the eighth century, Babylon in the seventh and sixth centuries, the Persians in the middle of the sixth century—and all of them are instruments of Yahweh's actions in history (Isaiah 10; Jeremiah 27; Isaiah 45). In the framework of Yahweh's salvation history for Israel they have their role to play as instruments of his judgments, [[347]] and then as objects of his judgment because of their *hybris* against Israel (Isa 10:12ff.).[14] In the breakup and decline of the great empires, Yahweh shows that he is Lord of world history. World history, too, is understood in its continuity and finality from the point of view of salvation history.

In Jeremiah an entirely different motive for interest in world history appears. In the legal proceedings in 2:10f., where Israel is accused of apostasy from Yahweh, we read, "For cross to the coasts of Cyprus and see, or send to Kedar and examine with care; see if there has been such a thing. Has a nation changed its gods, even though they are no gods? But my people have changed their glory for that which does not profit" (RSV). It should be noted with what zeal the prophet urges, as it were, research expeditions and study of source materials in the general history of religion. "See, send, examine, see!" He challenges them to compare Israel with the nations of the West as well as with those of the East in order to bring to light the singular nature of Israel's apostasy from her God. Thus in the midst of the crisis of salvation history ethnological interest appears because Israel's unique nature comes to light only in the framework of the history of the nations.[15]

---

14. Cf. A. Alt, "Die Deutung der Weltgeschichte im Alten Testament," *ZThK* 56 (1959) 134ff.

15. The way in which a mandate for research in world history is present in the passage Deut 4:32–35 should be noted. It inquires back into the beginnings of human history and

Finally, however, prophecy sees that Yahweh is also carrying out his purpose in the Gentile world in an effectual manner, and in particular this is true in Ezekiel, where his special intention for Israel becomes a historical reality. "And the nations shall know that I am the Lord, when I shall be sanctified in you before their eyes" (Ezek 36:23; cf. 36; 21:4[20:48], on which see Zimmerli, BK, 13, 466, and Isa 40:5; 43:8–13). Previously Isaiah had already seen that in the end all nations would flow together to Zion and there receive the instruction and law of the God of Israel (Isa 2:2–5). Thus in the end, because of the uniqueness of God, the lines of the history of the nations and of Israel come together in a historical goal. [[348]]

(b) In a final expansion, the universal interest of the prophets reaches out over the history of the nations into the history of nature. Second Isaiah recalled to mind the waters which were subdued in the days of Noah. Amos showed how drought, locusts, blight of grain, plagues, and earthquakes were intended to effect the return of Israel to the covenant demands of God (4:6ff.). Since the God of Israel, as the Lord who has at his disposal the ordered course of nature, is the sole one who causes even such natural catastrophes, these actions of his also are to be understood in relation to his continuous and goal-directed conversation with men. He who rejects this connection must prepare to stand naked before his God. In a different manner Hosea shows in a breathtaking sequence that Israel's faulty consciousness of history has consequences that are cosmic in scope. If there is lacking in the land that knowledge of God which is possible in Israel, then the first result of all is a destruction of community life. But in the constantly increasing use of force even life on earth itself is threatened. The destroying fire that man in his incompetence for community has let loose brings death to the plant and animal world and even to the fish of the sea (4:1–3). On the other side, Second Isaiah can anticipate that even the wilderness plant life will exchange its thorns and thistles for cypresses and myrtles when Yahweh leads his people out into freedom (55:13). Unanticipated natural catastrophes as ell as unanticipated fruitfulness share in God's history with the nations. Here it is plain that the prophetic understanding of total reality as a continuous, conclusive historical context necessarily moves toward universal history.

We hold as a third conclusion: *In prophecy interest in universal history is aroused because the coming God of Israel is recognized as the sole Lord of all reality.*[16]

---

includes the whole extent of the world of the nations. The sources of interest in world history in the Old Testament are in need of a new historical and theological investigation.

16. The roots of the prophetic view of history which has been developed here are to be found neither in prophecy itself nor in the world of Israel's environment. They lie in the old Israelite's traditions [[footnote continues on next page]].

[[349]] Finally, in this connection two things must be underscored. First, that such interest in history is, as it were, a by-product of the prophetic proclamation of the coming God. Because the speaking and acting of the God of Israel is related exclusively to ascertainable, this-worldly occurrences, total reality is included on the basis of the prophetic theology as history in the sense developed here.

Second, it must be said that nowhere in the prophets is a plan presented for history. All their zeal is directed to assault each contemporary situation from the point of view of the coming God. It is in this zeal that they proclaim that no hearer can understand their God if he does not at the same time understand reality as history determined by him and directed to him, as his conversation, first with Israel, but finally drawing in the whole world of the nations. Intimation is always of more value in prophecy than a clear statement.

II

It is not possible for us here to follow the working out of the prophetic understanding of history.[17] But we would yet like to ask whether our relation

---

1. The prophetic view of the unity and continuity of history presupposes the exclusive nature of the Yahweh faith as it is manifest from the beginning, particularly in the Sinai tradition. Yahweh's jealousy forbids in unsurpassable strictness the worship of other gods. This basic presupposition underlies even the oldest historical sketch in the salvation history Credo (Deut 6:21ff.; 26:5ff.).

2. This confession of the early saving deeds of Yahweh in the Exodus from Egypt and the occupation of the land of Canaan shows, from the first, contacts with world history. The God of Israel has shown his strong hand in dealing with the might of Egypt as well as with the previous inhabitants of Canaan. The presuppositions of the prophetic view of the universality of history are contained in such primitive confessions of Israel, not only in respect to the still limited role played by the history of the nations in the history of salvation, but also in reference to the certainty that natural events are included, as for example, the east wind at the Red Sea (Exod 14:21).

3. Already in the ancient Credo there are intimations of the goal-directed nature of history. Yahweh's actions do not really take place in the course of the natural year, but they are an irreversible sequence in the free field of history. So the two basic facts of salvation history are from the first united toward a goal: "He brought us out from there, that he might bring us in, to give us the land which he swore to give to our fathers" (Deut 6:23; cf. Lev 25:38). Thus there are at least hints of the finality of the prophetic understanding of history in the early traditions.

On the basis of these suppositions it was possible for the true writing of history to begin long before the time of the great prophets. Cf. G. v. Rad, *Ges. Studien zum AT* (1958) 152ff.

17. The first fruit of the prophetic understanding of history lies in the so-called Deuteronomic history. Cf. M. Noth, *Überlieferungsgeschichtliche Studien* (1943) 1–110. It exists in its time and in its environment as a singular document of genuine history writing within world literature. This is so in several respects:

to history, which has become problematic, must not share the fate of cut flowers because we can no [[350]] longer draw nourishment from the roots of the prophetic understanding of history which we have sought to recognize. I shall inquire in three directions.

1. How is the concept of a *unity* of history possible for us? It presupposes that the contingent (that which is always more or less a surprising occurrence) and the coherence of history have the same origin.[18] Otherwise, our historical understanding would be dissolved into episodes, or at best into cultural cycles. Or, on the other hand, through imminent regularities which appear to be discernible, the contingent events are in danger of not being recognized. Then free research into total reality is endangered. The certainty that in the reality of the world the conversation of God with Israel, and through Israel with humanity, takes place and that

---

1. In its will and capability for following the whole history of Israel for some seven centuries from the time of Moses to the time of the author in the Babylonian Exile.

2. In its conscientiousness in dealing with the literary sources that had been handed down and were now collected and edited, and in its respect for what actually happened (cf. M. Noth, op. cit., 108).

3. In the compactness of its conception, which with all respect for the traditions and individual facts grasps such an extensive history as a unity and presents the continuity of this history in a convincing manner.

This unitary concept is possible because the author, in the details and in the total picture, recognized the correspondence of the proclaimed Word of God and the actual happenings. The whole history, including the period of the monarchy, is comprehended in the words of Moses in Deuteronomy. (Cf. the conditions attached to the promise of Nathan in 1 Kgs 2:3f. to 2 Kgs 23:2ff.).

The goal of this history is not to make the present intelligible to the reader as God's judgment, much less to explain it as the final termination of salvation history. If this were the goal it would be impossible to understand why again and again times of apostasy, of judgment, and of the continuation of the salvation history are presented according to the new ordinances of Yahweh (cf. especially Judg 2:11–22; 1 Sam 12:6–25). Rather, we can discern the intention of bringing the contemporary generation to return to the Word of God, which had been long since proclaimed and was now substantiated through history. At all decisive turning points of the course of history this intention is apparent. In this connection it is to be noted in addition to the passages already mentioned that the main catchword "repent" occurs over and over again in 1 Sam 7:3; 2 Kgs 17:13; 23:25, above all, in direct address to the exilic generation in 1 Kgs 8:46ff.; Deut 30:1–10; 4:30f. The dovetailing of Deuteronomy with the Deuteronomic history in the introductory and concluding sections of Deuteronomy must be subjected to a new literary-critical investigation, especially for chapters 4 and 30, in consideration of the concern of the historical work for proclamation.

In the presence of the recognized continuity and the proclaimed intention of God's dealings in history, universality moves into the background, if the connection of the history of Israel with that of the neighboring nations is left out of account. The universal goal of God's dealings with Israel is indicated only once in passing (1 Kgs 8:41–43; cf. 9:7–9). From the theological starting point, however, it comes to the astonishing proclamation of a program of research in universal history, as mentioned above in note 15, in Deut 4:32–35.

18. Cf. W. Pannenberg, *KuD* 5 (1959) 280ff.

to this extent reality is not to be understood as unified, goal-directed history, is basic to the origin of historical thought in the prophetic writings. It is saying too little to say that either God or even man is the subject of history.[19] Contingent happenings are rooted in the freedom of God's conversation with man; the continuity of all history, however, is rooted in the supreme, inclusive faithfulness of God. That is a prophetic certainty. It is in accord with this that our generation must attempt anew to conceive of the unity of history in our own thought forms. Otherwise, it faces the dilemma either of honorably renouncing[20] an [[351]] understanding of the unity of all of history, or, on the other hand, with postulated laws of evolution or other world views which are always founded in only a *portion* of reality, of endangering the freedom of research into the *total* of actual events.

2. But how is the *recognition* of the unity of contingent happenings possible? Reinhard Wittram says in this connection:[21] "If the question of the beginning of world history is not decisive, then the end of world history is by no means an object of historical science, but the quest for it is decisive for our comprehension of history." What then? A contemporary says, "Since we cannot conceive of the end, in our world views we have obstinately held fast to the moment."[22]

For prophecy, as we saw, recognition of the continuity and finality of history was possible only because the Word of God for Israel was for them an unsought-for, even feared, but yet decisive event. In this Word future history broke into their present in a recognizable way. Basically this future Word corresponded with the actual events of past history in all areas of reality. Thus it provided the basis for an approach to the possibility of recognizing the finality of all of history. But only an approach!

For us to be able to carry this out, the end of history must be [[352]] recognizable, that is, not only future history, but also the *novisimum extremum*. Primitive Christianity asserted that according to the prior prophetic word, the final Word of God was given when Jesus of Nazareth appeared in history.[23] It was a certainty of early Christianity that in his words and

19. Thus, for example, R. Bultmann, *History and Eschatology: The Presence of Eternity* (1957) 143, passim.

20. For Bultmann's consequences, op. cit., 154f.

21. Op. cit., 135.

22. R. Hülsenbeck, "Der halbe Mensch," *FAZ* 20, 1 (1960).

23. The historic connection between the prophetic and the early Christian kerygma cannot be understood without the connecting link of Apocalyptic. The relationship of the latter to history is often underestimated. (See Dietrich Rössler, *Gesetz und Geschichte in der spätjüdischen Apokalyptik*, Heidelberg Dissertation, 1959, VLG.d.Ev. Erziehungsvereins, Neukirchen.) The relationship here is to be sought in the fact that the God of Israel is more and more spoken of as the hidden one (Isa 29:14; Jer 15:18; Isa 45:15) and at the same time with

deeds, in his death, and decisively in the Resurrection of the Crucified One from the dead, the end of history, if not "anticipated," was nonetheless made discernible; indeed it had been entered upon, in that this was the end of God's conversation with man. Thus according to the Christian confession, in Jesus of Nazareth the end of history has become an object of research in the midst of history.

The early Christian recognition of Jesus of Nazareth as the final Word of God is indissolubly connected with the recognition of his historical connection with the Old Testament salvation history. We theologians are confronted in our generation, in view of the sundering of disciples in the generation of our teachers,[24] with the great task of grasping first of all the theology of the Old and New Testaments in a new, historical-critically oriented hermeneutic consideration in terms of the historical distance of each Testament from the other, but also in their continuity and analogy. Our Old Testament theology would be false if alongside the historical distance from the New Testament we ignored the aids to understanding which are supplied in the New Testament analogies and the New Testament completion of God's history with Israel. In the same way, our New Testament theology is largely only half true, because it fails to recognize the [[353]] historical bonds that tie it to the Old Testament. These bonds must essentially be made more decisive than those which tie it to contemporary Judaism and Hellenism. So we must work toward a new outline of historically oriented *biblical* theology, which the coming generation must then recognize as its task.

For in biblical theology the scientific presuppositions are present which make possible the recognition of the unity and goal-directed nature of all of history, provided that the eschaton of all history, which is implied in the Old Testament and to which witness is borne in the New Testament, has in principle become subject to historical investigation in the history of Jesus of Nazareth. It is not that belief in God supplements reason in the recognition of reality, but that it rather liberates it for an objective view of data which are historically comparable to each other. At the same time, unbelief runs the risk of partially distorting this view and thus becoming semi-realism.[25]

---

increasing emphasis as the coming one. Jesus himself understood his message "as the last Word of God before the end" (H. Conzelmann, *RGG*, 3rd ed., Vol. 2, 668).

24. R. Bultmann has kept us back from conversation with the Old Testament science of the last thirty years. As W. Zimmerli has set forth above, pp. 89ff. [[not reprinted here]], Bultmann's essay "Prophecy and Fulfillment" (see above, pp. 50ff. [[not reprinted here]]) is an example of what untenable scientific consequences this leads to. Cf. also, above all, G. v. Rad, *Theologie des Alten Testaments*, Vol. 2.

25. Cf. the important references of W. Pannenberg, op. cit., 276f., to Luther's discussion of the evidence of Scripture in *De servo arbitrio* (WA, 18, 607ff., etc.).

On the whole, our generation is threatened from the left by a refusal to recognize the unity of history, from the right by the postulate of a goal of history at the expense of total reality, and above all, by the exclusion of the history of Israel and of Jesus of Nazareth from the exploration of total reality. This generation, therefore, is vigorously asked whether it will expand the historical research limitlessly and whether it can recognize the goal of history and with it the unity in the singular phenomena of prophecy and of Jesus of Nazareth, without which *human* existence is not really possible.

3. But have we not learned that God is not to be seen in the process of world history? Have we not just learned, as Christians or as nihilists, to reduce history to the authenticity of existence?[26] [[354]] Have we not fortunately dissolved the totality of history into existential accomplishments?

Due to the renunciation in principle of universal history we are obliged to abandon critical comparison and with it the question of truth. Therefore the necessary and inevitable step of existential philosophy and existential theology must not remain the final step. After philosophy, through the impulse given it by Kierkegaard, took the commanding position, theology is now called upon to lay anew its weight of biblical theology on the scales.[27] Can our generation then hold fast to the separation of the existential accomplishments from universal history at a time when world history first begins to take place as an empirical unity?[28] The pupil of Huizinga, Theodor J. G. Locher, professor of general history in Leiden, stated in a lecture in Mainz in 1952, "Our age is now faced with the mighty task of giving its historical background to the *one world*, which we must bring to realization amidst all its diversity or perish."[29] I believe that we are faced with the question in all its acuteness of how we intend to make the one world a reality and exist in it today if we cut ourselves off from the roots of our historical thought. Prophecy, which repeatedly addresses its hearers, does not thereby succumb to a pointilism, which is at present our greatest danger. It addresses men in an irreversible and unrepeatable context of events, in which God's conversation with the hearer takes place. In

---

26. Historicity as "responsibility for the heritage of history in respect to the future" (Bultmann, *History and Eschatology: The Presence of Eternity* [1957] 143); cf. F. Gogarten, *Der Mensch zwischen Gott und Welt* (1956) 388ff.; and, fundamentally, M. Heidegger, *Being and Time* (1962) §74 (The Ordinary Understanding of History and Dasein's Historizing) and §75 (Dasein's Historicality and World-History), e.g., 442f.; "Real historicity understands history as the reoccurrence of the possible, and realizes therefore that a possibility reoccurs only when by fate existence is momentarily open for it in its predetermined repetition."

27. While we are canonizing Kierkegaard's necessary contradiction of Hegel, we have already been attacked from the opposite direction.

28. Cf. H. Heimpel, "Der Versuch, mit der Vergangenheit zu leben," *FAZ* 25, 3 (1959).

29. Quoted by R. Wittram, op. cit., 128.

this the objects of our natural science are just as much involved as the dealings of human polities. Interest in universal history stands and falls, as we saw, with the certainty that the address of the Lord of all history is heard in the midst of history.

Wherever scientific research no longer deliberately cuts itself off from the biblical origin of our understanding of history, but remains open to total reality, it experiences how the source of a new passion of the academic disciplines for one another springs forth, just as certainly as the university cannot be separated in its [[355]] origin from a confession of the Lord of all history. In 1789, Schiller could say in his already quoted inaugural address in Jena, "The Christian religion has so manifold a part in the present form of the world, that its appearance is the most important fact of world history. But neither in the time in which it appeared, nor in the nation in whose midst it arose, is there a satisfactory basis for explaining its appearance." To be sure, this basis can be found only in the Lord of all history, to whom the prophets bore witness and whom the New Testament presupposes. Schiller already saw clearly the threatened separation of our sciences. He said, "Where the hireling (he who separates his scientific specialty from all others) divides, the philosophic spirit unites." Can the philosophic mind manage to do this unless its interest draws a sustenance and strength from the roots of our historical thinking?

At the outset we said it was an alarming sign of our time that interest in history has become discredited. Can we expect anything else from our contemporaries who are oriented in terms of natural science and technology, as long as anything less is looked for in history than the address of the Lord of the whole of reality, anything less than the exhortation and the appeal of the Lord of the future?

[[265]] What emerges strikingly from a comparison of Hosea with the other eighth-century prophets is Hosea's extensive reliance on Israel's past traditions. Indeed, backward reference is *the* preeminent characteristic of Hoseanic proclamation. A selection of these traditions forms the heart of Dwight R. Daniels's 1990 study, which represents a revision of his Hamburg University dissertation, completed in the summer of 1987 under the direction of Klaus Koch [[266]] of the Protestant-Theological faculty.

Daniels's intent is to investigate Hosea's use of and relationship to Israel's early traditions from their origins with the Patriarchs until the entrance into Palestine, whereby the following questions comprise the framework of the study: Can one speak of "salvation history" in Hosea? What is the relationship between past, present, and future for Hosea? Is it a relationship of continuity or discontinuity? How is Hosea's use of historical tradition to be evaluated?

The author approaches these questions in two steps: The first step is (a) to give an overview of research on the themes "God and history in Old Testament theology," "history in the preaching of the prophets," and "history in Hosea" (pp. 1–21); the second step is (b) to inquire into the growth and development of the book of Hosea (pp. 23–31).

The author critically presents the theme "God and history in Old Testament study" according to the sometimes quite distinct positions of

Reprinted and translated with permission from *Biblica* 73 (1992) 265–70. The review is of Dwight R. Daniels, *Hosea and Salvation History: The Early Traditions of Israel in the Prophecy of Hosea* (BZAW 191; Berlin: de Gruyter, 1990). Translated from German by Peter T. Daniels.

G. von Rad, F. Hesse, R. Rendtorff, B. Albrektson, and W. Zimmerli, emphasizing that they all agree on the goal of Old Testament study as the representation of its theological content, though they differ considerably on how that goal is to be achieved. They all operate with the concept *history*, but they interpret it differently.

In the author's opinion, the quest for "history" has consequences for dealing with the prophets, since they knew Israel's history. How do *history* and *word* interact in them? Reacting to the contrary positions of G. von Rad, G. Fohrer, M.-L. Henry, R. Knierim, and J. Vollmer on this theme, the author maintains that in the prophets the preaching of the word must not be allowed to be played off against history. The question whether *word* or *history* is primary in the prophets is a false dichotomy, since without knowledge of history the prophets would never have been able to organize the word. Here one must take into account a historic-superhistoric overall process which, following K. Koch, he calls "metahistory." The author understands this as the interaction of the following components: empirically observable events (economic, ritual, and military causalities); human behavior; and the powers of nature and society.

In his examination of Hosea, the author wishes to show that the historical traditions constitute a fundamental component of Hosea's preaching. He also wishes to take into consideration Hosea's view of Israel's history as well as his evaluation of Israel in his own time. *Both* absolutely must be included. Within Hosea research (O. Procksch, E. Sellin, J. Rieger, G. von Rad, H. W. Wolff, W. Rudolph, J. Vollmer, H.-D. Neef), no consensus regarding this topic has been achieved, since the concept of *salvation history* and the debate over the continuity versus the discontinuity of the historical tradition in Hosea remain open.

[[267]] Finally, the author wishes to investigate how Hosea's knowledge of the historical traditions of Israel can be reconciled with recent findings in Pentateuch research (H. H. Schmid, J. Van Seters, R. Rendtorff, E. Blum), according to which before the seventh century B.C.E. no continuous presentation of the history of Israel existed.

Since Hosea's preaching extended over a period of some thirty years, it is unavoidable, according to Daniels, that not only the question of authenticity but also the question of the redactional process be posed. He concurs with the thesis that the final form of the book of Hosea is a Judahite product, as can easily be seen from the Judahite insertions in 2:2 [1:11]; 4:15; 5:5, 10, 12, 13, 14, and so on. This would show that the book was "complete" before the Judahite insertions. Perhaps it came into existence around 722 B.C.E. After the Assyrian invasion Hosea and his disciples probably would have headed south. As for the three major parts of the book of Hosea (pp. 1–3, 4–11, 12–14), he proposes that chap. 3 is by Hosea himself, and chaps. 1–2 come from his disciples; Hosea himself would be the editor of 4–11 and 12–14.

The centerpiece of Daniels's book is the presentation of the Hoseanic concept of the history of Israel (pp. 33–110). In the author's opinion, Hosea divides Israel's history into four periods: (1) Patriarchs, (2) Exodus–wilderness, (3) Canaanization, (4) renewal.

The author elucidates the first, patriarchal period on the basis of a detailed exegesis of Hos 12:3–15[2–14] (pp. 33–52). Hosea harks back to the Jacob traditions because of the identity of the name of Israel with Jacob and the nation. The prophet appears to know only these traditions but not the Abraham and Isaac traditions. He not only takes into account the traditions preserved in Genesis but modified them as well. Whether he accessed them in oral or written form can scarcely be determined. Hosea's position regarding Jacob is ambiguous. The latter is neither judged nor praised, although in Jacob's deeds an undertone of deception and malice is always detectable. These characteristics, latent in Jacob, break out openly in Ephraim at the moment of the encounter with Canaan. Hence the author translates the verb *ʿqb* in 12:4[3] 'drive out/deceive' and rejects a direct connection to Gen 25:26a.

The second period, the Exodus and wandering in the wilderness, is reflected, according to the author, in Hos 13:4–8, 6:7–10, and 8:1–3 (pp. 70–92). For Hosea this is the period par excellence, since here a harmonious relationship between Yahweh and Israel prevailed. It began with the Exodus under the leadership of Moses (11:1; 12:10[9], 14[13]) and reached a sudden end with Israel's arrival at Baal-peor. A tradition must be presupposed in which the motif *grumbling* was unknown.

At this time Yahweh established a covenant with Israel (6:7, 8:1). Since in 8:1b 'covenant' and 'law' (*tôrâ*) are found in parallel, it is possible to conclude that Hosea knew of a covenant between Yahweh and Israel. The 'law' for Hosea comprised both ritual and secular regulations (6:7–10), which were preserved, transmitted, and administered by the priests. Because Israel had broken [[268]] this covenant and thus had become unfaithful to Yahweh, it was on the verge of collapse. Hosea's use of the marriage image was only possible given the background of his understanding of the covenant. Since Israel had been thrown into a condition of need because of the encroachment of foreign powers, there was also a connection between the lamentation over privation and the transgression of the covenant. Possibly the appeal to renew the covenant was issued in the context of ritual observations with the background of the national catastrophe.

The third period, Canaanization (pp. 53–70), began with the events at Baal-peor (9:10–13, 11:1–7). This is where Israel's straying from its God commenced, and after entering the land it intensified (8:11, 12:12). Yahweh's endeavors to halt the straying by calling prophets were futile. The bounty of the land caused Israel to grow so proud that it forgot its God (13:6). The horrible consequence of this hubris was the loss of the land.

The author postulates the fourth period, renewal, on the basis of 2:16–25[14–23] (pp. 92–110). Since these verses cohere well with Hosea's world view, they probably come from Hosea himself. Here the prophet speaks of a covenant between Yahweh and Israel (2:20[18]) that was concluded after the return from the exile in the wilderness (2:16[14]). It is clear from 2:20b[18b] that more is here intended than a covenant between Yahweh and the animals, since the removal of weapons from the land clearly goes beyond what one would expect in a human/animal society. Reminiscences of the covenant formula are clearly recognizable in 2:25b[23b].

The author uses the two concluding chapters (pp. 111–16, 117–30) to assess the contribution of the historical traditions in Hosea. Since they attest to Yahweh's acts of salvation toward Israel, one may legitimately speak of *salvation* traditions and *salvation* history. The continuity of this salvation history does not depend on Israel's conduct but exclusively on Yahweh's will respecting his people. The concept *salvation history* must not be limited to a particular period of Israel's history. According to Hosea, the climax of this history is the salvific relationship of Israel [[*sic*; read "Yahweh"?]] to his people in the land. Israel, however, remains far distant from this goal, since through its straying from God it has rendered the salvation traditions powerless. Therefore Hosea prophesies an exile in the wilderness, from which the foundations of a new, lasting covenant between Yahweh and Israel can be laid.

The author's work is an important, ground-breaking contribution to Hosea studies. Its themes are presented in agreeable, nonpolemical language and contrasted fairly with diverging opinions. He shows convincingly that Hosea divides the history of Israel into four periods and that the historical traditions considered here stand at the heart of Hosea's prophecy. He attains this goal by means of careful exegesis of the text that consists of translation of the text (with detailed text-critical considerations), form-critical observations, and commentary. Also to be mentioned are the intelligent contextualizing of the themes in the [[269]] wider scientific discussion of Old Testament theology and the fine, detailed bibliography (pp. 131–45). The author's observations on the topics (1) *covenant* in Hosea and (2) *Hosea and Pentateuch research* merit special attention.

The author has convincingly shown that Hosea knows the concept *covenant* and that *covenant* in Hosea refers to the relationship between Yahweh and Israel. This is conclusively demonstrated by the careful exegesis of 6:7 and 8:1. Thus the thesis—very influential within Prophets studies—of *covenantal silence* in Hosea (L. Perlitt et al.) is improbable.

The conclusion of the investigation, that Hosea could already make reference to a continuous representation of the history of Israel, must be taken more seriously in Pentateuch studies, which have hitherto found this doubtful. The thesis that Israel's history-writing began only with an exilic Yahwist needs revision.

Criticisms of the study's conclusions arise on the following points: Can a negative portrait of Jacob really be drawn from Hosea 12? Is the translation of ʿqb in 12:4 as 'drive out/deceive' correct? Is it correct to detect an undertone of deception here? If Jacob is already a cheater from the womb, then why does Hosea ascribe so much value to the statement that Israel's fall began with its entry into the civilized land (cf. 13:6 et al.)? In any case a negative picture of Jacob cannot be drawn from Gen 25:21–28! Does not the use of the Jacob tradition presuppose that, to Hosea's audience, it must have been unambiguous? The author's theory that Hosea refers to a Jacob tradition that is unknown to us is a stopgap [[*Verlegensheitslösung*]].

Problematic is the theory that the covenant tradition in Hosea is closely bound up with rituals of covenant renewal (8:1, 2:25[23]), which in specific gatherings were arranged for the people at the shrine. The passages cited in support do not point clearly enough in this direction. The naming of the *shofar* [['ram's horn']] in 8:1 suggests, rather, a reading in terms of an imminent judgment, which Hosea is announcing. Further, 2:25 does not allow us to conclude definitely that the Temple was the location of the event.

The author conspicuously chooses not to engage other traditions evident in the book of Hosea. Thus Hosea's references to the Decalogue or a protoform of the Decalogue (4:1–3 et al.) go unmentioned. Similarly the possible connections of Hos 6:7–11a to Judg 12:1–6 and Hos 5:1 to Gen 31:43ff. and Deut 33:18–19 pass unremarked. Exegesis of these passages might have exceeded the limits of the investigation, of course, but a brief mention of these references or a short explanation of why they were omitted from the discussion would have been in order.

In the section on the growth of the book of Hosea (pp. 23–31), a more detailed exposition of the interesting observations would seem to be necessary. The difficult question about the redaction of the *entire* book of Hosea can hardly be set forth in a few pages. This very question involves important preliminary considerations that bear on the overall assessment of the book of Hosea.

[[270]] These critical inquiries, however, do not lessen the author's achievement and the valuable place this study has earned in Hosea research. [[Corrigenda for a few typographical errors omitted.]]

History and Historiography: The Royal Reforms

GARY N. KNOPPERS

[[178]] The history of royal reforms can mean at least two different things—the study of the history of royal reforms within Chronicles or the study of royal reforms within Chronicles as a means of writing ancient history. In the first case, one approaches Chronicles as an object in itself, a coherent work of history. In the second case, one approaches Chr's work as an avenue to the past, albeit an indirect one, an aid to reconstruct various incidents either in the history of Judah or in the history of post-exilic Yehud.[1] The two approaches are related; indeed, the modern, critical study of Chronicles has often confused them. But they are distinct

Reprinted with permission from *The Chronicler as Historian* (ed. M. P. Graham, K. G. Hoglund, and S. L. McKenzie; JSOTS 238; Sheffield: Sheffield Academic Press, 1997) 178–203.

Author's note: I am most pleased to dedicate this essay to the memory of Raymond B. Dillard. I first met Ray when he was a visiting professor at my seminary in 1981. The love Ray had both for his students and for his subject matter, Chronicles, was very much in evidence. After receiving my doctorate, I came to appreciate Ray's scholarship, collegiality, and leadership in another setting, the Chronicles, Ezra, Nehemiah Section of SBL.

1. By Chr, I mean the author of Chronicles. Both S. Japhet ("The Supposed Common Authorship of Chronicles and Ezra–Nehemiah Investigated Anew," *VT* 18 [1968] 330–71; "The Relationship between Chronicles and Ezra–Nehemiah," in J. A. Emerton (ed.), *Congress Volume: Leuven, 1989* [VTSup, 43; Leiden: Brill, 1991] 298–313) and H. G. M. Williamson (*Israel in the Books of Chronicles* [New York: Cambridge University Press, 1977] 5–70) have forcefully argued against the single authorship of Chronicles and Ezra–Nehemiah. Some of their arguments have been challenged by J. Blenkinsopp (*Ezra–Nehemiah: A Commentary* [OTL; Philadelphia: Westminster, 1988) and D. Talshir, "A Reinvestigation of the Linguistic Relationship between Chronicles and Ezra–Nehemiah," *VT* 38 (1988) 165–93. I believe that more than one author is responsible for Chronicles, Ezra, and Nehemiah, but I do not deny some connections between them.

enterprises.[2] The first approach is a legitimate investigation by [[179]] itself, because it involves pursuing questions of literary structure, historiographical conventions, and ideology. But pursuing the second approach
necessitates giving some attention to the first. Evaluating the historical
importance of royal reforms in Chronicles involves understanding Chronicles as a specific kind of literary genre—a history. Chr's history, as a continuous narrative, tells us first of all about the writer's own compositional
technique, style, and ideology.[3] The value of this literary work for reconstructing the history of pre-exilic Judah and post-exilic Yehud is, therefore, linked to a knowledge of its structure and *Tendenz* [['inclination']].

In this essay, I will give some attention to both approaches—Chronicles as an example of ancient historiography and Chronicles as an indirect witness to the history of Judah and Yehud. Given the general nature
of the assigned topic and the limitations of space, this is not an appropriate occasion to discuss a great variety of individual figures and incidents.
I will try to alert readers to relevant scholarly evaluations of particular
episodes, but a full discussion of royal reforms would require a book in
itself. To do justice to the complexity of the primary material and various secondary treatments, this essay will deal primarily with non-cultic reforms during one particular period, the eighth century.[4]

Chronicles and History

The editors have requested that I address the different ways in which
modern scholars have construed the relationship between Chr's portrayal
of royal initiatives and history. Before proceeding to a discussion of royal
reforms within the eighth century, it will be useful to address these preliminary issues. Reviewing the scholarly treatment of the [[180]] distinctive
nature of royal reforms will illustrate the problems and challenges that
one encounters in employing Chronicles to reconstruct ancient history.

---

2. S. Japhet, "The Historical Reliability of Chronicles," *JSOT* 33 (1985) 83–107; M. P.
Graham, *The Utilization of 1 and 2 Chronicles in the Reconstruction of Israelite History in the Nineteenth Century* (SBLDS, 116; Atlanta: Scholars Press, 1990); J. W. Wright, "From Center to
Periphery: 1 Chronicles 23–27 and the Interpretation of Chronicles in the Nineteenth Century," in E. C. Ulrich et al. (eds.), *Priests, Prophets and Scribes: Essays on the Formation and Heritage of Second Temple Judaism in Honour of Joseph Blenkinsopp* (JSOTSup, 149; Sheffield: JSOT
Press, 1992) 20–42.

3. In maintaining this position, I wish to distance myself from the influential notions
that Chronicles primarily tells us about the pre-exilic period or the post-exilic period. What
we primarily derive from Chronicles, or for that matter any other historical writing, is what
a given author thought about a particular subject.

4. For issues of cult, see most recently, J. W. Kleinig, *The Lord's Song: The Basis, Function
and Significance of Choral Music in Chronicles* (JSOTSup, 156; Sheffield; JSOT Press, 1993).

The Nature of Royal Reforms in Chronicles

When one studies the nature of royal reforms in Chronicles, one must immediately distinguish these from DtrH's conception of royal reforms. In Kings royal reforms are virtually synonymous with cultic reforms. Noncultic reforms are occasionally mentioned, but almost as an afterthought. Kings mentions, for example, the cities that Asa built (1 Kgs 15:23 [MT]), the ivory palace and cities that Ahab built (1 Kgs 21:39), and how Hezekiah "made the pool and the conduit" (2 Kgs 20:20). But in each case, this information is conveyed on the concluding formulae for these monarchs.[5] The main attention of the Deuteronomist lies elsewhere. Assuming a normative (Deuteronomic) mandate for *Kultuseinheit* (cultic unity) and *Kultusreinheit* (cultic purity), the Deuteronomist constructs an elaborate system of religious regression and reform in the histories of the northern and southern monarchies. Two principal Israelite regressions and ten Judahite regressions mark the histories of the two kingdoms.[6] Despite periodic attempts at reform by monarchs, such as Jehu in Israel and Asa, Jehoshaphat, and Hezekiah in Judah, most of these twelve regressions are decisively countered only by the radical measures of Josiah in the late seventh century (2 Kgs 23:4–20). In the Deuteronomistic construction of history, Josiah's enforcement of orthopraxis and removal of heteropraxis redress not only the causes of Israel and Judah's declines, but also the principal reasons for the division itself.[7]

In comparison with the Deuteronomist's interest in cultic regression and reform, Chr exhibits a comprehensive perspective toward the ways [[181]] in which Judahite kings improve conditions within their realm. The shape and contours of royal reforms in Chronicles evince considerable diversity.[8] When one reads Chronicles after having read Kings, one has to redefine "reform." Royal reforms in Chronicles are martial, administrative, judicial, geopolitical, and cultic in nature. Having established the united monarchy as the golden age in Israelite history, the time in which normative institutions take shape, Chr pays great attention to how Judah's best kings rejuvenate their nation. If the creation and consolidation of

---

5. In this regard, the formulaic introduction to these notices is relevant, "The rest of (all) the deeds of RN . . . , are they not written in the Annals of the Kings of Judah / Israel . . . ?" (1 Kgs 15:23; 21:39; 2 Kgs 20:20).

6. H.-D. Hoffmann, *Reform und Reformen: Untersuchungen zu einem Grundthema der deuteronomistischen Geschichtsschreibung* (ATANT, 66; Zurich: Theologischer Verlag, 1980).

7. G. N. Knoppers, *Two Nations under God: The Deuteronomistic History of Solomon and the Dual Monarchies*, vol. 1, *The Reign of Solomon and the Rise of Jeroboam* (HSM, 52; Atlanta: Scholars Press, 1993); vol. 2, *The Reign of Jeroboam, the Fall of Israel, and the Reign of Josiah* (HSM, 53; Atlanta: Scholars Press, 1994).

8. R. H. Lowery, *The Reforming Kings: Cult and Society in First Temple Judah* (JSOTSup, 120; Sheffield: JSOT Press, 1991).

national institutions under David and Solomon establish a normative standard or form for later generations to emulate, the attempts to later Judahite kings to reestablish these institutions constitute reforms. But Chr's reforming kings are not mere conservators of a static ideal; they modify earlier policies, creatively adapt to new circumstances, and introduce new programs. Many, but not all, of Chr's best kings lead their people to recovery and renewal after times of decline and apostasy. Such monarchs renew their domain by building fortified cities, fortifying existing cities, appointing officers, amassing large armies and equipping them, stationing garrisons, constructing towers, and rebuilding city walls.

Chr's independent perspective is all the more surprising, since the Chronicler, as is well known, used a copy of Samuel–Kings to compose his own work. Because Chr's work exhibits broader historiographical interests in narrating the history of the Judahite monarchy than the Deuteronomist's work does, the additional reforms that Chr ascribes to Judah's kings cannot be dismissed for historical reconstruction. This is especially true when one compares both Kings and Chronicles with a variety of ancient Near Eastern royal texts. Chr's keen interest in geopolitical and martial reforms is broadly consistent with the concerns of many ancient Near Eastern royal inscriptions and dedicatory texts.[9] The [[182]] narrow focus on cult in the Deuteronomist's depiction of monarchical history is, therefore, exceptional. King Mesha of Moab boasts:

> I took 200 men of Moab, all of its leaders and I led them to Jahaz. And I took it, adding it to Dibon. I built Qariho, the wall of the Fore[sts], and the wal[l] of the acropolis. I built its gates and I built its towers. I built the palace and I constructed the retaining walls[10] of the reser[voir for the sp]ring in the mid[st] of the city.[11]

---

9. Two classic studies on kingship in the ancient Near East are R. Labat, *Le Caractère religieux de la royauté assyro-babylonienne* (Études d'assyriologie, 2; Paris: Adrien-Maisonneuve, 1939); and H. Frankfort, *Kingship and the Gods: A Study of Ancient Near Eastern Religion as the Integration of Society and Nature* (Chicago: University of Chicago Press, 1948). See more recently K.-H. Bernhardt, *Das Problem der altorientalischen Königsideologie im Alten Testament* (VTSup, 8; Leiden: Brill, 1961) 67–90; S. N. Kramer, "Kingship in Sumer and Akkad: The Ideal King," in P. Garelli (ed.), *Le palais et la royauté (archéologie et civilisation), 19 Rencontre assyriologique Internationale* (Paris: P. Geuthner, 1974) 163–76; and G. W. Ahlström, *Royal Administration and National Religion in Ancient Palestine* (Studies in the History of the Ancient Near East, 1; Leiden: Brill, 1982) 1–25.

10. The masc. pl. construct, כלאי can be understood in two different ways—as 'both' (cf. BH כלאים, Ugaritic כלאת) or as 'confining, retaining things' (cf. BH כלא). In the former case, one would translate, 'the double reservoir for the spring'. K. A. D. Smelik, *Converting the Past: Studies in Ancient Israelite and Moabite Historiography* (OTS, 28; Leiden: Brill, 1992) 65.

11. I follow the reconstruction of *KAI* 181.20–24 (כלאי האשוח.למ]ין); see also H. Eshel, "The QRHH and the Wall of the Ya'aran in the Mesha Stele," in A. Ahituv and B. A. Levine (ed.), *Avraham Malamat Volume* (ErIsr, 24; Jerusalem: Israel Exploration Society, 1993) 31–33.

Given its particular nature, interests, and date, Chronicles presents a series of literary and historical paradoxes. Its history of the monarchy is heavily dependent upon Samuel–Kings; yet Chronicles is a very different history.[12] Chr narrates what one expects to see Judahite kings doing, given the tenets of ancient Near Eastern royal ideologies; yet Chr writes during the post-exilic period, when that monarchy no longer existed. Chr lavishes attention on military, administrative, and geopolitical affairs; yet there is considerable historical distance between the time of his writing and the events that he portrays. With the exception of the chapter that he devotes to the demise of Saul (1 Chronicles 10), Chr's history of the monarchy begins, continues, and ends with an exclusive focus upon the deeds of the Davidic dynasty. Yet Chr writes at least decades, probably centuries, following the collapse of the Davidic kingdom.

Assessing Chr's Historical Reliability

[[183]] How, then, does one appraise the historical reliability of Chr's claims about the activities of various monarchs? Modern commentators have approached this question in quite different ways: making inner-biblical comparisons, invoking extra-biblical sources, treating Chronicles as a work of theology or exegesis, applying the criterion of verisimilitude, and appealing to archaeology and epigraphy. Each of these approaches has its strengths and weaknesses. Contrasting Chronicles with various earlier biblical texts, especially Samuel–Kings, calls attention to the particular assumptions and features of each work. One can learn a great deal about Chr's account of Sennacherib's invasion (2 Chr 32:1–23), for instance, by taking careful notice of how he has abbreviated, edited, rewritten, and supplemented the materials in his *Vorlage* [['source']] (2 Kings 18–20).

But comparative biblical analysis also has its shortcomings. To begin with, the application of this approach has been uneven. Comparative studies have often worked to the detriment of Chronicles, because many of its changes over against Samuel–Kings are thought to represent tendentious alterations of an authoritative *Vorlage*. This is unfortunate. Chr does, of course, sometimes alter his *Vorlage*, but comparative studies should pursue broader questions as well. What do the differences between these works say about the compositional technique, historiographical assumptions, and ideology of the respective authors? What do the similarities between the texts say about the composition of history in ancient

---

12. How much Chr's *Vorlagen* of Samuel and Kings resemble the MT of Samuel and Kings is disputed; see W. E. Lemke, "The Synoptic Problem in Chronicler's History," *HTR* 58 (1965) 349–63; S. L. McKenzie, *The Chronicler's Use of the Deuteronomistic History* (HSM, 33; Atlanta: Scholars Press, 1985); A. G. Auld, *Kings without Privilege: David and Moses in the Story of the Bible's Kings* (Edinburgh: T. & T. Clark, 1994).

Judah and post-exilic Yehud? If comparisons are used simply to reflect upon Chronicles, they mystify DtrH—effectively treating this work as history itself, rather than as a narration and explanation of the past. In short, comparisons should teach us how to read both texts.

Second, inner-biblical comparisons are of limited value for historical purposes, because scholars are contrasting one indirect, secondary source with another. The task of historical reconstruction still remains. Moreover, there is much unparalleled material in Chronicles. Some of this additional material may be attributed to Chr's interpretation of his biblical sources.[13] Nevertheless, arguments that much or even all of this [[184]] unique material represents Chr's exposition of his *Vorlagen* [['sources']] have not been, in my judgment, successful.[14]

The appeal to extra-biblical sources serves two complementary functions. The supposition of Chr's access to such ancient materials—either unused or unavailable to the Deuteronomists—explains his unparalleled material. Second, because Chr used such putative sources, his history is a reliable witness to pre-exilic realities. However defensible, the invocation of extra-biblical sources also has its limitations. To begin with, commentators sharply disagree about the nature and number of such sources. One has to ask whether a given source employed by Chr was reliable and complete. If so, one has to inquire further whether Chr abridged, rewrote, or supplemented these materials. One has also to determine, inasmuch as this is possible, whether the author has applied a source to the proper historical context. Finally, one has to study how Chr has (re)contextualized the materials that he purportedly uses.[15]

Viewing Chronicles as primarily a work of theology or exegesis shifts the whole question of historical reliability to the post-exilic age.[16] In this

13. See, for instance, T. Willi, *Die Chronik als Auslegung: Untersuchungen zur literarischen Gestaltung der historischen Überlieferung Israels* (FRLANT, 106; Göttingen: Vandenhoeck & Ruprecht, 1972); P. R. Ackroyd, "The Chronicler as Exegete," *JSOT* 2 (1977) 2–32; M. A. Fishbane, *Biblical Interpretation in Ancient Israel* (Oxford: Clarendon Press, 1984); K. Strübind, *Tradition als Interpretation in der Chronik: König Josaphat als Paradigma chronistischer Hermeneutik und Theologie* (BZAW, 201; Berlin: de Gruyter, 1991).

14. See my review of K. Strübind's *Tradition als Interpretation* in *CBQ* 55 (1994) 780–82.

15. To take one example, most commentators agree that the list of fifteen named, fortified cities built by Rehoboam in Judah and Benjamin (2 Chr 11:5–10) reflects an extra-biblical source: S. Japhet, *I & II Chronicles: A Commentary* (OTL; Louisville, KY: Westminster/ John Knox, 1993) 663–67. But scholars debate whether the listed fortifications should be attributed to Rehoboam, Hezekiah, or Josiah. On Chr's contextualization of this material, see my "Rehoboam in Chronicles: Villain or Victim?" *JBL* 109 (1990) 423–40.

16. P. R. Ackroyd, *I & II Chronicles, Ezra, Nehemiah* (TBC; London: SCM, 1973); R. Mosis, *Untersuchungen zur Theologie des chronistischen Geschichtswerkes* (FTS, 92; Freiburg: Herder, 1973). In P. Welten's view, Chronicles anticipates certain features of apocalyptic writing: *Geschichte und Geschichtsdarstellung in den Chronikbüchern* (Neukirchen-Vluyn: Neukirchener Verlag, 1973).

line of interpretation, Chronicles does not provide any new and trustworthy information about the pre-exilic period, apart from that which can already be gleaned from Samuel–Kings. If Chronicles can be classified as a history at all, it is a highly paradigmatic history that reflects life in Yehud. The merit in this approach lies in the links that it recognizes between Chr's work and the context in which it was written. [[185]] Some aspects of Chr's coverage relate more to understanding the author's ideology and post-exilic conditions than they do to understanding pre-exilic history.[17] To take one example, the organization of Uzziah's army (2 Chr 26:11–13), like Jehoshaphat's (2 Chr 17:14), is according to a predominately post-exilic social institution: ancestral houses. References to the בית אבות are found only in Chronicles, Ezra, Nehemiah, and the Priestly writing.[18] There are other features of Chr's work that clearly reflect his own ideology. The incredible numbers in the armies of Uzziah and other monarchs, for example, are a meaningful indication of Chr's thought but are not taken by historians as accurate information about either pre-exilic or post-exilic life. Nevertheless, it seems reductive to attribute all of Chr's unique material to literary invention or theological reflection. Not all of Chr's claims about the history of the Judahite monarchy can be shown to mirror post-exilic life or the programmatic interests of the author.

Another criterion of historical credibility is verisimilitude. Some scholars have defended, for example, the (pre-exilic) historicity of Chr's claims about Uzziah's reforms (see below) by pointing to the limited and hence plausible nature of these reforms. Others have pointed to events in the international context of Uzziah's tenure as lending credence to Chr's assertion that Uzziah engaged in some military and geopolitical reforms. The attraction of this criterion is readily understandable.[19] Uzziah's reforms are geographically confined. But the application of verisimilitude can be complicated by other factors. Because the narration of Uzziah's reforms evinces stereotypical Chronistic vocabulary and style, some commentators are skeptical that it has much at all to do with events in the eighth century.

17. G. N. Knoppers, "Jehoshaphat's Judiciary and 'the Scroll of Yнwн's Torah,'" *JBL* 113 (1994) 59–80.

18. E. L. Curtis and A. A. Madsen, *The Books of Chronicles* (ICC; Edinburgh: T. & T. Clark, 1910) 33 (#104). In contrast, the expression בית אב [['ancestral house']] appears only once in Chronicles, Ezra, and Nehemiah (Neh 1:6). See further J. P. Weinberg, "Das *beit ʿabôt* im 6.–4. Jh. v. u.Z.," *VT* 23 (1973) 400–414; J. Blenkinsopp, "A Jewish Sect of the Persian Period," *CBQ* 52 (1990) 5–20; P. Dion, "The Civic-and-Temple Community of Persian Period Judaea: Neglected Insights from Eastern Europe," *JNES* 50 (1991) 281–87.

19. But it is completely rejected by T. L. Thompson, *Early History of the Israelite People: From the Written and Archaeological Sources* (Studies in the History of the Ancient Near East, 4; Leiden: Brill, 1992) 388.

To summarize, there is no doubt that Chronicles betrays the time in [[186]] which is was written and the particular ideology of its author. But one important question remains: to what extent is Chr's presentation of the monarchy shaped by his own present context, his exposition of Samuel–Kings, and his ideology? Does Chr's history, however much it reflects the ideology of its author, a particular rhetorical structure, and its own time, engage the pre-exilic past? On this matter, scholars are sharply divided. One way to address this question is to turn to the last criterion of historical credibility—the witness of archaeology and epigraphy.

The Appeal to Archaeology and Epigraphy

The advantage of this approach is its focus upon the degree to which Chr's unique claims correspond to our present knowledge of the material remains of pre-exilic Judah, if they indeed correspond at all. Recourse to archaeology and epigraphy does not deny the role of Chr as either a theologian or an expositor. Nor does it exclude the application of other criteria, such as comparative biblical analysis and verisimilitude. Rather, this approach seeks to determine, inasmuch as this is possible, the degree to which Chr's account of a particular reform coheres with information gleaned from ancient Near Eastern epigraphy and archaeology. Although I will be employing this approach in assessing Chr's account of eighth-century reforms, I am well aware that recourse to archaeology and epigraphy also has its problems and limitations.[20] Comparing biblical claims with material evidence is a rather complicated matter. Ancient material remains, unearthed by the archaeologist's spade, are not self-interpreting, and archaeologists differ in their assumptions and methods. In addition, many sites have not been excavated; the identity of others is in dispute; and in dealing with excavated sites, archaeologists can differ in their methods, dating of strata, and interpretation of material finds. To complicate matters [[187]] further, archaeological excavations illumine broad periods in Israelite or Judahite history, but they have not attained such technical sophistication that ceramic assemblages can be dated to particular generations. Hence, the material remains from ancient Judah do not

---

20. R. North, "Does Archeology Prove Chronicles' Sources?" in H. N. Bream, R. D. Heim, and C. A. Moore (eds.), *A Light Unto My Path: Old Testament Studies in Honor of Jacob M. Myers* (GTS, 4; Philadelphia: Temple University Press, 1974) 375–401; S. L. Dyson, "From New to New Age Archaeology: Archaeological Theory and Classical Archaeology—A 1990s Perspective," *AJA* 97 (1993) 195–206; W. G. Dever, "Archaeology, Texts, and History-Writing: Toward an Epistemology," in L. M. Hopfe (ed.), *Uncovering Ancient Stones: Essays in Memory of H. Neil Richardson* (Winona Lake, IN: Eisenbrauns, 1994) 105–17; S. Bunimovitz, "How Mute Stones Speak: Interpreting What We Dig Up," *BARev* 21/2 (1995) 58–67, 97.

easily lend themselves to forming a precise commentary on a biblical author's claims about a given monarch.

Despite these limitations, the use of archaeology and epigraphy may shed some light on the extent to which Chr's depiction of royal enterprises may be used to write the history of pre-exilic Judah and post-exilic Yehud. Because historical reconstruction is linked to a knowledge of the structure and *Tendenz* of a given work, I will first comment upon Chr's presentation of three reforming monarchs. My study will then address how archaeology and epigraphy illumine eighth-century Judahite history and whether the distinctive claims of Chronicles comport with historical reality, as best one can presently construe this.

Eighth-Century Royal Reforms

Chr presents three Judahite monarchs of the eighth century as reformers: Uzziah, Jotham, and Hezekiah. These rulers implement a variety of administrative, geopolitical, and military measures that renew their realms. The detail that Chr accords to non-cultic reforms of Uzziah and Hezekiah, in particular, is remarkable. In contrast, Kings lacks any record of comparable activities for Uzziah and contains only a terse mention of non-cultic reforms for Hezekiah.

Uzziah

The Deuteronomist's brief portrayal of Azariah (Uzziah) presents him as a minor figure (2 Kgs 15:1–7), but Chr presents this monarch as a major reformer, whose fame extended all the way to the entrance to Egypt (2 Chr 26:8). Uzziah rebuilt "Elot" and restored it to Judah.[21] Uzziah also "built cities in (the area of) Ashdod and among the Philistines" (2 Chr 26:6). If the MT is not corrupt, this building [[188]] activity should probably be associated with Uzziah's successes against the Philistines, Arabs, and Meunites (2 Chr 26:6–8).[22] Chr does not specify which cities Uzziah built.

Most of Uzziah's attention is directed toward the south and southwest, but some of Uzziah's construction activity is directed toward Jerusalem itself. He "built and fortified towers in Jerusalem by the Corner Gate

---

21. The MT of Chronicles consistently reads אילות [['Eloth']] (2 Chr 8:17; 2 Chr 26:2), whereas Kings features two forms: אילת [['Elath']] (2 Kgs 14:22; 16:6) and אילות (1 Kgs 9:26). The LXX of Chronicles has Αἰλάθ [['Ailath']]. Another issue is the (re)builder of Elat. The subject of 2 Kgs 14:22 is uncertain, but H. Tadmor and M. Cogan argue that the most likely referent is Azariah: *II Kings* (AB, 11; New York: Doubleday, 1988) 158.

22. Some commentators favor emending the MT (and LXX) of 2 Chr 26:6 from ויבנה ערים [['and he built cities']] to ויבז הערים [['and he plundered the cities']]; W. Rudolph, *Chronikbücher* (HAT, 21; Tübingen: Mohr, 1955) 282.

(שׁער הפנה), by the Valley Gate (שׁער הגיא), and by "the Angle" (המקצוע; 2 Chr 26:9). Like David, Abijah, Asa, and Jehoshaphat before him, Uzziah commands an enormous army (2 Chr 26:11–13). Unlike most previous censuses, Uzziah's census mentions those specifically responsible for the muster (2 Chr 26:11). But as was the case with Jehoshaphat's muster, Uzziah's muster depicts ancestral heads (2,600) as having responsibility for his large army (307,500). Like Rehoboam before him and Hezekiah after him, Uzziah supplies his troops with an arsenal. In addition to "establishing for them, for all the army, shields, spears, helmets, mail, bows, and slingstones' (2 Chr 26:14), Uzziah developed new weaponry by "making devices, sophisticated devices (to be placed) on the towers and the corners in Jerusalem to shoot arrows and large stones" (2 Chr 26:15).[23]

Chr's Uzziah also enhances the condition of his royal estates. The subject of royal estates also appears in Chr's depiction of David's reign. 1 Chr 27:25–31 contains a list of officials (שׂרי הרכושׁ), who administer extensive crown properties,[24] and Chr's description of Uzziah's royal estates resonates with the description of David's patrimony, though Uzziah's holdings do not match the variety and extent of those [[189]] ascribed to David. Commensurate with the geography of his military triumphs, Uzziah's royal properties feature the south and southwest. Uzziah "built towers in the wilderness (מדבר) and hewed out many cisterns, for he had large herds in the Shephelah and on the plain (מישׁור) and vinedressers in the hills and the fertile lands."[25] Uzziah, Chr explains, was "a lover of the land" (2 Chr 26:10).

Jotham

In Kings Jotham is a monarch who is rated positively, but of whom little is said (2 Kgs 15:32–38). Chr also evaluates Jotham positively but adds more material about his reign. In Chronicles Jotham continues the pattern of

23. The MT of 2 Chr 26:15 has ובאבנים גדולות [['and great stones']]. The Syriac lacks much of this verse (through גדולות).

24. Y. Aharoni, *The Archaeology of the Land of Israel: From the Prehistoric Beginnings to the End of the First Temple Period* (Philadelphia: Westminster, 1982) 15–16; O. Borowski, *Agriculture in Iron Age Israel: The Evidence from Archaeology and the Bible* (Winona Lake, IN: Eisenbrauns, 1987) 28; V. Fritz, *Die Stadt im alten Israel* (Munich: Beck, 1990) 136–37. I view most of 1 Chronicles 23–27 as an integral part of Chr's work; see S. Japhet, *The Ideology of the Book of Chronicles and Its Place in Biblical Thought* (BEATAJ, 9; Frankfurt am Main: Peter Lang, 1989); and J. W. Wright, "The Legacy of David in Chronicles: The Narrative Function of 1 Chronicles 23–27," *JBL* 110 (1991) 229–42.

25. The MT of 2 Chr 26:10 adds אכרים (farmers), but I follow the LXX[AB] (*lectio brevior*) [['shorter reading']]. On the geography, see Y. Aharoni, *The Land of the Bible: A Historical Geography* (Philadelphia: Westminster, rev. edn, 1979) 345–56. Borowski argues that the towers were most likely built for the protection of agricultural workers and produce in these territories (*Agriculture*, 106).

public works begun by his predecessor, Uzziah. Consistent with his *Vorlage*, Chr asserts that Jotham built the upper gate of the temple (2 Chr 27:3//2 Kgs 15:35), but Chr attributes other construction and fortification activities to Jotham as well. Like Uzziah, Jotham did not confine his building initiatives to Jerusalem. Jotham built extensively on the wall of the Ophel, established cities in the hill country of Judah, and built fortresses and towers in the wooded areas (חרשים; 2 Chr 27:3–4). Chr does not specify which cities in the Judahite hill country Jotham established.

Hezekiah

Chr devotes more attention to Hezekiah than to any other king, except David and Solomon. Hezekiah is clearly one (if not the chief) of Chr's favorite monarchs in Judahite history.[26] Although the Deuteronomist's coverage of Hezekiah's reign is also extensive and highly laudatory, the foci of the two accounts diverge considerably. Indeed, it is remarkable how Chr can mention so many major events addressed by his *Vorlage* [['source']]—Sennacherib's invasion, the speeches of his officers, the prayer of [[190]] Hezekiah, the intercession of Isaiah, the destruction of the Assyrian camp, Hezekiah's illness and recovery, and the visit of envoys from Babylon—yet present such a different account of Hezekiah's tenure. To begin with, his treatment of these events appears in condensed and varied form. Chr's interests lie more with Hezekiah's reforms and restoration, following the unprecedented evil imputed to Ahaz (2 Chr 28:1–27).[27] Whereas the Deuteronomist devotes only two verses to Hezekiah's cultic reforms (2 Kgs 18:4, 22), Chr devotes three chapters to the restoration of the temple (2 Chronicles 29), the celebration of the passover (2 Chronicles 30), and Hezekiah's other cultic initiatives (2 Chronicles 31). Only then does Chr deal with an event that dominates the Deuteronomist's coverage: Sennacherib's invasion (2 Chr 32:1–23). Chr also ascribes to Hezekiah considerably more non-cultic reforms than does the Deuteronomist.[28] Chr situates most reforms to Jerusalem's physical plant before Sennacherib's invasion (2 Chr 32:3–6) and most royal initiatives in Judah thereafter (2 Chr 32:27–30). But Chr's chronology of events is not entirely clear.[29]

26. Ackroyd, *Chronicles*, 179–89; Mosis, *Untersuchungen*, 189–92; Williamson, *Israel in the Books of Chronicles*, 119–25; M. A. Throntveit, "Hezekiah in the Books of Chronicles," in D. J. Lull (ed.), *Society of Biblical Literature 1988 Seminar Papers* (SBLSPS, 27; Atlanta: Scholars Press, 1988) 302–11.

27. E. Ben Zvi, "A Gateway to the Chronicler's Teaching: The Account of the Reign of Ahaz in 2 Chr 28,1–27," *SJOT* 7 (1993) 216–49.

28. 1 Chr 4:39–43 also mentions a movement southward by the Simeonites during the reign of Hezekiah.

29. Chr's arrangement of Hezekiah's royal reforms is somewhat schematic (see below). The construction of Hezekiah's conduit, for example, is mentioned in both DtrH (2 Kgs 20:20)

Consistent with his portrayal of Judah's premier reformers as progres-
sives—kings who uphold the legacy of the united monarchy while successfully enabling their nation to surmount new challenges—Chr presents
Hezekiah as a strong leader. Hezekiah explicitly prepared for Sennacherib's campaign against Jerusalem by initiating a program of public works
and urban mobilization (2 Chr 32:1–8). After taking counsel with his officers and mighty men, Hezekiah and a large force stopped the flow of
springs outside the city, as well as the wadi that [[191]] flowed through the
land (2 Chr 32:3–4).[30] For Chr good government is not only reactive, but
also proactive. Hezekiah took strength "and rebuilt the breached wall and
raised towers upon it" (2 Chr 32:5).[31] Hezekiah's repair and fortification of
Jerusalem's wall resemble the actions of two other eighth-century reforming kings: Uzziah and Jotham. But Chr's Hezekiah does not limit himself to
rebuilding the old wall. He is also said to have built "another wall outside
it" (2 Chr 32:5). Another Hezekian public works project consisted of
strengthening the millo of the City of David (2 Chr 32:5).[32] Chr later mentions that Hezekiah also closed the upper outlet of the Gihon spring and
directed the waters down to the west of the City of David (2 Chr 32:30).

There is a clear logic to this pattern of defensive preparations. Having
rebuilt the Jerusalem wall and constructed a new wall outside it, Hezekiah
ensured a continuous flow of water for the inhabitants within these walls.
He then equipped and mobilized Jerusalem's defenders: "and he made
weapons and shields in abundance" (2 Chr 32:5). Hezekiah personally
organized Jerusalem's defenses by appointing "battle officers over the

---

and Chr's history (2 Chr 32:30) after Sennacherib's invasion. But historians unanimously
agree that this defensive action must have taken place prior to the siege of Jerusalem. On
a-chronology in ancient Mesopotamian historiography, see H. Tadmor, "The Campaigns of
Sargon II of Assur: A Chronological-Historical Study," *JCS* 12 (1958) 22–40, 77–100; idem,
"The Inscriptions of Nabunaid: Historical Arrangement," in H. G. Güterbock and T. Jacobsen
(eds.), *Studies in Honor of Benno Landsberger on his 75th Birthday* (AS, 17; Chicago: Oriental Institute of the University of Chicago, 1965) 351–63; J. Van Seters, *In Search of History* (New Haven, CT: Yale University Press, 1983) 61–62 [[repr., Winona Lake, Ind.: Eisenbrauns, 1997]].

30. It is unclear precisely what stopping the flow of water in the wadi designates. The
most common explanation is that Chr is referring to rivulets in the Wadi Qidron. Thus,
Ackroyd, "Chronicler as Exegete," 11; H. G. M. Williamson, *1 and 2 Chronicles* (NCB; Grand
Rapids, MI: Eerdmans, 1982) 381. The reference to stopping the flow of springs outside the
city is usually taken to involve the Gihon: Japhet, *Chronicles*, 982–83.

31. The MT reads, יבן את־כל־החומה הפרוצה ויעל על־המגדלות [['and he built up all the wall
that was broken down and he raised up on the towers']]. The LXX adds καὶ πύργους [['and
towers']] after הפרוצה, which may be an assimilation toward 2 Chr 26:9, 15. At the end of the
last phrase, the Tg. and Vg. reflect a slightly different and superior version of the Hebrew, עליה
מגדלות [['on it (i.e., the wall) towers']].

32. In enacting this physical reform, Hezekiah harks back to the time of David (1 Chr
11:8). Unlike the situation in 1 Kings (9:15, 24; 11:27), Chr does not attribute any (re)con-
struction of the millo to the time of Solomon.

people" and by exhorting them to stand firm in the face of "the Assyrian king and the horde that is with him" (2 Chr 32:6–8).

In Chronicles Hezekiah's geopolitical initiatives go beyond bolstering Jerusalem's defenses. After providing his much-abbreviated version of Yʜwʜ's humiliation of Sennacherib and his forces, Chr depicts additional Hezekian accomplishments and initiatives.[33] Instead of focusing [[192]] on defensive reforms, Hezekiah is able to pursue broader economic and political initiatives. Prosperous Hezekiah "made treasuries for himself for silver, gold, precious stones, spices, shields, and every kind of splendid vessel" (2 Chr 32:27).[34] The king built "storehouses (מסכנות) for the yield of grain, wine, and oil, as well as facilities for every kind of cattle" (2 Chr 32:28). In Chronicles royal wealth is an indication of divine blessing, and as a number of commentators have observed, Hezekiah's assets rival those of Solomon.[35] Hezekiah also "made cities for himself and (enjoyed) flocks and herds in abundance, because God gave to him vast possessions" (רכוש, 2 Chr 32:29).[36] Chr does not further specify the locations of these treasuries, storehouses, and cities. Nor does he situate Hezekiah's flocks and vast possessions.

We have seen that Chr ascribes reforms to particular monarchs and periods that he wishes to exalt. The scope and nature of these reforms belie some influential conceptions of Chr's work as narrowly religious or theological: "a cultic history written by cultic functionaries especially for the use of cultic personnel."[37] All three kings—Uzziah, Jotham, and Hezekiah—are resourceful builders and energetic administrators over Jerusalem

33. 2 Chr 32:21–22. The reason why Jerusalem survives varies in the sources embedded in the Kings narrative and identified by B. Stade, "Miscellen 16. Anmerkungen zu 2 Kö. 15–21," *ZAW* 6 (1886) 172–83. In the B1 narrative (2 Kgs 19:7, 36–37), Yʜwʜ causes Sennacherib to hear a rumor and return to his own land, where he is assassinated. In the B2 narrative (2 Kgs 19:35), a מלאך יהוה [['angel of the Lᴏʀᴅ']] kills 185,000 Assyrian troops. Chronicles contains short, albeit more vague, references to both: Japhet, *Chronicles*, 988–92.

34. Instead of the MT's מגנים [['shields']], the LXX has καὶ ὁπλοθήκας [['and armories']]. The Vg. reads *et armorum universi generis* [['and arms of all sorts']]. Rudolph reconstructs מגדים [['excellent things']]: *Chronikbücher*, 312.

35. See also 2 Chr 32:23; Williamson, *Chronicles*, 385; R. B. Dillard, "Reward and Punishment in Chronicles: The Theology of Immediate Retribution," *WTJ* 46 (1984) 164–72; idem, *2 Chronicles* (WBC, 15; Waco, TX: Word Books, 1987) 252–61; M. A. Throntveit, *When Kings Speak: Royal Speech and Royal Prayer in Chronicles* (SBLDS, 93; Atlanta: Scholars Press, 1987) 121–25.

36. In spite of the textual corruption at the end of 2 Chr 32:28 (MT, ועדרים לאורות [['and flocks for pens']]; LXX, καὶ μάνδρας εἰς τὰ ποίμνια [['and folds for sheep']]), I see no compelling reason to excise ערים [['cities']] at the beginning of 2 Chr 32:29. Pace Rudolph, *Chronikbücher*, 312.

37. W. Riley, *King and Cultus in Chronicles: Worship and the Reinterpretation of History* (JSOTSup, 160; Sheffield: JSOT Press, 1993) 24; cf. R. L. Braun, "The Message of Chronicles: Rally 'Round the Temple,'" *CTM* 42 (1971) 502–14.

and Judah. Each amply uses his resources to enhance the living conditions of his people. Hezekiah, in particular, is lauded for his preparations for and response to a severe international crisis. However [[193]] one views the nature of Chronicles, this work evinces broad geopolitical and military interests.

Historical Considerations

The past century has witnessed archaeological excavations at various sites, while the last decades have witnessed archaeological surveys of different regions within Judah. It will be useful to compare analyses of the material remains from the eighth century with Chr's account of royal reforms during this same period. Such a comparison yields, I would argue, mixed results. To begin with, it is sometimes unclear what conditions a Chronistic text reflects. The date and nature of the military technology that Uzziah introduces to the wall of Jerusalem can serve as an illustration. If Chr is envisioning catapults, as some scholars think, the reference (2 Chr 26:15) is anachronistic, because extrabiblical sources do not mention catapults until at least the fifth century B.C.E.[38] But Yadin argues that Chr is not describing ballistic engines but wooden frames built upon towers and battlements, like those depicted on Sennacherib's reliefs of Lachish, on which defenders could stand to their full height while wielding their bows or casting down heavy stones.[39]

In some cases, comparison between material and written remains plays an important, but penultimate, role in the reconstruction of history. In describing Uzziah's fortification of Jerusalem's wall, Chr may have in mind redressing the damage done by Jehoash of Israel during the reign of Amaziah (2 Chr 25:23//2 Kgs 14:13), as many commentators claim.[40] But Chr's description of Uzziah's fortification is [[194]] difficult to appraise historically, because it resonates with features of Nehemiah's description of

38. Ackroyd, *Chronicles*, 169; S. Herrmann, *A History of Israel in Old Testament Times* (Philadelphia: Fortress Press, 1981) 240; D. B. Redford, *Egypt, Canaan, and Israel in Ancient Times* (Princeton, NJ: Princeton University Press, 1992) 327–28. Fourth-century B.C.E. historian Diodorus places catapults in the fourth century, though Williamson identifies similar devices in Persian sources earlier than the fourth century: *Chronicles*, 337–38.

39. If Y. Yadin's reading of the biblical and iconographic material is correct, there is no chronological problem inherent in Chr's depiction of Uzziah's military technology: *The Art of Warfare in Biblical Lands in the Light of Archaeological Study* (New York: McGraw-Hill, 1963), vol. 2, 325–27.

40. Williamson, *Chronicles*, 336–37; Dillard, *Chronicles*, 206; A. Mazar, *Archaeology of the Land of the Bible 10,000–586 B.C.E.* (ABRL; New York: Doubleday, 1990) 446; G. W. Ahlström, *The History of Ancient Palestine from the Palaeolithic Period to Alexander's Conquest* (JSOTSup, 146; Sheffield: JSOT Press, 1993) 626–27.

Jerusalem's ruined (Neh 2:13–15) and rebuilt walls (Neh 3:1–32).[41] As constituent features of Jerusalem's walls, the Valley Gate and the Angle are only mentioned in post-exilic sources,[42] although references to the Valley Gate in the first passage (Neh 2:13, 15) presuppose the pre-exilic existence of this gate.[43] To complicate matters further, not much is known, archaeologically speaking, about the course and nature of Nehemiah's wall. Nevertheless, the very resonance between the testimony in Nehemiah and Chr's description of Uzziah's modification to Jerusalem's defenses is useful for historical reconstruction. Most scholars agree that Nehemiah's wall, whatever its precise line, encompassed the old City of David and did not surround the Western Hill, which shows no traces of occupation during the post-exilic period.[44] Given the consonance between Chr's description of Uzziah's fortifications and Nehemiah's wall, one can better understand the force of Chr's presentation. Uzziah, Chr tells us, fortified portions of the wall surrounding the City of David. If this understanding of Nehemiah's wall is correct, there is no evidence in Chronicles that Uzziah either built or fortified a wall encompassing the Western Hill.[45]

Not all comparisons result in ambiguous conclusions. Uzziah's expansion to the south and southwest may serve as the first example of how archaeology can illumine a biblical text and contribute positively to the reconstruction of Judahite history. Chr's description of Uzziah's royal estates resonates somewhat with our present knowledge of development in the Judahite Shephelah during the eighth century. The number of towns in the Shephelah during this period was [[195]] unprecedented. According to recent archaeological surveys, the Judahite Shephelah reached a settlement and demographic peak in the eighth century with about 275 sites, occupying a total of 250 hectares.[46] By contrast, most of the sites in the

---

41. Welten, *Geschichte*, 63–66; Williamson, "Nehemiah's Walls Revisited," *PEQ* 116 (1984) 81–88.

42. The Valley Gate appears in Neh 2:13, 15; 3:13, while the Angle appears in Neh 3:19, 20, 24 (together with הפנה [['corner']]), 25.

43. Williamson, *Chronicles*, 336.

44. K. M. Kenyon, *Digging up Jerusalem* (Nashville: Nelson, 1974) 180–87; idem, *Archaeology in the Holy Land* (London: Benn, 4th edn, 1979) 306–8; N. Avigad, *Discovering Jerusalem* (Nashville: Nelson, 1983) 61–62.

45. Pace E.-M. Laperrousaz, "Jerusalem la grande," in S. Ahituv and B. A. Levine (eds.), *Avraham Malamat Volume* (ErIsr, 24; Jerusalem: Israel Exploration Society, 1994) 138–47.

46. Y. Dagan, "The Shephelah during the Period of the Monarchy in Light of Archaeological Excavations and Surveys" (MA Thesis, Tel Aviv University, 1992; Hebrew with English summary); A. Ofer, "Judah," in E. M. Meyers et al. (eds.), [[*The Oxford Encyclopedia of Archaeology in the Near East*]] (New York: Oxford University Press, [[1997]]) 3.253–57]]. I wish to thank Professor Ofer for making a copy of this paper available to me [[prior to its publication]].

Judahite Shephelah were destroyed by the end of the eighth century. The most famous example of such massive destruction and depopulation is, of course, the damage inflicted upon Lachish (Stratum III). The surveys indicate that only about 40 built-up sites, occupying a total built-up area of 80 hectares, existed in the Shephelah during the late seventh and early sixth century. Hence, the total built-up area of the Judahite Shephelah decreased about 70 percent from the eighth to the seventh and sixth centuries.[47] The assumption is that at the end of the seventh century, as a result of Sennacherib's campaign, this territory was lost to Judah.[48] It is, therefore, highly relevant that Chr mentions an eighth-century monarch as the only king in Judahite history with extensive agricultural interests and holdings within these specific areas. Chr does not make such detailed claims for kings either in the ninth century or in the seventh and early sixth centuries.[49]

A second example of how the material remains, when coupled with Chr's history, can shed some light on pre-exilic history involves the construction activity in Judah ascribed to Uzziah, Jotham, and Hezekiah. Archaeological excavations and surveys disclose a large increase in the number of towns and fortifications in the Judahite hill [[196]] country during the eighth century.[50] Public works projects included walls, water systems, and fortifications.[51] The eighth century also witnessed an impressive

47. Ofer, "Judah"; I. Finkelstein, [["The Archaeology of the Days of Manasseh," in *Scripture and Other Artifacts: Essays on the Bible and Archaeology in Honor of Philip J. King* (ed. M. Coogan et al.; Louisville: Westminster/John Knox, 1994) 169–87]].

48. For example, I. Finkelstein, "Environmental Archaeology and Social History: Demographic and Economic Aspects of the Monarchic Period," in A. Biran and J. Aviram (eds.), *Biblical Archaeology Today, 1990* (Jerusalem: Israel Exploration Society, 1993) 59.

49. As we have seen, Chr also attributes substantial building projects and wealth to Hezekiah (2 Chr 32:27–29), but Chr does not specify the geographical locations of Hezekiah's agricultural holdings.

50. Y. Shiloh, "Judah and Jerusalem in the Eighth–Sixth Centuries B.C.E.," in S. Gitin and W. G. Dever (eds.), *Recent Excavations in Israel: Studies in Iron Age Archaeology* (AASOR, 49; Winona Lake, IN: Eisenbrauns, 1989) 97–103. The interpretation of the material remains from a few of these sites is disputed. According to Mazar, Khirbet Abu et-Twain is one of several fortresses and towers in the Judahite hills and Shephelah dating to the eighth and seventh centuries (*Archaeology*, 453–55). But K. G. Hoglund dates this site to the fifth century: *Achaemenid Imperial Administration in Syria-Palestine and the Missions of Ezra and Nehemiah* (SBLDS, 125; Atlanta: Scholars Press, 1992) 191–94.

51. A. Mazar, "Iron Age Fortresses in the Judaean Hills," *PEQ* 114 (1982) 87–109; Na'aman, "Sennacherib's Campaign," 5–21; Y. Shiloh, "Underground Water Systems in Eretz-Israel in the Iron Age," in L. G. Perdue, L. E. Toombs, and G. L. Johnson (eds.), *Archaeology and Biblical Interpretation: Essays in Memory of D. Glenn Rose* (Atlanta: John Knox, 1987) 203–45; D. W. Jamieson-Drake, *Scribes and Schools in Monarchic Judah: A Socio-Archaeological Approach* (JSOTSup, 109; The Social World of Biblical Antiquity Series, 9; Sheffield: Almond Press, 1991) 81–106; G. Barkay, "The Iron Age II–III," in A. Ben-Tor (ed.), *The Archaeology of Ancient Israel* (New Haven, CT: Yale University Press, 1992) 332–34, 369.

increase in the settlement of Judah.[52] Archaeological surveys in the Judahite hill country conducted by M. Kochavi and A. Ofer reveal a peak of 88
sites with a total built-up area of about 85 hectares in the eighth century.[53]
Ofer estimates that the total built-up area for all of Judah in the eighth century was 470 hectares.

Given the stylized and generalized nature of Chr's descriptions and
the dating of material remains to broad eras rather than to specific generations, archaeological analysis does not prove many of Chr's specific
claims about Uzziah, Jotham, and Hezekiah. But there does seem to be at
least some congruence between the Chronistic notion of Judahite expansion and fortification in the eighth century and current [[197]] analysis of
the archaeological record.[54] Such congruence does not make Chronicles
merely an important witness for the reconstruction of Judahite history—
among the historical books, Chronicles is practically our only witness.
Aside from the mention of Hezekiah's water works in Jerusalem, there is
no indication in Kings of non-cultic reforms among eighth-century Judahite monarchs.[55]

Chr's account of Hezekiah's reforms in Jerusalem comprises a third
example of how Chronicles, when coupled with epigraphic or archaeological analysis, can elucidate ancient Judahite history.[56] A variety of archaeological discoveries pertain to Hezekiah's activity in Jerusalem. The
most famous is the Siloam tunnel inscription (*KAI* 189), discovered in
1880, commemorating the completion of this conduit. Both Kings and
Chronicles, in different terms, ascribe this engineering feat to Hezekiah
(2 Kgs 20:20; 2 Chr 32:30). Palaeographical analysis of the Hebrew script

52. Mazar, *Archaeology*, 438–62; B. Halpern, "Jerusalem and the Lineages in the Seventh Century B.C.E.: Kingship and the Rise of Individual Moral Liability," in B. Halpern and
D. W. Hobson (eds.), *Law and Ideology in Monarchic Israel* (JSOTSup, 124; Sheffield: JSOT
Press, 1991) 19–34; Jamieson-Drake, *Scribes and Schools*, 48–73. In this context, the generalizations of Thompson (*Early History*, 409–11) need to be revised.

53. The results of A. Ofer's "The Highland of Judah during the Biblical Period" (PhD
dissertation, Tel Aviv University, 1993; Hebrew with English summary) are conveniently summarized in his "Judean Hills Survey," *NEAEHL* (1993) 814–15.

54. More difficult to appraise is Chr's assertion that Uzziah built towers in the wilderness (מדבר 2 Chr 26:10). Only in the seventh century does one see permanent settlements
flourish in the Judean desert. The seventh century is also an important period for the Judahite Negev. When compared with the previous century, the number of sites and total built-
up area nearly doubled: Ofer, "Judah."

55. Prophetic texts (e.g., Isa 22:9–11) are another matter.

56. J. Rosenbaum, "Hezekiah's Reform and Deuteronomistic Tradition," *HTR* 72
(1979) 23–43; Ahlström, *History*, 697–701; Japhet, *Chronicles*, 977–83; B. Halpern, "Sybil, or
the Two Nations? Archaism, Alienation and the Elite Redefinition of Traditional Culture in
Judah in the 8th–7th Centuries B.C.E.," in J. Cooper [[and G. Schwartz]] (eds.), *The Study of the
Ancient Near East in the Twenty-First Century* (Winona Lake, IN: Eisenbrauns, [[1996]]). I wish
to thank Professor Halpern for making a copy of this paper available to me.

generally comports with a late eighth-century date but is insufficiently precise to be of more help in dating this inscription.[57] Given the discoveries on the Western Hill (see below), however, one need no longer be skeptical of Chr's unique assertion that Hezekiah brought the waters of the Gihon "down to the west of the City of David" (2 Chr 32:30).[58]

Other important archaeological finds, unearthed by Avigad in the [[198]] Jewish Quarter of the Old City, shed light on the history of eighth-century Jerusalem. One of these is the remains of an ancient city wall, seven meters thick, which Avigad dated to the late eighth century on the basis of stratigraphy and pottery analysis.[59] The discovery of this so-called Broad Wall, as well as a variety of other structures and artifacts, indicate that the settlement of Jerusalem expanded to the Western Hill in the pre-exilic period. These finds also give new credence to the view that at least part of the plateau of the Western Hill was encompassed by a fortified wall.[60] Isa 22:9–11 and 2 Chr 32:5 are the only biblical writings referring to two Jerusalem walls.[61] Excavations of ancient Jerusalem and other sites in Judah yield other important evidence. The discovery of למלך [['for the king']] jar impressions, 44 of which stem from the Jewish Quarter alone, testifies to significant royal involvement in the administration of Jerusalem and Judah. To be sure, there is ongoing debate about the precise purpose of these jars.[62] But the two-winged sun and four-winged scarab are

57. Note especially the shape and stance of the *waw, yod, kap, lamed,* and *qop* [[letters of the Hebrew alphabet]]. See further the three articles by F. M. Cross entitled, "Epigraphic Notes on Hebrew Documents of the Eighth–Sixth Centuries B.C.," *BASOR* 163 (1961) 12–14; *BASOR* 165 (1962) 34–46; and *BASOR* 168 (1962) 18–23; and L. G. Herr, *The Scripts of Ancient Northwest Semitic Seals* (HSM, 18; Missoula, MT: Scholars Press, 1978) 79–152.

58. Cf. North, "Archaeology," 375–79.

59. Avigad, *Jerusalem,* 45–60.

60. Avigad, *Jerusalem,* 31–44; Y. Shiloh, "Jerusalem," *NEAEHL* 2 (1993) 705–8; H. Geva, "Twenty-Five Years of Excavations in Jerusalem, 1967–1992: Achievements and Excavations," in H. Geva (ed.), *Ancient Jerusalem Revealed* (Jerusalem: Israel Exploration Society, 1994) 5–7.

61. One could argue that Chr employed Isa 22:9–11 in his construction of Hezekiah's reign, but two features of the Isaianic presentation should be noted before one leaps to such a conclusion. First, Isaiah 22 does not explicitly attribute the construction activity to Hezekiah. Second, there are important differences between the two texts in question. Isa 22:9–11 mentions that the Jerusalem wall was refortified and that a basin was constructed between the walls to collect the water of the old pool (cf. 2 Chr 32:30). 2 Chr 32:5 mentions not only the refortification of the city wall, but also the raising of towers upon this wall and the construction of another wall outside the old one. Hence, even if one allows for the possibility that Chr understood Isa 22:9–11 as alluding to Hezekian activity, this still would not be sufficient to explain the particular details of Chr's presentation.

62. N. Na᾽aman, "Sennacherib's Campaign to Judah and the Date of the LMLK Stamps," *VT* 29 (1979) 61–86; idem, "Hezekiah's Fortified Cities and the LMLK Stamps," *BASOR* 261 (1986) 5–21; Avigad, *Jerusalem,* 43–44; Mazar, *Archaeology,* 455–57; Halpern, "Jerusalem," 23–26.

clearly royal emblems. Hence, the existence and diffusion of these impressions in the late eighth century, continuing to some extent in the early seventh century, bear witness to the influence of a central administrative or military organization. The strongest biblical evidence for such an administrative [[199]] reorganization and consolidation of power comes, as we have seen, from Chr's presentation of Hezekiah's reign.

The final example of how Chronicles may be used in historical reconstruction involves explaining the surge in Jerusalem's population during the eighth and seventh centuries. The excavations of Kenyon have documented the expansion of Jerusalem on its eastern slopes in the late monarchy, while the excavations of Avigad have documented the expansion of Jerusalem on the Western Hill in the eighth and seventh centuries.[63] Although there is some debate whether this population swell began in the eighth century or somewhat earlier in the ninth century,[64] there is broad agreement that waves of refugees fleeing the Assyrian campaigns against the northern kingdom contributed to the increase of Jerusalem's population.[65] But Kings never mentions any such migration from the north to Jerusalem. In contrast, Chronicles depicts northerners migrating to Judah sporadically throughout the history of Judah (e.g., 2 Chr 11:13–17; 15:9). Chr also depicts the involvement of northerners in covenant renewals and Jerusalem-centered feasts, most prominently the passovers led by Hezekiah and Josiah (2 Chr 30:1–27; 35:1–19). Because the reclamation of Israelite people and land is such a clear programmatic interest on the part of the Chronicler, one cannot be sure what historical reality lies behind each of Chr's individual descriptions.[66] But it is remarkable that these descriptions exist at all. In this context, the invitation to the celebration of Hezekiah's national passover is especially relevant (2 Chr 30:6–9).[67] By appealing to those northerners who survived the Assyrian conquest [[200]] to journey to Jerusalem, Hezekiah's message effectively counters the repeated assertion of Kings that the northern population was either killed

---

63. Kenyon, *Digging up Jerusalem*, 129–65; Avigad, *Jerusalem*, 54–60.

64. Avigad, *Jerusalem*, 54–55; M. Broshi, "The Expansion of Jerusalem in the Reign of Hezekiah and Manasseh," *IEJ* 24 (1974) 21–26. Cf. Barkay, "Iron Age," 364–68.

65. Refugees from the Shephelah and the countryside of Judah probably also contributed to the increase; see Halpern, "Sybil." For a dissenting view, see Thompson, *Early Israel*, 410–11.

66. G. N. Knoppers, "A Reunited Kingdom in Chronicles?" *PEGLMBS* 9 (1989) 82–84; "Reform and Regression: The Chronicler's Presentation of Jehoshaphat," *Bib* 72 (1991) 504–24; " 'Battling against Yahweh': Israel's War against Judah in 2 Chr 13:2–20," *RB* 100 (1993) 511–32.

67. Japhet, *Ideology*, 189–91, 318–20; Williamson, *Israel*, 110–31; Dillard, *Chronicles*, 252–61. I disagree with Williamson, Throntveit, and Dillard, however, that Hezekiah's measures permanently reunify the (former) northern and southern kingdoms: "A Reunited Kingdom," 74–88.

or exiled (2 Kgs 17:6, 18, 20, 23; 18:11), only to be replaced by Assyrian sponsored emigrants (2 Kgs 17:24–33). Chr's very wording of Hezekiah's appeal presupposes that some Israelites survived the Assyrian campaigns and remained in the former northern kingdom. Inasmuch as historians wish to support with textual evidence the notion that some northerners survived the Assyrian conquest and that others contributed to Jerusalem's growth, they must turn to the indirect witness of Chronicles.

We have seen a number of instances of correspondence between administrative and geopolitical reforms during the eighth century and current archaeological and epigraphic analysis of this era. Given the great skepticism that characterizes much scholarly discourse on the relationship of Chr to the pre-exilic age, these correlations are significant. It would misrepresent the data, however, to suggest that such resonance tells the whole story. Archaeological and epigraphic analysis not only illumines, but also greatly complicates the use of Chronicles as a source for reconstructing Judahite history. In his description of Hezekiah's reign Chr, like the Deuteronomist, narrates a miraculous deliverance of Jerusalem. My primary interest is not the divine spectacle, which presents its own set of historical and metaphysical issues, but the impact of the Assyrian campaign upon Judah.

Both the Assyrian western campaigns and Hezekiah's response to those campaigns profoundly affected the social life of Judah.[68] Sennacherib's campaign, in particular, inflicted great damage on many of Judah's cities.[69] He asserts that he decimated "46 of his [Hezekiah's] strongwalled cities, as well as the small cities in their environs, which were without number."[70] Similarly, according to 2 Kgs 18:13, "Sennacherib, king of Assyria, came up against all of the fortified cities [[201]] of Judah and captured them." The Assyrian king's invasion is associated with the systematic destruction of Judahite border fortresses.[71] Mazar credits Sennacherib with taking Lachish (III), Ramat Rahel (VB), and Timnah (Tell el-Baṭash [III]), and perhaps also Beer-Sheba (II), Gezer (IIB), and Tell Beit Mirsim (A2).[72]

68. F. J. Gonçalves, *L'expédition de Sennachérib en Palestine dans la littérature hebraïque ancienne* (Ébib, ns, 7; Paris: Librairie Lecoffre, 1986); J. M. Miller and J. H. Hayes, *A History of Ancient Israel and Judah* (Philadelphia: Westminster, 1986) 353–63; Halpern, "Sybil."

69. See Gonçalves, *L'expédition*, 102–36; Halpern, "Jerusalem," 34–49; Ahlström, *History*, 665–707, and the references listed in these works.

70. D. D. Luckenbill, *The Annals of Sennacherib* (OIP, 2; Chicago: University of Chicago Press, 1924) 32–34.

71. Aharoni, *Archaeology*, 253–69; Tadmor and Cogan, *II Kings*, 223–25.

72. The date and cause of the destruction at some sites, such as Beer-Sheba (II), Gezer (IIB), Tell Beit Mirsim (A2), Arad (X–VIII), Tell Halif (VIB), and Bet Shemesh (IIC), are disputed; see Aharoni, *Land*, 387–94; Mazar, *Archaeology*, 416–40; Ben Tor, "Iron Age," 328; Ahlström, *History*, 707–16.

The Assyrian king was apparently also responsible for the marked depopulation of many parts of Judah at the end of the eighth century, either through devastation or deportation.[73] Ofer's recent archaeological surveys suggest that Sennacherib killed or exiled most of the inhabitants of the Shephelah and about 50–70 percent of the inland residents. Because of the systematic destruction and deportation, Stohlmann speaks of a "Judaean exile after 701 B.C.E."[74]

The impression of devastation caused by Sennacherib's campaign, gleaned from archaeological and epigraphic sources, contrasts sharply with the picture offered by Chronicles. Chr frames his version of Sennacherib's campaign (2 Chr 32:9–21) with material that presents Hezekiah's reign in a very positive light. In addition to detailing Hezekiah's extensive preparations for a defensive war (2 Chr 32:1–8), Chr portrays the aftermath of Sennacherib's invasion as a time of rest (2 Chr 32:22). In Kings and the Annals of Sennacherib, Hezekiah renders hefty tribute to Sennacherib. But in Chronicles tribute for YHWH flows to Jerusalem, as do precious objects for Hezekiah (2 Chr 32:23). The Chronicler also adds material describing Hezekiah's impressive public works and riches (2 Chr 32:25, 23, 27–30). For Chr, wealth, tribute, and rest are sure signs of divine blessing.[75] Given that Sennacherib only encamps against the fortified cities [[202]] of Judah, "thinking that he would capture them" (2 Chr 32:1), Chr's Sennacherib does little, if any, real damage to Jerusalem and Judah. Hezekiah and his people weather the Assyrian storm extremely well.

By comparing Chr's presentation with other sources, one can see the degree to which Chr's programmatic interests affect his description of Hezekiah's reign. The author's particular brand of royalism leads him to include various notices about Hezekiah's reforms and prestige, but this same impulse also leads him to present a completely one-sided account of Sennacherib's invasion. Like the Deuteronomists, Chr accentuates Jerusalem's survival, the annihilation of Sennacherib's forces, and the humiliation and death of Sennacherib himself. But the Chronicler, even more than the Deuteronomists, draws a veil over the depopulation and massive transformation of Judah at the end of the eighth century. In describing

73. Aharoni, *Archaeology*, 253–66; Mazar, *Archaeology*, 544–47; Halpern, "Jerusalem," 30–34. Sennacherib's own deportation figure is fantastic: 200,150 (Luckenbill, *Annals*, 33).

74. S. Stohlmann, "The Judaean Exile after 701 B.C.E.," in W. W. Hallo, J. C. Moyer, and L. G. Perdue (eds.), *Scripture in Context II: More Essays on the Comparative Method* (Winona Lake, IN: Eisenbrauns, 1983) 147–75.

75. J. Wellhausen, *Prolegomena to the History of Ancient Israel* (Edinburgh: A. & C. Black, 1885) 203–10; Japhet, *Ideology*, 150–76; Dillard, "Reward and Punishment," 164–70; R. L. Braun, "Solomon, the Chosen Temple Builder: The Significance of 1 Chronicles 22, 28, and 29 for the Theology of Chronicles," *JBL* 95 (1976) 581–90.

this aspect of Hezekiah's legacy, the author of Chronicles occludes the pre-exilic past. Chr's presentation of Judah's history during the Assyrian crisis tells us much more about Chr's ideal of Davidic kingship than it does about the immense transformations that occurred in the demography of Judah at this time.

Conclusions

To return to the issues raised at the beginning of this essay, Chronicles is historically important in two different ways—as an example of history and as an indirect means of reconstructing history. The first should not be underplayed or underestimated. Chr's history provides commentators with insight into how someone, who was much closer to the period in question than modern authors are, construed the history of Judahite royal reforms. How a civilization takes account of itself is important evidence on its own terms. As to the question of which history—pre-exilic or post-exilic— Chronicles reflects, the answer may not be a case of either/or, but both/ and. Chr's history inevitably reflects a certain rhetorical structure, the author's own post-exilic context, and the author's programmatic interests. Writing about the past is never done in a vacuum but is always influenced by the witness's own circumstances. Chr's account of royal reforms has to be approached cautiously and critically. It is also clear, however, that the unique evidence of Chronicles, when compared with archaeological or epigraphic evidence, [[203]] is occasionally of some value for historical reconstruction. Chronicles is not a treasure trove of information about pre-exilic history, but it does interact with pre-exilic history.

In this regard, one of the advantages of Chronicles for historical reconstruction—that it relates to both the pre-exilic age and the post-exilic age—is also a disadvantage. Chronicles as a post-exilic construction of the pre-exilic past complicates the history of both Judah and Yehud. Such complexity does not justify, however, scholarly neglect or ignorance. In approaching Chr's account of royal reforms, commentators need to be aware of a variety of issues—their own assumptions and commitments, the limitations of their methods, relevant literary questions (form, structure, style, and author's *Tendenz*), and historical matters (possible relationships of Chronicles to other sources, inscriptional evidence, archaeological remains). But scholars should engage the witness of this extensive ancient history. A discriminating understanding of Chronicles enables contemporary scholars to write more sophisticated, nuanced, and balanced histories of both ancient Judah and post-exilic Yehud.

Part 6

The Future of Israel's Past

The Future of Israel's Past: Personal Reflections

V. Philips Long

In the introductions to the the earlier parts of this volume, I interacted fairly fully with the content of many of the reprinted essays and at times also with some of the essays listed under additional reading. Taken together, these introductions give an indication of some of the strengths and weaknesses in current studies of Israel's past, and my comments and caveats along the way suggest on-going concerns. In this concluding chapter, my aim is to draw together some threads and to try to discern patterns in the weave. Looking to the future, I will even venture to suggest some patterns that I would like to see appearing more prominently as the weaving continues. If, as we often hear, the discipline is in crisis (or, to put it slightly less dramatically, in a state of flux), the time seems ripe for such suggestions.

Part of the difficulty in "doing history" is the fact that it involves many different subdisciplines and distinct areas of research. Even a quick overview of the essays included in this volume (and how many issues have hardly been touched!) is sufficient to confirm that the historical study of "ancient Israel," like historical study in general, is a "field-encompassing field." Perhaps a good way to begin our final reflections is by pondering this oft-repeated adage.

The Future of a "Field-Encompassing Field"

While the study of Israel's past is as deserving of the label "field-encompassing field" as any other, it is not the only discipline to which the label is affixed; other recipients include, for instance, theology and jurisprudence. Indeed, an analogy is often drawn between the aims and objectives of jurisprudence and of historical study, for both fields involve similar kinds of evidence gathering and logical analysis.[1] Simply put, "historical knowledge is based upon evidence in just the same way the deliberations of a jury are."[2] When a trial is conducted in a court of law, the aim is to establish beyond a reasonable doubt what must have happened in the past in regard to a particular issue (for example, a criminal charge). Absolute proof is seldom, if ever, possible. In pursuit of this aim, the judicial process focuses attention both on verbal testimony and on material evidence. Verbal testimony is collected for the most part from witnesses who are called to testify, who are required to answer certain direct questions, and who are subjected to cross-examination. The pool of witnesses will not be limited to eye-witnesses only (what we might call primary sources) but will include any who, for whatever reason, are regarded as having information of potential pertinence to the case (we might call them secondary sources). The goal of the examination and cross-examination of witnesses is, first, to *understand* their testimony as well as possible (to discern *truth claims*) and, second, to *judge the veracity* of the testimony (to decide *truth value*). Testimony that is incoherent—that is, not self-consistent (based on a common-sense approach to what constitutes consistency in normal human speech)—will be immediately suspect. Even entirely coherent testimony may be distrusted if (1) the witness is not of reputable character or (2) the scenario described by the witness is deemed impossible by those conducting the examination—here the "background beliefs" of the jurors will influence their judgment regarding the plausibility of some claims. (For instance, if a witness claims to have detailed knowldge of a crime simply because he dreamed about it, some jurors will immediately view such a scenario as impossible; others may be more open to the paranormal; all should be cautious!) Assuming a witness of reputable character who delivers testimony that is both coherent and not "impossible," the initial inclination will be to believe the witness, pending assessment of other evidence.

Testimony provided by witnesses under examination constitutes direct verbal evidence. Indirect verbal evidence may also be available—tape-recorded conversations, a ransom note, personal letters, words scrawled on a wall, and so on. Such evidence, though verbal, may not speak directly

---

1. See, e.g., S. Toulmin, *The Uses of Argument* (Cambridge: Cambridge University Press, 1958), esp. 94–145; and also the discussions of the judicial analogy in V. A. Harvey, *The Historian and the Believer* (New York: Macmillan, 1966) 43–64; J. A. Soggin, *A History of Ancient Israel* (trans. J. Bowden; Philadelphia: Westminster, 1985) 20; and J. M. Miller, in this volume, p. 359.

2. B. Halpern, *The First Historians: The Hebrew Bible and History* (San Francisco: Harper & Row, 1988) 13.

to the question under investigation but can still be used as part of a cumulative case advocating a particular reconstruction of events. The unintentional character of such evidence means that it sometimes carries great weight. In a sense, this evidence falls somewhere between verbal and material evidence.

Material evidence per se is nonverbal: a weapon, a spent shell, a corpse, a bloody glove, a DNA sample, and so on. Such material evidence, though highly significant, is not self-interpreting. To discover its significance, expert witnesses may be called—a ballistics expert, a coroner, a glove manufacturer, a scientist, or others. These experts provide guidance in how to interpret this or that piece of material evidence, but they are generally not called upon to suggest a grand synthesis (and would likely receive a censure were they to attempt to do so). Only when all available evidence, of all sorts, is collected and considered is the jury in a position to render a verdict. (Indeed, the emergence of new evidence can lead to reconsideration and even reversal of earlier judgments.)

The threefold task of conducting the examinations, putting all the pieces together in a coherent explanation of "what happened," and seeking to persuade the court belongs to the lawyers. In a legal trial there will typically be at least two reconstructions of "what must have happened," each the reconstruction of an opposing lawyer. The competing reconstructions are motivated by each lawyer's desire to build the strongest case from the available evidence for the side he/she represents. Recognition of this fact has not led jurists to the conclusion that they are involved in a purely subjective or self-serving exercise. Unlike the state of affairs in some other intellectual spheres, in jurisprudence common-sense still holds sufficient sway to insist that at most one of two opposing scenarios can be in accordance with "what *actually* happened," and it is the court's responsibility to decide which.

Even this rudimentary description of the judicial process is adequate to confirm that jurisprudence is a field-encompassing field. While no analogy is perfect, the similarity of the processes described above to the work of historians is obvious.[3] The aim of historians, like jurists, is to establish beyond a reasonable doubt (not to prove) what must have happened in the past concerning a particular issue.[4] Depending on what issues interest

3. For fuller discussion, see my *Art of Biblical History* (Foundations of Contemporary Interpretation 5; Grand Rapids: Zondervan, 1994) 184–94.

4. Some today writing on Israel's past insist that the Old Testament's testimony is to be trusted only insofar as it can be proved through external verification (for example, most recently, N. P. Lemche writes: "the biblical text cannot in advance be accepted as a historical source or documentation; it has in every single case to prove its status as a historical source" [*The Israelites in History and Tradition* (Library of Ancient Israel; Louisville: Westminster/John

them, historians can write quite different histories of the same period: political, economic, environmental, intellectual, cultural, religious, and so forth. These various areas do not of course exist in isolation from one another; each is in some respects influenced by the others. And though it may be a worthy objective to try to do justice to all of them, it remains the case that most histories are written with a more limited set of questions in mind. Like jurists, historians seek to reconstruct the past not in its entirety but as it pertains to specific questions they are asking. This means that written histories are partial and perspectival. Each individual work falls short of exhaustive coverage, but it can still be called a history if, to recall Deist's definition, it presents "an explanation of the meaningful connectedness of a sequence of past events in the form of an interested and focussed narrative" (in this volume, p. 380).

In terms of the central concern of the present volume, it should by now be apparent that historians who explore Israel's history writing or seek to write Israel's history approach their task with many different concerns and goals. Depending on what these are, certain kinds of evidence may weigh more heavily than others. But insofar as there is interest in *human* history and not just natural history, all historians (like responsible

---

Knox, 1998) 29]). It is not at all clear, however, what form this verification would have to take in order for some to be convinced. One need only consult L. L. Grabbe's brief discussion of the "Berekyahu b. Neriyahu" seal, an apparent external verification of "Baruch son of Neriah" (Jer 32:12, etc.), to see how difficult it might be "verify" the biblical testimony to those disinclined to accept it; Grabbe writes: "One could even argue that the seal actually contradicts the book of Jeremiah, for why would a major official in the bureaucracy hire himself out as a mere amanuensis to a controversial prophet? In other words, the author of Jeremiah may have simply appropriated a famous name while creating a fictional narrative" (L. L. Grabbe, "Reflections on the Discussion," in *Can a "History of Israel" Be Written?* [ed. L. L. Grabbe; JSOTSup 245; European Seminar in Historical Methodology 1; Sheffield: Sheffield Academic Press, 1997] 191–92). R. P. Carroll warns of the danger of "the 'old credulists'" using "a *totalizing transfer mode* here to read into the name on a bulla the whole story of Jeremiah and Baruch as found in the biblical book of Jeremiah" ("Madonna of Silences: Clio and the Bible," in ibid., 97). Of course, one cannot look to a single bulla/seal to confirm the entirety of the biblical testimony (and even an "old credulist" would not suggest that one should), but again one wonders what kind of "verification" is being demanded. Even were something quite striking to be unearthed, one fears that some, rather than be convinced, would simply choose the it-could-be-a-fake escape route (see Carroll's assessment of N. Avigad's presentation of *Hebrew Bullae from the Time of Jeremiah* [Jerusalem: Israel Exploration Society, 1986]: "They cannot be counted as serious evidence for anything because who knows which are faked and which are reliable?" [Carroll, "Madonna of Silences," 97]). In essence, the verificationist approach appears to be saying that every item of testimony must be externally verified, and *no verification of individual items will ever suffice to justify confidence in the testimony as a whole*. About all that one can say to such an approach is that, were similar standards applied in a court of law, virtually no case could ever be decided.

jurists) must give attention to the two major classes of evidence mentioned above: verbal and material.

For the historian of ancient Israel, verbal evidence will come in the form of the written word, whether in the biblical corpus or in ancient Near Eastern texts. Direct interrogation and cross-examination of witnesses will not be possible in the same way as in a court of law, since the witnesses are not "live" and cannot be required to answer direct questions. Nevertheless, depending on the questions a historian may be pursuing, texts that evince a marked antiquarian bent may come close to direct testimony if they happen to treat matters central to the modern historian's interests. This may partly explain why the theological historiography of the Bible is weighted rather differently (or should be) by theistic, as opposed to nontheistic, scholars. Often the biblical and extrabiblical texts will come closer to indirect verbal testimony, inasmuch as they were not written with the specific concerns of the modern historian in mind. Whatever the case, the same kinds of questions will need to be asked in deciding which "witnesses" are to be trusted. Is the "witness" (biblical or extrabiblical text) of reputable character? Does it tell a coherent story? Are its claims not impossible? And does its story square with available material evidences? Whenever such questions are asked, the penchants and presuppositions of individual scholars begin to have their influence (a fact of which the best scholars tend to be aware). As noted earlier, a text may strike one scholar as a "crazy patchwork" of sources and another as a coherent source (much depending on one's literary competence, sensitivities, and training). Or a textual claim may strike one scholar as quite plausible and another as utterly impossible. In deciding these matters, philosophical and metaphysical core convictions inevitably become involved, as indeed they do when the "character" of a biblical or extrabiblical text must be judged.

In regard to material evidences, the future will likely see an increasing variety put forward for consideration. With the prominence of an ever more sophisticated "new archaeology" and an array of social science approaches, the future may develop greater and greater ability to put flesh on the bones of the skeletal historical storyline. How the storyline itself is arrived at will vary from scholar to scholar. Will it be provided by the ancient texts (biblical and extrabiblical), by sociological models, by modern (political) ideologies, by personal prejudices, or by some combination of these? Given the specialization involved in many of the disciplines involved in the field-encompassing field of history, experts will often be called as witnesses to make sense of the data. Historians themselves will continue to play roles analogous to "opposing lawyers," conducting their examinations, formulating their reconstructions of "what happened," and seeking to persuade the jury (the academy and the reading public) that their particular reconstruction of events is the more probable. As recent events amply demonstrate, rhetoric will likely have as important a persuasive role in doing history as it does in arguing a court case. To be eschewed in this regard is argument that consists of little more than rhetoric or that becomes ad hominem.

The future will also undoubtedly see continued debate regarding the weight to be assigned to different kinds of evidence (textual, material, environmental, and so forth) and to different explanatory models (whether idiographic as in traditional histories' focus on great individuals and events, or nomothetic as in the social sciences' focus on more general features or "laws" of historical process). While some scholars will continue to pursue "one-sided approaches,"[5] the majority will likely prefer eclectic approaches that draw on many different methods in the hope of doing greatest justice to the widest array of evidence. The majority will also probably remain resistant to overtures that would virtually remove the biblical texts from the evidentiary mix, though the debate over the Bible's role, already hot, will likely get hotter. As Grabbe has recently remarked, "It seems clear that the question of the biblical text will continue to dominate many future discussions."[6] It may be hoped that in the course of these discussions the future will witness a greater awareness among scholars of how their core beliefs affect their scholarship and a greater willingness to let this be known. After all, as Harvey has observed,

> all our judgments and inferences [including historical ones] take place . . . against a background of beliefs. We bring to our perceptions and interpretations a world of existing knowledge, categories, and judgments. Our inferences are but the visible part of an iceberg lying deep below the surface.[7]

This is as true of the "nonreligious" as of the "religious" scholar, and the sooner this fundamental truth is accepted and made discussable, the sooner honest debate and understanding (if not agreement) may come to characterize the historical study of ancient Israel—a field, as we have noted, deemed by many to be in crisis. These last observations well introduce the

---

5. See S. Herrmann, "Observations on Some Recent Hypotheses Pertaining to Early Israelite History," in *Justice and Righteousness* (ed. H. G. Reventlow and Y. Hoffman; JSOTSup 137; Sheffield: Sheffield Academic Press, 1992) 115.

6. Grabbe, "Reflections on the Discussion," 193. Barstad is innocent of overstatement when he writes that "the most important question seems to be whether or not it is possible to write a history of ancient Israel on the basis of Old Testament historiography" (H. M. Barstad, "History and the Hebrew Bible," in Grabbe [ed.], *Can a "History of Israel" Be Written?* 37).

7. Harvey, *The Historian and the Believer*, 115.

first of two hopes that I entertain for the future of the discipline—whether either will be realized is anyone's guess. Let us look at them more closely.

Two Hopes for a Field in Crisis

Increased Openness among Scholars about the
Existence and Impact of "Background Beliefs"

In his 1985 survey of the state of "Israelite History," Miller concluded that "probably there is no other area of biblical studies so obviously in need at the moment of some fresh ideas based on solid research."[8] And Whitelam has stated that "a debate on methodology is extremely important."[9] My own contention throughout this volume and elsewhere has been that, while methodological debate is certainly welcome, the debate needs to move to an even deeper level, beyond the question of *methods* to the prior question of *models*—what are the reality models embraced by scholars, evinced by texts, and inherent in methods? In this volume we have heard from Deist that "human involvement in any process of interpretation is accompanied by interests" (p. 386), and we have been challenged by Maier's insistence that every historian is obligated to give an account of his/her philosophical and religious assumptions (p. 201). If present trends be any guide, the future will see resistance to this obligation in some quarters. We have heard Davies, for instance, after querying whether Whybray may not be "driven by reactionary conservatism or religious attachment to Christian scripture," remark, "I would rather not debate on this level, lest we bring scholarship as a whole into disrepute" (p. 190). If, however, as Davies admits in the same context, "no scholar should deny that non-scholarly motives are present," it stands to reason that scholarly communication and understanding could be furthered by openly acknowledging such motives and making them discussable. Whether the discussion would "bring scholarship as a whole into disrepute" would depend on the ability of scholars to treat each other with respect and to disagree agreeably. Surely nothing is gained by simply burying real points of disagreement and then acting as if the only points of disagreement are, say, methodological or a matter of personal scholarly (in)competence. Perhaps if scholars were more forthcoming about *their own* core commitments, there would be less temptation to characterize (or caricature) one another in terms that might indeed bring scholarship as a whole into disrepute.

8. J. M. Miller, "Israelite History," in *The Hebrew Bible and Its Modern Interpreters* (ed. D. A. Knight and G. M. Tucker; Philadelphia: Fortress / Chico, Calif.: Scholars Press, 1985) 23.
9. K. W. Whitelam, "Recreating the History of Israel," *JSOT* 35 (1986) 63.

To suggest that scholars be more candid with one another about "what makes them tick" is not exactly a "fresh idea," but it is one that has not yet been consistently put into practice. And so it may be hoped that the future will see more scholars willing to give at least some indication of the background beliefs that accompany them as they seek to write their histories of Israel. As Degenaar rightly observes: "Theoretical self-reflection raises historiography to a higher level, for the historian can now take into account his (hidden) assumptions, and he can become conscious of the fact that there are various interpretative strategies by means of which historical meaning is constituted."[10] This will not come naturally to many traditionally trained historians (and biblical scholars) since, as Barstad notes, "many historians have felt that what is going on in philosophy is more or less irrelevant to what they themselves do."[11] As he goes on to say, however, "as long as these same persons in their very practice also *make* methodological statements based on epistemological and ontological presuppositions, they simply cannot pretend that philosophy is irrelevant. They are all in fact *practicising* some sort of philosophy, and it would certainly not hurt their work if they had realized this."[12]

Adoption of the Biblical Worldview as "Interpretive Strategy"

A second "fresh idea" also relates to the issue of worldview but not in the same way. Whereas the first hope is that scholars will become more self-reflective and forthcoming about how their worldview figures into the full range of their interpretive motivations, the second relates more specifically to the worldview evinced by the Bible. One may debate, of course, to what extent it is legitimate to speak of *the* biblical worldview, but as long as the delineation of it is restricted to basic contours—God exists, he is the lord of history, and so on—then the designation seems fair enough. In keeping with Norbert Lohfink's call for an approach to Israel's history that pursues its subject within biblical categories,[13] my second suggestion is this: whatever may be their personal view of the world and of history, all interpreters should adopt, if only as a methodological principle, the *biblical* worldview for the purpose of determining the historical *truth claims* of the biblical texts. If the biblical texts claim, for example, that those who were to become the nation of Israel were delivered out of slavery in Egypt

---

10. J. Degenaar, "Historical Discourse as Fact-Bound Fiction," in *Facts and Values* (ed. M. C. Doeser and J. N. Kraay; Dordrecht: Nijhoff, 1986) 76.

11. Barstad, "History and the Hebrew Bible," 48.

12. Ibid.

13. N. Lohfink, "Gesellschaftlicher Wandel und das Antlitz des wahren Gottes: Zu den Leitcategorien einer Geschichte Israels," *Dynamik im Wort: Lehre von der Bibel, Leben aus der Bibel* (Stuttgart: Katholisches Bibelwerk, 1982) 119–31.

and subsequently entered Canaan by a process involving military conquest, or if they claim that Jericho was razed (or, if we may cast a glance at the New Testament, that Jesus was raised), then historians should acknowledge that *in terms of the biblical worldview actual historical truth claims are being made*. Whether modern historians are prepared also to accept the *truth value* of these claims will depend, of course, on the degree of common ground, if any, between their own worldview and the texts'. But at least they will not mistake their skepticism regarding the veracity of the claims as grounds for denying that historical truth claims have been made in the first place.[14]

To see how this methodological adoption of the biblical worldview might look in practice, we may consider what Meir Sternberg has to say about the biblical notion of *inspired* narration.[15] Sternberg explains that in biblical narrative the narrating persona is always privileged, that is, omniscient. This privilege (omniscience) is not to be explained in terms of the "quasi-inspirational model" of modern fiction but in terms of the "inspirational" model at home in the Bible.[16] Sternberg does not insist that interpreters must *believe* the Bible's inspirational model. He is quite aware that "opinions about the Bible's real-life authority show infinite variety." His only insistence is that we recognize that "personal opinion about fact or faith is one thing, and interpretive strategy another." Thus, "intepreters must either invent their own biblical text or grant the storyteller all the storytelling authority (divine and otherwise) he enjoys in cultural context." In short, "to make sense of the Bible in terms of its own conventions [that is, rules of grammar and inspirational model], one need not believe in either, but one must postulate both." The writer is "omniscient historian," and the Bible is neither "inferior history" nor "superior fiction."[17] Rather, "with God postulated as double author, the biblical narrator can enjoy the privileges of art without renouncing his historical titles."[18]

To summarize: in the foregoing paragraphs I have expressed the twin hope that the historical study of ancient Israel may in the future be advanced (1) by scholars being more self-aware and forthcoming about how their own core beliefs affect their scholarship; and (2) by scholars more

14. On the importance of distinguishing truth claim and truth value, see the 9th rule of reading articulated by Mortimer Adler and Mark van Doren in *How to Read a Book* (rev. ed.; New York: Simon & Schuster, 1972) 142–43: "You must be able to say, with reasonable certainty, 'I understand,' before you can say any one of the following things: 'I agree,' or 'I disagree,' or 'I suspend judgment.'"

15. M. Sternberg, *The Poetics of Biblical Narrative: Ideological Literature and the Drama of Reading* (Bloomington: Indiana University Press, 1985) 73–83.

16. Ibid., 76–77.

17. Ibid., 81.

18. Ibid., 82.

clearly distinguishing between, on the one hand, their responsibility rightly to discern the truth claims in the sources and, on the other, their personal response to these claims (that is, their own beliefs regarding the truth value of said claims). Both of these considerations are related to issues of worldview and background beliefs. As I have contended throughout this volume, these "reality model" issues are of great importance if scholarly conversation and understanding are to advance. Once the foundational issues have been aired, we shall be in a position to enter more intelligently into methodological discussions. Perhaps a good motto would be: "Let consideration of models precede application of methods." From my own perspective as a theist, there are certain methodological adjustments/enhancements that I would like to see. Here I shall mention but three.[19] The first will likely encounter resistance from nontheists, but the other two may find more general welcome.

Three Methodological Suggestions

Re(de)fine the Canons of the Historical-Critical Method

In his highly instructive discussion of *Divine Revelation and the Limits of Historical Criticism*, W. J. Abraham asks whether the believer may not continue to believe and yet still lay claim to the title of historian.[20] Abraham argues that an affirmative answer is possible, provided that the three chief principles of the historical method (that is, criticism, analogy, and correlation) are appropriately defined. The principle of *criticism*, for instance, can and should be defined not in terms of systematic doubt but in terms of a thoughtful appraisal of the evidence in keeping with its source. (Little would ever be accomplished in a court of law if "systematic doubt" were rigorously applied to all witnesses no matter how unimpeachable their character, how coherent their story, and so forth.) What kind of criticism should be applied to the Bible will very much depend on scholars' opinions regarding the Bible's character. For those who regard the Bible as either not at all interested in history (thus devoid of historical truth claims) or as hopelessly incapable of conveying historical information (thus devoid of historical truth value), skepticism toward the possibility of drawing

19. I develop these suggestions more fully elsewhere, so my treatment here will be very brief; see my essay "Historiography of the Old Testament," in the forthcoming volume entitled *The Face of Old Testament Studies: A Survey of Contemporary Approaches* (ed. B. T. Arnold and D. W. Baker; Grand Rapids, Mich.: Baker, 1999) 145–75; and see also my fourth chapter in *The Art of Biblical History*.

20. W. J. Abraham, *Divine Revelation and the Limits of Historical Criticism* (Oxford: Oxford University Press, 1982).

historically valuable information from the Bible will indeed be the appropriate "critical" attitude. But for those who do not share these views, "systematic doubt" may be "the most inappropriate procedure imaginable for dealing with the Bible."[21] Concerning the principle of *analogy*, Abraham argues for a broad, rather than a narrow, definition, whereby plausibility is not judged solely by analogy to the historian's own personal experiences or those of his/her contemporaries but where reasonable arguments can be made for belief in occurrences with which the historian may have no personal acquaintance[22] and where, not only may the present serve as a key to the past, but the past may also serve as a key to the present.[23] Finally, in regard to the principle of *correlation*, Abraham argues for a formal rather than a material definition. According to the material definition, historical change can be brought about only by natural causes or *human* agency. According to the formal definition, agency is defined as *personal* agency, not merely human agency, and thus God is allowed back into the picture.[24]

Restrict the Claims of the Social Sciences to Their Proper Functions

Briefly stated, the social sciences are well suited to deal with *general* features of societies and cultures, but they are usually ill suited to pronounce on *specific* events and individuals. Their rightful function, then, is to provide background information against which the specific actions of individuals and groups can be better understood. As Halpern puts it, the chief function of the social sciences is to describe "the abiding institutions and patterns of culture, against which the quicker movements that catch the scholarly eye are visible."[25]

As long as practitioners recognize the proper role of the social sciences in addressing background concerns and in writing "history from below," their studies provide a valuable service. It is only when they begin to minimize the role that individuals can play in bringing about historical change or to make pronouncements on the likelihood or unlikelihood of

---

21. G. Maier, *Biblical Hermeneutics* (trans. R. W. Yarbrough; Wheaton, Ill.: Crossway, 1994) 24.

22. Abraham (*Divine Revelation*, chap. 5) uses the example of a remote people being convinced through reasonable discussion to believe in a moon landing, even though such an event is completely foreign to anything they personally have known.

23. For full discussion, see ibid.

24. Ibid., 108. For a rebuttal to the objection that, since for God anything is possible, allowing God a role in historical process jeopardizes historical study as a discipline based on probability judgments, see my aforementioned essay, "Historiography of the Old Testament."

25. Halpern, *The First Historians*, 122.

specific events that they may exceed the limitations of their chosen method and may wittingly or unwittingly find themselves writing histories that bear a greater resemblance to their present concerns than to past realities. I have written at some length elsewhere[26] on this potential danger, and so I will not belabor the point here.

Rethink the Consequences of Modern Literary
Criticism on Doing History

Although Wellhausen-style literary criticism is hardly extinct, it has been increasingly challenged in recent decades and, in the minds of many, seriously undermined. This has far-reaching implications for the historical study of the Old Testament, for, as Hayes instructed us at the outset of the present volume, "the primary influence on Wellhausen's reconstruction of Israelite *history* was . . . the results and consequences of his *literary* study of the Old Testament" (p. 36 in this volume; my italics). For too long scholars have failed to see, or perhaps to admit, that the results of newer literary approaches often have a direct bearing on the results of older literary criticism.[27] Briefly stated, there needs to be increased exploration of how the legitimate results of modern literary studies of the Bible (that is, studies alert to the artistry, the poetics, the literary workings of biblical narratives) bear upon historical questions and at times challenge prior historical-critical judgments. Various essays in the present volume, not least the essays by Barton and Klement, lend credence to the claim that "we should not only ask what new insights the literary perspective gives us today, but also ask how far the absence of that perspective in the past invalidated the methods, and therefore the conclusions, of the scholars concerned."[28]

Conclusion

In the preface to this volume, which is now at its end, I indicated that in part 6 I would only be able to hazard some guesses regarding what developments in the study of Israel's past the future is likely to see. I noted also that the same optimism that prompted me to take on this project in the

---

26. Long, *The Art of Biblical History*, 135–49.

27. See, for example, R. W. L. Moberly's insightful discussion of "The Relationship between the Study of the Final Text and the Study of Its Prehistory," in his *At the Mountain of God: Story and Theology in Exodus 32–34* (JSOTSup 22; Sheffield: JSOT, 1983) 22–27; see my *Reign and Rejection of King Saul: A Case for Literary and Theological Coherence* (SBLDS 118; Atlanta: Scholars Press, 1989), esp. 7–20.

28. D. R. Hall, *The Seven Pillories of Wisdom* (Macon, Ga.: Mercer University Press, 1990) 110.

first place might resurface in my attempts to divine the road ahead. What I have written above confirms these judgments. My projections about what the future may hold are as much an expression of what I would like to see as of what I have reason to believe we shall see. The field at the moment is widely divided, and as long as scholars themselves remain divided in their beliefs about "life, the universe, and everything" it will remain so. Historians of fundamentally different worldviews, if they are consistent, will build their houses (their historical reconstructions) on distinctly different foundations. These houses will, in turn, be occupied by communities that feel at home in them. Nontheists will understandably feel uncomfortable in houses built on theistic foundations, thinking them to be built on sand, while theists will understandably feel uncomfortable in houses built on atheistic foundations, thinking them likewise to be built on sand. These assertions presuppose, of course, that scholars and their scholarship are marked by consistency—in other words, that there is a match between the model of reality each scholar embraces and the methods he/she employs. As we have already noted, however, consistency between foundation and superstructure has not always been the hallmark of the discipline. Little wonder scholars are sometimes ill at ease in the houses they build, not recognizing that there is a mismatch between the "below-ground" portion (that is, their core beliefs) and the "above-ground" portion (their specific scholarly practices). The question this raises for the future study of Israel's past is whether the discipline as a whole and individual scholars in particular will show the courage to dig down a bit and reinspect the foundation upon which they have been building. If the foundation is cracked, perhaps it can be mended. If in places it must be demolished and rebuilt, then let the process begin, for, though it may seem an unnecessary delay in the erection of the superstructure, if the foundation is not sound, anything built on it is doomed in time to collapse under its own weight.

INDEX OF AUTHORITIES

INDEX OF SCRIPTURE

Scripture is indexed according to Hebrew chapter and verse divisions; where the English versification differs, English chapter and verse are supplied in brackets.

Hebrew Bible

605

New Testament

Deuterocanonical Works